For my wife Jean, and our children

Preface

The Calvinist Temper in English Poetry

The idea of this book is to present a set of literary critiques on a body of material which has never before been considered as a unity. A few writers are drawn from the 16th century (most notably Spenser), some from the 17th (Marvell, Taylor, Milton), more from the 18th and 19th. No important distinction is made among English and American writers, for reasons that will be shown within. What the writers are claimed to have in common, of course, is a supposedly similar Calvinistic religious background. In some instances (Smart or Coleridge), this fact of Calvinism will have to be proven. For most of the others, with the possible exception of Cowper, the fact is known, but the relevance has been ignored in the past. Even with Cowper there has been remarkably little written on the Calvinist influence on his poetry, as opposed to his life, on which perhaps we have too much. In all the cases the success or failure of the theory hinges on the success of the explications.

A larger issue, the existence of the Calvinist literary tradition on theoretical grounds (think how strange this sounds!) will not be insisted on, except by implications. We are working on the principle of a *zeitgeist* influencing the sensibility of writers, however, and on the assumption that if the *zeitgeist* has universal and unchangeable notes, these will create permanent marks on the sensibility of all under the influence of that *zeitgeist,* even allowing generously for the uniqueness of the temperaments and personalities of poets, for the strictly literary influences of a given age, and for numerous other philosophical and social influences upon the writers. The minimum that must be shown is that the Calvinist influence is the dominant one on a given writer, or at least upon certain poems by that writer, and that this influence appears in similar or identical fashion upon writers of different ages and countries where the Calvinist religious view is found. Less than this there is no case at all. Thus the writers in this study have been carefully chosen with this limiting point in mind. These are writers in whom we can allow for wide and extreme influence outside of Calvinism, but in whom the Calvinist influence not only dominates, but also colors, the others and ultimately integrates the writer's total imaginative apprehension of the world.

The first section of the book is given over to theology and to history, which may dismay the literary student. He is to be reassured that this grounding in fact and history is necessary, not an indulgence of the author. Books which search out origins in this way are often accused of being non-literary. Such accusations stem from a very superficial view of literary criticism which does not care to seek out the roots of an author's imaginative world, and, in an instance such as this one, from a hidden dislike of the religious sphere itself, as opposed to sources of inspiration in, say, the political, social, or biographical. This bias disfigures the academic mind and should long since have yielded to impartiality. My reasons for going into these forbidding areas are more scholarly than polemical, however. The assertion of my argument is so unusual that for the careful reader, and certainly for the theologian, whom I hope to number in the audience, it must be proven. Then again, the history and theology which bind this argument together are somewhat obscure, except to the theologian, so some of what is given is on the grounds of preliminary information. But there are also certain links, some historical, some theological, which the author has had to work out for himself in order to establish the metaphysics of Calvinism and show the unity of sensibility of the Calvinist vision. Some of these links or insights may be useful to the theologian *per se,* or, if they are questioned, the author is anxious to have them set down in clear form, so that the criticism can be meaningful. The historian or theologian of Calvinism, to give an important instance which will be all-pervasive in the following pages, has been too quick to concede that Calvinism lacks an aesthetic, or, if he has claimed an aesthetic, the case has been made on weak or feeble grounds. Puritans smashed windows and broke statues, but this fact is not very important if we know and can make use of the fact that the Calvinist sensibility is mainly a matter of ear and intellect. I hope that the theologian will be pleased with what he reads, and that it may revise his opinion of Calvinistic aesthetics for the better. To the literary reader, for whom the book is primarily intended, I hope Part One has some meaning and interest, and I advise in advance that the arguments and explications of the later parts are only valid and perhaps intelligible on the basis of Part One. The method here is zig-zag and by cross-currents, from ideas and traditions to sensibility and poetry, but then back from poetry to the ideas and traditions. This is allowable in an intellectual continuum, the existence of which we prove as we move along. For the theologically-minded we might also say that a poem may well show or be the intellectual link between two facets of doctrine or dogma formerly thought to be discontinuous, inconsistent, or simply puzzling. It is a two-way street. If this seems to be promising too much, I hasten to add that I mean only that the theoretical and practical parts are logically and internally connected, and not merely chapter variations on a given theme.

I am indebted to an enormous range of authors — historians, theologians, and critics — for whose help in specific areas of analysis, many debts are happily mentioned in the text and notes within. For personal insights and aid I am happy to mention professors John Smith, Kathleen Coburn, Walter Ong, S.J., Basil Wiley, and Frederick A. Pottle. There is a negative aspect to this study, directed towards certain types of rationalist theorists of literature and critics of religious poetry, an aspect that will arise when necessary for clarification of specific points, since the main purpose is not to clear up older confusions but rather to make a positive contribution to an obscure and troubled area. In the closing stages of writing, John New's *Anglican and Puritan* and Norman Pettit's *The Heart Prepared* were especially valuable. Though written with different purposes in mind, those books and this one are mutually supportive except in a few matters, and will lay the groundwork, it is hoped, for a new and more informed view of the subject than has in the past prevailed.

Summer grants from the Brown University stipend fund, an English department Bronson research fellowship, and a grant from the American Philosophical Society have materially aided this work. The work was begun in 1961—62 under a Morse research fellowship from Yale University to Cambridge University in England. I wish to thank the staffs of St. Catharine's, Emmanual, and the University Library at Cambridge for help on many occasions with Puritan source materials.

I would also like to thank Michelle Massé, Stephen Murray, Patricia Steenland, and James Catano for their help in preparing this manuscript.

James D. Boulger

Because of his illness and subsequent death in July, 1979, Professor Boulger was unable to revise or correct the typescript and galleys for this book. Editorial changes have been limited to points of consistency or usage.

Michelle A. Massé

Table of Contents

Introduction

The Calvinist Temper

The view of poetry, of the place of historical background in criticism, and of the relationship of theology to literature will become clear in the course and method of this study. An introduction is not a replacement for the specific tasks that lie ahead, but as an outline of purpose it does have some use in giving an overview of the theme of the book. It will deal generally with the group of topics studied at length in the book and give the reasoned principles which are the guidelines making the book a possible venture. First there is the nature of poetry and the place of religious poetry in this context, then the place of history and of literary history in the study of such poetry, and finally the specific literary methods that are appropriate for a study of a special kind of religious poetry within the defined historical and literary framework.

We may take it as axiomatic that all good poetry arises from some successful combination of themes and means of presentation. This prosaic statement is not meant to remove the mystery and power from the many literary terms of our day which are more exciting and more specific than simply "means of presentation." It is merely a starting point for a working definition. Even less does it intend to separate theme or idea from literary means. Yet inevitably it is the case that critics are not able to talk very clearly about individual works without at least a theoretical division of terms, and it is this acceptable tradition that is followed in the comments on theme and presentation here with a particular eye to the problems of religious poetry.

The theme or idea in religious poetry is some body of theological material, or attitude towards such material, or an attitude towards other ideas and themes influenced profoundly by a theological and religious view. In the most basic sense, then, if there is a problem with theme in religious poetry it is the old issue of poetry as philosophy or as didactic material in a specific form. The presiding view of twentieth century criticism holds that merely philosophical or merely didactic poetry is almost always not very good poetry, even if the philosophy is very appealing (or "true" for some readers), or the moralism very sound, that is, re-inforcing the reader's own experience with life and reality. Most literary critics still hold that "beauty" and "pleasure," (the aesthetic dimension considered from the most abstract and intellectual to the most basic and physical) are the grounds for calling poetry an art, an art not identical with philosophy, theology or other abstract disciplines which pursue truth for its own sake. Another commonplace we must accept, which makes difficulties for this study, is that much religious poetry, including a certain amount of what is to be called "Calvinist" or "Puritan" in these pages, shares the failings of types of philosophical poetry known as ideological and types of moral poetry called didactic. The worst poetry is both ideological and didactic with little interest in redeeming aesthetic means. This situation raises a problem for this study for which the literary solution seems at first at variance with the historical response. The historical view would seem to require an abundance of evidence, even and perhaps from "typical" or "bad" poetry to prove that persistent themes and ideas in a "Calvinist Temper" in poetry do in fact exist; a literary study, on the other hand, seems to require literary merit as expressed in many kinds of specific ways as the justification for consideration of any poetry in primarily literary terms. The answer to the possible dilemma lies in the extensive use of historical theology, devotional prose works, and the scholarly works which have discussed enough of the mediocre or plainly bad Calvinist poetry, such as Wigglesworth's *Day of Doom*, for fairly accurate determination of Calvinist-Puritan ideas and patterns. The devotional prose writings are sometimes interesting, and their weight, added to study of the original theology and the accounts of the mediocre poetry by literary predecessors, leaves no doubt as to the existence of a close connection in themes and ideas between the great mixed mass of the tradition in general, and the best of the poetry which alone will be the object of close study in the book. Thus the usual viewpoint of most literary studies prevails in the main body of the book, wherein poetry of merit is discussed within the angle of vision of the "Calvinist Temper." In the opening section, attention is given to questions of history, religious ideology and literary history, to ensure a coherent approach to the entire topic.

The opening sections involving history and theology, and the historical transitions, must justify their presence. Once the discussion of the individual literary figures begins, most readers will be on the familiar ground of literary criticism, with a special angle. For these readings the justification must be in the quality. One qualification in this study is that the readings have little validity or interest in themselves unless the connection between abstract themes in Calvinist-Puritanism and the poets and poems are clearly made. To ensure these necessary points, the first section is devoted to the theology and history of Puritanism and analysis of Calvinist-Puritan patterns in prose. Introductory transitions between centuries or periods, or in a few cases between poets, in other words "literary history," also occur as the means to establish the continuity between the tradition as defined and the individual major poet, and to take into account the mutations in ideas and themes resulting from the passage of time and conflict with outside forces. For the history of English Calvinism, theology and analysis of the prose, the author has for the most part done his own work, though gladly relying on the good work of others where it existed; the transitions and connections of literary history with the individual poets were more readily found in reliable available studies, and are always cited fully with gratitude. To those who would argue that primary history, theology, and sound literary history have no importance for serious literary criticism, I have no response, and no intention of setting about justifying these disciplines. For the success of using these different disciplines in one study, the answer must be in the book itself. Some preliminary comment should be given, however, for the choice of Calvinist-Puritanism as the source for themes and ideas in the poetry studied, and so in fact a little excursus into literary history, and about the literary methods to be used in the main body of the book.

Literary history in standard accounts does not now recognize a "Calvinist Temper in English Poetry." It recognizes only chronological ages, often attached to a great figure like Shakespeare or Johnson. It does recognize most of the poets studied in this book as at least partially under Calvinist influence, and all in some senses as religious poets. To establish some sense of continuity among these poets requires many kinds of evidence and judicious use of reliable literary historians whose intentions were far other than what is attempted here. This is not a new departure in modern literary study, where there have been various attempts at looking upon literary tradition in cross-section, with the best highly provocative and at least partially successful. By realizing the tradition of the "poem of meditation" (Martz), "the visionary company" (Bloom), "the great tradition" (Leavis) we do not thereby invalidate the "Augustan Age," "Age of Johnson," "Age of Wordsworth" and the like. We do, however, see literary history in richer terms. One of these newer views of tradition, the poetry of meditation developed by Martz, will be cited further within as a very important influence on this study. The intellectual histories of scholars such as Miller, Fairchild and many others also have many uses which are cited in the proper places.

This introduction concludes with a brief and rather abstract look at the various specifically literary methods that come into play in showing that there is a "Calvinist Temper" in English poetry, and that the poets studied in this context do belong together if seen in this particular light. For the problem of a Calvinist temper related to the poets chosen for the study, both historical and literary analysis and techniques are required. The theology must be studied, and at the same time the themes of theology analyzed in a reasonable body of Puritan prose and poetry, the propriety for inclusion of each poet presented, and a literary analysis of at least some major works of each poet offered, this last and most important being concerned both with thematic and "aesthetic" materials and in their intertwining to make good poems.

Biographical materials will be of very limited importance in the study. For most of the poets the relationship between the Puritan themes and at least some important poems is evident in the texts of the poems, without need of biographical appeal. Only where it is supposed or known that Calvinist influence upon the poet would now be disputed by serious readers of that poet, even with the evidence of the poetry at hand, will biography become a minor issue, as in Coleridge and Wordsworth. Occasionally biographical matters about the better known Calvinists such as Cowper and Byron will help illuminate meaning in a poem, a process this writer has always regarded as a proper critical maneuver if wisely used. I doubt that many readers will find much to object to in the spare usage of biography envisioned within. More likely to raise problems is the matter of paraphrase of texts, which often is boring and always open to the charge of "reductionism." Many books otherwise valuable in various ways have been hurt by it. To show an intelligent reader how to get from one to ten is the obstacle it creates, but sometimes this is necessary to point out what may or ought to be the obvious, to ensure the presence and consistency of a major pattern. "Theme" books cannot avoid some of it if the theme is to be explained and proven to be the important link the author claims to have found among the poets. I know no way around this problem except to keep paraphrase at a minimum, presenting as much detail as necessary in the early sections and poets, and relying on allusion wherever possible thereafter. Paraphrase may be a valuable substratum and not a "heresy" if it prepares soundly for more direct, aesthetic discussion of the best poems. For religious poetry these discussions in essence become an interpretation of symbols, metaphors, and other poetic devices as vehicles for the religious "allegory" described in the total structure of the book, that is, Calvinist-Puritan religious symbol and allegory. Allegory is considered here in the sense described by recent students of the subject, mentioned in detail in proper place within. In this sense it is not sharply separated from "symbolism" in many instances, not a mechanical four-tiered structure, and definitely not mere didacticism. With the success or failure of the readings given to the symbols and metaphors as a developing Calvinist-Puritan religious pattern of "allegory" this book stands or falls, since here is its central purpose as literary study. Some attention will also be paid in the contexts of specific poems to many of the devices and terms normally associated with literary criticism − verbal texture, ironies, dramatic techniques, prosody, and so forth. They are present as variables in the poets studied, some obviously associated with all good poetry, others with the special interests of an age, and a few the favorite techniques of a given writer. Clear examples of the later are the irony of Marvell and the strange prosody of Smart. A look at such devices is of course necessary in the consideration of the unity of any individual poem, the one aspect of modern literary criticism accepted by all.

If it seems strange to stress the necessity to cite chapter and verse in the development of the argument of a book of this sort, one must remember that this work is not "myth criticism," or the newer practice of using the ideas of Freud or Jung to allow any kind of divination to be accepted as serious literary study and criticism. "New Criticism" forced people to look at texts, and was therefore therapeutic at a certain time in the past. We now have more to learn from careful scrutiny of poets in their historical and cultural contexts than from abstract critical methods and theories. Literary history has been for too long neglected in our attempt to understand literature.

To ignore the perplexing requirements of seeing a poet in his true historical and cultural context is to allow criticism to become a form of fantasy, a fiction in itself perhaps as interesting as the literature it purports to criticize, but not of much service in understanding literary texts or history.

PART ONE

The Patterns of Calvinism: The Sixteenth Century

I. The Background

Calvinism: General Characteristics and Operating Force

The *Institutes of the Christian Religion* of John Calvin, his other writings, and the writings of other early theologians of the Swiss and French schools are of necessary yet remote interest in the study to follow. To be sure, the important doctrines unfolded in the *Institutes* are the guidelines for all the later thinking of the English school of Calvinists, and therefore the precise theological nature of these doctrines must be understood by the student of English Calvinism and Puritanism. But the differences are as crucial as the similarities. Pure Genevese Calvinism was an abstract system, in practice a system of rigorous religious ritual that Calvin intended. Although the early French and Swiss Calvinists were more relaxed and open to aesthetic impulse than popular history has allowed, there was little place in the original abstract Calvinist scheme, partly because it was pursued so abstractly, for the aesthetic and imaginative as such. There was the theory, there was the practice, without an imaginative bond to give a living sense of the system. *Les Hugenots* was written out of the impulse of the classical tradition and of religious persecution in France; but nothing like the English literary outpouring of the years 1570–1660 can be matched in the other Calvinist countries, including the neighbor to the north, Scotland, where the system became more fully entrenched than in England. In England, especially during the great Cambridge days of the last decade of the 16th and first decade of the 17th centuries, the theory and practice of Calvinism became an integrated and whole way of life, fully imaginative, what some of the commentators call the "inner drama of the spirit."[1] This drama was total, encompassing the world and all areas of experience, and that is why it was open to imaginative interpretation as was later the Calvinism of New England. Very few historical or critical commentators have been able to approach this drama, bringing the perspectives and categories of Calvinism proper, without drying it up, or missing the intensive imaginative life into which Calvinism was transferred in its English phase. Haller,[2] on the English side, and Miller,[3] on the American, have managed to do this to some extent, to convey some sense of aesthetic and emotional appeal in the system, but their interest was mainly historical and not in the aesthetic as such. Nevertheless their work is closer to the spirit of living Calvinism and Puritanism in England and America than any that has yet been done, and therefore their work is the cornerstone of mine, which attempts to probe further into the aesthetic and imaginative side of Puritanism for its own sake.

Calvin's intellectual and methodical presentation of the truths of the Christian religion is the ultimate source of any later phase, religious, political, aesthetic, economic, of Calvinist manifestation. This is necessary to state in a study whose purpose is not to dwell long on the logical arrangement and intricacies of Calvin's system for its own sake. There are countless studies of this subject, many of which can be recommended to the reader for illumination of one point or another in the system. In this section the doctrines of Calvin which were later important for the aesthetic side of Calvinism will be emphasized. In the following section some emphasis will be given to the system itself. These include the nature, power and sovereignty of God; the conception of original sin and of man's depravity; the process of salvation or "secret operation of the spirit," the passing from damnation, to election to justification to sanctification to glorification, which later became central to the English Puritan drama; and election itself in relation to double predestination, about which perhaps, taken alone, too much has been written apart from the total process. The doctrines not particularly of importance for aesthetics would include Calvin's Christology, his doctrine of the Church and church discipline, the nature of the two sacraments and authority of the Bible. There is some negative importance here, however. The de-emphasis of Christology and of the Eucharist in Calvinism (compared with Roman Catholic or Anglican or even Lutheran practice) leaves lacunae in the imaginative world of the scheme of redemption in Calvinism which must be filled by other sources. One of these sources is prayer, made powerful in Calvinism by the support of the emphasis upon the doctrine of the Holy Sirit. Perhaps the only major aspects of Calvin's system which are unimportant for our purposes, either positively or negatively, are the sections on doctrine and discipline of the Church and authority of Scriptures about which Calvin and all his followers in all countries wrote endlessly. Here we enter the political and economic aspects of Calvinism, on which so much has been written, and which this writer happily leaves to others.

Some writers have stated that Calvin's one purpose in writing the *Institutes* was to expound and defend the nature and sovereignty of God, his "honeur and segneurship," reflecting some peculiarly French notion of honor. Like most sweeping statements or half-truths of a cute sort, this statement has some value, although the French honor part cannot be taken seriously. Calvin, like Aquinas before him, began his treatise with a long section on the power, nature and sovereignty of God, perhaps in contrast to the Lutheran emphasis on the doctrine of justification by faith, which in emphasis at least is man-centered. The Anabaptists, heretics and the practices of the Roman clergy of the day are also always in Calvin's mind when he writes on the primacy and power of God. It is important, then, to recognize that Calvin never intended any doctrine or part of his system to be emphasized or even considered apart from the opening thesis of the *Institutes* on the power, nature and sovereignty of God. If the importance of this doctrine is remembered and kept in mind, one cannot go wrong in making a general assessment about the meaning of Calvinism or about its impact on the religious life of England in later times. Naturally, as history and the inevitable human situation tell us, the system was broken up, distorted, given emphases not intended by Calvin in his own day and later by Calvinist and enemy theologians alike. The distortions and their impact are as important for the history of Calvinism and for the religious sensibility which it generated as the pure system itself, the reality. Perhaps this brief analysis of the dynamics of the system, its strengths, its weaknesses, and its loopholes for outward movement, will explain what I mean.

Since Calvin's system is a system, the most complete and logical since Aquinas', one doctrine should follow logically upon the other. The power and sovereignty of God leads to the weakness and smallness of man, then to the severe doctrine of original sin, and so on. At this point I am not concerned with all the logical connections, which I think are clear enough in Calvin himself. I am concerned to point out that a purely logical analysis of the sort usually undertaken by theologians will miss the emphases, not intended by the logic of Calvin's argument, which are also all important in assessing the meaning of Calvinism. Calvin's section on Christology, for instance, is impeccable taken separately, and denies none of the traditional status given to Christ as God or man in Catholic Christianity. Yet the unusual emphasis upon the power of God in Calvin does in effect limit the previous emphasis upon the person of Christ in traditional Catholicism. The doctrine of the sovereignty of God creates a vertical relationship of man to God almost to the neglect of the Mediator. This leads in turn to the weakness in the sacramental system in practical Calvinism, since the rituals of the Eucharist are related directly to Christology. Calvin made a good deal of the doctrine of the spiritual presence in the Eucharist, and although it is obvious that there is a psychological de-emphasis in moving from transubstantiation to the idea of spiritual presence only, there is no logical reason in the *Institutes* for complete de-emphasis of rituals attached to the Eucharistic sacrament. In practice, as a matter of fact, there is a certain amount of Eucharistic worship in the Calvinist tradition, the poetic meditations of Edward Taylor and Richard Baxter being outstanding instances. But the logical and practical de-emphasis of the Eucharist and Christ in favor of the idea of the sovereignty and power of God leads other Calvinists to a direct and dialectical relationship between man and God, with prayer, not a sacrament, as the mediator.[4] This may be called the Hebraic side of Calvinism, for the focus is upon the Old Testament, and in its institutional manifestation is recognized as the importance of the word and the preacher in the Protestant tradition.

The items of the Calvinist tradition as presented in the *Institutes* which fit logically together and carry traditionally an equal amount of emphasis in the writings of the English Puritans are the sovereignty of God, the depravity of man and hence the power of original sin, the process of salvation in the series − sinfulness, election, justification, sanctification, glorification − prayer (in its limited function), and mild devotion to the Eucharist as the spiritual presence of Christ. These work together to give a world view which is at once religious, wholesome, sane, and a high form of Christian contemplation. The items in Calvin's system important for the Church and for the social functions of religion, the authority of the Bible and of the Church, are logically connected to the above by Calvin but are not important for religious sensibility and the inner life as such, and hence have no bearing upon literature. The doctrine of authority of Scripture as related to the doctrine of the Holy Spirit and the inner life of the Spirit stands apart in a peculiar way as the weakest link in Calvin's logical chain, leading later to some great disasters in Calvinism. Calvin undeniably did emphasize the Holy Spirit in the *Institutes*, but not in a way that would decrease the sovereignty of God or the prominence of Christ as mediator. But this was a decided re-emphasis in relation to Catholic tradition which led in the following century to the complete breakdown of the idea of authority in the Scriptures, to the left-wing Puritan and Quaker doctrines of the inner light and raising of the Holy Spirit to an eminence above the other persons of the Trinity. In this sport of Calvinist tradition the entire drama of sin, election, justification etc. is completely eroded. Spiritual hubris does away with authority and even sin, giving first Quakerism and then the pantheism and general notion of spirit in the world that opens up the Romantic movement. In this work we are in the main not dealing with the aberrations of the doctrine of the Holy Spirit, but it is well to point out that the germ for all this is in Calvin himself, as followed by those who grasp the emphasis of a doctrine apart from its logical position in the system. This collateral line, as it were, will be useful for us in pointing out something else, not widely recognized, that within the framework of what is undeniably the Calvinist center it was still possible to create distortions in the system and the sensibility by overemphasis on any one of the several central doctrines of the system: power of God, original sin, election, predestination, proper place of the Spirit. Indeed, our work would be rather dry and fruitless if these overemphases, isolations and distortions had not occurred, for the central system in its pure form gives us essentially one drama, one artistic vehicle, and that is of ineluctable triumph. This drama and its explanation will be a main interest here, but we shall note also the byways and desponds of those who heightened God at the expense of man, or original sin at the expense of election, or the happy few who seemed able to begin the process of salvation at justification and proceed quickly and surely to glorification. In short, we are dealing with a highly complex central system, having a number of almost necessary subordinate or auxiliary systems branching from it, and several genuine heresies lurking within it as seeds of its possible destruction. In the late sixteenth to the mid-seventeenth centuries we get the central system in its healthiest form; in Cowper, Coleridge and Dickinson there are some of the most interesting byways; the Spiritist heretics such as Fox and the Quakers prepare the ground for the sensibility of at least one great Romantic, Wordsworth, and possibly for others.

In order to understand the aesthetic impact of the central system of Calvinism upon the English Puritans and later Calvinists, a brief analysis of the central doctrines in the *Institutes* follows, more specific than the general and historical description given thus far. As with what has been given in the general historical area, the guiding principle of selection will be those doctrines later to have greatest impact for sensibility and aesthetics, not an attempt to describe the system in its entirety of relationships.

II. Background

The Institutes *and Calvin's System:*
Brief Analysis of Central Points

It is necessary to subject only the main doctrines of the system important for aesthetics to analysis for our purposes. This is an aesthetic study within a given historical framework, not a full theological discussion of Calvin's system, or of the historical and social effects of that system, or the kind of modern re-interpretation that might serve the needs of reformed churches today. The reader of this study may have interest in all these matters, for which a bibliographical note mentioning books of special merit is appended.[5] The basic analysis in this section, then, will be of those doctrines in the *Institutes* with important implication for aesthetics later unfolded in the Puritan tradition. Another mode of analysis, emphasizing the obscurities and matters of logical debate in Calvin's system, particularly about election and predestination, need not be the focus of this study. In the light of the later history of Calvinism, particularly among the English Puritans, this analysis will follow up the general statements in the previous section and emphasize the doctrines and lines of thought in Calvin's system which later had the greatest impact upon the aesthetics of imaginative writers under the influence of Calvin. In the instances of Calvin's views of election, predestination, effectual calling and justification, the aesthetic consequences for literature were as enormous as the moral and theological consequences in other areas of life. But this was not always the case. His doctrine of prayer (*Inst.* III, 20)[6] was vital to poets of the Calvinist meditative tradition in the 17th and 18th centuries, yet not distinctive or decisive in the history of theological controversy. Conversely, the entire fourth book of the *Institutes*, on the Church and civil government, which had the greatest social and political consequences of any of Calvin's writings, and generated the greatest number of written responses and controversies throughout the period of historical Calvinism, that is, from Calvin's age to the early 19th century, had little direct effect on imaginative life and writing within the Calvinist-Puritan tradition, if we take into account the minor exception that the influence his views on the doctrine and discipline of the sacraments and on the value of music in the service had upon the writing and singing of hymns, a special minor branch of poetry to be considered later with Watts.

Several important, and in a sense obvious, but for that reason often neglected, aspects of the relationship between Calvin's writings and "Calvinism" and especially "Puritanism" should also be brought to light before looking briefly at the central tenets of the *Institutes*. In reading Calvin's theology, it becomes clear throughout that he intended his writings to be taken as one whole, especially the final and perfected volume of the *Institutes*. He did not expect his doctrines to be questioned of re-interpreted, as they were inevitably in the later history of Calvinism, and certainly not found puzzling or objects of learned speculation in theological seminaries. Calvin reasons meticulously through each doctrine by his own logic to his own conclusion, citing precedents, scriptural texts and adversaries. When he has finished a topic, the doctrine is settled, to become a member in the chain of reasoning which is his system. He did not expect doctrines, such as predestination or election, to be held up separately as belief or to be discussed in a vacuum. This is especially so because the system was intended as a network of beliefs held by a community of believers, the Christian community of faith. Justification might be a major stumbling block without election, and election certainly was that without predestination and justification, but within the community of belief these snares that might lead to shipwreck (one of his few literary metaphors) led rather to assurance. It became historically the case of course for many of Calvin's doctrines to be taken up in isolation by various groups, for them to be the subject of savage inspection by religious controversialists in many ages, and for some members of the Calvinist-Puritan community in England, and New England particularly, to lose the sense of Christian community and church discipline that Calvin always stressed in his writing about doctrines. Abstract theologians, poets and other imaginative writers especially were likely to view Calvin's doctrines in isolation from an active community of church worship. These practices gave rise to the many peculiarities and even monstrosities that have passed by the name of Calvinism in theology, history and literature. Calvin, essentially a pious and practicing preacher, would no doubt have deplored most of this progeny, but we need not look upon the situation with similar eyes, as long as the distinction between Calvin's writings and its influence is held in view. Some of the historical and literary effects of Calvinism may be more interesting in the history of humanity than the writings of Calvin himself, a point to keep in mind especially in the question of our special subject, the literary sensibility generated in history by Calvin's writings.

For if any one thing is clear from a general reading of Calvin's theological writings, it is his lack of interest in the aesthetic, his distrust of the imagination (shared by most of his scholastic, Catholic adversaries) and his preference for a literalistic, legal reading of the Scriptures over what had become a very relaxed medieval attitude. This point is so overwhelming, and has been so fully accepted in the common notions of "Calvinism" and "Puritanism," that it is made only in passing. Calvin, like his favorite theologian Augustine before him, approved explicitly only of music, and that as edification for church service and worship. But the point must be accepted only to be refuted in a more meaningful sense. As Calvin's doctrines were capable of being pulled away from the system to form strange new configurations in Puritanism and in the lives of individuals, so also an aesthetic sensibility grew up about his essentially theological and literalistic picture of the world. This, we acknowledge by hindsight, was inevitable, as we know any powerful, original picture of man's place and of man's self, whether theological as in Calvin, or scientific as in Newton, will affect profoundly the imaginative picture of men who accept such theories as belief. Every "world picture" is a possible aesthetic; every original theologian, philosopher or scientist a man of imagination in this special sense. Since the middle of the 18th century there have been attempts at purely aesthetic views of the world, of imagination as the highest potency or maker, and the rejection of science and especially theology as the giver of the basic picture. Though Calvin would have rejected the notion that he was presenting an imaginative picture (potentially, at least), and not literal theological truth (while conversely the special science of aesthetics and literary criticism in the modern period has held both theology and literalism in contempt), we must not blind ourselves to the truth of the fact that what Calvin presented as a reasoned chain of arguments from Scriptures and as literal truth was actually a highly imaginative and special world picture, as many others before and later. When, in Puritan England and New England, whole societies took up this

picture, or parts of it, as truth and as the guide to their lives, it was
inevitable that special imaginative colorings would be given to
doctrines such as election, justification and the rest, since every
society has its share of people of high imaginative talent of this
derivative sort. It is a paradox then that Calvin, who despised
imagination, was more imaginative in the fundamental sense than any
of the Calvinist poets and writers who accepted his views, but it is a
familiar paradox, also true of Augustine, Aquinas, Kant and Newton.
Even the most powerful writers, who twisted and sometimes
transformed the system of Calvinism to their own ends — Milton,
Byron, Coleridge — maintained a fundamental debt to their source.

In examining the major doctrines with the aesthetic possibility in
mind we can be brief, since the actual unfolding into the aesthetic
realm in every case happened at a later stage of the historical
development of the Calvinist-Puritan sensibility, and we intend in the
later discussions of periods and individual writers to point out all
these flourishings of the Calvinist literary temperament. Therefore
hints of what is to come and the possible attitudes towards the
doctrines, some of which Calvin did see and rejected, others which he
did not see at all, will be the aim of this little excursus through the
major positions in the *Institutes*.

The most significant doctrines in Calvin's *Institutes* fall into three
classes, for convenience presented here in increasing order of
importance. In the first group we can place doctrines that were crucial
for Reformation Protestantism yet not in the judgment of history for
the intellectual and aesthetic life of subsequent centuries. Calvin's
doctrines of church discipline, worship and civil order, or Book IV of
the *Institutes,* fall here. In the second are grouped doctrines whose
weight has been greatest in the intellectual and moral realms, and also
important for the aesthetics of Calvinism: God's power, governance
and providence; testimony and secret operation of the Spirit; Christ as
Redeemer and his fulfillment of the justice of the Law. Most
significant are the doctrines which have both influenced profoundly
the direction of Protestantism and the intellectual, moral and aesthetic
lives of generations of men, to wit, original sin and freedom of the
will, justification by faith, election and predestination, effectual calling
and vocation. As stated earlier, a special category must be established
for those doctrines and attitudes of Calvin which were significant for
aesthetics alone in the 16th—17th century historical period: his view
of prayer, special respect for music, dislike of allegorical reading of

Scripture, and approval of aural communication of the Word and hence of the aural in general over the visual and other sensuous or imaginative means of presenting the relationship of God to man. Except for the chapter given to prayer (II, 20) the other points are merely mentioned in passing by Calvin. Summing up, the first class of doctrines has no literary importance. On the other hand the "special category," while directly aesthetic and important for establishing the acceptance of some literary and other aesthetic forms in Calvinist societies, takes up aesthetic matters in passing and is not dogma and doctrine. Our brief survey of the aesthetic implications in the doctrines of Calvin can be restricted, then, to the important doctrines in classes two and three. We are to note several matters in this survey, namely, the prominence of each doctrine in the total system, its uniqueness in Calvinism, the degree to which it was possible for this doctrine to be wrenched from the system and viewed or taken in isolation, and finally, with hindsight of course, how far a doctrine might take hold of and influence imaginative men.

Calvin's awesome view of God's power, governance and providence as theology is a straightforward doctrine, the most prominent and the cornerstone of his system (I, 5, 13, 16). As his commentators say, he was concerned chiefly to maintain the dignity and sovereignty of God. Yet it was this doctrine, which surely no other Christian group could seriously question, that led to logical consequences from which many other theologians did shrink or which they found unacceptable – election, reprobation, predestination, calling, and so on. Since as a platitude all could find God's power acceptable, this central viewpoint of Calvin was not discussed separately, wrenched out of context. It could and did lead to pious moralizings in divinity, dull moralizings in poetry, proper ejaculations in prayer, and to a somber and serious hymnology. The same generalities hold for Calvin's most important explicit Christian doctrine, Christ as Redeemer and his fulfillment of the justice of the Law (II, 12–17). As the first was his major deduction from the Old Testament, the second was from the New. Again it was a position acceptable and indeed required of all Christians at the time of the Reformation, and in itself led to pious moralizings, dull moralizings, proper ejaculations and a somber hymnology. Calvin's "use" of it, in soteriology, as his "use" of the majesty of God in election, is another matter.

The third doctrine in this group presents a special problem and is indeed the most puzzling doctrine in Calvin and the entire Protestant tradition. Unlike the doctrines mentioned previously, this one was not shared with Catholicism. The idea of the testimony and secret operation of the Spirit, which appears throughout the *Institutes*, is never satisfactorily defined, and was destined to be torn away from Calvinism and Puritanism, to become the decisive doctrine of the sects to the left, Anabaptists, Quakers, and Levellers. It fell into disrepute for this reason among later Calvinists and Puritans, who yet could never fully reject it. Spirit is indeed an obscure and vexing issue within Calvin's system and Protestantism. The doctrine of the Spirit was needed as an alternative to the Catholic belief in Church authority in the question of the surety of the Scriptures. The authenticity of the Scriptures, the appeal to the individual conscience, and the need for generally acceptable readings of Scripture often led in contradictory directions. Why are Calvin's views more valid than those of Jack the Journeyman, if there is no church or historical authority to appeal to? The answer was the "testimony and secret operation of the Spirit," but even Calvin's usual logic, rigor and scrupulous precision of definition did not rescue this doctrine from obscurity, a failure later to have a profound impact upon the history of Puritanism and the sects to the left of it.

The more peculiar doctrines of Calvinist-Puritanism, such as election, and justification by faith, might be abhorred or disputed by adversaries, but were at least available in logical form for inspection and argument. Controversies about these doctrines also arose within the Calvinist-Puritan tradition, but these revolved around a commonly accepted position. With the doctrines of the Spirit it was otherwise. The Journeymen Jacks of the 17th century were unsatisfied with Calvin's testimony, preferring their own. This important doctrine, which was essential to the Protestant view of interpretation of Scripture, remained vague and therefore subject to vast difference of interpretation within Protestantism and to ridicule from without, by "Papists" and humanist writers, especially the dramatists. It was an all-pervasive belief that could not be explained logically. As such it is subject to no precise definition or explanation helpful for Puritan aesthetics. It may sometimes be the source or undercurrent of confidence in a writer, but where it appears directly as defining principle, we are moving from Calvinist-Puritanism to the "left" spiritual tradition.

This doctrine of the testimony and secret operation of the Spirit is vexing for other reasons. It stands as the counterpart of the Catholic doctrine of authority and historicity as the guarantor of the validity of Scripture and the possibility of coherence in its interpretation (I, 7). The term "proportion of faith" is used to state this specific purpose. Yet since Spirit is such a vague and indefinable term, we cannot be sure that the guarantee means anything more than that for Calvin the Roman Church, existing historically somehow in error, was capable of miraculous renewal by reformers endowed with the correct testimony and operation of the Spirit. This idea of Spirit also plays a role at crucial points in the unfolding of other, more characteristic Calvinist doctrines, such as freedom of the will, justification by faith and effectual calling. These were the supreme doctrines in their effect upon the emotional and imaginative lives of Calvinists, and thus this idea of the Spirit is an important factor, if not the direct and shaping force, of aesthetic and imaginative responses to these doctrines among Calvinist poets and writers. But the line must be drawn faithfully to the facts of the history of the sects. At the point where doctrines of the Spirit become the central operating principle, and the formal shaping principle of religious writings, we pass from Calvinist-Puritanism to Quakerism and other sects to the left of Puritanism. It is admittedly a hard line to draw and discipline to keep in either theological or literary analysis of Calvinist-Puritanism, because the doctrine of the Spirit was indeed very important to Calvin and his English followers, and seems at times to have served as a final obscure explanation when no other explanation was available. This point is more difficult to grasp at first in Calvin than in later writers, since his firm legal and logical surface hides it more effectively than do the more emotional writings of the English Puritan successors. But nevertheless, there it hides, a non-logical appeal to the existence and power of the Spirit.

In a way fatally vague for the connection between religion and literature, this doctrine of the Spirit was destined to survive the transition from religious to secular society. A later subject of this book, an example or two will suffice here. Diffused almost beyond recognition, the "spirit" appears as the source of vitality in Smart, that which gives to his Anglicanism a vitality lacking in his time and to his religious life the integrity lacking at large. It appears again later in Wordsworth as the "spirit of the woods" in "Nutting," the sealed spirit of the Lucy Poems, and as the obscure "emotion" or imagination of much great Romantic poetry. Seeking for the spirit in self and nature the Romantics were carrying on the twin Puritan beliefs of "secret operation of the Spirit" and of effectual calling through evidences of election, sought and found however in the personal emotional life and in the life of nature rather than through Calvinist-Puritan religious and theological categories.

We turn now to the doctrines of Calvin which have traditionally been viewed as having given Calvinism its uniqueness as a theological system and view of the world. These are also the ones having the strongest impact upon the emotional and imaginative lives of the English Puritans and other followers of Calvin. Though all are inter-related, it is possible to group them in logical clusters that are emotionally and imaginatively, as well as intellectually, akin. The idea of original sin and freedom of the will form one; justification by faith, the major doctrine that includes in its orbit the question of the moral law, good works, and the place of prayer, forms another; predesti-nation is the third major doctrine from which flows Calvin's implications on election, reprobation, effectual calling and vocation. Though the traditional view that these doctrines give Calvinism its unique stamp has much justification, it can be accepted only with qualifications. That they had the strongest impact upon the Calvinist-Puritan sensibility can be accepted without question.

What is unique to Calvin is not these doctrines, but the pursuit of logical implications in the doctrines into difficult areas, and the connections of implications between the doctrines. His views of original sin, freedom of the will, predestination and election are those of Augustine and the conservative tradition in the early church. But because he pursued these views to logical limits (and apart from Church authority and sanction), it was necessary to invent radical means to preserve the traditional Christian view of salvation, and so he construed the "secret operation of the Spirit," effectual calling and vocation as balance or remedy for the stark effects of the grimmer doctrines. It was true that Calvin's Protestantism was destined to throw the individual desperately back upon himself, though Calvin and his immediate followers, with their powerful sense of church community, were not able to foresee this. Calvin's doctrine of justification by faith essentially follows Luther's reading of St. Paul, pursued to extreme consequences. Nothing good is left to be said for the Catholic ideas of penance, confession, good works, posing for Calvin the very difficult problem of how to cope with the fact of sin in the justified. Calvin did not shrink from the belief that the justified are still sinners, and, in exchange for penance, confession, and good works, invents new notions of prayer, a new sense of strength in the Holy Spirit (the secret operation of the Spirit again in still another manifestation) and the firm operation of the sense of election in the justified. The rejection of good works as efficacious, of the non-elect and non-justified as capable of salvation, and of the possibility that God might not be limited to the one clear method of salvation as interpreted by Luther and Calvin from the Scriptures, all seem arbitrary and even capricious to the modern mind. Though that may be the case, the "system" made profound impact upon those who believed in it over a long period of time, and our purpose is to investigate the emotional and aesthetic implications of that belief.

On original sin, Calvin concludes,

Original Sin, therefore, appears to be an hereditary pravity and corruption of our nature, diffused through all the parts of the soul, rendering us obnoxious to the Divine wrath, and producing in us those works which the Scripture calls 'works of the flesh.' (II, 1—8)

He continues that man is "so totally overwhelmed" that "no part is free from sin," and that "whatever proceeds from him is accounted sin." The fallen intellect is allowed some natural potency for worldly endeavours, but is totally devoid of supernatural attainment and potency. The will is so bound by the slavery of sin that it cannot devote itself to anything good, but rather sins voluntarily, not with reluctance or constraint. In its unredeemed state it must sin, but it sins voluntarily. Propensity of the will to any good thing can be found only in the elect. Put another way, whatever good lies in the human will, is the work of pure grace. The prospect for natural man is grim indeed, though of course for the elect there would be another prospect and process. The sanctified will, by the benefit of election and justification by faith in Christ, receives enough grace to do good in the state of regeneration and to persevere through sanctification to glory. The non-elect, including Christians not "called," those not called effectively, the heathen of all ages, and all infidels, sceptics and atheists, remain in the natural state of original sin which leads them inexorably to deserved damnation.

In pursuing the implications of original sin, and also of predestination and election to the logical conclusion of excluding the heathen and infidels, even the good among them, as well as the sceptics, atheists and Christians not properly called, Calvin parts company with the only early Christian theologian for whom he had consistent respect, Augustine. Throughout the *Institutes* Calvin attacks Roman Catholic positions and those of other reformers. On most of the theological points which separated Calvin from his adversaries to the right and left, it is fair to say that the verdict of history places Augustine on his side. But even Augustine, who accepted most of the grim consequences of original sin and predestination, glossed over by most medieval theory and practice, insisted in such extreme matters as the implications of original sin and predestination, that the justice of God must be stressed over pure power and majesty, his arbitrary will. From Calvin's standpoint it is not unjust for God to condemn the good pagans of antiquity, since any salvation by election is God's gift. Augustine and the early church, closer of course to the pagan world, stressed God's justice in placing the *Imago Dei* in all men as grounds for possible redemption, and insisted that baptism of desire did save the good pagans. The act was of the individual as well as of God. The saving of the good Jews was another matter. On this Augustine and Calvin agree that this had been part of God's plan according to his secret will. Calvin's logic is narrower than Augustine's and his view more historically Christian in a biblical sense. The Jews are the people of the book, albeit the "Old Covenant." In the question of universal salvation as a possibility, Calvin's is decidedly a potentially darker view than even the most pessimistic form of Catholicism, and for this reason would later be called the most irrational form of Christianity by enlightened religious and non-religious minds alike. But it must be stressed again that within the scheme of salvation devised by Calvin, the darker possibilities on the whole were to and did give way to the more optimistic, giving the Puritan emphasis upon "calling," the doctrine of the Spirit, and so forth. On the other side of the ledger Augustine's grim views of original sin and predestination, although sweetened by the *Imago Dei* and baptism of desire in the cases of just pagans, led to the complex series of spiritual exercises known as monasticism, an attempt to conform man to the *Imago Dei* within, of which he was unworthy. There is no point in stone-casting here. As we will see in our study of the poets and great pose writers, Calvinism functioning successfully is generally optimistic in the 16th and 17th centuries. It grew darker in the 18th and early 19th centuries, when sceptical attitudes intruded upon the religious view of the world. It is pessimistic in Cowper, Coleridge and Hawthorne, even bleaker in Byron, Dickinson and Melville, and has been called a source of the demonic in certain 20th century writers, such as O'Connor and

Faulkner. Needless to say, Calvin and his 16th and 17th century followers would not have understood the later historical twists of their doctrines in the least.

This is a way of emphasizing again the crucial distinction between Calvin's view of his system and other ways of viewing it, with the above doctrine as the prime case in point, although a similar observation might be made concerning predestination, election or justification. Calvin's doctrines, taken in isolation or given different interpretations, are susceptible of the direst consequences for the emotional, moral and aesthetic life of man. Only in a chain of reasoning which places the individual in a positive position regarding election, grace, operation of the spirit, calling, justification and glorification, are these doctrines capable of positive interpretation, leading to a state of assurance and salvation. The fact that Calvin and numerous others after him were able to assume this positive position has led to some glibness and even to flippancy in discussions of the Calvinist process of salvation. The position is asserted that with a little prodding all good Calvinists managed to find effectual calling and moved successfully along the path to glory. While there is plenty of evidence that this happened to most zealous Puritans, it is an over-simplification of Calvinist thought and the facts of history. There are three objections to the simplistic view of Calvinism, herewith presented with the evidence for a more varied "Calvinist tradition" than seems to be allowed by the *Institutes* taken as theological logic.

In the first, it will be pointed out fully in the pages which follow that the process of "glorification" was not taken glibly by the most serious Calvinists, the preachers, poets, and intellectuals, even if the process was followed through successfully. Real agonies occurred in contemplating the "sin-state" (original sin), the need for grace and the Spirit, the all important questions of election, calling, justification and vocation, and in carrying out, if successfully called, the process of sanctification in prayer, acknowledgment of sin in the justified, and perseverance against temptations and despair. The evidence is in the works of Calvinist writers, which some students of religious literature have not taken trouble to read. The second objection is that the process was not inevitable. An individual could be blocked at some stage of development in the pattern, and some were so blocked at each stage. This phenomenon gave rise to intellectual, moral and aesthetic patterns in writers that Calvin himself had not contemplated. It would be unfair to state that these blocked patterns are more interesting than the accepted one, but they are at least as interesting. Again, the evidence is in writing to be assessed later. The third objection is not directed at students of 17th century religion and literature alone or even mainly, for the mistaken assumption applies to a larger group of critics and readers. This is the point that Calvinism can be found in diffused form, that is, mixed with other intellectual traditions, from the late 17th through early 19th centuries, and that one or more of these central doctrines of Calvin had decisive influence on persons, mainly poets and writers, who would not have been able to accept Calvin fully or literally. And further, that this decisive influence can be distinguished from the merely vague sense of Calvinist influence which is felt in many writers after the mid-19th century.

The Calvinist doctrine of original sin and the fallen intellect and will of man, then, was likely to strike terror into those who could not believe in their own election and the life of grace, and anxiety in those who could. For the former, life would become insufferably bleak and even perhaps unbearable; for the latter it would be fraught with temptations and trials testing whether election, grace and justification were really present, so that the will might perform those actions minimum for salvation. Terror, anxiety, scepticism, despair, assurance and glory were to be permanent features of the Calvinist-Puritan emotional pendulum. It was the peculiar feature of Calvin's system that it led to extreme states of joy and despair and so forth. The reason lies in the logic of his general argument concerning these major doctrines. What we have seen with original sin and freedom of the will applies also to election/reprobation, predestination, justification and calling. His arguments on all of these matters have a theoretical plausibility if we grant his premises on the power of God and the authority of Scriptures. From that perspective the arguments are legalistic enough, but only from that perspective. From the viewpoint of general law, equity and universal principles, Calvin's system is not fair or logical, for it denies both the power of the human reason to frame laws sensible for the person, and the power of the human will to determine its actions. The first attitude is embodied in scholasticism (later rationalism), which Calvin regarded as impudent. The second, usually called the question of "good works," when connected with justification, calling and grace, Calvin always denied on the grounds that thereby man sets up his own accounting system concerning his merit before God. In place of these affirmations of reason and will Calvin gives us faith, the secret operation of the Spirit, the search for signs, and the scrutiny of emotions and imagination in intense introspection. In short, a drastic reordering of priorities and a religious revolution which was bound to affect the sensibility and literary temperament of its followers. Radical Calvinism had only limited influence in Protestantism. The engrafted legacies of centuries of rationalism and tribalism were cast from the Judeo-Christian message for a brief period, only to reappear in the 17th century in the newer forms of scientism in the rational sphere and Arminianism in the theological, latter-day versions of the belief in rationalism and good works.

Calvin's thinking in general on the doctrines of predestination, election, calling and justification may be presented together for our purposes, since the principle involved and the emotional and imaginative effects follow closely the outline above. In each he argues from the power and majesty of God, the justness of his arbitrary power, and from his interpretation of passages in Scripture. His theoretical reasoning is always consistent with the premises, but such is not always the case with the use of Scripture. Of course scripture-juggling was a vice of both Protestant and Catholic divines in the Reformation period; Calvin is not guilty of the usual vices and dishonesties, but he is a victim of an inconsistency that was almost fatal to his system. Arguing as a New Testament evangelical reformer, Calvin should always have viewed the Old Testament from that perspective, that is, from the viewpoint of the atonement achieved and salvation possible in the life and death of Christ. In his arguments for justification by faith, and in his ordinances for the Christian life he achieves this perspective, making light of "good works," the commands of the Old Law, and other seeming commands of God countermanded by the New (III, 11–18). In his doctrines of predestination, election and effectual calling he departs from this standard, perhaps fatally. Though he acknowledges that such are speculative matters, and as such should be viewed only within the active scheme of Christian salvation, he departs from the spirit of the more evangelical parts of the *Institutes* to digress upon the mysteries of election, double predestination and reprobation (III, 21–25). It was consistent with his view of the power and majesty of God to do so, but not with the wisdom of a Christian preacher. The effect of his discussions of such abstract and speculative issues was to thrust the attention of the would-be believer, the person interested in his salvation, from the

Christian operational scheme of grace-justification-salvation, to direct contemplation of the mysterious will of an arbitrary God. Within his own scheme, Calvin's positions can be followed, since those who receive the necessary grace for justifying faith in Christ are the elect, and vice versa. But it is a major difference, having awesome emotional and imaginative, as well as intellectual, consequences whether one contemplates this process as a believing Christian or sees oneself in relation to it as an abstract speculator, Bible in hand without other guide. It is therefore acceptable to say, as scholars do, that some of Calvin's doctrine is oriented toward the Old Testament God of wrath and arbitrary power, from which arises a religious scheme based upon terror. Without the Jewish idea of the Covenant of the Chosen, such terror must be the lot of the would-be believer contemplating the possibilities of election, reprobation and effectual calling, and searching for "signs" of election in his own life and the world around him. Later a New Covenant would be provided by Puritan divines to relieve this terror, but for the individualist, or unusually sensitive person, a Smart, Cowper, Coleridge, Dickinson, Melville, it was always present. In fact, through these Calvinist doctrines of election, effectual calling and reprobation Calvinism survived the specifically Christian setting of Calvin's system, an inevitability that would have puzzled the founder.

In his consideration of election, calling and justification, then, John Calvin, though a Christian minister of the gospel, reminds his readers constantly that only the elect will be called and saved, that the elect are such by the mercy of God, since in his justice, by virtue of the fall of man and the effects of original sin, all deserve damnation. Where all deserve damnation it is foolish to talk of good works, merit, natural goodness, human virtue and intellect, and Calvin is consistent in thrusting aside and exposing all arguments and viewpoints based explicitly or implicitly on such views of human nature as the basis of the relationship of man to God. Though he speaks of grace, the operation of the Spirit, or faith in man's justification by means of the imputed righteousness of Christ, the terminology of his message as Christian preacher, what he really means, if forced to speak abstractly and in strict logic, is that God is arbitrarily merciful to a few sinners who deserve damnation, and allows the rest to receive their just reward. When pressed for a method to discern the presence of this arbitrary mercy, Calvin speaks with Luther of justifying faith by imputed righteousness of Christ, and in his own voice of effectual calling and signs of election (thus giving Calvinism both a God-centered consciousness and a Christ-centered consciousness, a marked distinction from the Christocentricity of Catholicism, Lutheranism and Anglicanism), but at bottom he must acknowledge that he is dealing with arbitrary mystery. It was this peculiarity of Calvinist-Puritanism, which left its stamp upon generations of men, poets and writers among them, that it dared to face this stark mystery directly, although it also often chose the method of the mediating Christian message and Church to assuage or cover it.

Predestination is the fundamental position at the heart of Calvin's system. By that he intends that God not only knows every man's destiny (which the Catholic tradition and scholasticism accepted), but also wills it, and that this will is just because it is the will of God. Election and reprobation follow from predestination. Calvin states that denials or equivocations on these matters are the contemptible sophistries of the schools. Such thinking had the good intention of saving the idea of the justice of God before the eyes of men, an intention that Calvin thought unnecessary and held in contempt. It is man who must accept God's will, not the other way around. In very abstract terms, Augustine and many medieval traditionalists actually accepted Calvin's view, but in practical terms imposed a softer more humanistic view in order to avoid the practical effects of the harsher one, which often were disastrous. Scope had to be given in any scheme geared for the commonalty of mankind to man's powers of will, and his ability to do good and to receive merit as his reward. Calvin's scheme denies such scope in its doctrines of justification by faith, freedom of the will, election and effectual calling. Though the first, which imputes justification to man by the formal cause of Christ's sacrifice and atonement, derives from Luther, while the others are of Calvin's own devising, a common thread of man's helplessness and worthlessness runs through them. To have the faith necessary for justification, one must have been given grace, for the faith cannot be merited as an act of man. To know that one is called, and is therefore of the elect, one must experience the secret operation of the Spirit, for no mere exercise of intellect or will can bring about assurance of calling or election. Thus in regard to the general doctrines it is the operation of the Spirit, and in regard to the Christian doctrines the free grace of God, about which the Calvinist believer must be attentive. Calvin did not foresee many of the psychological consequences of these positions. Since man is merely human, his human intellect and will were to become bound up with the operation of the Spirit in "evidences of election," "signs of religious affections," the operations of "grace," and so forth. The proper path outlined by Calvin from despair over sin through assurance to glory might be followed by the Red Cross Knight and Bunyan's Pilgrim. A too easy path to assurance avoiding the terrors of sin, reprobation and unworthiness was to be taken by many of the political and social Puritans in the 17th century. Worse still, except perhaps for literature and the varied sensibility it engenders, many Puritans would later ignore Calvin's warning not to contemplate election and calling apart from the Christian hope in justification by faith, and these were to give us the Calvinist-Puritan tradition of despair, irony and an almost modern view of human helplessness and meaninglessness. One outstanding fact is clear from all this. Whatever Calvin himself would have approved or denied, and in spite of the glib commentary in literary circles that Calvinism was detrimental to complex experience because it launched the believer too easily on the road to assurance and glory, Calvin's system gave rise to a complex and original viewpoint of man towards himself, one that was decisive in its influence upon many areas of life in the western world for several hundred years.

The Calvinist positions were, in fact, so other-worldly in their pure form that corruption was inevitable among the common lot of men, as Augustinianism, monasticism and Jansenism were corrupted in their turn by contact with the world. The basic doctrine of the majesty of God was one that all the religious-minded must accept but few could live with consistently. The saying arose in Germany that all good men should live as Catholics (free will, merit for good life) and die as Lutherans (imputed righteousness, acknowledgement of sinfulness in all and the power of God). In short, having it both ways, or recognizing the just insights in both systems on justification, merit, grace and good works. Coleridge in the early 19th century viewed "high Calvinism" as a sheep in wolf's clothing and extreme "free will" Arminianism as the real hidden wolf. If one seriously considers moving the idea of merit and good works from the counting house and the world to the soul and the conscience, there is much truth in this insight of Coleridge. Calvin's insight about the basic relationship of man to God cannot be regarded lightly by believers of any persuasion, though on the other hand his sweeping rejection of the scope of the human function in the economy of grace is a view that few can fully hold. Even in accepting his admonition to view election and calling solely within the confines of the Christian faith, many sincere believers were likely to fall into trouble, as the subsequent history of Calvinism proved. Though concentration upon the doctrine of justifying faith was likely to lead to proper assurance and sanctification, the problems inherent in calling and election were likely to lead in more dangerous directions. Calvin was aware of the dangers in calling and election, and warned against many circumstances, particularly the intrusion of human merit and intellectual speculation into the process of determining calling. He asserts that calling should not require unusual or impious speculation, but as usual, his interest is in preserving the glory and power of God at the risk of placing a terrible burden upon man.

This internal call therefore is a pledge of salvation, which cannot possibly deceive. . . . Here two errors are to be avoided. For some suppose man to be a co-operator with God, so that the validity of election depends on his consent; thus according to them the will of man is superior to the counsel of God. . . . Others . . . suspend election on that which is subsequent to it; as though it were doubtful and ineffectual until it is confirmed by faith. That this is its confirmation to us, is very clear; that it is the manifestation of God's secret counsel, before concealed, we have already seen . . . ratified with a seal. For what can be more absurd and inconsistent, when the Scripture teaches that we are illuminated according as God has chosen us, than our eyes being so dazzled with the blaze of this light as to refuse to contemplate election? At the same time I admit that, in order to attain an assurance of our salvation, we ought to begin with the Word. . . . (III, 20)

We see in this passage a movement back and forth between direct contemplation of the mysteries of election and calling, and the safer acceptance of manifestation of calling in justification by faith in Christ. Calvin *must* give the theoretical power of God its due, yet admonishes as to the dangers of vain and idle speculation apart from faith.

As it is erroneous, therefore, to suspend the efficacy of election upon the faith of the gospel, by which we discover our interest in election; so we shall observe the best order, if, in seeking an assurance of our election, we confine our attention to those subsequent signs which are certain attestations of it. . . . I call it seeking in a wrong way, when miserable man endeavours to force his way into the secret recesses of Divine Wisdom, and to penetrate even to the highest eternity, that he may discover what is determined concerning him at the tribunal of God . . . then he sinks himself in an abyss of total darkness. For it is right that the folly of the human mind should be thus punished with horrible destruction, when it attempts by its own ability to rise to the summit of Divine Wisdom. (III, 20)

Calvin is hereby opening the way for the most interesting ambiguities and an unexpected open-endedness in his system, for though this system prescribes rules and principles in the clearest possible order, it cannot prescribe method, that is, the exact experience of the would-be believer in relation to these rules and principles. It is true that later in the system there is an elaborate doctrine of the Church including method of worship, of reception of the two sacraments, of preaching, hymn singing, and so on. This emphasis on the community of believers in the Church was designed, and quite rightly, to occupy the religious life of believers and to relieve disquiet about speculative areas of their faith. However, as was said above, in the most serious areas of the intellectual and emotional life, the believer, if a person of intelligence and sensibility, was thrown back upon his own resources in seeking answers to the questions of election, calling and justification. The serious Calvinist-Puritan had to become more introspective than had the serious medieval Catholic before him. The latter, who also believed that Christ was the formal cause of justification, might yet believe in faith as an active virtue, in merit and good works, in infused righteousness, and thus could bring to the confessional a reasonable certainty that his debts and credits, if calculated honestly in conscience, were properly attributed to him on the divine scroll. It is true that Pelagianism, Arminianism and Jansenism, variations of the moderate and officially sanctioned scheme of Thomistic scholasticism, led to the consequences of *more* or *less* assurance than the scheme of Calvinism. But for the most part the mediating schemes of the Mass, penance, confession and transubstantiation of the Eucharist provided reasonable certainty for the believer who chose to believe. The mediation in Calvinism is by calling, justification and sacraments as "signs" of grace and election, and behind these signs lurked for many the abyss which Calvin at the same time encouraged and deplored.

   Calvin's response to his own dilemma of being God-election-intellect centered on the one hand and Christ-justification-emotion centered on the other is to give warning after warning to the dangers of contemplating predestination abstractly, while stubbornly clinging to belief in the necessity of the doctrine. This warning is always for the believer to turn from the abstract view of God to the Word and the life of the Church, but it is clear from Calvin's fascination with the subject that sensitive Calvinists were not likely to treat it lightly:

Therefore, if we dread shipwreck, let us anxiously beware of this rock, on which none ever strike without being destroyed. But though the discussion of predestination may be compared to a dangerous ocean, yet, in traversing over it, the navigation is safe and serene, and I will also add pleasant, unless any one freely wishes to expose himself to danger. For as those who, in order to gain an assurance of their election, examine into the eternal counsel of God without the word, plunge themselves into a fatal abyss, so they who investigate it in a regular and orderly manner, as it is contained in the word, derive from such inquiry the benefit of peculiar consolation. . . . Hence we conclude, that they are beyond all danger of falling away, because the intercession of the Son of God for their perseverance in piety has not been rejected. What did Christ intend we should learn from this, but confidence in our perpetual security, since we have once been introduced into the number of his people. (III, 24, 4)

The cleavage here is striking as to the consequences of the alternate paths. On the one hand, shipwreck, anxiety, dangerous ocean, fatal abyss; on the other, ocean, safe, serene, pleasant, assurance, consolation, perpetual security. Because of Calvin's stubbornness and tough-mindedness his followers were deprived of the possibility of stressing only the Christ-centered doctrine of justification, as did the later Methodists and Evangelicals in the 18th and 19th centuries. For although Calvin acknowleged, as any Christian must, the great emotional pull of belief and faith in Christ,

If we seek salvation, life, and the immortality of the heavenly kingdom, recourse must be had to no other; for [Christ] alone is the Fountain of life, the Anchor of salvation, and the Heir of the kingdom of heaven. . . . The persons therefore, whom God hath adopted as his children, he is said to have chosen, not in themselves, but in Christ. . . . But if we are chosen in him, we shall find no asssurance of our election in ourselves; nor even in God the Father, considered alone, abstractedly from the Son. Christ, therefore, is the mirror, in which it behoves us to contemplate our election, and here we may do it with safety. (III, 24, 5)

he is always finally forced to admit that man cannot by any emotional means or faith limit the nature of the inscrutable God.

"O man, who art thou that repliest against God?" For, as Augustine justly contends, it is acting a most perverse part, to set up the measure of human justice as the standard by which to measure the justice of God. (III, 24, 22)

Examples of this dilemma in Calvin's thinking could be multiplied by looking further in his chapters on election, calling and justification. In the latter (III, 11–14) where the emphasis is necessarily on the positive side, stressing justification by faith through the imputed righteousness of Christ, his method of argument is the reverse of that on election and calling. Most of the argument is given to stress on faith over works, the Spirit over the Law, and assurance over despair, and to the questions of immediate concern to the Christian believer. There is, from time to time nevertheless, clear acknowledgement of the theoretical precedence of election over justification:

No man, therefore, is properly founded on Christ, but he who has complete righteousness in him; since the apostle says, that he was sent, not to assist us in the attainment of righteousness, but to be himself our righteousness. That is to say, that we were chosen in him from eternity before the formation of the world, not on account of any merit of ours, but according to the purpose of the Divine will. . . . (III, 15)

How one achieved and maintained assurance, looking forward to calling, justification, sanctification and glorification while feeling at one's back the anxieties of election, the sin-state of original sin, and reprobation is a nice question, on which the system and history of Calvinism turns. Calvinism, like all great intellectual systems, was Janus-faced in the creation of its own dilemmas. The Calvinist-Puritan thought about and felt these dilemmas in what he considered to be the center of his being, that is, his conscience.

III. The Primacy of Conscience

[Conscience] may bee taken for a kinde of actuall knowledge in the minde of man: but to speake properly, this knowledge must proceede of a power in the soule, the propertie whereof is to take the principles and conclusions of the minde and apply them, and by applying either to accuse or excuse. This is the ground of all, and this I take to be conscience.

Perkins, *A Discourse of Conscience*[7]
2nd ed. Cambridge, 1608

In turning from consideration of the abstract doctrines of Calvinism as a system and theological force to consideration of the actual practice of the English Puritans, attention must be given to the primacy of the conscience in the Puritan tradition. Without attention to this point any study of the Puritan tradition would easily become a venture in the history of ideas and the fruitless effort that implies. In its range of ideas Puritan Calvinism is indebted to medieval scholasticism, to the other Protestant reformers, to the Renaissance, and later, to certain Enlightenment trends. Once can easily get lost in dealing with a great mass of ideas on the same subject seen from various points of view. Multiplying or refining analogies between the Calvinist doctrine of this and that and the Anglican or Catholic might easily lead us to believe that Puritanism as such did not exist. Certain studies of Renaissance ideas in relation to the Middle Ages have fallen into such embarrassment. On the other hand, one cannot merely rely upon history as the measure of the nature and existence of a tradition, for this easily leads to circular argument. It has also led, in the studies of Miller and Haller, to an exaggeration of Puritan uniqueness by taking up Puritan writers in the abstract and in a vacuum. Of this problem there will be more a little further on.

In order to be able to say that a tradition exists analytically, apart from history or reliance upon the works of other writers, it must be shown that a body of writing, and a group of men, existed at a given time and place with a qualifying difference in viewpoint about an entire set of ideas, even if all the ideas themselves existed in the same or almost the same form previously. Puritanism is such a set of ideas or tradition, historically and analytically. Analysis reveals both a startling similarity between the ideas of the Puritans and those of medieval scholasticism and other forms of Protestantism, and an important difference, or qualifying factor. This difference is the Puritan's proclivity to view conscience as primary in human activity, and to subsume all other forms of activity into that of the conscience. Previously existing ideas are thus given a new cast, and many later ones are successfully assimilated into the "system." This is the tradition which converted Calvin's abstract system from a purely logical theory into a living force for three centuries.

The primacy of conscience in the Puritan tradition can be demonstrated in both theoretical and practical ways. The practical, which will follow shortly, appeals to the experience and writings of the great Puritan preachers and theologians of the Cambridge period. The theoretical assumes for the moment that this work is known and has been analysed for its dominant theme. In the interest of clarity this dominant theme will be presented here.

The Puritan view of the conscience is best understood in relation to the medieval scholastic background. The contrast is wide enough to allow the clarity of difference to appear, yet the scholastic tradition is wide enough in its scope to provide the proper background of Puritanism. Briefly, the scholastic tradition had defined rather completely, for religious and moral purposes, the various uses of intellect, will, emotions, conscience, and consciousness. Each faculty is given its sphere, with intellect most important in the gaining of knowledge and truth, will and conscience in determining actions and the state of sin. Emotions were indifferent qualities, and lowest on the scale. They were suspect as the source of concupiscence unless disciplined by the intellect and the will. The great complications of scholastic faculty philosophy cannot be gone into here, except to say that they allowed generously for the complexities of man's mind and nature, yet insisted ultimately upon the primacy of the will as the arbiter of sin. The moral system based upon this philosophy and psychology was a generous and general one, framed for all men and allowing for the frailty of human nature. Within the scholastic moral system, not contradicting it but directing the choices of man much more closely was the counsel of the saints, in the writings of Hilton, a Kempis, the great mystics. In their views the direction of the intellect and the discipline of the emotions by the will and conscience assumed greater importance, leading at times to a good end, saintliness, and at others to a bad one, "angelism." Scholasticism allowed the saints to flourish as long as they did not disturb any cardinal principle, such as original sin or the disposition of the intellect to attain theoretical truth. Such disturbances occurred throughout the Middle Ages, and were usually successfully put down by reason or/and authority.

The English Calvinist-Puritan tradition historically is the child of one of the many medieval revolts against the scholastic doctrine of reasonableness and of coming to terms with the world. Everyone knows that Huss and Wycliffe, the crypto-reformers, contained in their doctrines the seeds of the Puritan and Protestant revolt. Following these men, the 16th and 17th century Puritans referred all ideas and doctrines to the aegis of the conscience, and further insisted that all men must follow the new moral path in order to be saved. Hence the most important terms in Puritanism are the conscience and "the saints." The latter has been much abused in English literature, from the time of Chaucer on.

If the function of conscience as the guide of the moral will was made supreme by the Puritans, it followed that the true and the beautiful were subordinated to the good, and were not to be followed for their own sakes. Yet the true and the beautiful were not ignored, for it was often necessary to ascertain whether something was true or beautiful in relation to the good. Intellect was kept busy here, searching out the true from the false in matters of truth and morality. The purely useful functions of the true, like the theoretical, were seldom given much individual emphasis, since the Bible existed as a guide as to what was true. Even more so was this the case with the beautiful − the aesthetic interest in art, nature and beauty in general. To the extent that the beautiful or the speculative might be moralized, it was received into the Puritan conscience and became its art. Otherwise, as the famous cases of Zwingli on the intellectual level and stained glass on the aesthetic indicate, the instinct of the intellect and the aesthetic could be ruthlessly surpressed. The Puritan imagination, in so far as it existed independently, was a moral imagination.

Will and conscience were the most important functions of the whole man. As regards the former, the major scholastic function of the will as regulator of the actions of man in the direction of the good was accented completely. A moral life must be a life of practically good actions. But the more important theoretical function of the will in scholasticism, as the arbiter of sin, was turned over by the Puritans to the conscience in general. Sin was no longer technically "in the will," but in the whole being functioning as conscience. The formerly indifferent passions and emotions (indifferent as regards good or evil before an act of will) became also functions of the Puritan conscience. In other words, the emotions and passions must be purified in themselves, just as the intellect must be disciplined to think along religious lines. Consciousness itself, apart from conscience, had no separate existence for the Puritan, since the sense of conscience became in fact the workings of the passions, intellect and will together upon matters of morality and of faith. Here was the real secret of the Puritan revolution, the unique contribution to the history of man's life on earth. The Puritan was no more likely to be interested in an abstract point for itself — the binomial theorem, for instance — than he was in the purely aesthetic beauty of an apple. Yet mathematics and the beauty of an apple were desperately important for him insofar as they were moral questions or touched upon questions of conscience. They were thus subject to the allegorical and moral treatment given to all areas of experience by the Puritans. In the Calvinist-Puritan system old ideas and new experiences found their place under the aegis of the conscience. Only those ideas and experiences extremely repellent to the moral and intellectual life of the Puritan's conscience were rejected completely. If stage-drama and certain liberal scientific ideas were rejected, at the same time music, poetry on serious subjects, and a good deal of psychology and philosophy of the day were easily assimilated to the Puritan view of life.

Conscience, then, was both the theatre and the final arbiter of the Puritan drama. Within this theatre there were many moods and forms, some prescribed, others more spontaneous. The prescribed were the famous and well-known stages in the path of salvation — sin-consciousness, election, justification, sanctification, glorification, about which more soon. These strictly religious moods and stages colored all the other or freer aspects of the Puritan's life, but the others had their own areas of hegemony. Most important were eucharistic worship, prayer, the active vocation in life, and meditation. These often appeared in mixed forms, and thus certain of the arts, especially music, diary-keeping, and the reading and writing of literature found their place in the life of the godly. Here was the

Puritan's excuse for art, a moralizing art to be sure, which could absorb much, but by no means all, of the spheres of common life to the hegemony of morality in conscience. The Calvinist-Puritan supposedly lived "out of" the world, but managed to adopt much of the world to his standards. Indeed, his purpose was to reform the world at large, for which much of the world has not forgiven him his pains.

It follows, then, that certain important ideas of the medieval-scholastic tradition appear in Calvinist-Puritanism in a new form. Puritanism rejected the scholastic codification of a general morality for all men which allowed a good deal for the laxity of human nature and for man's interests other than in the purely moral or religious. On the other side it also rejected the minority view of the Middle Ages, that certain individuals should secede from the world to attain a greater perfection of morality and feeling than the world at large could attain. The Puritan way was new in being a middle way, having elements of the saintly and mystical traditions (the discipline of intellect and emotions) and of the scholastic-worldly (laboring in one's vocation in the world). Its tone and moral standard is much more religious than that of the medieval world at large, and more religious than the norm of the successor religions of the Reformation period (a point not hard to prove, for on it rests the reason for religious wars and emigrations). Yet it is much less purely ascetic and narrow in its religious interests than the high strain of asceticism in medieval Catholicism or its counterparts today. Its devotion is *in* the world, and the major originality of the Puritans could be said to be the reformation of the conscience along the lines given above to make of it an instrument for the sanctification of every individual in the world. The heights of earlier sainthood, and the depths of the common spirit, are equally avoided. All are called, and theoretically capable of performing their duties on the road to sainthood. We are interested for our purposes here mainly in what the Puritans did with that worldly device, literature, and with what softening effects literature had upon the Puritans.

In presenting the characteristic moods and doctrines of the Calvinist temper in the 17th century out of the writings of preachers and theologians, one great error of many previous studies can perhaps be avoided if we understand the function of conscience in the Puritan's life. Writers have often claimed too much, or too little, for the originality of Puritan thought. This has been the case for two reasons. A really careful sifting of Puritan ideas in relation to medieval scholasticism has not been made, and what little has been done is not widely known by historians and critics. In the few cases where certain ideas have been viewed in a comparative way, or in relation to a permanent theological problem, Puritan originality has often been quickly diminished by the history of ideas pattern. To give some examples, Haller in *The Rise of Puritanism* writes at times as if no ideas or images of the Calvinist-Puritan tradition had existed before the Puritan movement. Wakefield, in his *Puritan Devotion*, by excessive quotation of Bishop Bayly's *Practice of Pietie*, a dubious source of Puritan devotion, tends to blur the distinction between the purely Puritan and other strands of 16th century piety. Martz and Ross, in ways practical and theoretical respectively, make excessive claims for the influence of Counter Reformation theory and devotion in 17th century England, to the diminishment of the influence of Puritan originality.[8] One must steer a careful course here, and the way to do so is knowing the value of sources and influences.

Yet the relationship of Calvin to his primary sources, medieval Thomism and Augustinianism, is clearly known, and available to those who take the trouble to seek out the proper sources. Few literary critics have taken this trouble. The situation concerning the sources of the Puritan imagination is more troubled, since the two best writers on the subject, Haller and Miller, tend to assume originality of ideas in what they have found in reading the 17th century material, not originality of purpose. Their expert shaping of this material has created a powerful "myth of Puritan origins" which is the starting point of literary (and indeed other) study of the Puritan situation. This impasse might have been already corrected if scholars in medieval philosophy and thinking had taken an interest in Puritan thought, which they largely have not done. Dom David Knowles, the great expert on medieval philosophy and theology in England, once stated privately that there was no influence of the medieval Catholic period upon the Puritans. These are areas of study, in England and America, in which feeling is still partisan on both sides, and has led unfortunately to lack of knowledge by one side of the other.

Since our concern is not primarily with Puritan origins or with medieval sources as such, there is space for only one important example here of the relationship between Puritanism and the medieval tradition, that between Haller's *Rise of Puritanism* and a fairly well-known book, Walter Hilton's *The Scale of Perfection*. Haller was perhaps the first to point out the recurring motif − initiation, election, justification, sanctification, glorification − in Puritan practical writing, upon which this and other studies lean heavily in describing the Puritan imagination in greater detail. He does not mention specific sources for this in medieval ascetic writings. Other writers hint that sources of Puritan imaginative patterns may be found in medieval mysticism, especially of the lower variety, but do little to support the point. A cursory reading of medieval mysticism suggests to this writer that a case can be made for the general appropriation of certain medieval ideas and images by the Puritans for their own purposes. What in mysticism is confined to a method or activity of the few, in the Puritan scheme becomes a general program for all the saints. There is therefore a difference of levels and of intentions. But in outline the medieval *via* of perfection is strikingly similar to that of the process of sainthood described by 17th century Puritan writers. Some differences toward theology and in personal viewpoint are acute, yet the common source of some of the abiding images of mysticism and of Puritanism in Scripture, especially St. Paul in, above all, Romans, and of an intention we at least in the 20th century would regard as similar, provide startling similarities. In Hilton's *The Scale of Perfection*, for instance, appears a passage which has both the journey image and the idea of movement from initiation through glorification.

And in what manner this is done, St. Paul rehearses thus: Quos Deus praescivat, &&. . . . Those whom God foreknew should be made conformable to the Image of His Son, those He called; and whom He called those He justified; and whom He justified those He glorified. Though these words may be understood of all chosen souls in the lowest degree of charity [the Puritans do not recognize this distinction: all saints are called to the same end] who are reformed only in faith; nevertheless they may be understood more especially of those souls that are reformed in feeling, to whom our Lord showeth great plenty of grace, and is much more busy about them for they are in a special manner His own children who have the full shape and the likeness of His Son Jesus.[9]

The primacy given to feeling over will and intellect in reformation or calling in Hilton's writings is common in the loose mysticism of the Middle Ages, that of Eckhart, etc. Scholastic doctrine placed such primacy in the will, next the intellect, with feeling or emotions lowest on the scale. Post-Reformation Trentine doctrine made the primacy of will and intellect severe dogmatic matters, under the pressure of heresy. The Puritan tradition on this point seems to have its source mainly in the medieval tradition of the ascetic strain. Yet it would be unwise and false to leap to a conclusion of excessive medieval influence (balancing perhaps the *sui generis* notions of Haller and Miller) without taking note of the fact mentioned above, that the body of medieval ascetic ideas was transformed in Puritanism by virtue of its doctrine of the primacy of the conscience. So transformed, these ideas become the vehicle of a sensibility which is both religious and worldly in expression and temperament.

No examination of the Puritan conscience and of the relationship of Puritanism to the Catholic past would be complete without mention of St. Augustine. There will be occasion later, in the section on Milton, to consider some specific influences of Augustinian sensibility in *Paradise Lost*; here the remarks can be general. The most direct influence upon Puritan writers comes from the importance of St. Augustine's thought to Calvin's theology. Calvin mentions Augustine often, and it is widely accepted that Calvin's doctrines of original sin and of election are heavily influenced by Augustine. Such obvious connections are less important for the development of Puritan literature than are the influences of Augustine upon Puritan sensibility. In part the Puritan emphasis upon the inner life and upon the primacy of conscience shows the influence of Augustine.

If the *City of God* influenced Calvinist theology, it was the *Confessions* that influenced the sensibility. This might seem strange at first, the *Confessions* being such a highly Catholic work in religious history, but the reason is not hard to find. The *Confessions* is written in the form of an individualistic discovery of the religious life; there are both moral and theological problems to be overcome by the searching soul. Augustine's search, unlike that of numerous medieval followers, is not done within the clear framework of the ritual and dogma of the Church, although the Church was his goal. The Puritan writers appreciated this point. Although they are notorious in their sermons for avoiding most classical and hagiographic reference, preferring the words of Holy Scripture above all else, Augustine is one of the few notable exceptions to this rule. Augustine's concept of the inner life of the memory (which the Puritans called conscience), and the use of this as a moral and religious force, was congenial to the Puritan temperament. A few illustrations from both sources will serve to make this clear.

Augustinian inwardness and individualism in religious quest are expressed unconsciously everywhere in his writings; perhaps this quotation from *De Magistro* expresses as succinctly as possible the appeal of Augustine for the Puritan view of life as a trial of the inner life and conscience:

> Our real Teacher is he who is so listened to, who is said to dwell in the inner man, namely Christ, that is, the unchangeable power and eternal wisdom of God. . . . [W]hen we have to do with things which we behold with the mind, that is, with the intelligence and with reason, we speak of things which we look upon directly in the inner light of truth which illumines the inner man and is inwardly enjoyed.[10]

Augustine's most famous exposition of this inner life is in *Confessions* X, viii–xxvi, his sections on the memory. It is not hard to show that what Augustine calls memory in these sections the Puritans later called conscience. Neither term, of course, is being used in its ordinary restrictive meaning; both terms are widened to represent the stage of the inner life where God is to be found. We have noticed the Puritans on this, and will again shortly in specific cases. Augustine answers the question in sections xxiii–xxvi, which state that man finds God through meditation on remembrances, that in a sense the memory containeth God. In later sections of Book X he goes on to discuss Christ and other Christian mysteries as following from this acknowledgement of the indwelling of God in the memory. There are other ways of knowing God in Augustine, of course, but this intensely personal and individual way of the time of his conversion was likely to appeal to the Puritans more fully than might the rationalistic proofs which were taken up by the scholastics in the Middle Ages. The intimacy and intensity of the inner life in memory mirrored in *Confessions*[11] become the trial or struggle of conscience of the Cambridge Puritans. Augustine's statement (X, xxv), "But why seek I now in what particular place of my memory thou dwellest, as if there were any places at all in it? Sure I am, that in it thou dwellest: even for this reason, that I have preserved the memory of thee since the time that I first learnt thee: and for that I find in it, whensoever I call thee to remembrance," is present in one way or another to most Puritan writers, with the name "memory" changed often to "conscience." Shy though they were of such practice, some Puritan writers even quote Augustine directly and with acknowledgement, although acknowledgement of a Catholic source went against the grain of 17th century polemical practice. Augustine's famous lines in X, viii, "*ibi mihi et ipse occurro, meque recolo, quid, quando et ubi egerim queque modo, cum agerem, affectus fuerim,*" are quoted directly by John Preston in his Sermons. The notion of the self meeting with the self in the inner mind or conscience and in the presence of God was congenial to the Puritans. The Calvinist-Puritan tradition found the general, inward-looking method of meditation in *Confessions* suitable to its own mood. It is not surprising that the Calvinist-Puritans accepted some, but by no means all or unalloyed, of Augustine's theology and moral outlook.

The moral outlook of Augustine could at times be very gloomy, as in the famous passage in the last book of *City of God* on man's life in this world. This point will be taken up again in our section on Milton's *Paradise Lost*, Books XI−XII. The striking theological similarities of Augustine and Calvin have been mentioned and are widely known. In areas of personal taste and aesthetics, lesser matters to be sure, the similarity persists. Augustine's meditations on memory, just as the Puritan's on conscience, lead inevitably in Book X of *Confessions* to moral matters, and we get this on the pleasure of hearing (xxxiii):

Again at another time, through an indiscreet weariness of being inveigled, do I err out of too precise a severity: yea, very fierce am I sometimes, in the desire of having the melody of all pleasant music, to which David's Psalter is so often sung, banished both from mine own ears; and out of the whole church too. . . .

This view was later to be echoed by Calvin in the *Institutes*. This problem of legitimate pleasure, of what may and may not be allowed, of what is good for the service of God in the world and what dangerous, was familiar to every Puritan preacher and writer. Marvell was to write one of his most interesting religious poems, "Resolved Soul and Created Pleasure," on this very subject of music which agitated Augustine. It is no wonder that the Puritans found in that saint of the pre-scholastic period and pre-medieval conformity to outward rule of the Church a prototype of much of their own experience. In X, xxii and xxiii Augustine sums up the meaning of the journey, the conscience, and the turning inward in a manner to which the Puritans later were to have no objection:

For there is a joy which is not granted unto the ungodly (but unto those only which love thee for thine own sake), whose joy thyself art. And this is the happy life, to rejoice concerning thee unto thee, and for thy sake: this is the happy life, and there is no other. . . . For a happy life is a rejoicing in the truth: for this is a joying in thee, who are the Truth, O God my Light, the Health of my countenance, and my God. This is the blessed life that all desire; this life which is only blessed, do all desire; to joy in the truth, is all men's desire. . . . For there is a dim glimmering of light unput-out in man: let them walk let them walk, that the darkness overtake them not.

Puritan preachers, writers and common saints spent their lives looking for this joy, and struggling against the powers of that darkness in the area of the conscience.

IV. The Central Drama and Its Implications for Art

It is the purpose of this section to show the development of Calvinism in its English phase, from about 1570 to 1660, especially in relation to the central drama of election and salvation. The important byways connected with the doctrines of depravity and election will be taken up in brief, but extensive development of these points will be left to the more proper place, their connection with the specific Calvinist peculiarities of Cowper, Dickinson, others. It is a definite fact that the pecularities and aberrations can be found and documented from the earliest period of Calvinism on, as we will do in the following pages, yet it is equally true that in the great period, 1570–1660, these pecularities were not primarily important for either the religious life or the sensibility of Calvinist writers. What *is* more important to show in this section is the inner life, the emotional possibilities and flexibility of appeal of the central doctrines as they are taken up, expounded and lived in the works of the most important theologians and preachers of the period, the men whose works would be known to Spenser, Taylor, Milton, Marvell. Included for illustration here are the writings of William Ames, Lewis Bayly, Richard Baxter, John Dodd, William Perkins, John Preston, and Richard Sibbes. The order followed shall be that of doctrines, not of writers and works. The chronology of the latter will be looked after in the notes.[12]

It may not be amiss to point out in a general and abstract way some of the qualities of spirit and feeling which the great doctrines elicit from these writers. Then it will be easy enough to fill in the details and to give illustrations, some remarkable for their warmth and power, from the best of the Puritan writers.

The leading doctrine of the power and majesty of God is not, as a matter of fact, one of the most productive of religious and artistic sensibility. This makes some sense. The awe, the respectful Hebraic negation of the name of God, is strong in Calvinism. But if the idea of God is approached indirectly there are positive results. Puritans contemplated the divine purpose in history and providence, they thought about the divine attributes in their relation to the world, they allowed in prayer an almost direct petition and talking with God, expressed commonly in the words "Abba father," an intimacy associated only with Christ or the saints in Catholic worship. They looked upon nature as the work of God and read his will and purpose in every nuance of the natural order. This gives to their reading of nature the well-known allegorical turn influential in Puritan literature.[13] All in all, although man's role in relation to the all-powerful God was supposed to be one of abject submission to his will and largely negative, the Calvinist, when he was not thinking exclusively about this point, managed to convey the majesty and power of God in symbolic and literary forms both intimate and artistic. Milton's is the only attempt to confront this God of power directly, with mixed results, as literary history tells us. We will pick up this point later. Whatever the case with Milton, other writers in prose and poetry were able to make a good deal of the intimate dialectic of Calvinist prayer, of the allegorical readings of nature, and of its symbolic reading of the divine purpose in every human action and thought. Artistic development here finds its fullest expression in Hawthorne and Melville, just at the end of the Calvinist era in America.[14]

The Calvinist doctrine of original sin and depravity is close to the center of Calvinist feeling and outlook. The logical source of the doctrine is clear enough in Calvin himself, and is followed carefully by the English Calvinist theologians. In a way the doctrine is the logical obverse side of the idea of the power and sovereignty of God, and this is how it was felt emotionally by the believer. In strict logic the doctrine of total depravity is an extension to its limits of Augustine's view of man's fall: Adam's fall was total into the state of sin. His will and intellect were totally corrupt. After the fall man is nothing, God is everything, which is fitting in relation to the doctrine of the power and sovereignty of God. The redemption of man by Christ does not wipe out the stain of sin or totally reinstate the will and intellect of man. Neither does it in Aquinas or general Catholic theology, of course. But the Calvinist metaphor of clothing or covering with the righteousness of Christ has a different meaning than the Catholic image of wiping away a stain. In Calvinist terms, the affront to God is irremediable, the power of Christ performs only a limited remedy. The role of the mediator is more decisive, especially in practice, in Lutheran, Anglican and Catholic theology.

In other words there is a haunting sense of depravity, called sin-consciousness by later theologians, in the conscience of the Calvinist. This may be, indeed the theologians insist it should be, an over-whelming sense of sin and depravity at first. A state of anxiety is the first motion in the Calvinist process of redemption. This anxiety or sin-consciousness is not to be confused with the post-baptismal cata-loguing of actual sins by the conscience common to Catholicism or high Anglicanism, sins to be itemized specifically in a confessional. The total state of sin-consciousness of the Calvinist is not the product of actual sins and in theory at least is a state that the Catholic or Anglican should never know. It results from the original sense of depravity in the individual derived in turn from the original sin itself present in full force in the individual. Logically and abstractly this state is associated with election, but personally it is connected intimately with the sense of sin itself, giving to the Calvinist con-science that attitude of mistrust of the self, that almost infinitesmal kind of moral calculus and examination of motive for which the followers of Calvin are renowned in fact and fiction. From this state three moves are possible, all recorded amply in the histories of Calvinist moral dialectics. If one remains in the state of total sin-con-sciousness and depravity it is a sign of non-election and leads to moral despair, possibly suicide. We shall have occasion to mention the numerous suicides in Cambridge in the 1580's and 1590's later on. This is the state of Red Cross Knight at the end of Canto IX (Bk. I, *FQ*) in the cave of despair, and the permanent state of the later life of William Cowper. Or one can move out of this state by a process of moral calculus in the conscience to the state of justification (also known as assurance of election) and then, by the same process in reverse (called backsliding in everyday language) fall back into the sin state. This happens to the extraordinarily sensitive or self-mistrustful persons who are still well within the range of normal personality. Viewed detachedly, this dialectical movement has rich artistic possibilities, as in the poems of Emily Dickinson, or Marvell, and the prose writings of Hawthorne and Melville. I am not saying that moral ambiguity is not found in some natures, especially artistic natures, outside of Calvinism, but I do believe that this phase of Calvinism gives the largest possible sanction in its intellectual scope and tradition for such ambiguity. It is behind the coolness of Marvell in relation to the other metaphysical poets as he assesses his religious motives and feelings in "Coronet" and "Dialogue" poems. It is the decisive element in common among the New England writers of the early nineteenth century.

The doctrine of election or non-election, trying to ascertain the will of God from the human point of view or what is called technically double predestination occupied the Calvinist-Puritan mind and conscience continually. It is connected logically to the doctrine of innate depravity as its corollary: if all men deserve damnation by virtue of original sin, then if any are to be saved, it must be by the will and goodness of God, his choosing of the unmerited few or elect. Election is an element in Augustinian theology, too, so what is peculiar to Calvinism is the assertion of the small number of the elect and the introduction into Christian thinking for this reason of speculation on one's election. In other Christian dispensations baptism, a striving for sinlessness, and good works make interest in election unnecessary. From the human point of view and of simple or merely God-centered election, election need not be a problem at all. Only the Calvinist interest in double predestination encourages (although the clergy often exhorted otherwise) this second guessing or assurance from God of election. On purely intellectual or theoretical grounds alone one could never determine one's election, but considering the Calvinist sense of odds the results were bound to be depressing. On practical grounds each individual had to settle the issue as best he could in his own conscience and feelings. Categorically, then, election in practice became tied to the doctrine of original sin and of justification by faith. In the Calvinist theorizing and practical divinity of the Cambridge period, 1570–1660, these three areas were usually considered together or even confused; the acute writers at least viewed these categories as a spectrum ranging from sense of sin to problem of election to feeling of justification. If one could feel justified and victorious over the depravity of original sin, one could conclude in favor of election, in the practical if not the ultimate sense. It remained for the New Englander Jonathan Edwards, far into the next century, to sort out all the problems concerning election in his great treatise, *Religious Affections.*[15] Meanwhile, and after for that matter, the doctrines and feelings associated with election gave rise to a rich and sometimes complex body of attitudes and to a deep sense of the inner life among those who fully followed the Calvinist-Puritan tradition.

The categories in the Calvinist drama of salvation then are as follows: the power of God, the decree of election, original sin, justification or assurance, sanctification, glorification. Thus far we have considered the first three and have seen how justification or assurance can be considered as part of the sin-election problem. It is rightfully a category in itself, however, and should at least be mentioned as such. In fact, though, the category of justification is so intimately bound up with the sin-election problem, the feelings the idea of justification provokes are so closely associated with what we may call the negative side of the Calvinist drama, that there is little said in most Puritan writing about justification itself. The properly positive states, or "assurance" states as 17th century preaching called them, are sanctification and glorification. Sanctification is the gradual lessening of the power of sin and the attainment of true freedom of the sanctified will in this world; glorification pertains totally to the life after death, the world of the saints.

Once the assurance of justification is felt, the road to sanctification begins. This process of sanctification is dwelled upon at length in all Puritan writings, so much so that assurance and sainthood came to be the mark of the Puritans among their enemies in the 17th century, a legend which dies hard even today. All the prayers, the singing, and the contemplation associated with Baxter, Bunyan, and the numerous diary keepers are aspects of the method of sanctification, and give us a rich source of truly devotional verse and prose literature, the famous *Pilgrim's Progress*, the devotional meditations of Edward Taylor, and the poems of Isaac Watts being a few famous examples. The apocalyptic sense that runs through Milton and Spencer has its source here, too. At its highest level sanctification corresponds to the Catholic mystical state of illumination, the third step on the *via mystica*. Both Catholic and other writers on formal mysticism consider Baxter, Bunyan, Fox and others as illuminative mystics.[16] But the writings of the Puritan preachers and theologians themselves tell us another side to this story. Assurance and sanctification are goals eagerly sought, indeed, it is sinful *not* to seek them, but there is no easy victory. The would-be saint is warned to conduct a daily examination of conscience for specific sins, and to consider his general state of justification regularly and earnestly. Backsliding, arrogance and torpor are constantly feared. Although there is no doubt good historical evidence for the stage Puritan and the Puritan merchant of the satirical tradition,[17] this is not the ideal image of the preacher or the image one gets from reading the sermons and discourses of the period 1570−1660. Surely it can be assumed that the best people, the people of intelligence and sensibility, tried at least to follow the careful and scrupulous exhortations of the preachers, that an inner life of Puritan spirituality was created, and that this life is reflected in the Puritan literary imagination. If this can be proven, one of the oldest ghosts in English literary and historical tradition will be laid to rest, and a new interpretation given to a large phase of English and American literature.

Glorification is of the next world, and is not a favorable subject for either preaching or literature. It is the promise at the end of the road of sanctification and is strictly speaking a visionary area. As we shall see, the great Puritan preachers approached it cautiously. Only Baxter succeeded in dealing with it fully and with dignity in *The Saints Everlasting Rest*. The hallucinations and excesses of popular preachers made this visionary aspect of Puritanism a laughing stock among the rationalistic high Anglicans. In literature Bunyan, Milton and Spenser deal with it rather successfully, in different ways. It is still present metaphorically in Wordsworth's visionary gleam and glowing skies, as in "Stepping Westward," and, in a strange distorted way, in Blake's prophetic books.[18] In American literature there is more of it in Melville than in Dickinson and Hawthorne. Glorification holds a unique and rightful place in the Calvinist scheme, leading to literature of a certain visionary nature, and is not to be found in any predominant place in post-Trentine Catholicism, in Anglicanism, or in 18th century deism or rationalism. It was not for nothing that Coleridge mentioned William Law in *Biographia Literaria*; the relationship Coleridge took so earnestly has been largely ignored until recent criticism, and I hope some later chapters of this study can set the record straight.[19]

The last two items important for the Calvinist religious sensibility are not in the same category as those considered thus far. Prayer is not a doctrine at all, but a means of achieving many of the above ends. The Eucharist properly speaking is a doctrine in Calvinism, but not one of first magnitude nor of the central drama. In effect it also is a means. The uses of prayer extend throughout the Calvinist drama; Eucharistic worship pertains only to the level of sanctification. Thus prayer is the more important of the two. The chief value of the Calvinist doctrine of the Eucharist, and of the type of meditation and worship of the sacramental sort that grew up around it, is that it provides an easy means of distinguishing facets of the Calvinist religious and artistic temper from the better known Anglicanism of Donne and Herbert, and the more available baroque Catholicism of Crashaw. The true center of the Calvinist inner life seems to be too arcane or intellectual for today's literary critics, but the doctrine and practice of the Eucharist is a touchstone, as it were, wherein the differences and similarities are more obvious. In polemical discussion this would provide a convenient point of departure, and later on we will have occasion to look into the various problems and representations created by the work of Louis Martz or Malcolm M. Ross and their attempted correction by John Smith and Gordon Wakefield.[20]

Here, where our concern is to introduce and describe the primary categories of the Calvinist experience, it need only be mentioned that the polemical area exists. The theoretical implications in the doctrine of the spiritual presence of Christ in the sacrament, the memorial presence as it was called, are also important. No doubt there was a lessening in outward and ritualistic fervor, in the variety and richness of sacramental devotions, with the demise of the doctrine of the real presence in Calvinism. An obvious case can be made, as it was by Ross,[21] for the lessening of attention to this sacrament and for a lessening of fervor in prose and poetry devoted to it as we move down the scale from Crashaw to Herbert to Marvell to Milton, i.e., Catholic to Anglican to Calvinist. But Ross and Martz see only one side of this spiritual equation. The Calvinist did not abandon dogma in the doctrine of the spiritual presence, but the diminishment of sacramental dogma allowed his energies to move elsewhere, as we have pointed out. Even the positive side is not without its interesting points. The abandonment of the real presence for the spiritual presence of Christ in the sacrament brought with it the requirement for more strenuous mental and inward activity on the part of the worshiper: we might expect a Calvinist meditation on the sacrament to be, for instance, more intellectual and introspective, less devotional and fervent, than its counterpart in Crashaw or Herbert. This is the case with Taylor, and, in a more ambiguous writer, Vaughan. To explain all this fully we must go into the problems of the supposed antithesis modern critics have worked out between poetry and mysticism, and the alleged analogy between good poetry and the "real," the tangible and factual. This valuation has given great importance to certain types of 17th century and modern poetry, and in some theoretical critics this value has been attached to the Catholic doctrine of the "Real Presence."[22] For this preliminary deduction we insist only on the existence of the distinctions themselves; between the doctrine of the real presence, the Anglican and Lutheran compromise called "consubstantiation" and other names, the Puritan doctrine of the spiritual presence, and, importantly for our later work the distinction which has been more often overlooked by literary critics, that between the Calvinist doctrine of the spiritual presence and the extreme Puritan or Quaker breakdown of this doctrine and its replacement by the idea of the Holy Spirit or the inner light. We can accept the historical fact that one doctrine did pass into the other, with great importance for literature from Vaughan to the Romantic movement; but this move was not historically necessary, or logically necessary, as I hope illustrations from the writings of Richard Baxter and a host of others will suggest. The standard belief that Protestantism inevitably led to transcendentalism, echoed by C. Feidelson in his *Symbolism and American Literature*[23] is not born out by a reading of Jonathan Edwards, Hawthorne, Melville or Dickinson. Puritan Protestantism remained Puritan Protestantism until outside forces, secular forces outside the system itself, well-known but unimportant to enumerate here, first corrupted and then brushed it aside. Until that time the safe thing to say is that various strands of Christian belief, the Catholic, Anglican-Lutheran, Puritan, and Quaker-inner light, moved along in parallel ways, with great importance for the literature of England and America from 1570 to 1860.

V. The Calvinist Writers: 1570−1660

An enormous amount of material is available to illustrate the various Puritan attitudes toward doctrine. For our purposes we shall restrict our choices to only the best work of the best writers of the Cambridge period (1570−1620) and to the great 17th century writers, who continued the Puritan tradition into the days of its decline. There is no logical or chronological reason, on the level of the spiritual problems themselves, for not including works of American writers here − Taylor's prose for instance; but American scholarship of our time has made so much of the uniqueness of the New England experience − this has become the dominant myth since Perry Miller's *New England Mind* − that a separate explanation must be attached to the consideration of American writers, as an introduction to the work on Taylor's Calvinist metaphysical structure.

The vigorous account of the inner experience of the English Calvinists given by William Haller in *The Rise of Puritanism* is still the best starting point for any historical introduction to the Puritan writers. Our intention may be more specific and analytic at this point in Puritan studies, but Haller's introduction to the main lines of Puritan thought as it picked up the Calvinist theology coming into England from Geneva in the 1560's and 1570's is a necessary starting point.

Election-vocation-justification-sanctification-glorification was more than an abstract formula. It became the pattern of the most profound experience of men through many generations. From this deep and personal experience grew both the epic and the varied forms in which it was experienced.[24]

The most powerful and lasting effect of the popularization of Pauline doctrine [by the Puritans] was to arouse the most active widespread interest in the inner experience of every individual human being. . . . Every man was either a convert or susceptible of conversion, and the inner life of any man, once converted, was fraught with daily possibilities for struggle and adventure. It followed that every man's state of spiritual health was the subject of acute concern to the man himself and of sympathetic curiosity to others.[25]

The devout Puritan turned his back on stage plays and romances, but only in order to look in his own heart and write what happened there.[26]

The Puritan faith invested the individual soul, the most trivial circumstances of the most commonplace existence, with the utmost significance.[27]

The test of the saint's conversion was, of course, to be seen in his perseverance in the faith, and faith must be continually active. Each day one sinned, each day one must repent, and each day one must be reconciled afresh to God, and each day one must . . . enter those circumstances in one's diary. It was of the very essence of Puritan self-discipline that whatsoever thoughts and actions the old Adam within has most desire to keep hidden, the very worst abominations of the heart, one must when one retired to one's private chamber at night draw forth into the light of conscience. To set them down in writing, albeit in secret "character," was a great help in this. They were the devil incarnate in men and could drag him down to hell. It was also of the essence of Puritan discipline that one should remember and record the good things that happened. These showed the saint that, bad as he was, God had not forsaken him. . . .[28]

These main lines of the Puritan experience show the intentions and interests of Puritan preaching, and suggest the result of this preaching upon the Puritan elite, that is, the creation of a strenuous moral life, an inner self consisting largely of a perpetual dialectic of conscience.

Of the enormous body of Puritan writing between 1570–1660 our selection must be most rigorous here. Haller, Miller, Knappen, Smith and Wakefield list ample bibliographies of the period, and countless other items could be found in an *omnium gatherum* way.[29] The selections chosen in the illustrations to follow were made on the principles of completeness, quality, economy. For completeness, obviously, the complete range of doctrines, in both their theoretical and practical aspects must be sampled. Quality means merely that a first-rate writer — Baxter, Bunyan, Perkins or Preston — has been used whenever possible for illustration of a point: ours is not the task of historical dredging. Unfortunately, there still must remain some areas in which illustration must be had from burlap writers. Economy is a wish rather than a fullfillment, I am afraid. The arch-pattern of Puritanism tends to repeat itself straightforwardly in every writer, as in what follows there will be a great deal of parallelism. It is important to remember that some parallelism is necessary since we are looking for individuality of response, and often the important nuance occurs in passages in which the actual thought is largely identical with the commonplace idea. Still, I have tried to eliminate all unnecessary duplication of idea and attitude.

In the brief summary of writers that follows, reference in the text will be given to the edition used in the illustrations. In all cases this is the earliest edition that was available, but no special effort seemed necessary to use first editions exclusively. For many works first editions are not available, while about others the situation is clouded. The most prominent Puritan writers in the first great wave were Ames, Perkins, Preston and Sibbes. We can add Dodd and Bayly to this list, and also some of the minor diarists whose work is personal and un-philosophical yet intelligent and useful. In the second wave are Baxter and Bunyan, possibly also Watts, if we wish to enter into the early 18th century. And of course Milton who in prose is a major figure, but not the towering genius of the poetry.

A. *Diagrams and Illustrations*
   of the Categories of the Calvinist-Puritan Experience

William Ames (1576–1633), the scholastic theologian of Puritanism, wrote the long and rather dry but useful *Conscience with the Power and Cases thereof* (1639), important as the major redaction of Calvinist theory by an English writer. Lewis Bayly, Bishop of Bangor (d. 1631), whose position as a Puritan is a matter of dispute,[30] is credited with the most popular religious treatise of the late 16th century, *Practice of Pietie* (ed. of 1628), which influenced both Puritan and Anglican devotion for over forty years by filling a much needed place in the moral life of the average man after the rejection of Catholic practice. John Dodd (*Ten Sermons*, 1610) is our one example of the dead level of Puritan thought and writing, wherein the piety is straightforward and homely, not intellectual. His work is useful for gathering commonplaces. Perkins (1558–1602), Preston (1587–1628) and Sibbes (1577–1635) are at the center of the Puritan tradition. We will look into Perkins' *A Case of Conscience* (1595), *A Golden Chaine* (1608), *A Treatise . . . whether a Man Be in the Estate of Damnation or in the Estate of Grace* (1608), *A Grain of Mustard Seede* (1608), *A Treatise of Gods free Grace* (1608), *Treatise of Mans Imaginations* (1613), *The Whole Treatises of the Cases of Conscience* (1613). Some of these works are theoretical, others practical as we shall point out. John Preston's output was even greater than Perkins' and from his works we will draw on *The New Covenant* (1634), *The Breast-Plate of Faith and Love* (1634), *Foure Godly and Learned Treatises* (1633), *Sins overthrow: or, a Godly and Learned Treatise of Mortification* (1635), *Three Sermons . . . Lords Supper* (1640), *A Heavenly Treatise of the Divine Love of Christ* (1640), *The Saints Spiritual Strength* (1634), *Sermons preached before his Majesty* (1634), *An Excellent Treatise of the Spiritual Death in Sinne* (1608), and *Two Treatises . . . Repentance; Combat of flesh and spirit* (1608). Preston gives us the greatest variety of theoretical and practical works of any the Puritan writers of the high period. Richard Sibbes' (1577–1635) important works fall into the practical area: *The Bruised Reede* (1635) and *The Soules Conflict with it self* (1625) are both crucial for the revelation of Puritan sensibility. The diarists Samuel Ward and Richard Rogers are not important for theology, but are fine illustrations of the impression the great Puritan preachers made upon the sensitive and intelligent laity of the day. They show the ground swell which is necessary for the growth of any vital movement.

The later writers, Richard Baxter (1615–1691), in *The Saints Everlasting Rest* (1st ed. 1650), and in various others of his monumental works,[31] Bunyan in *Grace Abounding* and other prose, and Isaac Watts in *Poems* and prose treatises, tend to show more direct literary and imaginative power than those of the Puritan heyday. This prose parallels the poetic development of Spenser, Marvell, and Milton and occurs in the period of Puritan control of the government but loss of forward energy. A similar situation will re-occur in the American 19th century, the outpouring of creative writing in the decline of Calvinism after Jonathan Edwards. Milton's prose writings logically belong here too, if we bear in mind that Milton is a special and complex case, and further, that his prose writings on the whole illustrate the tragic decline of Calvinist writings in the Puritans' day of power in their almost universal political outlook and interest. Milton recouped with his poetry, but others did not. The early Calvinist-Puritan writers had made personal exhortation and piety their main interest – the inner life. In Milton's prime the struggle was for power, then to hold power, and finally a rear-guard action for political survival. Only such unusual figures as Baxter, Bunyan, and Watts were able to remain outside of this political mainstream. In America, something more public and central happened, as Perry Miller has brilliantly shown, but our assessment of that in relation to English Puritanism is for a later place.

Practical examples from the Calvinist writers at work are now going to be given. Since the categories and moods of the Calvinist spirit which are closest to, and most important for, literature will be stressed, at the expense of others which are important in wider ways, a brief summary of the structure of the entire system is in order. The first chart is hierarchical in structure, showing the place and importance of all important categories from the viewpoint of Calvinism as a religious system and theology.

Diagram I

A. The Fundamental category —
   Power and majesty of God contrasted to the sinfulness of man. This is the basic Calvinist-Puritan insight.

B. The Abstract System —
   The Philosophy and Theology of Calvinism. *Institutes* and lesser presentations of the system.

C. The Psychological System —
   1. The primacy of Conscience
   2. The Categories of Grace.
      a. Sin-consciousness
      b. Election
      c. Justification
      d. Sanctification
      e. Glorification

D. The practical means of Grace —
   1. Prayer
   2. The Sacraments — Baptism and the Lord's Supper
   3. The Church (The Covenant)

E. Categories of the Secular life —
   1. Vocation in the World
   2. Church fellowship within the Covenant
   3. Meditation, reading and writing including diary keeping.
   4. Imaginative literature

This diagram of the total religious structure differs on various points from another possible diagram having the central interest of illuminating the relative value of religious categories for the literary imagination and sensibility of Calvinist-Puritanism. In the second diagram the primary categories would be taken for granted as the all-pervasive insight requiring particularization in various forms in order to be meaningful for literature. The power of God and sense of personal sin are the cornerstones of Calvinism, and we can point to their influence in every major work of Calvinist literature, but their presence needs further determination to give them literary relevance. So also with the abstract system of Calvin and his English theological followers. This must be known, at least in its major points, to reach any understanding of the literary temperament and imagination, but the study of the abstractions of theology alone will not reveal the literary sensibility. Consideration of the sensibility and imagination begins properly with the categories of grace, understood as unfolding in the primacy of conscience. The conscience is the stage, or the object, of much Calvinist-Puritan meditation, and hence of its devotional and wordly literature. But as such the conscience is too big a category, too much a matter of Calvinist epistemology, to be useful for literature. Two of the categories of religious means, prayer and the sacraments, figure in the making of imaginative literature, but the third, the Church or community, largely does not. Prayer obviously is personal and psychological with its setting in the inner life; the two sacraments – baptism and the Eucharist – being more psychological than formal and external in Calvinism than in other forms of Christianity, also lead to the personal, the internal, the devotional, and hence to the literary imagination. For obvious reasons, the Eucharist more than baptism figures in Calvinist devotions and poetry. On the other hand, the structure and life of the Church leads towards the sense of community and the external life of the Puritans, to the political and social realms not of concern in this study. There is a literature here, of liturgy, set prayers and hymns, well known and often studied for its own sake. This literature is not often of high imaginative or artistic quality, Watts', Smart's, and Cowper's hymns being among the few happy exceptions.[32]

Strictly speaking, the categories of the social life overlap with the internal categories thus far described. But each has its own special place if looked upon as external. Vocation is the gaining by the Puritan of his daily bread in the world, even though for the Puritan life was always lived before God. Meditation can be considered as a separate item of the Puritan experience, but in practice it was concerned with prayer, or thinking about one of the categories of grace, or prompted by reading or writing of devotional literature. The reading and writing of literature took various standard forms – the

Bible, of course, theology and sermons, perhaps devotional poetry and the keeping of a diary. Private ejaculations, the writing of poetry, and finally great literature such as *The Faerie Queene* or *Pilgrim's Progress* would be the final flowering here. This second chart, a structural diagram, takes into account the relative importance of the categories for literature.

Diagram II

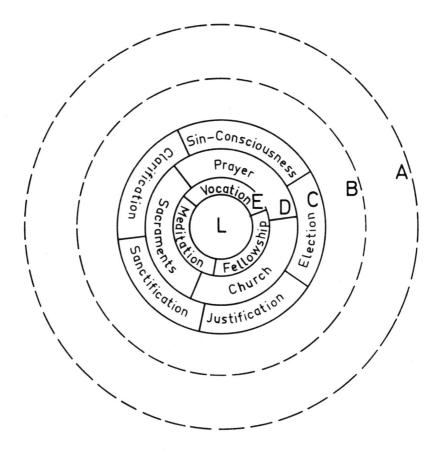

A. Fundamental category – Power and majesty of God
B. The Abstract System – Theology of Calvinism
C. The Psychological System – Conscience
D. The practical means of Grace
E. Categories of the secular life – Meditation, Vocation, Fellowship
L. (Also E–D) Imaginative literature

The two broken circles at the outer extreme of the diagram represent areas A and B of the hierarchical chart, the fixed and encompassing limits of the Calvinist-Puritan insight and theology. The completed circles C, D, and E, each with their set of categories representing certain phases of Calvinist mental or practical life, may be viewed as moveable wheels around the center, which is literature. This diagram, then, suggests the general structural relationship of literature to the feelings and moods of Calvinist life at large, and more particularly, which areas of that experience most directly affect literature and are thus useful for literary criticism. A mythic poet such as Spenser or Milton, or an allegorist such as Bunyan, might try to give the entire pattern and all the relationships in one work. He will not succeed in exhausting the relationships thereby, since the number and possible combinations within the system is inexhaustible by one vision. Nevertheless, the mythic poet will give some sense of the whole. The more particular poet (what we are soon to call "personalist" or "existentialist" Calvinist) will assume the two fixed circles of the Calvinist-Puritan experience, to concentrate upon some combination of C, D, and E in producing his own literature. Several possible instances may be of help as explanation here. A writer whose personal religious interest centered on justification and sanctification, and who in his personal life chose meditation upon the sacraments as his primary religious means, might write poetry which turned out looking very much like Taylor's. One with a consuming interest in formal theology (rare, to be sure), with special problems about election who chose prayer and the reading of the Bible and sermons as his personal means of devotion might produce the abstract literature of a Jonathan Edwards. Another, in despair about his own election, who favored prayer and sermons as his means of grace might well be a William Cowper, and so on. Let us hasten to add that great writers are not explained by such mechanical charts; only that their position within the Calvinist sensibility is somewhat defined. And it is perhaps needless to add that many practicing Calvinist-Puritans from before 1570 or after 1700 did not choose to, or could not, write literature in the strict sense of the word at all. Many contented themselves with writing sermons, diaries, or private ejaculations and meditations of varying quality. Still many more experienced the Calvinist sensibility and dialectic in a completely non-literary way. With these mute Miltons we have no concern, but to their brethren of the middle road, the sermon, diary and private meditation writers, we must turn to given examples of the breadth, nature and extent of the patterns described thus far in the abstract.

Some more words of caution about what follows. The diagrams above, and our method of fleshing them out with examples, do not intend to suggest crudely that $x + y + z = L$. They do not explain why one man can write and another cannot, or the nature and texture of a given work. But as a model explanation these can be useful in isolating accurately for analysis the factors which went into a tradition which has, as its great glory, literature of the first rank. Since most writing about Puritan literature has been vague or derogatory, perhaps this move to the other extreme is to some extent justified at this time.

The quotations and commentary will follow the structure of Diagram I, the scheme of overall religious pattern in Calvinist-Puritanism. The importance of various categories for literature is expressed in Diagram II. The outer circles representing overall categories central to theological study will have brief illustrations since neither variation nor intensity occur there. The shaded areas, or completely non-literary, can virtually be ignored. In effect, then, referring to Diagram I, the importance falls upon A–B (slightly), C 1 and 2 (a–e), D 1 and 2, and E 3. E 4 is imaginative literature itself, or L, not fundamental by any means in a theological scheme, but central to us. The diagrams, then, have two values, to clarify the method of choosing quotations and illustrations from the theological tradition, and to provide a means for transposing theological terms and emphases into literary insights and emphases. The latter will take place in this chapter only in an abstract and visual manner. In the readings which follow, it is hoped that a transformation more congenial to the literary student will be achieved.

To allay the reader's suspicion of theological categories pressed seemingly into the service of literature let us look first at the writings of John Bunyan, particularly *Grace Abounding*. This is a chronological anticipation, yet since Bunyan was among the very few Puritans who was both a conventional writer (sermons, diaries, tracts, etc.) and an imaginative one, his situation is useful in getting under way. The other examples in this section are mainly drawn from tract and sermon writers who were not interested in imaginative literature. Our poets, Milton, Taylor and Marvell, if not Spenser, wrote religious prose, but not of the centrality of Bunyan's. The nature and importance of the doctrines for sensibility must on the whole be established indirectly.

With Bunyan this is not the case. We can move from sermon writing to the imaginatively theological *Grace Abounding* to the purely literary *Pilgrim's Progress*. Although the latter will not be directly approached in this study, there will be occasion later to say some things about Bunyan's theory of allegorical style in its relationship to Puritan thought, to the Bible, and the work of the poets. Here we are interested in the area of *Grace Abounding*, the middle area between theology and sermon on the one hand and pure imaginative vision on the other. The point is that the essential categories that have been worked out theoretically, and will be shown to reappear consistently in writings of Puritans from Ames to Baxter, are present in *Grace Abounding* in a half-theological, half-imaginative way. It is proof that Calvinist-Puritanism bridged this gap in its own sensibility, and *Grace Abounding* nicely rests between theology and artistry.

As should be expected on the basis of the two diagrams, *Grace Abounding* does not deal specifically with the outer categories, A and B. Calvinist theology and the primary Puritan insight of God and man must be assumed as causes and hidden forces behind the work. For Bunyan, this is the *zeitgeist*, needing no proof. The attention is given to the conscience, the drama of salvation, the primary works of meditation and prayer, leading to but not into the inner circle of Diagram II, imaginative literature. The last leap is not made in *Grace Abounding*, for this would require the untypical literary sense in and for itself, which Bunyan quite consciously shows in the poem introducing *Pilgrim's Progress*. *Grace Abounding* is semi-literary and not necessarily intentional preparation for literature by exercise of the Puritan imagination and sensibility. Ames, Preston, Perkins, Sibbes and Baxter, earlier to or contemporary with Bunyan, went this much of the way in their works. But a good deal of their energy was devoted to First Principles (A) and Theology (B). Other writers could begin even farther along than did Bunyan, relying upon a developed theology and sensibility, and give us the poetry of Spenser and the 17th century.

Henri Talon in *John Bunyan: The Man and His Works*[33] has given an analysis of Bunyan's Puritan sensibility which may serve our purpose here. With the other writers and the development of the categories we must proceed directly. Talon's work places Bunyan's sensibility for us very well. He notes that Bunyan's theology must be derived from his works indirectly, and derives a theoretical Calvinism from the workings of Bunyan's imagination. He also notes a paradox or clash in Bunyan of natural optimistic bent with the gloomier Calvinist notions of salvation, and sees rightly the source of Bunyan's energy and imagination in this clash. This is also true of other Puritan writers. His remarks on the structure of *Grace Abounding*, and its relationship to the central pattern of the Puritan drama of salvation is most interesting for our purpose. As to the work itself,

There is no trace of 'constant progress' in *Grace Abounding*. Indeed, the superficial reader might well be upset by the irregularity of its rhythm, by the contrary waves that sweep the author's spirit, by the fear that he is never going to make any headway. Yet there is an advance, though the goal is never reached, for, as Bunyan says in his allegory, conversion is a "progress" which has no end on earth. *Grace Abounding* admirably illustrates this perpetual becoming, precisely because its author is faithful to the truth of life.[34]

This statement is at once a confirmation and a correction of historian Haller's pattern of the Puritan drama given earlier. The pattern is there to be discerned in an overall way, it is true in idea, but mere presentation of its historical existence belies the complexity of its operation in any Puritan life, not to speak of the lives of the imaginative and the creative. The intensity and importance of the inner drama, which could, as Haller comments, turn a man from the world and the stage drama of his inner life, is an almost inevitable vehicle for literature in the man of more than common imagination. As Talon says of Bunyan, the Puritan need for public confession of his inner life becomes almost unbearable:

His sins, as we have seen were often nothing but a sort of perversion of his need for expression. . . . But their shadows still lingered in the dark recesses of his soul, so he had perpetually to shed more light on that deep dwelling-place; he perpetually had to unburden himself and repeat himself. Repeat his reasons for believing, reassure himself that faith alone justified and that Christ's blood really had been shed on purpose to wash away the sins of His miserable creature, John Bunyan; repeat the comforting texts that Jesus whispered to him; pick up the Bible again because its sacred words offered inexhaustible enlightenment. Even when he was addressing others he was really talking to himself, and throughout the whole length of his work there runs this hidden moving personal dialogue.[35]

Such description applies with equal validity to the sermons and tracts of the Cambridge Puritans, to the other 17th century writers, and, *mutatis mutandis*, to the poets. On this score Talon senses the special imaginative grip of the Puritan vision upon Bunyan, leading him finally to create, not merely participate, in the drama.

Bunyan never ceased to recreate his life and to marvel at his destiny. There was a treasure hidden in every nook, and each had to be explored. His memory was an enchanted palace to him, for he could have said with St. Augustine "There also meet I with myself" (*ibi mihi et ipse occurso*). It was a precious palace, and more precious still the memories it contained. The human adventure engraved on its walls has become immortal through him. Curiously enough, Bunyan never imagined heaven or hell without reference to the earth. The joys of paradise and the torments of hell were perhaps nothing but the heightened memory of our joys and torments on earth.[36]

The stuff of Bunyan's vision in *Grace Abounding* is the great central drama taking place in conscience: election, vocation, justification, sanctification, glorification. In all true Calvinist-Puritans it was existential as well as theoretical and theological; in some, like Bunyan, it became imaginative in *Grace Abounding* and literary in *Pilgrim's Progress*. Talon concludes his account of this phenomena on a very equivocal note, one which we must take into account in what follows. For him, Bunyan the Puritan has the ideal sensibility for the writer of literature:

Hence everything predestined Bunyan to write: his apostolic ardour, his restlessness that had to be appeased, his sensibility reaching out for human contact, his imagination bent on realising its dreams, and his soul avid for self-contemplation. And always there was his fervour, compelling him to proclaim his faith, his love, his faults, all his victories, and to seek in prayer the directing inspiration of his life.[37]

With our categories we could prove this sensibility in detail in the case of Bunyan, a remarkable example of the practical-imaginative Puritan type. Yet if we did, Talon's account would leave us with as problem, for he concludes, referring more to *Pilgrim's Progress* than to *Grace Abounding*, that

Thus Bunyan achieved a task which, according to Edward Dowden, is always difficult for Puritans. He gave to ideas and feelings the body and plastic form which alone can interpret them artistically to the outside world. We know the penetrating analysis in which the author of *Puritan and Anglican* contrasts the Puritan dualism of visible *versus* invisible, the sensory sphere *versus* the spiritual sphere, with the Catholic conception which unites them in a universal sympathy and understanding.[38]

Bunyan remains a mystery for Talon in passing to the inner category of literature from the categories which prepare for it so well. But must this Puritan sensibility of conscience remain a mystery, a sport in our literature, on the authority of Dowden's early study, and the recent studies of Ross, Martz and others who echo it? Talon's close understanding of the relationship of sensibility to literature in Bunyan, and his tantalizing begging of the question, might lead to other, more analytic, responses to the question.

B. The Categories of the Calvinist-Puritan Experience

1. Power and Majesty of God in Relation to the Sinfulness of Man

This category of the Puritan experience is so widely accepted by all the writers either explicitly or implicitly that it is perhaps pointless to quote excessively in proof and illustration. Without this basic intuition the Calvinist-Puritan sensibility could not be said to exist and its presence is so internalized in most writers, especially the imaginative ones, that it is difficult to find specific illustrations that will not seem fairly vague. For the starting point, then, we can do no better than cite the opening paragraphs of the *Institutes*, Calvin's justification for his theology as a whole:

True and substantial wisdom principally consists of two parts, the knowledge of God, and the knowledge of ourselves. But, while these two branches of knowledge are so intimately connected, which of them precedes and produces the other, is not easy to discover. For, in the first place, no man can take a survey of himself but he must immediately turn to the contemplation of God, in whom he "lives and moves;" since it is evident that the talents which we possess are not from ourselves, and that our very existence is nothing but a subsistence in God alone. These bounties, distilling to us by drops from heaven, form, as it were, so many streams conducting us to the fountainhead. Our poverty conduces to a clearer display of the infinite fulness of God. Especially, the miserable ruin, into which we have been plunged by the defection of the first man, compels us to raise our eyes towards heaven, not only as hungry and famished, to seek thence a supply for our wants, but, aroused with fear, to learn humility. For, since man is subject to a world of miseries, and has been spoiled of his divine array, this melancholy exposure discovers an immense mass of deformity: every one, therefore, must be so impressed with a consciousness of his own infelicity, as to arrive at some knowledge of God. Thus a sense of our ignorance, vanity, poverty, infirmity, depravity, and corruption, leads us to perceive and acknowledge that in the Lord alone are to be found true wisdom, solid strength, perfect goodness, and unspotted righteousness; and so, by our imperfections, we are excited to a consideration of the perfections of God. . . . The knowledge of ourselves, therefore, is not only an incitement to seek after God, but likewise a considerable assistance towards finding him.

On the other hand, it is plain that no man can arrive at the true knowledge of himself, without having first contemplated the divine character, and then descended to the consideration of his own.[39]

Nowhere more fully than in this opening of the *Institutes* is Calvin both so lucid and so magisterial. Most of his English followers tend to hurry over such fundamental and psychological materials to begin treatment with theological points or with the practical problems of personal salvation. Perhaps with some justice they feel that Calvin has had the word on so basic a point. Even in a theoretical work such as Perkins' *A Golden Chaine* (1608) there is little of truly fundamental assumption, since the author states clearly that he follows Beza and Calvin on such matters. Quoting Ephesians 1.11 and Mathew 10.29 Perkins is interested in connecting the notion of God's majesty with the specific doctrine of predestination and providence. "Therefore the Lord, according to his good pleasure, hath most certainely decreed every thing and action, whether past, present, or to come, together with their circumstances of place, time, means, and end. Yea, he hath most justly decreed the wicked workes of the wicked. For if he had not willed them, they should never have bene at all. And albeit they of their own nature, are and remaine wicked; yet in respect of Gods decree, they are some wayes good: for there is not any thing absolutely evil."[40] The Calvinist concern with God's honor and grandeur is not dwelled on as in Calvin himself, but it is a peg to establish the point of predestination, or the practical working arrangement between God and man.

Although the preachers are usually intent upon more specific and practical goals, usually concerning election and the process of salvation, the diarists tend to brood upon the power of God and their own sinfulness. Such brooding, as in the cases of Ward and Rogers in their diaries produced by Knappen,[41] is usually kept within the bounds of ordinary prudence. However, it was possible for this to get out of hand if the doctrines of election and predestination were improperly understood, as they often were. The Cambridge suicides, or the rejoicing of the Catholics of Lancashire,[42] could then be the unlooked for result. As has been stated earlier, this doctrine or more basically central idea or attitude is the one without which Calvinist-Puritanism cannot exist. There are many possible emphases and distortions within its confines, but without it a Puritan sensibility could not be defined. In the 18th century in America a troubled

Jonathan Edwards was really asking the same questions, with more subtle and newer tools of thought, when he wrote at the beginning of his treatise *Religious Affections* "There is no question whatsoever, that is of greater importance to mankind, and that it more concerns every individual person to be well resolved in, than this, what are the distinguishing qualifications of those that are in favor with God, and entitled to his eternal rewards? Or, which comes to the same thing, What is the nature of true religion?"[43] To emphasize this point in Calvinism-Puritanism may be to carry coals to Newcastle indeed, but there are some prudential grounds to do so softly. After Calvin, through the end of the 17th century no writer, poet or preacher, would have felt it necessary to dwell in this overwhelmingly obvious area. However, in the 18th century and later this basic awareness becomes a way to distinguish the truly religious writer amid a welter of alien forces. It also, as in the case of Edwards and later Emily Dickinson, provides the common mark with their English brethren which may help to reduce the exaggerated claims of American uniqueness put forth by some contemporary historians and literary students. We shall try to show that the American sensibility in its fundamental aspects has the same 16th and 17th century sources as the English. The many differences we are more than eager to point out; these are differences on various points within the fundamental category, and exist as vividly between English practitioners as between English and American.

This section may well close with quotations from the pen of the great Puritan court preacher, John Preston, who devoted the first portion of his work, *The New Covenant or the Saints Portion* (1634), to the question of "God's All-Sufficiency." In doing so he was, of course, merely producing a commentary on Calvin's opening book of the *Institutes*. Preston in the 1610–1620 period was preaching these doctrines to the royalty and powers of London:

. . . likewise he accounted *faith to him for righteousness* because *faith* does sanctify & make a man righteous . . . let a man believe, that God's all-sufficiency, which is the Covenant, for *justifying faith* is but a believing of that part of the Covenant, and enabling a man to keep the other part which is requird. . . . It knits his heart unto the Lord. It sanctifieth a man *throughout*, it makes him *peculiar* to the *Lord*, it makes him *wholly* to him. This is the nature of *faith*.[44]

So much for a clear account of the most primary of the requisites of Puritan sensibility.

2. The Philosophy and Theology of Calvinism.

In a literary study of this sort, philosophy and theology as such may be necessary as an assumption, but redundant as a category, since the important writers of the imagination begin with categories of experience, not with abstract definitions. Be that as it may, some little attention must be given to the matter here, as a point of clarification. The key to the question is the *Institutes* itself and Calvin's other writings. Calvin did his job so thoroughly, and was armed with so many contemporary commentators and allies, that there was little incentive to this sort of endeavour in the English tradition. Most of the preachers, as well as the writers, hardly concerned themselves with first principles at all; rather they plunged into the practical problems of election and salvation as personal issues. The diarists and imaginative writers dramatized various aspects of the system according to their abilities and personal proclivities. In the heyday of Calvinism in England (1570–1660), there is always somehow the assumption that the reader or listener has a grasp of the whole, has read Calvin perhaps. Attempts at total synthesis were largely of a confessional nature, such as the Westminster Confession of 1595. Confessions, as brief statements of doctrinal belief, add little to either theology or imagination. A notable exception to this general practice was Perkins' *A Golden Chaine, or The Description of Theologie* (*Armilla Aurea*, 1590, in Latin).[45] This brief work (a little over 100 pages), compared to Calvin's, hits upon the high points of Calvinist theology for the English reader. It is explanatory in nature and frankly derivative from Calvin. Perkins was essentially a preacher, but evidently felt that an argumentative and polemical commentary on Calvin's system was necessary in the atmosphere of the 1590's. The book was much republished and Perkins turned thereafter to practical divinity, of which more later. His judgment in this matter was sound. There was more need for preaching and polemic than for fundamental rethinking of theology in the world of the competing religions of the 17th century. Only in the 18th century, when Calvinist doctrine was challenged by dangerous outside forces of science and rationalism, did speculation become inventive again, in the vaguely mystical and inward writings of William Law (for example, *The Spirit of Prayer*, 1749) and of course in Edwards' daring *Religious Affections* (1746) and *Freedom of the Will* (1754). Thus fundamentally Calvinist-Puritan doctrine in the dogmatic period remains that of the *Institutes* and the numerous commentators on doctrine or the effects of doctrine. As an influence on sensibility abstract theology tends to cancel out, or is represented in, the more specific and immediate areas of Calvinist concern, that is, the conscience, the road of salvation, and the practical means of grace in daily life.

3. The Primacy of the Conscience

The conscience in Calvinist-Puritan experience has two roles. One is traditional, as the seat of judgment or moral calculus as to what is right and wrong. This aspect was inherited from the medieval Christian system, and is reflected in such a book as William Ames' *Conscience with the Power and Cases thereof* (ed. 1639). This work and others like it show how inevitably the new moral system succumbed to prudence and convention. Several illustrations will be given from it, as a point of contrast with the more unique Puritan view of conscience as the center of all moral and religious experience. The latter is found in innumerable writings, among which the most interesting are Perkins' *A Case of Conscience, the greatest that ever was . . .* (1595) and Sibbes' *The Soules Conflict with itself, and Victory over it selfe by Faith* (1625). This version of the conscience as a witness is often allusive, since the Puritan's assumption about it is so firm and so casual that he often moves back and forth between conscience and some specific moral or doctrinal matter. In the long run, however, its importance must be acknowledged as giving the special tone to Puritan writing, the unique scrutiny and self-searching that is found in Milton, Marvell and far later in Cowper and Dickinson. On the other hand conscience as a general category embracing the activities of such diverse functions as election or sacramental meditation has not the same meaning as the "Spirit" or "inner light" of Quaker and other left-wing 17th century sects. It does not replace or refute all other witnesses, whether of doctrine, scripture or reason; it is not a final and irrational arbiter. In fact it leads to a greater, not a lesser intellectualism, which was the bone and marrow of contention in Puritan-Quaker disputes as we find them in Baxter's works or in Barbour's recent book.[46]

Returning to Ames' *Conscience with the Power and Cases thereof*, we find an enlightening and in some ways amusing introduction. He and his parishioners have found the heady general views of conscience given by Perkins and others unworkable in practical moral affairs:

And indeed, if such things were handled in the meetings of Preachers, according to the variety of Cases that fall out, and the more remarkable decisions set down in writing; the children of Israel should not need to go down to the Philistines (that is, our Students to Popish authors) to sharpen every man his Share. . . .[47]

Ames will try for a compromise that preserves Puritan principles yet maintains the exact judgment of the Catholic system: "The Papists have laboured much this way, to instruct their Confessors. . . . But they are without the life of this Doctrine: and death is in their pot."[48] Next Ames does the most significant thing of his entire treatise, at least for our purposes. He refutes the definition of conscience given by Perkins in *A Case of Conscience* and *Discourse of Conscience* (1608).[49] He does this in full awareness that Perkins' definition of the general conscience has been central to the Puritan experience of conversion and the religious life:

The most grave Divine, William Perkins, who only of our countrymen hath set forth a peculiar Treatise of Conscience, doth place it among Faculties; and he doth so define it, as he putteth for the general nature of it a part of the Understanding, that is to say, as he explains himself, a natural power or faculty. He gives this reason of his opinion, namely, because the act of Accusing, Comforting, Terrifying, && cannot be ascribed to the Conscience, if itself were an act. Besides Master Perkins maketh Conscience, Understanding, Opinion, Knowledge, Faith and Prudence to be one kind or sort. . . .[50]

Ames finds that Perkins' definition of conscience is too general. With Perkins dismissed, Ames falls back upon the medieval-Catholic view of the conscience as the specific faculty of the practical judgment "proceeding from the Understanding by the power or means of a habit" (p. 3). For those familiar with Catholic theology, the rest of Ames' treatise can be anticipated: he deals with doubt, scruple, prudence, laxity and evil and the other general problems in the scholastic manner. Legality and minute concern with the moral law replace Puritan inspiration:

An act of Conscience is a reflex act of the Understanding, whereby a man understandeth, and with judgment weigheth his own actions with their circumstances. It is commonly called *Consideration*, or *meditation on our ways*. It is called in the Scripture, *A respect* or *beholding* by the mind. . . . The *cause* of the *Reviewing* of our actions ought to be, First, a care to please God in all things. Secondly, a fear of sinning.[51]

And so on. In the second part of the treatise Ames becomes more interesting as he tries to reconcile all this scholastic scruple and legalism with the doctrines of election and justification. But assurance and legalism do not sit well together, and what emerges is a kind of horrifying Catholic-Puritanism, in which even the memory of any sin is a possible source of damnation. "First, past sinnes are not to be forgotten. No, not those which were committed in youth. This remembrance of former sinnes is profitable, to humble us. . . ."[52] In practice, then, falling into any sin may be a judgment against the individual, a sign of his lack of faith and election, unless complete repentance in the judgment of conscience is undertaken for each sin. The more standard and comfortable Puritan notion, we shall soon see, holds that temptation and even constant falling may be a sign of God's interest and salvation. In Ames' legal view satisfaction of the law in conscience is the only hint of salvation:

. . . by what motives may a man be stir'd up to labour for Sanctification? If he consider, 1. that without holiness no man shall see God. 2. That there can be no true Faith or justification or adoption without sanctification, i.e. 1. A reformation of all the powers, and faculties of the whole man. 2. A respect to all the Commandments of God. 3. A constant care to avoid all sin. 4. A walking before God. 5. A combat between the flesh and the spirit.[53]

The scholastic and especially monastic goal of perfect sanctification, with conscience as the constant judge, looms into view here: "Now we shall make a progress in Sanctification 1. If we exercise our selves dayly to a more perfect denying of sin and of the world, and of our selves, and to a more earnest and serious seeking of God and his kingdom. . . ."[54] Ames becomes inconsistent at the end of his treatise by stressing election and assurance, two qualities that certainly do not follow from the casuistry and moral perfectionism of the scholastic view of conscience. These inconsistencies are unimportant, however. Ames' work is interesting for the light it throws by contrast upon the more consistent Puritan view of conscience as the central arena for the drama of salvation.

For this view of the conscience as a general area of the mind usurping all others in importance we might turn to any of the great Puritan writers. For reasons of brevity Perkins and Sibbes will suffice. Perkins, as Ames noted, tried to give a succinct theoretical view in his *A Case of Conscience* (1595) and *Discourse of Conscience* (1608). Sibbes, as a practical and devotional writer, is more general, repetitive and imprecise, yet it is this method of overlapping the conscience itself with many of the aspects of salvation that is common to much Puritan writing.

In reading over Perkins' treatise, *A Case of Conscience*, we can understand again the perplexity of religious argument in the Reformation period. By the scholastic standards of Ames, Perkins is not treating cases of conscience at all, which would be specific moral matters and sins. Instead he is talking about election, predestination, justification, sanctification — in other words, the staple ingredients of all Puritan religious writing, whether practical or theoretical. But there is an inner logic here, if not one which makes sense to the outside world. The drama of personal election, upon which all else hangs in Puritan theology, is acted out in the conscience (the terms "understanding" or "consciousness" might be clearer, but were rejected by the Puritans as unreligious terms). For conscience in this sense, the terms "Spirit," "Spirit of God," and sometimes even "faith" were used, but some attempt, not always successful, was made to distinguish the human agent from the divine means involved in the knowledge of election. Perkins says:

This is that Jesus Christ, which came by water, (Sanctification signified by the legall washings) and blood (imputation of Christ's righteousness, or the sprinkling of his blood:) not by water onely, but by water and blood: (because Christ worketh both justification and sanctification together:) and it is that spirit (a man's owne conscience inwardly purified) that beareth witness: for that spirit is truth: (that is, that the testimony of the spirit of adoption, certifying us that we are the Sonnes of God, is true).[55]

The conscience does not become the Spirit of God, as in the Quaker view, but it is the ultimate human referent of this Spirit. This is important to understand when reading, as in Perkins' treatise, the usual swift movement from election, on to vocation, justification, sanctification, and glorification. Although logically one is grounded upon the predecessor, psychologically each and all are grounded upon that assurance of conscience about which Perkins has been quoted. These Puritan treatises seem wayward in a sense, if compared to more formal orthodox theology, because they return often and abruptly to the starting point. But this is logical and necessary within the system, which is, unlike Ames' and that of the scholastics he admired, not legal in basis. There is no confessional or organized hierarchy to appeal to in cases of conscience, only guidelines of one individual to another. After twenty pages on election, for instance, Perkins returns to the inner testimony for proof:

Therefore the Apostle saith, that we have received the spirit of adoption, by which we crie Abba Father: as though he should say, this testimonie of the spirit is altogether so sure, by which he beareth us record that we are the sonnes of God: that presently without doubting, we can call upon God, and crie Abba Father. And all the Elect have this testimonie, being made the sonnes of God by Faith, and being revived by the holie Ghost: and ingrafted into Christ.[56]

And he returns to this point again later, in sections on sanctification and glorification. Since the Puritan edifice was not legal in basis, it was always capable of quick collapse if not shorn up by the fundamental sense of election in the conscience. Catholic polemicists had been quick to see this weakness and to apply the needle, to which Perkins and many others would make this answer:

In a word, godly writers have proved against School-men, that they which are indued with true faith in Christ, cannot be ignorant of it.[57]

There were the seals of faith, the signs and marks of election, of which more soon. Perkins presents many of the important ones in this treatise. The important point here is that the special place given to conscience, the wide if vague place it holds in Puritan theology, is absolutely necessary if the Puritan system is going to work psychologically and be upheld against Catholic scholastic argument. It was Ames who committed the logical error, in thinking it was possible to hold the fundamental positions of reformation theology and have the minute legalistic clarity of the scholastics. But with this foundation in the expanded conscience, the psychological system of the Puritans follows easily enough:

Therefore it must needs be, that all they which are elected in Christ, must also at length effectually by called and drawn to Christ. *After an effectual calling followeth Faith, the effect of predestination, which is said to be peculiar unto the elect.* And without which, (as the Apostle saith) it is not possible to please God.[58]

That is, it follows in theory. In practice the road from election to salvation was often found to be too easy or too hard. For a writer like Perkins, giving a theoretical account, it is only necessary to add an injunction to the conscience that life is a perpetual warfare (p. 44) against sin and Satan to avoid easy assurance, and to remind the weak and wavering conscience that predestination can never be said to indicate the damnation of the individual:

For if predestination (as Augustine witnesseth) be a preparation to the blessings of God, by which most certainly they are made free, whosoever are made free: therefore whosoever feeleth himself freed through these graces of GOD, may be assured and certified of his predestination.[59]

This is fine in theory, but if the theory is one that by nature zigzags between theology and psychology, what about the cases of individuals? There were questions here which gave a life's work of writing to men of practical divinity, such as Richard Sibbes.

Sibbes tells his readers in the prefaces to *The Soules Conflict* (1625) and to *The Bruised Reed* (1635) that his purposes in writing are purely practical. If it were not for the difficulties experienced by souls in practicing the Calvinist system, there would be no need for his or other commentary. But the conscience needs constant shoring up, else despair replaces the process of election-justification-sanctification-glorification.

Some, and none of the worst, Satan prevailes withal so far, as to neglect the means, upon fear they should (being so sinful) dishonor God and increase their sins: and so they lie smothering under this temptation as it were bound hand and foot by Sathan, not daring to make out to Christ, & yet are secretly upheld by a spirit of faith, shewing it self in hidden sighs and groans to God. The more Sathan is malicious in keeping the soul in darkness, the more care is to be had of establishing the soul upon that which will stay it. . . .

God knows that as we are prone to sin, so when conscience is thoroughly awaked, we are as prone to despair for sin; and therefore he would have us know that he setteth himself in the Covenant of grace to triumph in Christ over the greatest evils and enemies we fear, and that his thoughts are not as our thoughts are, that he is God and not Man. . . .

Two things trouble the peace of Christians very much; Their weaknesses hanging upon them; and, Fear of holding out for Time to come.[60]

Inevitably Sibbes must touch all the bases of the Puritan theology in order to present a thorough picture of the election-glorification cycle and to show the relationship of assurance and despair. In both treatises, as Perkins has done in his theoretical work, Sibbes returns time and again to the nature of the conscience, to the fact that the Puritan theology and its complicated ways of salvation may collapse at any time that the conscience weakens to despair and sin. He also sees the constant danger of returning to the legalistic Catholic system as a recourse from the "war of the members and the spirit." The preacher must constantly shore up the Puritan view of conscience:

The child of God when he seeth that his troubles are mixed with Gods displeasure, and perhaps his conscience tells him that God hath a just quarrell against him, because he hath not received his peace with his God, that this anger of God puts a sting into all other troubles, and adds to the disquiet.[61]

Election itself is a cause of anxiety of conscience, but conscience must not be allowed to lapse into a "natural kind of Popery."

Another cause of disquiet is, that men by a natural kind of Popery seek for their comfort too much in sanctification, neglecting justification, relying too much upon their own performances.

No wonder why Papists maintain doubting, who hold salvation by works, because Satan joyning together with our consciences, will always find some flaw even in our best performances.[62]

There was clearly a tendency, pushed flagrantly to its conclusion by Ames, to revert to the Catholic scholastic view of conscience and sin, at least in practice. This would give an emphasis in the religious life to the problem of sanctification, expressed in meditation, prayer, and various sacramental rites. The Puritan center should be, as the preachers tell their faithful, more inward, with the center always on the enlarged and general notion of conscience (which we may call understanding, or even, in a limited sense, inner light). The result is a more intellectual and speculative kind of religious experience, in which many of the standard elements have their part (election, justification, sanctification, the forms of worship in the Church) but in which the center is the conscience with its enormous responsibility to provide a balance between wise assurance and wise doubt. Thus for good reason the practical works of Perkins, Preston and Sibbes seem to be moving endlessly in the same circle, in a sense no further advanced on the last page than on the first of any treatise, or from one treatise to another. Each treatise is a renewal of the problem of the new life of the conscience, just as each man in his own life was expected to attend to this renewal from one moment to another. This attentiveness to the conscience as the foundation of the moral being accounts for the tone and intensity of Puritan writing of all kinds, and is quite different from the casuistry and moral calculus of Ames and the Catholic-scholastic writers on "cases of conscience" and the weighing of sins as external deeds.

As with the other categories, many further quotations could be given relating the importance of the general conscience to specific doctrines and moods in the Puritan sensibility, from Sibbes, Preston, and a host of others. This will not be attempted, but it is hoped that the reader will note, in the sections devoted to specific doctrines, how often the relationship to the general conscience is made.

4. The Cycle of Salvation: Election, Vocation, Justification, Sanctification, Glorification.

In the following sections the examples will be more numerous, as the religious material tends to fall closer to the immediate experience of literature. To facilitate the aim of drawing religious experience closer to the imaginative and literary, the above cycle, which is found in the standard Puritan preachers, is rearranged for literary relevance into the following: *a.* Sin-consciousness-Election; *b.* Vocation-Justification; *c.* Sanctification (Prayer, Lord's Supper, Meditations); *d.* Glorification. The reasoning is as follows. Election as a formal doctrine has little relevance for poetry and literature, but great importance for theology. Sin-consciousness and guilt have great importance for Puritan literature, yet strictly speaking are aberrations in formal theology (i.e., these states should not occur as often as they do). The two appear together in the practical works of the Puritans, since one is almost always related to the other, and in imaginative literature the dramatic presentation of despair always has the shadow of predestination behind it. Vocation and justification figure very slightly in imaginative writing, and thus will be slightly represented here. Vocation strictly speaking is the Puritan's place in the world, and, unless he is a writer, this has no literary importance. Even if, as in the case of Emily Dickinson, the writer makes a good deal of "vocation" it turns out to be a Calvinist peculiarity of little importance. Justification is more important in Lutheran and low Anglican theology than in Puritanism, since the important matters of faith and belief implied in justification are really subsumed into election and predestination by Calvinists. In Calvinist writings justification becomes a form about which there is not very much to say, and little of practical importance in the leading of the religious life. Its theoretical aspects are covered by election, and the practical by sanctification. Puritans speak of it, however, since it is in the Pauline cycle.

I include prayer, meditation and the sacraments under sanctification, because without them it too is a relatively empty term. The preachers are mainly interested, as we have seen, in distinguishing Calvinist sanctification from Catholic piety and casuistry, and in assuring their followers that sanctification does follow election and justification. But in practice the process of sanctification is the practice of Puritan piety, and that of course is found in meditation, prayer, and various sacramental devotions within Puritan safeguards. Glorification stands aone, with the best and most sustained treatise being Baxter's *Saints Everlasting Rest*, and in literature perhaps the final sections of *Pilgrim's Progress*, *Paradise Lost* and some cantos in *The Faerie Queene*. General meditation will be considered under a separate heading.

a. Election

With good historical reason the average student of Puritan literature considers the Puritan obsession with sin-consciousness and with the doctrine of election as the central concern of the Puritan movement and of individual lives. It is no doubt the most written about of all Puritan religious experiences, and does not diminish in importance between the time of Perkins' *A Case of Conscience, the greatest that ever was* (1595) and Edwards' treatise on the same subject, *Religious Affections* (1746). The ultimate source for this doctrine in the Puritan tradition is the *Institutes*, Book III, chapters xxi—xxiv, on election and predestination. Calvin had St. Augustine behind him and quotes freely from his great predecessor in these chapters. Calvin's statements, as always, are clear and orderly, and as always leave something to be desired as a basis for religious practice:

The covenant of life not being equally preached to all, and among these to whom it is preached not always finding the same reception, this diversity discovers the wonderful depth of the Divine judgment. Nor is it to be doubted that this variety also follows, subject to the decision of God's eternal election. . . . [T]he very obscurity which excites such dread, not only displays the utility of this doctrine, but shows it to be productive of the most delightful benefit. Predestination we call the eternal decree of God, by which he has determined in himself, what he would have to become of every individual of mankind. For they are not all created with a similar destiny; but eternal life is fore-ordained for some, and eternal damnation for others.[63]

In chapter XXIV Calvin does not wince in reciting the great numbers of the damned. He does leave the matter of individual election and assurance open, as befits a general tract. It was the problem of all Puritan preachers and writers to show the justness of these doctrines for life in general and for the individual life. The Christian life begins with the sense of personal justification and the question of election, from which all else — the Church and the sacramental life — must follow. Election was talked and written about by everyone, from preachers to writers to common people, and is the religious term which appears most overtly in the writings of Milton, Melville, Dickinson and others. It is the one concept that literary critics are likely to deal with, whether as religious reality or as metaphor.[64]

According to all the preachers following Calvin, the new life of the Christian begins in acknowledgement of the overwhelming sense of sin in the individual, the need for justification, and the search for election. Unlike the Catholic system, experience preceeds belief in Calvinism. The preacher must make the hearer believe that the doctrines are true of course, but it is more important to make him believe that they are true for him. The ubiquity of election doctrine in Puritan thinking. has led some writers, especially literary men, to take a rather simplified view of it. One often comes across the sneering remark, to the effect that those who sought election and assurance always found it. This is simply untrue to the actual experience as reflected in recorded documents. They very fact that every Puritan writer traversed the same ground, and that many reiterated the same positions in many works, is not grounds for assuming simplicity of situation. There were many traps and nuances in the movement from sin-consciousness to election to justification, and they are all mentioned in one writer or another. If the road had been easy and unsubtle, the preachers's job would have been completed in handing out Calvin's *Institutes* and the Bible to the congregations. Instead, Jonathan Edwards was going over the same ground, in *Religious Affections* (1746) for an audience as bemused as that of the early preachers. Some Puritans accepted sin-consciousness as the beginning of the way, but could get no further. Others could be persuaded of justification and conditional election, but not of sanctification, as "backsliding" into sin raised doubts of justification or election. The preachers were hard-pressed to make the most of good works of the spirit as a relief of anxiety without themselves falling away from the doctrines of election and justification. No wonder that Sibbes calls man the "bruised reed" and that the "spiritual combat" became a most familiar term in Puritan life.

These words of Calvin are seminal to all discussions of election by the Puritan writers:

Paul, therefore, justly reasons from the passage of Malachi which I have just quoted, that where God, introducing the covenant of eternal life, invites any people to himself, there is a peculiar kind of election as to part of them, so that he does not efficaciously choose all with indiscriminate grace.

In conformity, therefore, to the clear doctrine of the Scripture, we assert, that by an eternal and immutable counsel, God has once for all determined, both whom he would admit to salvation, and whom he would condemn to destruction. . . . In the elect, we consider calling as an evidence of election, and justification as another token of its manifestation, till they arrive in glory, which constitutes its completion. As God seals his elect by vocation and justification, so by excluding the reprobate from the knowledge of his name and the sanctification of his Spirit, he affords an indication of the judgment that awaits them.[65]

It was the duty of every Puritan-Christian to meditate, with the help of preaching and Scripture, upon the application of these passages on election to his own life. "Faith, indeed, is properly connected with election, provided it occupies the second place." This turning of Calvin from both Catholic and Lutheran views of faith and belief set in order a new reorientation of the religious experience.

Perkins' *Golden Chaine* and *A Case of Conscience* have been cited in other connections. They too have a good deal on election as part of the total theological process. For the present purposes such general treatises will be overlooked in favor of particular ones dealing more exactly with the problem of sin-consciousness and election. From Perkins there is *Estate of Damnation or Estate of Grace* (*Works*, 1608) dealing with the problems directly, and indirect presentation in works on conscience, and on imagination. Preston and Sibbes deal with these issues indirectly in most of their work, and directly in *The Breast-Plate of Faith & Love* and *The Soules Conflict* respectively. Again there is room only for the direct references. And finally, this great tradition leads to and ends with Edwards' famous *Religious Affections* (1746), the last authentic theoretical Puritan document.

In Perkins' *A Treatise tending unto a Declaration, whether a Man be in the Estate of Damnation, or in the Estate of Grace* all facets of the sin-election theme appear, and one might say that all treatises between this and Edwards follow Perkins, although actually all are merely following out the implications in Calvin. Perkins takes up all the subtle logical and psychological implications of the doctrine, not always in the most subtle manner. All men are of course guilty of sin after Augustine's doctrine of original sin, but for the elect, sin-consciousness is the first and necessary "sign" of election, while for the reprobate it is a sign of damnation:

The reprobate may have all externals, but not the secret cause of salvation. Wherefore, this knowledge which the reprobate receiveth from nature, and from the creatures, albeit it is not sufficient to make him do that which shall please God: yet before Gods judgment seat, it calleth off al excuse, which he might alleadge, why he should not be condemned.[66]

The reprobate hath oftentimes feare and terrour of conscience: but this is onely, because he considereth the wrath and vengeance of God, which is most terrible.[67]

This was a fine line to draw, yet it was necessary for the Puritan preacher to continue it through all the stages of salvation, since the habits of the reprobate tended to shadow the piety of Elect:

In this thing the elect and the reprobate differ. The reprobate *generally in a confused manner* beleeveth that Christ is a Saviour of some men: and he neither can nor desireth to come to the particular applying of Christ. The elect beleeveth that Christ is a Saviour of him particularly. The reprobates faith may perish in this life, but the faith of the elect cannot.[68]

So also on perhaps the most tricky point of all, one on which Puritans were often defamed and ridiculed by outsiders, the sins committed after election. These sins must not be allowed to be interpreted as evidence of backsliding in the elect:

And herein the elect and the reprobate differ: for the elect are somewhat reformed in every one of their sines. But the Reprobate, though he be amended in many faults: yet some one fault or other, he cannot abide to have it reformed: and by that, in a vile manner the devill wholly possesseth him.[69]

It is obvious that the sincere application of this double sense of sin and of election-reprobation would occasion much anxiety in the individual. Perkins goes on to allay this by presenting a rather clear and simple definition of the elect, clear and simple, that is, until one tried to apply it to oneself:

The Elect are they whome God of the good pleasure of his will hath decreed in himself to choose to eternal life, for the praise of the glorie of his grace. For this cause the Elect onely are said to have their names written in the Booke of Life. Whom God electeth, them he *calleth*. . . . God by his holy spirit indueth them with *true saving faith*: a wonderfull gift, peculiar to the elect.[70]

Faith becomes the first mark of election, and this treatise, like the numerous that preceded and followed, becomes a recital of "marks" of election. With or without these aids, the individual interested in his salvation was given a great deal to think about, and, if he wished to be pessimistic, an insoluble point to ponder, whether as election (psychological) or as predestination (philosophical). Only one thing was really clear: that the lack of any sin-consciousness at all was a mark of reprobation. This mark did not help the individual Puritan distinguish himself from other Christians or in deciding whether, among Puritans, he was of the elect.

In the enumeration of the "signs" of election, there is always a Scylla and Charybdis for the Puritan to contemplate. Saving faith in the elect is not the same as the false beliefs of the Papists. A diligent conscience is often a mark of election, "The godly man *from his youth suffereth the terrours* of God" (p. 364). But extreme grief and terror is the product of false imagination, as Perkins says in this treatise and elaborates in another on the imagination and its evil ways. A natural, worldly grief is evil, and if carried too far becomes a sign of reprobation, not election (pp. 364–365). The fine line is always drawn, as in this definition of "holy desperation" as opposed to a mere wordly terror of the power of God:

holy desperation: which is, when a man is wholly out of all hope ever to attaine salvation by any strentgh [sic] or goodnes of his owne: speaking and thinking more vily of himselfe than any other can doe. . . .[71]

So also true sorrow for sin is distinguished from "natural melancholy" (p. 365). A kind of holy assurance without hubris is the equilibrium that the religious person is supposed to seek:

Therefore when an humbled sinner comes crying and knocking at his mercie gate for the forgivenes of sinne, either then or shortly after the Lord worketh in his heart a lively assurance thereof.

The Elect being thus joyned unto Christ, receive three wonderfull benefits from him, *Justification, Adoption, Sanctification.*[72]

At this point Perkins, and all the preachers who followed him, turn the tables on the argument. Scandalized by Catholic polemics and by notorious examples, the preachers attack faint-conscience and backsliding in the elect, going so far as to say:

The first [sign of faith] is a perswasion, that a mans owne sinnes are pardonable: this perswasion though it be not faith, yet it is a good preparation to faith: for the wicked cutte themselves off quite from Gods mercie.[73]

A strong sin-consciousness is the prerequisite of a sense of election. But the preachers are anxious to get the sinner away from this thought and along the road of justification and sanctification. The sense of assurance and sense of sinlessness of the elect, even in their sins, was an all-too-glib answer of the preachers. But their dilemma, if not always the logic, can be appreciated if we recall how many Puritans, including some famous writers, were troubled with the scruples surrounding the doctrine of election.

To be fair to Perkins and the other preachers, it must be stressed that assurance was defined as a kind of ideal, Janus-faced state in which both a sense of sin and sense of election could live together:

> No Christian attaineth to this full assurance at the first, but in some continuance of time, after that for a long space he hath kept a good conscience before God, and before men: and hath had divers experiences of Gods love and favour towards him in Christ.
> By means of this speciall faith, the Elect are truly *joyned* unto Christ, and have an heavenly *communion* & fellowship with him; & therefore doe in some measure inwardly feele his holy spirit mooving and stirring in them. . . .[74]

If such modest assurance were not possible, it would have been impossible for the preachers to evoke a life of sanctification for the saved; yet the states of assurance and sanctification are troubled in Puritan theology and psychology because of the peculiar basis in election and the conscience. All positive states are possible boobytraps for the Puritan sensibility; in speaking of the good or pacified conscience, another mark of election, Perkins must add quickly that it has its opposite, the dead conscience of the unelect reprobate.

> The slumbering & dead conscience is much like to the good conscience pacified, & many through ignorance take the one for the other.[75]

Some anxiety must remain in the state of assurance or sanctification, enough to show the sting of conscience, as in Sibbes' *Bruised Reede* and Preston's *Breast-Plate of Faith and Love,* which talk equally of problems of election and the life of sanctification. But too much anxiety is theologically dangerous and morally scandalous. Many more quotations can be given on the various facets of this point, but I hope now two at least are clear, both much misinterpreted in literary study of the Puritans. The total operation of sin-consciousness was a complicated matter, subject to further complications of an aberrational nature in the individual. Also, while the preachers stressed assurance against the dangers and terrors of fearing non-election, this assurance, as has often been implied or stated,[76] was more a hope than a reality. It was hope against irreligious despair, but was subject to constant temptation and scrutiny. To demonstrate this completely we have only to mention the number of treatises which concerned the state of assurance-sanctification as a speciality. The Perkins treatise from which we are quoting here is essentially about election, although it brings in other matters towards the end. A treatise on sanctification proper, of which there are many, is essentially a treatise on methods of prayer, sacramental meditation, and the like. Between these two, the beginning and the end of the way as it were, are a special Puritan class of sermons and works on the tremulous states called assurance, or justification extending into sanctification. These commonly have a warfare term in them, such as "breast-plate" or "bruised" or "combat." Constant temptation of the most appalling kind is an effect of Calvinist theology that we cannot blink at, for this helps to define its intellectual and inward bent, and its cautious (compared with Anglican or Roman practice) handling of the areas of the devotional life. In Perkins' words, after election is assumed, the following state occurs:

> Nowe followeth the spirituall exercise of a Christian in his manifold temptations, which are in this life inseparable companions of grace. The reason is, because the devill hateth Christ with a deadly hatred, and sheweth this hatred in a continuall persecution of his members. . . . Now therefore as soone as Christ Jesus beginneth to shew any token of his love to any man, the devill contrariwise sheweth forth his enmitie, and stirres up his fellow champions the flesh and the world to ware against him for his confusion. And furthermore the Lord in great wisedom permits temptations to the last end of a Christian mans life to trie his faith, to purge . . . to humble . . . to quicken and revive the graces of his spirit.[77]

Catholic and Anglican analogies can easily be found for this matter of temptation. The difference remains in the appalling consequences to the Puritan once he loses his sense of the state of assurance and election. Perkins' treatise on election and reprobation is repetitive after this point, outlining in detail the temptations, trials and combats of the saint. The works of Preston, Sibbes and others on the same subject cover the same ground in almost the same way, and there would be no need to present excerpts from their work at all, except to show the point of the almost exact reduplication of language, attitude, and fervor on this important subject.

In Sibbes' *Bruised Reede and Smoaking Flax* (1635), the basic dilemma of the Puritan life is approached from a pastoral viewpoint:

> The ground of this mixture is, that we carry about us a double principle, Grace and Nature. The end of it is especially to preserve us from those two dangerous Rocks which our natures are prone to dash upon, Security and Pride, and to force us to pitch our rest on Justification, not Sanctification. Our spiritual fire, is like our ordinary fire here below, that is mixt. . . . From this mixture it is that the people of God have so different judgments of them-

selves, looking some-times at the work of grace sometimes at the remainder of corruption.[78]

Sometimes in bitterness of temptation, when the Spirit struggles with sense of Gods anger, we are apt to think GOD an enemy, & a troubled soul is like a troubled water, we can see nothing in it. . . .[79]

In spite of the troubled nature of the life of the saints, Sibbes too holds that the sense of assurance in the elect must overbalance the senses of terror and of sin:

This prevailing of light in the soul, is, because together with the spirit of Illumination there goeth (in the godly) *a spirit of power*, to subdue the heart to truth revealed, & to put a taste and relish into the will, suitable to the sweetness of the truths, else a mere natural Will, will rise against supernatural truths, as having an antipathy & enmity against them. In the godly, lively truths are conveyed by way of a taste, gracious men have a spiritual palate as well as a spiritual eye.[80]

The remainder of the *Bruised Reede* more properly concerns sanctification than election, yet there returns throughout the treatise the constant reminder that the religious life is a spiritual combat, and the hint that no Puritan, while he should cling to the sense of election, can afford to become complacent about it. Again, this treatise gives a different view of the Puritan religious experience than one would derive from reading some of our contemporary literary works on 17th century religious literature and tradition.

John Preston, like Sibbes, is primarily a preacher rather than theologian and commentator on Calvinist doctrine, yet his works too are scattered with references to election, assurance, faith, seals of election, sin-consciousness, and those special words used by Sibbes and later Jonathan Edwards, *excellence* and *taste*, referring to the spiritual life. In *Foure Godly and Learned Treatises* (1633), Preston stresses the necessity of an overwhelming sense of sin-consciousness as the preparation for the awakening of the religious life:

So in men that are spiritually dead, there is no beauty, no vigor, they have death in their faces: they may have painted beauty, which may be like the living. . . .

Christians having the treble Law, the Gospel, the Law of nature, the moral Law, *shall be condemned for all three*; and among all Christians such as have had more means, and better education, the greater shall their punishment be.

Thirdly, for the death that is opposite to the life of joy, the degrees of it are more sensible: Some have legal terrors, the beginnings of eternal death; others have peace of conscience and joy in the Holy Ghost, the beginning of eternal life . . . in those who are spiritually dead there is a life of understanding by which they themselves may know that they are dead.[81]

After such a gloomy beginning, Preston, like the others, takes great pains to chart out the grounds of election and to exhort his hearers on to justification and sanctification. His work is emphatic and fuller of allusion and metaphor than the others, but essentially he follows the same line, except for personal nuance of expression. In his longest collected work, *The New Covenant or the Saints Portion in Fourteen Sermons*, he preaches the usual self-searching which leads to the feeling of being "called":

> . . . he cannot say he feares God, and nothing else: for there are many things that he feares more than God, so he cannot say of his love to GOD, that, that is right, it may be, it is misplaced, though many other things may be right in him, he loves riches, he loves credit. . . . So that, if God and thee should come in competition, he would be ready to violate his conscience towards him, rather then to part with these: And so his grief, that is not principally for sin, there is somewhat or other, that you shall find him failing in, there is not an integrity in the subject.[82]

The usual marks of election are sought out in these sermons, and also in Preston's other long work, *The Breast-Plate of Faith and Love* (ed. 1634), where the marks of election are considered specifically in relation to justifying faith and grace. If Preston's work on election has any distinguishing mark it is the tendency, warned against by Perkins and most other Puritan preachers, to strive for literal perfection in this world, not, as many Puritans believed, to take the word for the deed:

> Now, I say, when a man is so entire, when there is such truth in him, that bring him to what touch-stone you will, let him be brought to the light, he knowes his workes aright, he is not afraid, let GOD himself look into his heart, that hath pure eyes, that can reach every cranie of it, to who every thing is naked, yet he shall find him true: that is, he doth every thing (if GOD look to the most inward retired thought) in GODS sight, he approves to him, such a one hath a perfect heart.[83]

But he spends a good deal of space, as do his brethren, in explaining the difference between sin in the elect and sin in the unregenerate. The Puritan tendency to stray in practice into the Catholic view of sanctification was usually countered by dogmatic reminders (to themselves as well as listeners) of the arbitrariness of election and the precedence of justification over sanctification in reformation religion.

b. Vocation and Justification

Vocation and justification are Puritan doctrines peripheral to the formation of literary sensibility. Only to the extent that "calling" encouraged constant meditation and performance of religious duties does it have some bearing, although, as is well known, Calvinist-Puritanism encouraged vocations in the world to such an extent that ridicule and the "stage-Puritan" were the results. Sibbes in *The Soules Conflict* expresses the classical view of "calling" succinctly and clearly:

The like may be said for our *particular* calling, wherein we are to express the graces of our Christian calling, and *serve one another in love*, as members of the *state* as well as of the Church, therefore every one must have 1. a calling, 2. a lawful, 3. a useful calling, 4. a calling fitted for his parts, that he may be even for his business. . . . Most of our disquietness in our calling, is that we trouble our selves about Gods work. Trust God and be doing, and let him alone with the rest.[84]

The doctrine of vocation or calling had the good purpose of sanctifying life in the world, as few in Puritanism were called to constant meditation, prayer, or to the office of preacher. There is little in the poets, except for Milton's "On his blindness," directly on the subject of "calling." For the political and economic study of the Puritan movement, as everyone knows, "calling" is vitally important and has become a controversial subject. In bringing sanctification to the world, instead of confining it to a monastic system of retreat from the world, Puritanism ran the risks of being overcome by the world. With the decline of piety and theology in the 18th century, there is no doubt some justification for the image of the Puritan as the somber and close counting-house man who reserves his religion for Sunday. But this image did not apply to the literary man, even in later days, and is of little concern to this study.

It is for a more precisely theological reason that justification by faith is relatively unimportant for Puritan literary sensibility. As a theological point in Puritanism (unlike its place in other Protestant denominations), it falls between election and sanctification, and generally is swallowed up by these giants in the consideration of the preachers. Not that discussions of faith, saving faith, the nature of faith, or the theology of divine satisfaction behind the doctrine are missing from the writings of Perkins, Preston, Sibbes and others. It is just that such an enormous weight in the Puritan drama of redemption is placed upon sin-consciousness and election in the first instance, then a necessarily great amount of time given over to the process of sanctification and the minutiae thereof, that justification, after brief and proper treatment, is usually ignored as a point of consciousness. Its one vital use, as many preachers found, was as a constant reminder that discussions of the state of sanctification were in constant danger of "lapsing" into Papist thinking, the kind of moral perfection through works that Puritanism was supposedly in revolt against. Preachers discussing such matters as prayer, meditation, and sacramental devotions had constant need to remind themselves of this fact. Preston in *The New Covenant* puts the matter succinctly enough:

... if a man would have his conscience purged from dead works, let him labour for faith, whereby he may be justified, let him labour to be sprinkled with the blood of *Christ* ... that eternall Spirit, that shall purge and cleanse his conscience from dead works.
The best way ... to change our hearts ... is to grow up in the assurance of the love of God to us in Christ, to get assurance of pardon and forgiveness, to labour to be partaker of the Covenant of Grace; your hearts will then be softened, when you have received the spirit, that hath wrought in your hearts a disposition answerable to the Law without, when the Law is put into your minds.[85]

This doctrine of justification was needed as a reminder both against the arrogance of good works faithfully performed, and against the despair of good works unperformed or of sins committed. Thus while justification is handled early and succinctly in most Puritan tracts, it keeps cropping up in general ways throughout any discussion of the means of sanctification. It qualifies the Puritan views of sanctification, and of prayer, sacraments and other good works, and as a pivot in the system tends to prevent the means of sanctification from attaining a life of their own, as they often do in Catholic and Anglican pratice and literature. There is the usual wariness here in referring everything back ultimately to the initial problem of conscience and election.

It would be possible to conclude this section on vocation and justification, as well as that on election for that matter, with selections from the writings of Jonathan Edwards, particularly *A Treatise Concerning Religious Affections* (1746).[86] Here are given the famous twelve signs of election, a thoughful compendium by Edwards of his learned reading of 16th and 17th century Puritanism. Edwards wrote this treatise as a result of the disasters of the "Great Awakening." He has concerns not present to the earlier Puritans, such as the dangers of emotionalism and the epistemology of Locke. Yet essentially it is important for our purposes to note that the basic structure remains intact here in the mid-18th century in New England. A 16th century Puritan would be able to find his way around in Edwards' work. Edwards was, of course, called retrograde or reactionary in his own day and in the history of American thought. This does not matter for our purposes, which are to show that the sensibility we are trying to define through the use of 16th and 17th century materials remained intact for a long enough period to be of influence upon a remarkable group of late 18th and early 19th century writers in England and America. The evidence presented in this chapter is not confined in usefulness to the immediate period 1570–1660, although its use is most obvious in that period. *Datis dandis*, it will serve to illumine the works of Cowper, some Romantics, and the New England writers.

c. Sanctification

Sanctification and its attributes comprise by far the largest single area of the Puritan mental life, as it is for all intense religious experience. This point has been lost upon such writers as Martz and Feidelson, who occupy themselves only with the intellectual side of the Puritan sensibility. Gordon Wakefield's recent *Puritan Devotion: Its Place in the Development of Christian Piety* deserves great praise in helping to restore some sense of balance here, although it is wanting in two respects. Most important is the connection of Puritan piety to the intellectual and theological side of the movement, which the present work tries to achieve. Second, and important for a literary study, is the analysis of the literary sensibility of the movement, which was not Wakefield's province to attempt.

To maintain the sense of the first in discoursing of Puritan piety and devotion, it is important to remember the place of sanctification in the Puritan scheme. The preachers always maintained the sense of its derivation from election and justification, its closeness to the problem of the conscience. This was less necessary in dealing with the theory of sanctification itself or with its first fruit, prayer, than with the other usual areas of sanctification, such as sacramental devotions, church practice, and general meditation. To make this point, the areas will be handled accordingly, with prayer and sacramental meditations falling under sanctification, and general meditation and church practices (also called Covenant theology) given separate consideration. The latter, Covenant doctrine and church order of worship, deserve no more than mention, since this political and public side of the Puritan movement contributed little to its imaginative literature. For the specific notion of sanctification we find enough material in the writings of Perkins, Preston and Sibbes. With prayer, sacraments and more general areas of Puritan worship, a wider variety of material must be called upon.

Sanctification is viewed by Perkins, Preston and Sibbes as the "regenerate" state. Except in general treatises dealing with the entire cycle, it is treated separately as a matter of the soul or of the conscience. Such titles as Perkins' *Cases of Conscience*, Sibbes's *Bruised Reede* and *Soules Conflict* and Preston's *Three Sermons on the Sacrament* indicate the pastoral nature of the problem of sanctification. There is general agreement that sanctification is a desired end, that it is not easy to achieve (hence the problems of sin and of bad conscience which arise in the state), and that devotional methods, properly used, are helpful in achieving the state. Ritual is looked upon with suspicion, of course, but a general imitation of Christ and close discourse with God (the calling upon "Abba Father") are encouraged. Above all else, the preachers strive heroically to maintain a view of the process of sanctification which is congruent with the doctrines of election and justification. The dangers of the faithful falling into the Catholic view of works and sanctification lurk everywhere, and some, like Ames in *Cases of Conscience*, succumb. Despair of attaining a reasonable degree of sanctification is another great issue for the Puritans, and here the preachers constantly remind the faithful of the relationship of election to sanctification. It is lawful to despair of sin before election and justification, but unlawful thereafter. The sins of the elect do not prevent sanctification, and legal, literal sanctification of all sins and evil tendencies is impossible. This attitude may be called "the sinning of the just" out of context, but in context it is a reasonable notion following upon election, and one which toned down the spiritual agonies and strivings from their level in counter-reformation Catholic practice. The elect must strive in sanctification, but always act and feel as if this state, after justification, has been minimally achieved. This attitude had some of the "double think" and Janus-faced quality in it which has been noticed of all 17th century English religious practice; nevertheless it was not an invitation to hypocricy or indifference, as the tone of the writing indicates. It wished, on grounds satisfactory to its own premises, to promote sanctity among the faithful without causing the consternation, despair and perhaps excesses of the Catholic counterpart. As Martz and others have shown,[87] many Catholic devotional treatises, properly purged and edited, were circulated among the Puritans and Anglicans of the 17th century. From the viewpoint of the Puritan preachers, there is nothing clandestine or immoral about this, as long as Catholic "legal" theology and "heretical" devotional practices are surpressed.

Perkins discusses sanctification briefly in his theoretical works. In *A Golden Chaine* (1608) he defines it thus:

The third degree, is Sanctification, whereby such as beleeve, being delivered from the tyrannie of sine, are by little reneued in holines and righteousnes. ... The mortification of sine, is the first part of sanctification, whereby the power of sine is abated, and crucified in the faithfull.[88]

He continues to sketch the process of sanctification, one side of which is warfare against the devil and sin, the other the holy means of a good life. Imagery common to Puritan literature appears here, such as "spiritual armour," "girded," "breastplate," "shield of faith," "helmet of salvation" and so on. "The warriors, are the tempter, and the Christian souldier [the victim of the temptation]. ... The Tempter, is the prince, or his helpers. The Prince is Satan and his angels, which are spirituall wickednesses, in high things. His helpers are the flesh and the world."[89] Assaults against faith, election, and conscience, as well as actual sins, make the life of the saint one of constant temptation. Therefore the positive means of holding out against these assaults are prayer and petition, religious observance and meditation. A good portion of Perkins' later works are devoted to spelling out the spiritual war that occurs in striving for sanctification. His *Treatise of Mans Imaginations Showing His natural evil thoughts* (1613) deals with the various natural evil proclivities in man which war against sanctification. After listing the usual temptations of the flesh, of the world and of spiritual despair, he presents the ancient idea of a "holy imagination," an imagination disciplined by meditation. Contrary to popular views, the Puritans did not try to supress the imagination totally, but rather as other Christians did, tried to make it a positive force. Perkins' longest practical or devotional work is entitled *The Whole Treatise of the Cases of Conscience, Distinguished into Three Books* (1613). It is significant, for reasons already explained, that study of the sanctified or devotional life would be called "cases of conscience" by a Puritan writer. It begins with a definition of the state of sanctification, which stresses again the idea of spiritual combat:

Most sinnes are partly from the will, partly against it. Of this sort are the works of the man regenerate which are done partly with his will, and partly against his will, being partly good, and partly evil. . . . There are in man after regeneration, two contrary grounds or beginnings of action: to wit, natural corruption, or the inclination of the mind, will, and affections, to that which is against the Law . . . and a created quality of holiness, wrought in the said faculties by the Holy Ghost, termed the Spirit. And these two are not several but joyned and mingled together, in all the faculties and powers of the soul. Now between them there is a continuall combat, corruption fighting against grace, and grace against corruption . . . there must necessarily flow from the man regenerate contrary actions. . . .[90]

This is bravely put, and what follows is a paradigm of exhortation and advice which is duplicated in the other preachers. The efforts of sanctification must never obscure the effects of election and justification, falling into the old "Papist" calculus of the moral life. Prayer, religious services and sacramental devotion must never become "works," as in the Papist scheme. Yet voluntary confession of sins to a friend or minister is even cautiously advised to the squeamish of conscience. Most of the tracts are devoted to specific items, such as prayer, the Lord's Supper, and group meditation. On the surface Perkins' presentation may be hard to distinguish in some places from Catholic practice, except for the restraint and down-to-earth quality of the language. But sprinkled through the work are attacks on Papist errors, to remind the reader of differences, and a hedging attitude towards all devotional practice, based upon the doctrine of election, that is typically Puritan and intellectual in quality.

Sibbes' two main works, *The Bruised Reede and Smoaking Flax* (1635), and *The Soules Conflict with it self* (1625) are essentially about sanctification, although other matters enter from times to time, as in all Puritan tracts. *The Bruised Reede* follows Perkins in calling the "regenerate" state a state of conflict, contraries and spiritual warfare, a struggle allowed by God and not to be confused with the struggle over election, which, if carried on too long, becomes impious. Both works have a good deal on prayer and the sacraments, which will be deferred to the proper place below. *The Soules Conflict* has a fine presentation on the heights and delicacy of the spiritual combat in the state of sanctification, something to keep in mind in reading Marvell, Dickinson, or, in a secularized way, Hawthorne:

There is yet a further degree of conflict betwixt the sanctified powers of the soul, and the flesh, not only as it is seated in the baser parts, but even in the best faculties of the soul, and as it mingles it self with every gracious performance (as in David) there is not only a conflict betwixt sin and conscience, enlightened by *a common worke of the Spirit*; but between the commanding powers of the soul *sanctified*, and itself *unsanctified*, between reasons of the *flesh* and reasons of the *spirit*, between *faith* and *distrust*, between the true light of knowledge, and false light. . . .
As in the conflict between the higher parts of the soul with the lower, it clearly appears, that the soul doth not rise out of the temper of the body, but is a more noble substance, commanding the body by reasons fetched from its own worth; so in this spiritual conflict, it appears there is something better than the soul it self, that hath superiority over it.[91]

This passage sets the stage for the high drama of the soul, such as is found in Marvell's dialogues and *Paradise Regained*, between, that is to say, refined forms of good and evil. For this combat, meditation is necessary to ensure survival: "The life of a Christian should be a meditation how to unloose his affections from inferior things; he will easily die that is dead before in affections" (pp. 158—9). Sibbes defines the Puritan attempt at sanctification in its most attractive form:

The setting of an excellent idea and platform before us, will raise and draw up our soules higher, and make us sensible of the least movings of spirit, that shall be contrary to that, the attainment whereof we have in our desires. He will hardly attain to mean things, that sets not before him higher perfection. Naturally we love to see symmetry and proportion, even in a dead picture, and are much taken with some curious piece. But why should we not rather labour to keep the affections of the soul in due proportion?[92]

There follows a long meditation on the power of sin and concupiscence even in the elect and justified, ending with the follwing:

Hence it is that the *old man* is never tired in the *works of the flesh*, nor never drawn dry. When man cannot act sin, yet they will love sin, and act it ever again by pleasing thoughts of it, and by sinful speculation suck out the delight of sin; but because they want strength and opportunity to commit it; if such would not leave them, they would never leave sin.[93]

Here we have the temper of religious Puritanism indeed. Assurance is of election and justification, to prevent despair, but this by no means prevents the endless self-scrutiny of the would-be sanctified man. There are valuable insights in these attitudes for the study of paradoxes in the Calvinist religious poets. Imagination, for Sibbes as for Perkins, is a dreadful scourge of the natural man, unless it too can be disciplined through meditation to aid in the eternal fight on this earth:

Without the fight of which there can be no *sound repentance* arising from the deep and through consideration of sin; no desire to be *new moulded*, without which we can never enter into so holy a place as heaven; no *self-denial* till we see the best things in us are enmity against God; so high praising of Christ, without whom our natures, persons, and our actions are abominable in Gods sight; nor any solid peace settled in the soul which peace ariseth not from the ignorance of our corruption, or compounding with it, but from fight and hatred of it, and strength against it.[94]

Sibbes continues in this vein for many hundreds of pages, in the course of which he shows the efficacy of prayer and sacraments for the continuance of the sanctified life. But the conflict is one primarily of the total moral life, which, we have seen, is called by the collective term "conscience" in Puritan discourse. Faith, sin, the inner light of the spirit and the eternal struggle are all somehow inextricably wound in man sanctified:

And as sin causeth a distance betwixt God and us, so the guilt of sin in the conscience, causes further strangeness, insomuch that we dare not look up to heaven, till God open a little crevise to let in a little light of comfort (at least) into our soules, whereby we are by little and little drawn neerer to him. But this light at the first is so little, that in regard of the greater sense of *sin*, and a larger desire of *grace*, the soul reckons the same as no light at all in comparison of what it desires and seekes after. Yet the comfort is, that this dawning light will at length clear up to a perfect day.[95]

We can see that Sibbes' role was primarily that of a physician of the soul.

John Preston's *New Covenant* (ed. 1634), *Sinnes Overthrow, or, A Godly and Learned Treatise of Mortification* (1635) and *Three Sermons upon the Sacrament of the Lords Supper* (1635) follow the pattern set by Perkins and visible in Sibbes. The general treatment of sanctification appears in *New Covenant*, with the negative elements of sin and despair in *Mortification* balanced by the exhortations in *Three Sermons* to methods of devotion, especially prayer and the sacraments. As there are no significant variations on the theme, the excerpts from Preston, except those later on devotional practice, will be kept brief.

So that, my beloved, to have a purified disposition, to have a heart and a spirit ready to cleanse it self, this is to have a perfect heart: So that a godly man, he may be many times defiled with sin & uncleanliness, he may have his heart many times muddy and impure, he may have it clouded and overcast with passions and unruly affections, but yet it cleares up again, and he comes out of them all with more brightness, and with more clearness and pureness of heart.[96]

This is the typical Puritan view of sanctification as modified by the doctrine of justification. "I deny not that there may be many relapses into the same sin, though the heart be perfect and sincere . . ." Preston adds just after the above. There is collapse into wickedness in the reprobate, but only tension in sin in the sanctified. Preston's discussion does have a general drift into speculation upon freedom of the will, as he notices the force of irresistible sin and of irresistible grace. "The Spirit, the regenerate part, though it might and would always get the better, were it upon equal terms with the flesh; yet, when the flesh shall get the hill . . . in such a case, upon such a disadvantage, he is overcome, and falls into sin" (p. 256). But this aspect is not stressed, as it was to be later by Jonathan Edwards, to become a primary metaphysical problem in its own right; Preston believes traditionally in the methods of devotion that can induce the state of sanctification. The *Treatise of Mortification* was written to prescribe these means:

if you would have your sinnes mortified, . . . get spiritual joy. But this may seem a strange thing to mortify corruption by; a man or a woman would rather think that this were a meanes to increase sin: but it is not so . . . when the heart is not regenerate it is full of sorrow, and joy in this estate encreaseth sin. But when the heart is turned from sin to Grace, that is, heavenly disposed, there is a pleasant Object represented unto the eye of the Soul, as Christ, Justification, Remission of sinnes, and Reconciliation: and hence ariseth a spiritual Joy in the soul.[97]

He later employs the image of the journey and the narrow way:

for we must know that the way to heaven is not a broad footway, where many footsteps appear, as a path-way is to a great Citie; but it is a narrow way, and therefore we must journey hard; besides, there are not many going that way; and therefore we must not give ear unto the opinion and speeches of the multitudes.[98]

Bunyan may well have read these lines and others like them in the work of the generation before him. Preston also urges the practice of *contemptus mundi*, somewhat slackened from its medieval ardor:

so it is with a Christian that is humbled and cast down under the sense of the wrath of God for sin; tell him of any thing in the world in the most learned and excellentest manner that possibly you can, yet nothing will satisfy him but the love and favour of God in Christ, he can relish nothing but heavenly things; nothing will quench his thirst but the imputed righteousness of Christ.[99]

Like the other preachers, Preston intersperses his view of the hard life of the sanctified Christian with notions of the damnation of the wicked in the next world, and if in this world too, so much the better. In discussing meditation Preston, like the others, often falls into meditation himself. Meditation is the primary act of the state of sanctification. We shall see later how the diarists, in attempting to set down the daily life of sanctification, often fall into acts of meditation. Preston also, as befits a great Cambridge and court preacher, asserts the special importance of the preaching of the Word in the sanctification of the preacher and the listeners. The life of sanctification should be a life of cautious joy, never of despair, and not admitting of complacency:

... so it is with sin, if thou suffer thy heart to be spotted but with one sin, it will work carelessness in thee, so that hereafter thou wilt not much care what sin thou commit, nor how thy soul is soiled; therefore it behoves you to keep your hearts from every sin, and to make conscience of little sinnes.[100]

1. Prayer

Prayer in the Puritan tradition has three main divisions, only one of which is our concern in this place. Formal or "set prayer" involves the public worship of the Puritans and is strictly speaking justified as part of Covenant theology. In practical usage, this aspect of prayer becomes the question of formal order in church service. Horton Davies in *The Worship of the English Puritans*[101] has taken up all areas of this point, and Perry Miller has discussed its relationship to the theology of the Covenant.[102] A brief space will be given to it later. It has not seemed to this author that formal prayer and order of worship contributed much to the imaginative life of the Puritans, and hence to their literature, except in the special area of devotional hymns.

Informal prayer, private in nature, was favored by the Puritan divines, as we are told by Gordon Wakefield in his excellent *Puritan Devotion*, and as we may read ourselves in the writings of Preston, Perkins, Bishop Bayly and many others. Formal or merely memorized prayers were suspect of Popery. This attitude presents us with the problem of distinguishing informal prayer from meditation, which was not done sharply in the Puritan tradition. For our purposes, then, any general meditation on the religious life, and all meditations on the sacrament of upon the role of Christ, will be considered under meditation rather than as informal prayer. In treating informal prayer we will follow the strict definition given of it by several preachers as the first sign of repentance and of sanctification, the ability to talk to God and to call upon him as "Abba Father."

Perkins presents this idea succinctly at the beginning of his *A Case of Conscience* (1595). The ability to pray is a sign of election and the beginning of sanctification:

Therefore the Apostle saith, that we have received the spirit of adoption, by which we crie Abba Father: as though he should say, this testimonie of the spirit is altogether so sure, by which he beareth us record that we are the sonnes of God: that presently without doubting, we can call upon God: and crie Abba Father. And all the Elect have this testimonie, being made the sonnes of God by Faith, and being renewed by the holie Ghost: and ingrafted into Christ.[103]

For the Puritan, then, what prayer accomplishes as a work of devotion is relatively unimportant in relation to the fact that prayer is possible at all. It is the link of the regenerate man to God. The reprobate cannot pray effectively. In his *Cases of Conscience*, a more purely devotional work, Perkins expands this definition to explain the function of prayer as a bridge between election and sanctification:

Every petition must proceed from a lively sense and feeling of our own wants, and of our spiritual poverty. For without this, no prayer can be earnest and hearty; and consequently become acceptable unto God. For example, when we pray that Gods name may be hallowed, we must in making that petition, have in our hearts a sense of the corruption of our nature, whereby we are prone to dishonour the name of God.[104]

Clearly prayer is a means of sanctification. But prayer, like every other means of sanctification, is subject to abuses in the manner of the Papists. Perkins prefers private prayer over set or public worship, but condones the latter as a moderating community force (pp. 66ff.). Private prayer can tend to the idolatrous, unless careful rules are followed, which Perkins explicitly sets out:

Prayer is to be presented to God, in the name, merit, and mediation of Christ alone. For we ourselves are not worthy of any thing, but shame, and confusion. Therefore we cannot pray in our own names, but must pray only in the name of Christ. Our prayers are our sacrifices, and Christ alone is that Altar, whereon we must offer them to God the Father. For this altar must sanctify them, before they can be a sacrifice of a sweet smelling savour unto

God. Hence it is, that not only our petitions, but all other things, as Paul wisheth, are to be done in the name of the Lord Jesus. . . . Thus we have the first question of conscience resolved touching Prayer; that then the prayer is acceptable to God, when he that prayeth observes, as much as in him lyeth, all these conditions before in, and after prayer.[105]

From this passage in Perkins we can easily see that the matter of private prayer becomes tied in with sacramental and general meditation. The general guides for prayer are the Scriptures and good points in a godly sermon. The Puritans never developed any of the elaborate methods of mental prayer found in Ignatius and other Counter Reformation writers, but they did spell out their attitude more fully than many modern literary critics tend to believe. The devout life of sanctification within Puritanism was not entirely an intellectual process, as the writing of Martz, Miller and others tend to suggest. Gordon Wakefield's useful book stands as necessary corrective on this point.

An Elizabethan Puritan bishop, Lewis Bayly, in his extremely popular *The Practice of Pietie*[106] is more explicit than any other writer of the 16th century on the subjects of prayer and meditation. He approves of and uses "Master Perkins" as a guideline on the subject of private prayer, but one cannot believe that Perkins would have approved of the Bishop's sometimes florid Elizabethan style. Be that as it may, he is essentially a Puritan writer, and leads to the more openly devotional Puritan work of Baxter and others in the 17th century. Bayly opened the way for a more lively imagination about spiritual things than is found in Perkins, Preston and Sibbes. In their writings the joy of the religious life seems to be purely theoretical.

Most of Bayly's book is devoted to techniques of meditation and sacramental veneration, and we will deal with these aspects under those headings. He reaches the subject of prayer about one third of the way through the book. Bayly approves of spontaneous over set prayers, yet ironically his work is devoted to manufacturing spontaneous prayers for the faithful, as in the following:

Consider, how Gods *mercy* is renewed unto thee every morning, in giving thee (as it were) *a new life*: and in causing the *Sunne*, after his incessant race, to rise again to give thee *light*. Let not then his glorious light burn in vain: but prevent rather (as oft as thou canst) the *Sunne rising*, to give God thanks: & kneeling down at thy bed-side, salute him at the Day-spring with some devout Antelucanium or Morning Soliloquie . . . containing an humble confession of thy *sinnes*, the pardon of all thy faults, a thanksgiving for all his *benefits*, and a craving of his gracious *protection* to his Church.[107]

Examples of "set prayers" are given for morning, evening and other occasions. These are not "Papist" prayers to be memorized by rote, but rather examples to encourage the spontaneous outbursts of the individual. Some of these prayers are no more than recitation of Calvinist dogma:

> I render unto thee from the *Altar* of my humblest heart . . . for mine Election, Creation, Redemption, Vocation, Justification, Sanctification, and Preservation from my childhood until this present day and hour. . . .[108]

Pages of this ordinary kind of piety follow, obviously directed to the pious unlearned. Some rise to the level of sacramental and personal meditation:

> Oh let us feel the power of Christ's death, killing sin in our mortal bodies, and the vertues of his resurrection, raising up our soules to newness of life. So we beseech thee inspire thy holy spirit into our hearts, that by his illumination and effectual working, we may have the inward sight of feeling of our sins, and natural corruptions, and that we may not be blinded in them, through custome, as the Reprobates are.[109]

For the more intelligent and imaginative, a general rule is given:

> But in hearing, apply every speech as spoken to thy self, rather by God than by Man: and labour not so much to hear the words of the Preacher sounding in thine ear, as to feel the operation of the spirit, working in thy heart.[110]

The section on prayer ends with an example of a private evening prayer, after which Bayly continues to the subject of more severe mortifications to obtain sanctification:

> O Holy, holy, holy, Lord God of Sabbaths! Suffer me, who am but dust and ashes, to speak unto thy most glorious Majesty. I know that thou art a consuming fire: I acknowledge, that I am but withered stubble. My sinnes are in thy sight and Satan stands at my right hand, to accuse me for them. I come not to excuse, but to judge my self worthie of all those Judgments which thy Justice might most justly inflict upon me, a wicked creature, for my sinnes and transgressions.[111]

2. Lord's Supper and Sacramental Meditation

In a time of great theological division, none more fierce than that involving the sacraments, it is not surprising to find the Puritan preachers devoting much of their energy on this subject to matters of definition and polemics. Each tried to give a clear and workable definition of the sacrament to the faithful. But there was also some time for discussions of devotional practice, and Bayly devotes much of his *Practice of Pietie* to sacramental meditation. A difficulty appears in Puritan writings in distinguishing clearly between sacramental meditation and general meditation on the subject of Christ, a difficulty not present to the same degree in Anglican devotion and obviated in Catholicism by the doctrine of the Real Presence. Simply put, a meditation on the Lord's Supper might well be specific in Puritanism, but it might just as easily become a more general meditation on Christ's spiritual presence in the world. In this section both types of practice will be included, with some attempt made to show what, if any, distinction is made by a particular writer. The importance of this distinction will be made clear later as we examine sacramental meditation in Marvell, Taylor and Baxter.

It being obvious that sacramental meditation depends upon apprehension of sacramental doctrine, no writer could afford to discuss purely devotional matters, even Bayly in *Practice of Pietie*. Bayly, Perkins and others hearken back to Calvin for "true" views of the Lord's presence in the Supper, and grounded in these, approach the more personal and meditative qualities of sacramental reception. It is proper then to put succinctly what Calvin and Calvinism's view of the sacrament was, with the help of Wakefield's fine summary in *Puritan Devotion*.[112]

On this subject Calvin lacks some of the usual clarity and forthrightness with which he had handled the doctrines of original sin and election. He is forthright against transubstantiation to be sure, and against any form of devotion and worship directed to the consecrated sacrament itself, which he views as idolatry. More perplexing are his positive statements. He asserts Christ's presence in the sacrament, yet asserts freely that the mode of his presence is a mystery.

Let our faith receive, therefore, what our understanding is not able to comprehend, that the Spirit really unites things which are separated by local distance. Now, that holy participation of his flesh and blood, by which Christ communicates his life to us, just as if he actually penetrated every part of our frame, in the sacred supper he also testifies and seals; and that not by the exhibition of a vain or ineffectual sign, but by the exertion of the energy of his Spirit, by which he accomplishes that which he promises.[113]

The presence of Christ is at the time of the saying of the words and receiving of the sacrament, which gives an inevitable psychological element to Calvinist thinking of the sacrament not necessarily present in Catholic and other theories which claim sacramental efficacy *ex opere operata*, in the sacramental elements themselves.

I say, therefore, that in the mystery of the supper, under the symbols of bread
and wine, Christ is truly exhibited to us, even his body and blood, in which he
has fulfilled all obedience to procure our justification.[114]

Exhibited is the crucial word here. Christ descends in spirit from
heaven, yet remains in heaven: "We say that Christ descends to us
both by the external symbol and by his Spirit, that he may truly vivify
our souls with the substance of his flesh and blood" (IV, xvii). Christ
is present spiritually, but compared to Catholic doctrine that attaches
his presence to the elements of bread and wine, there is a "real
absence" also, as it was called in the theological jargon of Calvin's
day. But the question was not, as polemics have taught too many on
both sides to believe, of presence or absence, but of the manner of the
presence of Christ in the sacrament. Calvin at least saw this as the
issue:

The only question between us, therefore, respects the manner of this
presence; because they place Christ in the bread, and we think it unlawful for
us to bring him down heaven. . . . Let us hear no more of that calumny, that
Christ is excluded from the sacrament, unless he be concealed under the
bread. . . . If any one inquire of me respecting the manner, I shall not be
ashamed to acknowledge, that it is a mystery too sublime for me to be able to
express or even to comprehend; and, to be still more explicit, I rather
experience it, than understand it.[115]

A doctrine such as this may seem to involve a difficulty of real
presence vs. real absence as grave as the difficulties involved in transubstantiation. Whatever the logical problems, it satisfied a need of
certain Protestant thinking for the day. Perkins, Preston, and Bayly
talk a good deal of the reception of the sacrament and of proper
sacramental meditation, but for doctrine they are content to hearken
back to Calvin and often quote him. The experience Calvin
mentioned was shared by his followers for several hundred years, and
required strenuous psychological and rational participation in the act
in order to bring about the act. In the long run many have held that
this rationalistic element was theologically disastrous for Protestantism. In the words of Nuttall, "the Puritan movement was rooted in a
repudiation of the sacerdotal system. . . . In relation to the sacraments
there thus remained in many Puritans' minds something of an unre-
solved tension. . . ."[116] For our purposes it need only be noted that
the Calvinist doctrine of the sacrament gave rise to a distinct tradition
of meditation on the sacrament and upon certain aspects of the life of
Christ associated with the institution of the Lord's Supper. Literary

historians and critics have often confused or downgraded this heritage in writing of religious poetry and other literature.

It would be possible, but tedious, to trace the development and acceptance of Calvin's sacramental theories by the English Puritans. All the important writers quote or cite Calvin at some point in their writing on sacramental doctrine. Perhaps, then, Gordon Wakefield's useful and authoritative summary will suffice as a general judgment on Calvinist sacramental theory:

> The Puritan preoccupation with redemption allows Vines to say that the Supper exhibits Christ in but one of His aspects, though that the most precious, i.e. as dying. He will have no reference to the Resurrection and Ascension in the Sacrament. There can be no repetition of what was done once for all on Calvary, and, as Owen says, the whole glory of the Sacrament is in the work which a triumphant Saviour has finished for man. . . . There is a kind of psycho-physical parallelism in some of the Puritan explanations of the mystery of the Eucharist.
>
> The realism of Puritan sacramental teaching is qualified by the Reformed understanding of the "eschatological distance" between Christ and us. Christ is in heaven at the right hand of God; we are upon earth. The sacraments anticipate the Parousa; they do not precipitate it as the false doctrine of Transsubstantiation would imply, thus overthrowing the very nature of a sacraments.[117]

Wakefield draws four clear points of Puritan doctrine on the Supper from study of the English divines: a. The Lord's Supper is related to redemption rather than to creation; b. The Lord's Supper is related to the sacrifice of Calvary; c. There is a reverent agnosticism about the precise manner of Christ's sacramental presence; d. The "realism" of Puritan sacramental teaching is qualified by the Reformed understanding of the "eschatological" distance between Christ and us. Upon this doctrine the divines and their followers erected a system of sacramental devotion, including meditation upon the worthiness of the receiver, the nature and effects of the gift, and some aspects of the Christ who gives himself in this sacrament.

Bayly begins his account of sacramental meditation with a reference to Calvin's account and to 1 Corinthians 11.25. He paraphrases Calvin thus to his own satisfaction:

> Hence it is, that in the same instant of time that the worthy Receiver eateth with his mouth the Bread and Wine of the Lord, he eateth also with the mouth of his Faith, the very Body and Blood of Christ; not that Christ is brought down from Heaven to the Sacrament, but that the holy Spirit, by the Sacrament, lifts up his mind into Christ; nqt by any local mutation, but by a

devout affection: so that in the holy contemplation of Faith, he is at that present with Christ, and Christ with him.[118]

Bayly divides the act of receiving the sacrament into three parts, as do all the other Calvinist writers: preparation, meditation, and action in practice. Preparation is an examination of conscience, meditation the devout feelings at the moment of the reception, and action in practice a general wish to reform based upon contemplation of the gifts of Christ. This latter often trailed off in Puritan practice into general meditation on the merits of Christ; such meditations are dealt with here since in Puritan practice they are almost always connected with reception of the sacrament.

Steps in preparation include contemplating the worthiness of the sacrament, the unworthiness of the individual (p. 531), and minute examination of conscience. In Bayly, the meditation upon reception tends to follow a regular theological line:

he bestoweth upon the recipients all saving graces, necessary to attain eternal life; a the sense of Gods love, the assurance of our Election, with regeneration, justification and grace to do good works: till we come to live with him in his heavenly Kingdom.[119]

The Puritan doctrine of grace tends to reduce man's role in the reception of the sacrament, and almost to equate Christ with faith:

It is not our Faith, that makes the Body and Blood of Christ to be present, but the Spirit of Christ dwelling in him and us. Our faith doth but receive and apply unto our soules those heavenly graces which are offered in this sacrament.[120]

Viewed this way, there is no encouragement for Puritan meditation to emphasize the bodily Jesus or the actions of Calvary in the vivid Counter Reformation manner. The believer lifts his heart upward to a Christ in heaven, and is sustained by Christ as the informing Word of faith:

A true persuasion as of all these things, whatsoever the Lord hath revealed in his Word: so also a particular application unto a mans owne Soule, of all the promises of mercy which God hath made in Christ to all believing sinners: and consequently, that Christ and all his mercies do belong unto him as well as to any other.[121]

For as ours is the same supper which Christ administered: so is the same Christ verily present at his own Supper, not by any Papal transsubstantiation but by a sacramental participation, whereby he doth truly feed the faithful unto eternal life: not by coming down out of heaven unto thee, but by lifting thee up from the earth unto him.[122]

Such a view prepares the way for meditation upon Christ as redeemer and as personal savior, not usually to a reenactment of Calvary. It is safe to say that Bayly's type of general meditation with heavy emphasis upon theological points such as faith and justification found favor in Puritan circles; the penitent might think of his sins and of his redemption at the same time, with general after thoughts upon the mystery of Christ himself:

> After thou hast eaten and drunke both the Bread and Wine, labour that as those Sacramental signes do turn to the nourishment of thy Body, and by the digestion of heat become one with thy substance: so by the operation of Faith and the Holy Ghost, thou maiest become one with Christ, and Christ with them: and so mayest feel thy Communion with Christ confirmed, and increase daily more and more.[123]

Bayly does not go on to a general Christological meditation, but others did. In following the pattern in other writers, the general outline will be assumed, so that what they add to the structure of Bayly's meditations on the sacrament may be emphasized.

John Dodd in *Ten Sermons* (1610), Perkins in *Cases of Conscience* (1613), and Preston in various works take up the theological question of the sacrament, devout preparation and reception, and sundry meditations on the various benefits of Christ. It is typical of Puritan thinking that Perkins should class the sacrament as a case of conscience. Part of the reason here is to emphasize Calvinist doctrine and attack Papist errors, as in the following: "And the administration being ended, Christ is no more present in the bread and wine. And in the very act of celebration, he is not carnally, but spiritually present" (68). Perkins is briefer than most on the use of the sacrament, having more a negative than a positive aim. He strongly emphasizes examination of conscience for sin, as do all the Puritans (p. 81). This is preparation. His distinction of preparation, receiving and use is exactly that of Bayly. As did Bayly, Perkins speaks strongly of a man's belief in justifying faith, as well as in his own unworthiness. In other words, both preparation and reception of the sacrament become rallying points for the prime articles of the Calvinist confession of faith. In his section on use Perkins outlines a skeleton meditation of the significances of Christ, but it remains only that. Perkins is much more at home in the worlds of abstract theology and polemics. Thus he continues in *Cases of Conscience*:

> 1. which we see two signes to be received, we must call to mind that Christ is our perfect Saviour, that is, both bread and water of life.

2. we must remember, that Christ was ordained and appointed by God, to be our Mediator and Saviour.

3. we are to meditate of Christ, that was crucified for us, and broken, both by the first death, and paines of the second, whereby life and righteousness was procured unto us.

4. the giving of the elements into the receivers hands offers unto our meditation, this much: That God doth truly and really give Christ, with his merits and efficacy, to every believing receiver. [124]

But others were willing to flesh out this third aspect of sacramental meditation. Preparation remained about the same, an examination of conscience in detail; after 1600 the theology of reception could become more relaxed, but in some ways the emphasis upon faith and grace was built into the system. In Preston, Dodd, or in some 17th century writers like Baxter whom there is no need to quote, more play and room are allowed for the general postcommunion meditation. This also finds its way into the poetry of Taylor and others.

Dodd spends little time on the theology of the sacrament, assuming that his listeners and readers have had proper training:

Oh, but Christ is in heaven, and we are in earth, and how can we then eat his body and blood? Faith hath a long and an high reach, and the spirit of Christ hath as great a reach, to convey the same unto us: and our communion with him is not carnal but spiritual. [125]

About half of the sermons are devoted to preparation or minute examination of conscience. Two aspects do not follow the path of Perkins and Bayly, one relatively unimportant to us. Dodd, as a practicing clergyman, is concerned not only with the worthy conscience but also with the outward demeanour of sinners. The subject of "fencing the table" from sinners and the reprobate, which was to loom large in 17th century and New England Puritanism, so much so as to determine the external ordering of the Congregational Church, is given its due here. More important for our investigation of the inner life of Puritanism is the way in which Dodd includes signs of election and searching for faith as a part of preparation. Thus a specifically sacramental meditation could range over the most important grounds of the Calvinist view of religion; Dodd moves quite easily from discussion of personal sins (pp. 121–127) to that of evidences of faith:

How then may we certainly know that our hearts are sincere and upright before the Lord? . . . if we carry an inward hatred of this evil disposition that is in us. He that feeleth but a little faith, a little love, a little repentance, and would, with all his heart have them increased: and on the contrary, findeth much deadness, much impatience ... but would most willingly have these corruptions diminished; these very desires if they bring him to the conscionable use of the meanes, are evident signes of a faithful and well-affected heart.[126]

Dodd is almost off here seeking general signs of election, but brings himself back to the relevance of all this to the reception of the sacrament. The Puritan was forced to stress over and over again the appropriateness of the analogy: inward faith and outward reception of the Lord:

and as we with our bodily hand to receive the outward elements, so let us by the hand of faith lay hold of our Lord & Saviour & of all his merits: assuring our selves that as the bread & wine are made one substance with us, so is Christ Jesus in a spiritual manner made one with us, & we with him.[127]

Put more succinctly, Dodd say, "For the word must give life and strength, before the Sacrament can nourish and increase the same" (p. 121). On the use of postcommunion meditation Dodd is not very expansive, but does manage to stress the general merits of Christ:

We shall not meet the Minister only at the Lords table, but God himself in his own person; this may comfort the hearts of those that have examined their souls, and lamented their sins, and have a true desire to be reconciled unto the Lord, and to obtain such mercies as do belong to penitent persons, they shall receive according to their hearts desire and expectation ... the Lord of Glory will manifest his presence in giving to every one as he knoweth the integrity of their hearts.

Be covered through the righteousness of Christ, which maketh us as righteous here, as we shall be when we come to heaven, though we cannot see it so clearly, or apprehend it so fully.[128]

For Dodd the basic notions concerning Christ are theological, not historical or imaginative. Consequently his view of meditation is a rather limited one.

Preston's work on the sacrament and on Christ begins in this same limited way. In *The Breast-Plate of Faith and Love* (5th ed. 1634) his discussion of the sacrament is merely part of the more important topic of justifying faith. Even examination of conscience for individual sins is subordinated to the general search for faith and election:

Now if any of you will offer to come, and yet have not given up your selves to *God* in good earnest, you receive your own condemnation, you are divorced from *Christ*, and married to the World; and this is to receive the Sacrament unworthily. The maine end of the Sacrament is to increase faith; and salvation is ours by faith: therefore we should come with boldnesse, and lay hold upon the promises of it.[129]

Actual reception of the sacrament is also combined with the search and assurance of faith:

For the present occasion of receiving the Sacrament. What is the end of the Sacrament, but to preach faith? The Sacrament preacheth that to your outward senes that we doe to your understandings; it presenteth to the eye that which we now preach to the eare: for what is the Covenant of *God* in the Gospel but onely this? *God* offers *Christ* unto you freely, as the Bread and Wine is given unto you. . . . Now in the Sacrament both these are done: when the Bread and Wine are offered they are but a resemblance of the offer of *Christ*. Indeed there is a blessing in it: for it is *Gods* Ordinance, it increaseth this grace of faith. And againe, there is a bond on our part wherein we tie our selves to obey *Christ*.[130]

We notice here the limitations placed upon a general sacramental meditation. The sacrament is coordinate with the Word as received in preaching; grace is not restricted to the sacramental situation. In the process of sanctification the sacrament is a very important means of achieving grace, although there are others. Preaching and listening to the Word, prayer, and general meditation or "holy thoughts" are equally important.

In his *Three Sermons upon the Sacrament of the Lords Supper,* Preston is again concerned primarily with preparation, and on this occasion reprobation and fencing the table also loom large. He is also concerned, naturally, with proper definition, and takes over the familiar ones of Calvin, Perkins and others.

So in the Sacrament, except these words were from the Lords owne mouth that delivered it, this very delivering of the bread and wine, being a signe to you of the forgiveness of your sins, except the Lord has thus intended it, there had been no force in it.[131]

Preston also tells the pious to remember in the movement of reception the Covenant of the Lord. His language becomes quite strictly theological at this point, as was Bayly's:

It is a Covenant that consists of these three things or points; Justification, I will forgive thy sins; Sanctification, I will make you new hearts and new spirits; and the third, All things are ours; that is, I have made you heires of the world, heires of all things. . . .[132]

But there is also in this tract a general widening of the area of meditation, a more general interest in the personal relationship of the individual and Christ than in the other writers:

Christ is my chiefest treasure. I will parth with all therefore, I will part with liberty, with life, with goods, with credit, with pleasures, with profits, with whatsoever is neer and dear unto me, rather than I will part with the Lord Jesus. If this be thy hearts resolution and mind, then Christ is thy chief treasure. . . .[133]

There is a great warmth here, but it is not Counter Reformation dwelling upon the human nature of Christ. Nevertheless, there is a true interiority, an intimate association of Christ with the inner life, that is reminiscent of Augustine's *Confessions*. It is certainly not the mere abstract apprehension of God often ascribed to the Puritans. And who is to say that it is potentially less interesting for literature than Counter Reformation or Anglican practice?

So every man that is in Christ, he hath the comforts of the Spirit, the meditation of the privileges that he hath in Christ, the hope of Gods favour; These are his appointed food, these are the things that his soul feeds on in secret. . . . By this thou shalt know whether thou settest up Christ, as the chief Commander in thy heart or no, whether thou givest him thy chief throne, whether thou exaltest him for God in thy heart; you know when you exalt him for God, every thing then yields, if in truth he be set up for God in thy heart. . . .[134]

The "chief Commander" image will return to our notice in study of Marvell's poems and *Paradise Lost*.

A late work of Preston's, *A Heavenly Treatise of the Divine Love of Christ* (ed. 1640), was considered by Helen White worthy of treatment as mystical writing.[135] In relation to any standard definition of mysticism and of 17th century mystical writing, this is perhaps an overstatement, since Preston's book is solidly grounded in Puritan theological and moral teaching. Yet it is a movement towards what we find in a greater degree in Baxter's devotional works, that is, towards a free and imaginative embracing of various Christological ideas with warmth and feeling. Preston does not set this work in the form of sacramental meditation or connect it directly with reception of the sacrament. But it is obvious that such a turn of mind grew out of the third sacramental act, contemplating or meditating the use of the sacrament, which we have seen in the practice of Bayly and Perkins. The key to such a turn is the replacement of those constant terms, duty and sin, by the term love in contemplation of Christ:

Now do not deceive thy self; thou lovest the Lord, thou will say, but is this love *to his person,* or *to his Kingdom,* his goods? When thou presenteth Jesus Christ alone to thy self, canst thou then love him? It is true, Christ is a great

King, that can do much good or evil in the world, and so many may love him. But canst thou answer this question. *Lovest thou me?*[136]

After this opening, Preston warms to his subject:

If you love the Lord, Holy-daies and Sacrament-daies would be as Feastdays, and Wedding-days, for then you meet with God more neerly. Do you then put off your coming to the Sacrament, and would you not come neer it for speech of some, and yet will you say that you love the Lord: where love is, there is delight.[137]

There is a mystical touch here and there, without mystical flight. The sober Puritan is always in control:

Your love must be built upon his Person. If you love his, and not him, you will be unstable in your love. If thou lovest him in his Person, thou changest not, for thy love will be constant. But if thou love him for that he hath done for thee . . . thou wilt change thy love to him. Thou wilt then do as Job, receive good from the hand of the Lord, and also evil. . . . Sometimes God hides his face from his children, and *writes bitter things against them*. If then thou canst love him, thy love is on his Person, a constant love.[138]

Here we notice several things which help in understanding Puritan devotion. The warmth and imagination are controlled by both biblical authority and by the use of the term "Lord," which refers equally in this passage to Christ and God as Father. There is no dallying with human imaginations of the body of Christ or with images of Jesus the man. Such a direction would be against the grain of Puritan sensibility.

The little treatise ends with a "Soliloquy of a Devout Soul to Christ," which may, like so much other 17th century English piety, be based upon a continental source. If it is, Preston has been careful to weave proper doctrine on justification and faith throughout. But the imagery and sentiment is so naturally Puritan that the work may be entirely original. First there is an impassioned opening, reminiscent of Catholic meditation on the Lord:

Shew me then where thou liest at this my noone. Nowe thy sun doth shine upon this my tabernacle, and I have some time to behold thy beauty, that I may be in love with thy person, where then shall I find thee? If I look to *mount Tabor*, I see thee in glory, and I cannot but love thee for that. If I look *to the garden*, I see thee lying on the cold ground, sweating *drops of blood* for me, and I cannot but love thee for that. If I look to Golgothe, I see thee nayled *to the Cross*, and thy heart broached, that I may drink thy blood and live, and I cannot but love thee for that. If I look to mount Olivet, I see thee ascending *farre above all heavens*, and I cannot but love thee for that also.[139]

But then this humanizing tendency is restrained by a conclusion that mixes impassioned imagery with sound Puritan doctrine:

I may not run from thy love, *thou art my Lord.* I dare not, *thou art my Jesus.*
If thou live, let me know thy love to me. If I live, let me feel my love to thee.
Oh shed it more in my heart, that as in believing in thee my person is justified
so in loving thee my faith may be justified, and in having faith working by
love, I may so constantly walk in thy presence, that with comfort I may sing
with the Bride, *Come Lord Jesus, come quickly.* Even so, Amen.[140]

Such is Puritan meditation on the sacrament and on the divinity and humanity of Christ. Contrary to literary cliché, it is not merely dogmatic and intellectual; but it is fair to say in agreement with tradition that Puritan meditation and devotion never abandoned dogmatic and Scriptural sources for the more heady and dangerous fancies of the human imagination, a focus some commentators call emphasis upon *logos* over *mythos.* Many tracts were written against "vain imagination." Reason, dogma, and Scripture were the vehicles for curbing vain imagination and curbing it in the service of God.

d. Glorification

For glorification in the Puritan tradition we need go no further than Baxter's *Saints Everlasting Rest.*[141] This book is a treatise on contemplation or meditation, and deals with all aspects of the Puritan tradition. It has two peculiar characteristics, however, one an open attack on the excesses of sign- and election-hunting by preachers and saints, and the other a rather open acknowledgement of Catholic continental sources for meditation. For these reasons some have taken it to be a sport in the Puritan tradition, which is too glib a view.[142] Baxter actually covers all the traditional aspects of the Puritan tradition, including election and the sacraments, before getting to his subject of "high" contemplation. If he cites St. Bernard and covertly uses Ignatius, he also cites Perkins' *Cases of Conscience* favorably. Like Perkins, Preston, Sibbes and others, he is trying to present a balanced picture of the Puritan tradition as a whole. Yet his constant need to counsel the saints against backsliding, despair, and searching for marks of election is revealing of the basic intellectual problem of Calvinism, abstraction from full leading of the religious life. Mistrust of the human faculties, especially the imagination, is responsible for this failing:

Oh, how many hundred professors of religion, who can easily bring their hearts to ordinary duties, as reading, hearing, praying, conferring, could never yet in all their lives, bring them, and keep them to a heavenly contemplation one half hour together![143]

No doubt it is the death of our heavenly life, to have hard and doubtful thoughts of God; to conceive of him as a hater of the creature (except only of obstinate rebels), and as one that had rather damn us, than save us, and that is glad of an opportunity to do us a mischief, or at least hath no great goodwill to us: this is to put the blessed God into the similitude of Satan. . . . When in our vile unbelief and ignorance we have drawn the most ugly picture of God in our imaginations, then we complain that we cannot love him, and delight in him. This is the case of many thousand Christians.[144]

Calvin's view of election and the power of error leaves much room for terror and despair; it was Baxter's chosen purposes to present an alternative of joy, without betraying Calvinist theology. Contrary to some opinion, Baxter is not a revolutionary from the tradition of Perkins, Preston and the others; he is simply more thorough and more specific, wears his continental sources more openly. But in this spirit he does manage to cover all the areas of the contemplative and meditative world, including glorification, which was always mentioned and seldom described by the earlier generation of Puritans. They no doubt had scruples of man's "vain imaginings" which Baxter, Bunyan, Spenser and Milton were able to overcome.

The meditation of heaven properly begins at about page 365 of the Orme edition. This method is Baxter's attempt to give body and substance to the idea of glorification of the saints. He begins in a general way that no Puritan before him could take issue with:

There it is that trouble and lamentation ceaseth, and the voice of sorrow is not heard. Oh! when I look upon this glorious place, what a dunghill and dungeon methinks is earth. Oh! what a difference betwixt a man feeble, pained, groaning, dying, rotting in the grave, and one of these triumphant, blessed, shining saints! Here shall I drink of the river of pleasure, "the streams whereof make glad the city of our God."[145]

But to make the meditation specific, and to avoid constant repetition of certain scriptual passages, the senses must be employed (p. 375) and analogy must be freely allowed (on pp. 380–84 he cites St. Bernard's doctrine of analogy to show that heavenly delights exceed earthly). This may have been squeamish stuff for some contemporary Puritans. In the manner of Spenser and Milton he next contemplates last things under the temporary species of earthly things:

O what rare and mighty works have we seen in Britain: what clear discoveries of an almightly arm; what magnifying of weakness; what casting down of strength; what wonders wrought by most improbable means; what bringing to hell, and bringing back; what turning of tears and fears into safety and joy; such hearing of earnest prayers, as if God could have denied us nothing that we asked! . . . But, oh! what are these to our full deliverance; to our final conquest; to our eternal triumph; and to that great day of great things?[146]

Baxter himself was not a sanguine millenarian, but we can imagine the effect his work would have on others who had come very close to merging the two kingdoms in the time of the Commonwealth. At the least Baxter was stirring up some idea of how glorification might be treated.

From page 409 to the end of the book Baxter gives his own sustained vision of glorification and heavenly contemplation. There is no need to quote all or even abundantly from this famous work. Even in this magnificent passage there remains the 17th century's heavy sense of sin and mortality:

Now blessed saints that have believed and obeyed, this is the end of faith and patience; this is it for which you prayed and waited; do you now repent your sufferings and sorrows; your self-denying, and holy walking? Are your tears of repentance now bitter or sweet? Oh, see how the Judge doth smile upon you; there is love in his looks; the titles of Redeemer, Husband, Head are written in his amiable, shining face.[147]

The Christ figure here becomes more human than Calvin would perhaps have approved of, even though the theology is sound enough. In Baxter there is the true ring of a soul lifting itself out of the ordinary life of human sanctification into a glorified existence even before death:

Is not the life a state of love? Is not the great marriage-day of the Lamb, when he will embrace and entertain his spouse with love? Is not the employment there the work of love, where the souls with Christ do take their fill? Oh, then, my soul, begin it here.

Why should I then draw back discouraged? My God is willing, if I were but willing. He is delighted in my delights. He would fain have it my constant frame and daily business, to be near to him in my believing meditations, and to live in the sweetest thoughts of his goodness, and to be always delighting my soul in himself. O blessed work; employment fit for the sons of God!

Nay, how many a weak woman, or poor despised Christian have I seen, mean in parts, but rich in faith, who could rejoice and triumph in hope of this inheritance: and shall I look upon it with so dim an eye; so dull a heart; so dejected a countenance? Some small foretastes also I have had myself, though indeed small and seldom, through mine unbelief, and how much more delightful have they been than ever was any of these earthly things?[148]

The *Saints Rest* is a treatise of glorification, heaven, and holy dying all in one. The fact of its existence, with the writings of Preston, Perkins, Spenser, Bunyan and Milton behind or alongside of it, is fit evidence that the Puritan tradition could lay aside its distrust of imagination long enough to construct its own visions of last things. It is important to stress that Baxter and Bunyan should be read along-side Preston, Perkins, Sibbes and many other Puritan divines. There is certainly development towards visual imagination and greater prominence given to glorification in the 17th than in the 16th century. This is development, not contrariety, as Coleridge would later put it. The earlier Puritans believed in, and explained, glorification in their sermons and treatises. But they did not devote much visual imagination to the last state, and centered their thoughts on earlier aspects of the cycle, usually coming to rest in sanctification with firm promise and belief in later glory. Ample illustration could be presented on these matters, but the need is not there, so long as the disjunction stressed by Martz and Kaufmann is rejected. We are dealing with a development of doctrine here in Newman's sense, not a new doctrine or departure. Baxter and Bunyan were as staunchly Calvinist as the Cambridge generations before them.

5. Meditation in General

Since the previous section has dealt with sacramental meditation and meditations on various aspects of the figure of Christ, the present section will be devoted to more general types of meditation, with one exception. This will be Bayly's examples of meditation on "last things," or the Puritan contribution to the lively 17th century subject of *memento mori*. For reasons that will be made clear, the extracts from Bayly's *Practice of Pietie* appear at the end of this discussion of meditation.

For more general meditation in the Puritan tradition we can turn to two valuable books of the previous generation, Knappen's *Two Elizabethan Puritan Diaries* and White's *English Devotional Literature 1600—1640*. Knappen's introduction gives his impressions of the diaries of Richard Rogers and Samuel Ward, while Miss White considers the Puritan tradition as a strand of 17th century piety. Both are valuable on the subject of meditation.

Knappen views the entire inner life of the typical Puritan as a meditation upon his own sanctification:

The most striking feature of the Puritan way of life revealed in these diaries is the overwhelming predominance of the ethical element. It was the good, rather than the beautiful or the true, which occupied the Puritan's mind.

The ideal state, which the Puritan was constantly seeking to attain, may be described by his own term "godliness." It is seen, upon analysis, to have consisted of an attitude of mind. When the writers are "staied," "settled" in course, "well-reasoned," having "fruteful" meditations and good thoughts, they are content, but when they are unsettled, "wanderinge," "roavinge," dull, dead, slack in hearing chapel talks, making "imperfite" prayers – in other words, unable to concentrate on the right things – they are driven to complaints and to self-accusation.[149]

Meditation became the primary weapon in the Puritan's army against self-doubt and general slackness in religious duties:

Thinking of religious matters meant meditating on God and the believer's relation to Him, the plan of salvation, the thinker's past conduct, the making of resolutions to do better, and such matters. Of mystical dwelling on the abstract qualities of the Deity there is little evidence. The Puritan thought rather in terms of his own conduct and God's opinion of it.[150]

Knappen shows surprise at the incessant cataloguing of sins and of the terrors of conscience. These things are to be expected in the hearers of Perkins, Preston and Sibbes. The diaries, such as those of Rogers and Ward, were merely further refinements of the general Puritan method of mental calculus.

Here belongs also the mention of the practice of regularly keeping the diaries themselves, the writing of which obviously served to keep the attention fixed on the goal. This device was apparently more effective than most other means. It interrupted incorrect trains of thought, and caused the writers to renew his resolution to live correctly.[151]

Knappen rises to a rather high and cheerful estimate of the Puritan sensibility from his examination of the diaries:

Briefly stated, it was the desire to experience the immediate feeling of satisfaction which came from approaching the ideal state of mind. Theorists might talk of a future life with rewards and punishments. The diarists, doubtless, believed in it, and preached it. But their writings are singularly free from any dwelling on such matters. ... In practice, these authors were otherwordly only in the sense that immaterial desires are otherworldly. For all practical purposes, the Puritan, even when "in good Frame," lived nine-tenths or more of his time for the joys of this world. They were spiritual joys and not material ones, it is true, but they were of this world in the temporal sense of the phrase. . . . What the Puritan lived for was the joy of having the right spiritual attitude here and now.[152]

We shall look at the evidence in Ward and Rogers shortly. But we should not ignore Helen White's findings in her search for 17th century books of meditation. Except for Baxter, and Preston in *A Heavenly Treatise of the Divine Love of Christ*, where Miss White allows that the Puritan tradition attains a high ideal of spirituality, her evidence of Puritan meditation is on the gloomy side. She finds the scars of searching for signs of election and the terrors of being damned in much Puritan private writing. One story is so good and so well told by Miss White that we will indulge ourselves in reporting the details:

On the other hand, failure of faith aroused a suspicion of whether or not one was of the elect. In some groups, particularly in Puritan groups, this consciousness of the possession of faith, this inner certainty of being of God's elect, was insisted upon with such literalness and fervor that it of necessity became a grave problem of the inner life, with sometimes almost tragic results.

A Brief Discourse of the Christian Life and Death, of Mistris Katherin Brettergh, . . . in the Countie of Lancaster . . . who departed this world the last of May 1601. With the manner of a bitter conflict she had with Satan, and blessed conquest of Christ, before her death to the great gloree of God, and comfort of all beholders. . . .

Under the best of circumstances this failure of the faith would have been distressing and somewhat embarrassing, but in Lancashire, from Elizabethan days a stronghold of Recusancy, it was a calamity. For if we can believe the account of the very lively "Postscript to Papists" with which the book opens, they did not hesitate to draw uncharitable conclusions from Mistris Brettergh's troubles. . . . To judge from the account, this was not only a great consolation for Katherin and her distressed friends [her final assurance] but also a neighborhood triumph for the Lord and the forces of truth and righteous-ness. . . .

This little drama must often have been played in those days of Predestination and Election and Justification by Faith alone, sometimes with a less happy ending. And often, no doubt with an audience as malicious as the Papists of Lancashire.[153]

Miss White's witty account is another reminder that serious study of the Puritan sensibility cannot rest with superficial views of despair or of assurance as the Puritan way. The very number of possibilities created a tradition as complex as the Anglican or the Roman Catholic in the 17th century.

Turning to the diaries of Rogers and Ward, there is evidence in abundance for an ultimately cheerful but eternally wary Puritan view of the struggles for sanctification in this life. Samuel Ward was a fellow of Emmanuel College, Cambridge during the great days of Perkins, whom he mentions in the diary. His diary is dull compared to Rogers', perhaps because of the nature of life in the college. Much of it is given over to religious gossip, such as the melancholia of another fellow, Mr. Benson, who thinks he has sinned against the Holy Ghost. This is no laughing matter, as we know from various sources that there were a number of suicides during the high Puritan period at Cambridge. Spenser, who was there, may have had such stories and events in mind in construction the Despair episode in *The Faerie Queene* I, although there are numerous traditional sources for the episode. Generally speaking, however, Ward's diary confirms the impression of Knappen, that meditation was a successful weapon in keeping up the spirit while not allowing assurance to become hubris:

Think how blockish men are that never think of God and ther salvation. Remember God's mercy toward thee, in gyving thee grace at the end of thy prayer to pray heartily unto thee, where as in the beginning thou wast blockish. . . .[154]

How ytt pleased God to deteyne the sense of my sinnes from me in my prayer, howsoever I called often for the sight thereof, but I must attribute ytt to myne owne wantes in prayer. How ytt pleased God to give thee some insight into the state of salvation att thy evening prayers. Thy concept of God, not as he is omnipotent, omnipresent, but most just, most good, most mercyfull.[155]

There is not much pleasure in reading Ward's extreme and constant accusations of himself; if he felt elect, he certainly did not feel sanctified:

My negligence in preparing me to the receyving of the Sacrament. My negligence in exhorting Nevinson to the revarent recyving of the Sacrament. My hardness of heart when I should have prayed. How, notwithstanding my heart was hard, yett ytt pleased God to give me some comfort in calling upon him. June 8, '95—.[156]

What is completely missing in Ward is any sense of joy, imagination or broadness of vision. Rogers, living in the world, has room for more scope and variety. He was a clergyman, married, living just outside of Cambridge, doing his rounds of study, preaching and holding conference with the godly and with sinners. During the time of the diary his wife dies, he has scruples about remarriage and about "rising" in the world, the Armada is defeated, and he is dismissed from his post for Puritan preaching. His career is more that of a low-keyed John Bunyan on the journey of the spirit than of a Fellow cooped up in a "godly" college, as was Ward. Nevertheless, the outer world is relatively unimportant to Rogers compared to the inner. His interests are essentially similar to those of Ward and of other Puritans, perhaps a little better expressed and with an eye for worldly detail. He tells us of constant moral preoccupation, conferences with other clergymen, meditations and the distractions preventing them, a trip to Cambridge with his wife during which too much talking ruined the planned "set" meditation, worries about appearing too worldly or too abject. Most interesting are his set pieces or general meditations on his life and resolutions to reform it:

And looking backe, I acknowledge that my course hath been farre unbeseeminge one who hath so long given name to the gospel and that not after a common manner. Oh what had become of me if god had put me to my plundge in many trials as he might have done? For I had been utterly unable to have stood.[157]

Meditation and diary keeping prevent the struggle against sin to be completely lost:

But this after noone I felt a strongue desire to enjoy more liberty in thinckinge uppon some vain things which I had lately weaned my selfe from. Me thought it great bondage to be tyed from delighting in such thinges as I tooke pleasure in, and if I had not either written this immediately, or by some other means mett with it, I had allmost been gone from this course and become planely wicked and idle as before.[158]

We see the impulse here to formal meditation controlling the will by exercise as in Catholic practice, but the result remains individual and spontaneous. At times the result was spontaneous joy and well-being:

Among other meditations this was one in this month: that I beholding how graciously the lord hath hedged me in on every side, what sweet knowledge of his will, in comparison of that which I was like to have attained to, he hath given me, and other blessings, good will and a good name with the godlier sort, communion with them and such manifold comfort in my life and with his people, with liberty in my ministry. . . .[159]

It would not be fair to leave Rogers in this Puritan euphoria of spiritual joy, for we know that these great moments were few and dearly bought. Another good passage rising to imaginative crescendo tells us that in his life he had found the exhortations of Perkins and others to be true, that even for the luckiest of men the spiritual combat never ends:

In my retourne home my minde by the way was taken upp in veery heavenly sorte, receiving not a little that the lord has so enlarged mine heart as that mine olde and accustomed dreames and fantasies of things below were vanished and drowned. The meditations of mine heart were such as caryed me to the lorde, and full graciously reasoned me against my coming home. Yet ceasinge but a little from good doing, some way I began to waxe colde, the which grew upon me by reason of lingering after Barbara wherewith I feared that I should be enforced to remitt somewhat of my former covenant, which to thinke was as grevious to me as it was comfortable to hope for the continuance of it. And although I found gracious deliverance againe, yet I see that I shall be without special grace, in great danger. But thus it must be till our synnes be better looked to and their strength better diminished in us.[160]

Such was the vision, the struggle, and the reward of a man we may safely call typical of the Puritan movement at its height. No great thinker or intellectual, and no great sinner either, by objective standards, Rogers comes through to us not as a plaster saint or stage Puritan but as a man of sincerity, character, humane faults and ordinary interests. What lifts his life above the ordinary in his diary is his adherence to the Puritan code and his willing and imaginative participation according to his sensibility in its vision of life. Neither Ward nor Rogers, unfortunately, gives us a meditation on the subject of dying, no doubt because their diaries close before their time of death. So we must supplement this study of primary sources for meditation with the more calculated art of Bishop Bayly on the subject of holy dying, Puritan style. Miss White's material on the Katherin Brettergh scandal makes it clear that Puritan meditation had a strong necessity to come to grips with the subject of dying in the Lord.

In some ways Bayly's thoughts on dying in *Practice of Pietie* are typical of Elizabethan and 17th century *memento mori* literature, but he is urged by the times, the times of the Puritan preachers and of subjects like Katharin Brettergh to give this subject a Puritan cast:

It is found by continuall experience that neere the time of death (when the Children of God are weakest) then Satan makes the greatest flourish of his strength: and assults them with his strongest temptations. For he knoweth, that either he must now or never prevaile; for if their soules once get to Heaven, he shall never vex or trouble them any more. . . .

If Sathan tell thee that thou hast no faith, because thou hast no feeling: meditate, 1. that the truest faith hath often times the least feeling, and greatest doubts; but so long as thou hatest such doubtings, they shall not be laid unto thy charge; for they belong to the flesh, from which thou are divorced. . . .

That thy salvation is grounded, not upon the constancie of thine obedience, but upon the firmness of God's Covenant. Though thou variest with God, and the Covenant bee broken on thy behalf, yet it is firm on God's part; and therefore all is safe enough if thou wilt return. . . . He hath locked up thy salvation, and made it sure in his owne unchangeable purpose; and hath delivered to thy keeping the keyes, which are Faith and Repetance. . . .[161]

Notice in all this a firm grip is kept on the theological nature of the problem. There are no gruesome pictures of the grave and the decay of the flesh, as in Donne and Counter Reformation *memento mori* literature. "For whom God loveth, he loveth to the end, and never repenteth of bestowing his love on them who repent and believe." But Bayly can do better than repeat digests of sermons to the dying Puritan, and rises to one of the typical Puritan visions of the glory of dying in the Lord:

Listen, O drooping Spirit, whose Soule is assailed with waves of faithless despair; how happy were it to see many like thee and Hezekiah . . . rather than to behold many who die like beasts, without any feeling of their owne estate, or any fear of Gods wrath, or tribunall seat, before which they are to appear? Comfort thyself, O languishing soul, for if this earth hath any, for whom Christ spilt his blood, on the Cross, thou assuredly are one. Cheere up, therefore, thy self in the All-sufficient Attonement of the blood of the Lamb, which speaketh better things than that of Abel.[162]

In this rather sober Puritan language of joy we can catch echoes of the later triumphs of assurance in Spenser, Taylor, Bunyan and Milton. Despair and fear of election are the final snares to be triumphed over. Some may prefer the more grisly details and keener psychological soundings of Counter Reformation or Anglican 17th century death literature, but there are legitimate reasons for seeing something of energy and courage in the Puritan's bout with the final meditation on death. It is as if the energy of despair and fear of election build up to a final fury which suddenly snaps in a last moment of assurance of salvation:

Meditate on these Evangelicall comforts, and thou shalt see, that in the very agony of death, God will so assist thee with his Spirit, that when Sathan looketh for the greatest victory, hee shall receive the foulest soile. . . .[163]

This, at least, is what was supposed to happen at the end. That it did not always occur this way we know from the documents and the fact that pious meditations such as Bayly's and many good examples could not remove the fact that each struggle was individual, each saint had to pass through the last trial alone, and therefore that much preparation and meditation in advance were required to achieve the victory.

VI. The Covenant and Federal Theology

According to Perry Miller,[164] who has written extensively on the subject, the Covenant of Grace was invented by the Puritan divines in order to give a more rational appearance to the Calvinist scheme of redemption than it had in the original, theoretical scheme of Calvin and the early Puritans, without at the same time falling into the traps of Arminianism or Antinomianism. It is a scheme in which God limits his arbitrary power to bargain with man in a contract or Covenant. For man to keep his side of the Covenant is a way to provide assurance of salvation. We find a good deal about the Covenant in Preston's *The New Covenant or the Saints Portion* (1629), where the last five sermons concern the subject of the Covenant. According to Miller, Preston's work was deeply influential upon the New England Puritans in developing the "federal theory" or collective covenant. Miller sees a diminution of piety and immediacy of religious experience in its Puritan form as the legalism of the Covenant replaces the personal, "murky" confrontation of men and God in the Calvinist scheme. He allows that this was a New England, not an English phenomenon, and it is certainly true for instance that in Preston the legalisms of the Covenant do not impede fervor and immediacy of religious doctrine. Nor is this statement to be accepted of the American Puritans without qualification, at least before the opening of the 18th century. There are spirits such as Taylor and, later, Edwards that refute the too wide and easily held assumption that Puritanism drifted easily into rationalism and complacency.

However, the consequences of the covenant are not the concern of our study. The fact that some form of individual and collective covenant was invented both in England and New England is important. The general covenant, in England at least, never replaced the importance of the individual experience, but it did help to divert the Puritan religious experience away from extreme individuality and "new light" doctrine. Even in its milder English form the collective idea of covenant insured the establishment of churches and the existence of forms of public worship. Again, the English Puritans did not go so far as the American federal theologians, who finally demanded public witness and churchgoing while looking with suspicious eyes upon interiority and individuality, but the notion of collective covenant did constitute a drain upon individual depth and piety. All the writers we have observed approve of private and spontaneous prayer over public, formal and set prayer, yet all must in the end also approve of forms of public worship in order to preserve a church. Horton Davies has given a thorough account of the various forms of Church order devised by the English Puritans in Europe and in England.[165]

This aspect of the movement is of interest to us only in a negative way. It shows the amount of energy and imagination that went into making Puritanism successful as a group activity. If we also add in passing the amount of ingenuity and energy given over to purely political issues, such as Milton's tracts, or compare the spiritual writings of the Puritans with their political interests, the point becomes obvious. Whatever the Puritan tradition has left us of imaginative worth and as evidence of the inner spiritual life, it is no doubt little compared to what was possible. The perhaps necessary drive to the political and the outward in the mid-17th century damaged by default the kind of spirituality and imagination this book is trying to describe. Perry Miller may overstate his case in *New England Mind* when he drives home the political and rationalistic elements in the Puritan tradition in New England at the expense of the inward and pious. Edward Taylor and other like spirits were lurking in the valley beyond the better-known political clergymen and magistrates in the Bay Colony. In England the tradition of piety, of Perkins, Preston, Sibbes and the others, held on more tenaciously in Bunyan and Milton, and into the 18th century, despite the triumphs and failures of the Commonwealth. Yet if Puritanism missed its chance of full inward development, it still has more of the inner and imaginative life than Perry Miller or conventional literary history credit it with having.

VII. Puritan Style

Now that we have seen something of the structure of the Calvinist-Puritan sensibility and its potential for operating as imaginative literature, a few words should be said about style itself as a transition from the world of the literal to the world of the imaginative. This is the one subject of the total area which has received a good deal of comment, much of it to the point. Yet our method cannot allow us here simply to refer to Sasek's *Literary Temper of the English Puritans*, to Walter Ong's *Ramus: Method, and the Decay of Dialogue* or to Louis Martz's introduction to *The Poems of Edward Taylor*.[166] Our approach requires that we give attention to much of the usual ground of studies of Puritan style − allegorical vision, dialogue, the "plain style," diction, biblical analogues − yet the method developed thus far suggests that these factors cannot be viewed as externals or as aspects of a general subject divorced from the intellectual and theological vision. If this study has any value, it is to prove such a point. On the other hand there is no wish to obscure the usual meaning and methods of handling the issue of style. To this purpose certain aspects of style will be talked about briefly here in the conventional way, deferring more serious consideration to the analyses in the sections which follow.

It is my conviction that the inner vision of the Calvinist-Puritan writers and their allegorical cast of mind does not receive just treatment viewed *ab extra* as another aspect of style. As the heart and soul of the Puritan literary experience, analysis of this cast of mind cannot exist apart from individual texts. But it is possible, if only for clarification of our present study in relation with the usual methods, to say something about the more common aspects of style which unite the Puritans to other writers of the age. This usually amounts to a consideration of diction, the "plain style," dialogue or dramatic method, and the relationship of literature to the Bible. Sasek, Ong, and Martz, mentioned above, and Lily Campbell[167] have handled these subjects in various ways. While it may be dangerous to suggest some inevitability or completeness in following their schemes here, later chapters will provide different viewpoints by entering the complexity of individual writers.

The plain style is most often attributed to Puritan preaching (and to doggerel literature) by critics and scholars of the 17th century. In itself this is not usually intended as a derogatory term, but rather to indicate a conscious turning of the preachers and other prose writers of Calvinist-Puritan cast away from the classical and especially Ciceronian models so sought after by Renaissance classicists and continued by the Anglican preachers of the 17th century. It is customary to compare the prose style of any random Puritan with that of Donne, Herbert or Andrewes, well-known for erudition, wit, quotations of Church Fathers, baroque and compex syntax. In such a context even the more fiery parts of Preston, Sibbes and Perkins seem a bit drab. This may be accepted, as long as one remembers that Donne and Andrews were exceptional stylists, and that the plain style is not to be held synonymous with dullness and conformity to a low common denominator. Sasek has pointed out ably[168] that the Puritan scholar and preacher knew his "heathen writers," and was fond of quoting or artfully alluding to the more acceptable of the classics — Plutarch, Tacitus, Seneca, and even Horace, Virgil, and Juvenal. As Sasek has done this work thoroughly, there is no need to go over it again, except perhaps to remind the reader that Perkins' *Armilla Aurea* (1590) appeared in at least three Latin editions by 1612, as well as twelve English editions. Perkins' Latin style is simple and vigorous, reminding one more of medieval scholastic Latin style than of the ornate and complex style of Erasmus and More. Perkins and the Cambridge preachers were addressing themselves, at least until the opening of the 17th century, to a cultivated and serious religious audience. If they eschewed the dazzling techniques of Donne and Andrews, it was not on account of ignorance. In such inherited techniques of the early Renaissance the Puritans, for better or worse, saw both vanity and obscurity. The new method of the plain style fulfilled the requirements of seriousness and directness of communication urgently required by the times. Peter Ramus had pointed out the way, so they thought, to distinguish what was good in Aristotelean-Quintillian rhetorical theory from the baubles and frippery added during the 1000 years of the schools. Walter Ong's book traces the development and gradual influence of Ramist technique upon literary style in the 16th century.[169] The result in England was a hardy and functional prose, erudite, witty if necessary, which tended on the whole perhaps a bit too much toward rigorously schematic logical division of subject, parts, sub-parts, divisions, ones-twos-threes along the way. The preacher always wished his audience to know exactly where he was in discourse, and resisted the temptations to wander or to display his own rhetorical knowledge. Admitting all this, it is still possible to say that Puritan preaching and writing, and later literature, was capable of attaining a spartan form, an elegance and depth all its own. The game of comparisons has too often been used to diminish its value in relation to the Anglican tradition. The work of Sasek and Ong should help to temper this view.

Toward the close of his *Ramus: Method, and the Decay of Dialogue,* Ong makes the interesting suggestion that the Ramist technique, enforced by the abstractions of Descartes, led to a decay of liveliness in writing and preaching and to a decline in the drama in the 17th century. This suggestion should have some bearing upon Puritan literary technique in particular, considering Ramus' background and the eagerness with which the Cambridge Puritans adopted his revision of medieval rhetoric. Unfortunately, like all large cultural theories, this one is difficult to prove in practice. The tendency away from dialogue which shows clearly by the early 18th century may have had obscure origins in Ramism and in the Calvinist-Puritan attitudes, but this does not show very largely in 16th and 17th century work. The Puritan feeling against stage plays was a moral rather than aesthetic matter. Many Puritan sermons and prose writings, and much doggerel poetry, employed the "dialogue technique," which was of course a standard rhetorical topos with sanctions going back to Plato directly and to the Bible indirectly. If Ramist logic and rhetoric thinned out the richness of prose style, it did not prohibit the use of a time-sanctioned topos. It is interesting in this context to note Bunyan's defense of the allegorical method in *Pilgrim's Progress* over the dialogue method of writing. *Pilgrim's Progress* has much dialogue, of course, but it is not a dialogue or *débat*, the form used by Marvell, Taylor, and the metaphysical poets. In his introductory poem Bunyan defends his choice, and of course refers to the New Testament for sanction. Interestingly enough, he realizes that dialogue is the most popular form for the kind of literature known as religious, and seems,

in the abstract, to hold nothing against the use of the dialogue method
by other religious poets and writers:

I find not that I am denied the use
Of this my method, so I not abuse
Put on the words, things, readers; or be rude
In handling figure or similitude,
In application; but, all that I may,
Seek the advance of truth this or that way
Denied, did I say? Nay, I have leave
(Example too, and that from them that have
God better pleased, by their words or ways,
Than any man that breatheth now-a-days)
Thus to express my mind, thus to declare
Things unto thee that excellentest are.
I find that men (as high as trees) will write
Dialogue-wise; yet no man doth them slight
For writing so; indeed, if they abuse
Truth, cursed be they, and the craft they use
To that intent; but yet let truth be free
To make her sallies upon thee and me,
Which way it pleases God; . . .

In the 18th century William Law, who found stage plays immoral,
employed the topos of dialogue for some of his meditative works. The
truth seems to be that the Puritan writers such as Bunyan, Milton,
Marvell and Taylor, and the educated preachers of the 16th–17th
centuries, felt free to use most literary means available to convey their
points and visions. While the plain style and allegorical vision were
the Puritan literary methods par excellence, with sanction in the Bible
and in the Puritan's own view of reality, a good deal more freedom of
choice existed in practice than any clear-cut stratification of traditions
would seem to allow. Ong's thesis concerning dialogue, then, runs into
difficulties among the 17th century Puritans, not to speak of the
difficulties raised by the presence of Shakespeare or Donne. For the
Puritans, their special form of prayer as a talking with God or "Abba
Father" could easily be transformed into a literary method of dialogue
in sermon, prose piece, or poem.

The diction of the Puritan writers in general, studied by Sasek and
Martz, can be handled in connection with the authority of the Bible in
Puritan life and writing. Both subjects will be treated briefly here, as
external aspects of the Puritan literary tradition.

Again, it is important to strike a balance between a neat theory and
actual practice. We would expect all Puritan writers of whatever cast

to be influenced by biblical modes, styles, and diction, and this is the case, especially among the preachers given to extended quotation of texts as illustration or proof. It would be natural for these preachers to weave their own style into a biblical pattern, so that in some instances it is difficult to discern where the preacher leaves off and the Bible begins. Enough is known generally about the language of the "Godly" to let this point pass without illustration. Lily B. Campbell's *Divine Poetry and Drama in Sixteenth-Century England,* cited above, has shown the power and authority of biblical tropes and styles upon all English writers of the time, and the frequency of imitation of biblical themes and stories. An important point this book reminds us of, however, is that before the Authorized King James Version, the influence of the Bible upon English style was not as strong as later, in either Puritan or Anglican tradition. Most of the sixteenth century work consisted of translations or free renditions of Greek or Latin versions of the Testaments. In this as in many other areas, the existence of a Latin-oriented culture among the educated cannot be minimized. Only in the 17th century, with the spread of Puritanism among the lower classes and the popularity of English translations of the Bible, can an authoritative biblical diction in English be said to exist.

The work of Sasek on the Puritan preachers and Martz's writing about Edward Taylor help dissipate the easy assumption, which the reading of primary sources completely dispells, that Calvinist-Puritan writers were completely Bible-ridden in their work and outlook. In this area the propaganda of the stage writers against the "Godly" has taken all too well, and many believe the Calvinist was capable of mouthing only biblically-inspired cant. But the Puritan knew the things of daily life as well as the next man, and he often followed an unlikely profession which lent words and phrases to his vocabulary. If he was a University man, he also knew the classics, and thus was able to lard his work with apples and beer on the one hand, and Seneca and Horace on the other. Reading the Cambridge Puritans at length is not the most exciting literary experience possible, but it is nowhere near as dull as many would expect on the basis of the popular legend about the Puritan sensibility. As Sasek and others have pointed out the range of Puritan diction inside and outside of the Bible very thoroughly, this material will not be repeated. We will only add a few examples from the works of John Preston which may open some eyes to the range of Puritan interests in the late 16th and early 17th centuries.

If the studies of Martz and Sasek have shown that the Puritan preacher and writer could use the commonplace and everyday as well as the biblical and theological in his work, that his avoidance of the high style did not prevent a wide range of appropriate allusion to the world of culture, these few examples from Preston's *Sermons* may add another and even less expected note. If quotations of the ungodly Greeks and Latins, and the suspect early Catholic Church Fathers sometimes crept into the writings of the best Puritans despite their abjuration of all worldly devices and splendor, what about the most ungodly playwrights, between whom and the Puritans there was no love lost? Now admittedly Preston, as a favorite of James I and chaplain to the young Prince of Wales, of good family and court connections, was not the usual Puritan type of Milton, Spenser and Oliver Cromwell. It is yet surprising, in his formal sermons given at Lincoln's Inn and at court, to find indirect references to the Bard of Avon, no friend to his cause at the time of Preston's rise to fame (1605−1616). We do not have to conclude that Preston actually attended the condemned plays, but we must admit he had an eye and an ear for the best popular language of the time. In *The New Covenant* (ed. 1634) there are three references to the Bard, as follows: "It will strengthen you *against that expense of spirit*" (p. 61−2); "for, when all is done, *you shall find that but labor lost*" (p. 71); "he that hath the lower part given him to act, *while he is on the stage of this world*" (p. 133).[170] *Four Godly and Learned Treatises* (ed. 1633) has: "that which is best in the end . . . is to be chosen above all things else. *That is well which ends well.*"[171] We cannot expect a Puritan writer to go so far as to give the Bard credit for his words, as Preston does for early Catholic or pagan writers of antiquity, but the keen indirectness with which Preston molds Shakespeare's language to his purpose for a cultivated audience may help somewhat in re-evaluating the entire question of the Puritan attitude toward and use of literary language.

Preston may also be thinking of Donne in one of his rare extended figures, rare not because of paucity of imagination in the preacher, but for reasons of propriety. In the following we may detect traces of Donne's famous twin-compass image. Perhaps there is a common source of which this writer is unaware:

Faith is like the part of the compass that goeth about and doth the work; and love is that cementing grace whereby we are more knit unto the Lord; they have both their office and their place; you know love is an uniting affection, therefore this is the definition of it. *It is a desire of union with that it loves.*[172]

If *Songs and Sonets* is the source of this, we may respect Preston's reticence in citing it.

So much for diction and imagery viewed abstractly. This section on style has been kept very short in keeping with the writer's belief that the Puritan imagination should not be studied externally and apart from total contexts, but it agrees with Sasek and others who have found a wide range of learned, common and interesting allusion in the Puritan writers.

VIII. Conclusion of Part One

In attempting to reform the feelings of all men and to bring their lives under the discipline of conscience, the Puritans were attempting what most men, and even Christian tradition at large, has considered well-nigh impossible. One may grant that an occasional saint in the Middle Ages achieved this end, and even that some Puritans and latter day followers of the tradition — Law, Wordsworth, etc. — followed the path in their own peculiar ways. Such an admission does not also admit the wisdom of monasticism or Puritanism as systems for men at large. Worldly and common sense notions aside, there is the Christian view of original sin to cope with here. Puritanism felt it could afford to scorn the common sense of scholasticism and its Greek and Roman forebears, but it must, and did, take seriously the wrestling with the devil known as sin. The doctrines of election and justification were mighty weapons in the war against Satan, which, Calvin felt, would never be won by scholastic rationalism and the external reliance upon sacraments.

Our interest here has not been to assess Puritanism historically, or judge its social value as a force in modern life. Many conflicting assessments are available on these scores. We recognize that back-sliding and hypocrisy became commonplace in individual Puritan lives, and that, as Perry Miller has pointed out,[173] the New England federal theology or Covenant of Grace was in effect a betrayal of the inner and personal meaning of the Puritan experience. In England the saints lost their battle with the world; in America they won control of the wilderness at the loss of their inner integrity. All these facts, however, are irrelevant to the existence of the inner experience and drama. The actual existence of practicing Puritans from Cartwright to Milton and Bunyan and on to the reforming Edwards of the 18th century is our concern. They and their writings are the basis of the

Puritan-Calvinist imaginative experience, of the Red Cross Knight's journey, *Pilgrim's Progress*, Edwards' meditations and Wordsworth's attempt to reform feeling in the early 19th century. The failures of the Puritan psychological experience are important too – Cowper, Coleridge, Dickinson, and the little known 17th century suicides are desperate cases. External failures of the merchants and political leaders also follow an understandable and traceable path, but one not of great concern to us.

In presenting this series of personal responses of many Puritans of the period 1570–1660 to the various modes of the Puritan psychological quest we have followed an analytic rather than a historical or topological approach to the issues. In brief, it has been shown what the analytic possibilities are, including the negative or undesirable effects, in the modes of the Puritan experience. In presenting this rich variety at the core of the Puritan experience we have also suggested from time to time the limits of that experience, analytically speaking. While these limits are various and at times personal, three important ones can easily be diserned. On the one hand, Puritanism was capable of lapsing into a narrow version of scholasticism, a religion of the letter rather than of the Spirit. This tendency appeared early in Ames' *Cases of Conscience,* which sits in judgment over the moral trials of the saints. Covenant theology was the terminus of this sort of thinking with its peculiar mixing of Puritan ideas and scholastic methods. Far to the other extreme, Puritanism had within it the seeds of disintegration through incoherence of thought and method. The doctrines of the inner light and of the Holy Spirit have their place in orthodox Puritanism, as we have seen; nonetheless, these doctrines had a tendency to break loose from the core of conscience and to stand alone as in the practice of the Quakers. There were good Puritan answers to the doctrines of the inner light and Holy Spirit, as the writings of Baxter attest, but the frequency with which this road was travelled also attests to a tendency in the Puritan inner drama to mistake the promptings of the emotions for those of the Holy Spirit. Perhaps, for some, sanctification of the emotions came too easily and was mistaken for the promptings of the flesh. Barbour's book on the Quakers[174] documents all these arguments between Puritans and Quakers with great care. The third limit and danger of disintegration was more external, the forces of the rationalistic spirit upon Puritanism. This Perry Miller has taken note of in *The New England Mind: The Seventeenth Century*, but I do not

agree that secular rationalism was an inevitable outgrowth of
Puritanism. The Puritan intellect was highly trained to deal with
matters of faith and with theology on an abstract level. It would not
naturally turn secular so long as its primary interest was moral under
the hegemony of conscience. Edwards' intellect shows that the
orthodox direction of intellect was intact fifty years after the
"rationalistic enlightenment" among Puritans had begun, and the
same cast of mind appears strongly in Wordsworth, Coleridge,
Dickinson, Hawthorne, and Melville in the next century. What we
can say, more justly on the evidence, was that in historical fact
the majority in Calvinist-Puritanism succumbed, as did the most
enlightened spirits in Anglicanism or Catholicism, to certain Liberal-
Enlightenment forces, but it did not create, or lead to, these forces
itself. To say such is a confusion in the history of ideas, the source
of which lies mainly in a certain sort of American hagiography.
Even to acknowledge, as we must, that this third outside force, not
scholastic rationalism or the inner light heresy, brought about the
demise of the tradition after the mid-18th century (except in some
final literary flourishes) is not to admit a logical connection between
the two forces. In the sections that follow we shall stay within the
bounds of the tradition as described, analyzed and illustrated in this
chapter. However it is desirable and will be possible in the
introductory comments to the various periods and authors of the
Puritan tradition to state the changing relationship of Puritanism to
the various outside intellectual and historical forces mentioned here.

PART TWO

The Patterns in Poetry: 1580−1700

I. Introduction

We know that Spenser spent his college years (1569−1576) at Pembroke College, Cambridge, at the time when the Puritan revolution in its theological stage was first beginning to manifest itself in strength. Milton's Cambridge years (1625−1632) were spent at Christ's during the waning period of Puritan influence in the University. Fletcher's monumental *The Intellectual Development of John Milton*[1] lists some of the standard Puritan preachers and scholars of the period between Spenser and Milton (1576−1632) as part of the required reading for either term time or summer vacation. Included in the list are Perkins, Preston, Sibbes, and the others who made Cambridge the intellectual stronghold of the Puritan party in the Church during the later years of Elizabeth and the entire reign of James I. The main lines of the development, rise, and fall of the Puritan intellectual movement in the late 16th and early 17th centuries, the various parties and contentions among themselves and with ecclesiastical authorities, have been presented at some length in books English and American.[2] The only aspect of the Puritan tradition and influence yet slighted is the relationship between the Puritan intellectual and social view of the world and the artistic sensibility of the time: particularly the sensibility of the great poets − Spenser, Marvell, Taylor, Milton, among others − who were closely influenced in education, intellect, and temperament by the Puritan ideal. There are many reasons why this influence has not been taken seriously. First, of course, the notorious reputation of the Puritans in relation to the arts in general. Scholarship of the past fifty years has tempered the common view here considerably, but unfortunately the results have not become widely known or recognized, at least among literary critics, where they might bear fruitful results.[3] As significant in preventing investigation of the Puritan sensibility in at least the major writers is the presence of so many other better known, and in most instances better liked and understood, influences. With Spenser and Milton these are enormous, yet even in the case of Marvell or Taylor there are other traditions − metaphysical or meditative-contemplative − to appeal closer to the range and interest of the literary scholar.[4] In what follows I hope to show awareness and appreciation of a great deal that has been done in the way of placing these writers in one tradition or other, and at the same time to point out a legitimate strain of the Puritan sensibility in their work which is important for the vision of the author and on the other hand not found in other contemporary authors uninfluenced directly by the great Puritan intellectual awakening of the period.

Our 16th and 17th century explorations will be of Spenser, the metaphysical Puritan tradition (Marvell and Taylor) and Milton. Puritan prose literature which qualifies as great − *Pilgrim's Progress* and the writings of Richard Baxter − will enter the discussion as general background and in illumination of specific points. If the discussions are successful, the relationship among Calvinist theological points, Puritan patterns of thought, and the imaginative attempts of writers will be made clear.

The reader may wonder why Spenser is the only 16th century poet of Puritan tendency to whom attention is given in this section of the study. The answers are various. We have given a good deal of attention, perhaps too much from a purely literary point of view, to Puritan prose writers, even to those of the third or fourth rank, in establishing the premises of the Calvinist-Puritan sensibility. If we were to devote equal attention to all of the minor Puritan poets of the 16th century, and with the exception of Spenser and possibly Sidney (to the extent that he was Puritan in his poetry), they are all relatively minor, the study might turn into a commentary on minor Puritan poetry, which is decidedly not the intention. Lily B. Campbell, in *Divine Poetry and Drama in Sixteenth-Century England,* has devoted proper attention to the minor Puritan writers of the time.[5] As for Sidney, while there are certainly Puritan influences in his poems, this writer seriously doubts that he may be called Puritan in any decisive sense, as is manifestly true of Spenser. The general atmosphere in Sidney is major Elizabethan, that of Shakespeare, Marlowe and the other dramatists, great and small. Waller and other minor poets have received the attention they deserve.[6] The rationale for this book almost demands that the study of the poetry begin with a decisive major figure, in order to justify all the required preliminaries we have passed through. At a later stage, when the Calvinist-Puritan tradition thins out in the 18th century, there is justification for including the relatively minor Watts, the curious Smart, as well as the pivotal prose writer Law, along with the only major writer of this type of poetry in the 18th century, William Cowper.

At the risk of presenting the reader with information which is widely available in intellectual histories of the period,[7] a few words must be said about general 17th century intellectual history and the place of the Calvinist-Puritan movement in this period. We were heretofore concerned with the growth and pattern of the Calvinist tradition itself, and with its English manifestations in a definable sensibility. For the major part of the study the concentration will be on the writers who present some important literary aspect of the tradition, with some attempt to describe interrelationships and development of religious language and imagery. Between these two areas of concern, there is a large area of historical connections and intellectual history which is strictly speaking not our province. Other books easily available supply this link, among which the most outstanding may be Haller's classical *The Rise of Puritanism* dealing with all phases of 17th century Puritan tradition and the more recent Milo Kaufman's *Pilgrim's Progress and Tradition in Puritan Meditation*,[8] which considers closely such prose writers as Bunyan and Baxter, so important as a backdrop for a study of the major Puritan poets. Use of these sources will be made indirectly in what follows on the poets. For a short space here we must, however, look at the intellectual history of the period more directly, to give an immediate background to our concerns. This background will be of the period extending from the time of Spenser's greatest writing to the close of the 17th century, and is intended not as original historical reading but as a way of understanding the development of the Puritan sensibility in the complexities of the 17th century situation.

The opening chapter established the nature of the Calvinist-Puritan movement in the 16th century, but did not show its influence or importance. For this purpose a more objective and historical stance is needed, that of chronological and intellectual history. The work of Haller and Knappen has provided the vantage point for such evaluation, against the background of more general views of intellectual history as given by such writers as A. O. Lovejoy, Basil Willey, and E. M. W. Tillyard.[9] As a historical force Calvinist-Puritanism developed in the period 1550—1600, reached its zenith of intellectual and political strength from 1600 to 1660, and became recessive after 1660, continuing its major influence as a contributor to certain strains of Enlightenment thinking and as a force in itself in New England. For the purposes of this study the political and social ascendency of Puritanism is not of great importance, as our interest is in its moral and intellectual influence upon the sensibility of creative individuals. This is a valid distinction. Yet it would be a mistake, and a cause of misunderstanding, not to have as a background the history of the political fortunes of the movement during the period, its relative importance from one generation to another in the great arena of ideas and politics that was England from 1580 to 1700. This history has psychological implications in dealing with the writers; although as a system Calvinist-Puritanism may be seen to have general and immutable features, so that Cartwright (1570) and Edwards (1750), Cowper (1780) and the 19th century Evangelicals belong to the same tradition of thought, it does make some difference whether the movement is struggling for ascendency and mixed with English Elizabethan patriotism (as we find it in Spenser), if it is temporarily dominant (in the mid-17th century in Milton, Baxter and Bunyan) or if it is in political and intellectual decline as in the entire 18th century and early 19th century except for the Colonies.

Haller has proven abundantly in *The Elect Nation* that the temporary victory of Puritanism in the 17th century had its basis in 16th century history as well as ideology.[10] The great Cambridge reformers and preachers, whose establishment in England of the Calvinist intellectual views and sensibility we have studied, needed the cooperation of history and the skill of a great popular ideologue such as Foxe to bring their message to the center of the English consciousness. Strictly speaking, the fires at Smithfield, the providential death of Mary and coming of Elizabeth, the victorious years 1570 to 1600 in English history, the practical deification of Elizabeth by the English people, have little to do with Puritanism as an intellectual movement. Quite rightly, indeed, Anglican historians and scholars can claim the greatest Marian martyrs as their own, although there were numerous Puritan dialecticians among the burned who spoke most successfully against the Marian Inquisitors. The queen was no friend to the Calvinist-Puritan cause in either its theological or its political aspects. But history contrived, with the help of polemicists and propagandists such as Foxe, to give the Puritan views and English history a striking coincidence during the last part of the 16th century. The Saints were a "chosen people," on the authority of Scripture, "elect" individually and destined collectively to bring the kingdom of God to perfection on earth. England, by virtue of the "Tudor myth" had also steered a miraculous course from the time of Henry VIII to the triumphs of Elizabeth over Catholicism and Spain. There was similarity enough between the purely religious myth and the purely political myth to allow the two to be insinuated by the Puritan preachers as a double and coequal work of providence. Foxe's *Book of Martyrs* and numerous lesser historical and religious works show this wondrous connection, though not always with great clarity or logic.

Elizabeth and her councillors, while they believed little of this and loathed the political aspirations of the Puritan party in state and Church, allowed the Puritans their spiritual combat with the Anglican establishment during the 1570–1600 period on the wise grounds that the Puritans were a lesser danger than the Catholics, would be vital in a national emergency, and hopefully could be brought around to the general English Church compromise in time. Only the last premise proved to be wrong, as Elizabeth and her councillors miscalculated the force and sincerity of the Puritan ideology. From the Puritan point of view, this era was one of hope and combat: that is, they naively hoped to reform by prayer and preaching the entire fabric of the English state, including the great Queen and her ministers and bishops. They had not yet turned to the idea of arms as a necessary alternative. This is the historic background for Spenser's Puritan sensibility in *The Faerie Queene*, where the pure Puritan religious strain appears occasionally, but is more often entwined with the patriotism of the Tudor myth, adulation of the Queen and pride in the accomplishment of Elizabethan England.

The period 1600–1660 was both the triumph and disaster of political Puritanism. From the literary point of view, the disaster was not only political. The best minds, theological and literary, were turned from their native directions to politics during the crisis of the Puritan movement in England. Milton and Baxter wrote as much political material as that in the areas of their natural genius. Only Bunyan, semi-educated and at the bottom of the social ladder, and Taylor, later to find security in New England at the Restoration, could develop a normal Puritan sensibility in those times, which might later function undivided. Marvell's Puritanism was more marginal and sceptical than that of any other major figure, and could function in its own peculiar way during and after the Civil War. His writings, and Baxter's after the Revolution, are portents towards the Puritan sensibility of the 18th and 19th centuries, inward and non-political.

The events of history from 1600 to 1660 made no longer possible the mixed Puritan sensibility of Spenser, which had been able to combine successfully Puritanism, Englishness and a good deal of the older medievalism. The vision of the kingdom of the saints and the wishes of a substantial portion of the English people could no longer be taken even by wishful thinking as compatible. Milton could not give the Stuart kings the adulation Spenser bestowed upon Elizabeth and which the Puritan preachers and writers tried to bestow upon the scholarly James I. The new "chosen people" reluctantly had to consign a good deal of the chosen island to Satan. The established Church, that "shadowy and empty Rome," showed greater stamina and sense of identity than the Puritans of the Elizabethan period believed possible. Even in temporary defeat in the field of arms it survived, with its own myths and sense of history. Hooker, Andrewes and Donne had accomplished their tasks very well. The "little Rome," the tool of the state and of subservient men like Parker, did not fade away under Puritan polemic or victory in war. Baxter and Milton believed in the rule of the saints before 1640, not as Fifth Monarchy or millenium men, but as believers in a kingdom of God coequal with the state. Their disillusionment during and after the Protectorate, if we read carefully enough, was not merely with the forces of Satan or the royalist enemy, or even with the triumph of Charles II in 1660. The problem was an inner one. Cromwell had achieved the grand design by force of arms, yet the Congregationalists, Baptists, Quakers, Presbyterians and the minor sects of the "inner light" turned this victory into a tower of Babel. Whatever the varying modern opinions of the success of the Commonwealth and the Protectorate may be, it was a bitter defeat for those who held power. The rule of the spirit became the rule of chaos. The doctrine of individual election, so central to Puritan religious sensibility, and fought for so valiantly in the spiritual struggles of the individual life, became in its collective form a nightmare Trojan horse for the Puritans. It gave the confidence that led to victory, but such collective confidence also led to smugness, dissension and illusions about the nature of the human constitution. Ironically enough, the Puritans, obsessed with sin and quick to note the sinfulness of man and need for repentance, fell collectively into a view which defied the Augustinian basis of Calvin's original insights on human nature and sin. After 1660 Milton and Baxter recoiled from this collective hubris, and Puritanism as a collective movement became again a passive, wary and individual matter of theology and sensibility. The year 1660 is the last important division for English Puritanism. The American date is somewhat later, but not as late as many historians are inclined to put it. In an intellectual sense and as a social force it reaches only to the time of Jonathan Edwards in the mid-18th century.

After 1660 English Puritanism produced no further thinkers of the calibre of Milton and Baxter. The Puritan tradition lived on into the 18th century on the capital of their declining years. A Bunyan or Marvell might flourish mildly in the declining sunset years, but no new power was forthcoming to keep the movement at a high productive pitch. The cases of Richard Baxter and John Milton after 1660 prove this point poignantly. As both will figure later in this study, the points here will be brief.

Milton forsook his literary career to promote the kingdom of God under Cromwell. He wrote mountains of polemical pamphlets and state papers, and on Cromwell's death sent out frantic pamphlets defending the Commonwealth ideal and the elect nation. Reading them carefully, we catch the hint of despair about the Commonwealth idea even while it is bravely defended against the outside world. This failure of hope, abetted of course by the excesses of the Restoration, led to his revised view of the Puritan myth of history, which appears in the last two books of *Paradise Lost*. Times have changed since Foxe's *Book of Martyrs* and Spenser's ecstasy over Gloriana. Loyally enough, Milton attributes his change of heart to the evils of the Restoration, but it is obvious that the practical experience of the Commonwealth also helped. *Paradise Lost* stoutly maintains the central Puritan idea of individual election (Bk. III), and the historical and biblical idea of a favored few in history beginning with Abraham and reaching the saints of the 17th century, but it rejects group and national election leading to a millenium or kingdom of God on earth. Instead we get the static Christian reading of history that had been devised by Saint Augustine in *City of God,* the theory of the two kingdoms and history as weighted by the force of original sin. The great points are divinely controlled and out of man's hands. There are ups and downs as the elect or the damned struggle in the arena, most of history is a dark passage, and the controlling forces are not in the hands of the saints. This is no more pessimistic than medieval Christian history, but a remarkable recession from the high water mark of Puritan hope of controlling history and, so to speak, determining on earth the hand of God. On another level, Milton's far-ranging speculations on the cosmos and the Trinity in *Paradise Lost* bespeak the death-knell of intellectual Puritanism to come after the Glorious Revolution. Puritanism, except for the remarkable exception of Edwards in America, had outrun its intellectual sources, and was to be a recessive possession of minor writers, Watts, Smart and Cowper. One gets the impression while reading the 16th century Puritan sermons and polemics that that time was one of genuine intellectual and emotional exuberance in the new freedom from scholastic and Catholic control. The Cambridge preachers and theologians felt satisfied and free within the bounds of a theology which allowed more personal freedom and freedom of speculation than did the earlier tradition. With what impudence and zeal did they refute the doctrine of the Real Presence in the sacrament, or of the Pope's authority, even at the threat of the stake. The Puritan version of Calvinism was an authentic imaginative release, a liberty of exploration of conscience for those who embraced it. In the early 17th century, how they attacked with delight the authority of king and bishop. But in *Paradise Lost* Milton, the greatest successor to this tradition and its greatest poet, is out of this territory much of the time. We know that he read the Puritans with zeal at Cambridge and believed their religious and political vision for most of his life. But there are numerous other contributions to his thought, varieties of Renaissance skepticism and humanistic thought the Puritans could not accept. We view this struggle in the last book of *Paradise Regained*. His boldness and intellectual freedom are leading to the world of Newton and Locke, and, despite himself no doubt, to the deism of the 18th century, which he would have deplored, although some critics think otherwise.

Richard Baxter's was a humbler and more pious mind than Milton's, and thus his reaction to the failure of the Commonwealth to which he had dedicated his hopes was of a lesser scope. Also, he had had his troubles during the rule of the saints. An essential religious personality, as Milton was not, Baxter after the Restoration helps us to see what will happen to the Puritan movement in retirement and decline. After the Glorious Revolution Puritanism takes an inward turn, a reversion from a world given over to secularism and Satan. Catholic recusants had done likewise after the Elizabethan triumph one hundred years earlier. The inward piety and personal devotion in *Saints Everlasting Rest*[11] is directed towards the individual, or at most to the congregational witness to the word of God. The direction here is followed by Watts, Smart and Cowper in the 18th century, though less so by the forceful and gregarious Methodist preachers. Baxter, an upright, narrow but profound man of God and religion, had been treated badly by all sides in the great upheavals of 1630–1660. The reformist saints of the Commonwealth no less than the returned Anglican victors of 1660 had found him a difficult man. His problem was that of ideals and principles held against the sway of the world. He could not live easily under the rule of the saints as practiced during the Protectorate, 1650–1660, nor could he turn with many of his fellow Englishmen to the cynical and easy-going ways of the post-Restoration period. With crises over, the older church of Parker and compromise with the world soon obliterated most of the traces of the Anglican piety of 1600–1640, the years of Donne and Andrewes, in a new and permanent settlement of the Elizabethan variety.[12] Baxter's isolation and solitude after 1660, the inwardness of his later works, prefigure the isolation and recessive nature of the Puritan movement and all earnest piety and religious feeling after the opening of the 18th century. To the mockeries and worldliness of Swift and Pope, the gentle Watts, Smart and Cowper were going to appear minor figures indeed in the history of 18th century thought.

If history is told by victors and survivors, this is true of intellectual history, too. In a well-balanced view, such as Willey's *Seventeenth-Century Background,* there appears what seems to be an inevitable march of intellectual history from the scholastic overlays of the early century to Locke and Newton at the end, ushering in the age of deism and rationalism. No doubt, with hindsight, that was the way it was. But primary documents tell us another story. History is not inevitable to the participants, and for long periods the Calvinist-Puritan sensibility seemed to be winning in the 17th century. A viewpoint such as Willey's does not convey this inner or limited sense of history. Also, movements such as Puritanism or Catholicism, which lost their places at the center of the English mind in the 17th century to moderate Anglicanism and later to deism, received a bad image but did not die out. Some movements, it is true, like Rosicrucianism and hermeticism, and the millenarian sects, died in their time, for all real purposes, though capable of revival at a later point in history. But movements like Calvinist-Puritanism, which in fact expressed its force in

the sensibilities of religious writers into the early 19th century, cannot
be said to have died suddenly, even if they were far from the center
of power and intellectual prestige after their apogee. Intellectual histories written to telescope the past into the present, to connect our
thought and science to the past, or to reinforce the bias of the present, tend to diminish the richness of history and of thought by concentrating mainly upon the dominant or forward-looking theory or
school of a given era which makes progress seem "inevitable." Literary
history especially must also be written from another point of view,
since it is questionable if literature is progressive. This point of view
will account for important minorities, in this instance for the rich
residue of Calvinist-Puritan sensibility after 1700 as well as before.

Despite the clear emergence of the Calvinist-Puritan ideology with
its attendant sensibility in the 16th century, followed by its brief
triumph in the 17th, which we have related in these pages, there are
those who deny not only the Puritan sensibility but even the Calvinist
ideology, or at least deny it much importance except in the political
field. The Georges[13] worked entirely within the premise of a general
Protestant tradition in the period and deliberately played down major
distinctions within Protestantism except for a few minor matters. William Halewood's admirable book[14] distinguishes 17th century religious
poetry sharply from the muddled thinking of much 20th century
criticism of it, but generally follows Martz and Gardner in not being
very concerned about distinctions, satisfied with the majority middle
way of the Anglican establishment. John New[15] performed that necessary task again admirably in a recent monograph (necessary again
because literary students do not know or ignore the excellent work
of previous generations of historical scholars), and his definitions of
the lines of difference between Puritan and Anglican and Catholic on
all major theological points are lucid and can be accepted with the
cavil that his refusal to recognize predestination as a major Calvinist-
Puritan hallmark is curious. Norman Pettit[16] moves beyond the level
of theology and ideology, assuming the originality of the Puritan tradition, in order to make the most valuable recent contribution to
these studies, in which the patterns of Puritan sensibility are outlined
and elaborated. The Puritan stages of election and salvation are
assumed in Pettit's discussion of "preparation," that is, the standard
form of sin-state, vocation, election, justification, sanctification and
glorification we have discussed in the previous chapter. Pettit considers preparation before and after election, and thus his scheme is

an elaborate pattern of thoughts and devotions within the standard movement. He devotes much space to the logical problems and quibbles among the divines of the first generation of English and American Puritans regarding the propriety of preparation before or after election, and notes the degree of fudging of the issues that went on. Opinion ranged from the irresistible call, once and final, as on the road to Damascus, to elaborate preparations (assuming prevenient grace) during all the stages, but particularly those before election is secured. Such logic-chopping is of minimal interest for the sensibility and poetry; but the fact of the existence of many positions within the Puritan community is of vital importance to us. The poets and others had choices within the Calvinist scheme of salvation, and preparation took various forms. The Pauline was the most dramatic and final, but limited for art; on the other hand the various preparations before election were important for the sensibility of Marvell, while those within sanctification were equally so for Taylor. Since this book stresses the variety of the Puritan sensibility against the lockstep caricatures of much literary history, Pettit's findings, though he limits focus upon theologians, is a welcome addition to our knowledge. Our discussion of the various strategies of Spenser, Marvell, Taylor and Milton will point out how valuable it is to have this sophisticated sense of Calvinist-Puritan tradition at our disposal.

II. Spenser

A. The Immediate Background

It may be supposed that a movement, both fervent, new, and intellectual in quality, would not escape the notice of the leading men of sensibility of the late sixteenth and early seventeenth centuries. Puritanism escaped no one's notice. Some writers were decidedly against its ideology. Shakespeare and other Elizabethan dramatists ridiculed Puritanism throughout their works. In the next century the metaphysical poets, with the exception of Marvell, and all the Cavaliers, avoided or protested against the movement. Anglicanism by that time found itself capable of supporting its own intellectual and literary traditions, in the work of many fine theologians, poets and prose writers. Nevertheless, other important writers, beginning with Spenser and Sidney in the sixteenth century, were Calvinist-Puritan in spirit. In the next century there were many more. In the opening section we found that Calvinist-Puritanism is a very wide area, allowing, within the system or sensibility, many variables. Some writers were impressed with the political and moral qualities of the Puritan preaching. In this way it became incorporated into Spenser's myth. The purely political aspects are mainly nonliterary, yet Milton managed to unite theology and politics in much of his writing. The theological and devotional sides of the movement appear in Taylor, Marvell, Bunyan and Baxter, with Taylor and Baxter particularly trying to develop the devotional potentialities in the Puritan theology as rivals to Catholic or Anglican practice. In all these varied efforts, there is mingling of the Puritan strain with some other or others, as befits the seventeenth century, the nature of the poetic sensibility, and the marginal character of the Puritan movement in England except in the years 1640–1660.

It is this mingling, and non-literary character of much of Puritanism itself, including many of the sermons, that has caused critics' hesitation in approaching this subject except in purely theological or political terms. Yet evidence of all sorts points to the existence of a Puritan sensibility in literature, a tradition of writers who are identifiable as having much in common, as metaphysicals, Elizabethans or Augustans are identifiable. In discussion of traditions one runs the risk of viewing poetic qualities mechanically, and the greater risk of over-simplification by isolation from other contributing sources. There is also the risk of being old-fashioned in approach. One can plead the writers' and readers' knowledge of other readings, sources and opinions of the major and lesser figures. One can also plead innocent in advance of attempting to force great figures like Spenser and Milton on any Procrustean bed. Puritanism is an important aspect of their work, but not all of it.

The case of Spenser will be given some polemical thought, however, so that, *datis dandis,* such thought may be ignored when similar problems arise in the cases of Milton, Marvell and Taylor. The reading and reputation of Spenser, like all other great figures in English literature, have not been immune to changes in 20th century critical taste.

The reputation of Spenser fell sharply with the decline of interest in moral readings and in allegory during the heyday of textual or new or iconic criticism, whatever one wishes to call it. Also, with a declining interest in and knowledge of old-fashioned historicism, the meaning and method of Spenser's own historicism fell into obscurity. Recently allegory has been rescued from oblivion by virtue of its connection with myth, and it is inevitable that a myth criticism will raise the opinion of and interest in Spenser. A modified historicism is having its comeback too, as we notice the recent awareness of the Tudor Myth in explicating many political aspects of Spenser's allegory. The Puritan movement, as Haller has shown in his study of Foxe's *Book of Martyrs,*[17] has connections with the Tudor Myth, and Spenser was capable of successfully using both in his appraisal of the historical and religious situation of England. Some recent commentary has stressed the social and political patterns in *The Faerie Queene,* relating them to the overall mythic conception, which is fair enough. The moral and religious aspects should not be left to the disregard given to older allegorical readings, however. In making the connections Spenser blends Puritanism with Tudor historicism, drawing the line at certain ultimate aspects of both. It will be our purpose to show the nature, and the restrictions, of Spenser's Puritan strain in *The Faerie Queene*.

If we bear in mind the tenor and quality of the Puritan sermons of Spenser's Cambridge years, our first reaction to the appearance of this strain in *The Faerie Queene* is to notice the restraint, the caution with which the poet introduces Puritan themes into his great work. There were the Queen and the court to consider, but a good deal must be attributed to Spenser's own Renaissance sophistication. His belief in the Puritan-Protestant view of salvation is in earnest, but he was not intent in driving home an either/or method to a corrupt political and moral society, as were the Cambridge and London preachers during the period. His wide-ranging knowledge of the Renaissance found its place in his work, as well as the Renaissance notion of instructing and teaching together. In seeking after *omne tulit punctam, qui miscuit utile et ducile,* Spenser allows to the surface of his poem a grace and complexity which the preachers, with their "plain style" and Ramist premises, would have frowned on, and which even Bunyan, the most homogeneous of Puritan allegorists, would have found digressive baubles on a moral tale. Spenser's New Testament and Puritan morality and theology appear from time to time in striking and unmistakeable form, as in I,ix–xii and II,xii; at other times it is buried deep in the layers of political or mythic allegory, and at still others, one suspects, not present at all, when Spenser becomes interested in his medieval-Renaissance story for its own sake and its enchanting characters. Recent critics have rightfully emphasized the textual complexity, the dramatic flair, and the contrapuntal nature of some of the narrative from the main theme, in Spenser's poem. These qualities, also found in Milton, are welcome in a great and subtle work. One aspect of the poem seems at times to conflict with the Puritan-Protestant intention of the total theme. This is not, as often stated, the sensuousness of Spenser, the allure and attractions of the flesh and the world for which he has so often been berated, (and lately praised). Such elements fall quite easily within the spiritual combat of the Puritan writers, their keen and realistic appraisal, following St. Paul, of the powers of the flesh. The sermon writer or theologian found it inappropriate to dramatize such combats except in abstract terms, but we have seen Richard Sibbes in *The Bruised Reede* devote an entire treatise to the powers of concupiscence. If his language was almost always abstract, the tone, to say the least, was high-pitched and emotional, suggesting obviously a real personal and existential problem of spiritual combat. Today only an abnormal person or a hypocrite would accuse Spenser of overstating the allure of the world, the flesh and the devil. For those who decry his ultimate resistance to such things, his knights' victories over these forces, one can answer that psychological modernism is not an absolute standard which ought to be allowed to twist or belittle the values of the religious Puritan past. This theme of faith, hope and charity in Puritan terms recurs in Marvell, Taylor and Milton, and will be seen as one of the consistent patterns in Puritan aesthetic sensibility. The only area in which Spenser's vision of reality as reflected in allegory does seem to conflict with Puritan sentiment is in the political and historical: he seems much of the time to accept the Tudor English myth of the state.

Of course others, such as Foxe, had done the same. But there is a difference between the Puritan's earnest hope that church and state may share one destiny, and Spenser's revelling in the Tudor myth and Gloriana. The Puritans never lost awareness, in their constant admonishment of Elizabeth and James I, that the great work had yet to come about, that the kingdom of the saints, with the help of the monarch, had yet to be completed. Spenser seems willing to leave some division, call it platonic or mythic, between the actual successes of England under Gloriana and apocalypse. In not urging that the two be more fully brought together, Spenser may be considered either as more smugly Elizabethan or as more traditionally Christian. If we compare the historical myth in the last part of *The Faerie Queene* with the last books of *Paradise Lost,* Milton's view of history after the failure of the Commonwealth, we see that Spenser is more worldly than traditionally Christian in his reservations about the Puritan millenium.

In fact, Puritanism is the only element which keeps Spenser within the bounds of religious sensibility at all. It is the moral and religious sensibilities of Sir Guyon and the Red Cross Knight that do this, giving a limited relationship of the individual to the Almighty. One is tempted to believe that he perceived the underlying arrogance of the full vision of the saints, and how they would later deny limitation in their reach for power in the Commonwealth period. Spenser is too cautious and non-political a Puritan to fall into the trap Puritan history later set for Milton. His is not the Renaissance secularism of Machiavelli or Shakespeare, but his worldly picture of the glory of Elizabethan England is a heady one. On the whole Spenser's Puritan religious and moral sensibility restrains Renaissance humanism, while his humanism releases some energies held too fully in check by Puritanism.

Spenser obviously felt that the purification of the individual, the church, and the state could proceed hand in hand, according to Foxe and the Tudor legend, and indeed the events of history until 1600 seemed to assure this view. The Puritan preachers restrained their demands under Elizabeth during the period of the Catholic and Spanish threat. Their hopes for an enlightened sovereign and a purified church lasted through the reign of James I and even into that of Charles. The Puritans destroyed the church and state under Charles in despair of reforming either. Such a mood is far from the spiritual and temporal optimism of *The Faerie Queene*. Spenser was sanguine of spiritual and temporal goals, since he did not view Puritanism as a political force to be carried to its limit, but as a moral force for the individual and national purification, as we get in the Red Cross Knight and Sir Guyon. The disillusionments of later years — of presbytery being Pope writ large, a Pope in every parish, and finally, every man his own Pope according to his inner lights, which spelled the end of organized religion as well as of the organized state except under tyranny — are hidden deeply in the mists of time at the writing of *The Faerie Queene*.

No writer on *The Faerie Queene* can ignore the debt we all owe to C.S. Lewis's *Allegory of Love,* a work which made the best Spenser criticism of our present age possible. My agreement with the spirit of Lewis's work is almost total, though I am nevertheless extremely conscious that his interpretation of the religious allegory differs essentially from what will be presented here. Of what is fundamentally Christian there is no doubt, and our mutual disagreement with certain modernists is almost total. Lewis views the Christian allegory specifically as Anglican and the political allegory as an upholding of the Elizabethan compromise. In the latter area our interest is minimal, and the difference of little moment, since Puritan political thought in the later 16th century was still in harmony with general Elizabethan, though in an avant-garde position. Frank Kermode and many other distinguished traditional critics of Spenser agree with Lewis's estimate of Spenser as medial Anglican man. It is enough at this point to admit that a case for more specific Puritan modes of theological thought in Books I and II is something of a radical departure from this tradition of criticism which must be tested in the pages to follow.

B. Spenser and Puritan Method

If one approaches *The Faerie Queene* from a purely aesthetic view-point, not regarding its supposed occult or ultimately mythic mean-ings, one is impressed by the fact of two strains of sensibility within the work. *Cave* our modern "mythic" critics, one of these strains is overwhelmingly moral, and encompasses most of Books I and II. It is also in structure fairly strict allegory, as that term was used before the appearance of the contemporary myth criticism of Frye.[18] There are lighter strains and more wayward uses of myth in I and II; there is moral complexity which is not moral ambiguity, and virtuoso dra-matic action. But the essential ground-structure is the product of a mind which springs from the same tradition as Bunyan, a mind more innately cultivated and more widely read than Bunyan's, to be sure, yet basically Reformation-Puritan. We cannot imagine Shakespeare, Donne, or, later, Pope writing in this manner. This is a matter of sensibility, not ideology. In Books III–VI the ideology of the poem does not change radically, the allegory persists, a sense of final unity is maintained. The ideology is, however, looser than in I and II, the sensibility more relaxed and open to influences outside a religious world. There is freer, more playful myth-making, more loose ends in the moral and meaning, a lessening (on the whole but with obvious exceptions) of intensity. The Puritan strain which was dominant in I and II has to share the center of attention with many others.

In I and II there are also many other strains, to be sure. Spenser is not Bunyan or a Puritan poet of the New England wilderness. These strains are absorbed into the dominant Puritan ideological and aesthetic structure which gives the Books their unity of purpose in the same manner as certain congenial strains of thought were absorbed by the Puritan preachers themselves. Spenser at Cambridge would not have been taken by doctrines and a way of life which allowed no possibilities for the natural man or for the imagination. Our modern bias against religious sensibility and ideology, which often goes by the name of humanism, or appears as a defense of the imagination, would not have been understood by Spenser, as we may hazard that he would not have understood certain contemporary readings of his work. Puritanism could be seen, towards the end of the 16th century, as a liberating intellectual movement, liberating the intellect from Catholic dogma, the body from minute ascetic practice, and the imagination from the "medieval" style of writing. Other views, such as those taken by Shakespeare or Marlowe, provided further liberation, but we must not fall into the error of equating the Calvinist-Puritanism of that time with the sterile, negative, and unartistic attitudes of the 19th century descendants of the Puritans in England and America, whose Calvinism is merely vestigial, moralistic, almost tribal. Spenser inherited the positive thrust of Puritan moral and intellectual life and devised literary methods that are taken from the literary tradition of the Renaissance and also consistent with Puritanism.

In a general way the victories of the Red Cross Knight (holiness) and of Guyon (personal morality) are, for the sixteenth century, imaginative victories as well as religious or prudential. In our modern sense, they are not prudential or proscriptive at all. They may seem so to 19th and 20th century readers who have inherited, and most likely rejected, the Puritan way as a formula for moral life and for success. In the 16th century this way was a path of discovery, a journey into largely unknown and dangerous territory of the soul. The medieval and Catholic way had been destroyed by Luther, Calvin and the polemics of the Marian period, except in its most universal features. The confessional and sacramental life of the Church was gone, and with it many of the applications of inherited morality. The Puritan preachers and Spenser realized that some inherited moral forms, going back to Aristotle and Plato and the Roman moralists, must not change essentially in the Puritan world. Thus Spenser can use Aristotle's theory of the virtues, and Ames' *Cases of Conscience* reads much like any Catholic work of its time, aside from the rather inappropriate anti-Catholic polemics, considering how much scholastic casuistry is silently appropriated. The change largely comes in giving imaginative shape to this material through the image of the journey and through the drama of the individual conscience discovering holiness or morality. We miss the whole point of Books I and II if we do not share in the dangers of the way, the dilemmas and obscurities in the search for holiness and moral meaning in the new religious world of the late 16th century. The Catholic-scholastic road, long travelled, had been largely abandoned. The Puritan way, trod throughout the 17th century, would in time come to seem dull and well known in its turn, after Bunyan and Milton. Our danger in reading Spenser, then, is in projecting back into the work our sense of anticipation, of knowing it all, of having seen many times the end of the journey. The journey is dramatic and dangerous, if we will take a little trouble to see how Spenser presents it to us.

We must remember the eagerness and heady calls of the Puritan Cambridge preachers in starting their flocks on this way in the late 16th century. In attacking the "dead works" of the Church and proclaiming the need for a new journey, a new way of salvation, they did not promise success to their followers or themselves. New guideposts on the way had to be discovered, and the way itself, for reasons of Calvinist ideology, would always be less certain and more an individual affair than in Catholic Christianity. The need for signs, emblems, and new dramatic presentation of the theological life is Calvinism's greatest incentive to imaginative literature. The intellectual despair of the Red Cross Knight and the moral severities of Guyon's journey must be read in the context of the Cambridge sermons, Calvinist ideology, and the effects of these phenomena upon the intellectual elite of the time. The suicides of the Cambridge period were as real as the triumphs of faith, and the rejoicing of the Catholic community of Lancashire over the final despair of a Puritan is an indication of the hazards of the journey.[19] The only constants in this religious world were a few dogmatic principles, the necessity of making the journey, and the allegorical vision or sensibility as the means of making it successfully. Spenser unites these three in the first two books of *The Faerie Queene,* for the first time in a major literary work. The Calvinist principles in these books are easy, all too easy perhaps, to discern. In isolation they are easily subject to ridicule as allegorical oversimplifications. I mean such things as the symbols of faith, hope, predestination and providence that are sprinkled throughout the Books. Book I, canto x is thick with them. The journey, in its larger significations, is so obviously taken over from medieval and Renaissance literary practice, with the general mythic associations of which our day is so fond closely behind, that modern readers are easily allowed to jump over, if they will, the local reformational significance of this structure. Spenser remembered the Cambridge preachers' exhortations to shake off the Catholic delusion, and then the natural man, to begin the great trial of faith, leading to salvation (or perhaps disaster). We have the writings of Sibbes, Preston and Perkins, among others, behind us on this point. He and his generation knew the necessity, and the awesome consequences of undertaking this journey. "Reformation without tarrying" was more an individual than a political cry in the 16th century. It became a general social cry in the 17th century as the Puritans gained strength and confidence. With our knowledge of this coming Puritan confidence, or over-confidence, we are in danger of reading Spenser in terms of it. There are great moments of confidence in Spenser, greater than in English poetry before, in the culminating cantos of each book. But it does injustice to the dramatic structure of the Books, especially I and II, to insert a later Puritan smugness into the encounters of the Red Cross Knight and Sir Guyon, which are truly dramatic, as Harry Berger's recent book has wisely emphasized.[20] The reasons for the dramatic possibility are in part literary, of course, Spenser's ability to create character and action; but the underlying reasons, which are necessary for any work of great art, are the Puritan views of the dramatic confrontation of the individual man with his fate in a Calvinist framework of predestination or rejection. Pushed from the moorings of the ethics, habits, and probabilities of scholastic thinking, the individual Puritan began his journey in dramatic encounter with the problem of his own sinful nature. He was encouraged to read signs along the way, as do the Red Cross Knight and Guyon (or Palmer for him). This indelible feature of radical Protestantism was being followed two centuries later by Wordsworth in his encounter with the Highland Reaper or the blind beggar (*The Prelude,* Book VII). Reading of a series of signs in tandem constituted a dramatic action or allegorical presentation of reality. Spenser used this mode for reasons intrinsic to his purpose and beliefs, not because it was a fashionable medieval device. Signs were of the greatest importance, even until the time of Edwards, in religious awakening, because Calvinism had cast doubt upon the older systems of religious certainty. With the Red Cross Knight and Guyon, religious man begins his journey towards inner integrity and God as if for the first time.

It was no doubt congenial that allegory both fitted the requirements of Puritan sensibility and had ancient and recent literary precedent. The allegory provided the drama and the surprises along the way; the journey itself is the central metaphor and reason for the existence of the work. Puritanism in theory and practice encouraged reading all events allegorically. Historically, this is the reason for the vogue of the genre in the 16th and 17th century. If one believes that nothing happens by chance, that providence as the will of God determines everything, and that the will is not free to effect a non-contingent act (one not related to the will of God), then, whether or not one is a Calvinist-Puritan, one will think allegorically. Mental events fall under this scrutiny too, indeed, are the most important of all. Many writers and peoples have thought this way, and have written allegorically, outside of Puritanism. Puritanism merely provides some specific answers to the problems which occur in the dramatic series, calling them doubt, election, vocation, justification, sanctification, and glorification, as we have seen in our first section. Spenser inherits most of this ideology. But the allegorical frame of mind as such can be found in widely different cultures; Virgil obviously has it, as fate and the gods are read into all the events of the *Aeneid*. Wordsworth's, a latter-day or decayed Puritanism, attached allegorical significance to the most (seemingly) insignificant events. His problem was in finding intellectual meaning for the natural movements of his own sensibility. Unlike Spenser, he must leave a great deal more as inscrutable and mysterious. This is an advantage with the modern reader who mistrusts allegory and its significations, and seems to leave Wordsworth more "open-ended" than Spenser. No doubt he is, yet we are too prone to assume the significance in Spenser without having followed the drama in its legitimate forms. The Puritan has a terror of portents and a fear of misreading events (God's will) that we seldom give him credit for.

The Puritan's ability to invest his life with profound dramatic significance and to read minutely the psychological, physical and natural phenomena in and around him, made of him a natural allegorical artist, and the art of allegory the primary Puritan form of full literary communication. These facts did not change down to the days of Byron and Hawthorne, whose concern with inner significance and inner revelation is widely known. It lives a more shadowy yet no less important life in the works of Coleridge, Wordsworth and Dickinson. Yet this natural artist of allegory often fell into dangers inherent in the outlook and method, dangers often enough emphasized to have made Puritanism no friend of accepted literary tradition. The primary danger is abstraction, which takes two forms. The first is the vice of the theologian, to endow and limit certain abstract terms with enough meaning to inhibit any further imaginative process. Unless made totally exclusive, as the Puritans were in no position to make it among their 16th century followers, this practice merely makes for arid and dull theology, not for the tradition which has given us *The Faerie Queene* or *Moby-Dick*. Abstraction is seen in more dangerous form (for literary purposes) in the sermons of some Puritans and in the works and diaries of their followers. This danger is the limiting of allegorical concern to narrow areas of life, to the Scriptures above all, and so producing too narrow and obvious a pattern of readings.

Another form of this, found in preachers and followers, is too facile a moving from the concrete event or thing to the abstract signification, a habit which obviously slights the richness of reality and leads inevitably to restriction and repetition of significances, a hardened and dogmatic tradition hurting the individual sensibility. As all these habits are those of common men, of men in the mass, and above all else of successful and over-assured men, these are the failings of the mediocre in the 16th century and of the Puritan "establishment" thereafter. Yet there are enough possibilities here, taken all around, to make one acknowledge that abstraction is an inherent danger of the Puritan sensibility and allegoric-dramatic method. In Spenser, the 17th century meditative writers, Hawthorne and others, it provides intellectual structure and a search for meaning which lifts these works above the contingencies of contemporaries. Enough is given to the individual case to engage the interests of the "realistically" disposed reader before the hunt for significance begins. Some modern critics, hunting for patterns and inner significances everywhere, do not bring the "realistic" caveat to bear upon these writers; their complaint is not of abstraction itself, but of, perhaps, simplicity of abstraction, too quick a jump from x object to y significance beyond the resonances of x object or the influence of the intermediaries n. Now if the pattern is pre-arranged by theological law, this is all too likely to happen, and in some spots Spenser does not avoid the dangers of reader anticipation of significance beyond present dramatic action. Call this a dangerous kind of literary predestination, if you will. In Hawthorne, Edwards, Melville, or Dickinson where the imaginative mind is so complex and the theology loosening its bonds, allowing for new "discovery" within a general frame, the problem does not occur. Spenser and the 17th century writers faced this as a literary problem, no different in some respects from the problem of fate that faced Homer, Virgil and the tragedians. How to gain artistic interest in an ineluctable drama?

As Cedric Whitman has been helpful in explaining Homer's method,[21] so Harry Berger has with Spenser's, even though Berger does not make much of the Puritan aspect of the allegorical tradition in Spenser. Spenser managed to be true to his Puritan aims and ideals, at least in Books I and II, and also to write a work of literary interest and discovery, not merely another Puritan moral tract of the journey and the drama of salvation. Without such structure *The Faerie Queene* is merely a pastiche of pretty passages, sensuous experiences and tendentious moralizings. To read Spenser whole, one must see the allegory and the morality, the theological abstractions and the concrete dramatic cases, the accomplished poetics and the versification, and the intellectual keenness and rigor. Above all, one must allow for the dramatically unexpected, for various alternatives, within the general Puritan allegorical framework. This is the difference between the Puritan way as a theological guide or absolute, and as material for imaginative literature.

This is not the place for another full reading of *The Faerie Queene,* of which there have been several very good ones in recent years.[22] Our method will be the consideration of certain episodes and instances to show the Calvinist temper at work in Spenser in the midst of other materials. Without being in the main mechanical, Spenser managed to dramatize allegorically the most important psychic states of the new Calvinist temper in Books I and II. Renaissance myths and ideas, classical authors and general Christian themes lend richness to this scheme without overwhelming or diverting the main Puritan thrust in Books I and II.

This method of reading Book I is decidedly a return to the tradition of Ruskin, Padelford, Woodhouse and Allen, away from the medieval allegorizing and the psychological myth-making of much modern criticism. The debt to Berger's sense of immediacy and dramatic psychology amply acknowledged, the sense of the center of Spenser criticism in this analysis derives from Greenlaw's great *Variorum,*[23] adding to it the perspective of the Calvinist temper of this book. Waters' recent book on the symbolism of Duessa in Book I[24] is also a welcome addition to traditional criticism, and it is appropriate to begin the analysis with a short comment on his work, since the book deals closely with many scenes and characters important in describing the Calvinist-Puritan pattern in the book.

Waters' thesis is that Duessa represents the Roman Mass, Archimago the Catholic Church in England, the movement of the poem the removal of these elements and the triumph of Protestantism in the person of the Red Cross Knight. He cites many Elizabethan divines and polemicists to make his points. The explications and proofs are convincing about Archimago and Duessa, not so sound in the assertion of Spenser's adherence to the "general Protestant tradition," but correct in holding that Spenser is more militantly Protestant than some modern criticism allows, if we substitute "Calvinist-Puritan" for "general Protestant." A main source for Waters' citations of the

Duessa-*missa*-mistress tradition is Bishop Jewel, a notorious Puritan. In short, though this is not the place for a detailed critique of Waters' thesis, the positive thrust can be accepted – Spenser's allegory is positively Protestant and robustly anti-Roman. But the positive Protestantism is essentially Puritan in overall aspects, perhaps not in some minute particulars where the term "general Protestant" is acceptable. Duessa as *missa*-mistress-whore is patently and deliberately offensive, as a Puritan polemicist would want her to be, and often presented her. Why then should the positive theology be as Waters describes it, the general compromise of the Anglican settlement? Waters does not take note of the complexity of the place of the Puritans in the 16th century in making his citations, and we can certainly excuse a literary student for carrying on the assumptions of the Georges, Halewood, Martz and Gardner and overlooking the scholars of Puritanism such as Knappen, Haller, New and Pettit. The Puritan case, especially in literary circles, is always in danger of obscurity and diminishment among literary students who cannot overcome the bad clichés to look at the documents afresh and let them tell their own story. Waters' book is a welcome return to the traditional historical-critical locus of Spenser studies in 16th century and religious backgrounds, and gives us a valuable reading of Duessa and Archimago, as these reflect the anti-Catholic and anti-papal beliefs of Reformation England.

C. The Calvinist Temper in the Poems

Spenser's religious sense is most fully developed in *The Faerie Queene*, Books I and II, and in the "Hymn of Heavenly Love." There are some other religious passages in the complete poems, none very crucial. Moral allegory is important in these three works: Book I and the "Hymn" are religious; Books I and II political and historical also. Book II has usually been considered moral rather than religious, so it is one purpose of this commentary to show a religious aspect in some parts of it supporting the moral allegory. A religious level, both generally Christian and specifically Puritan, gives interest for this study. The general framework of moral and religious thought and pattern will be sketched swiftly in each work, as preparation for concentration on aspects of the Calvinist-Puritan themes.

The moral-religious outline of Book I has been widely accepted. There are real difficulties with the political allegory, not of concern here, beyond the link Waters has shown between Duessa, the Mass, anti-Catholicism and Puritanism. Red Cross, as untried Holiness, is guided by Una (Truth) whom he does not really understand or appreciate. The moral set of episodes occurs when Holiness misunderstands Truth, allowing evil to separate them. Red Cross, not prepared for his trials, stumbles and falls in the Castle of Orgoglio. Meanwhile Truth is buffeted about, yet cannot really be harmed or beguiled by her tormentors. At several points these episodes have religious and Calvinist aspects, in preparation for the clearly religious second half of the book. After freedom from Orgoglio's and Duessa's power, the Knight becomes a formal pilgrim rather than a duped wanderer. The episodes from that point until the end are the Christian allegory of salvation, grace, redemption and a glimpse of glory, the Calvinist scheme presented in a sophisticated informal order. Calvinist symbols and ideas give intensity and richness to the universal framework. No serious reading disputes the religious presence in the total book. The value of Calvinism, except as historical anti-Catholicism, is not usually noted or accepted.

In Book II the theme is primarily moral. The few religious aspects are generally Christian. The Calvinism resides in the intensification of the morality in the person of the Palmer and in the nature of certain episodes. Though there is less to write about in Book II of explicit Puritan doctrine, there is enough to discern the importance of Calvinist-Puritanism in the allegory and meaning. The "Hymn of Heavenly Love" is a Christian religious poem in the widest sense, to which the Puritan doctrine of grace perhaps adds an important aspect. The complications in this poem are introduced by the rich medieval context rather than by allegorical method. In fact, except for these medieval subtleties, which would be better known to Spenser's readers than in our own day, the poem is straightforward and catholic in its Christian doctrine. In such matters as number of the sacraments it is Protestant but the doctrines dwelled upon are those accepted by all branches of Christianity. Its very directness in contrast to the allegorical method of *The Faerie Queene* plays an important part in interpreting Spenser's Christian method in the more obscure and difficult poem; it is largely in such a context that the "Hymn" will figure in this discussion of Spenser.

The "Hymn" provides a framework for Spenser's conception of the Christian religion. Though late, and presented with repentance for his early "sinful" works, we may assume this viewpoint was with

Spenser all his life, or at least from his university days. (The place of
"dalliance" in the poetry will be considered with *The Faerie Queene*.)
This firm Christian outline might have been before Milton when he
worked on *Paradise Lost*. It lacks detail, deliberately, to remain
generally acceptable to all Christians. The medieval tendency towards
contemplation informs the poem in a delicate way which does not
turn the poem away from its central theme. In the last three stanzas
this contemplation blends with the Puritan idea of glorification to
provide a proper climax for the poem. This is the one special Puritan
aspect of the poem, deserving some slight stress. The poem is a clear,
common and acceptable exegesis upon the biblical account of God,
the Trinity, creation of the angels and man, the fall of the angels and
man, redemption through Christ, his suffering and teachings, man's
need to love him, his sacrament and the Christian life, vision of divine
things and contemplation of the Divine Idea. Nothing in the poem
on these subjects is unusual or difficult, and that very fact makes it
useful in reading the "dark conceit" of *The Faerie Queene*. The final
stanzas blend the language of Christian contemplation with the language of Puritanism. This language helps us to recognize the presence
of Puritan glorification in the parts of *The Faerie Queene* to be closely
studied. Here are the lines, slightly excerpted, with emphasis given
the words which directly or by implication have Calvinist theological
resonance:

> Then shalt thou feele thy *spirit* so possest,
> And *ravisht* with devouring great desire ...
> With *burning zeale,* through every part entire,
> That in no earthly thing thou shalt *delight,*
> But in his *sweet and amiable sight.* ...
>
> Whose *glorious beames* all fleshly sense doth daze
> With *admiration* of their passing light,
> Blinding the eyes and lumining the spright.
>
> Then shall thy *ravisht* soule inspired bee
> With *heavenly thoughts,* farre above humane skil,
> And thy *bright radiant* eyes shall plainly see
> Th' Idee of his *pure glorie,* present still,
> Before thy face, that all thy *spirits* shall fill
> With *sweete enragement* of celestial love,
> Kindled through *sight* of those faire things above.[25]

The Calvinist-Puritan effect in these lines is cumulative rather than
precise. All the words were common in the religious language of
other traditions. Yet the density is unmistakable, especially when also

noted is the direction of the passage towards glorification, perhaps the Puritan's favorite theme. All Puritans wrote about the "spirit," "zeale" is an attitude attributed to them by friends and enemies, words such as "delight," "sweet sight," and "glorious" occur in abundance through their literature. More particularly, "ravisht" reminds of Edwards' "relish," "glorious beames" and "sweete enragement" of his term "excellency." The "heavenly thoughts" of God's "pure glorie" are ideas repeated and expanded in Baxter's *Saints Rest*, and the entire theme of spirits, delight, sight, radiant eyes, pure glorie sets the way for the great triumphs of light and sight in Milton. Without recourse to any specific doctrinal idea Spenser is working well within the triumphal side of Puritan tradition in this grand climax of adoration of the Divine Idea. The entire poem and especially the conclusion may serve as an aid in reading much 16th and 17th century Puritan religious poetry as well as Spenser's own best-known works, and also, looked upon in this way, as a fine example of how Puritan Spenser is in his highest religious flights.

Book II is the next appropriate place to turn in reading Spenser within Puritan tradition. Book II is above all else moral, as the commentators have stressed. Berger has shown the conflicting and then conjoining classical and Christian ideas of temperance and continence throughout the book, beneath which is a subtler struggle between pagan and religious (God-centered) ideas of creation and purpose. These conflicts and resolutions occur at all levels, in the fable, the character, the imagery and the sententiae. The moral resolution is very specific, as Guyon triumphs by grace unknown to him despite his weakness of mere classical temperance (*sophrosyne*); the religious assertion is more general, in that the shape of the universe is shown to be God-given, not naturalistic and earthy, instanced in the triumph of Arthur over Maleger, or grace over original sin. The action proceeds from dim to clear recognition of this vision, and such awareness is the real source of development in the poem. This view is congenial and acceptable as preliminary to reading the Puritan sensibility in the poem. Thus in the early cantos, where the various moral and religious perspectives are deliberately, that is, dramatically, obscure, specific Puritanism does not appear at all. The narrator describes the fable while dealing out moral cards rather indiscriminately, as in this sententia on the burial of the dead:

> Palmer, quoth he, death is an equall doome
> To good and bad, the common Inne of rest;

> But after death the tryall is to come,
> When best shall bee to them that lived best:
> But both alike, when death hath both supprest,
> Religious reverence doth buriall teene,
> Which who so wants, wants so much of his rest:
> For all so great shame after death I weene,
> As selfe to dyen bad, unburied bad to beene. (i, lix)

The classical view of death, Christian sense of salvation, and pagan motives for burial are given in order, with only a slightly greater emphasis upon the second. Some would no doubt argue that there is no special precedence, and while this is too modern an interpretation of Spenser's sober theme, it is easy to accept the idea that there is no domination or subsuming of the other themes by the Christian at this point. It is quite true, as Berger points out throughout his book, that the narrator's perceptions achieve clarity as the fable develops, and do not lead a moral life of their own, predetermined and over the head of the story. This may be seen as another way of putting our earlier point in the last section, that the Calvinist quest was open and exciting in the 16th century despite the logical difficulties theoretically presented by high-flying double predestination. By the middle cantos, especially Phaedria's pleasure island and the Cave of Mammon, the hierarchical pattern begins to be discerned, earthly-pagan, moral-classical and Christian-religious. The defeat of the first and the subordination of the second to the third occur in Alma's Castle and in the Bower of Bliss. Hints of a Puritan sensibility likewise begin in the middle cantos and are clearly dominant at the end. These have largely gone unnoticed, or have distressed critics even as wise as Berger who view them as faulty excesses of the poem or of Spenser the man. Other critics have found in them a challenge for ingenuity in finding reasons to exonerate Spenser of such a charge. Our aim regarding Book II can be a modest one: to demonstrate the presence of Puritan sensibility in the book though not its Calvinist theology. It is not a vice but rather a heightened quality of the moral and religious structure discerned by traditional Spenserians such as Lewis and Berger. Puritan sensibility in Book II lies in the poetical context, enhancing, not debasing it, as it has been some modern critical fashion to deplore. Even enlightened traditionalists are a bit afraid of the old bogey of beauty-hating and statue-smashing Puritans in dealing with Guyon and the Palmer in the last canto, almost willing to admit that to be Puritan is to be narrow or perhaps even evil. In complete contrast to this situation, Book I is primarily religious allegory, as all traditionalists agree, containing within its fable the primary Calvinist-Puritan doctrines as well as its general sensibility. The general allegory has received clear and precise treatment many times, beginning with Ruskin. In the Greenlaw *Variorum* there is a consistency in interpretation on the moral level and in the general Christian meaning, no matter how far the authors stray from each other in reading of individual symbols as religious, not to speak of the notorious differences in interpreting the political allegory. In our commentary on Spenser's Puritan ideas in Book I, the value of knowing the Calvinist-Puritan ideational tradition studied in Section I of this book will be apparent. For Book II the approach must be indirect and perhaps more tactful. Sensibility is sometimes hard to articulate, sometimes not. In either case the reasons for proceeding from Book II to Book I seem valid. The deeper level of Puritan penetration and Calvinist doctrine in Book I is best appreciated in the light of the aesthetic sensibility revealed in Book II.

A closer look at the meaning of Calvinist sensibility in Book II will show that it is largely descriptive until the final canto, the Bower of Bliss. In that canto everyone has noticed a firm Puritanism, in the popular sense of the word, that most readers have found repellent in the fiercely negative actions of the Palmer. But it is a mistake to isolate the Palmer's "puritanical" actions in the final canto from milder episodes and descriptions in earlier ones. The Palmer is described sternly and favorably in canto i:

> Him als accompanyd upon the way
> A comely Palmer, clad in black attyre,
> Of rypest yeares, and haires all hoarie gray,
> That with a staff his feeble steps did stire,
> Least his long way his aged limbes should tire:
> And if by lookes one may the mind aread,
> He seemd to be a sage and sober syre,
> And ever with slow pace the knight did lead,
> Who taught his trampling steed with equall steps to tread. (i, vii)

Canto vi has a dramatic contrast between his values and those of the lass of pleasure, Phaedria. This episode requires further discussion below. After it comes the second most important incident in Book II, Mammon's Cave. We may assume with most sophisticated readings that what is revealed here is the yearning and ironic tension of the mind regarding riches. If we add the idea of the Puritan mind, the episode gains greater interest, since everyone knows Tawney's theory and most believe it, though fewer know that the early Calvinist-Puritan response to money was never so clearly positive as now widely believed. Guyon's faint does raise the question that it comes closest of any temptation until the Bower to be his "worldes blis." Puritan preachers were as disturbed by the use of money and the problem of usury as any other Christian group at the beginning of the capitalist era. It was their 18th and 19th century heirs who were more complacent, a point not relevant for early Puritanism, Spenser, and *The Faerie Queene*. About the episode of Maleger it seems best to follow Berger's ingenious interpretation. Maleger represents sin, earth and radical evil, hence some "original sin" operating below the level of the fable of temperance. The point is a general Christian one, not particularly Calvinist-Puritan. Arthur is not a Calvinist figure, as is the Palmer, and the evil Maleger embodies does not have a special Puritan cast. It is the one shared by the entire Christian world view of the time. Arthur as a figure of Christ or simply as the manifestation of God's power deals with, but does not overcome completely, this phenomenon of nature and man before any specific redemptive process may even begin. There is a parallel situation in Book I, cantos vii and viii, in a context in which the religious symbolism is much clearer, and the preparation for the Puritan way in cantos ix—xii. Similarly, in the Bower itself, the religious aspects are less manifest than in Book I. The action is more negative and therapeutic, with neither the Palmer nor Guyon rising to become a great figure. Guyon remains within the positive limited sphere of classical virtue, the Palmer within the negative, the cautionary yet necessary role of Christian prudence. Together they can confine certain types of evil and base impulses which are harmful to the spiritual life and often destroy it. The ambience of canto xii is Puritan rather than merely generally Christian in the forcefulness, zeal and conviction of its purpose. Berger commits one of his few errors of tact in his otherwise excellent commentary on the religious implications in Book II when he says, regarding the destruction of the Bower by Guyon and the Palmer's imperviousness to Acrasia (not shared by Guyon, most readers, and Berger, as "natural men"):

This is a Puritan frenzy, described by Watkins as "growing moral uneasiness which finally, intensified by self-distrust, smashes beauty like a looking glass." In this moment Guyon accomplishes his Stoic quest. But at the same time

he reaches the more profound goal of the Christian quest: he awakens to
the consequences of Original Sin within himself.

The Palmer's conquest appears to owe more to the gifts added to his nature
and to the immunity of his nature, the product of his allegorical function:
"prudence belongs directly to the cognitive, and not to the sensitive faculty."
Therefore he is old, wise, Puritanical; his understanding of lust is abstract
rather than existential.[26]

In both the quotations, the use of "Puritan" is adjectival and within
the popular meaning of the term today. It is an excess of the stoic
norm in Guyon, provoking an awakening of a Christian sense. In the
Palmer it is proof of supernatural powers and graces not given to
mere mortals. Like the Phaedria and Mammon episodes, this one
requires closer scrutiny, for we cannot allow the terms "Puritan" or
"excessive zeal" to obscure the difficult fact that we are faced here
with another instance of the possible accommodation of evil within
a Christian scheme. How much of it can be accommodated before
the acceptance becomes connivance and collaboration? An old question
indeed, and it does little good to label a worrisome attitude towards
the problem as mere "Puritan frenzy."

Such ultimate questions and difficulties can temporarily be set aside
as we turn back to the first serious Puritan episode in the poem,
Phaedria's pleasure island. Even the sternest critics of the poem have
allowed themselves some delight with Phaedria, more than Guyon
does. The Palmer need not have worried about his protégé when he
was denied admittance to the island. Phaedria and her island pleasures offer some difficulties to the temperate mind and the Puritan
sensibility, lightly handled and overcome by the determined Guyon.
Phaedria is sensuousness clothed as art and delight, thus is perceived
quite rightly by Guyon not as moral evil so much as irrelevant frivolity. He can afford to be kind but firm with her. Her attractiveness
is not real power (Mammon) or eroticism (Acrasia). In her song,
with its nicely twisted version of the parable of the "lilies" of the
field, her one serious aspect as a possible menace is brought forward
– the use of time. The song suggests less evil use than waste of time.
But for the Puritan, to waste one's time on frivolity is a kind of evil
too far beneath contempt to become serious temptation. Taking oneself seriously, in the Calvinist-Puritan tradition, is incompatible with
spending precious time on pleasures, even upon most of the legitimate
ones, and certainly not Phaedria's preference for lazy bones. Guyon
courteously allows her to display the pleasures of her island, firm in

his inner reserve of resistance to the pleasures she has to offer and
to her winsomeness. He rejects the theory of pleasure and time presented guilelessly by Phaedria with courtesy:

> But he was wise, and wary of her will,
> And ever held his hand upon his hart. . . . (vi, xxvi)

The Palmer, had his presence been thought necessary, no doubt would
have dealt harshly with poor Phaedria, and needlessly so. Spenser is
making a fine point here, one also made by previous and later Puritans, including Milton, that simple pleasures are not wrong, are even
delightful under certain circumstances, as Phaedria herself is delightful. Music and song especially are legitimate pleasures in their place,
less open to the dangers attendant upon the eye and the will. Yet
there is simply no contest of priorities if a conflict arises between
any pleasure and the better – some goal or end – use of time. In this
not too serious contest politeness marks the tone, even after the rude
interference of Cymochles. Guyon is on a serious journey in which
he will confront more deadly perils than Phaedria, making it easy for
him to place her in a proper context, not overreacting to her light
temptations. As he leaves the island, they are where they began the
discourse, he courteous and modest in rejecting her offers, she finally
well pleased to be rid of one totally immune to the delights of folly.

The lightness and pleasantness of Phaedria appeals to the callow
Cymochles more than to the serious-goaled Guyon, though Guyon's
refusal of her pleasure contains some tacit admission of certain indifferent delights. These are indifferent delights that do not affect the
world for good or ill, and so are often unimportant to one on Puritan
pilgrimage. The light aesthetic pleasures of Phaedria pale before the
erotic demands of Acrasia, who, no matter how perverted in manner,
represents a deep natural instinct. This contrast between Phaedria
and Acrasia is obvious, and the Bower episode is filled with indications of the contrast between the playful and the destructive. Between
the two episodes is Mammon's Cave, by no means some mid-point
of the others, but a temptation of quite different order than Acrasia's,
though as powerful. In one respect it is more powerful. Lust is a
positive object, with a goal of clear limits: that is, after achievement
it can only be multiplied in repetition. Mammon's Cave may be a
museum piece, alluring and static as Acrasia's Bower in appearance,
but with a promise of use, in Mammon's subtle and tempting words.
Riches as a means to achieve action may promise good, delusive good,

or evil according to the nature of the individual tempted. Mammon knows his man to the extent of emphasizing the delusion that riches might be used for ends that appeal to the Puritan mind, hoping to catch Guyon in the old dilemma of means and ends. It is true that Mammon does not stint from the lesser delights of vanity, pomp, and miserliness, or from displaying the sheer aesthetic joy in the presence of shining beauty. We have perhaps been too fully trained to despise such displays as vulgar or juvenile, so missing the primitive significance of the beauty of gold as well as its uses. In that respect Spenser's allegory hearkens to the medieval and romantic past.

The central temptation remains the good aims to which riches may be put in attaining Puritan goals, and these do not escape Mammon or Guyon. This is the serious temptation and reason for his faint, a force acting far below all the pantomime of medieval action. The symbolic demon waiting to kill him if he releases his hold upon virtue and clarity of purpose is real enough, a quite effective allegory of contemporary and modern import presented in medieval guise. If Guyon should confuse means with ends towards riches in his goal, or yield to the temptation of means by embracing Mammon's aid in his quest, thus seeming to make the attainment of noble goals so much the easier, he will die morally. Money is not an ultimate evil; it may be an immediate good. Whatever else it is, it is always morally ambiguous, and that is why Guyon faints as the dumb show passes before his eyes. In his mind he knows too well the possible allegiance of riches with worthy aims, how worthy aims are so easily corrupted by the use of riches, and the very mobility from ideals they are likely to inspire. Gold is not corruption itself, unless hoarded away for aesthetic pleasure only, yet it is a part of the mysterious web of corruption of the most grand schemes of nobility, purpose and knightly ideal. For the Puritan it ranks above courtly love and unchastity as having the most dangerous universal potential, because it can play such a great part in the world, with all sorts of results. Collectively, gold allied with power in the 17th century assured first the success then the total failure of Calvinist-Puritan social hegemony. Individually, the identification of election with tangible success in the 18th and 19th centuries drained whatever spiritually had remained in Puritanism after the cataclysm of the 17th century, giving rise to the Tawney thesis of Puritanism and capitalism.

Thus Mammon presents a great and peculiar moral crisis for Calvinist-Puritanism, collective and individual. Guyon's faint, though only implicit failure, is more damaging than his later weakness in the Bower. The Bower, after some hesitation, is destroyed. Mammon is overcome only in a temporary way, as Guyon reaches the upper world gasping for breath. We might also speculate on the absence of the Palmer from Mammon's Cave. Phaedria did not invite him to her pleasure island in a situation where, as it turned out, he was not needed. In the Cave he was badly needed. One reason for his absence might well be the inability of Calvinist-Puritan values, positive and forceful as they appear in the Palmer, to come to terms with wealth, which is so easy to rationalize in connivance with positive goals for the world. Good causes need wealth as well as bad ones, as was seen in the 16th century alliance of the Puritan preachers with whatever noble families would embrace the cause. Since Mammon and the Palmer do not meet, Puritanism remains essentially spiritual with a danger averted. This is Spenser's subtlety of method and way of protecting spirituality, having known the corruptions of court and wealth in his own poetic career. Much later Puritanism seized power, then lost it, and finally identified election with worldly success, thus saddling itself with the modern cliché – true to an uncomfortable degree – which links Puritanism, individualism and capitalism. Long after Guyon's faint in the face of a temptation he resisted, to be rich and successful became *the* sign of election, merging practical Puritanism and capitalism in the modern world, and driving persons of spiritual dimension like Emily Dickinson out of the fold. Guyon's faint and the Palmer's absence from the Cave are a preludium to the phenomena that will be the ultimate temptation and destruction of Calvinist-Puritanism in the centuries to come, more dangerous ultimately than the sensual tensions faced in other parts of Book II, or the theological battles fought with pagans, Catholics and Anglicans in the theological arena of Book I.

But in the particular context of Books I and II sensual tensions and theological battles are more immediately perceived as dangers to religion and life than are the temptations of the Cave, for many reasons of Reformation and English history, so that the Bower, not the Cave, is the logical culmination of Book II. The perspective of later developments gives us an ironic insight into the dangers of the Cave not apparent at the time, though, as I have stated, Puritan preachers of the 16th century were not unaware of the dangers of Mammon. The episode of Arthur and Maleger is typical of these theological-moralistic concerns, and so logically is in direct line with the isle of Phaedria and the Bower. We have already alluded to Berger's ingenious and valid explanation showing how Maleger represents some image of original sin and radical evil, while Arthur is a deliberately vague symbol of grace or manifestation of God's power. The purpose of the episode is to distinguish a religious world order from a natural pagan one, setting the stage for the specific Christian and Puritan allegory of the Bower. The House of Temperance, over which Arthur and Maleger quarrel, stands between the unformed pagan materialism of Maleger and the Christian view gradually manifest in Arthur and Guyon, fully so in the Palmer. The House of Temperance is the best that formal pagan (classical) virtue has to offer, and this *sophrosyne,* confronted by the full power of evil and sensuality in the Bower, is not enough. At that point where Guyon falters the issue is clear enough: there is need for the mediation of the Palmer. The Palmer does not represent Puritan frenzy or unreal supernaturalism, as Berger suggests. If we see with Berger that Arthur's victory over Maleger is a victory of the religious view over unformed naturalism, and that the House of Temperance is superseded by the Christian graces Arthur and Guyon begin to have in the last cantos, then we also might accept that the Palmer has something specific, some Puritan Christian virtue, lacking in all the others, and this something is absolutely necessary to cope with the evils in and surrounding Acrasia. This at least is the point that we will try to make in this analysis of the Bower of Bliss, holding that its Puritanism is not mere superstition or a kind of hostile repression almost as repugnant as the witch herself, but an integral part of the redemptive process which superseded the natural virtues in the complex interrelations of Arthur, Maleger, Guyon and the House of Temperance preceding the climactic Bower episode.

The central fact of Acrasia's Bower is lust, surrounded by general sensuousness and enhanced by art. C.S.Lewis made one significant argument in supplying a motive for Spenser's powerful depiction of lust in the Bower, the many-pointed contrast between the descriptions here and those in the Garden of Adonis, the sterility here and the fecundity there. But Lewis carried the argument against the Bower too far, or made it too easy to exalt the Garden over the Bower. This argument, that art is artifice in the Bower and natural in the Garden, and even in the Bower lust is inactive (therefore less threatening), was placed in perspective by Berger, whose analysis of the artistry and rather kinetic lust in the Bower has the evidence of the text to support it. It is not possible to dismiss the evil power of the Bower in such an easy fashion.

Berger introduces a deeper argument, centering upon the inability of the knight of Temperance to resist the full evil of the Bower with the restraints and powers of classical temperance alone. His weakness awakens his sense of sin, hence is an opening for a Christian perspective on the final scenes. Only with the aid of the Palmer can the full force of Acrasia be restricted and controlled. But at this point Berger's argument begins to fail, for he ascribes the Palmer's victory to Puritan frenzy, age, supernatural attributes and pure rationality, as we noted in the quotation cited above. There is a better possibility that some positive quality is added to the general Christianity by the Palmer's Puritanism. If this is so, it also gives greater symmetry to the end of the episode, which otherwise seems to have negativism about it and a lowering of intensity disappointing to critics and readers. Hence a theological inquiry into the Palmer's power and meaning would seem to be in order here. If Spenser's sensuousness is not merely ornamental, nor its purpose only prurience, as all sound critics now agree, then we might take some steps further to show how this is so, if the Palmer can be resurrected as a positive character. No light exaggeration is intended in this: the Palmer has received a bad press even from Spenser's staunchest supporters. In the following reading of the Palmer's character as a Nun's Priest or Richard Baxter or some other Puritan saint, the purpose of the sensuality of Acrasia is to demonstrate by its opposition and overthrow a stronger positive force − Puritan Christian virtue. The overthrow and cleansing must be accomplished to ensure the liberation of something else − the process of sanctification. Of course this is done allegorically here, a symbol following the example of Christ proving that it can be done. Lust in actuality is never excluded from the sanctified, but it is dealt with, made manageable, as in the capture rather than destruction of Acrasia herself, whereas all of her allures and accoutrements of the senses, the positive spurs to lust, are destroyed.

To put the Palmer's actions in correct perspective, there must be a reconciliation among the three versions of him − the very honorific description mentioned above (I, vii), his very moderate and sober actions in the cantos that follow, in giving advice to Guyon which helps him to see through temptations, and the offensive (to many) manner in which he continues the aim of the destruction of the Bower after Guyon has faltered. His manner and actions in the last canto at first seem out of place, yet they really are not. It is Guyon who over-reacts, perhaps becoming conscious of lust in himself and of his "fall," signalled by an intensity of destructiveness. Some of his actions are not objectively motivated by any standard, and we need not import Freud to agree with Berger that acute anxiety and self-awareness are involved here. Only when Berger, in the tradition of Spenser critics before him, calls this "Puritan frenzy" according to the popular label is it an issue. It is fair to call the Palmer "Puritanical," as Berger does, only if we remember that he continues to be calm, "careful" through-out the last canto, including the climax in the capture of Acrasia. In other words the reconciliation is not a real problem if we notice that it is Guyon, the classical hero of Temperance, not the Palmer, repos-itory of Puritan-Christian virtue, undergoing change in Book II. There is another kind of limitation in this reading which we have already accepted. Book II gives us a Calvinist-Puritan sensibility (point of view) rather static on the whole, whereas Book I is kinetic and dra-matic. The first is helpful in understanding the second, or in other words, Book II is profitable to read and understand before Book I.

A certain *gaudium spiritus* runs throughout 17th century Puritan-ism, the joy depicted in Sibbes' *Bruised Reede* as the state of sanctifi-cation and in Baxter's *Saints Everlasting Rest*. Its presence is not to deny Puritan gloom, terror of sin, and certain actions for which the Cromwellians later became infamous. The later characteristics are denoted as Puritan fanaticism and are what most readers will call to mind while reading the description of the Bower's destruction, despite the alluring yet ugly picture of lust there presented. But the Puritan also combatted the temptations, especially those of the flesh, with vivid imagery and imagination of the joys of sanctification and of glorification. The life of the spirit could be vivid and palpable, the sense of heaven more real and enjoyable than anything fleshly lust had to offer. It is true that the Palmer, like Chaucer's Nun's Priest, is a man of few words, giving both characters a seeming coldness and remote intellectual quality in the initial portraits. From Baxter, Bun-yan, Sibbes and others we can fill in the implied qualities, certainly known to Spenser and not indifferent ones to the creator of the House of Holiness and the Garden of Adonis. In the previous section many quotations for the various Puritan categories were cited, giving little need to multiply examples. The following from Baxter's *Saints Rest* should suffice to make this positive side of Puritan values clear:

There is in a Christian a kind of spiritual taste whereby he knows these things, besides his mere discursive power; the will doth as sweetly relish goodness, as the understanding doth Truth, and here lies much of a Christian's strength.

The liveliest emblem of heaven that I know upon earth is, when the people of God, in the deep sense of his excellency and bounty, from hearts abounding with love and joy, do join together, both in heart and voice, in the cheerful and melodious singing of his praises.[27]

Variations and changes on this theme were to be heard from the middle of the 16th until the middle of the 18th century in English, from the Cambridge Puritans to Edwards. One point in the Bower of Bliss episode was to show that lust could not be overcome merely by Temperance — it is too powerful a driving force in man's life. A far more subtle and implicit aspect is that it is never overcome by mere negativism, since Acrasia is caged, not destroyed. The outward paraphernalia of lust can be temporarily abolished, yet it would be a small matter for a freed Acrasia to set up another Bower with new accomplices and victims. The only positive balance to lust is love — marriage on the mundane level as Lewis's book proved, and on the higher, love of the things of the spirit, of sanctification, finally of God. This process requires use of imagination as well as rational intellect. Spenser and Baxter are among the few Puritan writers having both in large supply.

Any reader of this book will be familiar with the standard allegorical readings of Book I and perhaps also with the aesthetic and historical arguments for and against allegory, or more specifically, the lengths to which allegory may be carried in reading the poem.[28] A rather bold assertion about the nature of Book I as allegory in relation to Calvinism is going to be made now, assuming that the book as an example of moral and religious allegory is not seriously questioned. Cantos i–iv present a conflict between the natural (pagan) world and emerging Christianity still weakened by (papal) superstition. Except for Una's steadiness, all is confusion. Cantos v–viii give us the emergence of a Christian world in a presanctified state, wherein Arthur is less Christian grace than a surrogate of God's power. In ix–xii Christianity triumphs with Red Cross's recovery. His recovery follows the familiar Puritan pattern of the 16th century divines, and in this aspect the allegory is religious, Christian and Puritan. The pattern is the usual: sin-state, election, justification/ vocation, sanctification, glorification. The historical-religious, moral, psychological and other levels that have interested critics are surely in the poem, as a part of the triumph that is generally Christian and specifically Puritan. The Christian pattern has been doubted by few and is not new. The emerging Puritan cast in the final cantos has seldom been accepted, though occasionally noticed, despite the specific religious qualities and doctrines involved. The conclusion to Book I has both the sensibility noted above in Book II and the more rigorous theological aspects of Puritanism that enable us to call it Calvinist. That is why Book II was discussed previous to Book I, in the hope that the display of general Puritan sensibility might prepare for the presence of sensibility and formal patterns in the first book.

Puritan sensibility appears in the tone of the narrative many times before the formal theology makes its appearance in canto ix in the notions of despair and election. Waters' book on Duessa takes up these points. Although the lion in canto iii is often taken as a symbol of the Henriac reformation, there is a particular ferocity in his havoc upon Corceca, Abessa and Kirkrapine that is more in keeping with Puritan iconoclasm under Edward, and the later Puritan desire to perform the same offices upon the "half-way" Anglican establishment of Elizabeth, than with the spirit and actual practice of reformation under Henry and Elizabeth. This same ferocity appeared in Spenser's tract on Ireland and was later a regular sign of Puritan religious activity in England and Ireland. Anglican reform always held the aim of gradualism and compromise, although results often went further than expected. Calvinist-Puritan reformers, almost from the beginning, viewed extirpation and destruction of Catholicism as necessity, and later, with just a little more reluctance, force came to be viewed by them as necessary in the creation of a true Church in England. Whether is remains historically impossible, as it now seems, to pin down the episode to either Henry's or Edward's reign, is no matter of great importance. The episode is Puritan in tone and attitude.

The stripping of Duessa in canto viii is another instance. Waters' case for Duessa as *missa*-mistress, the Mass and the whore (Catholicism) was alluded to above. It is a good historical speculation and need not be repeated here. His general point, with which many commentators in the *Variorum* agree, is that the episode signifies the removal of Roman Catholic power from England in the reign of Elizabeth. Duessa (the Mass), Orgoglio (Spanish military might), the Dragon (the Catholic powers), and Archimago (priesthood) are the enemies conquered by Arthur and Una, thus allowing holiness to flourish through the true Church. The episode is less obviously Puritan than the earlier one in tone, less of zeal for removal and more of rational justice. Yet as I mentioned earlier in passing, Waters lumps writers of Puritan tendency such as Bishop Jewel with establishment writers in displaying the animus against the Mass in Protestant circles between 1560 and 1590. It is at least unfair to hold Spenser to moderate Elizabethan views on the evidence in the canto or in the theologians and polemicists cited by Waters and in the *Variorum*. Establishment and Puritan views were identical in this period on the subjects of Queen Mary, Spanish power, the Catholic menace. If Duessa is strictly the Mass there is also little argument possible on that score either. But if her imagery also includes the aura of beauty and pomp of formal ritual, then the ruthlessness of her exposure is a Puritan tendency, as there was no desire in Elizabethan establishment thinking to remove these qualities, once these were separated from the theological and political association with Rome. One might see some degree of Puritan attitude in the thoroughness of the stripping and exposure of Duessa without accepting fully the historical assertion that Duessa is the Roman Mass. Since no specific historical allegory is called for in this reading of Spenser, not much can rightfully be claimed about episodes lacking specific theological content. Yet the episodes in cantos iv and vii give off some indefinable aura of Puritan zeal, something we should not expect of a writer of Elizabethan establishment opinion, which, by the time Spenser was writing *The Faerie Queene,* was already as afraid of Puritan thoroughness and threat of destruction to itself, as of the external power of Rome. The kind of reformation prepared for in cantos iii through viii is the thorough Puritan kind, hidden partly in allegory, of course, given Spenser's public position. However, his full sympathies reveal themselves occasionally. These episodes set the frame for the cantos of Puritan sensibility and theology in cantos ix—xii.

Before proceeding to the religious allegory and meaning in canto ix a look at the function of Arthur in the two cantos is in order, since many critics have viewed Arthur as a symbol of grace in cantos vii and viii. His helmet and shield with their blazing light are cited as proof of this, not to speak of the narrator's commentary referring to Arthur as Heavenly Grace and Una as steadfast Truth. Nevertheless, Arthur is not dramatically a Christian presence. His origins are pagan, clearly connecting him with Merlin, fairyland and pagan Britain. It is fair to view him as a symbol of God's will and providence, as a fiat or *deus ex machina* necessary before the Christian process of salvation can begin. His words to Una are characteristic of reason: "Flesh may empare," quoth he, "but reason can repaire." His deeds of the will are characteristic of the mysterious will of God which infuses itself into the world to bring about the good. Keep also in mind that after the battle was won over Duessa and Orgoglio, Arthur's quest was revealed as that of a lover, and that his gift of friendship to Red Cross is a magical box within which is a wonderful liquor for the healing of wounds. All these characteristics and deeds are consistent for a knight connected with Merlin, magic and the misty English pagan past. Red Cross's gift is the New Testament; his is the Christian way, the quest for holiness. Spenser is not inconsistent and contradictory in such contrasts of commentary and events. Arthur performs a similar function in his fight with Maleger in Book II, another cleansing process and introduction to a more religious world than the one to which he himself belongs. As a symbol and agent of God's providence he need not know it or be identified with the religious allegory and drama, as are Red Cross and Guyon. His existence in the poem is on its own plane, just as the commentary exists on another, influencing, but not determining by any means, the central actions, the journeys which carry with them their own gradual enlightenment. This enlightenment for Red Cross begins in earnest with the events of canto ix.

The fable in canto ix is among the most famous and memorable in *The Faerie Queene*. Red Cross is offered the opportunity of suicide by Despair after contemplation of his sins and shame. In Puritan theology this is the dangerous area of "sin-state," the recognition by the natural man of his depravity, which must precede the regenerative process. It is indeed a part of the regenerative process. Puritan tradition admitted a few examples of election/justification in the manner of St. Paul on his way to Damascus, but overwhelmingly believed that most individuals must pass through the dangerous states of doubt, despair of election, fear of personal damnation, and a time of feeling deserted and alone before a sign of election would appear. The proper handling of the state of sin became a sign of election. One sign of election is perseverance in the trial, which Red Cross with the aid of Una manages. For Puritans in actual life, a minister or converted friend performed this role. Election, justification and grace are not defined formally in this process, nor does Spenser attempt formal definition elsewhere in the poem. That the process was recognized in the 16th century as of the essence of Puritanism there can be no doubt. It was the practical, experimental replacement for the sacrament of penance in the Catholic system, more crucial to most individuals than differences in theology. The formal cause of salvation for all Christians may well be Christ, a reason why so much Reformation polemic seems curiously inflated to us. In the practical situation the Lutherans and Anglicans took greater risk than the Catholics in placing faith in Christ, and the Puritans an even greater in proposing to drop most of the old formal structures of the Church. The sects to the left of Puritanism theoretically were most dangerously free of all. Assurance and the Spirit played so large a role in their thinking as to offset the dangers of contemplating sin-state and despair of election alone. Only the Calvinists retained the firmness of the traditional Pauline beliefs while insisting upon a new spiritual way and process, the novelty of which is difficult for us today to grasp imaginatively. The Catholics of Lancashire supposedly rejoiced over the news of a Puritan dying in despair. These same Catholics would have cared much less or not at all about the soul of an Anabaptist or Quaker, because the latter lacked the Puritan pretensions to a Christian belief in common with other major groups. There was a mutual recognition among Catholics and the major Protestant groups broken away from Rome that sin, despair and possible damnation are real, and that the means of salvation must be taken seriously. Disagreement about the means is the history of Reformation polemic, of course, and not our subject here except for the Calvinist cast in Spenser. In brief we can say that the risk of despair was encountered by all traditions, and that in Puritanism the dangers are greatest in the first "movement," where institutional proppings are minimal. As some kind of safeguard this crucial movement was attached to election and justification, leading in a few instances to disaster, but in most, as the enemies of Puritanism never tire of reporting, to the expected movement through the states to glory. (Another possibility was the excessive scrupulosity about signs of election in later centuries, such as in Edwards.) Spenser brilliantly dramatizes this situation in canto ix. The theme is largely self-evident in the allegorical drama culminating in Red Cross's close brush with suicide. At its conclusion comes an explicitly theological passage, tying the incident to the doctrine of election, as *the* first sign of election, that is, the overcoming of the temptation of despair.

> Come, come away, fraile, feeble, fleshly wight,
> Ne let vaine words bewitch thy manly hart.
> Ne develish thoughts dismay thy constant spright.

In heavenly mercies hast thou not a part?
Why shouldst thou then despeire, that chosen art?
Where justice growes, there grows eke greter grace,
The which doth quence the brond of hellish smart,
And that accurst hand-writing doth deface. (ix, liii)

Spenser is pointing to the ideal Puritan way in this passage. As we
know from history, there were Puritan suicides among the first generations of Calvinist followers in England, and no doubt many soon took
the notion of election too lightly, once the novelty of the doctrine
and the break with Rome had become past history. If one were
brought up in a Puritan household, perhaps one expected to be saved.
But as we saw in Section I, and as the controversial history of the
experience in New England of "conversion" was later to prove, the
ministers and serious religious in all generations continued to consider
the conversion experience all important, playing the role of baptism
and penance in the more structured churches. In treating Red Cross
as he does here, Spenser has a keen sense of the mean or ideal of
Puritan experience, and perhaps also of the experience itself.

Canto x concerns the process of regeneration leading to the state
of sanctification. With it Book I turns explicitly to the religious theme
promised in its title, from the outer world of gallantry to the inner of
spiritual renovation. Initially this change in the imagery and action
gives a problem of form, for it has been a matter of acute anxiety
to some commentators to find a Protestant theme of salvation clothed
in medieval — presumably Catholic — images. Where the doctrine is
explicit it is certainly Protestant, indeed Calvinist-Puritan, as it is our
special intention to prove. C.S. Lewis's argument on this matter is
useful, although not perhaps fully convincing.[29] Other critics had
pointed to the fact that the imagery for Faith, Hope, Charity, the
works of mercy, and so forth were Catholic and medieval in Spenser
because the Protestant imagination had not had time to develop itself
in the 16th century and catch up with its intellectual advances. It was
for Milton, Baxter and Bunyan to fully liberate the Protestant imagination. Lewis argues against this that it is of the essence of Catholicism to embody, of Protestantism to be abstract. Therefore if a Protestant poet intends to embody doctrine in imagery, the imagery inevitably seems Catholic, on account of Catholic historic priority and the
reader's expectations. If we were laying stress at this point in this
book upon a Protestant or a Calvinist-Puritan aesthetic, Lewis's argument would seem to be difficult to accept, and the historical one to

carry more weight in the history of Protestant literary development. But our concern here is only with Spenser, and so there is less need to worry about the general situation. Spenser was not primarily a religious writer or thinker. No one doubts his affinities with the medieval allegorical tradition, Renaissance humanism, or Elizabethan issues such as the Tudor myth. If the means of expressing Puritan sensibility in Spenser are medieval, including some symbols from medieval Catholicism, pagan Britain and other sources, we can rest easily with the mixture as long as the doctrine is Calvinist-Puritan, all that anyone would try to assert, and still something of a novelty to many minds.

In brief, canto x includes traditional medieval imagery thought of as Catholic, some doctrine that is generally Protestant, and important elements specifically Calvinist. The Puritan emerges from the general Protestant, and both are presented in emblems more or less medieval, and therefore calling to mind Catholic practice. But if we look closely we shall see that neither the imagery nor the commentary call to mind any doctrine that is specifically Catholic, that is, a point of reformation controversy. The opening preamble is one any Reformation church would agree to, despite their many factional disputes:

> Ne let the man ascribe it to his skill,
> That thorough grace hath gained victory.
> If any strength we have, it is to ill,
> But all the good is Gods, both power and eke will. (x, i)

Later on when Faith explains true doctrine it is expressed in terms common to all Christians. There may be a Protestant implication in the dramatic manner closely joining faith to conversion experience, the process Red Cross is undergoing in his regeneration. We might easily point out activities a Catholic imagination would include in such an experience which are notably omitted in his learning experience with Faith, Hope, Charity and the others. But there is nothing presenting sharp contrast or contradiction among Christian sects in the initial process. The conclusion of his experience with Faith and Hope is somewhat more special. In two theological areas the viewpoint is explicitly Calvinist: the depth and corruption of the original sin and the concomitant agony in wrestling with it, and the reverse of this, the joy and assurance of the finally cured conscience and convinced Christian. These must be quoted together as two of the great moments of the Calvinist-Puritan conversion experience. The imagery from stanzas xxv–xxix is at its most medieval in visual ideas, causing many a commentator to wince at the ashes, sackcloth, dieting, iron whips, and so on. But the theme of facing the depths of original sin alone and surviving to serene assurance is a feature of the Calvinist-Puritan tradition distinguished not only from the former Roman way, but also from the milder views, oriented towards sacraments and rituals, of Establishment or Lutheran traditions. Calvin and the Cambridge Puritans wrote abstractly and practically about this awesome contrast, the abjection of the individual before full sense of sin in himself, and his final conquest of it through faith and election, leading to assurance in religious vocation. This is exactly what happens to Red Cross, and Spenser here is certainly alluding to his knowledge of the Calvinist-Puritan tradition of his generation in these striking passages:

> But yet the cause and root of all his ill,
> Inward corruption, and infected sin,
> Not purg'd nor heald, behind remained still,
> And festring sore did ranckle yett within,
> Close creeping twixt the marrow and the skin. (x, xxv)

> Whom . . . they to Una brought;
> Who, joyous of his cured conscience,
> Him dearely kist, and fayrely eke besought
> Himself to chearish, and consuming thought
> To put away out of his carefull brest. (x, xxix)

He is then prepared for his specific quest or vocation in the world, one of religious and secular dimensions. But before this can take place, there is one more complication introduced by the contemplation of the New Jerusalem. Here Spenser shows the influence of the moderate Calvinist-Puritan viewpoint on the heady subject of glorification, almost an exclusive Calvinist doctrine in contrast to more orthodox Protestant areas considered thus far. He is in sympathy with the millennial urge, as were the Calvinist-Puritan theologians, but with them resists the doctrines of the spirit of the extreme sects to which even major elements in the central Puritan tradition in England were to succumb in the next century.

The heavy and specific medieval allegory which leads up to the Knight's contemplation of the heavenly city sets this scene in a general Christian frame derived from Augustine's *City of God* and the complex tradition of dualism between heaven and earth which is the legacy of the Augustinian strain in Christianity. There is nothing specifically Calvinist-Puritan in this aspect. The vision of heavenly bliss is quite conventional until stanza lvii, where the connection between heavenly reward and the chosen (elect) is made, with the allied stress that the glory is a reward only of persons like the Knight who have been "purged from sinful guilt."

> "Faire knight," quoth he, "Hierusalem that is,
> The New Hierusalem, that God has built
> For those to dwell in, that are chosen his,
> His chosen people purg'd from sinful guilt
> With pretious blood. . . . (x, lvii)

It would be unfair to confuse this stress with a full blown Puritan sermon on glorification or with a contemplative treatise such as *Saints Everlasting Rest*. The germ and direction are there, though Spenser skillfully avoids the dangers of "otherworldliness" associated with monasticism and with the millenarianism later to provide a trap for some 17th century Puritans. His Tudor allegiance to the temporal order saves him from the second hazard, general Protestantism from the first temptation. The two realms remain separate in time. The justified man must preserve his vocation in this world with only a glimpse of the glory of his final destination. In stanza lxiii the Knight is reminded of his temporal duty and need to return to Una and to his quest. The Calvinist-Puritan strain is at its gentlest, most moderate and becoming at this point. Spenser has seldom been given credit for his ability to balance his earthly alliance to Elizabeth's England, his general Protestant beliefs, and a Calvinist attitude towards the doctrine of glorification, which cannot be called a bias or disproportion because it hardly disturbs the other levels of allegorical meaning depicted by the figure of Heavenly Contemplation and the New Jerusalem. The full Christian and special Puritan resonances are both present in the vision and in the Knight's attitude towards the vision.

Cantos xi and xii return to the action of gallantry and the allegory of knighthood. The religious allegory of the two falls and restorations by means of clearly defined symbols of baptism and Eucharist have been noted by all critics and accepted, however deplorable such allegory doubtless remains to certain modern sensibilities. On this point the differences in emphasis between Ruskin and the *Variorum* commentators on one side, and contemporary myth or psychological critics on the other, tell us more about changes in general attitudes and literary techniques than they do about Spenser's poem. The religious aspects of Spenser's allegory for the mid-twentieth century must be alchemised into something other than it is in order to be palatable to some critical tastes, so it would seem. In a study whose aims are both historical and critical, modern taste is of little interest in itself.

The symbolism of baptism in xxix–xxxi and of Eucharist in xlvi–xlviii are unexceptionably Christian. They are Protestant only in the sense that two sacraments are accepted of divine institution, as in the "Hymn of Heavenly Love." The difference between Calvinist-Puritan and other Christian traditions on sacraments occurred on the plane of interpreting the sacraments as things *in esse,* or composites, or signs. Spenser is unmistakably Puritan in sensibility in some areas, Calvinist in theology in a few others, never abstractly doctrinal in such matters as sacramental mode, formal causes of grace, and the like. The Calvinism of viewpoint in canto xi makes one clear appearance in stanza xlv, before the two falls and restoration by baptism and eucharist. The double notion of God's predestination of the events to follow, and the election of the hero are the Calvinist ground for all that follows. As in the *Institutes* and the Westminster Confession, predestination and election are logically prior to consideration of sacraments and other points of Christian theology. This theology is sharply Calvinist in the *Institutes* and Westminster Confession, deliberately compromised (some would say confused) in the Thirty-Nine Articles. Spenser accepts the sharpness of the Calvinists on the fundamental issue, the vagueness of the Elizabethan settlement on the sacraments. In having this attitude he was one with the majority of English Puritans until the policy of the reign of Charles I, loyal to the civil government and a nominal subscriber to the Articles to the extent that a Puritan might give private interpretation of them. His essential Puritanism in the final cantos is parallel to that in the *Hymns,* of little importance where the difference between Calvinist and Elizabethan were not matters of polemical interpretation, resplendently Calvinist in areas wherein the traditions moved on different planes. In canto xi one short passage is a reminder that the Calvinist theology dominates all that follows:

> It chaunst (eternall God that chaunce did guide)
> As he recoileed backward, in the mire
> His nigh foreweried feeble feet did slide,
> And downe he fell, with dread of shame sore terrifide. (xi, xlv)

In canto xii, as in the brief section of the hymn quoted earlier, glorification is the area of Puritan tradition given emphasis by Spenser. It would not at that time give offense to other Englishmen. In the 17th century the latent dangers in this doctrine were to become all too apparent, when heaven was brought down to earth according to the rule of the saints. Glorification appears openly in canto xii in the celebratory scenes revealing Una's radiance and the glory of God.

Una is revealed in all the glory of Truth in stanza xxii. This glory is heavenly glory, an image of Truth as it will be known to man after the final revelation. Her sad wimple is the shroud of doubt and uncertainty afflicting Truth in this world, which has often overpowered those who struggle and stumble in search of Truth, like the Red Cross Knight. The final Puritan emphasis upon gaiety of vision, the struggle won, the gift of the glimpse finally offered after trial, easily outshines any darkness lingering from the struggle, as indeed it should in this triumphal part of the poem:

> The blazing brightness of her beauties beame,
> And glorious light of her sunshyny face
> To tell, were as to strive against the streame:
> My ragged rimes are all too rude and bace,
> Her heavenly lineaments for to enchace. (xii, xxiii)

Then it remains only to describe the betrothal as a human emblem of the Divine Unity. The major part of the description is devoted to the splendor of the earthly court, as usual in Spenser's allegorical method and dazzlement with Elizabethan pomp. Yet the occasion does not pass, but is dominated and climaxed by mysterious and palpable infusions of the divine presence and guidance. Una as revealed Truth and Red Cross as earned Holiness have the divine sanction, impressed almost physically upon the guests by the mysterious sounds of heavenly music:

> During the which there was a heavenly noise
> Heard sownd through all the pallace pleasantly,
> Like as it had bene many an angels voice
> Singing before the Eternall Majesty,
> In their trinall triplicities on hye;
> Yett wist no creature, whence that hevenly sweet
> Proceeded, yet each one felt secretly
> Himself thereby refte of his sences meet,
> And ravished with rare impression in his sprite. (xii, xxxix)

Book I ends on the strongest positive note of Calvinist-Puritan tradition, justly having balanced the depths of sin depicted in the early episodes and the terrible temptation of despair in canto ix with this joyful conclusion. We have seen this pattern in many of the 16th century Calvinist preachers and are going to see it again in the poets of this tradition throughout the 17th and 18th centuries.

III. Marvell and Taylor

After Spenser the next poet with a full Calvinist mythic pattern is Milton. But some of the lesser patterns, or perhaps partial patterns, are to be found in other 17th century writers, some of whom have not been thought to be particularly Calvinist. Among these writers the best are Marvell in England and Taylor in America. Lesser figures could be mentioned, but in discussing the poetry, we adhere to a method of selectivity, on the grounds that the opening chapter has given enough sense in the prose examples of the variety and number of the Calvinist possibilities. In these opening remarks, the purpose is to justify the selection of Marvell and Taylor as legitimate examples of the Calvinist temper. The only convincing proof, needless to say, is in the value of the explications themselves. But some historical clichés must be examined as a prelude to the discussions of the poetry.

With neither writer is the historical problem acute. The matter is rather to encourage an emphasis in these poets that all readers have acknowledged and only a few taken seriously. The Calvinist bent has always given way to more interesting or immediate concerns of the critic and appeal of the writers. Both have been considered religious writers, metaphysical writers, poets of meditation — Marvell a political satirist, Taylor an American frontier prodigy. These concerns represent the critical interests of the past thirty years. Yet, a certain vague uneasiness has accompanied these categories. Marvell and Taylor do not fit into a scheme of Anglican dogmatic and meditative poetry as do the usual accompaniers in this line — Donne, Herbert Crawshaw, Vaughan. Poetry of meditation is such a vague term that it can include almost any great "subjective" work of English poetry to the present day. Marvell as political poet or Taylor as American frontiersman exhaust very little of their potential. Marvell's best poetry is religious, not political. The obsession with the American imagination has caused critics of the Perry Miller school to go to great lengths to show the innate Americanism of the New England settlers, and it may be accepted that certain political and religious writers had gone a long way by the end of the 17th century towards establishing an American tradition in letters; nevertheless, Taylor does not fit easily into this rationalistic category. Uncomfortable as it may be for the exaggerators of early American tradition, of whom there are many in our midst today, Taylor reads solidly like an English Calvinist transplanted to an unusual scene in the wilderness. His vision is religious, not political or nationalistic, and while his imagery may contain a good deal of the local color of the wilderness, his wilderness is primarily a biblical trope and only secondarily the actuality.

To say all this is not to deny the usefulness of various focussed reading of these poets, or of readings augmented by neutral analysis of imagery and structure. It is to say that the central and unifying vision of each poet, and his relationship to a common source and tradition, is thereby lost sight of, leading to a fragmented view of the poet's total achievement. The metaphysical imagery, political or American concerns, other side issues, find their way into the total concerns of the poet's vision, which is Calvinist-Puritan in ideology. These are the major obstacles to a Calvinist-Puritan reading of Marvell and Taylor. Although further proof of the inandequacy of reading based upon these assumptions could be adduced from historical causes or by analysis of the criticism itself, it is not our chosen path to do this work. At the conclusion of the positive analysis in the framework of Calvinist categories, it will be apparent what and how far earlier criticism is justified. We expect and welcome overlap as well as illumination.

Marvell and Taylor will be called "existential" Calvinists here, to show their allegiance with the 17th century metaphysical tradition, and to suggest differences from the mythic and more fully patterned Calvinist vision of Spenser and Milton. The term is not meant to have any modern connotations, or to suggest an attempt to link these writers with the concerns and philosophic outlook of the modern existentialist writers. "Personalist" might be an easier term to use for the qualities to be noted, but "existentialist" suggests both the personal concern and the religious outlook which personalist does not suggest. "Metaphysical," another alternative, is misleading in the light of the numerous studies of the Donne tradition and the commonly accepted use of that word. If our viewpoint towards Marvell and

Taylor has any value, it will be in showing the qualities each shared with the metaphysical tradition, yet as a part of a greater and coherent Calvinist outlook. On the other hand, their relationship to the total Calvinist pattern, as seen in the theologians and the myth writers, is that of minor to major: they choose the items of the Calvinist pattern of greatest concern to themselves and give to these items a vigorous mixing of the personal viewpoint and sense of emotional involvement. The result is "metaphysical" or "meditative" poetry with a unique and qualifiying difference.

One more comment on the method of this section needs to be made. Allusions to Baxter and Bunyan have appeared in Section I of this study. If the study were restricted to the 17th century, rather than to the poetry of the Calvinist tradition in the widest sense, there would be a place in it for direct study of such great pieces of Puritan imaginative prose as *Pilgrim's Progress* and the *The Saints Everlasting Rest.* There have been interesting consideration of these works in recent years,[30] and the need to confront them directly in our context is not pressing. On the other hand, both these works provide extra-ordinary confirmation of the Puritan sensibility and Puritan religious categories in imaginative literature that it has been our interest to trace in the poetry. It seems perfectly legitimate in this chapter to refer to the prose of Bunyan and Baxter in the common theological framework of Calvinism. This method helps to establish the sense of the Calvinist tradition in the practice of a varied group of writers in the 17th century. It will also make a contribution to the theory of Calvinist-Puritan influence in English literature of a wider sort as the book progresses.

In order to make some such contribution the overall unity of the Calvinist-Puritan experience must be stressed. Martz's *Poetry of Meditation* separated Puritan theology and meditation from the Catholic and Anglican types, in a way largely unsympathetic to Puritanism and literature. Kaufmann, in a follow-up of Martz's methods but in a more sympathic context, *The Pilgrim's Progress and Traditions in Puritan Meditation,* is far more perceptive in writing about Puritan literature, and about the intellectual place of Puritanism in English history. But he insists upon isolating sharply the Puritan literary mind from all others, to some detrimental effect upon Puritanism and literature. These distinctions are not new, merely pressed with extreme vigor and clarity. In Kaufmann's view Puritan "meditation" (or merely the normal means of confronting scripture) prefers word over myth, understanding over imagination, aural over visual, command over event. It is not difficult to find Puritan documents to demonstrate such affinities, as Kaufmann does in abundance. In our first section we have noticed some Puritans (Ames, Perkins in *Cases of Conscience,* for instance) who fulfill the scheme laid out by Martz and Kaufmann. But there were others, such as Sibbes and Bayly, not so easily categorized. The problem increases as really imaginative writing is approached in Puritan tradition. Kaufmann has to say this about characterization in Bunyan:

Manifestly, Puritan piety and the hermeneutics with which it was organically related gave powerful impetus to a didactic conception of character which effectively wedded historicity to plain instructive import and generality of reference. Despite the nisus toward the allegorical in such an approach, the perils, and difficulty, in ignoring historicity of biblical figure or of neighbor helped to keep exemplary character a genuine hybrid, paradoxial and intriguing in its dynamic equilibrium.[31]

Or, in simpler language, from the rule books of Puritanism as Kaufmann has expounded them, Bunyan should have learned to draw wooden allegories with single moral meanings. Instead, the characters and other elements attain some complexity. Kaufmann is happy with this state of affairs from a literary point of view, yet this strange conclusion is drawn from assumptions which placed Bunyan squarely in Puritan tradition. On the movement of plot, his premise and conclusion are closer. He notices in *Pilgrim's Progress* the problem Berger struggled with in *Allegorical Temper* concerning Spenser, but without attempting a satisfactory resolution as did Berger:

The modern reader can perhaps be forgiven for his impression that in a pilgrimage that is in large measure the exfoliation of a Word once and for all delivered, events only seem to be happening. . . . the peculiar dynamics of his narative are indebted to the Puritan conception of reading the Word as static system. Not only is such a system present behind the action, but it is related to Christian and his pilgrimage as prevenient truth in the shape of Evangelist and the book.[32]

Later we are going to see something of this same quality in Blake's diffused Puritan methodology in his prophecies.

It would be pointless here to argue fully against the methods of Martz and Kaufmann. For Martz the interest in Puritan tradition was marginal. Though for Kaufmann Puritanism is central, his method of working out literary traditions such as meditation and imagination causes some problems. On one page he separates Calvin's doctrines

from English Puritanism (p. 54), yet in many other places the two are
equated openly (pp. 127, 245) or by assumption (p. 116). Despite
these and other inconsistencies that could be pointed out, Kaufmann
is well versed in Puritan tradition. He knows Bayly, Sibbes, Perkins,
gives a fine analysis of the meditative imagination in Baxter's *Saints
Rest,* leading to his main thesis, meditative tradition in *Pilgrim's
Progress.* For Martz and Kaufmann the keenest interest is in literary
assumption, only a marginal interest in the theology of the Calvinist
tradition.[33] The view point of this chapter, and throughout this book,
is exactly the reverse, however distasteful to some literary minds. The
existence of a common theology is the groundwork of all the rest. This
theology appears in abstract treatises (Calvin), homiletic writings
(the Cambridge Puritans), and in literature, in Spenser, Taylor,
Bunyan, Baxter and the others. Writing in poetic or fable form, the
imaginative writer introduces new attitudes into Puritanism by
definition, but not new doctrine or fundamental tradition. In the 16th
and 17th centuries the Calvinist-Puritan tradition was an abstract
system to which preachers gave a partial imaginative response, and
creative writers a fuller one. To talk about imagination and meditation
apart from or superior to doctrine is a mistaken strategy in relation to
Puritan writing, even though it is one that allows for much comparative analysis with other traditions. If we look upon Puritanism until
the 18th century as this kind of unity we may move from Marvell to
Taylor to Baxter to Bunyan − for instance, in their common interest
in the great themes of sin and glory − as a prime example of unity
within a common tradition. Our focus will more often be exclusively
upon the poets and their particular contributions and circumstances.

Andrew Marvell

Although the critical and literary world is well aware of Andrew
Marvell's political Puritan background, it has not been fashionable to
treat his poetry in a religious context. The reasons for this are many,
and fairly obvious. A specific religious context for Marvell is not easy
to establish, as is the Anglican context of Donne and Herbert or the
Catholic of Crashaw. The point is that Marvell's Puritanism is of a
cool sort, as are his political and "metaphysical" interests. The appeal
of such cool political and metaphysical views to the modern sensibility
has been strong, and it is just that the best Marvell criticism thus far

has been of his political poems[34] or of his "ironic vision."[35] The best of this criticism has also taken note of a Puritan strain in the political poems and the "metaphysical" or ironic vision of the most popular poems. With the exception, however, of Legouis' rather thorough exploration of the Puritan strain in Marvell's personality in his now classic *André Marvell: poète, puritain, patriote*,[36] the consideration of Puritanism, especially in any specific religious context, has been peripheral to the concerns of the most discerning of recent critics.

The question of the context of Marvell's Puritan sensibility and poetry is far more difficult than to name the poems in the Marvell canon which are religious and specifically Puritan in flavor. All the major students of Marvell have agreed on this point, perhaps because the number of such poems is exceedingly small in a rather limited canon. "A Dialogue Between the Resolved Soul, and Created Pleasure," "The Coronet," "A Dialogue between the Soul and Body," and "The Mower Against Gardens," comprise the very small group of clearly religious poems in theme. With a clearer sense of the Puritan context than has prevailed in the past, one might be adventurous and notice that "The Definition of Love," the Mower poems, and some aspects of political poems such as the Cromwell group fall within the Puritan framework of sensibility not of specific theological interest. The primary question is to decide what the Puritan frame of reference means in relation to Marvell.

Marvell's Puritanism was primarily political, as is abundantly clear in his letters and whatever else we know of his public career. From what we know of his temperament and personality — too little to be sure — he does not appear as the sort of man who would have embraced the rigors of the Calvinist religious experience in the manner of Baxter or Bunyan. Nevertheless, he was in Cambridge at a time when the Puritan influence was still very strong, of the pre-Civil War generation which included Milton and other Puritan luminaries. Political interest was stronger than religious in this generation of Puritan, who were turning away from the methods of persuasion used by the great Puritan preachers such as Perkins and Preston during the reign of James I. But the evidence is clear in the case of Milton, and strong in that of Marvell, that Puritan methodology and theological attitudes were not abandoned after the first great wave of Puritan influence from 1590 to 1625. We do not expect men of the temperament of Milton and Marvell to keep diaries of conversion experience, or to revel in simple religious visions with Foxe and

Bunyan. Yet their ideas of political reform, and hatred of the religious policies of Charles and Laud, obviously had a religious basis in a preference for the Puritan religious way, including the leading aspects of Puritan theology. In Marvell, we must find the evidence for the Puritan sensibility almost entirely in the poetry, for there is little in the prose that is helpful. This makes the discussion extremely circular, unless our knowledge of the Puritan sensibility brings with it some disposition to detect evidence of the Puritan strain in quite subtle contexts.

The overriding quality of Marvell's religious poetry is its disposition to hold the subject matter at arm's length, the same "coolness" or ironic vision that appears in his handling of all other themes. We cannot expect him to deal directly with the delights or the terrors of the Calvinist religious experience, as do Spenser, Bunyan, Taylor and even at times Milton. He writes about things from the viewpoint of one who has had such experience, but not of the experiences themselves. He does not give the impression of having passed permanently into the state of assurance, or of viewing the dogmas and personal experiences of the religious life as part of the process of sanctification. One might simply call him a secular person, as has often been done in modern criticism. He is that in some poems and moods, yet the religious poems are there, as a very peculiar kind of religious sensibility. It is the sensibility of the not-quite-convinced Puritan, convinced, that is, of his own election, who on the other hand has no decided feeling of ultimate despair and damnation. Such a one would not be inclined to write hair-raising poems on despair and damnation, nor on the other hand poems which explore the stages of assurance and sanctification in the person of Christ as mediator. He writes, since Marvell is this one, about religious subjects more peripherally and always circumspectly. He is always looking carefully over his shoulder and cares not to be "caught" in an unambiguous mood toward religious experience, for in his terms the unambiguous mood would be the compromising one. If all this seems a far-fetched and unlikely way to approach the clear categories of sin-damnation, election, justification, sanctification, glorification, the dramatic states of Puritan inner life, let the following defense be entered on its behalf. It is surprising that the 17th century Puritan tradition did not produce more men of the sensibility of Marvell, rather than the few that we know of. In historical fact, 18th and early 19th century New England gave what abundance there is of Marvell's kind of response to Puritan theology and practice — the circumspect, abstract, and rationalistic response of Jonathan Edwards, Dickinson, Hawthorne and Melville. Such detached, even sceptical (though not in the contemporary sense of the word), response to Calvinism was inevitable once the excitement and drama of the late 16th and the 17th centuries gave way to quieter times or to Puritan victory over worldly adversaries. All Puritans became familiar with the steps of the Calvinist way leading to the Calvinist temper. Spenser, Bunyan and Milton dramatized them all; the preachers described them and exhorted followers to the experience; Taylor explored the implications and possibilities of the assurance state or santification. It remained for Marvell to trip back and forth lightly over them all, never resting in one and reflecting all of them. Doubt and assurance, election and despair get into the tone of Marvell's handling of religious themes, where he deigns to handle them directly, and contribute a sceptical and calculating tone to his treatment of all themes. In brief, as a Puritan Marvell was not some sort of sport or freak in the tradition; he was simply far ahead of his time in his total response to the Calvinist theology and sensibility.

Before attempting a reading of the religious poems as such, it might be interesting to test this view of Marvell's Puritan sensibility in a more neutral context, yet one close enough to be relevant, the political poems in which Marvell the public Puritan partisan should be evident. The best known and the best of these poems of course is "An Horatian Ode," on Cromwell, supplemented by a small group of lesser poems on the same great figure. Marvell's ambiguity of viewpoint in his handling of Cromwell and Charles in the major poem has been noticed by all readers and has been made the central fact of the poem by many. How the religious sensibility of Calvinism contributes to this ambiguity has not been widely noted, and will be our interest here to describe.

We know from his two early poems, *Ad Regem Carolum Parodia* and Ππὸς Κάπολον τὸν Βασιλέα that Marvell thought little of King Charles I as a man or political leader. We also know from the self-abasing letter of 1653 and several of the longer and more perfunctory panegyric poems on Cromwell that Marvell held Cromwell in great awe as a man and as the political leader of the victorious Puritan party. In "An Horatian Ode" the situation is somewhat different, and more interesting. Charles and Cromwell both appear as portents in English history, or what the Puritans called visible signs of divine providence. In both there is a degree of appearance and reality.

It is the true definition of each, in which way each is a visible sign of the will of divine providence, which the poem attempts and wherein the real ambiguity lies.

In appearance, Charles had the right of divine sanction on his side — in traditional parlance of Anglicans and Catholics he is the political and human analogy of Christ, of the sun, and ultimately of God. We know that the Puritans did not accept the scholastic doctrines of proportionate analogy of being in this same way; the will of God was supposedly more inscrutable to human perception, as Calvin never ceased pointing out. In reality, Charles became an obstacle to the visible rule of the saints on earth, and in fact, at the time of the writing of the poem, he had been eliminated. For many rejoicing Puritans the elimination of this enemy as obstacle was the reality, the sign of the victory of God's elect nation on earth. But the poet, balancing this new rationale against the "great work of time," or the analogy of kingship and divinity in western European tradition, is not so confident. Is Charles as symbol of kingship only an appearance that has been fully and confidently destroyed by the actual experience of his execution? The answer for the poet — and we refer to a theological rather than merely a political answer — would quite easily have been yes if the poet had been able to accept the other major symbol of the poem as reality and not perhaps as appearance. This of course is Cromwell as the visible sign of the "election" of the Puritan religious faction as the power of the nation in the Commonwealth scheme. Despite Marvell's personal indebtedness to Cromwell, and his admiration of the man of power, the great fact of this poem is the ambiguity of attitude toward Cromwell as this theological "sign" of God's providence. It is easier for him to accept Cromwell as a portent of temporary human success in history, yet even on this score there are the famous doubts in the last lines of the poem. If we ask from the viewpoint of Calvinist sensibility how Marvell could be so sceptical of the great "sign" of Puritan election that was unequivocally read as triumph by almost all other Puritans of the day, the answer brings us back to Marvell's equivocal attitude toward the central Puritan intellectual conviction, that of personal election. If the individual cannot finally know whether he is to be saved or damned, as was felt by Marvell and a small minority of the Puritans from the 1580's and on, despite the urgings of the preachers and saints, then no public, historical portent of group election, such as Cromwell's great victory over Charles, could be read unequivocally. Here is an example of

individualistic Calvinist sensibility (a minority report to be sure) influencing decision away from the seemingly irresistible reading of
Cromwell's victory by the majority of Puritans of the time.

In fact, Marvell's intellectual uncertainty and moral ambiguity
harken back to intellectual dilemmas in the origins of Calvinism.
Concerning election and providence, Calvin had at one point stated
boldly:

While God is truly wrathful with sin and condemns whatever is unrighteous-
ness in men since it displeases him, nevertheless all the deeds of men are
governed not by his bare permission but by his consent and secret counsel.[37]

In other words, the will of God is inscrutable to men. Yet Calvin himself in his treatises on the Church and on justification had tried to
make the will of God more rational and acceptable to men, and the
Puritan preachers of the 16th and 17th centuries had gone further,
finally arriving at the New England idea of Covenant theology. In
the minds of most Puritans in 1650, Cromwell was a clear sign of the
Covenant and the working of the will of God in human affairs for the
benefit of his chosen people. For Marvell, remembering Calvin's basic
premise of God's inscrutability, Cromwell as a sign of providence
is not as easily received. Concerning individual election, Marvell's
doubts are also central to the dilemma of Calvinist-Puritanism on
the subject. Calvin had stated: "While the elect receive the grace of
adoption by faith, their election does not depend on faith but is prior
in time and order."[38] Puritanism had accepted this idea abstractly, yet
strived to create a "way" by which man could understand his own
position in the drama of individual salvation. This way became the
steps outlined by every major Cambridge theologian — sin-despair,
election, justification, sanctification, glorification. In the 1580's–1590's
period the way seemed hard and uncertain, as we know from the
many suicides at Cambridge and the journey in The Faerie Queene
I–II. It had become more broadly and confidently travelled by the
time of Milton, Taylor and Marvell, with the constant exhortation of
preachers and the seeming worldly success of the Commonwealth and
of Cromwell to provide momentum. But the problem of individual
election could never finally be resolved in Puritanism by a burst of
good feeling; abstractly, as is clear in Calvin, election precedes the
human process of the experience of salvation. That this is the major
problem is historically verified by the later phenomena of the Awakening in the 18th century, when Edwards was forced to restate all the

grounds for signs of election in *Religious Affections* after the confusions of the Awakening. Marvell was simply a 17th century Puritan who never gave way to his emotions and affections, despite the temporary stirring successes in Puritan history and his admiration for Cromwell. His ambivalence towards personal election is best viewed of course in the personal poems of religious experience rather than in a political context. But it is fair to see that Puritan doubts of an intellectual kind pervade all of his poetry; it is the source of the "ironic vision" that other critics have laid to more secular causes.

Marvell's other political poems, even those on the subject of Cromwell, do not extend as fully into his theological vision as does "An Horatian Ode." Much interest in the poems is given over to satire, or panegyric, or to local historical events of limited importance. This, however, is not true of one section of "The First Anniversary," the lines which relate the local history of Cromwell's success to its larger implications in time:

> Hence oft I think, if in some happy Hour
> High Grace should meet in one with highest Pow'r,
> And then a seasonable People still
> Should bend to his, as he to Heavens will,
> What we might hope, what wonderful Effect
> From such a wish'd Conjuncture might reflect.
> Sure, the mysterious Work, where none withstand,
> Would forthwith finish under such a Hand:
> Fore-shortned Time its useless Course would stay,
> And soon precipitate the latest Day.
> But a thick Cloud about that Morning lyes,
> And intercepts the Beams of Mortal eyes,
> That 'tis the most which we determine can,
> If these the Times, then this must be the Man.
> And well he therefore does, and well has guest,
> Who in his Age has always forward prest:
> And knowing not where Heavens choice may light,
> Girds yet his Sword, and ready stands to fight. . . .[39]

In these lines the poet has returned to the puzzling image of Cromwell given at the end of "An Horatian Ode" as one whose destiny it must be to struggle endlessly as a sign of the strange unfolding of the will of God in the 17th century. There is more sympathy and partisanship than in the earlier poem, for Cromwell is viewed against the Presbyterian and other obstructionists here, not the legitimate and pathetic Charles. Marvell sees Cromwell, and presumably himself, as of the elect in human terms:

Hence that blest Day still counterpoysed wastes,
The Ill delaying, what th' Elected hastes. . . .

The real interest in these lines is not in the human counterpoints, fascinating as these may be for students of 17th century history. It is in the contrast of Cromwell, the human stumbling figure groping in history, "And knowing not where Heavens choice may light," and the ideal situation figured in the earlier lines, "High Grace should meet in one with highest Pow'r." This figure should, of course, be Christ, although the "his" and "he" of line 134 are not capitalized. But we cannot be sure that it is to be Christ and not some later human figure chosen by God for his divine plan, to bring the "mysterious Work" of salvation and damnation to "the latest Day." Intellectual Calvinist thought can be very arch and ambiguous on many points of Christ's function in the framework of history and redemption, and it is commonplace that intellectual historians have noted a latent "Hebraicism" or Socinianism in Calvinist thought only partially dimmed by Christian tradition and piety. As another example of the same intellectual temper, at the end of the "Poem upon the Death of O.C.," Cromwell's shade joins Moses, Joshua and David, not Christ and the Christian saints who would certainly be found in any Catholic or Anglican 17th century poem on the theme of the hero's death. We are not trying to make the erroneous and crude point that intellectual Calvinism is a form of Judaism, as some have done. It is closer to Judaism than to medieval Catholic and Anglican thinking and sensibility, but it was shaped by a man who viewed the Old Testament through the New and through the writings of St. Paul above all others. It has its own axes and tensions, one of the most acute and intellectual being, as here in Marvell's placing Cromwell in relation to an ideal, the function of Christ. Calvin had written, "While we are elected in Christ, nevertheless that God reckons us among his own is prior in order to his making us members of Christ."[40] To the orthodox Catholic or Anglican mind this is pure Socinianism, although it obviously was not to Calvin, who devoted much of the *Institutes* to the question of Christ, the sacraments, and the Church. In "The First Anniversary" there is the same problem of intellectual Calvinism at work: the High Grace and highest Power *might* be Christ in his second coming; on the other hand, it might be some greater and later Cromwell with a clearer mandate of providence than Marvell was willing to concede even to Cromwell, a man whose clear election could bring to an end "the mysterious Work" so that,

> Fore-shortned Time its useless Course would stay,
> And soon precipitate the latest Day.

There is no doubt that at one point in the short history of the Commonwealth even brilliant intellects such as Milton's believed in the possibility of the visible rule of the saints on earth, which would shorten time and hasten the last judgment. Marvell, his judgment always cool, and intellect unwilling to give way to feeling, remains ambiguous on this point, and prefers to view Cromwell most often in his merely human and political aspects, as the greatest hero of the day. This is shown mid-point in the passage, where he falls back from the vision of the ideal and returns to the actual Cromwell:

> But a thick Cloud about that Morning lyes,
> And intercepts the Beams of Mortal eyes. . . .

These lines are an echo of Dante, *Paradiso* 1.88,[41] and have the effect of acknowledging the inscrutability, from the human point of view, of the will of God. It has been said, and is quite true, that the incipient Socinianism in the Calvinist view of Christ is not there for reasons of logic, or as a reaction to medieval devotional practice; it follows from the Calvinists' need to preserve the majesty and inscrutability of God and providence. It was, on the other hand, quite easy and human for individual Calvinists to fall into kinder and more optimistic views, as did the federal theologians or Edward Taylor. Marvell, however, was not the man to refuse facing intellectual problems on intellectual terms; he might evade the Calvinist dilemmas with wit or ambiguity, but never denied their presence.

The small number of poems by Marvell which are specifically religious have been accepted as such by all readers. The difficulty has been in finding a context in which the religious poems are meaningful. Marvell's political poems are meaningful in the great and obvious 17th century context of Crown vs. Commonwealth. The Puritan sensibility in them is an aspect of a larger theme. The larger context of the religious poems is not so obvious. It is no longer acceptable to say that these religious poems are "metaphysical," or of the "school of Donne," or even "poems of meditation." More exact terms, such as "religious pastoral" have been invented, and recently, in his very helpful book, *Marvell's Ironic Vision*, Harold Toliver has used the term "Puritan-Platonist" to explore Marvell's vision in the religious and other poems. His discussion helps to isolate some of the Puritan qualities of Marvell's religious poems, and may serve as an introduction to this discussion of the poems.

Toliver sees the Puritan-Platonist preoccupied with certain standard dichotomies of the Platonic tradition (soul-body, heaven-earth, spiritual-material, etc.) in the context of the Puritan sensibility derived from Calvinism. Calvinism tends to sharpen these standard dualisms, so that the ordinary poetical debates of other religious poetry become "dialectical contests," "oppositional calculus" — the spiritual combat of the Puritan preachers in a more intellectual and sophisticated setting than it usually was found. External nature must have place in a Calvinist religious poem but "nature is engaged on the periphery, around a fixed, inviolable intellectual center."[42] The Calvinist sensibility and outlook allowed the "Puritan-Platonist to explore his relation to nature without becoming too deeply engaged in it."[43] Sharp dialogue is an inevitable mode of the Calvinist poet with his suspicion of nature and of the self.

The view of Marvell as Puritan-Platonist, as Toliver develops it, applies to all categories of poems in Marvell. It needs still further sharpening in the direction of the Puritan contribution to be of use in the study of the specifically religious poems, that is, poems on commonly accepted Christian religious themes. Toliver states acutely what a specific Calvinist direction would add to the religious sensibility of the "Puritan-Platonist," to define the difference between, say, the religious poems of Marvell and those of the Cambridge Platonists, in whom of course the second term in the description carried greater weight than the former. If the Calvinist-Puritan term is the weighted one, the outlook becomes less optimistic:

Though Calvin does not reject nature or moral law as categorically as one might expect, he does move them to a peripheral and precariously balanced position; active moral and political life becomes a *sign* of inner health and possible election rather than a temporal pattern uniting nature to grace.[44]

This is a very important statement in helping to define Marvell's peculiarly Puritan outlook in his specifically religious poems; we can accept the more general term "Puritan-Platonist" as applying to his nature and garden poems, and to some extent the political poems, but the religious context needs this further sharpening. Finally, in speaking further of the religious poems, Toliver makes two more valuable related points. He notes that "many Puritans and most Cambridge Platonists would have denied the sacrificial function of the Eucharistic rite."[45] For those who denied forcefully, the eucharistic rite would not appear as a major subject for poetry. Marvell's religious poetry is certainly of this sort. For many other Calvinists (including Calvin himself and poets such as Edward Taylor and theologians such as the great Baxter) a "use" was certainly found for the Eucharist in the Calvinist scheme. This should not disturb students of Calvinism who are willing to see in it a complex human phenomenon rather than a few rigid, abstract principles.

Marvell, then, chose to restrict his subjects of religious meditations and poems, excluding some obvious ones such as the Eucharist. We may be sure he had good reason for his choices, remembering Toliver's related insight on the subject of the religious poetry:

Since Marvell chooses to work within restrictive modes and tries out contradictory positions in successive poems, it is tempting to ignore the coherence of that intellectual and spiritual tradition when reading individual poems. But we need to be aware of the parts of his mind that are *not* engaged by a particular work as well as what does appear.[46]

In our terms, in other words, the choices of subject matter and the modes of writing that we find in Marvell's religious poems tell us a good deal about his attitude toward the Calvinist religious outlook as a whole. What he chose *not* to write about is important in the sense that it shows the aspects of Puritan religious tradition that were not particularly meaningful to him − the states of sanctification and glorification, for instance, or sacramental devotion. The aspects he does choose all fall in the general areas of more doubtful states of Puritan sensibility − the inscrutability of providence, the sin-doubt-unworthiness syndrome, the question of personal election. The religious state is a question mark, an uncertain "sign" in Marvell's poetry, so we get poems staged as debates, as combats with doubtful winners, or as questionings of man's spiritual condition. In other words, the two dialogues, "The Coronet," and "The Mower Against Gardens" in that order.

"A Dialogue Between the Resolved Soul, and Created Pleasure" is the most obviously Puritan in locus of the religious poems. Toliver notices "the stock warfare metaphor of the Puritans" in the dramatic stances of the combatants, and behind the metaphor of warfare is a more basic Puritan idea − the soul is seeking signs of assurance of its own election by venturing combat with the world. The drama presented is mainly external, so that the soul seems inviolable at the start to many readers, but such is not entirely the case. The inner dialogue with itself, presumably resolved in favor of election and virtue, must be tested against the allurement of a still fallen world, attaining a "freedom that allows action within a generally hostile scene," as Toliver puts it. In other religious poems we are given a view of the inner dialogue, the soul at cross-purposes with itself, which is of greater interest to the modern reader. Yet there is some purpose in beginning the discussion of the religious poems in the arena of external combat, the spiritual combat for signs of election.

The purpose of "A Dialogue Between the Resolved Soul, and Created Pleasure" is in fact more interesting than the effects of the poem itself. This judgment is the reverse of the usual one, which sees little in the static purpose of the poem while granting artistic quality to the language. There is artistic quality in the language, but little originality in the dramatic arrangement of the temptations.

Returning to the purpose, it obviously is to show the steadfast quality of the Resolved Soul, which seems at first glance very uninviting as a literary subject. If we ask *why* this structure from the Puritan viewpoint, the answers are interesting enough. It is the need for public acceptance of the private sense of election won in individual struggle; assurance is somehow stronger if aided by public acclamation. Toliver wisely calls this curious factor "public opinion" becoming important in a religious movement which began in intensely private searching of the soul.[47] Other historical analogues would include the required public proclamation of faith in the "fenced" churches of New England, with the strange history of private written confessions, exclusions, and backslidings. The federal theology of New England, the open Covenant of general election of the people of New England, was the logical culmination of this attitude collectively. Marvell's poem and vision remain of the individual, yet the element of the Chorus in the poem is to function as "public opinion" or collective conscience of assurance in its applause for the Resolved Soul. Since the battle has, in effect, been won before the demonstration of the soul's prowess begins, the role of the Chorus has been questioned as superfluous by readers. The Chorus is not involved or swayed as a Greek chorus is; that could not be its function in Puritan poetry. It is a sign of public acceptance and approval of the Resolved Soul's victory over the world.

The structure of the temptations is traditional in most respects. The outline of the seven deadly sins appears very strongly, as would be expected in any Christian poem on temptation. Also traditional is the division of the temptations of pleasure into two groupings, the lesser or sensual temptations, and the greater or temptations of the spirit. The poem moves from perfume and ease at the sense end of the spectrum to power and intellectual pride at the other. Sexual lust and avarice fall about the middle, which again is traditional. If we look more closely there are a few nuances in the arrangement that justly can be laid to the Puritan sensibility.

The first temptation is in a way the most sweeping of all — external nature itself is opposed to the soul or spiritual principle:

Pleasure. Welcome the Creations Guest
           Lord of Earth, and Heavens Heir.
           Lay aside that Warlike Crest,
           And of Nature's banquet share:
           Where the Souls of fruits and flow'rs
           Stand prepar'd to heighten yours.
Soul.   I sup above, and cannot stay
           To bait so long upon the way.

Pleasure here offers all creation to the Soul as its proper domain. The rejection of this offer categorically is typical only of Manicheanism, extreme Augustinianism and Puritanism in Christian tradition: any Anglican or Catholic demonstration in this area would be quick to find a "use" for the creatures.[48]

But this poem is a demonstration or sign of election, not a literal sequence of actual temptations. Otherwise the rejection of nature categorically would have precluded much of the rest of the poem, though not all. The use of the creatures here is of a special Puritan sort, what Toliver points out as the Puritan's ability "to explore his relation to nature without becoming too deeply entangled in it."[49] The poem is literally a demonstration or sign, not an *agon* of the spiritual combat between nature and grace. Fortunately for the Puritan artistic sensibility, it was capable of deeper combat and exploration, but the reader should not miss the special Puritan aspect of this external combat in looking for deeper dialectics.

The other Puritan nuances in the ordering of temptations are more obvious and less important. Music closes the opening round of sensuous temptations, and this is unusual. The Puritan affinity for music is widely documented and understood, and affected both English and New England Puritans. A world view which associated most sensuous pleasures with sin was likely to turn to the least sensuous and most abstract and intellectual of the arts for the worldly solace it allowed itself − and so Marvell does here.

Placing the intellectual temptation last is the other Puritan touch in the poem. It is only an emphasis, for general Christian tradition usually placed the intellectual temptation after the power temptation, and considered both primarily matters of the spirit. Yet there was a choice, and Marvell here, Milton in *Paradise Regained* and other Puritan writers, follow the aristocratic wing of the Church tradition on this subject − Augustine, Aquinas, and scholasticism − rather than commonplace pastoral theology which for practical reasons gave greater weight to sensuality and avarice. This choice of virtually all the Puritan writers makes a good deal of sense if we know their history. Sensuality and avarice are the commonplace failings of all humans, the Puritans not excepted. But the Puritans were an intellectual and religious elite in the great period from 1580 to 1680, unequalled in energy by any other people on the scene. They discovered, as do all elites, that the emphasis upon use of the mind carries with it grave temptations. A Marvell or a Milton might have been tempted by art or vain speculation. For the ordinary and political Puritan it is disputation, the Puritan vice, which broke up the movement into sects, that comes quickly to mind. The danger in the collective Puritan religious outlook and sensibility was in creating a Tower of Babel rather than a Sodom and Gomorrha. Hence the Chorus, expressing public approval of the Soul's private war with temptation and by this approval making the success public and general, is at the heart of the meaning of the poem.

The "Dialogue between the Soul and Body" is perhaps the best known of Marvell's religious poems. It has been referred to as a metaphysical poem, a poem of "wit," as Cartesian, and even as Manichean. It is unusual enough in structure and style to justify the labor of epithet bestowed upon it. Its Puritan aspect is far too extreme to be seriously held as a norm of the Puritan sensibility, and no attempt is made here to claim much for the poem in this aspect. The normal sense of combat between flesh and spirit, the viewpoint of St. Paul favored by many Puritans, is carried here to witty extreme, so that "dialogue" between the adversaries is literally impossible. Not adversaries in spiritual combat, they are simply ironically different in some grim joke of the Maker. No spiritual resolution is possible either. As critics have stated, the fact that the Body has the last speech is not significant. Such combatants might go on talking at each other to no

purpose for ever, and that is the sense the poem gives. Only a Puritan
in the metaphysical tradition of wit would think to extend the lines
this far — if Soul (spirit) and the Body (matter) are opposed forces,
of different substance, and totally at war, what then? Not spiritual
combat, but total alienation, intellectual chaos, and despair for both
elements. The hint is that the "secret will" of God has possibly made
things this way. Anything is possible for God in Calvinism. God is
good but He is also arbitrary, although this Calvinist thought usually
drives a pious mind to the belief that God is arbitrarily good. Marvell
presumably believed this, as did most Puritans in the 17th century,
yet is witty and clever enough to explore some of the darker implications and possibilities of the system in this poem.

"The Coronet" is Marvell's poem most obviously on a religious
theme in the 17th century metaphysical and devotional tradition. The
theme was a favorite of courtly poets turning from the world — the
renunciation of worldly and sensuous poetry, expressed in devotion
to mistresses, for devotional verse with some attempt to convert the
purposes of one to the other. For some Elizabethan and Jacobean
courtly poets the transition was all too easy. For Donne it was a
source of tension and triumph, with worldly vigor finally lending its
energy to the powerful religious modalities of the Holy Sonnets and
the "Hymn to God my God." Marvell's poem shows the strain that
the Puritan perspective would place on this manoeuvre from the world
to the spiritual. If the purely spiritual realm of "The Resolved Soul"
is untainted, it also is not of this world. "The Resolved Soul" as a
poem is a model demonstration. "The Coronet" is of human reality,
which always remains tainted by human motive, that is, the effects
of original sin *clothed* by the righteousness of Christ, not "washed
away" by his sacrifice. Hence the "wreaths of Fame and Interest"
must be recognized as permanent and universal by the poet attempting a devotional attitude in verse.

This deep sense of original sin as a permanent stain upon human
nature and severe limitation of man's intellectual and moral nature
and aptitudes was shared by all the Reformed groups in the 16th and
17th centuries. It was not until Dutch Arminianism penetrated the
Anglican Church in the writings of Jeremy Taylor in the Restoration
period that a Reformed position on original sin appeared in English
which paralleled the optimistic Roman Catholic decrees of Trent.[50]
The darker view informs, and gives vitality to, the religious poetry of
Donne and Herbert as well as that of the Puritans. There is spiritual

presumption in devotional activities since the would-be worshipper must always ask two questions – Am I worthy to presume these acts? and, Does God alone or in Christ need them? In the terms of strict Reformation theological discourse the answer to both questions must be an emphatic *no*, for this theology had discarded some of the elaborate Catholic doctrines of grace and transubstantiation which provided a spiritual rationale for devotion. Such acts were works, not faith, and poems, too, would be viewed as works of spiritual presumption. And so they were, at least logically, by Puritans and profound Anglicans. Only some of the sting is removed by recognizing presumption as such, as Marvell does here and Donne in many poems. For the Calvinist-Puritan this presumption is compounded by the doctrines of God's secret will and of election. If a Puritan views abstractly, as Marvell most often does, religious devotion in poems becomes doubly presumptuous, from the viewpoint of man and that of God. The usual deference to the fact of presumption is not enough, as it is in Anglican poetry or even in the poems of less abstract Puritan poets, such as Taylor. It is for this reason that Marvell's one poem of what might be called personal devotion does not finally remain within the ordinary range of such poetry. It begins in this personal area, with references to secular ideals and the difficulty of judging the intentions of the inner self. The heart is found untrustworthy and confirmedly secular in its values. One cannot win the struggle against original sin by exercising devotion or by writing poems of praise:

> Alas I find the Serpent old
> That, twining in his speckled breast,
> About the flow'rs disguis'd does fold,
> With wreaths of Fame and Interest.

So the poet's focus changes drastically at that point. Devotion to and exploration of the human figure of Christ is forsaken almost as it begins. The spiritual poverty of the devotée cuts too depressing a figure to merit going on. Thus the drama shifts to the cosmic plane, where the Puritan is more at ease, where religious man can become *spectator ab extra* of cosmic drama. Christ the Saviour becomes Christ the triumphant God, and irremediable personal sin dramatizes itself externally as Satan. The end of this drama is clear for all time and for all to view. Christ will prevail over Satan and sin, and also, through the drama, some men will be saved. The drama is the primary sign God gives of election of those He wills to be the just. If one takes all this seriously, as the poet is doing here, one wisely waits on the sidelines for the sign in its reference to him, not presuming election by devotional practices and devotional poetry. Devotional practice is withdrawn from on deeper thought, as in the last lines,

> That they, [garlands, devotional poems, devotional attitudes] while Thou on both their Spoils dost tread,
> May crown thy Feet, that could not crown thy Head.

Such is the movement of the poem. The image pattern in which it occurs is not particularly difficult to follow or obscure in provenance, and has often been explicated by critics. The conclusion of the movement is significant, for in it Marvell has explained why he cannot write more devotional verse in the "Donne tradition." And in this strict sense of the term, indeed he never did.

The Mower poems, "The Mower against Gardens," "Damon the Mower," "Mower to the Glo-worms," and "The Mower's Song" are the final poems in the Marvell canon to be viewed in relation to Puritan sensibility. There is no clear Puritan theme, or even one specifically religious, in these poems; they are not religious poems in any intellectual sense. The obvious themes are love and nature, for which reasons they have been read individually as pastorals, or as nature poems, with heavy reference to Neoplatonic traditions and the verbal traditions of Greek and Latin pastoral. In treating this timeless pastoral theme in these poems Marvell shows a decidedly Puritan tilt of sensibility that would not be found in other 16th and 17th century pastorals. If the series is looked upon as a whole, the common themes of the group reveal the Puritan sensibility.

The most general theme is the contrast, at time specific and elsewhere implied, between the unfallen and the fallen states of nature and man. On the one hand are unfallen nature, Damon in pastoral ease, a tamed and toothless snake. This Damon is able to read nature as a mirror of his own thoughts and mind. On the fallen side are the garden, the artificial works of fallen man, Juliana, whose presence brings the sense of "heat" and sin, and, among lesser evils, the speckled snake. Writers on Marvell's pastoral poetry have pointed out much of this, so as a point of structure it need not be pursued. What is interesting from our viewpoint is the portrait of a confused Damon in a chaotic world into which sin has been introduced in the element of sexual desire. In many respects it is the traditional

Christian picture of the Fall, as the picture of the unfallen world is also traditonal, not "Romantic" as some readings have claimed. The Puritan *feeling* in the poems lies in the cumulative effect of this picture, not in any specific intellectual or theological pattern.

In "The Mower Against Gardens" the speaker seems to assign a sinister implication to man's corruption of the state of external nature. Artifical arrangements of flowers and gardens are an absolute corruption of original sin − no latitude is given to man's imagination and intellect in the fallen state. It is assumed he will corrupt further the state of depravity in which he deservedly finds himself. The speaker in "Damon the Mower" experiences grave distress in the thought of Juliana and "hot desires." He would prefer fleeing to some "cool cave" or "gelid Fountain," forbidden to fallen man except in memory. In both these instances the memory of a pure ideal makes accommodation with fallen circumstances impossible. Imagination and tact are not put to work upon fallen nature or the fallen sensual state; instead there is confusion and distress of mind in "The Mower's Song." The clarity and ideality of stanza I, the mind as pure glass or mirror of nature, gives way to chaotic feelings and anger towards fallen nature. Both "Damon the Mower" and "The Mower's Song" end in the mock-murder of nature and suicide. Sexual desire cannot be coped with in a fallen world, the mind disintegrates, and nature disappears in chaos. Such attitudes are certainly Puritan in temperament, in various senses of the word. The Puritan burning within himself against the fallen sense is a central fact of his psychological history. The proper intellectual and theological attitude open to him was of course to wait upon evidences of election and the final judgment of the world by God. Some Puritans chose, as we know, to create their own apocalypse; others chose to create their own hell of despair. Marvell presents this latter alternative in the Mower poems, limited in significance of course by the dramatic situation with its comic overtones. It is a form of the serious play found in all of his poetry. In the Mower poems he wears his Calvinism lightly, as he everywhere wears his learning lightly.

Marvell is a Puritan poet of omission as well as commission throughout his poetry. What he does not write about is as important as what he chooses to give to the public. His praise of Cromwell the Puritan leader is circumspect, to say the least, in the final image of "An Horatian Ode" of a cross forced eternally to be also a vigilant sword of personal accomplishment, since Cromwell's "sign" of election over the hapless Charles is clouded in ambiguity. Sacramental devotion and glorification are avoided completely by Marvell, as, on the other extreme, are non-election and unqualified despair. Marvell is a sceptic in his religious poetry, with a scepticism that makes sense only within the framework of Puritan thought and sensibility. He adds something unique to that sensibility, yet without its presence his unique tone of demure "prayer and praise" would not have been possible.

Edward Taylor

Unlike Andrew Marvell, whose most interesting religious poetry concerned the state of doubt and even at times of intellectual despair, Edward Taylor drew most of his poetic inspiration from the assurance phase of the Calvinist cycle. This is not an unexpected state of affairs in an ordained clergyman; what is really unusual in Taylor is the sustained set of meditations concerning the taking of the Lord's Supper which reveal at the same time the growing state of sanctification in the individual. Most Puritan literature, theological and literary, had emphasized the state of sin leading to awareness of election, calling and justification. Sanctification was discussed at length as a theological reality, especially in Sibbes' *The Bruised Reede.* It remained for Taylor to articulate the full sensibility of sanctification in Calvinism in a work of art, remaining within orthodox Puritan tradition and not giving way to extreme doctrines of the spirit. With this as his true purpose and milieu, it is not surprising that his more traditional Calvinist poem, *Gods Determinations touching his Elect,* treating the themes of election, reprobation and glory in a cosmic setting, is rather wooden in style and feeling, and not considered a major contribution to the poetry of Calvinism. What is of more interest is the fact that the *Meditations* are permeated with a sense of assurance and sanctification, to the point that many poems on the more traditional subjects of sin, election and justifying faith almost seem to be perfunctory and to lack the essential sense of immediacy that such topics need to give the ring of validity. But Taylor preserves the sense of sin in the sanctified about which Sibbes wrote in *Bruised Reede,* a kind of sin that need not have the frightening implications of the pre-election sense of sin found in most other Calvinist poets. Taylor, then, marks a sense of progression in the Calvinist temper, in a rich, well-modulated examination of the sense of sanctification in the just who are yet in the state of sin.

Taylor's choice of topics in the *Meditations* illustrates the range of his interest in the state of sanctification. His groupings are general in both series, and it would be wrong to suggest a rigorous progression through the Calvinist states from sin on one extreme to glorification on the other. There are clusters of poems on most of the themes, and one gets the sense of the overall purpose of the *Meditations* by noticing what states are slighted, as well as where the emphasis is in the chosen themes. Some of the meditations are not specifically Calvinist.

There are few meditations on the great trial theme of the Puritan life – the preliminary sense of sin, despair and worthlessness leading to the sense of one's election and justification. We assume that Taylor experienced these stages as a young man and divinity student. They appear in his prose works and formal confessions of faith. To explain the omission from the poetry we must remember two things, first that these stages had been much written about in Taylor's youth, by the Puritan divines, in *The Faerie Queene*, and elsewhere. Second, and more important, is the fact that the *Meditations* are a product of his years as a clergyman in Westfield, when any personal involvement in the election-assurance problem would have been diminished. *Gods Determinations* is an abstract discussion of these themes, but it would have struck a false note for Taylor to present as drama in personal, existential poems of middle age, anxieties he no longer felt as real.

Allowing for this slighting, all the states of the Calvinist temper are present in the *Meditations*, although, as must again be emphasized, in no systematic order. There are little clusters on the sin-hell theme, on justifying and saving faith, and on the utter worthlessness of the individual sinner before God. These are set among the overwhelmingly positive majority of poems having to do with one aspect or other of sanctification itself, so that the impression is rightly given that the sterner themes are written *about*, within the framework of the sanctified life, as in Sibbes' *Bruised Reede*. This makes them less fiery and interesting than otherwise would be the case, but as we shall see, they repay attention from this point of view.

The positive meditations are capable of two divisions, again of the most general sort and without a real hint of progression. The first, which comprises the great majority of all the poems, are meditations on some aspect of the person of Christ or upon the meaning of the Lord's Supper itself. Christ as mediator of sin, as Lord, as brother, saviour, in his endless typological appearances in the figures of the Old Testament, or in his mystical role as active presence in the human heart, is the subject of these meditations.

As Martz has pointed out in his introduction to the Donald Stanford edition,[51] Taylor shares the ground of the 17th century tradition of meditation with Herbert, Donne, Southwell and the various Catholic traditions behind them. This aspect of Taylor's imagination has been most emphasized in recent criticism. The other, and fewer in terms of numbers, division of the poems is more Puritan in aspect – such as the positive set of poems on the theme of glory and glorification (I, 19, 20, 21, 22; II, 73, 74, 75, 76). As a way of emphasizing the lack of systematic progression it might be pointed out that this glory sequence, which schematically should appear at the end of the second series, is instead mid-way in each of the two series. Also, as a reverse corollary, the few poems on saving faith and assurance, which schematically belong in the early stages of the first series, actually appear as 154 and 155 in series two. There is nothing to be disturbed about in this, as long as the *Meditations* as a whole are viewed as occasional exercises upon the taking of the Lord's Supper, having their plan and limits in the state of the individual meditator, in this case one exploring the full range of the process of sanctification.

The above short survey does raise a question as to how Taylor as a whole should be read. If he is a poet practicing the common 17th century form of meditation in a Calvinist-Puritan framework, both these factors must be accommodated to a reading of the poems. Martz and Stanford did this in their way, with Martz emphasizing the poetic qualities and the meditative tradition behind Taylor in his Foreword, and Stanford giving the biographical background and theological framework in his Introduction. Such division of labor was entirely justified under the unusual situation of Taylor's being a virtually unknown poet to the mid-twentieth century. It would not be justified to continue this method. Even on its own terms the division created needless blind spots, as in Martz's comparison of Taylor to the better-known Catholic and Anglican poets of meditation. This forced him to stress the lack of actual everyday experience in Taylor's work (a charge not fully founded in the texts, as shall be seen). Even were it to be true, it is largely beside the point in the framework of Puritan theology and sensibility. Taylor does make the most of the imaginative possibilities in the God-Christ-man relationship, as do Catholic and Anglican writers. But some of the other themes, such as sin, hell, saving faith and glorification, have their own Puritan locus and peculiar drama which are not primarily of this world − whether this world be the English countryside or the New England wilderness.

We miss the "palpable reality" of Donne in the Puritan treatment of these themes only if we expect it. But knowledge of the Puritan intellectual viewpoint and poetic sensibility should guard us against expecting such worldly direction in Puritan meditation upon these particular themes. Where the theme allows more general range of human interest, as in I, 45, on human frailty in general, the imagery can be earthy enough, and gives a vivid sense of the life of a man living in a small New England frontier town in a region recently claimed from the wilderness and the Indian:

> A Crown of Glory! Oh! I'm base, its true.
>   My Heart's a Swamp, Brake, Thicket vile of Sin.
> My Head's a Bog of Filth; Blood bain'd doth spew
>   Its venom streaks of Poyson O're my Skin.
> . . .
> Becrown'd with Filth! Oh! what vile thing am I?
>   What Cost, and Charge to make mee Meddow ground?
> To drain my Bogs? to lay my Frog-pits dry?
>   To stub up all my brush that doth abound?

Martz's statement that the "*Meditations*, one might think, could as well have been written in England − or in India, or in Egypt" is not true of the above, and many passages like it. They could only have been written in a frontier settlement situation. (Indeed, for what it is worth, large sections of northern New England differ little today from Taylor's descriptions of 17th century Westfield!)

An overemphasis upon "local color" in Taylor's poetry would also be misleading. Its use in various poems will be pointed out because it often enhances the poems and has been ignored by critics anxious to ally Taylor's poetry to European Anglican and Catholic traditions of meditation. The presence of "local color" in Taylor's poetry is inevitable, and not to be attributed to some mysterious American context of experience, the claim made about Puritanism and Puritans in New England by Perry Miller. If we bear in mind again that the Miller thesis deals mainly with social and intellectual trends among the Boston Puritans, not with the imaginative writers or "backwoods groups," some of the possible confusion clears itself up. Also it is a critical fact that Taylor has not been included in the American theories of scholars in American Civilization. Martz and Stanford emphasized the general 17th century religious nature of his poetry and the peculiar Puritan aspect, ignoring any special American thesis in their ground-breaking book.[52] Miller and other charters of the New England mind are willing to exempt the English-born Puritans and dwellers in the Connecticut valley from their thesis on the movement from Puritanism to rationalism,[53] and of course Taylor falls into both groups. In an important recent book which makes sweeping claims for the uniqueness and unity of major American poetry, Waggoner exempts Taylor to a large degree on the grounds of his English Puritanism and narrowness.[54] For all these reasons Taylor belongs to the tradition we have studying in this book. For those who wish to see a complete early cleavage between English and American Puritanism, the fact that Isaac Watts wrote a preface to a book by Jonathan Edwards, or that Emily Dickinson would naturally be familiar with both old and New England Puritan writings through her family heritage, are facts to be remembered.

One other mistake has recently come into view concerning Taylor's poetry. Unlike the problems raised by influence or American theories, the result of over-generalized thinking, this newer problem arises from false application of the minutiae of Puritan tradition. The point of view in this chapter on Taylor is that he drew most of his religious inspiration from the assurance phase of the Calvinist cycle. The *Meditations* are permeated with a sense of assurance and sanctification. The sense of sin is that in the sanctified, about which Sibbes wrote so eloquently in the *Bruised Reede*. The latest confusion about the nature of the *Meditations* arises from false application of Pettit's recent book on preparation in Puritan tradition, mentioned in the introduction to this section. Pettit's argument, applied to the theologians of 17th century New England, is irrefutable. He examined the two types of preparation, the first occurring before election in an attempt to induce the proper state for reception of grace and acknowledgement of election, the second the preparation of the elect, amounting to meditations within the state of sanctification. Some critics have tried to see both types of preparation at work in Taylor's poetry, and assign the seeming lack of organization in the *Meditations* to the general state of confusion in Puritan thought on the issue in Taylor's time. In his prose and in an overarching poem such as *Gods Determinations* Taylor certainly shows awareness of the first type of preparation and the need to struggle with the sin-state and despair of the non-elect, or, more accurately, pre-elect. He no doubt had shared the common Puritan experiences given in our previous section, and was aware of the remedy of "preparation" brilliantly analysed by Pettit. But the *Meditations* are a product of his years as a confirmed believer and clergyman, after any personal struggle with the election-assurance problem would have been long settled. The *Meditations* are not systematically consistent according to formal logic. The poems do not always conform to the curve of the formal pattern, though the formal pattern is the basic structure of the poems. If we take them for what they obviously are, a chronicle of the moods of the sanctified state in relationship to fundamental Puritan doctrines, biblical tropes, and above all else, the Lord's Supper, not as a unified formal tract, understanding them will not present insuperable difficulties for readers attuned to the various aspects of the Calvinist temper in poetry, the essential aim of this study.

Taylor's *Meditations,* then, are generally Christian with specific Puritan aspects. Many could have been written by any 17th century divine, such as the long series on Old Testament typology of Christ. These are among the most boring and perfunctory of all the poems. Another long series on the person and attributes of Christ, and on the individual soul in relation to Christ, are also generally Protestant Christian in cast with a scattering of Puritan doctrines. We could mistake some of them for Herbert but none for Crashaw. The Puritan doctrines are not their point, only a habitual instinct in casual references to saints, election, and the like. In other words if we read the entire set of meditations on Christ the Puritan note is unmistakable even though many individual poems might have been written by any Reformed 17th century Christian.

For the dicussion of Taylor in this chapter the poems of greatest interest are the ones with a specifically Calvinist cast. These are scattered at large among the more than three hundred poems in the two series. The fact that they appear in this manner rather than in a logical one has been mentioned above, with some reason given. Perhaps a more detailed explanation is appropriate now, as well as some general comments on Taylor's style, as prelude to analysis of the specifically Calvinist poems. It was pointed out that Taylor wrote meditations from within the sanctified state. He is not following a logical progression through sin-state, election, justification, sanctification and glorification. From the state of sanctification he occasionally looks backward to the earlier states, or forward to glory, but all the poems are written *in* the assurance state and most of them – on typology, Christ and the sacraments – are about it. The external facts easily account for this situation. The *Meditations* are closely allied to sermons and communion services taking their start in a passage from Scripture. They are private homilies following the church year, not the record of a soul in crisis or mere theological tracts. They are *ad hoc* in nature. A Puritan substratum pervades all of them, that is, the sense of the whole is overwhelmingly Puritan. But the strikingly Puritan attitudes occur only in subsets on various topics, which we will get onto shortly. It is understandable that these subsets occur at random over the course of all the poems, not concentrated in a particular part for logical reasons. The poems do not exist as a tract in Calvinist-Puritan doctrine. Yet the number of central Calvinist doctrines and attitudes canvassed in the subsets is significant.

On a different level, a similar mixture of Puritan style with other styles pervades the poems. A few poems are unmistakably "metaphysical" with reference or resemblance to Donne and Herbert. In Series I "The Experience" and "The Return" are of this order and in Series II number 18, "We have an Altar." These poems may strike critics as the product of Donne or Herbert in burlap, but in any event these direct metaphysical imitations are not very interesting or where Taylor's strength as a poet really lies. His frequent mention of "inadequacy" with words, as in II, 164, "Words are Dear Lord, notes insignificant," is also often a formal convention that does not aid the real strength of his poetry. In other poems his sense of words and language is more interesting and genuine, reflecting the deep Puritan distrust of ornament in dealing with sacred things. This passage in II, 36, is a fine example:

> My Metaphors are but dull Tacklings tag'd
>   With ragged Non-sense. Can such draw to thee
> My stund affections all with Cinders clag'd,
>   If thy bright beaming headship touch not mee?

The larger issue raised by this point of view can be seen in II, 54, "Untun'de, my Lord. My Cankard brassy wire's unfit to harp thee Musick." Here the distrust widens to include all the powers of the self. It is an attitude generated by Calvinist theology which we will see again in Watts and Cowper, and have seen in Marvell. Some critics have leaped to the conclusion that Calvinism and poetry are incompatible, since this problem is lodged at its center. So they should be, perhaps, in a world of pure theory and logic. Yet poets will be poets, and it is of formal and aesthetic interest to see how poets handled the problem, since historically in fact there have been Calvinist-Puritan poets, good and bad. (Excluded here is the question whether other types of poems may be greater or better, or Johnson's remark that religious poetry must be inferior because of paucity of topics. This question will be raised in the introduction to the section on the 18th century, a time when other types of poems began seriously to crowd out the religious.)

The overall style of Taylor's poetry is clearly Puritan and un-mistakably his own, despite the few close imitations of other meta-physical poetry. His vision and imagery derives from the language of Scripture on the whole, his wilderness is more often the biblical figure than his own surroundings, as others have noticed. Yet this point has been subject to exaggeration, to force an easy contrast with Donne and Herbert. His worst lapses in taste occur where he is imitating too closely his metaphysical predecessors, as in II, 18:

> Mine Heart's a Park or Chase of sins: Mine Head
> 'S a Bowling Alley. Sins play Ninehole here.
> Phansy's a Green: sin Barly breaks in't led.
>   Judgment's a pingle. Blindeman's Buff's plaid there.
>   Sin playes at Coursey Parke within my Minde.
>   My Wills a Walke in which it aires what's blinde.

At other times he can relate a Puritan religious idea or experience quite admirably to the world around him. There is no intention here to match one false estimate with another. Taylor's poetry is not riotously sensuous nor a feast for eye and ear. It is mainly abstract and intellectual in the Puritan grain, and only sensuous in the specific sense when using the time-honored convention of the Canticles in late meditations in Series II. These are of little interest in themselves or as poetry. More adequate and authentic are the references to swamp, bog and frog-pit in I, 45, mentioned previously, or to a "Hive of Hornets" in I, 40, to "Prisoners . . . Padling in their Canoes" in II, 78, or an entire stanza in II, 159, wherein a historic English visual scene is nicely juxtaposed to another from the actual wilderness where Taylor lived and wrote:

> He'l feast us now with such a feast as made
>   George Nevills Feast although prodigeous 't were
> With dainties, things all fat and . . . trade

Was but like th'indian broths of Garbag'd deer
With which the Netop entertain his guests
When almost starved, yea welcome Sir, its our Mess.

Taylor's style at its best is a successful blending of Puritan abstraction and biblical language with the actual visual world which any true poet must use. As a Puritan he is wary of this world's beauty, and so uses it sparingly, but to great effect, never lapsing into catalogues of things for their own sake. His worst lapses, and they are few, are close imitations of English metaphysical poets, from whom he no doubt learned a great deal about writing poetry, and perhaps the interest in writing poetry, but from whom he also differed markedly in theology and cultural milieu.[55]

The mixture of styles in Taylor's fundamentally Puritan poetry is a symptom of the similar mixture of themes. In both series there is a Calvinist-Puritan substratum but not logical or theological order, as in *Gods Determinations*, or Wigglesworth's *Day of Doom*. The Calvinism is a substratum because the theology is assumed. For this reason the actual majority of poems is not particularly Calvinist except for casual imagery. The poems on typology, on the nature of Christ, on the Canticles and personal prayer were mentioned above as works that might have been written by any 17th century Reformed Christian. If we removed the casual Calvinist imagery not central to their meaning, identification of them individually as by a New England Calvinist would be impossible.[56] But an ample minority of the poems are specifically Calvinist-Puritan, in subsets that are sprinkled throughout the entire body of both Series. These provide our major interest for analysis of Taylor as a Puritan poet. A brief outline of their nature will help to make their place in the *Meditations* clear, since their occurrence is not systematic.

Taylor writes of the sin-state a very few times (I, 26, 39, 40; II, 25, 77). The reason for this slighting was mentioned above – he writes of the sin-state in the justified, who cannot be allowed to forget that they are yet sinners. The preparation is not pre-election, as some have thought. He also writes sparingly of justifying faith (I, 44; II, 154, 155). That these poems are doctrinal reminders and not dramatic material is easily proven by their positions in the Series, towards the end in each case. Had the sin-state or justification been serious problems for Taylor these would have been conceived as meditation preparatory to election, logically proceeding the others. He is not being illogical here, but rather, like Sibbes in *Bruised Reede*, reminding the just and sanctified of their previous condition. In the spirit of these meditations we expect and get more on glorification than on the earlier stages. There are three extended series on this theme (I, 19–22; II, 73–76, 99–101, 158). The sanctified state looks towards the glorified as the next step in Puritan thought, as we have seen in Puritanism over and over again. Another long series (II, 80–82, 104–111) concerns sacramental meditation proper, on taking the Lord's Supper. These are written within the Puritan idea of sanctification, the growth in spiritual life of the sanctified man by contemplation of his closeness to the Lord through the sacrament. Taylor sometimes uses the term "sanctifying grace" in reference to this state, and many times the word "spiritual" in referring to the nature of the Supper and its effect upon communicants. These are among the most beautiful poems in the *Meditations*. In a handful of others there is a Puritan ambience in the language, brought about by the use of the word "spiritual" and others associated with it. I call this "ambience" because doctrine is not involved so much as a state of mind, an exhilaration also found in Spenser, Milton, Bunyan, Baxter and Edwards. It is the Puritan state of "joy," which, as we shall see, was later partly naturalized by Coleridge and Wordsworth. It is best simply to quote, not analyse, these passages, since they are greater than the poems in which they occur and more important for detecting the inter-Puritan connections described in this book:

> Oh! wash mee, Lord, in this Choice Fountain, White
>   That I may enter, and not sully here
> Thy Church, whose floore is pav'de with Graces bright
>   And hold Church fellowship with Saints most cleare.
>   My voice all sweet, with their melodious layes
>   Shall make sweet Musick blossom'd with thy praise. (II, 26)
> All fulness is in thee my Lord, and Christ
>   The fulness of all Excellence is thine.
> All's palac'de in thy person, and bespic'de.
>   All Kinds, and Quantities of't in thee shine.
>   The Fulness of the Godhead in respect
>   Unto the Manhood's in thy person kept.   (II, 46)
>   At Gods right Hand thou sits enthroned there.
>   The Highest Throne in brightest glory thou
>   Enjoyest. Saints, and Angels 'fore thee bow.
> Come down, bright Angells, Now I claim my place.
>   My nature hath more Honour due, than yours:
> Mine is Enthron'de at Gods Right-Hand, through Grace.   (II, 72)

The resemblance to similar passages in the other Puritan poets and prose writers is unmistakable, the joy of the saints contemplating the end of the Puritan journey and its final reward.

Taylor also devotes a few Meditations to straight Puritan doctrine. He contemplates the New Covenant, as do all Puritans (II, 78, 102, 103); strict sacramental doctrine (II, 108); the Church Militant (II, 135); Grace (II, 49); the power and majesty of God (II, 40, 42, 48); Christ as warrior-king (II, 159). Over a span of more than three hundred poems these doctrinal excursions are not excessive; indeed, though not providing the most inspirational themes or best poems, they are quite natural reminders, to Taylor and to us, of the source of the freer and more lovely meditations on personal themes. There was no likelihood of straying into idiosyncracy or heresy in Taylor, even though as true poet he spoke most often with his own voice. He viewed the world from his original sensibility, but was also the Puritan pastor of Westfield. In II, 68 he comes closest to the art of mental prayer in the continental sense. In that poem the spiritual, unseen world is the subject, where the actual sun is contrasted to the spiritual light of the unseen world. The poem is not tied to continental Catholic theology or mysticism, of course, so that the effect of the spirituality in it strikes as a dim precursor of Coleridge, Cowper and Wordsworth again. As with the Puritan ambience in the other poems cited above, quotation rather than analysis should make this aspect manifest:

> The Spirituall World, this world doth, Lord out vie:
>   Its Skie this Chrystall Lanthorn doth orematch.
> Its Sun, thou Art, that in'ts bright Canopy
>   Outshines that Candle, Darkness doth dispatch.
>   Thy Crystall Globe of Glorious Sunshine furld
>   Light, Life and heate in't Sundayeth the World.
>
>   Thy Shine makes Stars, Moons, Sunlight darkness thick.
>   Thou art the Sun of Heavens bright light rose in
>   The Heavenly Orbs. And Heavens blesst glories spring.
>
> How shall my Soule (Such thoughts Enravish mee)
>   Under the Canopy of this Day
> Imparadisde, Lightend and Livend bee
>   Bathd in this Sun Shine 'mong bright Angells play
>   And with them strive in sweetest tunes expresst
>   Which can thy glorious praises sing out best.   (II, 68 A)

Our purpose in the remainder of this chapter is to analyse the best poems of meditation which are closely Puritan in scope, on the sin-state, justification, glorification and the taking of the Lord's Supper. A few words will be said about the strictly dogmatic poems — on the Covenant, mode of Christ's presence in the sacrament, Calvinist doctrine of grace — the poems we may call "rhymed theology" which are not rich as poetry and largely exist as statement. They merely recall the basic theology analysed in Section I of this book.

The dogmatic poems or "rhymed theology" place Taylor solidly within Calvinist tradition. The one on sacramental doctrine (II, 108) is squarely based upon Calvin's own doctrine. So is II, 59, on the doctrine of grace, and the series on the power and majesty of God. The poems on the Church Militant and Christ as warrior-king have the combative imagery we saw in Preston and Perkins, the breastplate, armor, swords, of Puritanism nascent in struggle with the Establishment. For Taylor in the next century these are items of contemplation, fixed relations in his mind, place and time. The New Covenant series (II, 78, 102, 103) firmly adheres to the central doctrine which the Puritan divines drew from Calvin's theories. It was a rationale for Protestant breakaway from Rome and for reform, as well as the substitute for Roman authority and tradition. God had chosen a new people, had given them clearly revealed truth free from the corruptions of centuries, and a new Church. The Covenant is the doctrine of Puritan collective assurance, making battle with the Establishment possible and also the endurance of trials in a new wilderness. Taylor celebrates these points in the usual fashion. Since these theological poems are not very exciting poetry, an analysis of one will do for all. In II, 108, on sacramental doctrine, Taylor first sweeps aside the "false" doctrines of Christ's presence in the Lord's Supper: ubiquity, transubstantiation, consubstantiation. In our first section we saw how often the Puritan divines stressed Christ's place in heaven, with frequent citation of the phrase "Abba Father" as proof. Here is Taylor on this:

> The Bread and Wine true Doctrine teach for faith
>   (True Consequence from Truth will never ly)
> Their Adjuncts teach Christs humane nature hath
>   A certain place and not Ubiquity.

He is just as sure of himself, if a little coarse, on the Catholic and Lutheran alternatives. The commonplace Reformation polemic, with its nice tidbit, "The Pope's a whore," need not be quoted here. More interesting is his explanation of the true doctrine, the "spiritual" presence. He is following Calvin, but as we have found out, this was one of the most obscure points in Calvin's theology, one he constantly quarrelled about with other reformers. It is helpful to juxtapose Taylor's text with the lucid explanation of Calvin's doctrine by François Wendel cited in a note in the previous section:

> These Adjuncts shew this feast is ray'd in ware
>   Of Holiness enlin'de with honours Shine.
> Its Sabbath Entertainment, spirituall fare.
>   Its Churches banquet, Spirituall Bread and Wine.
> It is the Signet of the Kings right hande,
>   Seale to the Covenant of Grace Gods bande.

Wendell has written, "According to Calvin, the spiritual reality of the body and blood of Christ does not identify itself with the material elements nor find itself in any way included in them. It is given at the same time. . . . In fact, though Calvin always rejected the transfusion of the natural substance of the body of Christ, he did affirm, on the other hand, the communication by faith of the Christ and his benefits, considered as the spiritual substance of the body of Christ in the Supper. . . . Calvin . . . put the Christ and the elements separately into direct contact with the believer. . . . The Eucharist, then, is a means of sanctification for the elect who are already incorporated in Christ. It serves to complete or to double the action of the Word, with the aid of material or corporeal means appropriate to our frailty." This is as lucid an explanation of the Calvinist doctrine of spiritual presence as we are ever likely to get, and whatever one thinks of the "logic" of the doctrine, it is clear that Taylor accepts it and has the right feel for it. His plain lines of explanation would not detain us for a moment were it not for the crucial factor underlying them, that each sacramental act is a coming together of words, elements, the believer, and the spiritual presence of Christ. Thus this Puritan dogma provides the justification for sacramental meditation as part of the communion act, and is the bedrock of the poetically successful personal meditations on the Lord's Supper which provide so many of the very best of Taylor's personal religious poems.

In this analysis and commentary upon the very best poems of spiritual life in Taylor the Puritan process of regeneration, explained in Section I of this book and certainly known to Taylor, will be adopted for the sake of structure, even though there is a certain artificiality in doing so for Taylor. These poems are sprinkled among the rest, not in any logical order. As also has been stated above, the earlier phases of the process probably carried little conviction for Taylor at the time of writing the *Meditations*. His greatest ardors go to meditations of Christ, the sanctified state, and glorification, the last present for Christ and in the future for the saints. Nevertheless the following order provides a reasonable progression through Taylor's best Calvinist-Puritan poems. There are enough of these poems, and some the finest in both series, to offset the commonplace nature of the typological meditations and others on standard topics indistinguishable from their appearance in any meditative poetry of the 17th century. The sense of sin and the sin-state occur in I, 26, 39, 40; II, 25, 77. It is not the urgent sense of Bunyan's pilgrim, nor does it carry with it the despair of some Puritans unable to overcome it. The tone and content of these poems parallel Sibbes and a host of other justified sinners. Justifying faith, a *fait accompli* in the *Meditations*, receives its due importance in I, 44 and II, 154, 155. The sacramental meditations proper, which form the heart of Series II and the best poems by Taylor, flow from the sanctified soul contemplating the sacramental act of the Lord's Supper. In them we find the center of Taylor's heart and mind. He must look backward to sin, and forward to glory, but his deep and rich spiritual life lies in quotidian practice of this, for him, beloved ordinance of God and the Church. In the Calvinist reenactment of the spiritual presence of Christ, Taylor himself came to experience the paradise within for which all Puritans deeply yearned. His meditations on glorification are also extensive and authentic, both Christ's glory and the future glory of the saints. Glory for the earthly saint was by nature not a present state, rather one to be contemplated as in Baxter's *Saints Rest* and the last pages of Bunyan's pilgrimages. The number of poems on glory is almost as long as on sacramental meditations. It will not be necessary to comment on each poem in these two primary Puritan categories of Taylor, since there is such abundance. The best artistically will be singled out for discussion.

After reading the works of Preston, Perkins, Sibbes or Edwards on the sin-state, election and reprobation, the subtle poems of Marvell on self-doubt and assurance, or the poignant despairs of Cowper and the defiant ones of Byron, Taylor's meditations on sin, election and justification are not likely to strike the reader as powerful inspirational poetry. Yet they are not merely perfunctory. Taylor knew Calvinist-Puritan tradition, had had his conversion experiences in early life,[57] and was aware that in Calvinist thought justification and sanctification could become confused with human hubris, and that sinfulness exists in the just. It is well to have appropriate reminders of all this even among the most saintly of meditations on Christ, typology and the Lord's Supper. These few poems, then, are not only theologically sound and proper in the sacramental meditations; everything about them, including their restraint, paucity and placement in both Series, testify to the authenticity of Taylor's poetry and to the Puritan wellsprings of his urge to write.

The five poems concerning the sin-state (I, 26, 39, 40; II, 25, 77) follow a definite pattern. Each begins with self-accusation and general sense of sinfulness. The sins are not particularized, though often presented in vivid metaphor, the extremity of which has been deplored as lacking decorum by some critics. We may presume that Taylor has both the general sense of sin in man's weakened will and particular failings in mind, though about the latter he is more reticent than some of the Puritan diarists. "Its all defild, unbiasst too by Sin" (I, 26.11); "Undoe my Sin I did, undoing mee./ My Sins are greate, and grieveous ones" (I, 26.16–17); "My Sin! my Sin! My God, these Cursed Dregs" (I, 39.1); "Was ever Heart like mine? A sty of Filth, a Trough of Washing-Swill" (I, 40.2–3). Examples could be multiplied from every one of this set of poems. The strong language in these poems has led some to believe that Taylor is genuinely doubting his election and justification in *Preparatory Meditations*. There is only one line giving evidence supporting this assumption, and that is quickly retracted by the following line:

I wonder, split I don't upon Despare.
Its grace's wonder that I wrack not so. (I, 40.45–46)

This mention of despair does recall the Cambridge suicides, the glee of the Lancashire Catholics, the Red Cross Knight at a point in I, ix, and the attitude of Marvell. But it is immediately qualified and thence removed. Taylor's language is so vivid and his feelings so genuine that these poems have been confused with the sense of sin and despair which precede effectual calling. Thus it must again be stressed that these are sacramental meditations, written from within the growing state of Puritan sanctification. Even if we must grant a certain ambiguity in the use of the sacraments in Calvinism (in relation to election and justification), the general consensus of orthodox Puritanism held that the Lord's Supper was not an empty sign, rather a continual fortification for the elect and justified, granting freely that these elect remained sinners in this life. As Sibbes put the matter, one evidence of the state of sanctification is the continual presence of both repentance and sin in the just. A too easy conscience is a dangerous sign. But this is not the same idea as viewing individual sins as signs of damnation or non-election, or as capable of producing damnation in the effectually called. Taylor was an orthodox Puritan who could tread this fine line. His individuality is in the remarkable range of devotion he brings to the state of sanctification and to contemplation of the Lord's Supper. Some critics, not appreciating this intricacy, have connected Taylor's poems on sin and lack of assurance too closely to other traditions, forms of Arminianism in which any actual sin is potential damnation. All the sin poems end on a positive note, as grace, pardon, faith in Christ overcome the sense of sinfulness. In I, 26 the turning point is in the middle, at line 19. In I, 40 it comes much later, and softer, at line 49:

> Hope's Day-peep dawns hence through this chinck. Christs name
> Propitiation is for sins.

There is considerable variation among the others in this group, but not one without the turning to hope and positive themes. Taylor is too firm a Puritan believer to turn back to the original sin-state and unbelief after proceeding so far on the scale of salvation as to have the gift for continual sacramental meditation in assured yet humble sanctification. Taylor walks this high wire with Baxter, Sibbes, Bunyan and others. It is a strange and successful act in a few of these genuine and thoroughly tried Puritan saints. It has been explained invidiously many times, and in sympathetic yet foreign terminology by some good readers of poetry. The way to understand what goes on here is to read Calvin, the English Puritans, and the meditative Puritans in a continuum, as in this study.

In one poem of accusation there does seem to be some doubt about Taylor's state of mind. In II, 77 he may have tripped off the high wire temporarily, though the problem may be in following the metaphor of the pit to its extremes. He first speaks of a sense of assurance (we may call this election, not original innocence in which no Puritan believed) once held:

> I once sat singing on the Summit high
> 'Mong the Celestiall Coire in Musick Sweet. ...

The burden of the poem in images reminiscent of parts of *Pilgrim's Progress* expresses loss of grace and a pit of sin destitute of God's presence. Though election is not mentioned, he may be hinting at temporary loss of effectual calling. The turning point does not come until the last stanza, and the means is not the usual mild mediations of the other poems but irresistible grace given in the image of "the golden Chain of Grace," recalling Perkins' famous work on effectual calling of 1595.[58] This poem is dated 1707, rather late for a complete collapse of faith. One can only speculate that Taylor in this meditation is recalling a very early experience before his arrival in New England and conversion, or is being carried away by a metaphor, or suffering temporary lapse. There is no other poem in either series on sin, justification, grace or faith quite like this one in its intensity and perilous closeness to relapse, however temporary and despite the final rally. His poems on justification and faith are all quite contained, if strong, supporters of doctrine, as we now shall see.

The poems on faith and justification occur at I, 44 and II, 154, 155. These poems differ from the "doctrinal" ones in that the theology is affirmed, not argued. In attitude they are much like the poems on the sin-state (except possibly II, 77), written within the Calvinist idea of affirmation and the state of sanctification. The theology of "justification by faith" of Calvinism is an assumption of these poems. That is, justification arises by faith in Christ, not by any merit or works of the individual. In I, 44 Taylor writes of "Adherent, and Inherent Righteousness," assuming that the inherent is in Christ, the adherent in those who are clothed with His righteousness and therefore have saving faith. This point is more forcefully put later in the poem:

A Crown of Righteousness, a Righteous Head,
    Oh naughty man! my brain pan turrit is
Where Swallows build, and hatch: Sins black and red.

Sinful man deserves neither faith nor righteousness, yet is confident of both through justification by the merits of Christ. Taylor is so sure of these facts that celebration, not argument, is the final note of this poem. "Oh! Happy me, if thou wilt Crown me thus." "Thy Glory bring I tuckt up in my Songe." Happy is the man of such confidence in his faith and in Christ's grace. A poem such as this asserts the fundamental Calvinist-Puritan basis of Taylor's religion whence he goes on to write the poems for which he is more justly famous as an artist. Justifying faith is again celebrated in II, 154. There are echoes of Puritan works on this subject in "Golden twist" and "Glorious Breast plate," placing the theology implicit in the poem firmly in

Puritan tradition.[58] In the affirmations of this poem, so necessary to maintain the sense of justification which allows the process of sanctification to proceed, little attention is given to the difficult theoretical questions relating to faith and grace:

> Faith doth ore shine all other Grace set in
>   The Soule that Cabbinet of Grace up fild
> As far as doth the Shining Sun in 'ts run. . . .

Is faith another grace, only preeminently so? What is the cause of faith in one man and lack of faith in another? If God is all powerful, and Christ all merciful, man sinful and weak, then there must be "prevenient grace." It is not that Taylor was unaware of such issues, but that the poem is an affirmation of faith which justifies, it is the recording of a particular experience. Faith and grace together "seal(s) up fast" the soul to Christ and God. The "sealing of the spirit" was of course a favorite term of Calvin and of Puritans. One passage seems to place this doctrine in the more general Augustinian pattern advocated by Scheick, the mysterious unity of human intellect and will through the Word with God:

> Faith is the Curious Girdle that ties to
>   The King of Glory, glorifide with Grace
> The bundled beams of th'Sun, Gods Son that flow
>   In graces Sunshine on the Soul apace. . . .

The special Puritan doctrines of justification and faith work well in this poem with the general affirmations of the Augustinian tradition influential upon Calvin and all Puritan thought.

Taylor's final meditation upon justification by faith is more openly doctrinal than the others. The Scripture passage on faith and reprobation upon which Meditation 155 takes its start doubtless accounts for this, but there are other reasons. This is one of the final poems in Series II, most of which have assumed and explored the sanctified state. In this poem the poet pulls up short, to remind himself of the sound Calvinist doctrine which allows the moods of sanctification to have the ring of validity. Too long a dwelling in Beulah or Zion may make one too much at ease; the need to return to "saving faith," to test election and justification again, becomes crucial:

> Thou bidst me try if I be in the Faith,
>   For Christ's in me if I bee'nt Reprobate.
> A Reprobate my Lord, let not this come
>   On mee to be the burden of the Song.

Sacramental rites and meditations depend upon justifying faith, and to have assurance of this faith is to be effectually called (one of the elect). In a blunt yet hardy passage Taylor reminds himself of this bedrock of Calvinist-Puritan belief:

It [justifying faith] is the Grace of Grace begracing all.
  Usefull for Grace, for Sacraments and Prayer.
Religion is without it an empty Call
  And Zeale without it is a fruitless Care.
  Preaching without it's as a Magpies Chatter
And as a little tittle tattles Clatter.
Prayer without Faith is but as prittle pratle.
  Fasts and Thanksgiving are but barren things
And Sacraments without it but as rattles. . . .

His sweetest meditations and best poems are upon sacrament, prayer, preaching, calling and the like, linking this Puritan "saint" with the pious and holy of other traditions. These meditations are often better poems, and have had larger appeal than the Puritan ones to many readers of today, for obvious reasons. Yet when Taylor in the last stanza appeals "Lord give me Saving Faith," he is speaking within a tradition that only a Calvinist-Puritan might fully experience and understand. It is the premise making the sacramental meditations possible; otherwise they only could be empty signs not conveying the presence of Christ or the possibility of real devotion.

It remains nevertheless the overwhelming fact of most readers' experience of Taylor that the sacramental meditations proper (II, 80, 81, 82, 104, 105, 106, 107–111) and the general Christological meditations which are an extension of them, are the center of Taylor's poetry and its greatest strength. Scheick is correct to a point in linking these poems to the Augustinian tradition of Word, word, intellect, will, and *Imago Dei*. The theme of love is foremost in the sacramental and Christological meditations. The goal may well be the perception of harmony between Scripture, nature and reason. This regenerative process should help to produce in the hearts of the elect a sense of harmony of all things. As Scheick puts it, "with his will thus graciously turned, the saint's entire being, body and soul, again mirrors the divine image." And further, "In his thoughts, words and works – but particularly in his poetic words – [Taylor] strove to discern a clue to the moral state of his soul and to offer his whole being, his whole self, to God through the love of his heart."[59] There is an ambience, as Scheick implies in these words, connecting Taylor's poetry with poets of meditation of other traditions. But there is a qualification in this eternal drive of the religious spirit in Taylor by virtue of his being a Calvinist. The human soul in this life can never fully mirror the divine image, since justified man is only clothed with righteousness. Puritan thought is more pessimistic than other Christian traditions on this point of the sanctified fully coming to know God. But it is more positive in another sense. In Catholic and high Anglican tradition only those of special sanctity proceed along the *scala perfectionis*. Puritanism opened the way from sin-state to glorification for all, at least potentially. The final thrust of meditation on Christ in the Lord's Supper for a convinced Puritan cannot be "to discern a clue to the moral state of his soul," for such matters fall earlier in the cycle, on effectual calling and election. Taylor allowed into his imaginative life more expansion than most Calvinists, and this gives to his poetry a visual sense of closer contact with Christ than is found in most of the preachers of the Word who remained on the abstract level for the most part. But he could never forget that Calvinist-Puritan theology does not allow the sanctified to have final intimacy, or that such intimacy in other traditions is often painfully near perdition. Thus the Puritan is allowed to know less while also assured of a final election and justification. This state is not to be taken as hubris or easy assurance, so sacramental meditation finds its special place in Puritan devotion. It is a subtle point which has suffered often from simplification in literary studies. In Taylor's meditations on the Lord's Supper and Christ such difficulty was inevitably to appear, for not only does he seem to think in the images of non-Puritan visual tradition in some respects rather than in the *logos*-centered strictly verbal abstract ones of the divines; beyond that, as slightly sketched above, Puritan tradition did have real difficulty in relating the sacraments to election and justification by faith. Coleridge was to see this difficulty much later, in his prose writings and marginalia, while Emily Dickinson was to consider the subject absurd, at least in a surface way, yet making of it compelling poetry. More about them in later sections of this book. Taylor was one of the few Puritans immersing himself in sacramental meditation and exhibiting the state of sanctification throughout most of his work. To understand what he was doing, being Puritan and general Christian and true to both, an understanding of his meditations in the light of Puritan sacramental doctrine is required. Most of this can be accomplished while looking at individual poems after a few abstract statements set the focus.

Taylor was not a mystic, as were some 16th and 17th century Catholic and Anglican poets (though the greatest, Donne and Herbert, were not either), and there is no excuse for the tendency to relate or compare him too closely with Anglican and Catholic piety, as some critics have done. He held the general Puritan view of isolation in this world for the saint, but not avoidance of it, as his calling in the ministry attests. He did not attempt to bridge the gulf between the natural and the supernatural completely, as does the mystic who denies the natural world and renounces the natural man. He accepted the restless and troubled role even for the saint, as depicted in Sibbes' *Bruised Reede* and other works of Puritan piety and sanctification. Meditation on Christ and the Supper provided some bond between the natural and the supernatural, and occasional glimpses of the paradise within, though never full possession of it in this life. Contemplation of election, or even of justification, if carried on too long or too scrupulously, led many good Puritans to the abyss or over it. It was for that reason that Calvin and the Puritans placed such great value on the sacraments or "ordinances," for these were Christ's own promises of aid in time of temptation and mental distress. What distinguishes Taylor from other Puritan contemplatives is the amount of real practical attention he gave to sacramental meditation, which most other Puritan divines, with exceptions like Bayly or Sibbes, tended to assent to in the abstract without much experiential sense of the reality. This is a weakness in Puritan devotion for which Taylor provided the strongest counterforce. He is at ease with the eternal paradise and other such common tropes of hope and union, but in a Puritan context almost uniquely his own. He did not deny election, justification, the radical difference between inner and outer world, between this world and the next, or the powers of sin. These thoughts occur in his "reminder" poems that we have looked at thus far, the doctrinal and other Calvinist poems showing continual awareness of his tradition. In the sacramental and Christological meditations he is more able to mingle Puritan doctrine with his own deep piety, which some critics have felt is so deep as not to be Puritan except for surface points. The real question is this one — how does Taylor manage to unite the visual and contemplative range of meditation on Christ and the Supper with his firm belief in the Calvinist-Puritan views on the sin-state, election, calling, justification?

For Calvin and the Puritans the sacraments of Baptism and the Lord's Supper are seals and signs of the more essential doctrines of election, calling and justification. Instituted by Christ, they must have deep meaning in the Christian life. They must not be viewed as mere tokens and empty symbols. As seals they help to preserve the faith of the elect in a special bond with Christ; as signs they continually renew Christ's presence, his spiritual presence that is, in the Supper according to Calvin's definition. Taylor allowed himself more contemplation of the spiritual presence than most other Puritans, and also contemplation of the figure of Christ under many aspects that we have come to associate with other Christian traditions. He is not totally alone as a "spiritual Puritan," since this study has shown that a rigid distinction between Puritan *logos* and other Christian *mythos* is artificial in Puritan practice. Taylor certainly is one of the stronger practitioners of *mythos* and the visual among creative Puritan writers. His focus has shifted from election and justification in the sacramental poems to sanctification of the individual and glorification of Christ. Yet the meditations are set within Puritan theology, as when he refers, in several poems, to the fact that such sanctified joys are only for the elect. At the same time he shares as far as is possible in the general Christian piety of the Lord's Supper, even using the term "sanctifying Grace" in one poem (II, 104, line 70), a term having a Catholic theological ring for most modern readers.[60] The reminders of Puritan doctrinal basis are consistent throughout the sacramental poems, and his imagination, certainly vivid in its way, is restrained by Counter Reformation standards. He speaks of Christ's body and blood as redemptive many times, nor does the repulsive (to some) idea of Christ's blood sacrifice repulse him as he contemplates the ceremony of bread and wine. But he does not revive the passion in the lurid details of his Catholic continental contemporaries. The differences, what he leaves out of his meditations, are as crucial to his Puritan origin and imagination as the occasional positive allusions to doctrines, such as that only the elect can be sanctified through the sacraments and meditation. These interesting points, or potential conflicts if you will, that are resolved by Taylor into his art, will be kept in mind in the present discussion of specific sacramental meditations. It is interesting to note Taylor's ability to write seemingly in both a Puritan and a general Christian spirit to which no other tradition can make special claim.

The sacramental poems assume the orthodox doctrines of the Trinity and the Incarnation. In II, 44 Taylor contemplates the dual nature of Christ, which he calls "theanthropic." He attempts little metaphor in poems dealing directly with God, Trinity or the divine and human nature in Christ. On the other hand the sacramental poems stress the communion service, the bread and wine, the body and blood of Christ. Inevitably they assume the prior doctrines and occasionally allude to them, as "Theandrick Blood" in II, 111. The sacramental poems are distinguishable from the general contemplations of deity in several ways, focussing upon the elements of the Lord's Supper, and with freer use of imagination, metaphor, witty language. Theanthropy is the immediate assumption of these poems, though never the direct subject in the series of sacramental meditations proper (II, 80–82, 104–111). In II, 105 he comes closest to the subject:

> Hast thou unto thy Godhead nature tooke
>   My nature and unto that nature joyn'de
> Making a Union thereby, whose root
>   Too deep's for reasons delving toole to finde. . . .

But this subject leaves the poet tongue-tied, "Yet my poore Pipe can hardly stut a tune." The emphasis in this poem, though less so than in the others, is upon the practical aspects of the sacramental act:

> To show that he our nature took, he then
>   Tooke breade, and wine best Elementall trade,
> Designed as the Sign thereof.

This poem goes on to say things that are said better in other poems. Its point is that Taylor's Christology is orthodox by Augustinian and by Puritan standards, as critics have found in reading his "Christographia" and other prose. His poems on this subject and on the Trinity have no special Puritan flavor nor very much flavor at all. There is a blandness and sameness about them, a deep piety in attitude and monotony in execution. They are the theological basis of the sacramental meditations proper, which are quite different, firmly Puritan in outlook, strong and original in language. The language of these poems is zestful and free, the theology decisive and strong. Though the figures are not always successful or tasteful, as a group the sacramental meditations are the most appealing, and at the center of Taylor's religious and poetic world.

In these sacramental poems the central concern is with the spiritual presence of Christ's body and blood in the bread and wine. The manner of this presence Taylor calls spiritual, following Calvin, rejecting other alternatives against Puritan orthodoxy in the straight doctrinal poem II, 108, which was looked at briefly above. The meditation in

II, 106 is far more meaningful, for it contains the fundamental argument that the validity of the sacramental act lies in the faith of the believer as much as in the sacramental signs, the bread and the wine. "And spirituall food doth spirituall life require." Hence the need for faith and meditation in the act of the Lord's Supper, and also the need for words and praise. This poem, as others, begins with the struggle for words, his longing for "a new set of Words and thoughts hereon. ..." The place of words in relation to spiritual presence and metaphor arises in many poems, more apparent elsewhere than in II, 106, and so reserved for later comment. The fundamental argument in this poem concerns the meeting of faith and signs, the possibility for subjective error in the state of the receiver of the sacrament (as opposed to objective error, expressed in the doctrinal poem 108). Constant alertness and sacramental meditation are needed to maintain the balance of inner spirit and outer dogmatic significations. For the act to be truly spiritual, intellectual rigor must be allied to true faith:

> Life first doth Act and Faith that's lifes First-born
> Receiving gives the Sacramentall form.
>
> Hence its as needfull as the forme unto
> This Choice formation Hypocrites beg on.
> Elfes Vizzarded, and Lambskinde Woolves hence goe.
> Your Counterfeted Coine is worse than none.
>
> A State of Sin that takes this bread and Wine
> From the Signatum tareth off the Signe. (II, 106)

This is fine indirect argument for Puritan poetry as a necessary aspect of piety. Also there is more than a hint of the "fencing of the table" attitude, but the emphasis is positive, focussing upon attaining the spiritual rightness that accompanies proper reception and meditation upon the Lord's Supper. This poem is primarily significant in its personal note and concern with the proper subjective conditions for the spiritual, the most important concept in this study of Calvinist poetry. It touches upon another issue, the meaning of spirituality in the elect who yet are sinners, in the line "A State of Sin this Banquet cannot beare," a subtle and difficult matter for Puritans more fully explored in other poems.

The formal and practical consequences of Taylor's sacramental meditations are squarely within Puritan tradition, brought out in II, 107. Negatively, these aspects can be looked upon within the notorious "fencing of the table" controversy of 17th century New

England. Taylor's view is very positive, dwelling upon the values for the elect and the sanctified rather than upon the backsliding reprobates. The latter were subjects more worthy of sermons than sacramental meditation. Meditation II, 107 is a concise overview of the practical applications and consequences of the institution of the Supper. It begins with five stanzas of general theology of God's justice, man's fall, the Old and New Covenants and the Supper as the seal of the New Covenant. All this is familiar background. Stanza vii breaks new ground. Using scholastic terminology, from which Puritans never turned if controversy with Catholics was not at issue, stanza vii considers the four "causes" of sacramental institution. This is not a personal meditation, examining what spirituality and sanctification through the sacrament meant for Taylor. The consequences here are general and universal ones: what the institution of the Supper is supposed to mean for the Puritan church and as a general confession of faith. It is a mixture of Calvinist theory and 17th century New England practice.

> The Primall End whereof is Obsignation
>   Unto the Covenant of Grace most sweet.
> Another is a right Commemoration
>   Of Christs Rich Death upon our hearts to keep
> . . . . .
> And Secondary Ends were in Christ's Eye
>   In instituting of this Sacrament,
> As Union, and Communion Sanctity. . . .
> Of Saints Compacted in Church Fellowship.

Obsignation primarily means the sealing in the Covenant discussed in stanza six, but also a peculiar sign of grace. Without this sign in the Supper grace would have no special habitation in the Christian life, though always a general one. Hence grace and this sacrament are often closely equated or even used as synonyms in various of the general meditations on the nature of Christ, His presence, natural objects. Obsignation insures the presence of grace in the church and among the elect. Commemoration was Calvinism's answer to the Catholic doctrine of transubstantiation. "Do this in commemoration of me" meant to Puritans that Christ was present in memory whenever conjointly the elements were present and the words spoken. Christ also adds his spiritual presence (while remaining in heaven) for the moments of the service. The worshippers by following his words give their assent in memory to the Last Supper by its recreation. Thus a holy moment is possible without dwelling upon the elements themselves too specifically, or upon the realistic and, to Puritans, illogical aspects in a "real presence" doctrine. Calvin admitted that the presence was a mystery, one he wished merely to make slightly more rational and spiritual than in some other practice. Since Puritanism has been blamed (or praised) for the later evaporation of the strongest areas of the Christian faith such as this one, it is well to dwell upon the fact that commemoration was a powerful and spiritual, not a vapid and merely rational, area of drama in the Puritan version of the Lord's Supper. The devotion and poetry of Taylor and some others attest to this, admittedly a more difficult type of spirituality to maintain in practice by the very fact that man's memory and imagination were involved in its recreation, not only in its contemplation, as in the piety and devotion of other traditions. Of the third or "secondary" end of the Last Supper little explanation is required. "Saints Compacted in Church Fellowship" are the proverbial "visible saints" of New England history. This state was the highest earthly end of the Puritan dream, a prefiguration of the sweet society of saints in heaven sung by Milton, Watts, Cowper and of course by Taylor in other poems. The opportunity for the visible saints was more available in New England than in England, where even the Commonwealth period was filled with quarrelsome competing sectarians. In New England the ideal in practice gave trouble, leading to the "fencing of the table," the "half-way Covenant" and other political and social expedients. One may hope and surmise that Taylor and numerous other orthodox Puritans found peace together in Christ in this community of saints they had created together in their idea of the spiritual presence. This idea of "spiritual" was to have a long and complex literary history, as we shall see later studying 18th and early 19th century religious and Romantic poetry.

The poem ends upon one of the most subtle and misunderstood of Puritan ideas, the state of the sanctified in relation to sin. We have said that Taylor's *Meditations* were written within the state of sanctification, looking forward to glory and occasionally backward to earlier states. Others have thought that he always doubted his election and lived in daily terror of sin and damnation. Certain lines from some poems, particularly II, 106, if taken out of the entire context of sanctified meditation, would seem to bear out this view:

> A State of Sin this Banquet cannot beare
> A State of Sin that takes this bread and Wine
> From the Signatum tareth off the Signe. (II, 106)

The conclusion of II, 107, and passages from other meditations, clear up the central issue, continual assurance of the elect:

> But lest this Covenant of Grace should ere
>   Be held by doubting Saints all Violate
> By their infirmities as Adams were
>   By one transgression and be so vacate
>   Its Seale is food and's often to be usd,
>   To seale new pardons freshening faith, misusd.

Participation in the sacrament is a seal and promise to the saved and sanctified. Their "infirmities" and "transgressions" are not the state of sin of the non- or pre-elect, but the sins of justified sinners. Taylor admits with Sibbes and other writers on Puritan devotion that there is a continual struggle against sin in the elect, and that the elect sometimes fall. But the transgressions do not vacate the pardon guaranteed by the sacrament as a "Seale." In II, 80 this special power is called:

> It's Life, its quickening Life to very many,
> Yea t'all th'Elect. It is a slip up bred
> Of Godlike life, in graces garden bed.

Puritan doctrine offered assurance, but not final knowledge of the *Imago Dei* to the elect-sanctified on this earth. The abyss for the Puritan was not to be elect or called, a subject looming later in the poetry of Cowper. Regular participants in the Lord's Supper like Taylor had a reasonable sign that they were called and in the process of sanctification. Augustine and severe Catholic tradition offered beatific vision on one hand, and damnation for one mortal sin at any time on the other. The entire Lutheran-Calvinist theological revolution was aimed against that viewpoint. Puritanism in practice had many unlovely characteristics, particularly the separation of the elect from the reprobate with its accompanying cant and hypocrisy. However notorious such practices have become in the minds of historians and literary critics, its form of devotion and piety was genuine in some practitioners, among them Taylor, and should not be confused with other traditions having similar ends but quite different means. Puritanism at its best forced an intellectual strain upon spirituality and piety, perhaps thereby reducing the output without diminishing the quality. When Taylor writes in II, 111 of the effect of the sacrament:

> The Soule it quiets: Conscience doth not sting
> It seales fresh pardon to the Soul of Sin. . . .

it is within this subtle and tangled theological tradition allowing the presence of sin in the justified and the sanctified. No one can doubt his sincerity. This spirituality, loosened from its tenuous Puritan orthodox moorings, later gravitated toward secularity, finally merging with secularity in the nature poetry of Emily Dickinson. That is a much later part of the story we are telling here.

Many critics have concentrated on the style, poetic figures and language of Taylor's poetry. It is accepted now that his visual range was greater than his early discoverers had given credit for, and above a few more examples have been added of his sense of local color and vision in general. The problem of decorum remains, that is, the aptness of many of his poetic figures to the religious subjects. This question in the sacramental meditations proper cannot be separated from the doctrinal aspects of meditation on the Supper, because in them metaphor is used as theology and as language. As Taylor interprets Calvin's doctrine of the presence of Christ's flesh and blood in the bread and wine, it is an extended metaphor:

> Some other Sense makes this a metaphor:
> This feeding signifies, that Faith in us
> Feeds on this fare, Disht in this Pottinger. (II, 81.20−22)

Thus contemplation of the sacrament contains within it encouragement to make metaphor, or new language to express the spiritual presence of Christ in the elements. Taylor's hand-wringing over his ability to create new figures and metaphors in sacramental meditation is a deeply felt need, not mere poetic convention. It was also his way of overcoming Puritan shyness before language − approving the ornate and hyperbolic over the plain and concise of Puritan sermon literature. The number of sacramental poems containing a complaint about his inability to write is hence very significant − II, 81, stanza one; II, 82, stanza one; II, 105, stanza eight; II, 106, stanzas one and two; and other scattered references. The complaint arises out of Taylor's difficulty in finding adequate language derived from physical objects for a subject essentially "spiritual." Happily he could use the word "metaphor" as descriptive of the Calvinist doctrine of the presence − "Some other Sense makes this a metaphor" (II, 81) − and also many more times in the usual literary sense:

> My tatter'd Fancy; and my Ragged Rymes
> Teeme leaden Metaphors. . . . (II, 82.1−2)

This gave him proper license to bring the physical into the service of the spiritual, without however making the practical task, or the decorum in literary terms, less difficult for Puritan spirituality.

Taylor continually uses the word "spirit" and its variations to suggest Christ's presence in the bread and wine. For example in II, 81 the phrases "more Spiritfull than wine," "the Spirituall Life, the Life of God, and Grace," "The Spirituall Life, and Life Eternall view," "In Spirituall wise mixt with my soul," "Eternally when Spiritually alive," and "Set on our heads, and made our Spirituall Food," all appear within four stanzas. This is a slightly unusual density, but only slightly. "Spiritual" is one of the most frequently used words in Taylor's poetry, and highly concentrated in the sacramental meditations by the nature of his aim. What is interesting about Taylor, as a Puritan and a poet, is his refusal to remain on this comfortable abstract plane. Despite his anguish about words he was willing to risk *discordia concors* in search for physical objects to express the spiritual reality. In many instances the visual side of the metaphor or simile is apt enough in expressing the spiritual state of the narrator: the frog-pits, hornets, Indian canoes, George Nevills Feast pointed to above. *Discordia concors* is a serious problem in some of the sacramental meditations, perhaps because of the difficulties involved in Calvin's doctrine of the spiritual, "metaphorical" presence. To balance this innate abstractness of Puritan sacramental doctrine, Taylor stresses the physical in the vehicles of many similes and figures. In II, 80 the following figure is worked out in full, over three stanzas:

> The Soule's the Womb, Christ is the Spermodote
> And Saving Grace the seed cast thereinto. . . .

One can make an argument that decorum is preserved here despite the inclusion of Christ in the sexual metaphor. In some other instances his visualizations of the divine banquet must be called lapses in taste, though authentic in local color and the homely aspects of life around him:

> Christs works, as Divine Cookery, knead in
>   The Pasty Past, (his Flesh and Blood) most fine
> Into Rich Fare, made with the rowling pin
>   His Deity did use. (II, 81)

Or:

> Feed it on Zions Pasty Plate-Delights:
> I'de suck it from her Candlesticks Sweet Pipes. (II, 82)

. . .
>But Soule Sweet Bread, is in Gods Back house, made
>   On Heavens high Dresser Boarde and throughly bakd:

Or finally,

>   Thou Graces Egg layst in their very hearts
>   Hatchest and brudl'st in this nest Divine
>   Its Chickin, that it fledge. (II, 111)

The problem with these images is not primarily their homeliness and gaucherie. It is the distance from the spiritual element they are supposed to represent in vision, the extreme *discordia concors* instead of apt metaphor for the spiritual. In other instances in these sacramental poems things come together better. The Word, the words, the elect and the poet harmoniously express the doctrine of the spiritual presence in the bread and wine, and the effects upon the soul and conscience of a successful communion service and meditation. Such is II, 110, a coming together of the positive Puritan doctrines and attitudes with the appropriate words.

In poem II, 110 Taylor turns from his customary worry about words to imagine the Last Supper in an aural setting. Much has been written about the Puritan preference for the ear over the eye, the hymn over the word as a form of praise. The opening section of this book touched upon this phenomenon of the Puritan imagination. Sinfulness was more usually associated with the eye than with the ear. Baxter, Bunyan and Taylor were willing to work directly with the word and the eye. This poem demonstrates that Taylor also was at ease with the aural forms of Puritan meditation and prayer. It begins by offering a guarantee for aural worship in the Scripture and in the acts of Christ himself:

>   The Angells sung a Carole at thy Birth,
>   My Lord, and thou thyselfe didst sweetly sing
>   An Epinicioum at thy Death, on Earth
>   And order'st thine, in memory of this thing
>   Thy Holy Supper, closing it at last
>   Up with a Hymn, and Choakst the foe thou hast.

This tradition allows the poet to express harmoniously the significance of the Lord's Supper, as we see in stanza four, where the Word, the elect and the poet appear together. The poet is not, as in other poems, struggling with alien words or wondering if metaphor is a proper way to express the flesh-blood, bread-wine relationship in the sacrament. His poetry derives from a sense of election and sanctification as a member of a community sharing an aural tradition:

Dainties most rich, all spiced o're with Grace,
   That grow out of thy Grave do deck thy Table
To entertain thy Guests, thou callst, and place
   Allowst, with welcome, (and this is no Fable)
   And with these Guests I am invited to't
   And this rich banquet makes me thus a Poet.

As a poet his special duty must remain the using of words, but there is a merging of his special role and the role of the aural community, leading to great joy:

Joy stands on tiptoes all the while thy Guests
Sit at thy Table, ready for to sing. . . .

The poem culminates in a comparison of his poetry to musical instruments, the pipe, the golden trumpet and the cittern. The voice of the individual poet becomes one with the communal song and hymn singing, as the Puritan has found a place for poetry in both worship and sacramental doctrine:

Ile close thy Supper then with Hymns, most sweet
Burr'ing thy Grave in thy Sepulcher's reech.

The mood of joy in sanctification reaches in several sacramental meditations a climax looking beyond sanctification to final glorification. The perspective on Taylor's poetry taken in this chapter prepares for this step and also explains the presence of the numerous poems on glorification itself. The center of Taylor's *Meditations* is a sanctified state which allows him to look behind and ahead. There is also a connection between the theme of glory, emphasis upon the spiritual, and aural tradition and hymns. The endings of Meditations 104 and 105 convey some sense of this commingling:

Wash't in thy Vinall liquour till I shine
And rai'd in Sparkling Grace unto thy Glory,
That so my Life may be a gracious story.

And leade mee on in Graces path along
To Glory, then I'l sing a brighter song.

The glory sequences (I, 19—22; II, 73—76; II, 99—101) bring to a climax these intricate patterns of the Puritan imagination.

Meditation II, 109 is a transition poem between the states of sanctification and glorification. It is a sacramental poem because the focus clearly is upon the Lord's Supper, yet also one leading to glory by a different path. The unusual aspect of II, 109 is in the perspective, which has changed from the human angle of the other sacramental meditations to a divine level. Christ is the performer of the sacramental rite with the elect (those presently glorified) as the guests:

> But thou my Lord a Spirituall Feast hast dresst
> Whereat the Angells gaze. And Saints are Guests.
>
> Thou sittest at the table head in Glory,
>   With thy brave guests With grace adornd and drest.
>
> They'r Gods Elect, and thy Selected Ones. . . .

The narrator is present at the feast in imagination so it is for him a prelection of glory from this mortal world. The technique is close to that in Baxter's *Saints Rest* where the divine perspective is used to enhance the human world. There are similar situations in Spenser's final scenes, in the hymns and poems of Watts, and dimly in the transformation of heavenly glory in Blake and Wordsworth. The line

> "In Spiritual apparell whitend white"

has its later resonances in the innocent children of Blake and Wordsworth and in the imagery of a poem such as "Stepping Westward." Herein is the Calvinist-Puritan yearning for the final state of glorification while still struggling with the trials of the sanctified in this world. This perspective, like the aural one of II, 110, tends towards tranquility and harmony for the Puritan, however delicate and momentary. Grace and music join with this vision of the divine order to set the soul at ease:

> Lord Deck my Soule with thy bright Grace I pray:
> . . . .
> When that thy Grace hath set my heart in trim
> My Heart shall end thy Supper with an Hymn.

A reading of all the poems on glorification as a separate set (I, 19–22; II, 73–76; II, 99–101, and 158) may persuade the reader that too much tranquility and harmony are not for religious poetry, and that Johnson's insight, that awe before the presence of God does not induce variety and felicity of expression, has limited truth. In these poems Taylor seems overawed before his subject, and too contented with his awe. Early in the first series he invokes his customary awkwardness with words:

> I fain would something say:
> Lest Silence should indict me. . . .
> . . . though my attempts let fall
> A slippery Verse upon thy Royall Glory. (I, 21)

A real sense of anguish is not in the lines on writing poetry, as in the poems on more personal themes discussed above. On the whole the glory poems preserve decorum, have few intricate figures (and so few lapses in taste), are scriptural in language and develop the meditation from a close paraphrase of the scriptural passage involved in the title. Most are on the theme of Christ's glory from the viewpoint of triumphalism, having the Miltonic overview of the triumph of Christ over Satan and death (I, 19) and Calvin's joy in the final triumph of glory, the Lord's and the saints', over Satan and the wicked:

> Then Saints With Angells thou wilt glorify:
> And burn Lewd Men, and Divells Gloriously. (I, 22)

For the most part the attempts to praise the glory of the Lord lead to a sameness in many of the poems, a characteristic noted in Taylor's poetry by critics that is true here if not elsewhere:

> Glory was never glorifide so much,
>   She ne're receiv'd such glory heretofore. (II, 73)

This sort of tautology is repeated many times throughout the series. Christ's glory is compared to the sun, moon, stars and the saints in II, 99 and 101 with the same repetitious effect. A hint of a mystical sense gives some color to the text in one stanza in II, 158:

> nor endure
> To look upon it without dazling joy,
> Thy beaming Glory falling on its Sight
> Would make its Vision darke as dark as night.

But the poems are orthodox Christian in their restraint on this subject of praise to the Lord in his glorification, though perhaps for this reason lacking in color and variation.

The few poems on glorification which have special interest for this study examine the subject from the temporal state. Our "vile Bodies" of Meditation II, 75 are contrasted to the future promise of glorification for saints of the present world in Meditation II, 76. Here Taylor's poetry has a genuine ring of enthusiasm for the subject:

> And shall not I (whose form transformed shall bee
>   To be shap'te like thy glorious body, Lord.
>   . . . .
> Transported be hereat for very joy,
> Whose intrest lies herein, and gloriously? (II, 76)

Taylor also thinks of the saints who have already persevered, and they are praised indirectly by mention of their presence with Christ in his glory. Christ's celestial court is described, as in Spenser, by overt or implied comparision to the splendors of Renaissance kings (II, 21), with the Puritan saints enjoying in such settings their triumph in and over the world. Though he often uses variations on the word "spirit," as in the sacramental meditations, Taylor's poems on glorification are decisively orthodox, maintaining a keen sense of the difference between this world and the world of glory. The saint may look forward — "Upon my Soule thy Shining Image place" (II, 99) — while remaining firmly placed in this world. "Spiritual" does not become the full revelation of *Imago Dei* as in mysticism or the "inner light" of the unorthodox sects deriving from Puritanism. Yet the heavy emphasis upon the spiritual joy of the sanctified in this life and their later glorification in Christ's glory is as distinctly a Puritan characteristic as the doctrines of election and reprobation. Taylor's poems on glorification, a brief parallel to Baxter's *Saints Rest*, are to be expected of a Puritan whose concentration is upon the state of sanctification. The more drastic Puritan doctrines later influenced Cowper and Byron. These "spiritual" ideas were also to have strong effect upon English poetry, directly in the 17th century, indirectly later upon Blake, Coleridge and Wordsworth.

It may seem unfair to end this chapter on Taylor by discussing poems which were not among his best. Our purpose has been to bring out the underlying Calvinist pattern of his poetry, not to read the poems as a whole or consider the subject of Taylor's place as a major poet. In the course of describing this Puritan pattern in Taylor, his special strengths and weaknesses as a poet have been noticed. He is at his best in deep personal meditation using language appropriate to his time and place, and in sacramental meditations, reflecting the sanctified state of most of his life. The sin-state was only a past memory for him in the *Meditations*, and glorification, both Christ's and his own, an ideal and abstraction not of this life. Few writers have managed effectively with glorification as a poetic topic. Taylor was not a mystic, hence not fully at ease with it, yet he accepted the need to include the topic as a part of the full Calvinist-Puritan scheme of theology and personal redemption. His success is as great as that of any except perhaps Baxter and Smart within Puritan tradition; it would be superficial to compare his poems on glorification to Anglican or Catholic poetry of the mystical way, so great are the differences between the traditions from which the poetry derives its fundamental viewpoint.

IV. Milton

In moving from Marvell and Taylor to Milton we return to the full epic pattern of Calvinism found in Spenser, but with the difference that in Milton the pattern is presented both directly and fully for the only time in 17th century poetry. Milton presents special problems both for reasons of his magnitude and the voluminousness of criticism about his work. From Fletcher we learn of the Calvinist influence upon Milton's education, from McDill the patterns of Calvinism in his work, and from many others the variety of responses, within and without the religious perspective, to his work. Thus our task with Milton is not to assert or demonstrate the general Calvinist nature of his poetry, which is accepted by all readers who view him within the Christian tradition, and will never be accepted, it seems, by those who do not have or dislike the Christian tradition. It is the more narrow one of defining the basic importance of Calvinist-Puritanism for his poetry and to show his continuity in the larger sense in this regard with the other truly Calvinist poets of the 17th century and with the tradition generally. To carry out this task of finding and presenting the most specific and qualifying aspects of Milton's poetry that make him the most important Calvinist poet in the 17th century it may at first seem that all the poetry should be examined very carefully, but this is not the case. Poems that are generally Christian, or political, or informed by the conventions of classical or Renaissance traditions can be set aside. This would leave *Comus, Paradise Lost* and *Paradise Regained* as the core poems for study of the problem of Calvinism in Milton, and about them an enormous amount has been written, much with this problem in view and much of this very good indeed. Fortunately it is not an oversimplification to state that all the problems and interests that concern us appear in their most significant forms in *Paradise Lost*, Milton's greatest poem, and therefore *Pardise Lost* will serve as the center of our discussion of Calvinist-Puritanism in Milton. This is not to say that similar study of the other poems would be merely repetitious, or that the others do not deserve consideration for their own sakes. It is a question of proportion within the framework of this study to focus on those aspects in a giant such as Milton which are most harmonious with the lesser poets before and after him, and to do that with any proportion *Paradise Lost* can fairly be singled out as Milton's most representative poem, and the one in which the question of his Calvinism is most acutely raised, as well as happily being his greatest poem. This matter of selectivity was faced in Spenser, where fortunately the Calvinist temper appeared in recognizable form in the first two books of *The Faerie Queene*, and must be faced again in the copious works of Blake, Wordsworth and Byron. With Marvell, Taylor, Watts, Smart, Cowper and Coleridge, the problems of method and selection are of a lesser order, for reasons that have been or will be set forth.

Paradise Lost, then, will be our text in Milton. We will try to read it with both the perennial controversies and recent criticism in the background. Our argument has to do only with the nature of Calvinist-Puritan sensibility in the poem, how Calvinism influenced Milton as a Christian in writing this most Christian of epics. What Milton did with Calvinism and where he left it for others trying to write religious poetry after him will be the main focus of what follows.

In writing *Paradise Lost* Milton quite clearly intended to present a general Christian scheme acceptable to all Christian sects, and criticism has widely held that he succeeded. The Blake-Shelley heresy, revived in the 1920's by Saurat, has been recessive in the criticism of the past forty years. Most readers have felt that the minor heresies (corporeal nature of angels), or even the major (Arianism), have not prevented the success of the overall scheme of justifying the ways of God to man. On the other hand, neither have the few clear appearances of Calvinist dogmatics in Book III ("Some have I chosen of peculiar grace/Elect above the rest"), nor the idea of election in history in Books XI and XII been taken as excessively constrictive of the universal meaning. It has been generally conceded that the view of man, of the fall and redemption, of grace operating in the unfolding of a Christian pattern of history, articulates a pattern well within the norm of the general Christian view of things. The heresy hunting of Saurat and others in the 1920's has been nicely balanced by the neo-orthodoxy of T. S. Eliot, C. S. Lewis and their followers.

From the viewpoint of this study the work of another group of critics, the myth and architecture variety, who delight in pointing out structural patterns, light and dark symbolism, often laboring the obvious, while as often noticing what was before unknown because so obvious, has sometimes a certain convenience of illustration, yet is not central to our argument. This criticism, which saves Milton on the grounds of his style and architecture at the expense of ignoring his meaning or granting its trivial or fairy-tale nature, performs a useful but dangerous function for the poet. The work of Saurat or Lewis, diametrically opposed as it is in attitudes and assumptions, shares a common ground of belief in the importance of Miton's ideas, not to be found in the more sophisticated critics of form in the poem for its own sake. Lewis granted Saurat this much in his *Preface to "Paradise Lost."*

Recent criticism has been nudging closer to meaning and significance again, timidly in Greene's *Descent from Heaven,* and magisterially in the much controverted *Milton's God* of William Empson.[61] Both share the view that Milton's religious beliefs, which are mainly related to major Christian beliefs (minor heresies aside), are important for the poems. Greene's view is part of his total assumption that epic expresses the fullest and most important beliefs of an age; he has no quarrel with Milton's Christian beliefs except to the extent that these detract (as he thinks) from epic grandeur. Empson's attack on *Paradise Lost*'s Christianity is followed by a full scale attack upon Christianity itself, which he calls an evil religion. Greene rests content in viewing it inadequate for the greatest kind of epic. Both quarrel in a sense with Milton's God, but on different grounds. Greene finds him unconvincing and cold as a vehicle for the intended justification and hints at a possible scepticism in Milton's own beliefs in a personal God as the source of the difficulty. He cites Pascal's famous scepticism as background to Milton. God, in Greene's view, is not convincingly the Christian God, and somehow this finally detracts from the resolution of both God and man in the poem. This writer agrees with Greene's conclusion, but on different grounds.

On the other side, Empson, arguing that Milton's God, the full-fledged traditional God of Christianity, is evil, finds himself assenting to the final vision of *Paradise Lost.* He agrees that something is wrong with God in the poem, but where Greene says that God is not orthodox enough (perhaps) and hence weakens the poem, Empson feels this very inadequacy in Milton's God is his only redeeming feature.

Milton's scepticism, or liberalism, or what have you, results in a greater, not a lesser poem, as the evil Christian God which was Milton's material passes into a neoplatonic or Romantic diffuse Absolute by the end of the poem. Empson's argument is curious and in ways non-literary in interest, but its major point for the poem is one that must be contended with. He raises the existential issue most acutely again. Greene gives one the impression of feeling that Milton's Christian view is unfortunate for the epic structure, but of no great concern otherwise. Empson has at least renewed the point that meaning and existence are necessary aspects of Milton's epic structure.

There are aspects of Empson's argument, which though curious and perverse in interest, must be set aside in this context – his Trinitarian speculations leading to the accusation that Christianity is a lie as a form of thought; his anthropology, accusing Christianity of harboring the main vestige of ritual murder in the civilized world, and so forth. His point that bears directly on the structure of *Paradise Lost*, and upon its theology of God in the poem, is that the Christian God becomes something else, something better, in the course of the poem. The abstract philosophy and notion of God's abdication that Empson adduces as evidence can be set aside as curiosities lacking evidence in the poem. But he does notice the lack of dramatic and theoretical interest on Milton's part in Christ as redeemer, in the redemption, in the sacrifice of Christ, and upon Christ as a force in history. Apart from the obvious reason, Milton's Arianism, Empson sees Milton's dislike of the "human sacrifice," "debtor-creditor" scheme as the positive good in the poem, weakening the poem as a Christian poem, while making it a better, more moral poem.

This is the central issue which must remain before the eyes of critics of *Paradise Lost*. Ideas and structure cannot be separated in untangling the issues of the poem. Greene noted several of the ideational weaknesses in the poem, but lacking, it seems, theological awareness, he attributes the problem to some vague scepticism in the air in the 17th century (a scepticism Milton himself certainly did not hold). As Greene puts it:

But the *impulse* to epic weakened only when man found himself overawed by the void around him, when his assurance dwindled before an unknown and ever-expanding heaven. An epic poem, in its respect for human potentiality and domineering command of space, is a declaration, however qualified with tragedy, of metaphysical pride. "Quand je considère," wrote Pascal, "... le petit espace que je remplis et même que je vois, abîmé dans l'infinite immensité des espaces que j'ignore et qui m'ignorant, je m'en effraie." This sense of lonely isolation qualified that greatness, *grandeur*, which Pascal counterpoised against human wretchedness, and it has qualified progressively modern conceptions of greatness.[62]

But *Paradise Lost* is not the sceptical type of Christian poem, of which we have various examples in the 17th century. Some sort of strong assurance is at the heart of Milton's Puritan religion, and of his intention and ability to write a poem of such scope and power. Sceptical poetry is fragmentary and dialogic, such as Marvell's, or Pascal's *Pensées*. The weakness in the poem must be seen in terms of the theology itself, a point which Greene hints at but does not carry far enough in the right direction.

This weakening of heroic prestige is abetted by the severing of the traditional bond between hero and community. It is true that the Son considered as hero is a benefactor of the widest possible community in his defiance of Satan. But if we agree to limit heroic awe to the human sphere, then we must speak only of individual heroes, lonely men who mount the current of common perversity. Their goodness, as Milton describes them, stands over against the universal evil; no, more than this it outweighs the evil.[63]

The point missed here is the Son's role as Mediator in his human nature, or more exactly the lack of importance of this role. This lack is the very point noticed by Empson as a good in his reading of *Paradise Lost* as a less than fully Christian poem.

There is no doubt something missing in Milton's view of the Christian scheme if compared with other 17th century poems. Empson has put his finger on a valid point when he says that the Christian reader is put off by, then defends, Milton's God, while the "detached" reader feels instinctively happier in the company of Milton than in that of Donne, Herbert, Crashaw, etc. The extreme views of Saurat and Lewis on the issue of Milton's theology has perhaps done a great deal to lead most readers to willing acceptance of the aseptic detachment of archetype and pattern criticism, which assumes *Paradise Lost* is a frozen myth to be viewed mainly for its structure. Perhaps some use of 17th century theological material may be able to help us around this abyss of extremes.

What is peculiar in the nature of Milton's God is not accountable by 17th century scepticism or by Empson's notion that God is intrinsically evil. It is rather a quality that can be defined within the givenness of the Christian tradition itself, by recourse to Milton's major theological sources, Calvin's *Institutes* and the Puritan preachers of 1580—1640, and by analogy to other Christian traditions with a different development of the God-Christ relationship. Perhaps it would be admissable to present a distant analogy first, one which will show the divergence of Milton from the central tradition most startlingly, and also cast some light upon Empson's argument. In *The Brothers Karamazov* the long argument between Ivan and Alyosha leads up to this point (Bk. V, iii—iv). This long argument of Ivan against Christianity has presented, by the way, the case against Christianity as fully as Empson does, while the "Grand Inquisitor" section following carries it a few steps beyond.

> "No, I can't admit it, Brother," said Alyosha suddenly, with flashing eyes, "you said just now is there a being in the whole world who would have the right to forgive and could forgive? But there is a Being and He can forgive everything, all and for all, because He gave his innocent blood for all and everything. You have forgotten Him, and on Him is built the edifice, and it is to Him they cry aloud, "Thou art just, O Lord, for thy ways are revealed!"
>
> "Ah, the One without sin and His blood! No, I have not forgotten Him; on the contrary I've been wondering all the time how it was you did not bring Him in before, for usually all arguments on your side put Him in the foreground."[64]

Empson's view of Milton is ironic in the context of Dostoevsky, for he approves the very lack of the symbol of suffering, the God-Man in *Paradise Lost,* while at the same time praising Milton for excluding it. Empson even hints at, but does not define, a connection between the pattern of Calvinism and this exclusion, as the following notations signify:

> This is also where we get the stage-villain's hiss of "Die he or Justice must." God is much at his worst here, in his first appearance; but he needs to be to make the offer of the Son produce a dramatic change. I do not know what to make of his expressing the Calvinist doctrine that the elect are chosen by his will alone, which Milton has appeared to reject (l. 185); it has a peculiar impact here, when God has not yet even secured the Fall of Adam and Eve. One might argue that he was in no mood to make jokes; and besides, the effect here is not a sardonic mockery of Satan, which can be felt in the military joke readily enough, but a mysterious and deeply rooted sense of glory.[65]
>
> Surely the reason why Milton's treatment here seems cold, compared to a Good Friday service which is the natural comparison, is that no one throughout the long 'scene in Heaven' ever mentions that the Son is to die by torture. Even Michael does not describe the Cross to Adam as painful, only as 'shameful and accurst.' Death for a day and a half any of us might proffer, but we would find slow torture worth mentioning. . . . I do not know whether there is a standard explanation for this lack in the poem, and do not

remember to have seen it noticed. The reason for it, surely, is that Milton would not dirty his fingers with the bodily horror so prominent in the religion. . . . This steady blaze of moral splendor must I am afraid be called unreal but at least makes the religion feel a good deal cleaner. The Son regularly talks like a young medieval aristocrat to win his spurs, and like him is not expected to mention pain.[66]

Empson is so determined to berate the Christian God and find him wicked that he ignores this Calvinist direction in favor of ascribing to Milton liberal and humanitarian feelings in his avoiding the pain-sacrifice theme and in hinting at God's abdication or transference into the Absolute. Dostoevsky's Trinitarian theology is at least aware of the fact that the pain-suffering God as the answer to the metaphysical problem is so obvious as to be stock-response for both Alyosha and Ivan. If the context of this problem is now restricted to Milton's poem, and we assume that Milton is a firm believer (as Empson does and Greene does not) we can arrive at a different way to view the problem of Milton's God which affects both the structure and ideas of the poem, yet without involving one's own cultural or personal attitude toward Christianity.

The influence of Calvin's theology upon Milton's thinking and poetry has been usually misunderstood because interpreted in a narrowly dogmatic fashion. Milton's humanistic bent and classical education, his presentation of the sensuous if not the sensual in poetry, have stood as evidence against his being taken seriously as Puritan-Calvinist. Earlier sections of this book have cleared up these mis-understandings of Puritan-Calvinism in general, but the application of a more enlightened attitude toward Calvinism to the problems in Milton presents the most difficult and peculiar problem of all. There *is* the theological divergence between Calvin's *Institutes* and *Paradise Lost* on important matters. Calvin is a Trinitarian, Milton an Arian heretic. Less certain is Milton's heresy regarding the doctrine of election, which is denied at one point in *Paradise Lost* (III, 111–134) and asserted later (183–197), and again in Milton's view of history (Bks. XI–XII). One can also point out that Milton accepts the scho-lastic doctrine of freedom for unfallen man, and the doctrine of election for fallen man. He compromises Calvinism further by allowing the doctrine of free grace as well as election after the fall. But it is not usually recognized by literary critics that Calvin is a Thomist in his con-sideration of unfallen man, and that the essential differences between the general Christian tradition and Calvinism relate to the doctrine of grace and of original sin, not that of unfallen man. Milton wished to invoke the Thomist doctrine of predestination and free will before the fall, and the Calvinist view of grace and election after (while compromising this seriously) yet also to preserve the Calvinist ideas of God's grandeur and his justification in acting out the pleasure of his divine will. Add some minor heresies and the major one (Arianism) and one can understand why critics have called *Paradise Lost* a metaphysical bramble-bush. I can envision no way to make *Paradise Lost* theologically coherent within the premises of a given system, but I do think Milton's "mixed Calvinism" can be shown to have very subtle and important effects upon the poem which are usually, if noticed at all, ascribed to other causes. Calvin and Milton share the same feelings and attitudes about God, if not exactly similar theology. In the long run Milton the Arian heretic and Calvin the orthodox divine produce the same feelings in the reader as to the nature of God, a feeling quite different from that of other Christian positions or non-Christian positions. If we understand the emotional and rhetorical emphasis given to certain doctrines by Calvin and especially his English followers, the results are surprisingly similar to, and in fact lead to, the God of *Paradise Lost*.

One further point must be taken into consideration before continuing this analysis of the theological situation. The question has been raised as to what degree of literalness one should give Milton's theology, indeed, to the epic structure of *Paradise Lost* as a whole. The day of an easy answer to this question has passed, i.e., either that Milton fully believed in every detail of his epic as literally true, or that it is all fairy-tale. It is now popular to say that Milton understood the work as myth, and intended it to be taken as such. The definition given of myth is so sophisticated that it damages neither the reality of the story nor its quality as artifact.

The direct use of myth in a poem such as *Paradise Lost*, as distinct from oblique references to it in the mythic incidents of *The Faerie Queene* or *Pilgrim's Progress*, clearly implies a kind of literalness that we are not always prepared to allow a poet. Although Milton, like Spenser and Bunyan, would have laid stress on the "spiritual" significances of his story, and its continuing relevance to our own lives, he would also have insisted, as they would not have done in quite the same way, on the validity of its literal "appearances" as he presented them. . . . Milton claimed, not idly, that he was accurately depicting "things invisible to mortal sight," "things unattempted yet in Prose or Rhime." . . . [W]e must recognize . . . Milton's conviction that, allowing for the inevitable margin of error, he was portraying fact. The claim for the truth of events is absolute: these things happened; for the truth of the images − the poems's places and personages − less absolute, but still insistent that the qualities and potencies bodied forth in them are real.[67]

By calling Milton's form "literal myth" MacCaffrey and others of this school of critics manage to preserve both the reality (theology) and the structure (poetry) of the poem. But myth in this sense does not necessarily (or even likely) involve the reader's sense of belief in the myth. Nonetheless the myth school makes an important point which all critics must bear in mind, for a time will come in English literature (reflected later in this study) when the use of dogma and of religious objects in poetry will be purely metaphorical at the first level of interest, in Romantic poetry and 19th century American literature. With Milton, we are still dealing with words, whether called theology or myth, which intend univocally to describe the reality they point towards.

In reading over Calvin's doctrine of the mediator (*Institutes* ll, ix−xvii) one gets two strong impressions: the meticulous adherence to all the central doctrines of the medieval Church (including in xv and xvi the doctrines of suffering and atonement which Milton found so difficult to dramatize), and at the same time some lessening of the total importance of this Christology in relation to the doctrine of God presented earlier in the *Institutes*. This is mainly a matter of emphasis or feeling and not of theology. One could quote Calvin at length, and indeed in moments of high irritation, against the faintest traces of Arminianism in Christian doctrine or lessening of the necessity of full atonement in the writings of persons he would regard as heretics. There is certainly no jot of sanction in the theology of Calvin as such for the lessening of attention or fervor to various aspects of the doctrine of the mediator. Yet finally one senses in Calvin's writings (and more obviously in those of his followers) *some* lessening of importance of this doctrine in relation to earlier scholastic doctrine, not to speak of Counter Reformation Catholicism. This background gives some sanction for the even more difficult state of affairs in *Paradise Lost*.

Our proof here lies mainly in the explanation given in earlier sections of this book of the emphasis of Calvin's *Institutes* and of English Calvinism. From the time of the *Institutes* themselves through the youth of Milton at Cambridge in the early 17th century,[68] certain doctrines in the *Institutes* were preached or explained at the expense of others: power of God, human depravity, doctrine of grace over human nature of Christ, sacraments, church ritual. It would be a gross misstatement, the sort made in the books of Ross or Martz, to say that Calvinist-Puritanism is purely or simply this or that. The de-emphasized doctrines were also preached and spread, according to their place in Calvin's theology, but in the long run the effect of regular de-emphasis was felt. Preaching about the power of God the Father, and about the Word, did have its spiritual and "abstracting" aspect, often noted by historians of Calvinist-Puritanism. Its traditional form was to abstract from the human nature and suffering of Christ without being heretical. The reasons for so doing were not Arian or instinctive dislike for aspects of the Christian tradition, but rather its great concern with other, more immediate and supposedly most important aspects of the tradition. It remained for Milton to re-discover the Arian heresy in order to bring the theory in accord with the usual Puritan feeling. This point, of course, in no way endorses Empson's belief that Milton consciously eschews Christian barbarities, or that he, a high Calvinist on all doctrine pertaining to the nature of God, advocates His abdication.

Let us now turn to a closer look at certain texts in *Paradise Lost* to notice how the link between Puritanism and Milton works out in detail. When one returns to these theological texts after abstract criticism one is struck by their bluntness. It is this bluntness which is at the source of all the major problems relating to Milton's God, and to *Paradise Lost* in general. The bluntness has been assuaged by referring to Milton's various heresies (Saurat), by fancifully making Milton a rebel against God (Shelley and Blake), or more sophisticatedly by referring to Milton's "myth." But the heresies are negligible (except Arianism) and even this heresy is understandable within Milton's context of intellectual Calvinism. *Paradise Lost* as a poem of rebellion is only intelligible to compulsive rebels who have some irresistible reason or necessity to distort the text. Calling it "the Christian myth" only cloaks the issue. It surprises the reader by its explicit and knowledgeable presentation of the function of Christ in the scheme of redemption only if he has been lead astray by Empson or Greene in one direction or another. Yet the presentation, while Christian, is not centrally Christian. It has about it a good deal of the Calvinist austerity which makes the religion more other-worldly than is central Christianity, and therefore interferes with the actuality of Christ's presence in history. It is in defining the qualities of the austerity here, and not in Milton's more explicit Arianism or use of Calvinist dogmatics relating to free will, election, or grace (Books III and X), that the issue of Milton's theology in relation to the poem can most clearly be put forward.

Which hee, who comes thy Savior, shall recure,
Not by destroying Satan, but his works
In thee and in thy Seed: nor can this be
But by fulfilling that which thou didst want,
Obedience to the Law of God, impos'd
On penalty of death, and suffering death,
The penalty to thy transgression due,
And due to theirs which out of thine will grow:
So only can high Justice rest appaid.
The Law of God exact he shall fulfill
Both by obedience and by love, though love
Alone fulfill the Law; thy punishment
He shall endure by coming in the Flesh
To a reproachful life and cursed death,
Proclaiming Life to all who shall believe
In his redemption, and that his obedience
Imputed becomes theirs by Faith, his merits
To save them, not thir own, though legal works.
For this he shall live hated, be blaspheam'd,
Seis'd on by force, judg'd, and to death condemnd
A shameful and accurst, nail'd to the Cross
By his own Nation, slain for bringing Life;
But to the Cross he nails thy Enemies,
The Law that is against thee, and the sins
Of all mankind, with him there crucifi'd,
Never to hurt them more who rightly trust
In this his satisfaction; so he dies,
But soon revives, Death over him no power
Shall long usurp; ere the third dawning light
Return, the Starres of Morn shall see him rise
Out of his grave, fresh as the dawning light
Thy ransom paid, which Man from death redeems,
His death for Man, as many as offer'd Life
Neglect not, and the benefit imbrace
By Faith not void of works; this God-like act
Annulls thy doom, the death thou shouldst have dy'd,
In sin for ever lost from life. . . . (XII, 393−429)[69]

This passage lies at the center of Books XI−XII, the presentation of human history to Adam by the angel Michael. It helps to define the nature of Milton's history, while at the same time having its logical place within it. Milton's view of history, like that of any Christian view, is linear and relatively stable and predictable: from the fall to the apocalypse there can only be one major event, the infusion of the divine in the person of Christ. Even this does not change the course of human history. Whereas other traditions view history as rising action, or falling action, or circular action (eternal return), the Christian view must be relatively humdrum. Even so, Milton's history, given the nature of Milton's God and the nature and function of Christ within history, is more static and austere than, say, an Anglican or Catholic view would be. The elect appear in history on a narrow and predictable basis, before and after the coming of Christ. Large and vital civilizations — Egyptian, Roman, medieval Catholic — are consigned to obliquity. Continuing beyond the point where Milton takes us, we may assume that the Puritan period of the Commonwealth had been the latest upward curve, with the evil rule of the Stuarts coming before and after. The short upswing in history after the coming of Christ, and before the Roman Catholic Empire of the Middle Ages, shows that the divine event, while giving history its moral grounding, can only transform a slight part of it. The city of God is always ephemeral on earth, always a dim emblem of reality. The pattern can be reproduced roughly in the following diagram:

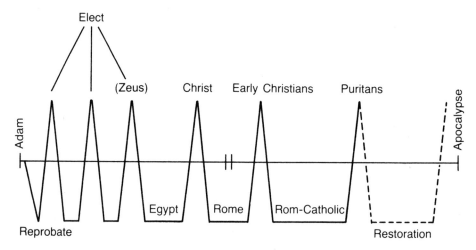

It is largely the Calvinist God, and the Calvinist view of Christ, that produces the pattern. Satan is the emperor of this world, the world of Egypt, Rome, medieval Europe, and contemporary England. The prototypes of Adam and Christ make their appearances as the elect with just enough frequency to illumine the will of God in history, but hardly compensate for the evil of the world from the human point of view. Aquinas and the medieval doctors had given a much rosier view of history, and even Augustine, a pessimist in regard to original sin, in whose footsteps Calvin followed, could write the *City of God*. These dark spots in Milton cannot be rationalized away from the human point of view, but the human point of view is what is precisely wrong if one wants to read the poem in the spirit in which it was written. Such comment renders *Paradise Lost* inadequate (Greene) or ridiculous (Empson). The problem must be seen from the perspective of Milton's view of God, of man's depravity, and of Christ's unique and limited role in history and as man.

In the passage quoted above which introduces Christ's divinity into history certain things are immediately noticeable. The debtor-creditor scheme in relation to abstract justice is present. Also the paradox that the law of justice is also a law of love. Most important is the fact of the crucifixion, the price of remission of God's abstract justice. Whatever one may have thought of Empson's view that Milton's refusal to portray Christ as suffering is established in the poem (based upon his reading of passages in Books III and VI), this passage certainly shows him to be in the wrong. The last point, leading out from the passage as quoted, concerns the effect Christ's sacrifice will have among men immediately after his death. The four points deserve separate commentary.

The first point may seem at first to be the most clearly Calvinist of all, the satisfaction of abstract justice by Christ's death. It is, and it is not. This is standard theology in all the Churches, Eastern and Western. What gives a Calvinist emphasis here is the insistence on this point in relation to the second point, the importance of love in the working out of salvation. "And by love though love Alone fulfil the Law" is a paradox in relation to the necessity of divine justice, and Milton prefers to leave it as such, rather than exploit it in the metaphysical tradition. The number of lines given to justice in relation to the brief mention of love is a fair indication of the Calvinist emphasis upon duty and rigor over love. Yet in fact Milton's allowance here of the theoretical primacy of love over justice is more lenient than Calvin's view. Calvin stresses the propriety and mathematics of the relationship more fully than does Milton. Looking at the problem from a different angle, one can see how other traditions, while holding the point of a divine mathematical transaction in theory, might stress the law of love and the human nature of Christ more fully than does Milton. This is the case with contemporary Anglicanism and of course Counter Reformation Catholicism. Milton does not dwell long on the mystery of divine love become human, as he did not earlier in his Nativity Hymn. Since he does not choose to do this, his acknowledgement of human suffering and pain in the crucifixion lacks its full positive force. He is legally and fully correct on the subject, *pace* Empson, of the suffering and humanity of Christ, but the human figure does not emerge fully enough to prevent the disappointment of critics who are looking for a hero in *Paradise Lost*. If *Paradise Lost* lacks a full human hero, and thus full epic scope, as Greene suggests, this is not to be accounted for in the character of Adam, but rather in the characterization of Christ. The full human characterization of Christ possible within the Christian framework would have implied, in Milton's eyes as it did in those of his Puritan forebears, some diminution in the scope of God as Father and arbiter of justice and providence. Here Milton's Calvinism shines through fully (in the form of Arianism, a logical step away from Calvin), and affects the view of man in history after the resurrection of Christ. Election and depravity operate to limit the number of the saved severely. Christ does not fully become realized as the sorrowful, suffering God-Man in history to whom all can turn; he does not operate in history in a way that is taken for granted as his function by characters in *The Brothers Karamazov*, believers and non-believers alike. His effective influence almost literally withdraws with him, lasting for about 100 years, except for the few elect, a class which in any case was appearing occasionally before the coming of Christ. God's world goes on as before, and Christ's appearance in it has the valid effect only of giving official sanction to a process fully in operation. The heinousness of Adam's fall, and its terrible effects upon human nature, demand many victims; Christ effectively saves very few, no more in fact than God has ordained from the beginning. He is allied in feeling and spirit if not in form with the just God and not with the suffering victims whom he technically has come to save. What would be the point, then, of elaborate ritual and worship of the God-Man in attempts to conform the will or reduce the power of sin? Better to sit still, trying to discern the will of God operating in the world and, hopefully, upon one's individual spirit. Human history from this angle can thus be viewed as a nightmare from which Everyman cannot escape, or as an edification of the elect, or as a working-out of the will of God. As the modern reader is not likely to view himself as one of the elect, he must resist the easy alternative of professing shock or horror at Milton's vision (and Calvin's): the wonderful working-out of the majestic and divine will of God. God is justified in *Paradise Lost* in the presentation of his majesty, power, and secret arbitrary will. All this is very foreign to the modern sensibility, but we must try to read the poem as written in the 17th century by an astute Calvinist-Puritan, and not substitute one of the many alternatives one encounters in reading contemporary criticism.

If the reader will permit a slightly unscholarly digression at this point, I should like to illuminate Milton's view of God by allusion to a contemporary analogy. The Puritan God is not a living force in modern Protestantism, but He lives on (or did until recent times), in modified form in traditional Irish Catholicism. The Jansenist heresies of the 17th century, as is well known, were imported into the Catholic seminaries of Ireland, and took strong root there. Even after the heretical formulas relating to free will, grace and original depravity died out in a Catholic setting, the spirit of Calvinist-Puritan teaching lived on in the attitude toward doctrinal points. That is to say, the full doctrine of the mediator and suffering Christ as human person was preached, but the humanizing and permissive effects which follow from such preaching were discouraged. Close behind the suffering, loving Christ stood the God of justice and hell-fire, the God of fearsome retribution. The doctrine of hell and a sense of human depravity regarding sins of the flesh were instilled early in the religious life, and led to confusions about the nature of Christ as the mediator. Such mixed doctrine allowed neither Milton's Calvinist sense of exaltation regarding the power and glory of God, accepting oneself as an unimportant agent in a divine drama, nor the personal exaltation and even sentimentality of Counter Reformation Catholicism, especially as manifested in Latin countries. James Joyce's early works − *Stephen Hero, Portrait of the Artist* and "The Dead" − are *loci classici* of this Irish syndrome which has received ample documentation of various sorts. In a sensitive artist this tradition tends to visions of hell rather than of heaven, as we have them in the conclusion to "The Dead" and in the Circe section of *Ulysses*. This is accounted for by the fact that "Irish Calvinism" accepts all too readily the power, justice and arbitrary will of God, without being able to share in the vision of his glory. Its other face is turned to the humanistic Lord, who is a suffering, rather static figure involved mainly in personal salvation or retribution. The Orthodox Russian or medieval Thomist sense of Christ as the living mediator in history is missing; there will be no transformation of the world by Christ. The drama is of the individual whose odds of salvation are as narrow as in Calvinism, without a doctrine of election

in his favor. The worst elements in all the Christian schemes are incorporated in Irish Jansenism. Yet, to the extent that it is a still
existing force in the modern community, it can provide us with a living
background for the Calvinist doctrine of Milton, and its forceful visions
of light, heaven, and the divine providence of God.

This analogy has been useful if it helps provide a sense of the
historical angle of vision in which Milton should be read. The primary
feeling one is supposed to get from the closing scenes of *Paradise Lost*
is of exaltation, because of the glory of God, the magnanimity of Christ,
and the luck and happiness of the elect. The viewpoint is actually that
of an angel representing God, that is, God's viewpoint. One must
share, however vicariously and intermittently, in the sense of election
in order to understand this view. Man must consider the mystery and
wonder of being involved in God's plan. Compared to the heavenly
vertigo of the final lines of *Paradise Lost*, Counter Reformation
Catholicism, with its emphasis upon the psychological and the personal, is a somewhat human religion. In Milton's final view man has a
privileged, unique ringside seat in God's moral amphitheatre:

> this act
> Shall bruise the head of *Satan*, crush his strength
> Defeating Sin and Death, his two main armes,
> And fix far deeper in his head thir stings
> Then temporal death shall bruise the Victors heel,
> Or theirs, whom he redeems, a death like sleep,
> A gentle wafting to immortal Life. . . .   (XII, 429–435)

> Then to the Heav'n of Heav'ns he shall ascend
> With victory, triumphing through the aire
> Over his foes and thine; there shall surprise
> The Serpent, Prince of aire, and drag in Chaines
> Through all his Realme, and there confounded leave;
> Then enter into glory, and resume
> His Seat at Gods right hand, exalted high
> Above all names in Heav'n; and thence shall come,
> When this Worlds dissolution shall be ripe,
> With glory and power to judge both quick and dead,
> To judge th' unfaithful dead, but to reward
> His faithful, and receave them into bliss,
> Whether in Heav'n or Earth, for then the Earth
> Shall all be Paradise, farr happier place
> Then this of Eden, and farr happier days.   (XII, 451–465)

This vision is the "world's great period," a moment of spiritual elation
not given to ordinary mortals. The air of *Paradise Lost* is rarified,

optimistic in the sense of sharing the viewpoint of the Almighty and rejoicing in his plan. It is the viewpoint of the elect, the saints, which can only be maimed or distorted by the various irrelevances brought to bear upon it by criticism. Medieval Catholicism (C. S. Lewis), Baroque Counter Reformation (17th century metaphysical specialists), epic traditions (Greene), and modern humanitarianism (Blake, Saurat, Empson) point out aspects of *Paradise Lost* that are in the poem, and important in some limited way. But Milton's high theme is Calvinist-Puritan in essence. The many varying readings of *Paradise Lost* in our time (including the detached "myth criticism" of MacCaffrey) suggest that this high theme does not strike a positive chord in modern man. Critics with a religious bent prefer the existential Christianity of Donne, or the humanized Catholicism of Hopkins and the moderns. On this issue two points should be made: dislike or detachment from Milton's religion is not necessarily the same emotion as dislike of Christianity in general. Modern Christianity is paradoxically more human *and* more aggravating than Milton's austere Calvinism. Further, for a reader sensitive to poetry and to theology, it is not necessary to believe or to reject Milton's Calvinist-Puritan religion in order to catch a glimpse of his imaginative vision, and through *Paradise Lost* to exalt imaginatively in the glory of God.

This reading of *Paradise Lost* may seem unduly restricted to the modern reader. Even if one grants the primary importance of the conception of God in the epic explained here, this reader will still view this reading as partial, showing the importance of the lines,

"I may assert eternal Providence"

but not at all

"Justify the ways of God to men."

He is not likely to accept the assertion of this reading that the justification of the ways of God to men is mainly accomplished in showing the grandeur and splendor of God, and man's privileged role in partaking of the divine scheme. The justification that seemed adequate and more than obvious to Miltion's 17th century Puritan audience no longer will suffice. The 20th century reader wants to see man justified in ways that Milton never intended, and the poet would have considered blasphemous any attempt to justify God from a man-centered vision. It is no wonder that attempts to read the poem that way led to the conclusion that it is in some ways inadequate.

Contemporary criticism has been occupied with the problem of Satan as villain or hero, with the humanity of Adam and Eve, and with humanistic speculation on the nature of God more appropriate to medieval Catholicism or modern existentialism than to the 17th century religion behind Milton. The view of Milton presented here is also resisted because it spoils the fun of reading *Paradise Lost* for some readers. But the fun and the glory of *Paradise Lost* are of different orders, and it is unfortunate that fuller understanding of the former has obscured modern man's already waning interest in the latter. The only point of the interest in all misguided criticism to the present study is the extent to which Milton encouraged misreading in the structure of the poem.

Milton unwittingly encouraged both the Satan reading and the humanistic reading of *Paradise Lost* by allowing both elements to eclipse God temporarily in the poem, Satan in I–II, and the first parents in IV and IX. He performed a very complicated maneuver in both instances, and readers have not let him off so easily as he no doubt thought would be possible. Satan *should* seem the Greek tragic antagonist, the Renaissance villain, the Romantic Prometheus, in the early books, while being actually the hissing snake, the evil minister of his final undoing in Book X. Adam and Eve *should* appear in the un-sullied heroic posture of primitive epic in IV, and as the all too human (but therefore much admired) parents of the race in IX and X, yet in reality remain the future elect, passive vehicles in the ineluctable mind of God, as the opening of XI reminds us:

> Thus they in lowliest plight repentant stood
> Praying, for from the Mercie-seat above
> Prevenient Grace descending had remov'd
> The stonie from thir hearts. . . .   (XI, 1–4)

Milton's performance in *Paradise Lost* is a complex game of appearance and reality, played by exacting but justified rules. God must remain at the center of all things. Many modern readers dislike this structure, indeed, feel that Milton has cheated them in investing so much human feeling in the portraits of Satan and of Adam and Eve, and yet finally not for a humanistic purpose. In the 17th century Milton's true purpose and meaning would have been understood and appreciated by the fit reader; by the 18th, the crypto-Deism of Addison, Pope and Johnson was uncomfortable with Milton's intimacy with God; with Blake and Shelley chaos set in, from which criticism has not fully recovered. In their various ways, the Empsons, Greenes, Lewises and even MacCaffreys are obscuring the main points by praising or blaming *Paradise Lost* for wrong or only partially correct reasons. Milton the master of frozen architecture is only a bit better than Milton the God-hater, or Milton the Renaissance Dante, or Milton the epic humanist. In this circumstance it is a pleasure to be able to quote briefly from a recent sober and clear analysis of *Paradise Lost*, Joseph Summer's *The Muse's Method*, which grasps the central point of the final books without allusion to the Puritan background.

Michael's last narrative provides the final trial of faith in the poem for Adam and the reader. It emphasizes Milton's conviction that the Christian faith could not be dependent on any dream of man's continued moral or spiritual progress; on the establishment of any particular secular government at any one time; on the incorruptibility of any tradition or institution; or on the external happiness, prosperity, or longevity of the faithful. It depended only on the providence and power of God.[70]

And at this moment we are released from the unremitting contemplation of the mass of human history and cosmic purpose – larger than man's mind – which the final hours in Paradise have involved. ... [W]e are left with that portion for which we are, by grace, responsible, with which we can and must come to terms: our own lives with our own loved ones, with the place and the way still to be chosen and found.[71].

It was this power and providence of God, and the cosmic purpose larger than man's mind, which had agitated Puritan preachers from the days of Whichcote until the close of the Revolution. We have traced the many strands of this complicated vision as it repeated itself in the works of many preachers, in frenzy, in burlap, or in ecstasy. Even in enthusiasm the cold prose presenting cosmic purpose makes dry reading in the 20th century. The Puritan preachers are at their best presenting the existential side of Puritanism, that reflected in the poetry of Marvell, Taylor, Dickinson and Cowper. The central Puritan vision of first and last things gets its only great presentation imaginatively in the writings of Spenser and Bunyan, and above all in *Paradise Lost*.

PART THREE

Religious Metaphor in the Eighteenth Century: Watts, Smart and Cowper

Malcolm Ross in *Poetry and Dogma* wrote that with Milton's *Paradise Lost* Christian dogma and symbolism in the 17th century reached a state of static equilibrium, to be followed in the 18th century by formalized decay.[1] This is less than half a truth in many respects, but an examination of the statement can well serve as an introduction to the 18th century religious poets – Watts, Smart and Cowper. A brief explanation of the decay of religious poetry in all traditions is a necessary prelude to consideration of the major religious spirits of the age.

If Milton is the unusual poet previous writing has shown him to be, exhibiting a high and visionary strain of the Calvinist temper in *Paradise Lost*, then Ross' statement is wrong on several counts. Milton is not representative of 17th century religious trends in poetry: if there was decay in religious verse and vision in the late 17th and early 18th centuries, the causes must be found elsewhere. It is more proper to ask why the existential personal Calvinist strain in Marvell and Taylor died out, or why the great religious prose of Baxter and Bunyan lacked successors. Dogma did harden, and individuals lost personal interest in the sense of religious mythic pattern as the century opened. The reasons for this sad state of affairs, after the fervor of the 17th century, are to be found both within and outside the religious community. Within the religious community a timidity of purpose and attitude arose owing to the rise of rationalism, and the decay of Puritanism politically. From without, and more seriously as regards Anglican poetry than Puritan, the spirit of rationalism lured away the best poetic minds of the late 17th and early 18th centuries into other spheres.[2] The poetry of Dryden and Pope, and the works of Swift may be called moral and Christian, but are not religious in the 17th century sense of the term. At that time only the unusual or the less than first-rate wrote and thought in the religious mode, Smart and Watts being two fair examples of the two categories. The religious musings of Cowper, and his nature poetry, are in part in this tradition, and in part the preliminary development of trends we associate in full measure with the Romantic movement. In Blake, the religious tradition again attains the level of the first-rate and also commences the Romantic movement.

From our viewpoint in this study it is not necessary, indeed, it would be tedious, to enumerate all the external causes for the decay of vital religious thought and poetry in the early 18th century. Our interest will remain focused on the area of religious poetry itself, allowing the intrusion of the external only where it shows itself to be a definite influence on an individual writer. An authentic religious prose writer like William Law is almost as important for the purpose of this exposition as the poets, and it is with regret that Law, for reasons of space, must be treated by allusion only, as were Bunyan and Baxter in the previous section on the 17th century religious-Puritan mode. A recent writer, David Morris, in a very able study, has pointed out the complexity in studying religious literature in the 18th century.[3] There were not only the well-known negative influences at work. Some positive aspects of the age helped to convert fervent subjective religion into a generalized objective religiosity. Deistic poems of great length and hymns were the result, including some by the poets of subjective and personal religious interest such as Watts, Smart and Cowper. Such religious poetry will not be studied further here, since it is properly associated with the mainstream of 18th century literature. What is subjective, personal and unusual in Watts, Smart and Cowper is of interest in itself, and as the bridge between earlier Puritan sensibility and Romanticism. Morris' specific views about these subjective religious poets, in relation to the dominant rationalist and generalizing trends of the 18th century, will be alluded to in more detail later in this section.

Isaac Watts

Watts (1674–1758) and Law (1686–1761) were roughly contemporaries as religious writers, the one a fairly successful but undistinguished poet, the other a popular prose writer and sometime mystic. Law found himself in *The Dunciad*, and justly so, for his popular exhortations against the theater, yet is remembered, and more justly so, as the inspirer of Coleridge. His works show remarkable development from the banal to the authentically spiritual, under the influence of Böehme. Watts' case is interesting as dramatizing the cleavage of religious theory and practice in the early 18th century, and is a much fairer example than Milton to test the case made by Ross regarding the hardening of dogma after the 17th century. The two writers, Watts and Law, may be viewed as contraries and in a way, religious unfortunates: Law having the mystic insight in the tradition of Protestant vision coming down from the 17th century, Watts the gift of poetry in a reasonable degree, and also a remarkably sophisticated theory of religious poetry, but somehow bound down and limited by the hardening and static conceptions of dogma prevailing in the early 18th century.

Passages could be quoted almost at random from Law's later works, *The Spirit of Prayer* and *The Spirit of Love*, to show his sense of the vital spiritual presence and the patterns of Christian thought of which 17th century religious poetry had been made.[4] In some works the language is his own, while in the later works it is often the language of Jacob Böehme. This merging of Law and Böehme is a matter of greatest importance in the Puritan religious tradition. Law taken alone is almost the direct line of Puritan thought from the 16th century through Taylor and the 17th century divines, and in this aspect leads directly on to Smart, Cowper and Wordsworth. In Calvinist-Puritan terms, Law preserved the two vital senses of the religious spirit: the sense of the pattern of Christian dogma in literary form (echoing clearly *Paradise Lost* in many instances) and an existential sense of personal confrontation with dogma and religious experience, verging into a mystical pattern at the highest levels. Law-cum-Böehme reflects the greater intellectual awareness of Milton, Spenser and Marvell, and keeps alive a tradition later to flourish in the mixture of the strictly religious and the arcane in Blake, Coleridge and Byron. Though diagrams are only rude approximations, the following indicates the above line of relationship in rough form (see page 264).

Watts' is a more directly poetic story. In the preface to his best religious poetry, *Horae Lyricae*, he submits an astounding analysis of the situation of religious poetry in his day, in which he sees not only the external problems of religious poetry in the 18th century, but also shows himself to be the unsuccessful heir of the 17th century religious tradition. He understands both the pattern of religious experience as

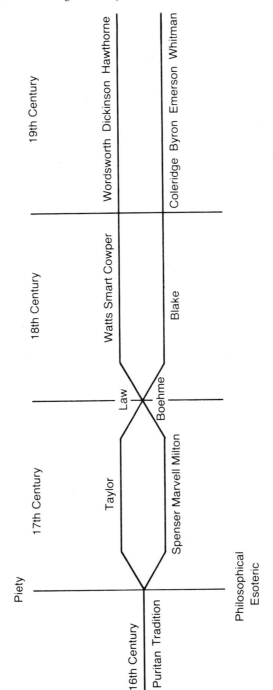

material for religious poetry, which is the tradition of Spenser and Milton, and the experiential confrontation with that experience, the tradition of Marvell and Taylor in Calvinism, and many others outside it. The paradoxical point is that his own poetry shows neither tradition powerfully: it is rather, on the whole, dogma versified, and influenced unconsciously by the rationalist, abstract tradition of 18th century philosophical thought.

This first quoted passage concerns pattern and myth in religious poetry. A brief section of the whole will be given, leaving out sections which demonstrate plainly that Watts was heavily influenced in his thinking by the success of *Paradise Lost*. With that success in mind, he complains heavily that "a Dryden, an Otway, a Congreve, or a Dennis" has not rather "furnish[ed] out a Christian poem than a modern play!" Why they didn't is obvious enough to us, yet we must agree, after reading Watts' account, that the potential materials for such poems were still available in the language and myths of the biblical world.

Now, while they paint human nature in its various forms and circumstances, if their designing be so just and noble, their disposition so artful, and their colouring so bright, beyond the most famed human writers, how much more must their descriptions of God and heaven exceed all that is possible to be said by a meaner tongue! When they speak of the dwelling-place of God, 'He inhabits eternity, and sits upon the throne of his holiness, in the midst of light inaccessible.' When his holiness is mentioned, 'The heavens are not clean in his sight, he charges his angels with folly. He looks to the moon, and it shineth not, and the stars are not pure before his eyes. He is a jealous God, and a consuming fire.' If we speak of strength, 'Behold he is strong: he removes the mountains, and they known it not: he overturns them in his anger: he shakes the earth from her place, and her pillars tremble. He makes a path through the mighty waters, he discovers the foundations of the world. The pillars of heaven are astonished at his reproof.' And, after all, 'These are but a portion of his ways: the thunder of his power who can understand?' His sovereignty, his knowledge, and his wisdom, are revealed to us in language vastly superior to all the poetical accounts of heathen divinity. . . . His transcendent eminence above all things is most nobly represented, when he 'sits upon the circle of the earth, and the inhabitants thereof are as grasshoppers. All nations before him are as the drop of a bucket, and as the small dust of the balance. . . . And to which of all the heathen poets shall we liken or compare this glorious orator, the sacred describer of the Godhead? The orators of all nations are as nothing before him, and their words are vanity and emptiness. Let us turn our eyes now to some of the holy writings, where God is creating the world. How meanly do the best of the Gentiles talk and trifle upon this subject, when brought into comparison with Moses, whom Longinus himself, a Gentile critic, cites as a master of the sublime style, when he chose to use it. . . .[5]

And so on. In contrast to this insight into the nature of highly patterned and mythic religious poetry, Watts' own work is that of a muted and not very glorious Milton. He was too involved in patterns of dogma to catch the liberating spirit of myth in his own work. Yet, his observations on personal religious poetry are even more exciting, potentially, as exhibiting insight into the life of the 17th century drama of the soul in the line of poets we have chosen to be in the Puritan pattern.

> The anguish of inward guilt, the secret stings, and racks, and scourges of conscience; the sweet retiring hours, and seraphical joys of devotion; the victory of a resolved soul over a thousand temptations; the inimitable love and passion of a dying God; the awful glories of the last tribunal; the grand decisive sentence, from which there is no appeal and the consequent transports or horrors of the two eternal worlds; these things may be variously disposed, and form many poems. How might such performances, under a divine blessing, call back the dying piety of the nation to life and beauty! This would make religion appear like itself, and confound the blasphemies of a profligate world, ignorant of pious pleasures.[6]

Watts was not able to attain this goal himself, but his attempts to do so are interesting enough to merit analysis. The goal and spirit of mythic poetry were simply unattainable in his work.

Law, Watts, Smart, Cowper and Blake were outside of the main 18th century stream of thought and writing by virtue of their religious commitments. It was a century that could consider three of these writers — Smart, Cowper, and Blake — insane, and laugh at the other two. Watts' hymns were a polite joke in the circles of culture and letters. Law was included in *The Dunciad* for his attacks on the theater in the *Serious Call*. Admittedly, Law was at his best in positive religious writing such as *Spirit of Prayer*, but one suspects that this side of the writer, if known, would have made little impression on the coffee-house wits. Law, Watts and Blake devoted themselves almost totally to religious writing and thought, Blake in the well-known private world of religious symbols he created for himself, Law and Watts in the mainstream of devotional and Puritan Christianity, which had become indeed a trickling brook in the 18th century. Smart and Cowper had been worldlings of sorts, and had written poetry under the two main 18th century influences, Deism and landscape meditation. *The Task* and other nature poems are still considered Cowper's best by general criticism, the *Olney Hymns* being taken as a lesser order. Smart's *Jubilate Agno* is considered his most interesting poem, and *A Song to David* his best, his other secular writings being of inferior order. Both poets have had the misfortune of being considered victims of religious mania or of being literally mad. Such charges are matters more of biographical than critical interest, but it is characteristic of the 18th century that the writing of religious literature in itself could be considered evidence of madness or at least of abnormality.

The question of deranged religious personality will not be considered directly in this study. Its importance is obvious enough for Smart and Cowper, and also arises to a lesser degree in writings about Blake and especially Byron, whose milder Calvinism and darker impulses have been described in psychological terms. The issues finally sort themselves out in a way that leaves room for personal and biographical discussion and a religious tradition, our interest obviously being in the latter only, unless some biographical or clinical point seems to demand attention.

In the 18th century the psychological issues relating to madness among these writers were not taken too seriously or probed deeply. Other reasons, pious or literary, were available to discredit the religious muse. Religious imagery which suggested an anthropological view of God was not encouraged by the deist mentality of the Augustans or the piety of Johnson. Johnson's uneasiness with Milton's figures in *Paradise Lost* was widely shared; he was echoing the feelings of Addison in *Spectator* a generation earlier. Johnson's pious and essentially shy and indirect view of the deity encouraged the landscape meditations of the major mid- and late 18th century poets, not the directness and morbidness of the religious poets. Meditation should be melancholy and general, not inward and morbid. Johnson would have noticed, and disapproved of, the inwardness and Calvinist bent even in Cowper's landscape poetry. His comment on Watts' religious poetry is intended to stand for the species, and no doubt would have been heartily echoed by most other critics and poets in the 18th century.

But his devotional poetry is, like that of others, unsatisfactory. The paucity of its topics enforces perpetual repetition, and the sanctity of the matter rejects the ornaments of figurative diction. It is sufficient for Watts to have done better than others what no man has done well.[7]

The chastiser of Milton's daring religious genius is not likely to approve the lesser muse of Watts in the same area, but we notice that he does approve of Watts' greater caution in handling the religious subject. The greater caution was the price of Watts' acquaintance with Locke and rationalism. Presumably the good doctor would have approved the similar caution of the *Olney Hymns*, their adherence to contemporary taste and frozen metaphor, and not Smart's *Jubilate Agno* and the daring religious impieties of Blake and Byron.

The standard of judging 18th century religious poetry must, by the nature of the subject, be difficult to define. It would be pointless to use the standards of literary history, either 18th century or modern, for these are not going to reveal anything we do not supposedly know. On the other hand, too defensive a standard is self-defeating, as one which sets too high a value upon the act of religious poetry itself. One could easily be engaged by a point of view especially congenial in a study of this sort, which placed great store upon poetic subjectivity, or on some kind of pure creativity on the poet's part in relation to dogma or religious pattern. In so far as such a point of view leads to freshness of perspective and excitement in religious poetry, it is a good standard. But its dangers are obvious too. This would easily make Blake the norm as the furthest extreme in such a process of subjectivity and originality. Smart would be passable, Watts and Cowper conventional, except for a few nature poems of the latter. We must remember that Blake's originality in religious poetry is partly within and partly without the range of Christian religious poetry, and Calvinist only by virtue of the connection with the "Holy Spirit" doctrine. It is religious because it takes its origin, in *Songs of Innocence*, at that very point where the extreme left-wing descendants of the Puritans, Quakers and other devotees of doctrines of the Spirit, pass over into Swedenborgianism and other antinomian versions of Christianity. We might also remember that the 17th century religious poets managed to convey a warmth and depth without resorting to excessive subjectivity or much formal heresy. The problem is the difficult one of defining the nature of religious poetry in the 18th century, then relating it to the Puritan tradition of which it is a part, a tradition hopefully meaningful in the larger context developed in the scope of this book.

This problem of defining religious poetry in the 18th century in traditional terms has been made easier by the fine distinctions and erudition in the first two volumes of H. N. Fairchild's *Religious Trends*.[8] His work is not helpful for the unusual case of Blake nor for the great Romantics, whom he disparages for lack of orthodoxy. This writer has discussed Fairchild on the Romantics elsewhere,[9] but his lack of sympathy with and failure to appreciate their religious kinship with Calvinism and Puritanism in no way invalidates his thesis about religion and poetry in the 18th century, the large contours of which are assumed in this introduction. As Fairchild so fully proves, Latitudinarianism, sentimentality and aesthetic emotionalism cut free from serious Christian belief are the overwhelming features of the poetry that can be called generally "religious" in the century. Watts, Young, Smart and Cowper are the exceptions, receiving the explicit label of "Divine" or "Christian" poets. There is no quarrel with this arrangement, but it must be taken further for our purposes. These poets are the exception to Fairchild's thesis and his abundant evidence that 17th century Protestantism and Puritanism led to, "decayed" in his strict Anglo-Catholic terminology, the religion and poetry of emotionalism and sentimentalism in the 18th century. But how explain the clear exceptions to this movement of lemmings in this *zeitgeist*? Fairchild demonstrates that all four maintained essential hold on Christian doctrine in its Puritan form, and this is the difference. This writer believes that Young is in the main stream of 18th century Anglicanism, and so need not be included in this study, though the case that Fairchild makes for the group is still valid whether Young is included or excluded. Certainly there are sections of *Night Thoughts* wherein the general melancholy and gloom can be seen as influenced by the Puritan funeral elegy of the 17th century, as Fairchild points out. Though this is the case it is the general features of Fairchild's argument that invite attention. This argument is the undersong of the main thesis of Protestantism collapsing into sentimentalism, and stresses the link between 17th century Puritanism, the four 18th century fugitives and survivors of the rationalist-sentimental deluge, and the great Romantic poets.

The thesis begins in a few astute observations in his consideration of Watts' poetry:

His ministry and his writings form a link between the zeal of the seventeenth and the revived zeal of the later eighteenth century. . . . Apparently he inherited from the seventeenth century certain Renaissance critical theories concerning the poet as a priest and seer who expresses sublime truths under the influence of poetic fury. . . . [H]e looks not only backward but forward to the romantic identification of the transcendental faculty with poetic genius. . . . As a child of Adam he is a weak and helpless worm, but as one of the elect he is a being of goodness, freedom, and power, full of "the glorious liberty of the children of God." A kind of intellectual antinomianism combines with his Platonic doctrine of the inspired rhapsode.[10]

Here is the link between Milton and the Romantics through Puritanism rather than despite it. In his consideration of Young, Smart and Cowper the point is developed or restated. These passages are chosen from the section on Young, agreeable to the point made above that there are Puritan elements in Young's fundamentally Anglican position.

> Young is no innovator in criticism. He merely develops the puritan view of religious, original, divinely-inspired, enthusiastic poetry which had been carried from the seventeenth century into the eighteenth by Dennis, Watts, and Blackmore. ... [T]he real situation, I believe, can more accurately be expressed by saying that both the theory of genius and the more obviously religious transcendentalism of *Night Thoughts* are parallel or cognate developments from the type of Christianity which Young inherits. Historically regarded both express, in their different spheres, the sense of inward freedom, goodness, and power which is felt by the "elect" Christian.[11]

Similar observations are made of the religious quality in Smart and Cowper, setting them apart with Watts and Young from the mainstream of 18th century poetry.

Two points must be made about Fairchild's observations on this subject. As all who are interested in the subject will know, Fairchild has been widely criticized for his firm yardstick of Anglo-Catholic orthodoxy throughout *Religious Trends* and for coming at his subject head-on, often with wit but seldom with subtlety, and, in the case of the major romantics, with great acrimony and even smugness. These points must be acknowledged, and also that these attitudes have done harm to the later volumes of the series. Regarding Puritanism in the 18th century, on the other hand, Fairchild has made and proven strikingly important observations which are valid about religious tendencies of which he profoundly disapproves. The frankness with which he puts forward his "value judgments" in no way invalidates his discovery of truth and facts, mainly that "Puritanism" in a general sense, and sometimes in more specific ones, is the vital link between religious poetry of the 16th–17th centuries and the Romantic movement. Close analysis of religious and poetic theory and attention to poetic practice show that this is indeed the case, so that the Calvinist temper might be seen to run through and survive a long period otherwise viewed as a hiatus or termination of its history.

Earlier in this chapter the recent book by David Morris on the sublime poetry in the 18th century was mentioned. Morris gave high praise to the intense personal poetry of Watts and Smart, though curiously Cowper does not figure in his account of the finest religious poetry of the age. The prevalent ideas of universality, sublimity and rationality dominate his overall viewpoint in treatment of religious poetry. His study leaves Watts in part and Smart at his best starkly in contrast with the main 18th century religious currents from Dennis to Burke, Johnson, Lowth and the Wartons. The complete account is a much more thorough version of the situation than that given in this section, but the aims are reasonably different. For though Morris writes on the personal subjective poems of Watts and Smart with approval and even warmth, his perspective never swerves from the important standard norms of 18th century literary history mentioned above to allow a closer look at the personal beliefs and the specific religious traditions that helped to make the best poetry of Watts, Smart, and also Cowper, so different and so interesting as religious poetry in a century not characterized by religious fervor. In the following comments on these three poets the personal and subjective religious factors will be stressed in various poems in the light of the Calvinist-Puritan sensibility. These comments are not intended as full explications of particular poems or studies of the poets, but rather as examples of the Calvinist-Puritan religious impulses, patterns, symbols and images, and as preparation for fuller treatment of these elements in some major Romantic poets.

In this study a certain point of view prevails, and this may be the right place to stress it somewhat in studying Watts, Smart and Cowper from a different perspective than Morris' able book, or many other studies of the 18th century. The 17th century had a widely shared sense of religious convictions, despite the endless controversies, and was a time when the amoral and irreligious formed a distinct minority. Eighteenth century values were hardly amoral or irreligious, but the trend towards secularism in all areas was apparent, as Morris pointed out. One result of this phenomenon was a new sense of difference or peculiarity in the religious mind in England, buttressed by the noble past (and Milton, of course), but more and more aware of its oddity. This minority sense of oddity has not been stressed in 18th century studies, though it evidently was shared by Watts, Law, Smart, Cowper, and later by Blake, Byron and the older Wordsworth and Coleridge. It is a belief in being different from the majority in feeling and idea, and also being right. Coupled with this feeling is a search for congenial allies, hopefully in an identical or similar religious tradition, but in fact wherever such might be found. Blake's attraction to William Law, the previous attraction of Law to Böehme, Coleridge's to Cowper, Law and religious esoterica, and other influences within this recessive tradition can be explained in this way. Abstract guidelines based upon literary theory, sublimity, rationalism and like concepts cannot provide a close explanation of the poetry which resulted from these feelings and yearnings. In introducing Watts, Smart and Cowper as self-conscious religionists, and co-religionists to a point, some interesting examples of interrelation come before us. Watts' knowledge of the American Puritan situation and the famous Edwards is the most fascinating. Colonial America is often − though not by American scholars − thought of as backward and dependent in the 18th century by modern students; for religiously fervent Englishmen like Watts, Cowper and the great Methodist preachers, the reverse was the truth.

The news of Edwards' work of conversion in Northampton soon reached the ears of Calvinist-Puritan dissenters in England, where by 1700 the descendants of the Commonwealth had become a quiescent minority with only the consolation of Watts as their celebrated divine and occasional poet. Watts rose to this occasion by getting out *A Faithful Narrative of the Surprising Work of God . . . by Jonathan Edwards with Prefaces, by Rev. Dr. Watts . . . of London.*[12] Watts' writing demonstrates the closeness of the theology of the English dissenters and the American colonists, and also a certain enviousness of Edward's success in the matters of piety and conversion in the new world. There is clear evidence in the little book of a living religious tradition of Calvinist-Puritan cast on both sides of the ocean. Edwards as theologian was far more brilliant and eccentric than Watts, but that hardly makes any important difference. An American Puritan poet, Samuel Davies,[13] also influenced by Edwards' more popular writings, contributed poetry remarkably similar to Watts' from his Virginia wilderness congregations.[14] William Cowper left among his books an autograph copy of one work by a famous early Puritan, John Flavel, *The Fountain of Life Opened*, (London, 1673). Flavel is better known for his influential allegorical work, *Husbandry Spiritualized* (London, 1669), which is in the mainstream of important formative Puritan literature. Many other examples of interrelations could be given, and some will be in discussing certain poems. All are intended again to point up the peculiar (if you will) focus of this book, to study traditions and connections that standard works play down or leave out, ultimately so that we might understand aspects of the Romantic religious poets otherwise totally obscure to the secular mentality.

To follow the Calvinist temper in Watts, Smart and Cowper the choice of poems must be rigorously selective, as there is no obligation in this book to add to the numerous full studies of these poets. Watts'

Hymns, Smart's Seatonian poems, the moralizing sections of *The Task* and other moralizing poems by Smart and Cowper are well within the province of typical 18th century religious verse studied by Fairchild, Morris and others. *Jubilate Agno*, once ignored and now perhaps overrated, at least by Romantic critics, is too strange and special a performance for this purpose, except in some remarkable passages. And if I may be permitted to so say, except for certain sections — not necessarily the strongly religious ones but such as the charming eulogy to Geoffrey the cat — *Jubilate Agno* is still not very much understood even by those who praise it fulsomely. Nevertheless this account leaves us a number of important poems to discuss, especially Watts' *Horae Lyricae*, Book I, Smart's *A Song to David* and personal religious pieces, the same type in Cowper, as well as many of the *Olney Hymns*. The essential criteria here are the personal, subjective and religious lyric with Calvinist-Puritan strain, so even the commentary on *Horae, David* and *Olney* must be selective. As will be noted in passing, there is much perfunctory decorative and typical 18th century conventional phraseology in all these poems, even though the best religious verse of the three poets also happens to reside in these poems.

To clarify the interest for this book in Watts, Smart and Cowper more specifically, the Calvinist-Puritan categories of experience mentioned briefly in Section I are helpful. These were 16th and 17th century categories, primarily of theology but also of poetic sensibility — the sin-state, vocation, election, justification, sanctification and glorification — within which we discussed the 17th century poets and Spenser. These categories offer no possibility of a procrustean bed for 18th century poets. Nevertheless we find traces of all of them in each poet, not in the order of the Puritan preachers or of Book I of *The Faerie Queene*, or in similar intensity in every poet, but the most important element in many cases. Watts gives the clearest pattern in *Horae Lyricae*, skipping only the early stages which would not be necessary for himself and his converted audience. The sin-state and the humility of doubt and conversion appear in some of his sermons and other prose. The most genuine poems in *Horae Lyricae* emphasize sanctification and glorification, but usually fail at the high Miltonic sublime. Smart, whose Puritanism is residual and present only in the integrity of his feelings, stresses sin, peculiar election, sanctification, and, somewhat unintelligibly, glory, and the idea of spiritual identification with Christ. Cowper most characteristically offers the sin-state, election-justification (almost, but not always, ambiguously allied to reprobation), sometimes sanctification, but seldom glory, with the exception of Book VI of *The Task*.

This is the proper way of looking at the best poems of these three poets as Calvinist-Puritan, but needless to say, it is a revisionary way. A more traditional 18th century and religious way of labeling and dividing may help to clarify matters for the reader, though ultimately I hope to show the interesting and useful intersection of the two sets of categories. In the more traditional terms of genre and 18th century study there are five types of religious poems in Watts, Smart and Cowper in which we are interested. (1) The deeply personal and anguished — Cowper's "The Castaway," sections of *Jubilate Agno* and "Hymn to the Supreme Being" and a rare poem or two in *Horae Lyricae*. (2) Poems of strongly theological cast with sincere power and unmistakable personal animus in favor of Calvinism — many *Horae Lyricae*, some *Olney Hymns*, traces in some sections of *Jubilate*. (3) Devotional verse within the structure of Church practice, occasionally showing some of the spirit of 17th century poetry of sanctification (Herbert or Taylor), but mostly perfunctory. (4) The mindless hymns of devotion sustained by music and by congregation participation that we associate with bad 18th century religious verse — unfortunately this is a faithful element in all three poets. (5) The visionary and Miltonic strain — Watts attempts this in some *Horae Lyricae*, fulfilling his promise in the preface without much success. On the other hand the best sections of *A Song to David* as well as the most unintelligible ones in *Jubilate Agno* are Smart's quite different results in attempted Miltonic sublime. Cowper avoids this strain in lyrics and shorter pieces, but it strongly influences Books V and VI of *The Task*, in a mode of verse both non-Miltonic and non-lyric.

For all the poems studied here, the task of sorting the strictly Calvinist categories and the conventional ones will be undertaken. For many poems this is obvious work. A poem like "The Castaway" is deeply personal, an anguished lyric, and also enmeshed in the Calvinist categories of sin-state, election and reprobation. Harder choices appear in sorting out *Olney Hymns* and *Horae Lyricae*, that is, the genuinely theological and Calvinist-Puritan, from conventional 18th century rigor and piety. Many critics have claimed that there is no such distinction. With the Miltonic sublime, at least, the test is always clear, whether we are dealing with a mere imitation of Genesis and *Paradise Lost* — which is what most 18th century sublime poetry, Calvinist and Anglican alike, amounts to — or with some genuine visionary and prophetic strain towards "last things," the glorification of the saints as found in *Saints Everlasting Rest* and authentic poetic works of this variety. The form itself can hardly be called Calvinist in the 18th century, since it had become generally Protestant and "Miltonic." Yet we may point out authentic strains in some Watts poems, in *A Song to David*, and the last books of *The Task* where the visionary impulse is again close to the Puritan original. In these discussions it is to be hoped that the individuality of the poets' styles will not be lost in any of the poems considered carefully; in cases where this seems to happen, let the reader remember that a variety of poems are cited as *exempla*, and only a few looked at for their own sakes, both to demonstrate the richness of religious poses and to number the interesting poems available to prove the not-obvious case made in this chapter: that a vital Calvinist-Puritan strain did exist in and survive the 18th century. While this is not an entirely novel and barren field of study, the point need not be made again that this outlook towards religious poetry in the 18th century, and the value of religious poetry for Romanticism to come, are hardly overworked in our present literary perspectives.

There are many nuances in the appearance of the Calvinist temper among the three poets as well as some real similarities and differences. All wrote deeply personal religious poems and also stultified conventional ones, but between the extremes there is no fair way to label any two poets. Any two are very close in some areas, drastically different in others. It seems therefore reasonable in this instance, as before in the brief summary of Calvinist-Puritan categories in the opening section, to have recourse to a diagram. In this diagram the usual religious genres and types appear along the top; along the side, above and beneath the names of the poets, appear the Calvinist categories and the most characteristic of them in each poet respectively. Badness as a quality is not accounted for, except under "conventional poems." The unusual syncopations of some categories of literary conventions and Calvinism in the case of Smart, and the few pertaining to the others, will be explained in the discussion of the individual poets and poems.

Isaac Watts is the proper poet to begin this specific investigation, both for reasons of chronology and logic. He is the only 18th century religious poet who continued the 17th century tradition of "devotional verse" in its full form, and received Johnson's displeasure for it. More centrally to our task, he wrote in all five definable 18th century religious categories — personal, Calvinist-theological, devotional, conventional, and Miltonic sublime — with different degrees of success. We

Sin State, Vocation, Election, Justification, Sanctification, Glorification	1 Personal	2 Calvinist Puritan Theology	3 Devotional	4 Conventional	5 Miltonic "The Sublime"
Watts Sin State, Vocation, Sanctification	yes	yes	yes	yes	yes
Smart Sin State, Vocation, Glorification	yes	no	yes	yes	yes (*A Song to David*)
Cowper Sin State, Election-Reprobation, Sanctification	yes	yes	no	yes	yes (*The Task*)

can easily isolate the poor conventional 18th century religious poem and hymn from the other types in his work. He also touches upon all the Calvinist categories of experience, three very seriously, the others lightly. And unlike the scattered and very different types of poems to be coped with in the complete works of Smart and Cowper, all these varieties of poetry are found in the scope of his significant volume, *Horae Lyricae*. In the brief allusions to Watts' biography and poetic theory earlier in this chapter, it is clear that he was very consciously a Puritan in life and aesthetic work, the most prominent in the early 18th century. Law's fervor comes from mysticism, which can be attached to any sect; Smart was unaware of his closeness to Calvinist-Puritan traditions, and rejects sectarianism in the very poem where it is most manifest (*Jubilate Agno*); and, as is best known, Cowper backed into Calvinism as a refuge from life and mental depression. Not so Watts, who may be called the leading preacher, writer and divine in the Calvinist fold in England in the first half of the 18th century, an admirer of his more intellectual American contemporary Edwards in America, and envious of Edwards' greater success in what they of course saw as their primary role, preachers and converters of souls.

The poems of clearly personal cast in *Horae Lyricae* include "Self-Consecration," "Confession and Pardon," especially "Two Happy Rivals," and several others. To them close attention must be given. There are a number of Calvinist-theological poems and hymns, as befits a teaching minister of the gospel, with titles such as "God's Dominion and Decrees," "God glorious, and Sinners saved," "Penitent Pardoned," and so forth. These may be impossible for practical purposes to distinguish for the modern reader from what will strike him as "conventional" poetic religious exercises, but a necessary and important distinction is needed here for the purposes of this study. Any poem that might have been written by some proper Anglican or even a well-meaning Deist or general Christian (Smart's Seatonian prize poems, for example) is conventional for this purpose and omitted from discussion. Admittedly, Calvinist-theological poems are also within a religious convention, but one it is our task to show flourishing in the 18th century. Watts also wrote poems of divine love to the Savior, after the 17th century models of Herbert and Crashaw, blending with the mode of earlier religious warmth enough conventional 18th century and Calvinist theology to distinguish them from high Anglican or Catholic fervor. These poems are given a separate place in some editions of *Horae*, with an apology for the throwback to an earlier era in at least one famous edition, with Southey's Preface.[15] Of course they are significant in stressing continuity in religious poetry from the 17th to the 18th century, or showing the complexity behind our comfortable historical categories, but not otherwise noticeable in this context. On the other hand, brief mention is not in order for his Miltonic or "sublime" efforts, among the best and the worst he wrote. If we recall his promise in the Preface to write in the subjective, individual style and also in the Miltonic sublime (God's purpose and grandeur in revelation and creation), then types one and five are clearly the most significant as poems. Type two, the Calvinist-theological, is usually not of much intrinsic value as poetry, though yielding to none in significance to the literary historian tracing the fortunes of Calvinist literature from Watts to Edwards and Davies in the Colonies, then back to Smart and Cowper in later 18th century England.

Watt's poems at their best give the impression of scaled-down 17th century works. (At worst, they are merely perfunctory convention, like all bad poetry.) We cannot assume that the effect of imitation is always unfortunate. Watts deliberately chose 17th century models —

personal-existential, Calvinist-theological, divine praises, and Miltonic
– as he openly proclaims in the Preface. The scaling-down may have
arisen from one of two sources: a conscious inability to equal Milton,
or lack of desire to imitate the excesses of the metaphysical and
baroque styles. If we compare his efforts with Milton's or the
metaphysicals', the sense of imitation is heavily present in both cases,
but the cause is different. In the first, honest emulation falls short of the
original; in the other, caution leads to a diminishment from the
baroque taste of the earlier period. But an equally fair judgement from
another point of view is that 18th century propriety had entered even
this most Puritan-sectarian breast. Even in the straightforwardly
doctrinal poems there are some curious things. Some are openly
Calvinist in the manner of Bunyan or the later *Olney Hymns*, eagerly
promulgating doctrine among the faithful. A larger number are
impersonal and very generally Christian in impact, and might have
fallen from the pen of any religious man, orthodox in fundamentals, of
the 17th or 18th centuries. The poems in all categories lacking
individuality or originality deserve little stress, while for conventional
poems, mentioning their presence will suffice. There are a reasonable
number of poems in every other group deserving commentary, enough,
it is hoped, to call into question Johnson's famous dictum on Watts in
particular and religious poetry in general.

Watts' personal religious poems have two tones, in one the clear
attempt to imitate the intimacy with religious things of 17th century
metaphysical poems, the second a genuine intimacy all his own, with
elements of reserve and the urbane that never become mere archness
and 18th century decorum. In structure these poems follow the
convention of dialogue poems with opposed speakers, or that of the
internal meditation, wherein the speaker communes with himself about
his innermost fears and hopes, both inspired by the religious
perspective of Calvinism. There is no innovation here. Both are
metaphysical traditions, and among the Puritans, Marvell, Taylor,
Baxter and Sibbes come to mind. Watts attempted also the sublime of
Milton, but not the allegory of Spenser and Bunyan. The fears and the
opponents are the usual ones – sin, death, Satan, despair vs. salvation,
resurrection, Christ, justification by faith. In ideas and structure, in
fact, nothing distinguishes any of these poems save one from the more
numerous Calvinist-theological poems, the "preaching" poems of
category two. They are distinguished by the intensely personal element,
the subjective *I*, which Watts announced as one vehicle for saving

religious poetry, but without following through successfully as often as he might, if his poems were to save the day for religious poetry. That they did not is perhaps accountable by the fact that there is so little of the authentic self in *Horae* relative to theological, conventional, devotional and Miltonic attempts. This is slight speculation, in the face of the massive drift of 18th century literature away from the religious mode. The one poem in which the dialogue or inner argument is not totally in religious counters is "Two Happy Rivals." In it the poet and parson argue out the eternal conflict between art and religion, that is, whether they are compatible in aim and in one person, and how far poetry may be the handmaiden of religion. Even this is not a new theme in religious poetry by Watt's day, but one handled by Watts in a decisively personal way, in his own voice.

It is a pleasure to read Watt's poems on the relationship between the muse and religion. The first really personal poem in *Horae*, "Self-Consecration," presents us with the character of a man of classical education renouncing the secular for the religious vocation of poet. In his enthusiasm of the moment one thinks that he is making an easy choice, but of course the poems in *Horae* are in the tradition of the classically educated Christian, except when Watts chooses to preach his Calvinist doctrines in verse. The second and greater poem renders the complexity of the situation, and its "happy" fruition, at least theoretically. The muse is free to range over secular subjects, or it may restrict itself to divine songs, Calvinist of course, or it may, at its most profound and penetrating, sing of the ultimate mysteries of the universe, which are indeed divine. In plainer language, there is room for *carmen saeculare*, personal existential poetry, and the Miltonic sublime in the range of the fully Christian poet. Final allegiance is not in doubt. As in mystical tradition, the final flight of religious intuition leaves behind even man's most noble human faculty of imagination:

> I will no more demand my tongue,
> Till the gross organ, well refin'd,
> Can trace the boundless flights of an unfetter'd mind,
> And raise an equal song.

Though we can never doubt final allegiance in "Two Happy Rivals," the poem comes closest to the expression of real tension and interest of all the poems, a concentrated version of the argument in the Preface, recapitulated earlier in this chapter and commended by Fairchild as the ultimate rationalization for Puritan poetry, the thread of theory linking Spenser and Milton with the 19th century — "O why is piety so weak, /

And yet the muse so strong?" Watts' response may seem naive enough, and ancient to boot: place the muse in the service of piety to infuse devotion with new vigor. After the inevitable movement from the merely secular interest to religious anxiety and exaltation, the sublime will overcome both worldly faculties, leading to the ecstasy of mysticism beyond the knowledge and despair of this vale of tears. This process explains also, in Fairchild's terms, how the vatic-prophetic and the Puritan ethos, which in some respects are ill at ease together, given the latter's suspicion of man's intellectual and moral capacities, came together in the 17th and 18th centuries. Early repressive ethical Puritanism had kept the imagination on short tether during the 16th and 17th centuries, Spenser forming the only significant exception. After the early 19th century, with suspicion of intellect and imagination again rampant from various sources, the contraction of the sublime again occurred. Byron and Coleridge struggle with these doubts, some religious in motivation, others not. Emily Dickinson and Hawthorne made the best of them, tempering imagination, reason and faith (piety) to all sorts of doubts and misgivings. Carlyle and Melville suffer more loudly and grandly but from essentially the same causes. Within the latter context, Watts seems downright complacent, and even the undoubtable personal turmoils of Smart and Cowper are anchored in a faith madness can shake only temporarily. But we cannot underestimate the sanction that religious ecstasy and ultimate aim gave to these poets. Constrained by their own pieties, they enjoyed a weapon against the contrary constraints of wit and proper meter in their vatic charge:

> Such is the muse: lo! she disdains
> > The links and chains
> > Measures and rules of vulgar strains,
> And o'er the laws of harmony, a sovereign queen she reigns.

It may not be too facetious a claim that, just as the active Puritans broke statues and killed kings by right of election, so the poetic-clerical brethren might cast aside secular rules and decorum. Ignorant rant and *Hudibras*, the satiric portraits from Butler to Scott, are inevitable end products of this attitude, but when coupled with knowledge of classical culture to provide obvious balance, we have the range of poets from Spenser to the early 19th century, who with different degrees of happiness and success struggle with the rivals of religion and poetry. It was a delicate game to be a successful Puritan poet, and as with all difficult games, few played it well. Watts, for instance, is a poor version of Milton because his vision seldom measures up to his outlines and expectations. His personal, less ambitious dialogue and "metaphysical" poetry is more often successful. A strange reason for the success of "Two Happy Rivals" is that we do not doubt that Watts will be successful in his projected Miltonic flights, so infectious are his enthusiasm and confidence:

> Shine from the sky,
> And call me high
> To mingle with the choirs of glory and of bliss.
> Devotion there begins the flight,
> Awakes the song, and guides the way;
> There love and zeal, divine and bright,
> Trace out new regions in the world of light,
> And scarce the boldest muse can follow or obey.

It is only by reading the directly Miltonic poems that we reluctantly accept his relative inadequacy as a visionary poet.

"Confession and Pardon," "Looking Upward," "Farewell" and "Pardon and Sanctification" strike a more personal note than do Watts' Calvinist teaching poems, and are not merely conventional, but the personal note differs from the attempted warmth of his 17th century devotional imitations. It is both more restrained and more authentic, yet less intense than in the poems already discussed. Some sense of Watts the man is in them, coming through the years and the conventions to us, and this is reason enough to consider them, though not to linger over them. The plainly conventional imitations of the 17th century metaphysical "divine love" poem and the 18th century teaching hymn need not be considered at all, except to note their existence in rounding out Watt's range. Most of the Calvinist-Puritan poems, and some of the Miltonic sublime, are not much better than the conventional in quality in Watts and Cowper, but have historical importance for the focus of this book. Since "Pardon and Sanctification" is the best and most representational of these personal yet not too intense poems, with heavy emphasis upon doctrine but not merely doctrinal, as are a good number of the Calvinist-theological and conventional poems, it is a fair poem for analysis of the balance of the doctrinal and personal which Watts can at times achieve.

The poem begins with a familiar description of the sin-state. The potential punishment of a vengeful God is sketched in a few brisk lines, bristling with the conventional ideas of "crimes," "hideous fear," "guilt," "hell flames" and "the eye of a revenging God." But of course there is justification by faith as the remedy, presented in the imagery of blood and washing away of sin so close to the heart of the evangelical movements in the 18th century and so repellent to modern men, even to most of the Christians who still accept the abstract doctrine. Then begins the familiar Puritan pattern of sactification, "conscience smiles within," and allusion to the struggle within the sanctified state against sin. The poem ends upon an imprecation against sin and Satan, not with a hint of glory. Watts has chosen to dramatize the sin-state, justification, and sanctification here, ignoring election and glory, and the full range of the cycle of sin and grace. This happens because his purpose is not merely to write an objective teaching poem, but rather one with stress. His desire is to dramatize what fear of damnation, sin, the sense of pardon, and struggle with sin in the redeemed state mean to the individual. Admittedly, he is not very successful. Though this poem is dotted with the personal pronouns, *my* (three times in stanza one), *I* (many times) and *me*, the poem is not convincing as deep personal statement, thought doubtless sincere. It cannot be compared seriously to "Two Happy Rivals" in personal resonances, and is light-years behind the best poems of the sanctified state in Taylor or Cowper's great "The Castaway" on the despair aspect of the subject. It is much like average Cowper in *Olney Hymns*. In another doctrinal poem of similar type, "Confession and Pardon," Watts tries for keener emotion by enlisting some 17th century clichés:

> O'ercome by dying love I fall,
> Here at thy cross I lie,
> And throw my flesh, my soul, my all,
> And weep, and love, and die.

Also this poem is longer and concentrates on the sin-state and the moment of justification, which gives it an initial advantage of intensity and depth. But the actual effect is a mixture of 18th century evangelism and 17th century fervor which does not hold together. By no means does the poem strike a false note or fail utterly; it is just that the two types of emotion do not mix, and are thus present in alternate patches throughout the poem. The sincerity is manifest but it is a tepid sincerity, gentle, muted, moving undisturbed to a predestined end. Again we see one of the central paradoxes of the Calvinist poet at work — he is at his best when progressing through the stages in real doubt and mystery, whether in the modes of allegory or personal experience, and conversely, almost always dull when too full of assurance and election. In the purely teaching poems, doubt is out of place, except as an abstraction. In the personal poems real doubt and mystery vary intensity and authenticity from poet to poet, from poem to poem in each poet. Spenser can be both a strong and a dull allegorist in *The Faerie Queene*, as we saw earlier in the book. The same is true of the poets who use the personal mode and all or some of the stages in the process of regeneration.

Watts' "preaching poems," a goodly number of the whole, are generally Christian with a heavy 17th century overlay, or Calvinist-Puritan, or merely redactions of Bible stories and the Psalms. "The Penitent pardoned," "Incomprehensible," "Sight of Heaven in Sickness," "Atheist's Mistake," and "Launching into Eternity" are examples of the first, wherein one can easily note the direct influence of Marvell, and occasionally other metaphysical poets. Since any good Christian pastor might have written them, their only importance is in showing the persistence of 17th century forms and attitudes into the religious mentality of the next century, which was a limited circle to be sure. In the extreme "Divine Love of the Saviour" group, set off in editions, this influence is even more direct. Of all these groups, the Old Testament redactions are the dullest and least inspired of Watts' poems, even when the Psalms are the source, though of course these poems were important for his pastoral work, another issue.[16] We need only look at examples of the class of poems treating Calvinist-Puritan doctrine in a generally impersonal way, choosing as usual ones which combine theological interest with some poetical merits.

"God's Dominion and Decrees," "God glorious, and Sinners saved," "Condescending Grace," and "The Infinite" are Calvinist teaching poems. In the two first the poet makes an appearance at the end, in a tepid unconvincing way merely as only another member of the flock. This is as it should be, for obvious reasons. Poems intended to express every good man's religious beliefs and feelings cannot linger over the peculiarities, whether joys or sorrows, of one man. Even the average poet is an unusual man by ordinary standards, and we know that Watts was a man of keen intellect and erudition who probably suppressed too much of both to accommodate himself to the kind of poetry he believed he should give to the world. Piety also no doubt held him in check throughout his life, except in the Miltonic flights, which fail for other reasons. At any rate these four poems, on God's power, glory, grace and mysterious infinitude (with other themes as additives) fairly represent Watts as Puritan preacher of the World through poetry.

"God's Dominion and Decrees" stresses Calvin's favorite doctrine of God's power and *bonne volonté* which leads inexorably to election. Watts is not squeamish in his echoing of this familiar and fundamental Puritan sentiment:

> Life, death, and hell, and worlds unknown,
>   Hang on his firm decree. . . .

The middle stanzas are standard cosmology using the argument from design and deep reverence for the Creator, without a hint of deism, and the poem becomes Calvinist again only when attention is paid to the mysterious will of God, where the language is bold and obviously Calvinist:

> His providence unfolds the book,
>   And makes his counsels shine;
> Each opening leaf, and every stroke,
>   Fulfils some deep design.

The tepid entry of the subject in the final stanza was mentioned, wherein the poet's humility is stressed, and his refusal to speculate on "double" predestination. Hope and piety are stressed over speculation, the signs of election are simply called fate and "gloomy lines." It is the pose Calvin recommended for the minister when he was not alone in his study, but out setting a good example for the faithful, and Watts had gotten the message duly set forth in the *Institutes* on this point.

"God glorious, and Sinners saved" gives far more to the former than the latter point. The praises, all conventional ones, are presented with gusto, and the groveling of guilty men, "rebellious worms" and sinners, extremely done by modern standards of taste. There is a good deal of the imagery of the Atonement, "dying Son," his "groans" to appease God's sense of offended justice, that repels the modern reader even more than it did Dr. Johnson. There is no aesthetic way to defend such diction, for this is not so much the abstract theology of the "divine spiritual economy" in itself, as the old theologians used to put it, but the baroque imagery, without the special cleverness of Crashaw or Donne, that creaks here from overuse in 18th century Puritan and Methodist poetry.

"Condescending Grace" and "The Infinite" are less personal and baroque. The first imitates a psalm, and there is a Hebraic ring to both poems, natural enough to the Calvinist mind apart from Christian aspects. From the early word "Eternal" to the last stanza, "Condescending Grace" could be any English paraphrase of a psalm. In the last stanza of "The Infinite" the stern Calvinist doctrine of grace mixes with the Hebraic vision of God, giving a strong, almost Gothic finality to the poem: "For nothing's found in Thee / But boundless inconceivables, / And vast eternity." This poem contemplates the nature of the Calvinist God without reference to Christ or the theology of regeneration. It has attempts at 17th century paradox and wit, but the effects are Hebraic and Calvinist, that is, awe and fear before the grim mystery and power of God. There are frequent echoes from Milton − "Boundless," "unconfin'd," "vast abyss," "ocean of infinities," "inconceivables," "vast eternity." It is not a directly Miltonic poem because tightness and metaphysical constriction, not amplitude and grandeur, are the structural aim, and so the poet makes of himself, though somewhat *absconditus*, a small rather than expansive man. Though not in the poem directly, he is a worried singer, not a vatic voice.

As for the direct 17th century imitations of Watts, dedicated to "Divine Love," and his otherwise conventional religious verse, these may be omitted from discussion, as will also be the conventional poems of Smart and Cowper, which are 18th century and evangelical in emphasis. Watts is vitally interesting as a Miltonic poet, or poet of "glorification," a category vital also to the other two poets, though Smart is less traditional in reliance upon Milton. Glorification is the last phase of the Puritan cycle, so it is fitting that the analysis of all three poets should end in this ultimate area of Calvinist Christian concern.

The Puritan category of glorification is now familiar to us from the early writers, and from Baxter, Bunyan and Milton in the 17th century. As Watts' Preface on divine poetry makes perfectly clear, for most 18th century writers this category and Milton were inextricably united. Only Smart in his peculiar way does not acknowledge the connection in his genuine moments of glorification, which occur in both *Jubilate Agno* and *A Song to David*. In Cowper the last book of *The Task* is closely concerned with glorification in a text heavy with Miltonic allusions. The reasons are obvious enough. We may believe that Baxter, Bunyan and Law made modest achievements in their glimpses of the sublime and glory, but they were largely forgotten in and after their day, and even in our own live in the shadows of Milton's achievements. Milton dealt boldly with first and last things, with heaven, hell and the cosmos, and with the individual's salvation within the vision of this mighty frame. Religious poetry has never been the same since, despite Johnson's strictures and Pope's sneers, and the best such poetry of later times has largely avoided the cosmic areas where Milton was strongest and comparison inevitable, by wisely turning to the existential or "metaphysical" alternative, as in Hopkins and many Catholic poets. Watts tried to be boldly Miltonic in some poems, whereas Cowper, more conscious of the burdens of learning, was more circumspect in Book VI of *The Task*. Smart easily outdistances both in *A Song to David*, no doubt because there, being entirely in his own element, he could be oblivious to Milton and almost all other tradition except the Bible.

Watts' excursions into the area of glorification can be viewed under three categories, which are by their very nature overlapping. The longer poems tend to mix the three: directly Miltonic imitations in theme and imagistic references to *Paradise Lost*; scriptural paraphrases of creation and other topics handled by Milton, which invite Miltonic comparison without especially being imitations, Watts having the Scripture directly in mind; glimpses of glory from the personal point of view, or glorification proper in the Puritan scheme, with examples such as *Faerie Queene* I, xii and the ending of *Pilgrim's Progress* for our reference as literary transferences of St. Paul, Calvin and the Puritan divines. Cowper follows this pattern also, with a different literary method, but Smart is wayward, requiring greater skill on the reader's part to see the patterns. For Watts we will look at some heavy-handed or bad poems, "Three Salvations" (political), "Law at Sinai" (more mixed in type and value), and "Day of Judgment" (almost pure Wigglesworth and unredeemable). Then there are some more reasonable examples blending the three modes, such as "Creating Wisdom," "Jesus only Saviour," and "God Supreme." Finally we will look briefly at some poems which do not attempt very much compared to the long Miltonic and biblical imitations, or are very successful in relation to the ones just named, but in which there are a few felicities to be gratefully and quickly pointed out.

"A Hymn of Praise for three great Salvations" is perhaps the most dismal long poem written by Watts. It is a stale rehearsal of the Tudor myth of the elect nation in its Puritan version, ground we have covered previously. The topics chosen are the saving of "our island round" from the Armada, the gunpowder plot and James II. Nothing special is added to the usual litany of bloody Rome, murdering Irish, Roman priests and the old serpent (Pope and Satan, as in Spenser) of 16th and 17th century lore. The poem ends on a tiresome encomium in the late 17th century political manner to the saviour, William of Orange, whose way is lined by angels and who nearly becomes one himself. The poem is bad not only in its narrow religious and political features but because it does not really seem to interest Watts. His interest in the politics of religion, especially in securing religious and social liberties for non-conformists, was lifelong, and of more genuine concern at the time than beating dead Papist horses, but it was not a subject of interest to him as a poet. In "Law at Sinai" and "Day of Judgment," Watts struggles with the sublime or Miltonic aspect of the religious muse, trying to achieve the promise of his Preface, for which we owe poems some respect and interest.

"The Day of Judgment" is the grim kind of Puritan poem which offends the modern reader by its content, in the manner of Wigglesworth's "Day of Doom." Though we are aware of passages in Augustine, Calvin and many Counter Reformation prose writers in which the pains of the damned are relished by the saved, to have them contemplated with joy in poetry has somehow always been more repulsive, for we can accept almost any feeling from a poet except love of the murderous instinct. After the lines,

Hark the shrill outcries of the guilty wretches!
Lively bright horror, and amazing anguish,
Stare through their eyelids, while the living worm lies Gnawing within
  them.

neither the good simile of the Baltic storm opening the poem, nor the Puritan note of redemption and the triumph of the faithful can do much to save the poem. The genuine joys of the blessed are always marred if the contrast is openly given to the fate of the damned; if the faithful revel in the sufferings of the damned, a lack of tact is committed which will at least ruin a poem in which such takes place. Watts is more often like Baxter, Law, and the more charitable Puritan saints, honestly exhibiting *gaudium spiritus* for the elect and the triumph over the evils of life, but sorrowing for, or at least ignoring, the damned. Only Milton might get away with something like this in poetry, and not even he more than several times.

"The Law given at Sinai" is very ambitious and reasonably success-ful in the round of Watts' attempts at the Miltonic sublime, that is, visionary poetry concerning God's grandeur from a cosmic rather than personal standpoint. There are finer passages in some of the shorter pieces but no other single poem comes closer than this one to the achievement of Watts' higher aim. Not that the poem, of course, does not suffer by comparison with Milton on creation and the other finest things in *Paradise Lost*; however, the presentation of God the Father in Book III, the war in heaven, and some of the poetry in XI and XII are places in Milton closer to the level Watts can achieve. A comparison is not the purpose here, except to set the range of Watts' abilities in relation to the predecessor he invoked in the Preface. The same abilities and range appear in " Creating Wisdom," "God Supreme" and "Jesus the only Saviour," the other reasonably successful attempts at longish poems in the Miltonic mode. Even with its flaws, the Sinai poem is the best example of Watts' striving originally to work on Milton's ground with less of imitation in the obvious sense than in any other single poem.

As stated, a close comparison of these poems with similar episodes in Milton is not intended. Still it is well to note the passages in *Paradise Lost* — with their main sources in the Bible of course — that either Watts directly uses, or where the events and images are so close as to call them inevitably to mind. One reason why "Law at Sinai" has superiority becomes apparent also by doing this, that is, Watts has more ample room to work with his material because Milton did less with that momentous episode in biblical history than with so many others. Book III of *Paradise Lost* involves the material of the other three poems, "Jesus the only Saviour" entirely, the others in the dramatization of God the Father and in the themes of justice, retribution and redemption. The long creation passage in Book VII is important for "Creating Wisdom" and "God Supreme," as well as for the less successful Miltonic poems to be glanced at cursorily in the close of this discussion. Since both the poems make some attempt at defining the mystery of wisdom and power in God, lines 150−172 of Book VII and God's difficult presentation of the creation of mankind's election and reprobation in Book III loom large in the background of the poems. On the other hand, though without question a source, the treatment of Moses at Sinai in *Paradise Lost* XII, 226−244 is rather slight, in a part of the poem often called perfunctory. The discussion of these final books in the previous section of this book makes it clear that this writer does not accept that judgment on the whole, but certainly agrees with the universal judgment of the greater magnificence of the earlier parts of the poem devoted to the mystery of God, retribution, the fall, the hymn to creation, and so on. This is the sacred and awesome ground trod by Watts in some of his other Miltonic efforts. Milton will not be quoted at length here in order to control and focus this discussion, the exception being this passage of

Moses at Sinai, which is valuable in making the special point that
Watts had greater relative freedom from Milton here than in his other
efforts:

> God from the Mount of *Sinai*, whose gray top
> Shall tremble, hee descending, will himself
> In Thunder, Lightning and loud Trumpers sound
> Ordain them Lawes; part such as appertaine
> To civil Justice, part religious Rites
> Of sacrifice, informing them, by types
> And shadowes, of that destind Seed to bruise
> The Serpent, by what means he shall achieve
> Mankinds deliverance . . . .
> > he grants what they besaught,
> Instructed that to God is no access
> Without Mediator, whose high Office now
> *Moses* in figure bears, to introduce
> One greater . . . .
>
> > > (*PL*, XII, 227–244)

This brief description based upon upon Scripture leaves Watts with
ample room for a poem of around 150 lines in which his confrontation
with the original can be more direct than in the other poems.

"The Law given at Siani" does not begin auspiciously. "Arm thee
with thunder, heav'nly Muse" is rant, followed by a perfunctory
account of the flight from Egypt, the Red Sea episode and the arrival
of the Israelites at Sinai. From that point until line 135, the announce-
ment of the commandments to Moses, the poem has its center. The
concluding paraphrase of the commandments is adequate, better than
the opening lines, but definitely a falling off from the central lines.
"Creating Wisdom" and "God Supreme and Self-sufficient" have the
same center, that is, to define, describe and work with the nature and
power of God, Calvin's presiding point throughout the *Institutes*, and a
great object in Milton, even though he condescended somewhat from
this high Puritan ground in offering to *justify* the ways of God to
man. There is a tension and fury in the Sinai poem from lines 50 to 135
in the description of the essence and action of God absent from the
more serene and complacent contemplations of wisdom and creation in
the other poems. This aspect sets the Sinai poem off somewhat by
itself. "Jesus the only Saviour" has a more Christian yet sublime topic,
handled in a somewhat legal and, to many readers no doubt, a colder
way than in other Christian traditions. It is reminiscent of *Paradise
Lost* III and to a lesser extent of the "Nativity Ode," having the

stubborn Miltonic-Puritan insistence upon thinking through matters of justice, retribution and sacrifice that others find repellent or minimize by restricting the viewpoint to the human and personal, wherein the individual may rejoice in his good fortune and God's grace without weighing the appropriateness of the "spiritual economy." It will be of help to comment briefly on "Jesus the only Saviour," Watts' best effort at a specifically Christological poem of glorification within the Puritan framework, before returning to the poems glorifying God as Father, power, lawgiver, etc., where he is at his best.

This subject, the objective contemplation of the sacrifice of the Son by the Father, provided difficulties for Calvin, Milton, and all Puritans. They are in *Paradise Lost* and the "Nativity Ode," and we expect to find them in Watts. There are several unbelievably bad lines, to be sure, such as:

Down to our world the Saviour flies,
Stretches his naked arms, and dies. . . .

but the real difficulty with the poem is in the stand-off occupation with vengeance, God's honor and glory, and his power as demonstrated through the eyes of the awestruck angels. Exactly as in *Paradise Lost* III no real dramatic sense of the Son as a person, or of his achievements, except as decreed by God, comes through with any force. With effort the poet says:

Low they adore the Incarnate Son,
And sing the glories he hath won;
Sing how he broke our iron chains,
How deep he sunk, how high he reigns.

But the focus of interest remains always with God the just and avenging Father, seeking atonement for Adam's transgressions. The Calvinist dimensions of election and predestination are present here in full force. If we look cursorily at Watts' Divine Love poems, a series of cloying 17th century imitations of Crashaw and Counter Reformation sensibility with such language as "embrace me," "sweet lips," "passions," "love knots," and so on, it is clear that Watts' apology for including them in *Horae* is not misplaced. They are indeed in the main poor imitations of a tradition in which Watts did not believe, one which humanized and sentimentalized the figure of Christ. Only two of the poems come off with any success, "Meditation in a Grove," where Marvell's cooler muse provides the source, and "A Preparatory Thought for the Lord's Supper," not imitated from Taylor of course, but in the tradition of Puritan preparations and meditations before taking the sacrament, which we studied in Taylor. Unlike the Counter Reformation materials, these are legitimate Puritan topics. But in any event the Counter Reformation poems stand in stark contrast to "Jesus the only Saviour" where Watts, being honestly Puritan at his religious best, has the usual Puritan difficulties in putting this viewpoint into poetry. The weak turning to the personal at the end of the poem gives a slight compromise which does nothing to resolve this Puritan dilemma:

> Raise me beyond the ethereal blue,
> To sing and love as angels do.

In Watts, as in other Puritans, Christology is best presented in the personal cycle of sin-state through glorification, not through attempts at objective vision of glorification. Like other Puritans, his cosmic vision is more at home with God the Father on Sinai, or in contemplating his supremacy and creative power, than in dramatizing the humanity of Christ "from above," as it were. Milton, except by his idolators, is thought to be weakest in the same areas, and for the same reasons – theological logic, not sudden diminishment of poetic skill.

To return to the middle lines of "Law at Sinai," in relation to Exodus 19−33, the cited passage from *Paradise Lost* XII, and Milton on God generally in *Paradise Lost*. In looking at the imagery we may consult the King James version, which was popular with Puritans in the 18th century even though 16th century Puritan versions were still available. The differences among the versions regarding imagery are slight in any case. Watts excludes all detailed references to Jewish law, where Milton had given one sweeping allusion to those details. His interest is in Moses, Sinai, God and the commandments. From line 50 to line 135 he heavily uses Exodus 19−20, and manages artfully to bring in important descriptions of God and Moses from later chapters, as we shall note.

It is helpful first to cite in paraphrase the language in the King James Exodus describing the descent of God upon Sinai. (The grammar and resonances of the King James are not an issue here.) He is preceded by the *voice* of a *trumpet* exceeding loud, the one that will call the last judgment, and by *thunder* and *lightnings* (which Watts was fond of in many poems). He comes in a *thick cloud*, He descends in *fire*, while Sinai in turn becomes a smoke, and *smoke* ascends from Sinai as the *smoke of a furnace*, to meet God. Later Moses drew near unto the *thick darkness where God was,* and a *cloud* covered the mountain. The glory of God abode upon Mt. Sinai, the sight of the Lord was like *devouring* fire; later God descended in the *cloudy pillar,* stood at the door of the tabernacle, and talked to Moses. I have italicized the images which Watts uses directly, paraphrases, or uses as a basis for originals, the ones to keep in mind in looking at Watts' version of this episode.

A transition section, iv, lines 41−51, briefly describes the terrors of the people at the approach of God, with the interest mainly in the trumpet of God which will proclaim also the end of time. The various reactions of the Israelites to the intercourse of God and Moses on Sinai prominent in Exodus are in fact played down, as Watts' interest clearly is in sacred events in this poem. In recalling the "trembling armies" and the "rails," "set bounds unto the people round about," he is merely being faithful to the setting. With the approach of God and the description of the mountain, sections v, vi, and vii, the poem has its center; viii is a nice personal and classical digression, ix and x the climax in the visualization of God and Moses, while xi, the supposed climax in the commandments themselves, is something of a let-down because the paraphrase is so literal, though it is not anti-climax or bathos, as some enemies of religious poetry might insist. Watts clearly felt, as many still do, that these divine injunctions and prohibitions needed very little help from the "little arts of simile," the "flowery things" that poets say. We can agree that a windy paraphrase of the commandments would have been a disaster, and it is lucky for the poem that Watts centered his energies elsewhere, on the movement, power, and mystery of God, and Moses' awesome reaction.

The description of God preparing to leave heaven in section v, and his swift passage to Sinai in vi are fine examples of Watts' method at its best, blending the language of Scripture with language from Milton and his own additions to this sublime subject. "Sapphire seat," "Adoring thrones," "A thousand guards before, and myriads in the rear," are directly or indirectly Miltonic, while "mighty pillars," "pitchy cloud," "His feet on solid darkness trod," refer clearly back to the Exodus account. The sources for "He breath'd, and sulphur ran, a fiery stream," and the very warlike,

> The winds in harness with the flames,
>   Flew o'er the ethereal road.
> Down through his magazines he past
> Of hail, and ice, and fleecy snow. . . .

are more general. Milton and the more warlike passages of the Old Testament must be included, of course, yet also classical sources, particularly descriptions of Zeus and Mars, cannot be discounted. We shall shortly note Watts' coy owning and disowning of the classics, less forthright in both cases than in Milton:

> Forbear, young muse, forbear;
> The flowery things that poets say,
> The little arts of simile
>   Are vain and useless here. . . .

which is followed by a passage exhibiting wide knowledge of classics, and preceded by a very artful simile in the classical and 18th century manner. This is the working of Watts' imagination, his commingling of sources with his own inspiration to create poetry in which there is sometimes more there than immediately meets the eye. Watts is not always the uninspired, dull, evangelical hymnologist he is usually taken for. For instance, in section vii there is more Exodus, Milton and some wit in the form of a simile that deserve to be untangled, for Watts is at his best here mixing his sources and traditions.

To understand the wit and the simile in section vii, the Exodus account, quit straightforward, must be kept in mind. Watts' wit is not ingenious by 17th century standards, but it has a classical complexity in relation to its source:

> And mount Sinai was altogether on a smoke, because
> the LORD descended upon it in fire: and the smoke
> thereof ascended as the smoke of a furnace, and
> the whole mount quaked greatly.

In Watts this is expanded as follows (section vii):

>   Sinai receiv'd his glorious flight;
> With axle red, and glowing wheel,
>   Did the winged chariot light,
> And rising smoke obscur'd the burning hill.
>   Lo, it mounts in curling waves,
>   Lo, the gloomy pride outbraves
>   The stately pyramids of fire:
>   The pyramids to heaven aspire,
> And mix with stars, but see their gloomy offspring higher.
> So have you seen ungrateful ivy grow
> Round the tall oak that sixscore years has stood,
>   And proudly shoot a leaf or two
> Above its kind supporter's utmost bough,
> And glory there to stand the loftiest of the wood.

Notice in the first three lines the expansions of God's grandeur from the simple "in fire" of the original to "glorious flight," "axle red" and "glowing wheel." Line four is exact paraphrase. Then the five lines of wit, stating what may be implied from the terse source, that the smoke, "gloomy pride," rose above the fiery mountain, "the pyramids to heaven aspire." Further expansion occurs in the "ungrateful ivy" and "tall oak" simile, a relatively uncomplicated Homeric type. Watts is using all the resources at his disposal to create a vibrant, brilliant picture of the scene for the reader. The "muse, forbear" palinode which follows is not to be taken seriously, nor the rejection of classical lore and style in the next fourteen lines which manage to display an easy knowledge of the history and language of Greece and Rome. "Lying Greece" has served him well, and he is having it both ways, as Milton and Marvell did before him, though less subtly. With the line "Behold the sacred hill . . ." midway in section viii a direct return to Scripture occurs again, and for the next thirty lines, carrying over three sections, Watts achieves the last major effects of the poem in displaying God's grandeur and Moses' feeling of astonishment and awe before it.

The last seven lines of section viii do not add to what Watts had already achieved on God's grandeur. The effect of the phrase, "it never bore / Infinity before" may even be slightly bathetic. He had simply reached the height of his power in earlier sections, so the effect is repetitious. Things become more promising in the next section where the effect of God's presence upon the people and upon Moses is visually presented. Here Watts ranges beyond Exodus 19–20 for sources, using chapter 32 (the Golden Calf) with the consequent destruction of the idolators, and perhaps chapter 33 (Moses' awe upon entering the tabernacle and upon seeing God indirectly). In any case the range of the section, with its "dying groans," "shrieks, and swoons," "darkness on every soul," and so on, is not found in Exodus 19–20, which proceeds abruptly from the descent of God to the commandments. Also the effect of God's presence upon Moses, prominent in other parts of the Exodus account of Sinai, is not important in the transition from 19 to 20, but Watts feels free to import the sources from later parts of the long account:

Moses the spreading terror feels,
No more the man of God conceals
    His shivering and surprise. . . .

In the short tenth section that follows, the last attempt is made to reveal God's power and grandeur, the real purpose of the poem, with better results than in section viii. Spaced properly from the earlier successes in sections v–vii, it is a last outburst of God's glory, succeeding partly because it follows the build-up of the effect upon Moses and the Israelites of God's presence. As with all the best passages, the mixture is Scripture, Milton and Watts:

> Hark! from the centre of the flame,
> All arm'd and feather'd with the same,
> Majestic sounds break through the smoky cloud:
> Sent from the all-creating tongue,
> A flight of cherubs guard the words along,
> And bear their fiery law to the retreating crowd.

After that, the commandments are somewhat of an anticlimax, as was said, yet one should not be too harsh with Watts' piety and literalness. He has been successful with his main object, to display God's grandeur and power, and the proper awe of people before it, in strong Puritan fashion.

"A Song to Creating Wisdom" and "God Supreme and Self-sufficient" may be read as companion pieces, neither having the intensity and Hebraic severity of the Sinai poem, but both among the best of Watts' attempts at glorification and the sublime. The latter and slighter of the two has an emphasis upon mystery which is not Hebraic, though it might be said to verge on the mystical in its rejection of scholastic-rational categories in contemplating God. The "Song" is very ambitious (for Watts a long poem) and attempts the Miltonic, the sublime, and Puritan mode of glorification in the high style.

"God Supreme and Self-sufficient" uses some language of traditional mysticism, such as "radiant flame," "heavenly light," and some of the language of paradox common in such contemplation:

> They are too dark, and he too bright,
> Nothing are they, and God is all.

But that strain does not run very deep, giving way to the traditional piety of praise of the creator through his works in stanzas iii and iv. The sentiment in the fourth stanza is the common contemplation of God's ever-eternal present, an aspect of the sublime mystery stressed in the opening stanza:

> The tide of creatures ebbs and flows,
> Measuring their changes by the moon;
> No ebb his sea of glory knows,
> His age is one eternal noon.

Shelley and Yeats, among many others, later pointed out this great contrast, from their atheistic, and so less serene, perspectives. It is the high point of the poem, which has a disappointing conclusion calling attention to the poem as a vehicle of prayer and praise, something that did not need to be done.

"A Song to Creating Wisdom" is in five parts, which for Watts is a poem of some amplitude. The viewpoint is cosmic, praising God through the creation, with sections given duly to the planets, the heavens, the storms of the lower air, the earth and the ocean. Heaven and hell or the underworld as theological placcs are not in the scope of this poem. It is a fine example of a poem Miltonic in essence, and to a lesser degree in form, but not a weak imitation. Watts confronts the material on his own, as he did in the Sinai poem, working in a Miltonic frame inevitably but with the freedom he set out to achieve in the Preface. A good example of this freedom within tradition occurs at the opening of Part II:

> Downward I turn my wondering eyes
> On clouds and storms below,

lines which evoke pleasantly but not slavishly the opening lines of various books of *Paradise Lost* wherein the poet in his own persona speaks of looking downward to hell, upward to heaven, then to the *media terra* of the new paradise. Much has been written on this aspect of Milton's art, his cosmic freedom. Watts here has some of it in a lesser way. As mentioned above, the areas of Watts' cosmic voyage seeking the wonders of God's creation are the standard ones. In Part III and the beginning of Part IV there is a little surprise when praise of earth becomes praise of Albion, but there is nothing jingoistic or political in the handling. As later in Blake, the pastoral, a certain mythology, and love of England blend easily:

> Tall oaks for future navies grow,
>   Fair Albion's best defence. . . .
> The bleating flocks his pasture feeds
>   And herds of larger size. . . .

After this, mention of the Thames and the Severn leads easily and delicately to consideration of the ocean in Part IV. This returns the tone to the high Miltonic conventions of the first two parts, on the high heavens and the lower skies, and is not noteworthy except for one small point, the diction of "finny nations" and "scaly monsters." If Watts never became a major poet, the reason was not his subject matter, as Dr. Johnson or today's anti-religionists believe, nor his range as a religious poet, demonstrably wide enough. His diction seldom has an original cast to it. Caught between the centuries, he mixed and toned down the characteristic energy and diction of both, just as in the world of politics and religion he presented the dissenting Calvinist tradition to the dominant Anglican and civil world in a genteel light, the best possible under the circumstances. No ranting covenanter or stubborn old Milton he, yet he did not accept the world on its terms in his life or poetry, and so was revered by the godly and reviled by wits in his lifetime. Perhaps we can detect his complacency, which he never carried to a fault, in the last stanza of Part V of this poem, and in the entire Part. It is a calm and rather unsatisfactory climax, glittering with generalities in a summary, "Thy glories blaze all nature round . . .," of all the beauty and power of the universe. It ends with mention of "softer passions" and "Jesus' face," appropriate elsewhere, but hardly the way to end a poem on God's glory, creating power and grandeur. Here as elsewhere Watts tends to include too much, the result is anti-climax, yet his effort on the whole meets with some success in this poem.

In closing the discussion of glorification in Watts a cursory glance at some half dozen other poems may be helpful. They do not add to the range of the poems discussed above, and are in all cases inferior to the best, but in mentioning them we pay some respect to Watts' persistence in his attempts in *Horae* to make the Miltonic sublime his own. "Nativity" and "Song of Angels" are on the Christ theme, weaker versions of "Jesus the only Saviour." In "Nativity," in the characteristic Puritan defect of coldness and legality with this theme, God and Christ both seem essentially concerned with mere pomp, not even with real power. "The Song of Angels above" tries to remedy the Puritan stance with humanitiy, but what comes through is sentimentality, of the later sweet, sickening evangelical kind. Watts seldom sinks to this level in his original poetry, but when he does we can hear the evangelical revival in the wings, and remember his career as hymn writer of poems filled with bad religious clichés:

> Jesus, the Lord, their harps employs,
>> Jesus, my love, they sing,

> Jesus, the name of both our joys,
>   Sounds sweet from every string.

The other four poems of any note are on the theme of God's power and glory, lesser versions of the poem on Sinai and on God's attributes we have seen. "Divine Judgments" has the Wigglesworth touch, but not as bad as in "Day of Judgment." "Creator and Creatures," "God of Thunder" and "Sovereignty and Grace" resemble "Creating Wisdom" and "God Supreme," though inferiorly, especially in structure. They are full of repetitions of thought, and at times in a style approaching bathos that no doubt tempted the Scriblerus Club to include Watts along with William Law in their jibes:

> His bowels, to our worthless race,
>   In sweet compassion move;
> He clothes his looks with softest grace,
>   And takes his title, Love.

These poems show Watts at a level of reasonable consistency and real mediocrity, and explain why he never succeeded in achieving the high and quite intelligent dreams of his Preface for religious poetry in the early 18th century. But that should not be our last word on Watts, which will be taken from the graceful and honest "Conclusion" to *Horae Lyricae*, lines in which Watts the authentic religious man and honest poet − in the senses of knowing his gifts and the place of poetry in his scheme of things − clearly shows to advantage:

> God is in heaven, and men below;
> Be short, our tunes; our words be few;
> A sacred reverence checks our songs,
> And praise sits silent on our tongues.

Christopher Smart

Christopher Smart's Puritanism resides in his two great poems, *A Song to David* and *Jubilate Agno*. He was consciously an Anglican and antisectarian, as is evident in many remarks, and that is why his formally devotional poetry is either in the tepidly 18th century Anglican or deist modes, lines of poetry not to be considered here for reasons stated earlier. The theological and other aspects of the Puritan tradition are openly present in the *Song*, his most highly wrought work, and to that poem we will devote adequate comments. In the *Jubilate*, which I deem incoherent as total poem in either the Callan or Bond edition, until some critic can make a convincing case for the contrary, there is much suppressed and indirect Puritanism in individual passages, often widely separated. The Puritan sense of close identification with Christ, with biblical prophecy, with the Spirit and a sense of prayer, all appear. Of course the same phenomena are present in the Anglican mystic Law, but Smart was not a mystic, and so could draw consciously only upon the public Anglican tradition of the 18th century. Inadvertently he drew upon the Puritans when his own tradition in the 18th century was found inadequate, which it was except for formal praise of an abstract deity.

Smart's poems do not relate very well to either set of categories for religion or poetry in the 18th century. He is concerned with the sin-state, vocation, and glorification in the poems, but in no definite order. Not overtly a Calvinist, Smart gives no special place to election, reprobation, justification and glorification, albeit many of his attitudes are easily translated into these terms. If we turn to the five clear types of religious poems in the 18th century, much less murky ground for Smart, there are also some difficulties not found in the range of 17th century poets, or in Watts or Cowper. His "Hymn to the Supreme Being" celebrating his recovery from illness is more personal than other poems in like mode addressed to the deity, but even a cursory glance back at Donne's great "Hymn to God my God, in my Sickness" reminds us of some 18th century impersonality. *Jubilate Agno*, in its most interesting religious passages, the only ones to be discussed, combines the deeply personal with the Calvinist-theological view of the self, a difficult point that must be proven by example and analysis here. There are no overtly Calvinist-theological poems for obvious reasons, nor poems deriving from a sense of the sanctified state, for in these instances at least, Smart belonged to the world of Dr. Johnson and other 18th century contemporaries rather than to the more stylized one of 17th century devotional, and theological poetry, for which Watts and Cowper show strong affinity. The Seatonian prize poems to the deity are Smart's contribution to 18th century religious convention, and no doubt belong to conventional poetry. His greatest single poem, *A Song to David*, is mainly Miltonic sublime with a strongly personal strain, in other words a blending of categories one and five. His other poems are not religious, or religious enough, to discuss in our present context.

Much has been written about Smart's life in relation to *Jubilate Agno*.[17] Our concern with *Jubilate Agno* is not with the life or the attempts to find a total structure and coherent meaning in the poem, only with the striking religious aspects.[18]

Since *Jubilate* is a series of statements, some poetical, some not, some clearly connected, others not, the religious quality in the poem is presented also through statement. There are four types of religious statement which recur throughout in no particular order or pattern. Taken together we can surmise that all his religious concerns are included in these four areas. The first is quite simple, showing the deep religiousness − not particularly theological − for which Smart is famous. These can merely be listed:

B 1, 89   For I blessed God in St. James's Park till I routed all the company.
B 1, 230 For all these things are seen in the spirit which makes the beauty of prayer.
B 2, 332 For by the grase of God I am the Reviver of ADORATION amongst ENGLISH-MEN.
D, 148   The Lord magnify the idea of Smart singing hymns on this day in the eyes of the whole University of Cambridge, Nov. 5, 62.
D, 219   The Lord pass the last year's accounts in my conscience thro' the merits of Jesus Christ. New Year by Old Style 1763.

The second group is more complicated, for he is somewhat contradictory in displaying his public sense of being a Christian. Smart was an Anglican and often berated the sectarians, the Papists, and foreigners, particularly the French. Several instances relating to the more Puritan sects will do for illustration.

C, 106   For I prophecy that there will not be a meetinghouse within two miles of a church.
C, 107   For I prophecy that schismaticks will be detected.
C, 135   For a hat was an abomination of the heathen. Lord have mercy upon the Quakers.

Smart's real views are not so narrow as this. In one passage he actually identifies with a Catholic martyr, attracted by what he saw as a similarity of their states:

B 1, 134 For I am redoubted, and redoubtable in the Lord, as is THOMAS BECKET my father.

In others he displays knowledge of and sympathy for persons and things associated historically with the Puritan cause. The one on Pembroke College should not be made too much of − "For Pembroke

Hall was founded more in the Lord than any college in Cambridge" –
though we may be sure he was aware of the praise of early Puritanism
indirectly bestowed in the statement; but the praise of Lewis Bayly,
coming at the end of the poem, cannot be overestimated in importance:

D, 43   Let Baily, house of Baily rejoice with Catopyrites of Cappadocia.
         God be gracious to the immortal soul of Lewis Baily author of the
         Practice of Piety.

We now know how important Bayly's work was for 16th and 17th
century Puritan thought and devotion, and no doubt Smart read it
avidly in his years of travail. The influence is not direct, yet Smart was
deeply attracted to the Puritan strain of thinking about the spirit and
piety while overtly attacking sectarians and Quakers and remaining
Anglican. Bayly's influence supplies part of the answer to this seeming
contradiction, since he was a bishop in the Church, but a Puritan bishop
before the rupture in the 17th century removed moderate Puritans
from the established Church. Smart's Puritanism indeed is related
much more closely than he knew to Pembroke Hall, and also to
Emmanuel College and the flowering of the Puritan strain in the
Church in the late 16th century.

   In the third, most significant group of passages his true, inner Puritan
spirit emerges, the one in which he identifies himself with Christ or with
the Spirit in Puritan fashion. It is true that there are intense passages of
this sort that might have been written by any good Anglican or
Catholic, a large number of them. Here are two cases in point:

B 1, 45   For I am a little fellow, which is intitled to the great mess by the
          benevolence of God my father.
B 1, 51   For I bless the thirteenth of August, in which I was willing to be
          called a fool for the sake of Christ.

Yet others can be singled out for the special quality of relationship of
self to God that we have seen in numerous Puritan poets and divines:

B 1, 3   For I am not without authority in my jeopardy, which I derive
          inevitably from the glory of the name of the Lord.
B 1, 20   For the word of God is a sword on my side – no matter what other
          weapon a stick or a straw.
B 1, 21   For I have adventured myself in the name of the Lord, and he hath
          mark'd me for his own.
B 1, 94   For the Lord is my ROCK, and I am the bearer of his CROSS.
B 2, 363 For a CHARACTER is the votes of the Worldlings, but the seal is
          of Almighty GOD alone.
C, 151   For Christ Jesus has exalted my voice to his own glory.

The Puritan language and thought-pattern is unmistakable in these and many others of similar import; it would be tedious to enumerate them for the reader of this book thus far, except to make the general claim that a sense of election and a view of the closeness of God in the Spirit, cornerstones of all Puritan religious thinking, are here in full force. A sense of election and a glimpse of glory, if not the formal looking for signs and the clear Puritan way from sin-state to glorification, was certainly vouchsafed to this strange tortured soul whose religious yearnings and desires could not be contained within the tepid Anglican tradition of his own time. In this respect only, Smart is closer to Bunyan and the earlier tradition of Puritanism than are the more theologically Puritan Watts and Cowper.

We may call the last group of passages Blakean, for in them there is a smattering of gnomic or unconventional thought, and an impatience with all orthodoxy. Perhaps Smart read Law or Böehme, for some of the passages are on the threshold of that type of mystical writing. It is not necessary to look for his inspiration in books, however, for his move in that direction is only general at best, and the insights are ones that we assume a man of Smart's religious depth and intensity certainly was able to discover for himself. His meditations on the Bible and other religious literature are probably the general "source," though they have a gnostic and Blakean ring to the modern reader, who is more familiar with Böehme and Blake than with 18th century religious poetry and literature, Puritan and otherwise.

B 1, 168 For due East is the way to Paradise, which man knoweth not by reason of his fall.
B 1, 195 For Newton nevertheless is more of error than of the truth, but I am of the WORD of GOD.
B 1, 292 The laws & judgement are impudence & blindness.
B 2, 329 For in the divine Idea this Eternity is compleat & the Word is a making many more.
B 2, 674 For it is not good to look with earning upon any dead work.
B 2, 675 For by so doing something is lost in the spirit & given from life to death.

The first passage obviously echoes Donne, Vaughan and other 17th century poets, and will appear again in Wordsworth. The others are like the early antinomian spirit in Blake, which will be brought up in the later chapter on Blake, who alone passed from left-wing Puritanism to antinomianism to a unique vision. Smart was his forerunner in this. Nevertheless these few passages are less characteristic and important for understanding Smart's contribution to Puritanism in poetry than are the groupings in One and Three, *A Song to David*, and the "Hymn to the Supreme Being." Tortured emotionally, Smart almost broke out of the confines of orthodoxy, but his intellect was not the daring kind of Blake, or even the quiet but adventurous William Law. He is a Puritan in his expression of religious emotions, and borrowed some of their intellectual machinery despite himself. In another sense, it is fair to say that he remained Anglican and orthodox.

As was stated above, most of Smart's religious poetry apart from *Jubilate* is conventional by any standard, and particularly outstanding (or the reverse, depending upon one's attitude) in examples of 18th century diction, abstraction in conception of the Supreme Being, and in platitudes. Only the "Hymn to the Supreme Being" and *A Song to David* escape this classification, the first being a good instance of Puritan piety somewhat toned down from the 17th century, the second a poem of glorification, both of God's everlasting glory and man's ability to participate in it under certain conditions.

The "Hymn" has its Hebraic stiffness in the three opening stanzas, and in places it, too, slips into 18th century generalities, congenital to the Seatonian prize poems on the attributes of the deity, in such lines as:

> All glory to th' Eternal, to th' Immense,
> All glory to th'Omniscient and Good. . . .

But essentially it is a Protestant-Puritan poem of devotion, the familiar 17th century type, wherein physical illness and recovery are likened to the sickness of sin and regeneration, though not so strongly or overtly as in Donne. Stanza vi is squarely within this tradition:

> But who are they, that bid affliction cease! –
>   Redemption and forgiveness, heavenly sounds!
> Behold the dove that brings the branch of peace,
>   Behold the balm that heals the gaping wounds –
> Vengeance divine's by penitence supprest –
> She struggles with the angel, conquers, and is blest.

In stanza vii some of the more specifically Puritan ideas occur, the despair found in *The Faerie Queene* I, the questioning diffidence of the tone of Marvell, and the absolute sovereignty of God's power:

> Yet hold, presumption, nor too fondly climb,
>   And thou too hold, O horrible despair!
> In man humility's alone sublime,

> Who diffidently hopes he's *Christ's* own care —
> O all-sufficient Lamb! in death's dread hour
> Thy merits who shall slight, or who can doubt thy power?

The sense is of overwhelmed weakness and sinfulness overcome by irresistible grace, a sense supported by the only later stanza which is specifically theological, number twelve.

> My feeble feet refus'd my body's weight,
>   Nor wou'd my eyes admit the glorious light,
> My nerves convuls'd shook fearful of their fate,
>   My mind lay open to the powers of night.
> He pitying did a second birth bestow
> A birth of joy — not like the first of tears and woe.

The "new birth" or second birth idea ran throughout the first generation of Puritan writers — Sibbes, Perkins, Preston and Dodd — we remember, and is an abiding Puritan theme. The steps from despair to glory are in the poem, some in syncopated form, some clearly, and glory in the form peculiar to Smart. After the regeneration note is struck, the last stanzas, xv–xviii, are given over to a catalogue of the grandeurs of God's world, such as precious gems, lions, whales and the glorious sun itself. *Jubilate* often broke down into a catalogue of such types, but here, as in the greater poem, *A Song to David*, the effect is integral, and closes with brief recapitulation of the themes of faith, love and forgiveness.

A Song to David is a much more massive poem than the "Hymn" in all ways, yet there are elements in common useful to point out in approaching the longer poem. Though one is extremely personal, the other seemingly an objective string of praises, underlying principles and surface techniques bind Smart's two best religious poems together. The brief allusion to Hebrew kings in "Hymn" widens into the central character of David; the emblems from natural and mineral worlds, relatively controlled in the personal poem, become the central means to express praise and prayer, loosely under "Adoration," in the major poem. The control is very evident on an ample scale, not the fragmented wildness of the lists in *Jubilate*. Smart succeeds in rendering what seems to be a cold, automatic catalogue into a vehicle for his own kind of major religious poetry, personal and impersonal at once. This aspect must be investigated carefully, for in its success the peculiar achievement of Smart as unusual poet resides, while it is also his way, crucial to our purpose here, of personalizing the Puritan category of glorification. No other poet in this study is so outwardly *non*-Puritan in form, yet inwardly exuberantly so, except Blake.

For a poem as long as the *Song*, with the difficult matters of its peculiar structure and method of achieving glorification to attend to, in the end both a victory of personal and impersonal poetry, perhaps a homely diagram of the gross structure is not out of place. This is merely a mnemonic device to hold the poem in mind, and will not be followed by a paraphrase of the content of each section. Analysis of the content at crucial passages hopefully will solve the problems raised above. Stanzas i−xxi characterize David as king, psalmist, man, and type of Christ, striking in this combination a better balance than most other Christian poets or Judaizing divines of the 17th or 18th centuries. The Book of the Creatures, a familiar medieval form of prayer and praise incontrovertibly proved by Martz and others as having been smuggled into 17th century Protestant meditative poetry, occupies stanzas xxii−xxxi. Then praise of God as founder and upholder of the world, in the mystical symbols from A to Ω follows, combining Revelation, neoplatonist and perhaps Cabala esoterica, but its effect in the poem is not arcane. From xxxviii−l we get Jewish-Christian moral precepts, with nothing new or out of the ordinary except that stanza xlviii, to which we shall return, is excessively Puritan in strain for an Anglican writer. Smart's special visionary quality and religious unusualness break the conventional mold again here. From stanza l to the end, the poem returns to adoration by means of Smart's peculiar method, the catalogue of beauty of the natural world, the animals, birds, flowers, with only one diversion, the reappearance of the "man of prayer" Puritan notion in lxxvii. The final stanza stands by itself, is difficult in syntax, and is supposed to draw together all the themes − David, prayer and praise, the Puritan ethic and devotion, and the climactic theme of glory in the conclusion of the catalogue. It obviously deserves special comment.

This discussion of the *Song*, in brief, will not be a full reading attempting to demonstrate the organic unity or full integrity of the poem. Smart's major commentators have done that to a sufficient degree.[19] Our course will be selective, choosing certain major and minor aspects, implied as such in the above summary, and emphasized now. Of major interest are the character of David, the ways in which emblems and lists − the seemingly tedious catalogues − are central to the method and success of the poem, how the poem succeeds in being personal and impersonal at one time, and of course how the poem is essentially Puritan. Of less interest are the Blakean connotations and the cabalistic esoterica in the A to Ω section. The artistry of the final stanzas, bringing all the themes together, Puritan and others, is a legitimate object of our concern.

It is not inflicting a fatal injustice upon the poem, nor is it to the detriment of the other fine aspects of the poem always stressed by commentaries, to put our interests in the terms of sin-state to glorification. The poem is not a Puritan meditation structured on the cycle, that is obvious. Some aspects of the cycle are attenuated, or missing or distorted in arrangement and stress. Yet the cycle is present in the poem, from beginning to end. The stanzas on David, i–xxi, which we may call part I, show traces of the sin-state and strong assertion of election. The state of justification is slighted as such, but its immediate consequence, sanctification, is stressed as the state achieved by David at the end of part I. The theme of sanctification is again taken up in part IV, xxxviii–l, with moral precepts extending David's sanctification to mankind, or at least the fellow-elect of mankind. As befits the tone of the poem and Smart's characteristic muse, glorification plays the largest role in the scheme, appearing in three parts, the catalogue of the creatures (II, xxii–xxxi), the mystical foundation of God's power (III, xxxi–xxxvii), and the long section on adoration (V, li–lxxxv). Thus glorification is given an esoteric meaning in the world, in the creatures and all the emblems from the animal, vegetable and mineral areas so dear to Smart's heart, and a less characteristic esoteric, slightly cabalistic one in the A to Ω section. The last stanza integrates all these ideas in the figures of God, Christ and David. Two more general themes become manifest in the last stanza, faith and predestination. Faith is the implicit theme of the entire poem, which is not one of proof or assertion, like the Seaton hymns, or of doubt and despair, as in Cowper. Predestination appears in the final, triumphant lines,"Determined, Dared, and Done." The unravelling of the final stanza will conclude the discussion of Smart's best poem by pointing out the complexity and artistry of these intermingled themes and symbols.

The long opening section on David stresses election and sanctification, with only one crucial reference to the sin-state, reminding one of David's past. The slight weight given this point is appropriate to the nature of this celebratory poem but even this is immediately followed by a shift to the positive side of things in the brief lines:

> Wise − in recovery from his fall,
> Whence rose his eminence o'er all,
>   Of all the most revil'd.   (xvi)

Much earlier the emphatic point had been made, "The man of God's own choice" (v). The chosen one then sings of his fellow-elect, in a passage cast in Hebrew and Puritan terms:

>   the Saint elect
>   For infinite applause . . .
> To rule the land, and briny broad,
> To be laborious in his laud,
>   And heroes in his cause.   (xx)

David is endowed in a summary with all the virtues of the elect, each of which is expanded in a separate stanza as a form of sanctification:

> Great, valiant, pious, good, and clean
> Sublime, contemplative, serene,
>   Strong, constant, pleasant, wise!   (iv)

There is no need to paraphrases these rather obvious expansions. After the opening twenty-one stanzas the sanctified saint is prepared to sing the glories of God.

Three sections of the poem have to do with glorification: first, of God in the world (II, xxi−xxvi), then the sources, "pillars" of God's power (III, xxxi−xxxvii), and third, the adoration by all things (V, li−lxxv). These sections are most characteristic of Smart's attitude towards the deity, and recall in a succinct and orderly way the lists in *Jubilate Agno*. Smart presents them in a far more skillful way in this poem. It was wise to introduce another theme, the moral theme, between parts III and V. There is an introductory stanza to both the world and the pillars, xxi and xxx. Between parts III and IV there is characterization of David as "scholar of the Lord," with a description of his harp as symbolic of his mission. It is also appropriate that an invocation − hardly a description − of God should appear between the rather mystical A to Ω section and the moralistic paraphrase of the Decalogue. This stanza may appropriately be called the center of the poem, which is a general Christian viewpoint, not one peculiar to Calvinist-Puritanism:

> There is but One who ne'er rebell'd
> But One by passion unimpell'd . . .
>   And saw the God in CHRIST.   (xxxix)

When Smart rings changes on the theme of glory we may see it as the
Calvinist stage of glorification. Joyful praise of the Lord is Smart's most
inner attitude, reflected and felt in much of his best poetry. This
attitude in Smart does not formally and consciously derive from
Calvinism for the historical and personal reasons previously discussed.
But it is fair to see in *A Song to David*, unlike other poems, a more
formal and concise ordering of the urge to glorification of God, which
in the *Jubilate* especially got out of hand. The ordering in the *Song* is
not strict − that is obvious. Yet there is enough ordering and spacing
of the theme of glory not to allow it to overwhelm the other fine parts
of the poem, the plateau stanzas of characterization and the conclusion.
It is not overreading to find this much of the Calvinist-Puritan spirit in
the total poem, if we keep in mind that Smart did not consider himself a
sectarian or consciously think in Calvinist-Puritan language.

Stanzas xl to xlix are a paraphrase of the Decalogue, which there is
no need of paraphrasing again. But we should ask an important
question of it, concerning its place in the poem. The logic in placing this
section between two sections on glorification and praise does not
appear in the section itself. This logic concerns the power of the word
and of song. David in the sanctified state is the proper person to
paraphrase the awesome words of Jehovah to Moses. Smart shares
Watts' high estimation of the central biblical passage common to all
western religious traditions. It is only much further along in the poem,
however, that he makes explicit the appropriateness of the moralistic
passages, curiously enough, midway into the following section on
adoration:

> And he, who kneels and chants,
> Prevails his passions to controul,
> Finds meat and med'cine to the soul,
>   Which for translation pants.   (lxiv)

The man of prayer and song provides a measure of controlling passion
and for making the good seem desirable. This central point is repeated
elsewhere, "Controul thine eye, salute success" (xlviii), "But stronger
still . . . the man of pray'r" (lxxvii). Thus the section on the Decalogue
is not an excrescence in the poem or a blot on the theme of praise and
adoration. Like the Puritans before him Smart felt both the controlling
power of music and song and the joy in living within the moral code.
Though its primary function is to reveal the power of God for its own
sake, the code is not presented as repressive. As a form of adoration,

the code liberates man if seen aright, through the proper use of word and song by the sanctified David. It is the function of David to turn "thou shalt nots" into sweet positive truths as the exuberance in Smart's lines attests:

Use all thy passions! — love is thine,
And joy, and jealousy divine   (xliv)
Work emulation up to heaven
    By knowledge and by zeal.   (xlviii)

Here surely is the "rhetoric of the spirit" of the 17th century Puritan anew, and the "relish" and "excellency" in divine things and commands which run through the works of Taylor, Edwards and other classical Puritan divines. Smart here is the inheritor of the tone of 17th century Puritan morality, and shares with it the view that morality is a joyful work of God. As we have noted this to be the area of the Puritan conscience and style of life least understood by outsiders, in fact much maligned then and now, it may be obvious why Smart's close connection with Puritan themes and attitudes has gone largely ignored even in this, his greatest poem, where the connection between Smart and Puritan tradition is most striking.

Towards the end of the long section of adoration (l—lxxv), Smart prepares for the conclusion by introducing more solemn notes into the hymn of celebration and praise of God through his works in this world. The idea of control of passion by prayer and song in stanza lxiv, referred to in connection with the moral theme, also stands out sharply as deeply thematic among stanzas otherwise monotonous in their happy purpose. The many stanzas on adoration have their special force. Smart is one of the few poets who can bring a catalogue of this sort to life, so that we respond to it as genuine poetry. But he also scatters other, deeper thoughts in preparation for the conclusion, biblical and Puritan echoes of the overall theme. "Hark! 'tis a voice — how still, and small" (lxvii); "But as for prayer, or e're it faints, / Far better is the breath of saints" (lxviii); and more fully:

But stronger still . . . the man of pray'r . . .
And in the seat to faith assign'd   (lxxvii)
Precious the penitential tear;
And precious is the sigh sincere;
Acceptable to God.   (lxxxii)

These are deliberately scattered as solemn notes in counterpoint with the ecstatic repetition of "Adoration," "Sweet," "Beauteous," "Glorious" and the catalogues that follow them in a nicely constructed musical pattern of major and minor moving to a perfect balance of rich themes in harmony at the end. The minor, sharply thematic, does not overtake the hosannas of praise, and there is no gloom in the final stanza. The controlling ideas gradually merge with the hymn of joy, giving shape to that joy in the total structure of the poem. Celebration and idea are united in perfect form, reminiscent of the ideal of 18th century music.

The final stanza is a little masterpiece in itself, at once the culmination and a miniature of the full poem. The explicit themes are brought to climax and the implicit made manifest. To explain this point requires quotation in full:

> Glorious, − more glorious, is the crown
> Of Him that brought salvation down,
>   By meekness, called thy Son:
> Thou at stupendous truth believ'd; −
> And now the matchless deed's atchiev'd
> DETERMINED, DARED, and DONE.

The literal meaning here is obvious enough. The litany of glory is concluded with the crown of Christ and with David himself as glorious singer. Also Christ is the son of David in the natural line, so the two are inextricably linked. But there is more matter in these lines, revealing the underlying themes of the poem. The central stanza of the poem, xxxix, "There is but One," as was pointed out, refers to God. God is the ultimate subject of the poem. Since Christ is the Son of God in the Divine Order,

> He from himself his semblance sent . . .
>   And saw the God in Christ   (xxxix)

and also the natural son of David, a reference to God in the final stanza is intended. The "Him" in line two is Christ, univocally, but the "thy" in "thy Son" refers both to David and to God. David too is a "son of God," made out here to be one of the first Christians, through his faith by means of prevenient grace, we may surmise. So regarding David the poem is about saving faith primarily and praise secondarily. "Thou at stupendous truth believ'd"-regarding Christ this concerns the means of salvation for all, his redeeming the world which David sings by the crown of salvation. Ultimately the poem's theme is the grand Puritan idea of God himself − his power, excellency, will, the A and Ω of the middle stanzas xxxi−xxxvii. The catalogue of attitudes in that

section reaches apotheosis in the final lines, "DETERMINED, DAR-
ED, and DONE," with equal reference to David (DONE), Christ
(DARED), and God (DETERMINED). David's faith and song,
Christ's act, and God's ultimate power are forms of the Puritan idea
about God, expressed from Calvin onwards, here in the word DETER-
MINED. So the poem ultimately, though somewhat covertly, concerns
predestination. David, Christ and the visible univere are all parts of
God's plan for praise of himself, the first (A) and final (Ω)
inscrutable mystery. Smart is cheerful about this mystery; some other
Puritans were not. But that is a matter of temperament, not doctrine,
and should not obscure the Calvinist temper and link with the past in
his best poetry, especially in *A Song to David*.

William Cowper

Cowper's Calvinism stands among the best documented in this study,
for along with Taylor, Marvell, Watts and Byron, the Calvinist
influences upon Cowper have been widely acknowledged and conceded to have played a prominent role in the formation of his life and
poetry. Cowper's Calvinism has even been something of a *cause
célèbre* because, unlike that of the others firmly within the tradition to
whom Calvinism was a given of background to be responded to in
various ways, Cowper embraced Calvinist Methodism mid-point in
his life and at a time when Calvinism in England was definitely on the
wane. His decision to follow the guidance of the reformed slaver
turned pastor, Newton, has been deplored by many biographers for
the sake of his mental health, but it is an important point that
Cowper's decision was a decided turn upward of Calvinism in England, for that particular moment and for the future, as it ensured that
such religious ideas and attitudes were to have an intelligent spokes-
man in verse and thus be given serious attention among the cultivated
classes for another generation. After Watts the English and American
situations had grown quite different. In New England Calvinism
maintained social status and gave the world Jonathan Edwards, the
religion's greatest mind since Calvin. But in England its fortunes sank
even more disastrously than those of religion in general in an
atmosphere where Smart could be considered deranged because he
prayed in public, and parsons were the objects of satire in novels and
plays. Calvinism was scoffingly dismissed to the lower classes and

produced no more straightforward poets or thinkers of high stature. Even its hold over the lower classes was largely removed by the Methodist revival, and it became the religion of the mercantile middle class, and never lost that image in later times. Nevertheless there was a strange alchemy in its dissolution as a vital force which led to Newton's and Cowper's Calvinist Methodism, to Blake's antinomian Swedenborgian views of the spirit, and to a general influence which was later to affect the poetry of Coleridge and Wordsworth. Byron received its influence in a more direct and traditional way.

Cowper is susceptible of more ample study from the viewpoint of Calvinism than the structure of this section calls for, but our purpose is to view Cowper within a range that includes Watts, Law and Smart, and to stress the continuities of a tradition. Since his general Calvinism has been widely noted, as mentioned above and in the books cited in the notes,[20] our pursuit of specific and narrower aims is justified, if the analysis brings out the essential importance chosen in relation to the Calvinist categories. This rigorous selection of poems includes many but not all the best-known poems – parts of *The Task*, "The Castaway," certain of the *Olney Hymns*, and some nature meditations.

Following both the order of the chart and a general sense of critical discussion we can see that Cowper's poetry ranges over the categories of sin-state, election/reprobation, and sanctification, if looked upon from a strictly Calvinist angle, and with types of poems we may call personal, Calvinist-Puritan, conventionally religious and Miltonic. "The Castaway," "The Shrubbery," "The poplar-field," "Yardley Oak," "Walking with God" and "Shining Light" are the deeply personal type, of which not all deserve equal comment. Similar selectivity will be exercised with the Calvinist-Puritan type. The conventional can be ignored, except for listing examples which show the type in contrast to others. Cowper did not write devotional verse of the older sort in the 17th century style, as did Watts. For the Miltonic sublime, there is really only *The Task*, in scattered passages and the final book.

"The Shrubbery," "The poplar-field" and "Yardley Oak" are religious poems of the quiet, meditative type with the persona of the shy man in retirement contemplating the timeless issues of time itself, the aging process, and the brevity of life and beauty. These are the themes of the classical moralists and had been incorporated into the general 18th century religious context of Anglicans and Deists for reasons of obvious congeniality and compatibility. They are not flatly moralistic in the direct 18th century way (though Cowper performed this feat also in his "Stanzas printed on bills of mortality," 1787–1790, 1792, 1793). These poems are set off from the merely conventional poem on time by the genuine interest in the object of nature in each poem. It would be pressing a point too far, and a lack of critical tact, to examine them in the Calvinist religious context, except that study of the more obvious Calvinist religious poems with nature as central object of meditation provides a certain context and insight into them, lacking if we merely bring the assumptions and knowledge congenial to the 18th century gentleman of Anglican, deist or classical attainments. For this reason we should study the directly religious poems under the heading of "personal" first, that is, poems such as "The Castaway" from the nature group and "Shining Light" and "Walking with God" from the evangelical. (With the other four categories, all the poems are more or less obviously religious in subject matter, so there is no special problem of need for indirection.)

"The Castaway" is perhaps Cowper's most famous poem and justly so. The long history of his relationship with Calvinist Methodism, and the turning to pillar of salt of the once happy encounter with the Unwin-Newton set, comes to a conclusion in its anguished lines. It is no longer fashionable, and justly not, to blame Newton and extreme Calvinist doctrine for Cowper's troubled last years. His insanity doubtless would have turned any doctrine inside out to seek the sour side, although it is certainly a heavy irony that fate provided him with a doctrine horrendously convenient to his self-destructive purpose in double predestination. Cowper's Calvinism is such a special case that its cultural importance should not be overemphasized in our enthusiasm for the qualities in the poetry. The Wesley brothers, Whitefield, Wilberforce, the hymns, great revivals, even the sturdy Reverend Newton are steadier barometers for the social and intellectual import of the religious revival in the late 18th century. Yet the aesthetic and intellectual power of the best poems derive from the interaction of Calvinism and Cowper's own mind, and there is a range and depth of Calvinist sensibility in his best poems of the Calvinist type that it is impossible to find in any other poet of the 18th century. We must return to Bunyan, Milton, Taylor and Marvell to find an equal to Cowper's achievement.

Cowper felt isolated, despairing and lost when he wrote this poem, in his personal life as well as religious attitudes. The key words, "hope," "home," and "friends" are balanced throughout the poem with the opposites, "despair," "sea," "outcast." The story of the lost sailor on Anson's ship is quite effectively appropriate for Cowper's own last years, even if theological aspects are not emphasized. But theology cannot be denied its central place here, even by the most blithe of modern liberal readers, who may only pity Cowper for his benighted views and era. Hope, despair, and loneliness are spiritual and psychological, no less than physical, conditions, and the poem, as one of its greatest merits, re-enacts the interaction of Calvinist theology, the sailor's death, and Cowper's state of loss throughout the poem. The last six lines, clearly Calvinist, are prepared for carefully in the events, natural scenery and personal attitudes manifest in all that precedes them.

Cowper's religious poetry, as we shall see in its total development, falls along all the phases of the Calvinist way, from sin-state to sanctification, even to a glimpse of glory in Book VI of *The Task*, but he tragically turned his back on Bunyan's final home for the Christian to the despair, rejection, and loss of religious life in the sin-state, unable to resist the final temptation in Calvinism wherein the sinner knows his own damnation, reading God's mind in his case. The terrifying lines bear quotation, though widely known:

> No voice divine the storm allay'd,
>   No light propitious shone;
> When, snatch'd from all effectual aid,
>   We perish'd, each alone:
> But I beneath a rougher sea,
> And whelm'd in deeper gulphs than he.[21]

Nature imagery, event, and theology of damnation merge beautifully in his stanza. No one has ever done it better. The effectual call, about which Edwards wrote so much and about which Cowper worried all his life (though not often at the surface of his religious poetry, often serene and assured) had finally and completely failed — God's purpose, as finally revealed in his case, was damnation for a deserving sinner. In our opening section there was comment on this possibility in Calvinist theology, its scandal before the world, as *accidia* or final despair is that of serious Catholicism. There were the Cambridge suicides, the glee of the Papists of Lancashire, and Spenser's artistic handling of the problem in *The Faerie Queen* I, ix, which we analyzed in Section II. Religious partisanship and "modern" liberalism are both beside the point in encountering this aspect of Calvinist experience. With the seriousness of final loss at its center, we owe it the respect that we owe all traditions that cope with the tragic in life.

Although there is much more to be said about the Calvinist center in "The Castaway," as the nadir of Calvinist despair, it is instructive (and only fair) to be able to view this powerful poem in a larger context of Cowper's response to Calvinism. In the *Olney Hymns* there are only a few deeply personal poems, one very serene, the others more cheerful than "The Castaway" in facing personal despair. They are "Walking with God," "Shining Light," and "Retirement." We can call these personal poems, though technically hymns, and distinguish them from other types of religious poems in the Olney group, because the personal is allowed to have its own voice, blended with the public theology of Calvinist Methodism and the Newton-Olney group. All the others are the public religious poems Cowper felt he owed to his community in the revival. In the personal poems the theology of assurance which the devout Calvinist was supposed to have conflicts with certain of Cowper's feelings – the urge to retirement, deep sense of loss, memories of his London past, love of God, and despair, in no particular order. Something authentic and dramatic goes on in these few poems which complements "The Castaway" and the more intriguing sections of *The Task*. With the moral-contemplative poems – "The Shrubbery," "Yardley Oak," and "The poplar-field" – these comprise the most valuable poems of the Cowper canon.

"Walking with God," the first of the *Olney Hymns* by Cowper, is one of his most serene religious poems. It is true that the poet's memory aches for past hours when his conversion was first accomplished, the moment of awakening to Jesus in assurance of justification, and also that a genuflection is made towards his own remaining sinfulness. But the compensations of a steady and proven faith are evident, and the calm, serene prediction that the friendship with God will grow closer still is conveyed fully in its steady, cheerful tone. Calvinism as urged upon Cowper by Newton and his Olney friends had saved the poet temporarily, in this, the most genuine poem of the assured state. The many poems teaching Calvinst-Puritan doctrine also derive from the sense of assurance and election, but there is the ring in them of the poetic schoolteacher that Pope unfairly assigned to Milton's God. "Walking with God" gives a glimpse, though only a brief one, of how it felt to be a Calvinist by Cowper the man, with some traces of the former London sophisticate, not the school divine, peeping through.

"The Shining Light" belies its title by immediately plunging into despair, a despair both genuine, as we now know, and stylized in familiar Calvinist-Puritan terms. Echoes of *The Faerie Queene* I, ix, Sibbes' *Bruised Reede*, Bunyan's Slough of Despond and numberless other Puritan *topoi* for this mood will occur to the reader of this book. The theology is quite conventional — the sinner deserves condemnation from the law and a just God; the glimmering light, representing Christ and salvation, marks the traditional path of the pilgrim in his war with despair. The poem begins on a genuine enough note, the despair merely stylized, but ends with conventional theology, in this case a happy blending of the two. One does not overpower the other or make the other seem unnecessary. In poems like "The Castaway" Calvinism is subservient to personal emotions; in most Olney hymns the reverse, with sometimes happy, sometimes other results. Here there is the balance also found in a few other poems, such as "Retirement."

"Retirement" expresses one of Cowper's deepest needs and desires in a religious context, the expression of which he is famous for in *The Task* and the meditative nature poems. The nature scene of general meditation on classical themes is also fit for prayer and praise of the Creator of all these wonders. Fortunately here, as in the best sections of *The Task*, physico-theological, loco-descriptive thoughts and diction of the usual 18th century type do not appear. The personal is allowed to predominate. God is a Spirit with whom the soul communes, the poet's solitary lays are prayers and religious poetry at the same time. It becomes a very private love poem to the Saviour, though without 17th century extravagance of tone or imagery. The urge for fame and audience is absent as long as the presence and friendship of God suffice for the mood and moment. The religious voice of Cowper is at its finest here, neither smug nor despairing. The modern reader no doubt, for unalterable reasons of time, will continue to prefer the agonies of "The Castaway" to this type of poem, which remains, nevertheless, among the best in 18th century religious verse. Fairchild pointed this out, distinguishing it both from "original" and mediocre poetry of the age, and his opinion was essentially sound.

The meditative poems focusing upon nature as the primary object, and secondarily through nature towards some sense of divinity are "The Shrubbery," "The poplar-field," "Yardley-Oak," "The Castaway," and *The Task*. The last two also have other, greater aspects, and so need not be considered in this place. Of the other three "The Shrubbery" provides the best example of Cowper in this mode, "The poplar-field" being rather obvious in statement of theme, "Yardley

Oak" too long yet unfinished, with the vices and virtues of *The Task*. All have heavy allusion to classical pastoral, which is overlaid in "Yardley Oak" with the Old Testament and Christian themes that so easily derive from pastoral. Though nature is observed in the poems, it is not looked into with delicate nuance as in *The Task*. The narrator is a very human figure distressed by the passing of time, his own life span, mortality as entwined in the slow decay of the natural world, and the natural world as the *work* of, not the particular *emblem* of, the Creator. The fact that all these areas of interest appear in the best and most representative of them, "The Shrubbery," allows the pleasant choice of giving close treatment only to that poem, with occasional allusion to similar qualities in the others. Had "Yardley Oak" been completed, our view of this series of nature poems might well have been of a different order. It comes closest to assigning a numinous deity in nature, but lack of completion leaves the most explicit assignment to the Druidic past in the half-hearted jest on ancient tree-worship:

> It seems idolatry with some excuse
> When our fore-father Druids in their oaks
> Imagin'd sanctity.

The subsequent allusions to oracular trees in classical Donona, to Jacob on time and man's decay, to Adam in Eden, partially retrieve the jest, and there is no doubt in my mind that a completed poem might have ended with a successful presentation of *numen* or spirit in the oak and all of nature, rising to an explicit Christian context and reference very much like that in *The Task*. But the poem is, alas, incomplete, and we must accept an intention unfulfilled and on the evidence of the poem, half-sportive in what we have of it.

"The Shrubbery" is a typical 18th century poem of its type in many respects. The narrator contrasting his gloom and despair with the sunny blessings of nature might as well be Burns, Thomson, Akenside, Shenstone or some other 18th century landscape poet. The source of the "care" and the "sorrow" remains a secret. This is a distinguishing but not a unique feature in this nature meditation. Usually such a poem is long enough to outline a general melancholia, or to make clear that the poet is a victim of love. The cause of Cowper's sorrow can be surmised as his religious crisis of the period. In poems of the same era he dealt explicitly with religious terror and despair in a framework of madness ("Lines written during a period of insanity,"

1763, "Song of Mercy and Judgment," 1764). The severe phase is over by the time of writing of "The Shrubbery," but the mood remains. Notice that the shades are "unblest," and that the poet contrasts himself with "saint or moralist." Such touches are not in tune with typical 18th century deist meditation on nature. The "affliction" is surely his continuing religious crisis, concentrating on mood and contrast with nature, not upon ideological content. While we are not free to read too widely into this vague and general mood, it is less likely that Cowper had any other content in mind, such as the classical *temporis acti, ubi sunt,* or deist gloom. In long poems like "Retirement," "Yardley Oak" and sections of *The Task,* he obviously exhibited the educated 18th century man's easy familiarity with these classical and neo-classical themes, but we may assume that "The Shrubbery" is more in the lyrical, personal vein of "The Castaway" and "Receipt of my Mother's Picture." Though the specific idea is suppressed, it is the essential Puritan one of belief in predestination ("sorrows yet to come") and damnation ("unblest," "soul less hurt than mine").

It is less easy to assign a specific quality or idea to nature in "The Shrubbery" than to the persona. The language has the real 18th century vagueness of deistic poetry, and is nowhere explicitly religious as in *Olney Hymns* or *The Task.* From the pressure of the religious and theological nature of *The Task,* the hymns, and Cowper's known views of the period, we can read into the description of nature in the poem a regard for the inner spirit of nature, for the Spirit or πνευμα as the breath of nature, or even specifically Puritan ideas. Yet it is critically unwise to do so. "Saint," "moralist" and "unblest" suggest a special presence in nature of the Spirit, one from which the narrator is effectively barred by his care and sadness. This can be taken as the Calvinist-Puritan nature of other poems. But it is not present in the language used to refer to nature — shades, glassy stream, silent bowers, moss grown alley — all perfect pieces of 18th century diction rendered more sensible than in other poets by the common sense of Cowper. The poet is the generalist here, muffling the religious distress into vague gloom, and the religious *agon* to moral platitude. These short lyrics are explicitly neither religious nor romantic. In other poems, as the ideas become more explicitly religious, so do the descriptions of nature appear more fallen, dark and ominous, driving man to shipwreck and other forms of destruction. These things are promised in the "sorrows yet to come" at the end of "The Shrubbery."

With the exception of the few poems striking the personal note discussed above, the *Olney Hymns* are exercises in poetic mediocrity. One attempts the Miltonic sublime without success, "The Light and Glory of the Word" (30); there are several of the personal too tepid to rise above convention; but the overwhelming majority of those devoted to doctrinal matters may be divided into the Calvinist-theological and the conventional. The latter merely express moral views or Christian doctrine in a way that any decent man might have done while the former reflect Cowper's conversion and Calvinism. In this group the interest varies from typological use of the Old Testament to express the pattern of life of the Puritan saint, to direct presentation of Calvinist doctrine on justification, grace, sanctification. There are no poems here (or elsewhere in Cowper) of formal devotion like Watts' "Divine Poems" after the 17th century manner. Cowper was too late in time for the baroque devotional style. But some shade of personal or devotional authenticity is lent them by numerous comparisons of the lost soul to shipwreck, drowning, being cast away, a kind of image with well-known sources in Scripture, Calvinist writing, and Calvin himself (*Institutes,* III, xxiv, 4), quoted in the first part of this book. We see this theme in Cowper leading to the great personal poem, "The Castaway," a poem of different level of power than the *Olney Hymns.*

The fairest way to distinguish the conventional from Calvinist-theological poems is by quoting a conventional poem which the reader will agree might have been written by any sincere Christian, and for contrast, discussing some of the theological poems that only a Calvinist could have written. There is no real claim for superiority of one group over the other, since the formally theological tends to be a mediocre poem in Cowper, as in Watts, Wigglesworth, Taylor or Davies, all motivated by the genuine desire to believe that Puritanism could be kept alive and healthy by means of the muse. Cowper's motivation is somewhat the same, with gratitude for his own (temporary) salvation also prominent. Historically such poems have the interest of showing the continuity of Calvinist thought in poetry, the seedbed of more valuable individual poems by the same writers. We do not intend to distort the value or quality in these exercises, as one could not in Wigglesworth's *Day of Doom,* or Taylor's *Gods Determinations touching his Elect,* their predecessors in the Puritan tradition of direct teaching through poetry in New England.

Here is "Self-Acquaintance," a typical conventional Olney hymn, quoted in full:

Dear Lord, accept a sinful heart,
    Which of itself complains
And mourns, with much and frequent smart,
    The evil it contains.

There fiery seeds of anger lurk,
    Which often hurt my frame;
And wait but for the tempter's work
    To fan them to a flame.

Legality holds out a bribe
    To purchase life from thee;
And discontent would fain prescribe
    How thou shalt deal with me.

While unbelief withstands thy grace,
    And puts the mercy by;
Presumption, with a brow of brass,
    Says, "Give me, or I die."

How eager are my thoughts to roam
    In quest of what they love!
But ah! when duty calls them home,
    How heavily they move!

Oh, cleanse me in a Saviour's blood,
    Transform me by thy pow'r,
And make me thy belov'd abode,
    And let me rove no more.

Notice that the religious conventions are not particularly Calvinist, indeed, are the ones found in 16th and 17th century Protestant and Catholic devotional works — "sinful heart," "tempter's work," "legality," "unbelief . . . grace," "cleanse me in a Saviour's blood." Without the intense personal note and sense of introspection of the best 17th century religious poets, the constant repetition of certain themes in religious poetry did give it a deservedly bad name in the 18th century. There are a number of poems of this sort in the *Olney Hymns*, the equivalents of the efforts of the Wesley brothers and others.

Without being in one sense any less conventional, another group of poems are more specifically Calvinist-theological in their attachment to Old Testament typology, and to the notions of the Covenant and the chosen people (the Puritan saints replacing the Jews, of course). We earlier encountered a good deal of this mentality in the late 16th and early 17th century Puritans in prose. Examples in the *Olney Hymns* are numerous: "Jehovah-Jireh," "Jehovah-Rophi," "Jehovah-Nissi," "Jehovah-Shalom," "The Covenant," "The Narrow Way," and others, of which the general characteristics are the same, and therefore susceptible of comment as a group. "The Covenant," of course, is the centerpiece, as we remember from Preston, Perkins, and Sibbes. The complicated theology of the New Covenant replaced the older one of God with the Israelites, and the false claim to authority and exclusiveness asserted for centuries by Rome. The *Hymns* do not give complicated arguments. They work by allusion to Old Testament sources and by assumption that the audience consists mainly of convinced and knowledgeable believers. In other types of poems the Calvinist-Puritan may wrestle with his personal doubts and sins, but in this set the Calvinist theology of the Covenant provides the general bedrock assurance for all. All the "Jehovah" poems operate on this assumption and general Christian typology, Old Testament characters and events representing the life of Christ and Christian theology, with Calvinist-Puritan interpretation of the latter. Thus the Puritan terms "Saints," "grace divine," "self-righteousness," "Jesus' blood," "gird me for the war," appear in harmony with familiar allusions to Jacob, David, Saul, Jonah, and with the general Christian gloss of these "types of Christ" which were centuries old at the time of the Puritan revolution. In one poem, not particularly Old Testament in cast, the Puritan absorption of Hebraicism is even stronger and more direct, in the need to view the world as a battleground for the saints. I quote stanzas i and iv, no doubt the kind of stuff that disgusted Swift and Pope, and later made even that sincere Christian, Dr. Johnson, very uneasy:

> The Narrow Way
> What thousands never knew the road!
> What thousands hate it when 'tis known!
> None but the chosen tribes of GOD,
> Will seek or choose it for their own.
>
> Cleave to the world ye sordid worms,
> Contented lick your native dust;
> But GOD shall fight, with all his storms,
> Against the idol of your trust.

The essential spirit of the Cambridge Puritans lives on in this writing, though the turn of phrase became less frantic and individual as discovery gave way to repetition. That Cowper and, to a lesser extent, Watts share much in tone with their "free grace" Anglican and Methodist neighbors, more than the surface of these hymns acknowledges. The sentimentalism of the 18th century did have erosive influence upon all religious traditions inherited from narrower, fiercer, but in many ways more manly times. Such sentimentalism does not peep through in this poem.

Another series of poems presents Calvinist doctrine in a strongly New Testament context as interpreted by Puritan tradition. The primary text is the letter of St. Paul from which Puritan divines deduced the famous cycle – sin-state, election/reprobation, justification, sanctification, glorification. There are other favorite passages familiar to the reader of Puritan tracts and devotional materials. Since Cowper did not write all of the *Hymns,* and since they are devotional, not theological, in intention (though *in toto* they do cover everything important in the tradition), methodical and full illustration is out of place. The tone and quality of the poems are evident enough in a few characteristic examples, the best available in quality. "O Lord, I will Praise thee" (8), "The Contrite Heart" (9), "Contentment" (19), "Light Shining out of Darkness" (35), "Welcome Cross" (36), "Afflictions Sanctified by the Word" (37), "Temptation" (38), "Not of Works" (64), "Grace and Providence" (66), "Longing to be with Christ" (later addition by editor) are titles suggesting a mixture of Puritan piety and devotion with Calvinist doctrine. Some are certainly also generally Christian, and remember again what was stated above, that the conventional Christian poems of category four and this Puritan strain, stressing piety based upon New Testament themes, differ little. A real distinction is present only in a few, to which attention for purposes of this study at least should be drawn. In striking the devotional note, a poem like "Welcome Cross" succeeds more fully than the more purely Puritan ones. Were it not for the "castaway" image in it, and the Puritan stress on the trials of the state of sanctification, the theme of suffering connected with the Cross would strike the reader more likely as Roman Catholic than Puritan in subject matter.

"Contentment" and "Longing to be with Christ" are in the same range as "Welcome Cross," that is, generally Christian with mild Puritan flavor. Several of the others have specific Puritan images or theological allusions without being doctrinal. "O Lord, I will Praise Thee" turns on God's anger (his "good pleasure" in Calvin's terms) and free salvation, the blessed state referred to very Calvinistically as "Zion." "The Contrite Heart" has the familiar 17th century paradox of the soul resisting the mercy and wooing of God, in this instance a weak shadow of Donne's powerful *Holy Sonnets*:

Oh make this heart rejoice, or ache;
  Decide this doubt for me;
And if it be not broken, break,
  And heal it, if it be.

Except for references to "thy saints" and "thy house of pray'r," so dear
to the Puritan heart, the poem is generally Christian. The doubt and
despair are not the serious Puritan type that precede signs of election,
or follow the sense of abandonment to reprobation. It is only the
normal doubt characteristic of the state of sanctification in the Puritan
cycle, as in Sibbes' *Bruised Reede* and Taylor's *Sacramental Meditations,* equivalent to the self-doubts of baptized, confirmed Catholics or Anglicans practicing the sacramental life. Not to have such
doubts would be arrogance, but their presence is not to be taken too
seriously; at this stage the soul is resolved. "Afflictions Sanctified by
the Word" mentions the familiar Covenant and chosen saints,
"Temptation" the recurrent shipwreck and castaway imagery of
Calvinism and Cowper. Only a Calvinist Christian could have written
such poems, yet on the whole, all Christians can share in their theology
and piety at some level. This is not true of the last three poems to be
looked at in this general area.

"Light Shining out of Darkness," "Not of Works," and "Grace and
Providence" are Calvinist-Puritan doctrinal poems of the strict sort
only Puritans wrote and responded to during the centuries of Puritan
tradition. Each one heavily emphasizes certain Puritan themes. In the
first the power and majesty of God, his arbitrary will, inscrutable
purpose and man's need to wait for grace are stressed over mercy and
the Covenant, but the overall outlook is cheerful:

Behind a frowning providence,
  He hides a smiling face.

This contrast between man's gloom and his joy in relation to God's
majesty is observed throughout the *Institutes*. The point that in
Calvinism man's intellect as well as will was weakened by original sin,
often overlooked or underestimated by commentators on the
intellectual side of Calvinism, is openly acknowledged in the poem, as
in Calvin and the English Puritan commentators. Later Puritan rationalists and some 20th century commentators have tended to tidy up this
matter. Cowper's authentic voice again reminds us of the real situation,
that basic Calvinism had not changed significantly from Calvin's day to
this among the faithful, only among revisionists and those moving into

Unitarianism. "Grace and Providence" goes over the same ground in a more lyric, supportive and confident vein: prayer and praise of the goodness of providence is the theme. It is true that "Satan's malice" is lurking always, and must be mentioned, but in this poem it is not very threatening. The poet feels strong enough to put in a good word for his own song, in humble tones of course, but unmistakably those of a careful student of Horace, one who values the muse and his own modest abilities justly.

"Not of Works" deserves little comment, except as typical of a group of directly preachy, theological poems on grace, sin, conversion, faith, and other points in the Calvinist scheme of salvation. They are uninspired dogmatizing, and hide in their assurance and false serenity the poet's own true feelings — his sense of despair and reprobation. He is performing in these exercises his public and communal function, being Puritan poet for the faithful flock, about as well as that task can be performed. Dr. Johnson's unfair comments on all religious poetry certainly apply to this species:

> Grace, triumphant in the throne,
> Scorns a rival, reigns alone;
> Come and bow beneath her sway,
> Cast your idol works away:
> Works of man, when made his plea,
> Never shall accepted be;
> Fruits of pride (vain-glorious worm)
> Are the best he can perform.

And so on, through another half dozen, laying out Calvin's doctrines in clear and no uncertain terms. But this is only a small portion of what Cowper and other Calvinist-Puritan poets had to offer.

In *The Task* there are elements of the Puritan religious spirit in the first five books, but these are intermittent and unsatisfactory and hardly a reason for reading the poem. The moralism is clear, uncompromising evangelicism; the descriptions of nature are variously delightful, at times stifled by 18th century diction, but occasionally brilliant and original, the stimulus of Wordsworth and Coleridge. These facts we now all more or less know and accept, having had them brought to our attention by Cowper's best critics and the best on the later Romantics. Only in Book VI does the religious aspect of the poem become serious and finally succeed in its own terms, though with the same fits and starts characteristic of the poem as a whole.

The account of Genesis (II. 348—372) is matter-of-fact, not very promising and in no way intended as a serious rival or echo of Milton. Examining the fallen world (II. 373—631), the mood turns to despair and defiance, a general preachiness seasoned by evangelical concerns reaching a narrow and sour low in contempt for the powers and future of poetry and in the ungracious line, "Messiah's eulogy for Handel's sake!" The almost immediate palinode to the memory of Handel's genius, "But hush! — the muse perhaps is too severe," does not hide the essentially Puritan contempt for those who toy with holy things and the Holy Book without giving serious thought to its real purpose and content (though few today would make such a judgment of Handel). It is only with the more than pedestrian bow to Milton and to the spirit of prophecy, with the thirsting for the end of time and this world (at least comparable to Books XI—XII of *Paradise Lost*) in lines 730—746, that an apocalyptic Puritan spirit of real poetry awakens in Cowper. From that point until the end, with little exception, we are in the familiar world of Calvinist-Puritan prose writing and poetry, and one could find not only the heavy influence of Milton, but also Spenser, Baxter, and Bunyan, and behind them the Cambridge Puritans, if source hunting were an important purpose. Cowper's copy of Flavel was earlier mentioned, and it is fair to assume that the Olney group would have been interested in early Puritan piety. But as usual, with few exceptions, the general themes and patterns are more interesting than specific verbal echoes of earlier writers, since a tradition, not isolated influence, has been presiding purpose of this book.

Milton is the one most dominant influence from line 747, "Sweet is the harp of prophecy," to the end of the poem, and the allusions to *Paradise Lost*, particularly to the final books, will be obvious to any reader. But it is narrow to make too much of the parallel, for Cowper himself wisely understates the relationship to Milton in order to place his final religious visions within a more general Christian context, demonstrable as a Puritan context:

> But, when a poet, or when one like me,
> Happy to rove among poetic flow'rs,
> Though poor in skill to rear them, lights at last
> On some fair theme, some theme divinely fair . . . .

The final poetic theme, fair and divine, is no other than the Calvinist-Puritan meditation on glorification from the individual and general points of view. In such company, Milton is the greatest artist, but only one of many practitioners Cowper is proud and anxious to join.

As an overall context for this final section, let me recall briefly the general position of the Georges, Pettit, New, Knappen and other commentators on Puritan tradition, on which all agree (not the points of theology subject to continuing debate), that is, the character of the Puritan saint and his vision. I will construct a succinct list, merely so that the appropriateness to the end of *The Task* will be obvious. The "saint" develops a certain isolation in the world, though not avoiding its demands completely like a Greek or Catholic hermit; he positively avoids the company of the ungodly, but chooses to reside in the company of a godly community, like Olney, over lonely Catholic asceticism. He views a gulf between the natural and the spiritual, which makes him always restless and troubled, but his quest for sanctity must be acted out in this world. He accepts the difference between the paradise within and outer reality, not seeking or inviting, but often provoking, by indifference to the world, the martyrdom the world can bestow. His model of Christ tends to make him meek, not militant, except during one historical period.[22] Enough trouble and martyrdom will seek him out if he is godly to prove his sanctification, for that is the nature of the world. In his vision of individual redemption, and in special and general glory, lie his consolation for the sufferings of this life.

All of this applies to Cowper's final lines, as it did to *Paradise Lost*, XI–XII, Taylor's *Meditations*, Baxter's *Saints Rest*, Bunyan, Law, Watts, even to Smart and Blake in their strange ways, as we have shown or will try to show. Here our concern is with the application of these themes to the great final lines of *The Task*, lines 747 to the end. In them a modern critic might find a systolic-diastolic pattern of rising and falling action, or expansion and contraction. The language is charged when the theme is Puritan in emotion and intellect, and falls when the poet returns to mere carping moralism. In the last twenty-five lines, the personal coda, a middle balance is achieved between high and low in the final just and modest presentation of the poet's view of his own character within the Puritan tradition.

The first upward sweep is in lines 759–765. As in all the strongest passages, Milton's presence is not oppressive in this glimpse of future glory. There is room for Baxter, Bunyan, and the Bible:

> Oh scenes surpassing fable, and yet true,
> Scenes of accomplish'd bliss! which who can see,

Though but in distant prospect, and not feel
His soul refresh'd with foretaste of the joy?
Rivers of gladness water all the earth,
And clothe all climes with beauty; the reproach
Of barrenness is past.

Cowper is at his best when working imaginatively with Genesis, the Prophets, or Revelation, never without intermediaries, for he is always a learned man. To read this side of Cowper correctly, that is, imaginatively, one must resist the temptation of minute citation, unless very crucial, and the indulgence of lengthy quotation, also a trap of Wordsworth commentary. As the passage moves to its conclusions at line 799 it weakens, becomes more conventionally evangelical. One can note eagerly an anticipation (also evangelical) of the early Blake in "Antipathies are none" (I. 777), but the tone and harmony cease to be staunchly Puritan in a set of lines like "Worthy the Lamb, for he was slain for us" where we hear unmistakably the rapturous music of the 18th century conventicle, whether Calvinist, Methodist, or storefront. At line 799 the sterner, older traditions and aspirations of the early Puritans return with obvious echoes from Calvin through the Cambridge group to the American Puritans and the English 17th century. Quotation must be resisted, but a minimum is necessary here:

See Salem built, the labour of a God!
Bright as a sun the sacred city shines;
All kingdoms and all princes of the earth
Flock to that light; the glory of all lands
Flows into her; unbounded is her joy,
And endless her increase.

The biblical allusions, and relatively quiet foretaste of even more powerful passages of similar splendor in Blake and Wordsworth, are there to notice also; but the temptation to minute particulars must be resisted. Even the lapse into dull and methodical biblical paraphrase from lines 804−17 does not ruin the handling of glorification in the passage as a whole. This perfunctory biblical paraphrase is easily compensated for by what comes next, one of the few passages on this theme in the poem equal to Milton in language and Puritan intensity. Cowper's diffidence, normally based upon a wise and accurate modesty, could be dropped when deeply moved, as by his own sins and damnation in "The Castaway," or here by the majesty and power of God and his final glory, the twin Puritan themes at opposite ends of the spectrum. Here resistance to quotation is not in order:

> Thus heav'n-ward all things tend. For all were once
> Perfect, and all must be at length restor'd,
> So God has greatly purpos'd; who would else
> In his dishonour'd works himself endure
> Dishonour, and be wrong'd without redress.
> Haste, then, and wheel away a shatter'd world,
> Ye slow-revolving seasons!   (ll. 818–24)

No one has more succinctly summed up the attitude of St. Paul, Augustine, Calvin or the burden of the last books of *Paradise Lost*, the burden of all Puritan thought — how God in his glory can endure this fallen world another minute — better than Cowper. The immediate contraction to pessimism with things here in the world is inevitable, the tragic duality of the Puritan (and all real Christian) experience. The drop here is to the general sadness of Puritan vision at its second-best, like Mr. Edwards in the woods, not with his spider, which in Cowper's case is the narrow carping he can easily fall into, and does a few lines further on. We can accept "Here ev'ry drop of honey hides a sting," and "From touch of human lips, at best impure" as more than moralizing but less than vision. Low grumbling and disgruntled moralizing follow in lines 871–95, the inevitable letdown, but we are surprised by the intervention of another powerful Calvinist-Puritan passage, lines 855–70, breaking into, but not removing the rhythm of the systole-diastole flow of the entire section.

> Come then, and, added to thy many crowns,
> Receive yet one, the crown of all the earth,
> Thou who alone art worthy! It was thine
> By ancient covenant, ere nature's birth;
> And thou hast made it thine by purchase since,
> And overpaid its value with the blood.
> Thy saints proclaim thee king; and in their hearts
> Thy title is engraven with a pen
> Dipt in the fountain of eternal love.
> Thy saints proclaim thee king. . . .

Calvinist ideas of God's majesty and glory, his seigneurship over the world by his own pleasure, the Covenant, and the eagerness with which the poet looks forward to God's vindication and the destruction of the wicked (a section which immediately follows), are apparent here. By placing the dramatic center of the celebration in the "saints," the heritage of English Puritanism with its particular love for that term receives an emphasis Cowper no doubt intends to be taken as an identification of himself with this ultimate glimpse of God's glory.

There is a grand coming together of Calvinist-Puritan traditions here. The movement is then diminished by still another of the long carping passages at things in the world as they now are (II. 865–905). Several allusions to conscience (l. 895), to the prophets (l. 899), and to "effectual work" (l. 904) give genuine religious zeal to the diatribe, enough to mitigate its essentially barren nature.

The final section of the book, lines 906–1024, is a modest but accurate self-portrait. Some of the attributes assigned to the portrait are specifically Puritan, others from the Cowper we have learned to know from earlier books of *The Task* and elsehere. The themes of retirement, of the man who makes his fate his choice, the poet who extolls contentment in humility, the sublimity of the natural world, and general contemplation appeared in the writings of a number of other 18th century gentlemen and poets, and indeed are stock 18th century themes. Only in intensity of real love of the natural world and of his predecessors and contemporaries can Cowper be said to excel.

The specifically religious and Calvinist-Puritan nature of his muse and character is intoduced with the word "contemplation" at line 924, for his contemplation is not primarily to be about things of this world, no matter how quietly or humanly splendid, but of

> a heav'n unseen
> And . . . glories yet to be reveal'd.

His thought of thoughts is the central Puritan one, presented in so many of the writers we have studied here, a variation of which is the title of a recent book by Martz, *The Paradise Within*. First duality, then warfare, then a paradise within, finally triumph over self, another way of describing sin-state, election-justification, sanctification and glory:

> His warfare is within. There unfatigu'd
> His fervent spirit labours. There he fights,
> And there obtains fresh triumphs o'er himself,
> And never with'ring wreaths. . . .

I am not going to quote extensively from writers cited previously in this book, or re-analyze any of these terms. This book is a total failure if such were necessary at this point. But it is interesting and important to notice the emphasis, assurance and finality with which the poet casts himself in this tradition, assuming, on solid grounds, that his reader (not necessarily his 20th century one) will understand the nature of the decision he has made and the identity found. Cowper later slipped back to the despair-state in his last insanity, giving us the great "Castaway" poem. These lines of *The Task*, from here to the end, should have the greater authority.[23] They are followed shortly by still another Puritan passage, this with its often accompanying Hebraic backdrop:

> Perhaps she owes
> Her sunshine and her rain . . .
>   to the pray'r he makes,
> When, Isaac like, the solitary saint
> Walks forth to meditate at even tide,
> And think on her [the world], who thinks not for herself.

In this passage silence, the still equanimity of the chosen figure, and the power of prayer combine to give reality to the "solitary saint" as persona, assured within himself. The power of prayer to affect the world is also a favorite Roman Catholic religious-poetic device, perhaps parodied in Keats' *Endymion* where Love is granted this power (I, 830−842), and more likely followed seriously in Coleridge's "Christabel," which emphasizes the mysterious powers of prayer and love. As for the "solitary saint," he is almost always an effective figure, even to non-believers of many kinds, just as to many believers the solitary saints who make up their own rules, such as Byron's Manfred, have deep appeal. Cowper in the coda of this poem has earned the right to claim the title in the traditional Christian terms, with an unmistakable Calvinist-Puritan flavor. The defense of chosen role and character tapers off after this high point, with some further peevishness towards the world and the great, and some special pleading for "idleness" on slightly worldly grounds. But the focus is not lost, as the "test of conscience" returns in line 998, and the biblical assertion that the fate of the world and all in it "is in his hand" (l. 1018). The concluding characterization of the poet as man of the world removed to retirement (the classical theme) and man of deep religious intensity and vision who has earned his right to the paradise within (the Puritan theme) is held in perfect balance, and the poem ends happily and successfully.

Cowper is best remembered for the striking despair in "The Castaway." With this judgment there can be no argument. "The Castaway" is a great poem, one which strikes only one note in the complex poetic vision of the Calvinist temper. In most respects, as this section has tried to demonstrate, Cowper shared this complex religious vision in the 18th century with Watts, Smart and Law, his true distinction being in his ability to compose the best religious poetry of the age.

PART FOUR

The Romantic Age: Blake, Coleridge, Wordsworth and Byron

I. Introduction and Blake

In turning from the 18th century to the Romantic movement we find that the deepening gulf between rationalistic assumptions and moral attitudes and feelings, which was growing throughout the 18th century and found full focus in Cowper, affects all the early 19th century writers deeply. The ways in which the writers reacted to the problem varied widely, and only some of the responses to the problem are clearly in the range of this study. The focus in the poet must be at least strongly religious or deriving from religious assumptions, which is the case with Blake, Coleridge, Wordsworth and Byron, but not with Scott, Keats and Shelley. If we were to consider American writers in this book, Hawthorne and Melville also fall within this tradition, where the center of the conflict over the problems of conscience and sensibility is in religious ideas and terms. In Emerson and Whitman, as with Scott, Keats and Shelley, though the problems of religious sensibility are present, the center falls elsewhere in more rationalistic and secular concerns. This may seem to be a fine line to draw for some of the poets, yet fine lines must be drawn in order to show that there is an authentic religious tradition in English poetry despite the great secular philosophical influences of the 18th and 19th centuries. Blake is the most unusual figure in this transition. A look at some other writers with similar problems though not in such acute form may help in understanding the crucial position of Blake. Hawthorne, Melville, and Dickinson are Americans who share some of these interests and problems; the English writers Shelley, Scott and Keats did not. It is good to note that similar intellectual and moral issues existed despite the imagined pseudo-barriers of oceans, new national identities, and the pigeonholes of historical scholars.

Hawthorne and Melville, American prose writers, fall outside of this study, yet both are essentially "Puritan" writers about whom much has been written from that aspect. A few remarks about Hawthorne's Puritan religious sensibility may illustrate the concerns common to early 19th century writers within the Calvinist-Puritan sensibility. A short comment on Melville will appear later in relation to Coleridge. On Hawthorne the conclusions of an important writer on American literature give acute focus on the problems of our interest.

Hyatt Waggoner, in his well-known study of Hawthorne, draws several important conclusions about Hawthorne's relationship to the Puritan tradition we would do well to ponder here, as giving firm guidance for studying Puritan influences in the 19th century.[1] He finds these dominant characteristics in Hawthorne as reflecting Puritan sensibility: belief in providence, without understanding its meaning; a doubtful faith; mistrust of individual motive and feeling; moral and intellectual ambiguity, and patterns in the work which reflect these attitudes. Put more succinctly,

But if his way of presenting the faith was more *reasonable*, less offensive to modern reason, than Bunyan's and Spenser's, it was also less *rationalistic*. Their faith may have been "false" in some of its elements, but it was a public, shared faith assumed to be objectively true, not needing to be validated, except in some ultimate and strictly personal sense, by the heart. Unlike Hawthorne, they did not see heart and head as in inevitable and unceasing conflict. (Hawthorne thought redemption, wholeness, would come only when the conflict ceased, when the two co-operated; but this was a wished for, not an experienced, state.) They could write more objectively because the dream that shaped their works did not seem like a dream; they were quite sure, indeed, that much of it was fact, not dream at all. Their symbols could have the kind of objectivity that is provided by known public referents. They could be, in their own eyes and those of their contemporaries who shared their beliefs, men of reason without committing treason to the heart.[2]

The axis of the reasonable and the rationalistic in relation to religious experience is a good one to test the continuance of the Calvinist tradition into the 19th century. It is not enough to consider intellectual and moral tension in themselves as the guideline here, for tension could be attributed to other objects or take other forms. The split between reason and the formerly reasonable systems of religious and philosophical faith encompassed all aware men. It can only be in the framework of given religious doctrine and tradition that we might say this struggle takes the form of the Calvinist temper, as it does in greater or lesser degree in Coleridge, Wordsworth, Blake, Byron, Hawthorne, Dickinson and Melville. Similar tensions of intellect and feeling occur in Shelley and Keats, or Scott and Emerson, with the intellectual axis deriving from other sources. Let us look briefly at the example of Keats.

Keats was most successful in holding together the 19th century tensions of intellect and feeling, perhaps because his interest was least bound by the traditional forms, religious or philosophical. He chose his beliefs carefully among pagan and Christian sources with an eye to what was good for poetry. There is tension, at times powerful, in his poems, but none that cannot be balanced or unified. There are no hereditary ghosts. Since religious elements and feelings always proved discordant in the 19th century, Keats chose to avoid problems which were never in any sense strongly personal. The tension is psychological, and the resolution purely aesthetic, expressed most often through the medium of myth.

On the other hand Coleridge and Byron are directly within the purview of the Calvinist temper, Blake and Wordsworth less obviously so. The difficulties Blake and Wordsworth raise will be taken up in introducing the poems to be read in a later part of this section. A few remarks here will concern only the most general conceptual problems.

Wordsworth is problematic because the question of his individualistic and visionary tendencies can be raised in any consideration of his poetry as religious. Yet also the fact of a strong residue of religious feeling in the poetry has never been disputed by serious critics. The shifts, if such there are, from the earlier "visionary" to the later religious awarenesses, can only be discussed in the contexts of specific poems of various periods. Byron is problematic and interesting in other ways. There is much in Byron clearly un-religious and non-Calvinist, and much of the outlook of the secular and cynical man of the world and of the 18th century. Classical models were always before Byron's eyes, as is well known, although his use of them is conceded to be less than slavish. This means that there are many works in the profilic Byron to which the statement quoted above by Waggoner on Hawthorne would not apply. Byron was not a writer of deep single vision as were Wordsworth, Blake and many others in this study. Yet Byron's Calvinist sense in some major poems cannot be dismissed. The biographical facts show a clear influence of Calvinist training in Byron's early life, and his rejection of Calvinist dogma as religious truth means very little in the context of artistic sensibility. As with the other major Romantics of some religious interest, and even a few earlier writers, it is a question of displacement, and discussable only by literary analysis. The greatest interest of course is in *Childe*

Harold's Pilgrimage and *Manfred,* with the religious closet dramas and some of the minor self-dramatic poems forming a backdrop.

It will not be difficult to show that both Coleridge and Blake are religious poets in some way. Although Blake is regarded as essentially secular in outlook and sensibility by some influential critics, such an opinion is rejected here, as it also has been by a number of critics who have come to Blake by a variety of means. The religious element is an essential aspect of his work, not merely a cast-off youthful heritage. The specific Calvinist influence upon Coleridge has not been previously noted. It is an intensification, in certain poems and at certain times in his life, of his by now well studied religious sensibility.

A difficulty of a general sort in writing about religious influence in the Romantic period is that of precise definition and exclusions. Until about forty years ago we were being told that Romanticism was inimical to precise religious doctrine, was essentially pantheistic. An antireligious tone was cultivated by some critics partisan to Romanticism vis-à-vis new critics and their favorite 17th century and modern writers. Now the situation has turned drastically, and we have the spectacle of learned Romanticists such as Wasserman and Abrams showing the inclusiveness of the Romantic spirit,[3] so that the Bible, the Fathers, Augustine and the patterns of German idealist thought are not incompatible, indeed make a mutual contribution to the Romantic mind. This new outlook is congenial to the aims of this study, if the critic is noting large general patterns, basic themes, and the most crucial historical relationships. If he is trying to be very specific, working with one traditional pattern such as Calvinism (though Catholicism and Anglicanism provide the same difficulties), these schemes are only useful as general encouragement. All Romantic writers, including Shelley, Keats and the continental Romantics, can be enfolded in the general embrace of universal cultural and historical religious patterns. Though many Romantic writers are excluded by the definitions and limits of this study, this writer readily allows for the general merits of the recent inclusiveness in Romantic criticism, and for the new awareness of Romanticism as central to western cultural tradition. This study, then, can be viewed as a specific instance of a general situation. When it began the general situation was not widely appreciated nor the overall patterns worked out. Calvinism was chosen as the specific perspective on account of its central importance for the English situation, not for its novelty or arbitrariness, and to remain true to this choice some poets had to be excluded. It is sufficient, I believe, to show that Coleridge, Wordsworth and Byron display in their central patterns the Calvinist tradition, and that in Blake, to a different degree, these religious patterns exist in the midst of other elements. The discussion of Blake can therefore be briefer than the others and more general, in fact a continuation of this introduction to the 19th century and an extension of the remarks made in the previous section when Blake's name inevitably appeared in the company of Watts, Law, Böehme and Smart. Blake raises an extreme example of the problems of religious sensibility in general and Calvinist-Puritanism in particular in the transition from the 18th to the 19th century.

The main problem is that Blake's originality is so extreme that his work falls outside of any normal sense of tradition, even if Böehme, Law and various other esoterica are invoked. There is certainly a religious sensibility working in the earliest and latest poetry, even if one dismisses the rebellious and political poetry between, but how to define this religious sensibility is a subject of controversy and real difficulty. Perhaps the earliest and the latest of the poems belong directly in a Calvinist-Puritan strain of the Christian tradition, giving a double problem of defining and placing Blake as the crucial figure at the turn of the century. Our purpose in looking at Blake is to ascertain what the situation of Blake can tell us about the relationship of poetry and religious experience at the threshold of the Romantic movement.

The Blake critics are not definitive on the question of the religious nature of his poetry. Harold Bloom insists that Blake is not a Christian, or even is anti-Christian. This has been a popular liberal view of Blake, sustained also by Alfred Kazin and more recently by Geoffrey Hartman. On the other hand Blake's use of the Christian Cabala and Böehme has given evidence for a general religious reading of the major poetry; and in one helpful case, E. D. Hirsch has successfully shown the historical influence of 18th century evangelical and Swedenborgian religious views upon the early poetry, particularly the *Songs of Innocence*.[4] However, the general note is one of confusion and controversy, as was brought out inadvertently in a recent *Festschrift*, wherein an incredible diversity of views towards Blake's Christianity appeared, with some contributors assuming atheism, others cabalism or gnosticism, and still others his "Christianity" ranging from a Puritan relationship to Milton to more general evangelical schemes.[5] In the light of Blake's complexity and the powerful response he evokes in readers some difference of opinion on this score is inevitable, but the basic disagreement whether Blake's poetry is "Christian" at all is merely another way of pointing to the uniqueness and cryptic nature of Blake's poetry. In this situation the constant allusions, in the critics who prefer to view Blake as Christian, to the low Church and Swedenborgian movements of the late 18th century are of some importance, since there certainly was an initial connection between Blake and such movements, which were the cutting edge or at least the most vital elements in the Christian experience in England at a time when orthodoxy had reached an extremely lethargic intellectual and practical state.[6]

The Swedenborgian churches, if not the esoteric doctrines, were akin to the storefront Christianity of today and appealed to the lower classes in London who had abandoned the established Church or been abandoned by it, and to the shopkeeper class deprived of a vital Calvinist-Puritan tradition yet still clinging to some vestiges of its "doctrines of the Spirit" in the new cults. Blake's native crankiness would have led him to Swedenborg, as it later turned him from the Swedish mystic, despite his affinities for the artisan class and dislike of the establishment. There were drawbacks for Blake in the Church of the New Jerusalem. In intellectuality and refinement its level was far below that at which Watts, Smart and Cowper had encountered Calvinism in the 18th century, or that which was available to Coleridge, Wordsworth, Byron and Dickinson in the next. This period, the last years of the 18th century, was the nadir of fortunes of all religious groups, as we know from Bampton and Boyle lectures and the charges of various bishops.[7] Yet the Quakers and millenarian sects of London and other large towns had managed to keep alive in extreme left-wing ways the basic Puritan forms of thought and practice from the 17th century, although by the late 18th century these were to be found only in very crude form. This residue of the wilder forms of 17th century Puritanism provided ready followers for Swedenborg's optimistic and imaginative visions of the Christian faith, and at one time William Blake was certainly an enthusiast of Swedenborgianism. Emotionally and psychologically, left-wing Puritanism, millenarianism and the Swedenborgian doctrines had much in common, and thus it was easy for Blake and others nurtured in extreme Puritanism to make the transfer to the more novel sect. Blake's early poetry has a strongly evangelical flavor, even when the dominant idea is original and heterodox. The difference between Blake and other followers of the New Jerusalem scheme was that the poet developed from this rather anarchic version of antinomian Christianity into his own original visionary world. And if we believe that Blake is the beginning of the Romantic movement we have the startling paradox that the rather crude millenarian and Swedenborgian movement, the last downward swing of institutional Puritanism in England, was also one of the more immediate inspirations for a poet and a movement which would, among its secondary effects, lead to a revival of interest in the established Church and Roman Catholicism. Thus the end of the 18th century in England found Christianity at the very depth of its fortunes, only to be revived spiritually in its various forms, including the Calvinist-Puritan, by the poets Blake, Coleridge, Wordsworth, Byron, and by others in America. This point is more important for our perspective than is the specific placing of Blake as a religious poet.

That Blake's starting point was Swedenborgian with its Puritan associations is not denied by any responsible critic; the question is whether the development of this peculiar sensibility in his poetry remains Christian, as we have it in *Songs of Innocence*, in the more rebellious works which followed, or if the frequent mentions of Jesus and more oblique use of other Christian symbols in the later writings have Christian meaning. It is not a question of holding Blake to any particular version of Christian orthodoxy, the mistake Bloom makes in his negative opinion of Blake's Christianity in *Blake's Apocalypse*.[8] On the other hand positive assertion will not do on the basis of mere feeling of a critic responding to Blake's poetry. It seems certain that Blake's Christianity in the later poetry, if his use of certain symbols and visions can be called that, has moved far from the antinomian-Swedenborgian basis of *Songs of Innocence*, about which this writer agrees with Hirsch in assigning some designation of "left-wing" Christian feeling and thought. The fact that no orthodoxy of any tradition can be cited for the later Blake leads Bloom and others to their exaggerated conclusions. But there certainly is real difficulty involved. Foster Damon in his original *William Blake: His Philosophy and Symbols* described the later Blake as a mystic of fundamental Christian type. It may be that Blake is this lone religious enthusiast, or in the general perennial mystical tradition, as another set of Blakeans has averred.[9] Almost everyone agrees to a Christian pattern of thought in the early poems, with the exception of the naturalists. The fact of Christian presence, and the kind of presence in the later works, are matters of doubt and disagreement. The kinds of antinomian Christian patterns in the early poetry, emphasizing "doctrines of the Spirit" and individual visions, are perennial, having appeared in Smart and Law, and before them in Böehme and the mystics. This gives a familiar context in which to read even the most difficult individual works. The symbols and visions of the later poems may be unique, or gnostic, or mystical Christian, or perhaps precursors of poetic expression in the modern era, the favorite view of the naturalists. All these positions have been put forward at great length. Thus it is justified to study only some aspects of the poetry in this chapter, concentrating on the Christian religious symbolism and possible Calvinist patterns in various poems from all stages of Blake's career. This approach is not systematic. Despite the amount of fearful symmetry devoted to methodological reading of Blake's work, this writer still very much doubts that such a system exists in Blake's poetry.

The works most naturally appropriate for discussion of Blake, Christianity and Calvinist-Puritan patterns are *Songs of Innocence, Marriage of Heaven and Hell, Milton* and *The Everlasting Gospel.* There are also important elements in *Jerusalem*, especially the Jesus figure, but since that appears in much the same light in *Milton*, some words will be said about the Jesus figure in *Jerusalem* in relationship with the other poems mentioned here, not in the total context of Blake's major epic. *Milton* has the advantage of being about the great Puritan poet and *Paradise Lost*, and so confronts us with Puritan pattern directly. *Songs of Innocence* has the Swedenborgian and religious background of the early Blake, dimly Puritan in its origins; while, as everyone knows, *Heaven and Hell* is important for Blake's initial rebellion against orthodoxy; and *The Everlasting Gospel* is a late return to snorts of defiance after the beautiful coherence of the traditional and individual ideas and visions in *Jerusalem.*

Placing Blake in a Christian and Calvinist perspective then presents major and minor problems. The minor concern aspects of his work that have been adequately and reasonably treated. The religious reading of *Songs of Innocence* makes sense over an ironic and naturalistic one, and gives a clear starting point for discussion of religion in Blake. To the naturalists can be conceded *Marriage of Heaven and Hell* and some of the minor political prophecies of little interest from the viewpoint here. When the naturalists such as Bloom, Kazin or Hartman read the late poetry as if it were by Whitman, Stevens or Ammons, their contribution can be ignored, since the distance from objectivity is obvious. The major problem, alluded to in our 18th century section and above in this introduction, is that Blake's poetry is both inside and outside religious tradition, as was his mind. A strictly Christian and Calvinist reading of the later poetry, the kind possible for Watts and Cowper, would be as dishonest as the naturalistic one, a literary form of axe-grinding. Yet unless the peculiar religious language and vision of *Milton*, and some of the symbols from *Jerusalem*, can be accommodated to the scheme of this book not much has been accomplished concerning Blake. This does not require another full explication of either poem; there have been enough of them. And of them only one, the most formidable and polemical, focusses the issues of greatest importance. Frye in *Fearful Symmetry* attempts a systematic reading of the kind with which this writer is not in sympathy, but his handling of the religious question in Blake is invaluable. Frye rejects the notion that Blake was an orthodox Christian or a traditional mystic, and yields to none in wry sayings and snorts of defiance concerning Christian orthodoxy, and so has been often viewed as a naturalistic reader of Blake. His followers may be, but he is not. In tone he champions the "rebellious" Blake, but in substance he is wiser. Frye claims that Blake transferred the symbols of Christianity into their true imaginative reality, away from the dead husks of orthodoxy, and his imitators have echoed this point. But Frye also maintains something far more complex, and true to the spirit of Blake's historical setting, mind, and the texts of the poems:

Blake is, therefore, trying to do for Milton what the prophets and Jesus did for Moses: isolate what is poetic and imaginative and annihilate what is legal and historical. This is also what he is trying to do for himself, and there will always be a curse on any critic who tries to see the Christianity and the radicalism of Blake as a dichotomy instead of a unity.[10]

This difficulty and fascination is at the heart of Blake's most significant poems, which arc neither orthodox nor naturalistic. Frye has a clear perception of this problem in Blake, perhaps the best though not the only critic who has seen this complexity of Christian usage in Blake. By wrestling with his own demons as often as explicating Blake in *Fearful Symmetry*, Frye is not always a sound guide, too much of an advocate of a reformed, illumined Christianity according to Frye to be always trusted. Yet he is the most learned critic of Blake we have had (some are learned, others critics), and few remember points like the above on the later poems, preferring to remember and emulate the snorts of defiance and gleeful wit in Frye's treatment of the *Songs of*

Experience, Heaven and Hell, other poems of rebellion. Let me cite
another quotation from Frye's discussion of *Milton* which is even more
sobering than the above, in its acknowledgment that a separation of
the problem of reading major Blake from the problems of Christian
religion, religious symbolism, and Calvinist tradition is simply impossible:

> ... there is much that is really good in moral good, when attached to the
> imagination and not made an end in itself. The moral law is the sub-
> conscious foundation of the imaginative life, as physical law is the sub-
> conscious foundation of the conscious vision. The artist who lives and dies in
> society without surrendering his imaginative honesty is of the class Blake
> called "Redeemed."[11]

No antinomian parting of morality from imagination in this. Frye
recognizes as we all must that Blake does play with the Calvinist
ideas of elect, reprobate and redeemed in *Milton,* but play is not
necessarily rejection. His transformations of the Christ figure and
Jesus, sometimes very human, at others divine, in *Milton* and *Jerusalem* raise the same issues. These ideas and images are inside the
poet, as they were in Milton before him. Frye exaggerates Blake's
rebellion and often is more exuberant than critical. At times he
sounds very much like Bloom and the other naturalists in his attitude
towards Blake's Christianity, referring to *Milton*:

> The religion will be the religion of Jesus, the Everlasting Gospel, and the
> language will be the tongue of Albion. Blake does not mean by one religion
> the acceptance of a uniform set of doctrines by all men: he means the attain-
> ment of civilized liberty and the common vision of the divinity and unity of
> Man which is life in Jesus.[12]

But Frye's vast knowledge of Christian tradition and of literature helps
him never to lose sight of the central fact that Blake's imaginative use
of Christian symbolism is reformed and displaced, not naturalized
completely and replaced. Frye is yet no friend of the more orthodox
Puritan tradition this book has dealt with thus far, and makes a
distinction between its strong and "bad" aspects in itself and in Blake:

> Milton is what may loosely be called a Puritan: he is a mixture of Christian
> vision with the sterility of moral virtue and rationalism. ... Puritanism was
> the ancestor of Deism in the sense that everything wrong with Puritanism,
> its vestigial natural religion, its Pharisaic morality, its scholastic rationalism
> and its belief in the infallible goodness of the conventional orthodox, had in
> the following century been precipitated as Deism. Los sees that Milton must

be on his way to reinforce, not the Deists, but the visionaries who have inherited the other half of Puritanism, its belief in the civilizing Word of God. . . .[13]

Granted that there are elements of truth in this version of historical Puritanism, it is very sweeping and simplistic. The strength of Frye's reading of Blake is that despite this handicap he never loses sight of the central fact about Blake's imagination in its Christian aspect, an imagination not merely mystical, merely naturalistic, merely Puritan in the historical sense; it was formed and continued Christian according to its own vision, just as *Milton* the brief epic is the continuation of the early Puritan visionary in the later one − in a reformed, rebellious, Puritan Christian Blake.

Reformed, rebellious, Puritan Christian Blake is a very elusive Blake, certainly difficult to pin down in many contexts. It is easier to work with the early Christian Blake of the *Songs of Innocence*, or with the rebellious Blake of *The Marriage of Heaven and Hell* in contexts which are authentically of one piece. (The view that Blake is ironical all of the time is rejected here.) When these simplicities disappear in the later writings, it is easier to construct a liberal-humanist Blake, a psychological Blake, or a gnostic-hermetic Blake than to face the complexities that actually occur in the major poems. Blake was reformed along general Protestant lines, no doubt; he was rebellious toward certain aspects of the traditional interpretation of the Judeo-Christian moral code, as many others have been; there are large influences of gnostic and hermetic writings in the imagery and patterns of the poems, and certainly no one denies that Blake is a liberal humanist if that merely signifies a decent man of humanitarian attitudes. He writes of Universal Humanity, the Human Form Divine, and the Humanity Divine Incomprehensible in *Jerusalem*, but also in the same climactic part of that poem of Visions of God in Eternity, and Jesus appearing as the Good Shepherd. It has been easy, and all too common, to remove the meanings of the symbols from the Christian meaning in Blake, to deny the force of "the Holy Spirit" in his view of poetry. The word "Incomprehensible" which appears along with the "Humanity Divine" towards the end of *Jerusalem* must be taken with some seriousness. I am not suggesting that the later Blake is merely a Puritan Christian Blake, but that he is more likely that enriched by much else than much else with that removed. It diminishes the poetry either to reduce him to his sources or to make him out more modern than he really is, however tempting that always is for any generation.

It may seem obstinate to pursue the religious theme in Blake in the light of what has been said, or admitted. The poet who wrote the introductions to the Jews, the deists and the Christians in *Jerusalem* obviously does not fall within orthodox patterns of thought, or even of the recognized, institutionalized forms of heterodoxy within the Protestant tradition. That is why claims upon him vary so widely and are so easily made, from naturalist to mystic, because the claims or refutations become involved with a complex symbolism of Blake's own invention and shaping. Unless the critic attaches meaning and system to all of these symbols as some do with gusto, very little can be learned specifically about the Christian symbolism in the later poetry. We can be confident that the Jesus images in *Songs of Innocence* have a Swedenborgian coloring, and are only softly unorthodox and antinomian. There is a public and historical referent for them; as Hirsch has shown, they are not merely private. To dismiss the later Blake as hopelessly unique in a religious sense solves no problem. He is unique, and also a religious figure of great magnitude, a link between the more orthodox Christian past and the many diffusions of the 19th century. Unlike some of the later diffusions, Blake's imagination was firmly rooted in the Bible, Protestant tradition, and Milton. His major Christian symbols, Jesus, the Elect, the Reprobate, the Redeemed, Rahab (the whore of Babylon) are not cut off from the past, no matter how reshaped and ironic they often appear in his mature work. A Calvinist Christian residue remains in them, and was not the least of his reasons for calling his autobiographical poem *Milton,* for this is an acknowledgement more conscious than some critics have admitted of a common Puritan heritage, both religious and poetic.

Even in *The Marriage of Heaven and Hell,* Blake's most antinomian work, the dramatization of Jesus as "all virtue" when he was breaking the Ten Commandments has been admitted as weak by some of Blake's greatest admirers. A common defense, with no doubt some validity, is that Blake in *The Marriage* deliberately exaggerates every aspect of the Hell side of things, in order to restore a balance lost by orthodoxy and conventionality. He seems to be saying that Jesus was all virtue because he broke the rules. Later on in *Milton* and *Jerusalem* his symbol of Jesus is far more complex. It becomes an imaginative vision of perfect unity of which the moral aversions of the early Blake form only an aspect. This is his most difficult Christian symbol, his ultimate one, and we may set it aside to examine first the more obviously ironical uses of Calvinism which help to explain it.

The Reprobate, the Elect and the Redeemed are classes Blake defines in *Milton* in inverted manner. The definitions have a clear surface meaning. Calvinism's Reprobates are the prophets antagonistic to organized society, not sinful as in orthodoxy. The Elect are really non-elect, the deluded followers of moral virtue and Satan in this world. The Redeemed are redeemed by the energies of the Reprobate away from the delusions and snares of the Elect, again a reversal of Calvinism and of Milton in *Paradise Lost* about the status of the great middle group of men in whom grace and nature struggle at length, and for whom the Elect, not the Reprobate, are the model. According to the various Calvinist commentators they can never be sure of election in this life, but before them always is the ideal of election and the fact of election in others. It is clear enough what Blake is doing with the categories. Though most of the commentators parse this pattern in the obvious way as here, his ultimate purpose is not easily certain in a poem of much greater variety and complexity than *The Marriage*. If his aim were mere inversion, then moral virtue (Satan – the Elect) must remain forever distinct from energy and imagination (the Reprobate). But as we saw in Frye, the casting out of moral virtue is not the purpose of Blake's mature writing. Moral virtue may often seem to stand in an antagonistic relationship with imagination, yet redemption means unification, not division. In other symbols, Blake-Los-Milton-Albion-Jerusalem, all redeemed, absorb Bacon, Newton, Locke, Satan, Rahab (the spectres, the evil ones in Blake's mythography) in a final apocalypse. The critics have given the details on these points, without settling the question of interest in this study, the place of the Jesus figure in all of this, or the real relationship of Blake's own religious vision to Christianity, Puritanism and Milton. Blake is too close to all these things to be removed by admirers who admire his rebellion and normal human instincts so much that they do not wish to see that his strength and his ultimate vision could only have come from the tradition described in this book, no matter how far removed in mere literal ways, as in the Reprobate, Elect, Re-deemed inversion.

The Jesus figure in *Songs of Innocence* is a symbol of innocence. In "The Lamb" the Lamb-Child-Jesus constellation is perfectly present-ed and given explicit meaning. Other poems of innocence diffuse these figures in the guises of shepherds, guardians, and kindly father figures.

This state is a low, simple innocence, the faith of a child, not presented to us for irony or mockery, as some critics think, but as the
psychological situation of the normal child towards the world, trust
built upon ignorance. (This does not mean that children are little
angels within their own scope, the early namby-pamby view of Blake
discarded by all serious readers.) The same might be said of the naive
Christian sects like the Swedenborgians. Though Blake did outgrow
them, he once experienced their version of innocence with its ground
in denial of sin and evil, the faith of children grown up but not mature.
Hence the violence of rejection in *Marriage of Heaven and Hell*. The
later Jesus of *Milton* and *Jerusalem* is the central figure in an
apocalypse struggling towards the assertion of a "higher innocence,"
a mature assertion of the unity and divinity of everything. Blake did
not fully succeed in this task, as his idolators believe. Yet without the
Jesus figure, a figure developed beyond innocence and rebellion to
maturity, the task would have been impossible. The later figure of
Jesus develops from the struggle, normally seen in Christianity as that
with sin, evil and limitation, which Blake presents in his own symbols
of Milton, spectres, Rahab, Satan, and so forth. The later vision looks
beyond the early innocence and the antinomian rebellion, not beyond
good and evil in Nietzsche's later sense, but to the kind of reconciliation always envisioned by mature Christianity. Calvinism made this reconciliation difficult by its uncompromising theology. As the inheritor
of this theology in one of its later versions, and an admirer of its
greatest expression, *Paradise Lost,* Blake's reconciliation of good and
evil, and all the other contraries that spring therefrom, is his own
version in his own invention and vision of the oldest of Christian
desires, taken for granted by the child or child-state, lost inevitably by
each adult, given up as naive and hopeless by most, or as a mystery
whose solution could only be in the next life. Blake's imagination
helped him to try to envision the solution in his mind and poetry, a
solution not fully possible for any writer in this world.

The Everlasting Gospel seems at first to contradict the idea of a
mature Jesus figure outlined in the previous paragraph. Its late date
(1818) and its seemingly outspoken antinomianism provide great difficulties. The date should lend authority over the earlier poems while
the rebelliousness, in the manner of *Heaven and Hell,* makes very difficult to demonstrate a better, mature Blake in *Milton* and *Jerusalem*
striving towards compromise between orthodox and heterodox religious views. The antinomianism and rebellion in *The Everlasting Gospel*

need not be given final authority. It contains, indeed, Blake's quality of rebellion without progression, similar to that in *The Marriage*. This presents a permanent side to Blake's mind, but not the only one. He reached the height of his maturity in *Milton* and *Jerusalem*, the latter a poem worked over for fifteen years after the first version. The extreme, simplified, rebellious Jesus figure of *Everlasting Gospel* should be regarded as an authentic outburst of basic emotion, and no more. It does his intellect and mature powers as an artist an injustice to place this poem as a last will and testament on Blake and religion, when the more complex, mature views are available elsewhere. Curiously, some admirers and detractors have been willing to assign great import- ance to *The Everlasting Gospel*. Its open presentation of the Jesus figure and the late date of the poem seem to lend irresistible authority to a simplistic view of Blake's religious ideas. The patterns of religious thought revealed in *Milton* and *Jerusalem* are more subtle and more just to the complexity of Blake. His shadows, spectres and the other limiting characters and symbols of his poetry often take origin in traditional religious concepts and struggle with the "redeeming" forces of rebellion and energy. *The Everlasting Gospel* merely defines the simplicities of rebellion and inversion of traditional values. The poem has no redemptive value and virtue because it is all assertion without struggle. It is important for rather obvious definitional content of one side of Blake; taken alone it is as much of a distortion as *Songs of Innocence* taken alone, or *The Marriage* read as Blake's final position on the contraries of energy and reason. As in *The Marriage*, its funda- mental weakness is the denial of moral good, or at least the part of moral good fundamental to existence and to the imagination. Rebellion is energy, and therefore imaginative in Blake, but the major prophecies show that unrestrained rebellion or mere inversion become as much a form of "Satan" as the more often maligned moral good of traditional definition. This very difficult reconciliation of moral good as the basis for imagination yet not the stultification of imagination and energy is attempted and partially resolved elsewhere. Blake manipulated the religious elements of his tradition with freedom and sometimes ruthlessly, as later did Joyce with Irish Catholicism, but neither achieved a complete freedom and indifference to them. Both realized this, though some of their critics have not, and both are greater writers than they might have been if the illusion of total liberation had been achieved. For such full liberation would have removed the center of struggle in their work, a center not in the liberal-humanist tradition as in Keats, Shelley, Whitman and so on, but in the imagination of the artist confronting the religious tradition in which his mind was formed, and which each came to know in depth, against ideas and values of other kinds.

A brief recapitulation concerning the position of Blake for this study is perhaps in order before offering any further analysis or conclusions. The evidence indicates that Blake was a Christian of a very unusual, original type. His poetry has a good deal of coherence and progression, with sources drawn from many traditions, but it is a mistake to systematize it in any one way. His own line from *Milton,* "There is a Moment in each Day that Satan cannot find," ought to be remembered by those who systematize his poetry, a line this writer would like to fancy was intended to insist upon the openness of his poetry. But if Blake was a Christian, as the evidence indicates, he certainly was not orthodox; that much may be granted to the "liberal-humanist" critics. He was always in revolt against orthodoxy, especially the more rigorous kind such as Calvinist-Puritanism. His own origins were in the extreme "doctrine of the Spirit" tradition, itself a breakdown of Puritan orthodoxy. The insights of his tradition go far in explaining the unique nature of the *Songs of Innocence*, written from a perspective within Swedenborgian and extreme evangelical views. This does not mean that he was at one with these views when he wrote the poems, or that as creator he did not stand outside of his creation. It does mean that the structure, symbols and sympathy in them could only have come from one who once was within the tradition. *The Marriage of Heaven and Hell* and the later *Everlasting Gospel* are revolts against traditional Christianity and his Swedenborgian naïveté of youth. This revolt is also carried out in some of the minor prophecies without benefit of traditional religious symbols. These poems have been much celebrated by the humanist critics of Blake, but their interest for this study is minimal. The Calvinist temper in Blake is most important and evident in *Milton* and *Jerusalem*, the first a direct response to *Paradise Lost* and Puritan heritage, the second with a complex Jesus figure growing out of that response. In these works there is no return to the simple innocence of the Jesus figure in *Innocence*, nor to the energetic revolt and snorts of defiance of *The Marriage* and *Everlasting Gospel*. The final complexity of Blake's poetic vision is influenced in part by his relationship with Puritanism, a relationship not diminished by its many negative aspects or by the inclusion in his final vision of cabalistic, hermetic and other unusual materials. Nor least of all his own originality. There is no wish in this study to exclude. Our assertions are that he was a Christian of some sort, and that his relationship with Calvinist-Puritan tradition was meaningful for his poetry. These points are necessary for the inclusion of Blake, even when our purpose is not primarily the reading of the poetry but the larger cultural aspects alluded to in the opening pages of introduction to Calvinism and the Romantic poets.

The obstacles to a Puritan Christian view of Blake outlined above are many. There are the misreadings of the naturalistic critics such as Bloom, for whom Blake is the precursor of Whitman and contemporary American naturalists. These same critics also wish to see Blake as the first poet-priest, in a role that would be demeaned by association with Christian religious poets of the past. Their views are antithetical to the one taken in this study. But the tone in much of Blake's poetry troubles many readers and presents a great obstacle to his acceptance as a Christian poet. The defiance of orthodoxy and convention in much of his poetry is a problem for new readers of Blake, but as was noted even in Frye, objective close reading of the meaning makes clear that Blake did not wish to separate moral life from imagination, only to re-arrange their relationship by new perception. Blake's high-handedness with orthodox notions in some poems may be offensive to the pious, or his freewheeling theological terminology and frequent inversions of terms, as in the Reprobate, Redeemed, Elect example in *Milton,* cause suspicion among those critics with theological training in Christian tradition He seems at times to be the unique theologian-priest of his own religion presented as poetry. His sources in gnosticism, neoplatonism, cabala and other hermetic traditions, some inimical to historical Christianity, have raised many obstacles. Only Damon and a few others, aware of all these complications, have been able to hold that Blake remained a fundamental Christian of a certain type. Blake was poet and creator enough to shape his materials to his own purposes. The conclusion that his vision was fundamentally Christian should not be deterred by the strange nomenclature of the poetic surface, another obstacle to his acceptance as a poet in the Christian tradition. On this point many naturalists and religious readers agree, and both are wrong.

Coleridge, a Romantic poet whose Christianity is not seriously disputed, also wrote of the Divine Tetracy, which he named Identity, Ipseity, Alterity and Community. His sources were similar to Blake's, his purpose to give fresh vision and interpretation to the idea of the

Trinity.[14] Blake's divine Tetracy consists of the Four Zoas, then of their emanations, spectres and so on. Their names, characteristics and functions have been described and analysed many times. The need now is not to go over this ground or to dispute certain assignments. But it is crucial to point out that this strange nomenclature, far more extensive and free than in Coleridge, and even more excessive in reliance upon "esoteric" source materials, is for that reason no less fundamentally Christian in final shape. Jesus and Satan are familiar to all readers; Los, Urizen and the "emanations" only to the special reader of Blake. Traditional heresies have been imposed upon this amalgam, to little purpose. His conclusions may look like objective pantheism to some, though it was a view he abhorred, or like subjective pantheism to others, a fairer equation, and one which plagued Coleridge in his relationship to Böehme and German idealism. Here the viewpoint of this study is in rare agreement with the gentlemen of the visionary company in stressing that Blake's work must be taken as poetry. The fairest traditional term for Blake is "immanency," the view that the divine spirit is in man. If this is so, then what Blake called "imagination" the Christian knows as "grace," grace as historically associated with the left wing of Puritan tradition, not a clearly defined dogmatic term of more orthodox churches. This exercise of grace-imagination does not imply the non-existence of God, Jesus, or the cosmos, things so many of the orthodox think Blake seems to be saying. The originality of Blake's poetry has been an obstacle no less severe than his constant critique of conventional and historical Christian terms and definitions, the most notorious being God the Father as Nobodaddy, the Son as empty Logos and the Holy Spirit as a vacuum, his proclamation in *The Marriage*. These obstacles have driven all but the most astute to the conclusion that Blake belongs with the naturalists who claim him as their own. What they do not see, and the naturalists wish to deny, is that imagination and grace are virtually identical in Blake's final vision, and that there is also a kind of predestination, in the mind of the poet as surrogate for God, which arbitrarily, in good Calvinist fashion, turns the two poems *Milton* and *Jerusalem* from despairing facts to affirmative conclusions. Such grace, imagination and arbitrariness towards the ultimate good are firm Puritan notions, analogues to the theology of Calvinist tradition. Blake differs only on one fundamental point with traditional Calvinism as found in the reformers, Spenser, Milton, Bunyan, Baxter, and so on. As a left-wing "spiritual" Christian, he rejects the notion of election and damnation of individuals, but accepts the ultimate Puritan goal of the cosmos. There is a paradise, a mysterious fall, a long dark night, a sudden and arbitrary turn and concluding affirmation in the major complete poems, *The Four Zoas, Milton,* and *Jerusalem.* Despair, discontinuity and defeat appear final only in the minor, lesser versions of his vision. Blake manipulates his symbols towards the traditional goals of Calvinist-Puritanism, sanctification and glorification. Along the way he chides Milton and theological predecessors for excessive negativism, while in a short late poem he chides his fellow Calvinist Byron for final, personal despair.[15] All that lives is holy for Blake, and all will live forever, not in the figment of imagination of one man or in a naturalistic paradise, but in a real eternity, that promised by Jesus, the dominant figure in *Milton* and *Jerusalem.*

Blake has been misunderstood from two directions, his real meaning is distasteful to much in the modern mind, yet some of his openness has been appreciated. On the other hand his complete freedom from legalism, his tone of defiance, and revisionism of religious tradition in his invention of original symbols have made religious readers and critics mistrustful of his purposes. His pattern is not that of Donne or Herbert, nor that of Hopkins and Eliot. Even as a Calvinist-Puritan, he is radical. But his reconciliation with his predecessor Milton and his alignment with Jesus in *Jerusalem* (though Los, Albion and much else that is pure Blake are there too) must not be taken lightly or dismissed. These crucial passages in his poetry ought to be the clue to a religious reading of Blake, a reading not revisionary but restorative, with the aim not so much to remove him from his present admirers, as to restore him to his own tradition, which has often rejected his work as strange and erratic. This larger cultural purpose is the aim of including discussion of Blake in this book and in this particular place, among the Romantics. The minute particulars must await another occasion. There is space here for the general outline of the argument and its fundamental points against other possible readings, a fair way to conclude this introduction to the nineteenth century and Blake.

A summary of basic positions on Blake and religion, put succinctly and fairly, looks something like this. The naturalistic view allows him to be the most liberated imagination of his day, yet still subject to some errors hanging over in the dead weight of Christian tradition. Many modern poets and critics instinctively see Blake in this way, as an aid to their own work. Bloom is the most thorough exponent of this viewpoint. In partial contrast, Damon and Frye define Blake's Christianity in the process of re-defining Christianity according to Blake. The result is a "Christian" Blake not recognizable within Christian tradition, except in the widest, definitionless sense. Calvinist-Puritanism is the whipping boy of Christianity in their readings of poems from *Heaven and Hell* to *The Everlasting Gospel*, that is, the element constantly cast out to purify Blake's real Christianity. Blake is a Christian in their eyes because he redeems himself from Calvinist-Puritan dogma and ethics, as well as from Catholic-type superstitions. For the other important group of Blake critics Christianity has little significance, except as a surviving cultural husk transformed by Blake into something entirely original. For these critics the key to Blake's thought is in various hermetic traditions, cabalistic, neoplatonic, gnostic, and so on. For the purposes of the cultural argument outlined here, the viewpoints of Damon and Frye are useful, since Calvinist-Puritanism is acknowledged as an essential element in his work by both, although obviously a negative one. The other types of criticism are too far from our interest to be of real use. In my own view Calvinist-Puritanism has a negative function to a point, but its presence is not entirely negative. As a firm aspect of Blake's cultural heritage it adds something to the Christian vision of his poetry.

We must now look at this Christian vision in the poetry more closely. If Blake had had no interest in Christianity, presumably the Jesus figure would not have loomed so large in the poetry, or indeed been used at all. (His ample invention of unique mythology is clear indication that he was not enslaved to the traditional for lack of invention.) Similarly, if the Calvinist terminology of election, reprobation and predestination had had little or no meaning for Blake, the poem *Milton* would not have been devoted to a critique and revision of the doctrines. There are two senses in which Blake is both a Christian and a Calvinist-Puritan. He is the first according to his own inspired imagination, the second by heritage rather than by belief. It weakens our understanding of his poetry to deny or minimize these two truths about the poetry. Taken together they form a cultural claim about Blake against the strictures of the orthodox and the evasions of the naturalists. To assert that Blake's Jesus represents a religious belief more specific than the universal humanism usually attached to it, yet less specific than orthodoxy, is a most difficult argument, requiring more attention to Blake's larger poems and religious symbols than is possible to give in this chapter. Some matters will be pointed to, without great detail, in order to make sense of the Calvinist presence in the poetry. Calvinist-Puritanism was a vehicle for Blake, one of the means he used to define his own Christianity and sense of apocalypse. Its presence was essential to his vision, though he rejected its literal doctrines. This is a modest, not a meaningless, claim. In the confines of this study we have not been concerned with the religious creeds of poets but in seeking the elements in one (Calvinist-Puritan) inherited religious tradition which help to define the poet's sensibility. For Blake this is most difficult, on account of the number of misunderstandings persisting on all sides. Indeed, the most fundamental task of all, the exact exploration of the Jesus symbol, has been sidestepped or subjected to large impositions of bias and outside assumptions by powerful advocates and heuristic critics of this or that version of humanism or modernism. Orthodox Christian critics, a helpful balance in other areas, have eschewed Blake or misread him narrowly or allowed the naturalistic claims to pass uncontested.

As usual, Frye has tried the hardest of any critic to reconcile the traditional, the naturalistic and imaginative in Blake's vision of Jesus and to view this as part of the total imaginative system. The traditional views, as also usual in Frye, suffer in the reconciliation, but with an advantage over naturalists in seeing that the fundamental term "Christian" must be used to be honest about Blake. Frye distinguishes the "creative" view of Jesus from its analogy, the literal history of the Bible and the Churches. Here is a fair quotation of his long and eloquent argument in the chapter on *Jerusalem*:

> The true Jesus is the present vision of Jesus, the uniting of the divine and the human in our own minds, and it is only the active Jesus, the teacher and healer and storyteller, who can be recreated. . . . In that moment the mystery of the Incarnation, the uniting of God and man, the attaining of eternity in time, the work of Los, the Word becoming flesh, is recreated, and thereby ceases to be a mystery. . . . We reach final understanding of the Bible when our imaginations become possessed by the Jesus of the resurrection, the pure community of a divine Man, the absolute civilization of the city of God.[16]

Against this eloquent vision are juxtaposed the "dead" body of Jesus, the memorial of the Eucharist, the literal history and the dogmas of the Churches, with Calvinist-Puritanism singled out for special scorn only because it was the orthodox form of Christianity best know to Blake. Some of these elements are now lightly held by modern Christians of various sects, others still dearly held, and a few still found necessary even by the very liberal "neo-orthodoxies" of our time. The exclusion of all these elements has never been accepted, even by the most liberal religious minds. Allowing the exclusion of all of them was called pantheism by Coleridge in reference to Böehme and Schelling, Protestantism decayed into transcendentalism by Brownson and American traditionalists, and disguised naturalism by some recent critics of Blake, the latter believing that he "writ better than he knew" and that the clinging to any Christian symbolism was merely a quaintness he could not slough off. Such severe dichotomy between the historical and the imaginative elements need not be accepted. Frye's Blake evaporates into vapidities, despite the persuasive rhetoric. Blake was critical of dogmas and churches and atrophied forms, to say the least, and sounds much like certain other Romantics and post-Romantics whose work drifted into pantheism or transcendentalism. But Blake differed from the others in his origins in the left-wing doctrine of the Spirit tradition, the residue of Puritanism which led him to Swedenborg and then to his own vision. We have related these doctrines to the *Songs of Innocence* earlier in this chapter. These insights and beliefs did not desert his imagination in the later prophetic writings. As suggested earlier, what kept Blake Christian and his Jesus some kind of real presence rather than the amorphous one described by Frye was the unity in his mind of imagination, the idea of the living Holy Spirit, and grace. The meaning of Jesus is not that the human becomes the divine and the reverse, or the co-extension of the divine man with the universe, absolute civilization and the other visions Frye extols. That indeed would be pantheism. Through the spirit, grace and imagination – Los and similar figures in Blake's pantheon – the mind of the poet grasps as much of the meaning of Jesus as can be known to man. Some of the mystery of the divine remains. If Blake claimed to know and see all, he would have been content with his own many creations, emanations, and ignored Jesus, the moral law, the traditional interpretations. He wished to give us greater insight into the mysteries connected with Christ the Logos and Jesus the man, was not content with the progress of his poetic predecessors in the Bible and Milton (the burden of *Milton* and *Jerusalem* as poems), and certainly claimed more grace, insight and imagination than any other man of his day. He was not shy before dogma and tradition, as is obvious. To say that his final vision is prophecy, fuller than any previous example in his own eyes, with a fuller sense of the meaning of Jesus, not full knowledge and identity, is to come closest to the truth about "Christian Blake." He had his few areas of humility, the most crucial being the belief that imagination and grace are the work of God through Jesus in man, and that even his work is only a glimpse of the last great apocalypse or eternity. He felt that he had improved on the Bible and on Milton, but not as the last prophet, only the best to his time. The work of the imagination, the spirit and grace is continuing in knowing the universe through the Divine Man, and it is not the lazy onlooker, deist or dogmatist, who helps forward this work, only the man of imagination, whatever his other earthly calling. If Milton did err, so Blake might err, in not seeing the full truth. Blake was not so smug as to think that he is to be called the last Christian. He may be one of the last true Calvinist Christians. Only someone who could reject orthodoxy yet not Christ, who could re-write Milton rather than view his ideology as "dated," could be a Christian in the manner of Blake's Christianity. It is a narrow line from there to naturalism and pantheism, and probably only one of Blake's intellectual heritage and imaginative gifts could manage to hold together such a complex vision.

As regards the peculiar doctrines of Calvinist-Puritanism, we have seen him having his fun with election and reprobation in *Milton* with all the usual ironic reversals. Yet finally he does not merely play with Puritanism; he is deeply Puritan in imaginative pattern. Everyone becomes elect in his vision, which is a clinging to the structure of Calvinism in an odd way that would have horrified Calvin and the orthodox, yet a proof of the point of this study: that he worked through his peculiar beliefs in traditional terms, and so Calvinism is an irremovable pattern in his major poem *Milton*. Similarly with predestination, a doctrine whose literal form he abhorred. This high Calvinist doctrine is woven through his poems *Milton* and *Jerusalem* in two ways. Mentioned previously is the arbitrary turning of each of the three great poems, *The Four Zoas, Milton* and *Jerusalem*, from a nadir of evil, darkness, Satan, Rahab the whore of this world, and so forth, to their opposites. This turning comes late in all three poems, with the arbitrariness noted by several astute Blakeans. Blake's vision is predestined to glory and triumphant prophecy given in his own terms, not the traditional Puritan terms we have seen in much of this study. It is the fusion of the Puritan heritage and the visionary mind which gives his poems this inevitable direction. This "predestination" is internal to Blake's imagination. There is an outer predestination in the achievement of the goal, the great moments of triumph and glory that end each poem. These are the passages of joy and fusion celebrated and quoted by many Blake critics, and need no repetition here. Our point is that they are, in his own very drastic and full measure, a repetition of the pattern we have seen in poets of more traditional Puritan type. I do not wish to force the analogy too closely, but the old "sin-state" corresponds to the fallen states of Satan and Rahab in *Milton* and *Jerusalem*, "vocation" to the poet's duty to hammer out the vision in the furnaces of Los, "justification" to the moment when the poet knows that his vision will triumph (as when Milton enters Blake's foot and other such assertions of the mantle of poet-prophet), "sanctification" to the descriptions of Beulah land and the many saved characters such as Rintrah and Palamabron which appear just before the climatic endings, these endings obviously corresponding to glorification. Suffused by the Holy Spirit and grace as Blake conceived them, these are the firm Calvinist-Puritan patterns of his major poetry. All together these do not make him a Puritan ideologist — to say such would be nonsense. But their presence complements the visionary Christianity to which critics like Frye respond and makes us accept the fact that Blake was in every real sense the Christian poet and visionary he claimed to be, no matter how defiant of orthodoxy, or rejected by its various forms in his time and ours.

This chapter has not attempted a full reading of Blake, only a cultural outline of Blake's place in Puritan tradition. The important fact affirmed is that he has such a place. To fill this outline requires more space and attention to minute particulars than the scope of this book allows. Full justice to Blake's Christian vision cannot be given without the required detail. Damon and a few others have pointed the way the mystic and the Christian in Blake coalesce. One day Blake may receive such a reading within the general Christian and Calvinist-Puritan guidelines of this chapter. For instance, "The Little Black Boy" has always been a stumbling block to literalists and to Blake's contemporary humanist admirers, for obvious reasons. Yet it is clear that Blake is not literal: there is no final black and white when all are set free from their clouds. All are predestined to perfection by eternal God, from a perspective which might be called mystical and reverse Calvinist. From Blake's perspektive this is not the reversal of Calvinism's predestination, but its correction and perfection.

II. Coleridge

In considering the poetry of Coleridge from a religious point of view, and particularly a Calvinist religious one, we must turn to his later poetry, that written after "Dejection: an Ode" in 1802 and especially to that written from about 1816 to 1834, the year of his death. Religious elements appear in the early poetry. In other studies this writer has considered the passage from Coleridge's Romanticism to his later career,[17] and also the marginal influence of the religious perspective upon even the best of Coleridge's early poems, "The Ancient Mariner" and the "conversation poems."[18] Only the early unsuccessful poem "Religious Musings" has not received adequate attention in this perspective, and will be the starting point of study here, for though an extremely flawed poem, it is one that contains in its mixed way many ideas and themes of Coleridge's best poetry and later thought, including a decidedly Miltonic-Calvinist cast.

The religious element is recessive in Coleridge's early poetry, merely mingling with his many other interests. It is also of importance to note that Coleridge's accompanying prose writings in the areas of theology and philosophy have earned him recognition as the most serious and important figure in early 19th century English religious life.[19] This is not of great concern here, though of rare achievement for a poet and certainly responsible indirectly for the religious power of his later poetry. We must content ourselves in this context with a discursive look at the quality and importance of Coleridge's religious poetry, particularly with the Calvinist aspects of this poetry, in a series of short poems stretching over some thirty years.

Coleridge emerges in his later poetry as a striking religious spirit of the early 19th century. This at one time may have been thought a rather bold statement, but recent study of his published and unpublished prose has tended to confirm the same interests.[20] What

distinguishes Coleridge's poetic vision from most other 19th century
and Romantic writers is his profound sense of the reality of God, of
sin, and personal guilt, with consequences thereof for self and world.
The concluding lines of "The Eolian Harp" are central for understanding Coleridge's religious vision:

> But thy more serious eye a mild reproof
> Darts, O beloved Woman! nor such thoughts
> Dim and unhallow'd dost thou not reject
> And biddest me walk humbly with my God.
> Meek Daughter in the family of Christ!
> Well hast thou said and holily disprais'd
> Those shapings of the unregenerate mind;
> Bubbles that glitter as they rise and break
> On vain Philosophy's aye-babbling spring.
> For never guiltless may I speak of him,
> The Incomprehensible! save when with awe
> I praise him, and with Faith that inly *feels*;
> Who with his saving mercies healed me,
> A sinful and most miserable man,
> Wilder'd and dark, and gave me to possess
> Peace, and this Cot, and thee, heart-honor'd Maid.[21]

We stop here only to mention the important words, which get into all
Coleridge's later discussions of religious questions and poems: "unregenerate mind," "guilt," "the Incomprehensible," "faith that inly
feels," "sinful, dark, and most miserable man." The religious aspects
of this poem have been brought out previously. In an even more
strikingly religious and Calvinist way, "Religious Musings" can offer a
starting point for study of Coleridge's early poetry and later religious
thought. In the private writings of his later life Coleridge developed a
theory, or at least a more abstract view, of these matters:

> Live begins in detachment from Nature and ends in union with God.
> The adorable Author of our Being is likewise its ultimate End.[22]
>   .. and further, on the score of consistency, I, S.T.C. aught to have taken
> time to put to myself the question, whether the essentials of the ascetic
> morality do not follow inevitably from my own views of Nature, God, and
> Man like the Moon flown off, but still reclaimed by the Sun circa 1830.[23]

This writer and others have tried to trace the fascinating career of
Coleridge the thinker, and have noted his growing accommodation
with traditional views in his later life.[24] The publication in our time of
Coleridge's speculations on divinity, the occult and the 17th century
theologians will show this career to have been even more fascinating

than previously believed.[25] For the present purpose we may focus entirely on the poetry, assuming knowledge of some of the readings of the best early poetry mentioned in the notes to this point, and begin our discussion with that potpourri, "Religious Musings," then turn to the discussion of the later religious poems which properly fall within the range of this study.

"Religious Musings" was published in 1796 as the strongest piece in Coleridge's first volume of poems. Few have argued the coherence of the poem, or even that it holds up as a unified statement. The adopted Miltonic style, often obscure and crabbed in performance, holds the poem together to the extent that it can be said to be one poem. Otherwise it appears to be an accumulation of Coleridge's current thoughts on religion, metaphysics, politics and philosophy. His views on these subjects would change in later life and writings, but it is remarkable how firmly these interests were all implanted in the young poet. After a vague opening, a long passage on redemption and the role of Christ is followed by one on the elect, which in turn leads to abstract, vague "pantheistic" musings on the Godhead, then to current politics, and finally to paraphrases of his favorite philosophers at that time, Hartley, Berkeley, and others. It is not our intention to consider any of these other interests in the poem except as they relate to the strong Calvinism of the early passage, which must be quoted in full:

> And *blest* are they,
> Who in this fleshly World, the *elect* of Heaven,
> Their *strong eye* darting through the deeds of men,
> Adore with *steadfast* unpresuming gaze
> Him Nature's essence, mind, and energy!
> And gazing, trembling, patiently ascend
> Treading beneath their feet all visible things
> As steps, that upward to their Father's throne
> Lead gradual — else nor *glorified* nor loved.
> They nor contempt embosom nor revenge:
> For they dare know of what may seem deform
> The Supreme Fair sole operant: in whose sight
> All things are pure, his strong controlling love
> Alike from all educing perfect good.
> Their's too celestial courage, *inly armed* —
> Dwarfing Earth's giant brood, what time they muse
> On their great Father, great beyond compare!
> And marching onwards view high o'er their heads
> His *waving banners* of Omnipotence.
> Who the Creator love, created Might

Dread not: within their tents no Terrors walk.
For they are *holy things* before the Lord
Aye *unprofaned*, though Earth should league with Hell;
God's altar grasping with an eager hand
Fear, the wild-visag'd, pale, eye-starting wretch,
Sure-refug'd hears his hot pursuing fiends
Yell at vain distance. Soon refresh'd from Heaven
He calms the throb and tempest of his heart.
His countenance settles; a soft *solemn bliss*
Swims in his eye – his *swimming eye* upraised:
And *Faith's* whole *armour* glitters on his limbs!
And thus transfigured with a dreadless awe,
A solemn hush of soul, *meek he beholds*
All things of terrible seeming: yea, unmoved
Views e'en the immitigable ministers
That shower down *vengeance* on these latter days.
For kindling with intenser Deity
From the celestial Mercy-seat they come,
And at the *renovating* wells of Love
Have fill'd their vials with *salutary wrath*,
To sickly Nature more medicinal
Than what soft balm the weeping good man pours
Into the lone despoiled traveller's wounds!
Thus from the *Elect, regenerate through faith,*
Pass the dark Passions and what thirsty cares
Drink up the spirit, and the dim regards
Self-centre. Lo they vanish! or acquire
New names, new features – by *supernal* grace
Enrobed with *Light*, and naturalised in Heaven.

(ll. 45–93; italics mine)

It is interesting to ask why this passage on the elect appears at all in the poem and stands where it does. The movement in thought from Christ the Redeemer to the nature of the Godhead does not contain the necessity for discussion of election. One answer obviously is the Miltonic tone and substance of the poem and the influence of *Paradise Lost* doctrines of election in Books III, XI, and XII. But it is important to see more here than a debt to Milton, namely, some inner necessity for Coleridge to include election in "Religious Musings," even though this belief, if it indeed was one at the time, would have been in contradiction with much of his thinking in the 1790's and much else that passes as philosophy in the poem. Though this is the case in this poem and much other writing of the 1790's, the picture is not all that clear, and the passage by no means totally isolated. Similar thoughts appear strongly at the end of "Eolian Harp," and in less obvious ways elsewhere. These lines on the elect and election deserve some close attention.

This passage displays a thorough knowledge of Puritanism, its Old Testament origins and imagery, and 17th century theological forms. It is thoroughly Miltonic yet not limited to Milton in sources. Coleridge obviously knew Puritan tradition and Calvinist theology at first hand, as he knew so much else. He no doubt also knew the progression from sin-state to glorification, the terms of which are scattered throughout the poem, though not presented methodically. The clearly Calvinist images are italicized above: the images are there but not the pattern. The passage is organized around the dominant idea of the elect, assuring glorification to come. The other states of the Calvinist cycle are not appropriate to the position of the passage in the poem.

The elect are the strong-minded few, as in Milton, who deserve glorification. The descriptive imagery helps to qualify these elect, whether taken from the Bible, *Paradise Lost,* or other Puritan sources. The elect are "blest," have a "strong eye," and they "Adore with steadfast unpresuming gaze." There is a forceful contrast between the fleshly world, visible things, all worldly things on the one hand, and on the other, the visions of the elect with their glory to come. The elect have the viewpoint of God; 'inly armed" against the world, "they dare know of what may seem deform / The Supreme Fair sole operant. . . ." No real need to justify the ways of God to man. But to enforce their difference from the world, there is the usual Puritan imagery of warfare, "waving banners," "Faith's whole armour glitters on his limbs." The sunny inner assurance of "solemn bliss" and "swimming eye" prepares for the glimpse of heaven, and in a more complicated theme, there is the usual double edge of Puritan vision — vengeance and terror towards the world, but a spirit of holiness towards God and things beyond earth's power: "meek he beholds / All things of terrible seeming. . . ." In these themes and images, the poet asserts the usual conclusions about the elect, that they are the just instruments of God's wrath against the wicked. Yet they remain holy and justified. There is no contradiction between "salutary wrath" and "renovating wells of Love," if seen through the peculiar Puritan lens of election. This may be Coleridge's reason for using the idea, his strategic reason that is, perhaps not his deepest one. The elect perform their traditional function of chastising the sin and evil of this world, and then they are allowed to pass to their eternal, just reward, in the climatic lines:

Lo they vanish! or acquire
New names, new features, by supernal grace
Enrobed with Light, and naturalized in Heaven.

In other words they are transfigured after witnessing and performing
in a world otherwise filled with sinners and evil, as decribed in the
larger portion of "Religious Musings."

Such are the Puritan elements in the passage, exceedingly well
organized around election. Acknowledging them does not automat-
ically solve a problem of inner meaning or authenticity for the passage. This is a problem which admits of no easy solution.

Even if all these Puritan elements in the poem are granted, most
critics and scholars would probably still evaluate the seriousness of the
Puritan element in the poem rather lightly. Many people are as yet
not aware of the deep religious nature in Coleridge throughout his
life; others would not place much importance upon any element in
such a rambling and inconclusive poem. That Coleridge was religious
is simply a fact that should be, and will be, better known as the
notebooks, letters and new biographies have their effect upon the
critical world. The other is a fairer point, and would be irrefutable
if "Religious Musings" were the only occurrence of Puritan-elect
notions in Coleridge. Calvinist religious thoughts appear mainly in
the later poetry and in the prose, while religious thoughts are
everywhere, it is true. But the important fact is that the Calvinist
thoughts in the poem and the later speculations are quite close, quite
consistent in nature. Psychological probing may help to get at the
motivation for such re-occurrence, and is available in George Whal-
ley's important and regrettably little known dissertation *Library
Cormorant*, in the University of London library. Notions of election,
rejection and self-abasement can be traced back to the traumas of
Coleridge's childhood and school life, to which the opium habit added
the idea of the un-free will. It is not the purpose of this book to trace
these patterns of his mind, only the patterns in the poetry as these
relate to the larger scheme of Calvinism in the nineteenth century.
The theology and tone of Coleridge's later religious poems have more
in common with the Calvinist tradition than with any other. This is not
to say, of course, that they are written within the framework of 17th
century theology. Like Cowper before him, Coleridge exhibits a
peculiar residue of Calvinist thought in his later poetry. Humphrey
House first pointed out the stylistic and tonal similarities of Cowper

and Coleridge.[26] It seems that these similarities derive from deeper religious ones.

This characterization of Coleridge's poetry, particularly the later poetry, may seem far-fetched to some. It is no longer Romantic poetry, yet not Victorian either, and certainly unlike the poetry of Catholic converts such as Hopkins or Eliot. Despite origins, it is not as firmly religious as 17th century religious poetry. We have the irate comments of H. N. Fairchild on the subject of Coleridge's religious verse as a proof of its elusiveness.[27] For one thing, Coleridge's effort was a virtuoso performance, unlike that of Cowper, who was a member of an evangelical group. For another, Coleridge's mind even in later life was never completely dominated by religious thought, strong though that became. There were always his flirtings with the cabalistic tradition, his uses of Jacob Böehme, and his love of neo-platonic speculation.[28] It would be ridiculous, then, to put Coleridge in a Calvinist procrustean bed. On the other hand, insofar as there is a religious drift in the later Coleridge and in the poetry, it is rather in the direction of Calvinism than anywhere else, even if Coleridge himself did not care for the name of the earlier Calvinist tradition. It was a basic Calvinist bent, not the latitudinarianism of the established Church of the day, that led him into the Church in 1827.

Coleridge's later views on original sin and the origin of evil were essentially Calvinist. Although these problems ultimately remained mysteries for Coleridge, the rational explanation which he gave of them was more in keeping with reformational Calvinism than with Catholic scholasticism or Anglican Arminianism.[29] Original sin, as in Calvin, is only intelligible if the will is acknowledged as a spiritual faculty absolutely distinguishable from everything in the natural world, animate and inanimate. Coleridge clearly acknowledged this in *Aids to Reflection* (pp. 284–85). Such a view of sin and the will tends to divorce man as a spiritual being from the undifferentiated manifold of the world. Coleridge also came to agree with Calvinists on the extent and the importance of the depravity in man's will and intellect as a result of original sin. The darkened intellect of the later religious poetry, having a categorical imperative in conscience, but shorn of the *analogies* in medieval scholasticism, bears some resemblance to Kant, but theologically it bears more to Cowper and the Calvinist tradition. The problems for Coleridge as religious poet also became the same ones that afflicted the Calvinists before him. The implied dualism of the position on sin and the relationship of man to God provides a

barren outlook (comparatively speaking, with Anglicanism and Catholicism in mind) for a religious poet, since nature, either as friend or
alter ego, or as the analogue of a personal Creator, can no longer
play a substantial role. Coleridge also shares the sceptical inheritance
of the 18th century Calvinists Cowper and Edwards, losing the 17th
century's early optimism within the Calvinist framework. Assurance
was no longer so easily had, either of the moral or intellectual variety.
In this modern Calvinist-oriented theology man is a spiritual being,
conscious of evil in himself and around him, of his darkened intellect,
and above all of his position as a alien in a world of matter and sense,
longing for his God whom he may know only partially, and this
through the resources of the internal, the spiritual, alone. What are
the prospects for literature, and especially poetry, here?

In trying to answer this question I am going to give readings of a
general nature for various of Coleridge's later poems. The readings
are not intended to be complete, but rather to point out a mood and
general attitude in particular contexts. The first readings are of
"Limbo" and "Ne Plus Ultra," poems which manage to have serious
religious concern and yet be rather sportive. By beginning here I hope
to avoid the charge of seeming to distort Coleridge's sensibility into a
foreign mold. A good deal other than Calvinist thought was feeding
into the later Coleridge, and these poems are fair indications of what
some of these irreconcilable elements are. As we move on to other
and more clearly religious poems, with Christian and Calvinist elements of one sort or another, the religious drift of the later poetry
will become more obvious.

"Limbo" (1817) and "Ne Plus Ultra" (1816) are religious and
speculative at the one time, giving to them a strange tone. The religious note is the open admission of an evil spiritual principle permitted by God, yet nevertheless functioning as a divisive, destructive
force in the world. Some of the ideas and imagery are theologically
sound, even in certain particulars strikingly similar to the presentation
of the idea of evil by Thomas Aquinas. The "Lurid thought is growth-
less dull Privation" of "Limbo" corresponds to Aquinas' standard
definition, "*Malum . . . neque est sicut habitus, neque sicut pura
negatio, sed sicut privatio.*" The general drift of "Ne Plus Ultra," that
ultimate evil is a permitted opposite of God, symbolized in the Christian tradition by Satan, is also orthodox enough:

> The Dragon foul and fell —
> The unrevealable,

And hidden one, whose breath,
Gives wind and fuel to the fires of Hell!

A certain element in the presentation of evil in "Ne Plus Ultra" is given in images familiar in Christian theology. "Sole Positive of Night/Antipathist of Light" resembles Aquinas' *"Dicendum quod unum oppositorum cognoscitur per alteram, sicut per lucem tenebra,"* and another interesting similarity occurs in the relationship between evil and prayer, where Coleridge's lines

Sole interdict of all-bedewing prayer
The all-compassionate!

express in substance the thought in Aquinas' *"Quae quidem peccata sunt quasi obstacula interposita inter nos et Deus."* The poems are interested in the Christian universe of values, where evil is handled metaphysically as a permitted privation of the ontological good, and morally as sin in the will of man, separating the creature from his home in the Creator. There is a pervasiveness of darkness and chastisement of the sinfulness of man throughout, with which the orthodox will agree. But there is also throughout both poems a sportive note, an extravagance in imagery in the way Coleridge handles the traditional concepts of privation, positive and negative nothing, and evil as metaphysical entity. There is a jocular tone and freedom from theological accuracy in his use of such elements as "Substance," "Fate-Night," "scorpion rod," which we do not confuse with the metaphysical wit of serious Christian religious poetry.

Other influences are at work upon these poems, extraneous to the religious traditions we are tracing. The theogony of Böehme and the idealism of Schelling were still very attractive to Coleridge in the 1810—1920 period, when he first turned away from his early Romantic mode in search of something more in keeping with his later convictions. Scholars and critics have discussed the theogonic and myth-making aspects of Coleridge's later poetry, so we may be brief here.[30] Such lines as "Ah! the sole despair/ Of both th' eternities in Heaven!" and "The Lampads seven/ That watch the throne of Heaven!" in "Ne Plus Ultra" have close analogies in Böehme's revelations on the nature of the Godhead and of heaven. And the presence of this perspective casts doubt on several ideas and images that would be purely orthodox in another context, such as "The one permitted opposite of God!" in "Ne Plus Ultra." The reader first presumes that God permits the opposite to exist, in other words, evil as *privatio entis* as in Aquinas and Christian orthodoxy generally. But if there are two eternities (and more) in heaven according to Böehme, there is also the serious possibility of an eternity of the opposite sort, evil and the eternal principle of ultimate negation, a form of Manicheanism which crops up in many cabalistic modes of thought as well as in Böehme. In the poems Coleridge seems to be attempting a mild flirtation with diabolic speculation in a framework of religious devotion and orthodoxy. The pull in two directions is a great strain, and Ridenour's ingenious attempt to forge these oppositions into a unity is not convincing;[31] thus the poems remain curiosities midway between the early Romantic Coleridge and the serious religious poems of his later years to which we now turn. In the later poetry the religious interest is no longer merely speculative. The symbol of the darkened world, for instance, which was always mitigated by light in the early Romantic poems, became important in "Limbo" ("By the mere horror of blank Naught-at-all") and in "Ne Plus Ultra" ("Sole Positive of Night, Antipathist of Light") and finally achieves dominant position in the later serious religious poetry.

In "Coeli Enarrent" (1830) the image of the darkened sky divides the "groaning world" of sin and physical evil from God. Man reads in anguish the Black-Letter starless sky as an "O" corresponding to his own pain and alienation. The stars, or light mediating between creature and Creator, no longer "alphabet the skies." In the poem "Reason" (1830) this image of alienation shifts from darkness to a mist "That stands 'twixt God and thee." This mist, like the darkness in "Coeli Enarrant," is contrasted with the "pure transparency" of the triumphant reign of pure reason. Now, however, there is a pessimistic reminder of the power of sin, evil, and error, and the words of Dante are included as a corrective to the presumptions of the reason and the expanding ego:

> 'tu stesso, ti fai grosso
> Col falso immaginar, sì che non vedi
> Ciò che vedresti, se l'avessi scosso.'
> (Thine own false fancies make thee blind; hence unperceived are things thou wouldst perceive, hadst thou but left thy vain concepts behind.)

It is no surprise that Coleridge turned to the great poet of the Middle Ages in his attempt to re-evaluate the power of the human reason; his gradual acceptance of Christian dualism had prepared for this step. But there is an important difference. The chief peculiarity in his theological reacceptance, the semi-dualism he inherited from Kant, served as a force denying him the possibility of becoming a Christian poet in the traditional sense, that of Dante or of the seventeenth century.

For a variety of reasons he was bereft as a poet of the usual consolations of the Christian, even after he accepted the orientation of the Christian tradition. Christianity on such highly philosophical "spiritual" grounds deprived him of the facility to use nature in poetry in the traditional way provided by the analogy of Being.

The communion of man and nature which had been so central to the early poetry broke apart completely in his Christian thinking, leaving a wide chasm between spirit and nature. Once man came to be conceived of as primarily spiritual, in the activity of his will, oppressed by the weight of original sin, the result was naturally a reorientation of man in nature. But Coleridge was not able to rehabilitate nature along the traditional Christian pattern. The problem of considering man apart from nature was at times too great, as in the poem "Human Life On Denial of Immortality" (1815), where the breakdown of spirit and matter in the old immanent unity finds man the "Surplus of Nature's dread activity," a "Blank accident! nothing's anomaly!" From the moment Coleridge began to think of spirit or soul as an entity *sui generis*, a supernatural occurrence in the material world, the formerly genial nature of inanimate objects and sensible things, carrying on the endless cycle of generation and decay, took on some of the horror present later in the poetry of the mid-Victorians. The following excerpt from a late notebook expresses a feeling much more in common with Keats' "Ode to a Nightingale" or Tennyson's *In Memoriam* than with his own or Wordsworth's earlier poetry.[32]

O nature! I would rather not have been − let that which is to come so soon, come now − for what is all the intermediate space, but sense of utter Worthlessness? Far, far below animals − for they enjoy a generic immortality having no individuation. But man is truly and solely an immortal series of conscious Mortalities, and inherent Disappointments.

The close connection shown here between interest in personal immortality and alienation from nature lends support to our general position. The sustenance which generations of earlier poets had taken from nature considered as the handiwork of God was denied to Coleridge; his scornful comments upon the old system of "natural theology," coupled with what we now know of his extremely sophisticated semi-dualism, tell us why.[33] The thinking Christian could no longer pursue his God through the analogies of nature. Henceforward Coleridge's poetry was to be written in two moods, one looking backward mournfully upon the days when nature had been his friend through the interpenetration of subject and object, the other looking forward, in hope but not enthusiasm, to the time when the soul would be able to free itself from matter for union with a highly intellectualized version of divinity.

The backward glance is expressed poignantly in "Constancy to an Ideal Object" (1825) and "Work Without Hope" (1825), where the breakdown of interplay between spirit and nature is complete. The nature described in the notebook entry, with its endless cycles, Coleridge now looks upon as a stranger. In "Constancy to an Ideal Object" all things in nature except man's thought "beat about" in the now harsh, detached expression of the poet, and in the cyclic process "veer or vanish." But here, instead of indulging in the self-pity of "Denial of Immortality" or the notebook entry, Coleridge, with emphasis on personal immortality, makes the puzzling difference between man and nature the point of a paradox. A single thought, unsubstantial, immaterial, is yet "The only constant in a world of change." The poet keeps the paradox alive by prescinding from all the metaphysical and theological relationships between spirit, thought and the world. In his overall attitude the permanence of thought, or the idea, is grounded in the unity of the Godhead, so that the pure ideas become more intensely actual than the world of matter and individual fact.[34] But this poem does not address itself to the spiritual mode of relationships; it considers man as a disaffected part of the formerly unified nature expressed in "Frost at Midnight." And in this respect the constancy of the ideal object of thought in the physical world is a paradox, because it is at once more and less than the physical world around it. "She is not thou, and only thou art she." The thought is a representation which becomes more permanent than the thing, in this case, the person, represented. The mingling of spirit with nature which occurred in "Frost at Midnight," for instance, the thought of the poet with the breath of the babe, no longer is able to take place:

> Fond thought! not one of all that shining swarm
> Will breathe on thee with life-enkindling breath.

The ideal, fixed mode of thought, the spiritual image, must remain detatched from the vibrant but mutable reality of nature, through a paradox which is emotionally enervating for the poet. It is interesting to note that the possibility of re-uniting thought with its object, man with nature, Coleridge with Sara Hutchinson, is expressed in terms of the nature imagery of the early poems "The Eolian Harp," "This Lime-Tree Bower"; the old symbols of interpenetration and unity of being in immanential monism recur in a backward glance:

> Home and Thou are one.
> The peacefull'st cot, the moon shall shine upon,
> Lulled by the thrush and wakened by the lark. . . .

But the present alienation of man as spirit in Nature involves the same image cluster as did the spiritually isolated Mariner in the early years:

> Without thee were but a becalméd bark,
> Whose Helmsman on an ocean waste and wide
> Sits mute and pale his mouldering helm beside.

Here the symbols of regeneration and isolation are not merged by the imaginative power as in the earlier poems. Man remains an isolated spirit in nature, the generative security of which offers no consolation to him. The question "And art thou nothing?" brings us back again to "Limbo," "Denial of Immortality," or "Ne Plus Ultra." Either man is a spiritual creature involved in an ontological complex with his Creator, essentially apart from nature, or else his highest nature is only the self-generated illusion of the rustic:

> An image with a glory rounds its head;
> The enamoured rustic worships its fair hues,
> Nor knows he makes the shadow, he pursues!

In his present mood Coleridge is content to let the paradox generated by his dissociated sensibility remain at the center of his consciousness. But there is no poetic fecundity in the "ocean waste and wide" of spiritual isolation. The either-or cannot be bridged by the exuberance of poetic imagination. Nor could it be, in Coleridge the poet, by the resurgent religious feeling of his later years.

The furthest point of spiritual isolation Coleridge reached is "Work Without Hope," where the meditation again is upon the individual estranged from the productivity and exuberance of nature. The poem moves in a tortuous elegaic manner and in the end seems to break off in despair, when the hopelessness in the dichotomy between nature and spirit has manifested itself completely:

> Work without Hope draws nectar in a sieve,
> And Hope without an object cannot live.

The poet as observing subject is completely cut off from communication with the objects, the living slugs, bees, birds of fertile nature. The key word in the first stanza is "seems." A barrier to immediacy of feeling between man and nature relegates the poet to the role of a mere onlooker.[35] The active projection of the mind upon the objects of nature, leading to the interpenetration and fusion of all things in "Frost at Midnight," no longer takes place. Nothing in nature corresponds to this paralysis of the spirit, for even the Winter, which might ordinarily be taken as an analogue of the torpid mind, "Wears on his smiling face a dream of Spring!" This is a further step from his position in "Denial of Immortality" or the notebook entry, since the horror expressed there at the impersonal participation of man in nature is now replaced by a spiritual stagnation, in relation to which even the former impersonal motions of nature would come as a welcome release. The word "seems" instead of "is" ("All Nature seems at work") indicates clearly the poet's hesitation to attribute any spiritual meaning to nature; he has become conscious of the "pathetic fallacy," a condition unthinkable in the mood and motion of "Frost at Midnight."

This spiritual isolation assumes a more general and universal status in the second stanza when the particular present scene is suddenly charged with symbolic values and associations drawn from Coleridge's earlier career. No longer engaged merely with a late February winter scene in 1825, the poet now views the sight of nature gradually renewing itself as a metaphor for the entire sweep of former imaginative life, when nature and spirit had responded to each other as reflex manifestations of the same reality. The amaranths, mystical flowers of eternal bloom, and the magic fount "whence streams of nectar flow" are drawn not from the present countryside, but from the misty land of the imagination, the landscape of "Kubla Khan" and "The Ancient Mariner." The word "ken" is used here in the sense "remember" rather than the usual "know" or "recognize," and in conjunction with the phrase "traced the founts" signifies that Coleridge is reproducing the hazy stream of ideas associated with the Romantic imagination, ideas whose objects transcend the ordinary bounds of objective space and time. But now it is only in the memory of the poet that such stirrings can be awakened, as in the poem "The Garden of Boccaccio" (1828), where a backward glance awakens temporarily but artifically the creative spirit of the early years.

The lines in "Work Without Hope," "Bloom o ye amaranths! bloom for whom ye may / For me ye bloom not! Glide, rich streams, away!"

refer of course to the deadness of external nature in the present spiritual void, but primarily indicate that the mythical sources of poetic inspiration in the mind's imaginative powers have dried up. And the following line, "With lips unbrightened, wreathless brow, I stroll," has more than the usual connotations associated with the happy pagan at home in nature. It should be read in connection with the closing lines of "Kubla Khan," with its enchanted poet:

> His flashing eyes, his floating hair . . .
> For he on honey-dew hath fed,
> And drunk the milk of Paradise.

Coleridge is referring to the sunny domes, the caves of ice, in short, the lost world of pure active imagination projecting itself upon nature. The spell cast by streams of nectar and honey-dew had long been broken; only in an imaginative flight of memory such as in this stanza could it be partially revived.

A baffling psychological situation appears to be that the fount of Coleridge's imaginative powers, the streams which nurtured his best poetry, the amaranths of eternal nature for the sight of which he still longed, were all deeply and inextricably bound up with the early years, the brightened vistas of that immanent universe in which all nature was the reflex of spirit, and spirit the conscious individual manifestation of nature. Whereas, sad to say, the alien spirit of later years, with the heavy Calvinist sense of spiritual will and conscience, was shut out from the nectar fount, and forced to pass through this world with wreathless brow instead of glittering eye. The alien spirit is the emotional counterpart of the spiritual will and conscience at war with matter and the evil principle, in a semi-dualistic universe under a personal God who could be recognized only in the dialogues of the still small voice, and never in the analogies of external nature. Coleridge could not revive the analogy or sentiment of Being from which Christian poets through the ages have drawn mythical and imaginative power.

Very illustrative religious poems of the alien spirit are "Duty Surviving Self-Love" (1826), "Forbearance" (1832), and "Baptismal Birthday" (1832), where all the tendencies thus far mentioned come to a head. Man is forced to look inward to the conscience which is the pure spiritual reality. The sense of sin is heavy, yet a feeling of the past glory in nature is great enough to forestall any movement toward spiritual tension between soul and body, or man and nature. The "idea" of God as purely spiritual wars against that anthropomorphic conception of deity which might lend the poem the personal human interest of 17th century poetry. Even the more feeble blessings of the 18th century non-Calvinist hymnological tradition, in which Methodist and Anglican alike cautiously but joyously praised their Maker through his words and manifestations in nature, were denied to Coleridge as a result of his long war against "Natural Theology," issuing finally in post-Kantian semi-dualism and religious Calvinism. This semi-dualism, with its austere conception of the relationship obtaining between man and nature, nature and God, man and God, did not allow the doctrine of proportional analogy common to the great Catholic and Protestant theological systems until 1700, and thus denied a universe of sacramental impact and the sentiment of Being. Christ remained primarily the symbolic manifestation of the "Divine Idea," or the Logos of neoplatonic tradition. In "Baptismal Birthday" (1833) we come the closest ever to Coleridge on his knees in prayer, but the habit of poetry was much more entwined with the habit of speculation, so that "Forbearance" and "Duty Surviving Self-Love" are unfortunately more typical and genuine expressions of his awakened religious consciousness.

This combination of isolated spirit and extreme interest in the conscience as an element *sui generis* culminates in a preaching tendency, which is also noticeable in the prose. The minor religious poems each tend to be little sermons directed by the self at the self. In "Baptismal Birthday" the result is somewhat more liberating than usual, as the "idea" of God manifested in Christ supplies a wider background for the trial of conscience. But wherever the background narrows to the extent that conscience reflects only a form of duty, then the sermons, as in "Forbearance" (on the theme "Beareth all things," 1 Cor. 13. 7), and "Duty Surviving Self-Love, A Soliloquy," tend to become mere vehicles of self-justification. The arrogant tone of righteousness, verging on defiance and quite uncommon in Coleridge, is a reminder that to a certain extent his cult of conscience is related, at least in part, through the common medium of Kant, to the cult of will represented by Emerson's "Self-Reliance" and to a great deal of Carlyle. The self-satisfied, conscious moralizing directed at the desertion by friends of the early years, in "Duty Surviving Self-Love,"

> Love them for what they are; nor love them less
> Because to thee they are not what they were,

shows that self-love has survived duty, or modified it into self-pity. "Forbearance," riddled with the same self-pity, advances to the further extreme of defiance, which indicates how close conscience as duty *sui generis* can aproximate self-will, in "Give him the rotten timber for his pains." More significant than the merely egotistical outlook in this poem is the deeper problem, the loss of community of feeling, or of the sense of mutual intercourse by analogy between man and man, or man and objects of nature within the context of a transcendentally good God. But the negative attitude of will or self-assertion is really abortive and tenuous in Coleridge. More often, in a poem such as "Baptismal Birthday," the movement is toward real communication between man and God through conscience in a genial ontological context in which the "idea" of God is manifested and made tangible to the human through Christ. The curious thing is that this positive Christian manifestation fails to make these poems good poetry.

In "Baptismal Birthday" the tone of stridency and somewhat hysterical straining to achieve union and immortality through Christ breaks down almost completely the interesting tensions of Coleridge's spiritual career; here particularly the doctrine of justifying faith is abandoned in favor of a complete surrender to the extreme Calvinist position. Complete surrender of personality and will, "Christ my all," "Eternal Thou and everlasting we," "In Christ I live," emphasis upon personal immortality, and alienation from nature go hand in hand. Paul on the road to Damascus always remained a dramatic alternative to patient seeking for signs of election:

> Let then earth, sea and sky
> Make war against me! On my heart I show
> Their mighty master's seal.

Spirit and matter are so sharply divided that in the pure interchange or blending of spirit there is no dialectic between man and nature, good and evil. Nature is merely abandoned to the enemy. The "idea" of God, which might conceivably have challenged the poet as it did the philosopher, is presented in commonplace fashion. "Baptismal Birthday" and "Self-knowledge" (1832) are good Calvinist Christianity but the lack of structure and tension shows that Coleridge has not been able to turn this religious interest into good poetry. Coleridge, on his own premises, was shut up within a semi-dualistic world of spirit. Alien to nature, and divided from God by sin, this spirit did not prove a fruitful source of great poetry to Coleridge.

The early poems, like "The Eolian Harp," "Frost at Midnight" and of course the "Wondrous Three," are Coleridge's best poetry, although to his later mentality they must have appeared as curious relics from the early years of optimism, the One Life and the universe of immanence. The real relationship between poetry and Coleridge's attempt to construct a religious philosophy can probably be summarized by the reminder that the little poem "Reason" is a mediocre expression of what the *Aids to Reflection* and *Opus Maximum* said in energetic prose. So also with the other late poems. It is no accident that a poem like "Reason" finds its way into the *Opus Maximum*, or that the flashing insights into the unity of being of the early poems are more likely to appear in his later prose.[36]

There may still be a good deal of scepticism about the propriety of calling this later poetry of Coleridge Calvinist in bent rather than merely vaguely religious, or the prelude of Victorian scepticism. For those who know also that every passage of admiration for the 17th century divines in Coleridge's unpublished prose can be matched by one for Kant, Schelling, or Jacob Böehme and the Cabalists, this scepticism may grow. Coleridge's was an enormously receptive mind, and we have no desire to define him except for the evidence in these poems. What he may be elsewhere is no concern of ours at the moment. If we see in these poems and in his religious prose a certain strain of Calvinist residue, the way the Calvinist mind would work in the early 19th century, we have done enough. It is a mind deeply religious, aware of the consequences of sin and guilt, and especially of the power of God in relation to man. On the other hand, it is on the whole a non-dogmatic mind, daringly speculative in certain areas, and not to be appeased by final solutions to religious problems. Given this combination, it is an uncertain and uneasy mind, in awe of God yet proud of intellect. In concluding this section, which points decisively towards Emily Dickinson and the dilemma of 19th century American Puritan tradition, I will present two passages from Coleridge's yet unpublished marginalia to various religious writers. In the first we see the Miltonic and visionary side of Coleridge's Calvinist inheritance, the optimistic intellect trying in the early 19th century to bring everything together as Milton had been able to do. In the second we see the sense of scepticism and inadequacy of religious vision which Coleridge and Calvinism had inherited from the intellectual changes of the 18th century. No 19th century Calvinist was ever to resolve the two sides of the tradition.

According to the Brahmen Theology, the Godhead is manifested in Nature in the trinity of production, destruction, and reproduction. Observe that its place corresponds to that of the Logos monogenos in the Christian triad. Now the properties of the Word are expressed in the terms, distinctive, evocative, separative, elective by selection. The word — the Logos — indeed hath life in itself, but still from the Father. Now in the idea of Life as in all other realities there are two Factors or Constituents, viz. the Ground, and the Form manifesting the Ground. Life is the one, or res unifica, manifested in the Many. In whatever subject, therefore, the Ground of Life is not, or no longer is, for that Subject Light ceases to be Light constructive and becomes Destructive. Light is beatitude of Spirits whose Will is the Will of the Father, and consuming Fire to all Iniquity. The distinctive becomes separative, and works in the forms of liquifying and pulverizing, as declared by scripture and nature. But further: every great epoch of reproduction (creative, regenerative, new birth) is preceded by a destruction. The world (avum aon) is brought to an end, a day of judgment takes place.

It is rendered highly probable by the recent investigations of Geologists that so it has been in each of the five great epochs enumerated by Moses as preceding the creation of Man. Holy writings present the two modes of Death above mentioned, the fluidific, a form of Death which is however the matrix of future life & the second, the pulverizing or incinerative Power, which reduces the substance to a harmony with Light. The Lamb, Agnus, the spotless, *agnos*, the consuming Fire and the purifying Water are one and the same with the Light of Life, the Living Light, whose indwelling Life is the alone true Light of Man. In the deluvial devastation, the figure of the Son, the Articulation of the word, is withdrawn; in the final conflagration the Will of the Ground is stirred up — the Distinctive Power no longer neutralizes its negative (minus Elect equals Oxygen) and positive force (plus Elect equals Hydrogen) but necessary it to itself the bitter will of the Ground shall oppose them in the fury of conflict, the dilative shall be the fuel of the contractive, and all shall be bound up in the utter darkness, sealed up in Death & have no place more.

Yet I doubt not, that God will be glorified therein. The flameless Fire burns inward: the Contraction is absolute . . . the Evil is incommunicable, hath no objective Being & by it's perfect absolute heterogeneity separated from the good, and may be the Hades, the hidden and dark ground of the glorified new earth. The enemy placed forever under the feet of the Blessed, the elastic Spring of their mystic Dance, the Rebound of their ever fresh Triumph — the reflection of the Light of the Lamb which maketh the City of God resplendent and filleth it with the reflexes of his Glory. So it may be & such are the forms which I seem to see dimly in the Mirror of Symbols, the laws and processes of corporeal world organic and inorganic, as interpreted by the Revealed Word.[37]

Birth is the passage of Being to Existence. The Potential becomes Actual. The potentiative cause, i. e. the actualizing agent, of our birth, into our present state of Existence, is the corruptible seed. Now a finite, conditional, and impermanent cause must necessarily manifest itself in a finite, dependent, and transitory Effect or Product. I confess, that I find nothing in Reason to authorize me, nothing in Scripture that requires me, to believe an actuality, or full existency, of the soul separate from the Body, even as I am utterly incapable of conceiving a Body without a Soul. Man, by necessity of his finite nature, at once potential and actual exists, as Soul and Body. The man in a mere potential Being you may call the Soul, but then recollect, that the moment this potential Being is actualized, the opposite mode instantly takes place and the unity of Man appears in the Diad or corresponding opposites, Soul and Body. Not that Soul and Body compose the Man, as Carbon & Hydrogen compose Oil, or Hydrogen & Carbon compose Alcohol, but rather as the Magnetic power realizes itself in the two Poles, attraction and repulsion. Hence, I hold that the Gospel first presented the true idea of Immortality – layed the first ground of future existence . . . whatever is, is necessarily, for it is, because God is, but it is not necessarily *actual*.

But even this is only the first & simplest view. The Problem expands when we take in, as we must do, the equally necessary terms of Multeity and Unity, as the character of every creature. For in God alone true unity. He alone is the One. The highest of creatures, the Angels even, are but *numbers*, i. e. multeity brought under unity. Now man is a number, and in his present state of lower Order. And it is this which renders the problem of our Immortality so difficult for the Reason, and which ought to make us so thankful for a Revelation. As natural men, we feel the underswell of our Multeity, of the complexity and dissonances of our Being, so manifoldly & intrusively as to perplex and unsteady our sense of the unity.[38]

The Miltonic visionary Calvinism in Coleridge is weaker than the sceptical and pessimistic. It is perhaps surprising that it survives at all into the early 19th century, at least in purely religious form. Others, but not Coleridge, were soon to give this visionary optimism a fully secular accommodation. These others, Shelley, Whitman, Emerson and Carlyle, are the descendents of the Calvinist tradition, but have departed from its theological limits. There must be that minimum sense of God, guilt, sin, and possibly regeneration, even if mixed with personal despair, that we find in the 18th century poets Smart and Cowper, and in Coleridge, Wordsworth, Byron, Dickinson, Melville and Hawthorne. Coleridge's place in this tradition is marginal, but without him we would be at a loss to define the actual continuation of Calvinist sensibility after the last strictly religious poets, Watts and Cowper. As a "minime-fideist" (one of the strange words from religious controversy Coleridge so loved) he helped the authentic tradition to survive into the 19th century.

Postscript: Coleridge and Melville

It is difficult to know where to place this small section in the structure of the study we are pursuing. Since one half of the relationship concerns Coleridge, while Melville, as an American Calvinist, appears only in passing in this study, a postscript to Coleridge seems a proper place, for the reasons given below.

The point of the Coleridge and Melville relationship for this study is a narrow one, admittedly, though extremely important. From the beginning of the poetic tradition of Calvinism from Spenser to Coleridge we have been reading poets who were ultimately believers in the tradition despite doubts, scepticism and sometimes despair. These factors vary greatly from poet to poet, but ultimately there was an assertion of faith. Such is the case in a less obvious way of Wordsworth, but not so of Byron, Hawthorne or Melville. These later writers worked more directly within the Calvinist tradition than did Coleridge or Wordsworth, but they lacked faith, and the difference is crucial for everything important about their works. As an analogy to Hawthorne was helpful in the introduction to this section in defining the general area of interest in the 19th century, so also will be some discussion of the religious similarities and differences between Coleridge and Melville as viewed in their handling of one very complex simile which each uses in his characteristic way as a religious analogy.

A source for the Plotinus Plinlimmon Lecture "EI" in *Pierre* has not to my knowledge yet been found. In the introductory portion of the chapter entitled "The Journey and the Pamphlet" there are obvious humorous references. "Plato, and Spinoza, and Goethe, and many more belong to this guild of self-imposters, with a preposterous rabble of Muggletonian Scots and Yankees, whose vile brogue still the more bestreaks the stripedness of their Greek or German Neoplatonical originals."[39] Carlyle and Emerson are certainly intended. German neoplatonic originals might refer to the idealist tradition of Kant, Fichte, Schelling and Hegel, or if the reference is to be taken more accurately and literally, to Böehme. It is widely accepted that Hawthorne and Melville read in all of these writers, and also in the English Romantic poets and the prose of Coleridge. The humorous introduction to the lecture, with mention of Three Hundred and Thirty-three Lectures, and "Being not so much the Portal, as part of the temporary Scaffold to the Portal of this New Philosophy,"[40] is not specific enough to lead to a particular source, but it is general enough in its satiric intent to refer to the "architechtonic" of any work from Kant's *Critiques* to Coleridge's *Aids to Reflection*. The main idea of the lecture, that there is a dualism between earthly time and morality on the one hand, and heavenly time and absolute morality on the other, is too generally a part of ancient and modern neoplatonism to require a specific source. It is only when we consider two further aspects of the lecture, the specific imagery of horologicals and chronologicals, and the bitter ironic twist that the lecture deduces from earthly/heavenly dualism, that we might entertain the notion that it is worthwhile to search for some specific source for the Plinlimmon material.

The four elements in Plinlimmon's thought are clock-watch time (horologicals), human mores or morality, heavenly time (chronologicals), and absolute truth or morality (Christ). If the analogy were more perfect the third item, heavenly time (chronologicals) would have been represented by the sun and other heavenly bodies, thus giving the analogy − clock-watch: sun-heavenly bodies : : human conscience-mores: Absolute truth. Melville refers to the "great Greenwich in the other [heaven]" for his eternal and immutable timekeeper, and thus muddies the image somewhat, although the idea in the analogy remains clear. The clock is an inaccurate version of "great Greenwich" or sun time, the conscience the same in regard to absolute truth. At this point Melville's ironic variations on the analogy begin, but before the full import of them can be understood, a look at other uses of the analogy in the idealist tradition can be helpful.

One possible general source for Melville's idea can be found in the *Table Talk* of Coleridge, which was first published in 1835. Though Melville and Hawthorne were readers of Coleridge's prose, the chances that Melville came across this item are admittedly slim, and the item itself only of the most general value for the thought of Plinlimmon:

Sept. 1, 1832. A philosopher's ordinary language and admissions, in general conversation or writings *ad populum*, are as his watch compared with his astronomical timepiece. He sets the former by the town-clock, not because he believes it right, but because his neighbors and his cook go by it.[41]

The two timepieces, the watch and the astronomical, are here, but "language and admissions" are far more general than conscience and mores. In another place Coleridge writes of this analogy with conscience and mores as the idea:

The more I reflect, the more exact & close appears to me the Similie of a Watch and Watches: the Sun & motion of the heavenly Bodies in general, to the conscience and consciences : : to the reason and goodness of the Supreme. Never goes quite right, any one: no two go exactly the same, they derive their dignity and use as being Substitutes and Exponents of heavenly motions, but still in a thousand instances they are & must be our instructors, by which we must act, in practice presuming a co-incidence, while theoretically we are aware of incalculable *Variations*.[42]

Since this note appeared in a private notebook of 1805, first published in 1895,[43] it was not a source for Melville, but the striking similarity in the terms of the analogy suggest a common source. Both Melville and Coleridge use the clock-watch / conscience part of the analogy; but Coleridge has "Sun and motion of the heavenly Bodies in general," where Melville has "great Greenwich," and Coleridge has "reason and goodness of the Supreme" while Melville refers specifically to the "heavenly wisdom of God" and to Christ. The present editor of the Notebooks of Coleridge did not look for a source for this entry, assuming it to be original with Coleridge, and to this writer's knowledge no one in Melville studies has pointed to a specific source for the four terms of the analogy as used in *Pierre*. If this common source can be found it will be possible to write with far more authority than is presently possible on the Plinlimmon section, yet limited as we are to our present information and taking Coleridge as a strong representative of idealism in its Christian variety,[44] we can see aspects of the Plinlimmon episode that are not apparent if the source is presumed to be vaguely platonic, and the purpose merely to poke a little fun at Carlyle and Emerson, transcendentalists outside of the Christian tradition for whom Melville had little respect.

In Coleridge's scheme the four elements present a perfect square of opposition. Two are physical images, two ideas, with the two ideas and the two images related directly, and each pair of image/idea related by analogy, that is, the clock-watch/conscience are human and imperfect, the sun-heavenly bodies/reason and goodness of Supreme and sun-time/conscience are divine and perfect. The watch/Supreme and sun-time/conscience form the opposites of this perfect square of opposition, opposites only implied in Coleridge and made explicit by Melville to attain his ironic purpose. The dualism of human/divine is accepted by Coleridge, but it is really a semi-dualism sweetened by faith in human/divine correspondence. Though the human conscience, like the human clock, must err in relation to the divine truth and heavenly motions respectively, and though no two clocks or consciences can be identical, therefore introducing an idea of relativity in all human calculations from the practical to the moral, the faith in the analogy as approximation of absolute time and absolute truth remains, as Coleridge concludes, ". . . but still in a thousand instances they [clock and con-science] are & must be our instructors, by which we must act, in practice presuming a co-incidence, while theoretically we are aware of incalculable *Variations*." This is certainly not feckless optimism; it is rather the severe and deep faith appearing in all of Coleridge's writings on the subject of religious belief especially after 1817.

Melville's square of opposition is not so neat as Coleridge's, and this is in a way unfortunate because he could have had his complexities and ironies without needless obscurity. The obscurity arises from his use of Greenwich in the clock-watch part of the figure. To make the point of the relativity of human time and watches, Greenwich is first set up as the absolute standard, from which clock time in "China" (standing for the variable mores of man) differs. But Greenwich is of course only a starting point for a standard of time variation based upon earth's rotation, and the idea of keeping Greenwich time in China is rather foolish if taken literally. Melville could have settled for the more obvious images and inferences in the imperfections of watches and consciences and have made his point. But it would not have been as startling. On the other hand the use of Greenwich as a (literally false) human absolute allows for the easy leap to the "great Greenwich in the sky," a mixed blessing, because this image obscures the total analogy, whereas the "Sun-celestial motion of the heavenly bodies" fulfills it explicitly. But when we think of the oppositions in this scheme, that is, watch/Supreme and sun-time/conscience, we see what importance the more obscure figure has for Melville's purpose. Mellville really wants the terms to be obscure at the edges and almost to blend into each other. The clock-watch time is both an absolute Greenwich in the world and the relativity of the twenty-four meridians, and also becomes the absolute Greenwich of the heavenly chronometer, Christ. Thus Plotinus Plinlimmon can state that while most men are horologicals, adhering to relative mores of their time and place, some men, by virtue of the identity of the divine and earthly Greenwiches, are chronologicals, absolutely opposed in principle to the human time (mores) around them and thus the world's martyrs. This quick movement back and forth between human watches and consciences on the one hand, and the absolute time (Christ) on the other, would not have been possible if the image of the sun and motion of the heavenly bodies had remained fully present and separate in Plinlimmon's analogy. Greenwich − first as human absolute in opposition to relative watch time, then as the "great Greenwich" which implies, but slides over, the sun-heavenly bodies image in the analogy, to take on the aspect of absolute truth itself, or Christ − is the middle term that occupies three places in the analogy at one time or another. Whatever the validity of the image, it clearly leads to the desired result. Melville does not want the result to be faith in the analogy of clock/conscience is as sun-motions/divine law, and acceptance of the inference that correspondence is possible despite relativity and that dualism does not lead to despair. In the Plinlimmon pamphlet dualism does lead to despair, because the absolute truth (Christ the Divine Greenwich) can be found occasionally in the world in the breasts of certain persons absolutely opposed to the mores of the society around them, a phenomenon prepared for by the introduction of Greenwich as a standard of time absolute in the human relative world. It is an act of verbal and visual legerdemain which allows Melville what he wants here, a chance to show the poignancy of the difference between absolute and relative morality in the world, and how this leads either to the despair and destruction of a chronological individual such as Pierre, or to the cynicism of virtuous expediency advocated by Plinlimmon, with its parody of idealism and sneers at Emerson, Carlyle, *et al.* in such lines as "by their very contradictions they are made to correspond."

In this loading of the dice in setting up the analogy Melville shows clearly that he lacks faith in the Christian idea of correspondence, as well as in the Romantic ideals of Identity of his time. He wants and achieves his own idea of extreme dualism, despair, and bitter irony. In showing how he does this, using the terms of contemporary idealism and the more perennial Christian variety, no adverse criticism is implied, except the one made above regarding the blurring of the square of opposition in the four-part analogy. That blurring was necessary for his purpose, but was also so drastic that it is difficult for the reader to follow his artistry. Byron and Dickinson, also lacking faith in correspondence and often reaching for cynical and ironic effects, use the ideas of idealism and Christianity by methods that are somewhat similar to those in the Plinlimmon episode, granting that each example of great artistry has its own uniqueness. If the common source for this analogy in Melville and Coleridge is located, it may lead to further illumination of Melville's artistry. If this source proves to be an 18th century one it may be important for understanding other aspects in the relationship between Christian religious belief, Puritan modes of thought, and the mutation to Romanticism in Wordsworth, Byron and Coleridge.[45]

Certainly this very close analogy in the thinking and imagery of Coleridge and Melville points out the influence of Calvinist tradition upon writers, their concern with dualism, the uncertainties of faith and the inquietude of the modern conscience as the ancient doctrine of analogy gradually lost its hold upon minds which were forced to question all dogmas. The desire to hold on to something positive is evident in Coleridge, the bitterness of being unable to do so in Melville. With the other ambiguous exception of Wordsworth, the path of Melville was followed by all the other writers of Calvinist background who had begun life with some kind of religious orientation and were not able to accept the kinds of idealism and optimism offered by Carlyle and Emerson. In many writers, particularly Americans, the religious residue was cast out early, so that it had no great influence on their work. Melville and Dickinson, despite bitterness and unbelief, retained the Calvinist heritage. That is why Byron, Melville, Hawthorne and Dickinson, though lacking belief, seem very close to Coleridge, Wordsworth, Cowper and Blake, who in their various odd ways retained religious belief, and all seem closer together than to fellow English or American writers of the 19th century whose rejection of religious influence was total.

III. Wordsworth

It is a common critical view today that Wordsworth's poetry is too mythic, visionary and individualistic to fall within even the most vague and diffuse religious characterization. Certainly it has been generally held that the appearance of religious words in his poems — spirit, spiritual, grace, motion, breeze, and others — has no particular religious meaning, at least in the great poems of the 1790–1810 period. The explanations given to these terms in their contexts are often philosophical, currently "visionary," and seldom religious. It would be idle to enumerate the various *isms* which have been held up as explanations of Wordsworth's poetry — in fact such an effort would be equivalent to rehearsing the history and causes of Romanticism as they are usually viewed by scholars. However, a good working knowledge of the usual sources given for Wordsworth's ideas is necessary in order to follow this argument and to assess its point of departure from the usual ones. German metaphysics, transcendental pantheism, Hartley's theory of association, Berkeley and Coleridge will not be mentioned explicitly, but they are always in the background.

Another point which must be made clear at the start in relating Wordsworth to the religious tradition of Puritanism is what poems one intends to use as illustration of the tradition in Wordsworth. There are some fine poems for which there is no place in this study. Many "lyrical ballads," other early poems, and *The Prelude* of 1805 fall outside the province of a study of Wordsworth's religious sensibility. In fact, had not Wordsworth changed his outlook sometime in the decade 1800–1810, allowing the possibility of a more religious view of life into his poems, it would be pointless to attempt the following commentary. He did change his outlook in part. The trouble for criticism has been to decide what it was he changed to. It is pretty well established that his earlier views were a synthesis of naturalism, personal mysticism, German metaphysics, and English psychological theory, given different emphases by various critics. Some have made the point that Wordsworth became a stoic, more or less a follower of Roman religion, after the warning of transcendentalism. Others have followed a rather obvious and literal path in taking his Anglicanism seriously.[46] The first way leads to the "Ode to Duty" and "Peele Castle" poems, and to the epigrams and later descriptions of nature. John Jones has made a good deal of Anglicanism in *The White Doe of Rylstone*. The latter view points toward the *Ecclesiastical Sonnets* and *The Excursion*. The availability of so much material after the great decade 1797–1807 is a problem, making generalization difficult and leading at worst to a compartmentallized view of the poet. While admitting that certain early poems are almost purely "Romantic," I suggest that another general group has a religious character that admits of no clear-cut type, and can, therefore, reasonably be discussed in the structure of this book. They are "spiritual" poems of some sort, but of what, no one has clearly made out. Included in such a group would be "Nutting," "Resolution and Independence," the Lucy poems, "Stepping Westward," "The Solitary Reaper," other shorter poems, parts of *The Prelude* of 1850 and *The Excursion*. Perhaps others of the very late poems and sonnets could be added to this list.

It may seem very rigid and artificial to look for a Calvinist-Puritan strain and a "rhetoric of the spirit" in some of Wordsworth's poetry when in fact the most contemporary of Romantic criticism and Wordsworth criticism have conceded both the general religious nature of Romantik poetry and of Wordsworth's poetry, repudiating the strictly humanistic bases of the earlier critical traditions mentioned above. It seems to be impossible to keep separate religion and Romanticism for very long. Though gladly conceding the wisdom of the general work of Abrams, Barth, McFarland and others on various aspects of religious tradition and Romanticism, the aim in this essay is somewhat different and more specific, to help us to see the force of one religious tradition in Wordsworth's poetry. This endeavour in no way implies that Calvinism is an exclusive force in the poetry, or that it appears in the form of strict and literal dogmas. To get a sighting on the function of this tradition in some of Wordsworth's poetry, it is wise to move from the general to the particular situation.

First, then, something should be said in brief about the general qualities of Wordsworth's poetry which may be called religious. Here several current myths must be set aside. One is that religious poetry in English is exclusively of the "metaphysical" variety, highly dogmatic in content, usually Catholic or Anglican. The main line of this tradition extends from Donne and Herbert through Hopkins to Eliot and Lowell. This fact may be granted, as long as the existence of a non-metaphysical, less dogmatic tradition is also granted, from Spenser and Milton to the American 19th century Puritans, in which Wordsworth would find a place. Our study exists mainly to point this out. Later on in this section a comparison of two religious poems by Donne and Wordsworth may suggest some breakdown in the exclusiveness of these categories. For now we may accept this division. Another myth, more central to Wordsworth criticism, concerns the false or misleading interpretations which have been given to Wordsworth's religious interests. For instance, his interest in Catholic practice and imagery has been largely ignored by critics who cannot find in it any connection with their naturalistic or philosophical readings of the poems. Admittedly, this interest is not easy to assimilate into a view of the later Wordsworth as orthodox Anglican. And yet Wordsworth was fascinated with the sense of solitariness, dedication, ritual, and holiness in Catholic ascetic practice, a fascination it held for no other Romantic poet. But was there something deeper? These lines from *The Prelude* (1850) are illustrative of the situation:

> And now a third small Island, where survived
> In solitude the ruins of a shrine
> Once to Our Lady dedicate, and served
> Daily with chaunted rites.
>
> (Bk. II, 62−65)

>   or the antique walls
> Of that large abbey, where within the Vale
> Of Nightshade, to St. Mary's honour built,
> Stands yet a mouldering pile with fractured arch,
> Belfry, and images, and living trees;
> A holy scene!
>
> (Bk. II, 102−07)

Other passages appear in IV, 323−38, and VI, 414−88. One can merely accept these lines as usurpation of the religious metaphor to express the artist's dedication to creative imagination, as is often the case in Keats and Joyce. This meaning *is* present in Wordsworth, especially in this passage in book IV:

I made no vows, but vows
Were then made for me; bond unknown to me
Was given, that I should be, else sinning greatly,
A dedicated Spirit. On I walked
In thankful blessedness, which yet survives.

                                    (Bk. IV, 334–38)

Yet one senses another and deeper feeling in these religious metaphors, a level of true spiritual import. The lines express both artistic dedication and true religious feeling. Critics have not been successful in articulating the religious feeling, although a great deal has been done with other religious images in Wordsworth's poetry. It has been more common, and easier, to note a religious spirit which is often called pagan or Roman, for want of more precise understanding. Wordsworth's religious feeling has been compared to the mild epicureanism of Horace's Odes, or to the stoicism of Seneca's prose. This is safer ground than a direct comparison with Anglican or Catholic orthodoxy would offer, but there is still a vital difference between the hard-lipped Roman resignation to death, accompanied by a mild epicureanism, as in Catullus' lines, "*Nox est perpetua una dormienda*," and Wordsworth's softer resignation and piety, which has about it a good deal of Christian resignation and cheerfulness. These lines, for instance, from "Glen-Almain,"

It is not quiet, is not ease;
But something deeper far than these:
The separation that is here
Is of the grave: and of austere
Yet happy feelings of the dead. . . .

have a tone, and express a dimension, foreign both to Catholic and Anglican explicitness on one hand, and Roman stoicism on the other. It is my belief that what Wordsworth draws upon to achieve his end in these poems is the English Protestant tradition of the Holy Spirit, in the self and in the world, which had been formulated in the 17th century by Puritans and Quakers. He is, of course, using their terminology metaphorically in the early 19th century; yet even conceding this, it is this terminology which allows him to create in certain poems his own unique views of the spirit, of piety, and of a sense of community among the living and the dead.

If this is the central point about Wordsworth's religious experience, and if the Catholic imagery and stoic viewpoint taken alone are misleading, then the burden of proof rests upon us, since it must seem odd that criticism has ignored such a central fact for so long. The reason here lies in the explicitness of so much of Wordsworth's source material, as opposed to his vague and devious method regarding the religious poems. The metaphysical, stoic or Anglican backgrounds can (and have) been traced with fair accuracy. The general Protestant spirituality shading off into Puritanism has not and cannot be traced in such a way. Wordsworth shows a certain mental deviousness in owning or even in understanding his religious sources, and toward taking a definite stand on religious matters. He is much more difficult to discuss in these areas than is his friend Coleridge, whose acknowledgement of sources and general level of intellectual awareness were much higher.

The *Ecclesiastical Sonnets* may serve to illustrate the problem of deviousness in Wordsworth's attitude toward explicit religious points. As his only extended work of a traditional religious sort, it might strike the reader as the most likely place to search out Wordsworth's religious opinions. It is, but the search is not an easy one, and leaves a good deal of ambiguity in its path.

The initial problem of the *Sonnets* is that while Wordsworth generally follows the traditional English view of ecclesiastical history in the main — that the present English Church and state are the mutual result of happy compromise — he is by no means doctrinaire in his acceptance of the establishment. He seems decidedly latitudinarian in relation to Spenser or Milton. He allows himself to see a great deal of appeal in Roman Catholicism, in the Puritans, in the American Pilgrim, in Laud and the High Church, in the latitudinarians and Milton, indeed in almost every area of English ecclesiastical history. Sometimes this respect is on aesthetic grounds, as with medieval Catholic practice, at other times it is the moral or social aspect of a group which he admires. But in every case he reluctantly follows the turnings of history which led to the domination of the Low Church establishment of his own day. Nevertheless he admired the dedication and austerity as well as the aesthetic appeal of pre-Reformation Catholicism, and his grief for the passing of the religious aspects of the old order is genuine. Only by reminding himself of the political implications of religious events in the 16th century can he bring himself to accept the demise of Catholicism in England. With the Puritans and non-conformists his praise is on other grounds, but his attack the same. The morality and social consciousness of the Puritans and Pilgrims, their allegiance to a sense of duty and the right (even if misguided) are what attract him in their religious life. The poems show relief when Puritanism passes into latitudinarianism, and when the descendents of the Pilgrims in America accept the Episcopal Church after the revolution. The two sonnets on "Eminent Reformers" (XXXIX and XL) express the typical "middle way" or "trimmer" view of the Anglicans that is reminiscent of the mood of Herbert or Hooker. The problem for anyone taking a serious interest in Wordsworth's religious views is that it is mainly the political and social middle way that he approves; there is little of specific religious or dogmatic matters in these poems. The way is left open for him to admire Catholic pieties and latitudinarian ideas, the convictions of the Puritans and Anglican religious modality, while rejecting the secular and political views which accompanied all but Anglican historical growth. Our view is that the *Ecclesiastical Sonnets* rather deliberately say very little about purely spiritual matters, and that only in the vaguest way. These lines from "Eminent Reformers" (XL) give us the typical view of moderation for which the established Church is supposedly noted:

> The truth exploring with an equal mind,
> In doctrine and communion they have sought
> Firmly between the two extremes to steer. . . .

Sonnet XXX, "The Point at Issue," comes closest (and this is not very close) to a position on matters of faith and dogma:

> . . . the Soul, freed from the bonds of Sense,
> And to her god restored by evidence
> Of things not seen, drawn forth from their recess,
> Root there, and not in forms, her holiness: —
> . . . .
> For Faith, more perfect still, with which the Lord
> Of all, himself a Spirit, in the youth
> Of Christian aspiration, deigned to fill
> The temples of their hearts who, with his word
> Informed, were resolute to do his will,
> And worship him in spirit and in truth.

Hooker, Andrewes and Herbert would find nothing to object to in the above, but they certainly would expect more than that on "the point at issue" and as a clarification of Anglicanism. Particularly Wordsworth's use of "Spirit" here would be met with suspicion unless modified further and defined. It is not helpful merely to say that Wordsworth is using layman's language here, as opposed to the

doctrinal explicitness of a professional: he has something quite definitely in mind in his definition of faith and spirit, a conception of the
Holy Spirit or inner light as the ultimate religious authority in man and
the refiner of his inner feelings. This is, to be sure, an element in
all Reformation doctrine, but to single it out as paramount or solely
important was the mark of the Puritan, the Quaker, and other
believers in the rhetoric of the spirit. In few words, beneath Wordsworth's acceptance of the Anglican Church and the middle way lies a
belief in certain doctrines rejected by the establishment yet central to
the Calvinist-Puritan and Quaker traditions. These doctrines in both
origin and structure, are more amenable to his earlier pantheistic
views than are Anglican dogmas of the Trinity and of authority. One
could point to Böehme or Law as possible transmitters of the
doctrines to Wordsworth, but source is not the important point. It is of
greater importance to explore the intellectual structure of Wordsworth's religious views in his poetry and in his 17th century
antecedents in Calvinist-Puritan thought. He, with his distrust of
Puritan politics and fanaticism, might have been surprised at the
parallels. These parallels are more a matter of feeling than of dogma,
yet the analogies, where they occur, are potent.

    We are dealing here with a splinter or sub-stratum of the main
Calvinist-Puritan modes of thought and feeling discussed in the other
chapters of this book. The ideas in question can be considered as
belonging to the "left-wing" of Puritanism, or as that part of
Puritanism which led to Quakerism, where they received full development. It was pointed out in Chapter I that Calvin's own ambiguity in
use of the terms "spirit" and "grace" led to this development. This
distinction is important, for we shall see later that certain central Puritan traditional modes of thought influenced Wordsworth to a lesser
extent. The chief doctrines and beliefs in question are the Holy Spirit
and the inner light. Some of the Puritan groups, in more explicit ways
than are given in Wordsworth's sonnet, turned from the Second Person
of the Trinity to the Third as a means of getting close to God and to
religious truth. Wordsworth is their spiritual heir. Such extreme views
were decidedly unorthodox, and were considered heretical even by the
staunch Puritanism of Richard Baxter.[47] The Spirit or Holy Ghost
dwelled within, according to extreme Puritans and Quakers, and had
primacy over sacraments and even the Word in the establishment of
truth and in reaching God. The sacraments, connected directly with the
Second Person of the Trinity, became less important as a locus of wor-

ship in Puritanism and were abolished by the Quakers. Dogmas connected with the sacraments were weakened accordingly; the locus of religious feelings outside the self widened to include all the world, specifically the natural world, and other selves, the saints. In extreme Puritanism even the Scriptures, "Bible as the religion of Protestant," fell before the onslaughts of the spirit within. All of man and the active universe became the dwelling of the spirit. Only one final line of distinction between this spiritual religion and fanatical madness was drawn, in the attitude toward rationality. For the serious and soberminded the spirit always remained rationality heightened, in practice a blending of the two. In the so-called "sects" of the 17th century, fanaticism welled up to drown and contradict the pattern of Puritan spirituality, in some instances in such startling ways that 17th century spiritual religion never lived down its bad reputation. The sober carried out the dictates and struggles of the spirit in prayer; the fanatics in levelling and shaking. In the best circles prayer replaced the sacraments as the center and best fruits of the Christian life and of the attempt to unite oneself with God.

This subject is fully presented in G. F. Nuttall's book, cited above, and more recently as concerns the Quakers in Hugh Barbour's *The Quakers in Puritan England*.[48] By comparing the findings of these studies with the information on the central Puritan tradition presented in our opening section, we can see what elements in the radical tradition would make a natural appeal to Wordsworth. On the positive side, there are extreme individuality in one's approach to God and to things of the spirit, the stressing of the inner spirit and the Holy Spirit, and a strong sense of assurance. On the negative side, one misses the strong Puritan sense of providence, of god as "outside," of predestination and of sin-consciousness, shared by Puritans and Calvinists from the beginning to Coleridge and Hawthorne. Later we will see that Wordsworth shared in these qualities too, but to a far lesser extent than in those of the optimistic side. This optimistic pratice could provide middle ground between his early natural religion and later formal orthodoxy. Wordsworth did not, and could not, leap immediately from his own nature-mysticism to Anglican orthodoxy. The period of transition, seldom recognized for what it was, left much good poetry. This group of poems might be called prayers in the soberest mood of the older Puritan rhetoric of the spirit. By defining them thus we come to understand their religious appeal in the absence of overt religious statement. Wordsworth shares the Spiritists' leaning toward the unorthodox and the heretical, their strategic ambiguity of statement, and their lack of dogmatic finality. We might, without being far-fetched, view them as a final flowering of the spirit and feeling of extreme liberal 17th century Protestantism, the *ne plus ultra* before the absolute secularism of Shelley and Keats. Spirit, the spiritual, individual feeling, solitude, loneliness, a dialogue with God, nature, and the confrontation with death are the *loci* of these poems.

There is no point in going further without some specific explication of poems. The poems chosen contain the religious elements and in most cases richly reward explication. These include the Lucy poems, "Stepping Westward," "The Solitary Reaper," "Resolution and Independence." Others, of lesser intrinsic interest for this purpose, such as "Nutting," "Peele Castle," "Ode to Duty," point out darker aspects of the Puritan spirit in Wordsworth.[49] Passages of longer poems appear only as illustrations to strengthen a generalization. At no time is any poem said to be this or that exclusively, and the great long poems, *The Prelude* and *The Excursion*, which defy chronology or other categories, are treated only in part. In dealing with these religious elements in Wordsworth's poetry, we do not wish to overstate the case or make them appear his overwhelming lifetime consideration, which they were not. On the other hand, our excuse for treating this phase is that it has been neglected in 20th century criticism.

Let us look first at the simplest poem in the group, "Lucy Gray, or Solitude," to test this view of religious feeling in Wordsworth. The story is a simple-minded ballad set firmly in the convention of the person whose spirit is said to return at night after death, or to roam the wilds and moors mysteriously. The analogues to such a ballad are legion. But Wordsworth lifts his narrative out of the commonplace in the final two stanzas. The first line, "Yet some maintain that to this day," is a ballad commonplace, but the expression "She *is* a *living* child" (italics mine) is not. It is faintly scriptural language and suggests both life after death and a living presence of the spirit in the 17th century Puritan tradition. Although it remains also the crude commonplace of preternatural folklore that one literally sees a ghost upon the lonesome wild, this commonplace is secondary. Wordsworth prefers to represent the spirit more indirectly, by song, a song that "whistles in the wind" in the final stanza. Here the spiritual or spectral is presented to the aural rather than to the visual imagination, as is always sound strategy in dealing with the supernatural in a sophisticated way. We might note also, although I do not insist on a direct relationship here, a connection between the Holy Spirit or Πνεῦμα, breath, and the whistling wind of the final line. The Πνεῦμα, or third person of the Trinity, represented community for the 17th century tradition and for Coleridge. It is a cheerful community which unites the living and the dead through the image of breath, wind, or spirit and I think it plays no small part in determining the ambiguous position of Wordsworth's use of spirit in the Lucy poems, somewhere between the crudely preternatural assertion of a literal ghost and the Christian belief in the afterlife. The ambiguity is maintained largely through the delicate poise of Wordsworth's language, of course, but also by these overtones of the dignified Puritan religious tradition of the Spirit in the living world.

The five Lucy poems proper were divided by Wordsworth in the edition of 1850 into two groups, poems of the affections, "Strange fits of passion," "She dwelt among the untrodden ways," and "I travelled among unknown men," and poems of imagination, "Three years she grew," "A slumber did my spirit seal." Wordsworth was not always so fortunate and accurate as here in the division of his own poems. "Strange fits of passion" is trite, "She dwelt among the untrodden ways" mildly but not offensively sentimental. The last stanza of "I travelled" rises to something higher:

> And thine too is the last green field
> That Lucy's eyes surveyed.

This is one of the many *place* (green field) − *time* (last) mergings in Wordsworth's poetry, a simple instance of the more complex activity of this sort in the "Intimations" ode.[50] But the poem is on the whole rather low-keyed and of the affections. It is in "Three years she grew" and "A slumber" that the imagination does its work of blending the literal and spiritual views of spirit and of the living with the dead.

The instigator or formal principal of the Lucy poems is Nature as a capitalized goddess who makes Lucy "A Lady of my own," and then mysteriously returns her to earth's diurnal course "With rocks and stones, and trees." This bald fact has given rise to the numerous interpretations of the poems as informed by 18th century mechanistic naturalism and pantheism.[51] I do not deny the presence of the naturalistic aspects of the poems, but I think these interpretations are incapable of doing justice to the human side of the poems. If Lucy is seen merely as a prop in nature's orderly and mechanical garden, she loses all human meaning, and thus the fusion of the human and the non-human by imagination, which is at the heart of the poems, becomes meaningless. Some critics have read these poems from this too literal and scientific (in a certain sense) point of view. Since Wordsworth called them poems of the imagination, we may assume he saw them as embodying something more significant and elusive than a literal naturalism. The attenuated but true spirituality in the poems, neglected in the naturalistic readings, is accounted for, I believe, by the influence of the tradition of 17th century spiritual religion upon Wordsworth's imagination.

The blending of the naturalistic with human and spiritual forces in Wordsworth's poetry has been taken account of perceptively by critics of *The Prelude,* "Tintern Abbey," the "Intimations" ode, but not, so far as I know, in regard to the Lucy poems.[52] The point is always the ambiguity between what is spiritual and what is physical, or between the clearly subjective and objective. Is the vapor in the Simplon Pass episode really vapor, a metaphor for spirit, both, or some *tertium quid* created by Wordsworth's imagination? However one wishes to put it, the fact of interaction and a confused blending among objects ordinarily considered to be of discrete classes also takes place in the Lucy poems, but in a rather more direct way, and with less confusion of syntax, than in *The Prelude* and elsewhere.

"Three years she grew" can be broken down, if rather crudely, into three groups of images conveying either the purely objective or natural, the purely subjective or human, and an elusive third which conveys the interaction of the other two. The force of all together gives the impression of Lucy's existence in a spiritual state quite close to the sense of πνεῦμα in spiritual religion.

In stanza two there are the contrasts of feeling in "law and impulse" and "kindle or restrain," impulse and kindle suggesting the human, law and restrain the totally naturalistic. The expression "in rock and plain / In earth and heaven, in glade and bower" is entirely human except for the odd appearance of heaven in this list, which here suggests not so much the other world as the not of this world. The lines "The Girl . . . Shall *feel* an *overseeing power*" give us both terms of the peculiar equation in this poem, that is, the human of "feel" and the totally detached and naturalistic "overseeing power." Only the sense of the middle state is missing here, but this appears strongly in the next stanza in the lines,

> And hers shall be the breathing balm
> And hers the silence and the calm
> Of mute insensate things.

The last line falls most heavily onto the naturalistic and ahuman side, but "breathing balm" is barely on the side of the obviously human, and "silence" and "calm" perhaps not at all. The effect is somewhat that of the opening stanza of "Ode on a Grecian Urn," although not so openly striven for. If this stanza has pulled the poem to the right of center toward the objectively naturalistic, the next section provides the restoration of the previous balance in the contrast between "motions of the storm" and grace (which here is both a human and a spiritual term) unified "by silent sympathy," where silent suggests the naturalistic and sympathy the decidedly human. This, then, is the most characteristic stanza in the poem, and the final three stanzas do not add anything to change the balanced achievement of the human and the totally other in some mysterious spiritual third state. In the final stanza we are left with "This *heath,* this *calm,* this *quiet scene,"* wherein the first term is physical, the second a state of human emotion, and the third a general impression or memory of the entire experience. The quiet scene exists neither in the normal world of everyday life nor in the naturalistic ahuman world to which Lucy presumably has departed, but rather conveys some state of spirit or grace, the result of the total experience, which is nourished and kept alive by memory and imagination. It is the Wordsworthian *tertium quid,* with many analogues in *The Prelude* and other poems, most usually called the mystical state by Wordsworthian critics, and religious contemplation by theologians. Here in the Lucy poems the manner is most purely that of the general mysticism or transcendentalism often associated with *The Prelude* and "Tintern Abbey."

It is more difficult so show the spiritual *tertium quid* in "A slumber did my spirit seal" than in any of the other poems under consideration. This is because the poet seems to have moved decidedly from the dialectic of objective into the purely objective, an imaginative leap, as it were, into the ahuman world beyond the spiritual. The spirit, or outer limit of the human sensibility, is "sealed." "I had no human fears" is said in triumph, but this triumph logically includes the destruction of human joys as well as of fears. Not being able to "feel / the touch of earthly years" is a large price to pay for what seems to be a numb and naturalistic eternity, a victory over death and fear at the price of life itself. Here Wordsworth *is* very close to the Roman stoicism often ascribed to him. The spiritual elements of the human condition "motion . . . force . . . hears . . . sees" are negated by simple denial, and instead there is only the motion of naturalistic laws, shared with objects ("rocks, and stones and trees") presented as extremely unhuman, in contrast to their more usual appearance in Wordsworth as highly colored with the sentiments of human perception and expression. The touch of the ahuman here has the quiet and positive finality of Yeats' "lack of breath" and "discourtesy of death" in "Major Robert Gregory." In both poems the spiritual is present only in the physical, and the body has achieved its naturalistic apotheosis in its envelopment by the laws of a purely physical universe. The imaginative feat here, as in "Gregory," is the lack of any sense of loss of the spiritual or of the human. The spiritual has seemingly generated its opposite, yet it is important to remember that this naturalism is felt as a spiritual presence in the poet's and reader's imaginations, and is not the literal naturalism of scientific intellect or everyday empiricism. One need only recall that natural science proclaims that the body is worth only a dollar in chemicals, or know the mood of Yankee empirical folklore with its laconic sayings, "When you're dead you're dead," or "At sixty you can take me out and shoot me," to understand how far Wordsworth's mood differs from literal naturalism. A faint halo of spiritual religion and doctrine of πνεῦμα supports even this extension of the mood of naturalistic imagination in Wordsworth.

The clue to a possible non-naturalistic reading is in the first line, "A slumber did my spirit seal." Wordsworth is here making use, and a rather precise use at that, of the Calvinist doctrine of the "sealing of the Spirit," the "assurance state" of Calvinist dogmatics. In this state the believer has passed beyond the doubts inherent in the earlier states of purgation and justification to a firm belief in the authenticity of what he takes to be the word of God, perhaps some specific interpretation of a scriptural text, or more likely the general state of assurance itself. The relevant passages in Calvin for this doctrine are in the *Institutes*, Chapter VII.

But I reply, that the testimony of the Spirit is superior to all reason. For as God alone is a sufficient witness of himself in his own word, so also the word will never gain credit in the hearts of men, till it be confirmed by the internal testimony of the Spirit. .... Some good men are troubled that they are not always prepared with clear proof to oppose the impious. ... as though the Spirit were not therefore denominated a "seal," and "an earnest," for the confirmation of the faith of the pious. .... Only let it be known here, that that alone is true faith which the Spirit of God seals in our hearts .... Herein God deigns to confer a singular privilege on his elect; whom he distinguishes from the rest of mankind.[53]

Wordsworth's line "A slumber did my spirit seal" must of course be taken metaphorically. He is creating his own meaning out of the earlier dogmatic terms. Yet the term "spirit" as used by Wordsworth must be understood in its relation to the older meaning. If the connotations in "spirit seal" do not carry in Wordsworth's poem any precise religious context — and I think they do not — at least they suggest the religious or spiritual overtones of the community of the spirit or πνεῦμα which disallow a purely naturalistic reading. It is a better poem for this spiritual dimension, allowing the blending of the spiritual and the naturalistic characteristics of Wordsworth's best poetry. A purely scientific reading denudes the poem of this richness and allows merely a flat naturalistic assertion. Perhaps this knowledge of the precise meanings of the spiritual terms will help exert a counterforce to the standard naturalistic reading of the poem.

For our purposes, "The Solitary Reaper" and "Stepping Westward" can be considered together. Structurally, they are much better poems, and infinitely more suggestive in their symbolism, than the Lucy poems, but ideationally they create the same spiritual *tertium quid* found in all the Lucy poems except possibly "A slumber did my spirit seal." Thus they are at the center of Wordsworth's religious and imaginative world, which explains the constant yet fleeting critical attention they have always received.[54] It is my point to define this interest more exactly.

The spiritual qualities found in the Lucy poems — nature, solitariness, silence, melancholy, strangeness, the suggestion of infinity and of some mysteriously spiritual state — appear in these poems in a way that is at once restricted to a unique place and time, and yet also infinitely rich in symbolic suggestion. Each has a central human symbol set in a defined locale: one is a human voice in solitude ("Stepping Westward"), the other is that, and also a human solitary in nature ("The Solitary Reaper"). The woman by the lake and the lass in the field do not attain any high degree of personality and individuality, yet they are more specific and powerful than the two Lucys'. We are interested in the persons as well as in the more important suggestiveness which they evoke in the poet. Though the persons are real enough, there is also a level of relationship between the observer and the girl or woman, between girl/woman and nature, and nature and the observer, which becomes wider and more comprehensive as the poems progress. The dramatic incident in each poem is important but does not limit the meaning of the poem. In other words, we are not in the world of Browning's character portraiture. There is the singleness and solitude in the pictures of observer and subject, but the mingling of things human with aspects of the natural and the spiritual is the dominant theme in the poems. So much for what can be said about the poems collectively. Individually there are enough differences to justify separate consideration. "The Solitary Reaper" has always been the more popular poem, justly so in human interest and structural richness. "Stepping Westward" is the more central and suggestive, leading us into the very heart of Wordsworth's domain of the spirit.

"The Solitary Reaper" is in a general sense a nature poem, meaning no more than that it is set in nature. What little there is of nature scenery in the poem takes its hues from the central symbol, the Highland Lass, and does not contribute the "rebound" effect of "Tintern Abbey" and parts of *The Prelude*.[55] It is the girl who attracts and holds the poet's and the reader's attention. The movement of the poem, carried out entirely in terms of this central symbol, is from isolation to communication between girl and narrator, to a world community suggesting some permanent spiritual presence in the world. At first loneliness and isolated individuality are the mark of both the reaper and the narrator, as the opening lines stress:

> Behold her, *single* in the field
> Yon *solitary* Highland lass!
> Reaping and singing *by herself*. . . . (Italics mine)

"Alone" and "melancholy" add to this picture in the first stanza. Perhaps her singleness is most poignant because the girl is performing what is usually a community project, harvesting, in a rural and primitive society. But one gradually becomes aware that she is not as lonely as seems to be the case at first glance. Although solitary, the figure of the girl is set in nature in such a way as to create a feeling of affinity, first between girl and nature, then between observer, nature, and the girl. She is in motion, reaping, cutting, binding, bending, and blending in with the nature around her; and through her song she binds not only the grain, but also the efforts of man and nature. The song is clearly a social symbol. It provides a bond between the observer and the girl, adds piquancy and zest to loneliness and solitude. The song of the Highland Lass makes the vale more profound and exerts the same influence on the wayfarer, whose soul is influenced by the song to the same depths of profundity. Through the song she communicates friendliness and human companionship in a solitary yet healthy situation of solitude (as opposed to the mood of the song in Keats'

"Ode to a Nightingale").[56] The music fills the vale and also the observer's heart with the message of human sorrow in a way that bridges the gap of strangeness between them, a strangeness of location, nationality, and language. The lonely traveller in the Highlands is quite willing to accept the melancholy and mysterious strain in this music as inevitable in life:

> Some natural sorrow, loss, or pain,
> That has been, and may be again?

The indirect, half-surmised communication of the full burden of human misery becomes a healthy bond between man and man, and between man and nature. Present or past pain and anguish are of subordinate interest to the song existing in an eternal spiritual present seemingly without end. Celtic music, as well as being melancholy, has about it an endlessness (technically there is no ending in the sense of western music and most pieces break off abruptly and arbitrarily or fade out slowly and imperceptibly), an effect which here blends with the endless horizon of the sky suggested by the inclusion in the poem of the far-off lands of Arabia and the Hebrides. Indeed, in stanza two all sense of loneliness and individuality seem to break apart in the mention of the two birds, which, combined with the girl's song, tend to promote universal friendliness and community, even though in isolation, throughout the world. Critics have noticed this.[57] Perhaps it has not been noticed how loneliness and individuality finally fuse with an overpowering sense of life in the spiritual journey conveyed in the endless song of the three singers. The speaker, observing the young girl, suggests in the imagery of the first four lines of this stanza, taken metaphorically, that he is half-way through his day-journey in the world of light; there is a hint of darkness and weariness in the mention of the nightingale and in the lines:

> More welcome notes to *weary* bands
> Of *travellers* in some *shady haunt* (Italics mine)

but the journey is on the whole a joyful, daylight one. The hint of darkness in the first analogy is more than offset by the lines describing the cuckoo, which of course metaphorically relate to the girl's youth in the poet's perfect designing of the narrator/girl/nightingale/cuckoo analogy.

> A voice so thrilling ne'er was heard
> In spring-time from the Cuckoo-bird,

Breaking the silence of the seas
Among the farthest Hebrides.

The youthfulness in "thrilling," "spring-time," and "Cuckoo-bird" obviously suggest the girl, and I do not think it farfetched to point out that the young-old, girl-traveller relationship is further maintained in the implied contrast between age and storied suggestions in "among Arabian sands," and the youth and newness of the song "Breaking the silence of the seas" in the almost unknown western isles, the Hebrides. Yet all these contrasts are finely balanced and in a sense almost merge to become, as Coleridge would say, "reconciled opposites."

The final picture is of a spiritual communication between two solitary beings on the *via* of life in a nature of unlimited space and amidst a timeless present eternity. Human consciousness is not limited, a thing apart and *sui generis*, as in Keat's evening mood in the Ode. Rather, consciousness fuses with πνεῦμα or spirit. The traveler, the maiden singing, and the countryside itself enjoy and share in Lucy's ahuman naturalistic eternity, "Rolled round in earth's diurnal course," but they also enjoy the advantages of a spiritual dimension barely perceptible in "A slumber." A strong sense of something spiritual is preserved after the experience:

The music in my heart I bore,
Long after it was heard no more.

This characteristic touch, preservation by memory of the imaginative experience, is similar to its many appearances in *The Prelude*. The difference lies in the fact that whereas meditation in *The Prelude* and "Tintern Abbey" is usually a turning of the mind back on itself in a humanistic self-communication, here there is an abrupt movement from almost stark isolation of the original scene to the rather mysterious and spiritual conclusion.

"Stepping Westward" comes closest of all these poems in defining the mood of spiritual religion. The mood is defined both explicitly-

And seemed to give me *spiritual* right
To travel through that region bright

— and by metaphor and situation. The subject of the poem is merely a voice, soft and courteous, saying something, not, as in "Solitary Reaper," a fully realized person and song. The central symbol is a human voice in solitude. All else in the poem seems disembodied and purely spiritual, the "strange land," the guests of chance, the echoes of the voice. Both the here and now — the lonely traveller in a strange land — and the hereafter, the *wildish, heavenly* destiny are deliberately indefinite. The scene is less restricted than in "Solitary Reaper," and with greater force of allusion. The purpose of the scene is to lead outward, away from the purely human. Nature and the human do not exist in and for themselves. At first, nevertheless, the influence of the sky and the sound of the voice impart a human sweetness to the scene of solitude. "Are you stepping westward" was said in a soft voice, by one beside her native lake, and becomes a greeting which generates a thrill of belonging for the traveller. The echo of the voice brings some inner profundity of feeling as in "Solitary Reaper." The greeting is the poem's social symbol. Yet the main point of the poem is not social and human, as in "Solitary Reaper." In the poet's response to the greeting,

'Twould be a *wildish* destiny,

we find the major theme, which is spiritual and outward. There is in it the sense of opening dimensions of space, time and eternity:

I liked the greeting: 'twas a sound
Of something without place or bound.

Life is a *wildish* destiny, a *heavenly* destiny, in a land without the usual sense of place and permanence, and the greeting which unites traveller, woman, and nature suggests no type of finality, but rather

Of travelling through the world that lay
Before me in my endless way.

In other words, there is an infinite process, a movement, a sense of infinity itself. The spirit or πνεῦμα appears here in the images of death, as in Lucy poems, and there is the same illusive yet cheerful victory over death through the spirit. The spiritual image of the glowing sky and the expression "heavenly destiny" turn the journey into death to a journey into light. The land is dark behind and at the poet's feet:

The dewy ground was dark and cold;
Behind, all gloomy to behold . . .

but ahead is the "region bright," made more amenable by the sweetness of the woman's voice. Life and light lead to eternity, and here present and eternity are one in a spiritual state created by imagination. Wordsworth comes closest here to naming and defining the realm of the spiritual, his own and the heritage of the Puritans, in

And seemed to give me spiritual right
To travel through that region bright.

Thus far we have discussed the interlocking metaphors in the poem, which contribute, in the manner of musical motifs, to the sense of spiritual quest. Behind these images and the specific scene of the poem lie certain powerful commonplaces and evocations of the meanings of words which Wordsworth has, unintentionally I think, called upon. He is dealing with the archetypes earth, sea, sky, darkness, light, as parts of the greater archetype of the journey. In this way a slight poem is attached to greater ones, and to the subconscious images common to them all. Satan's journey from hell to heaven (i.e. darkness to light) in *Paradise Lost,* II—IV, is just the most obvious analogue. I am not interested at this point in delineating the full meaning of the dark journey,[58] but would like to call attention to the point that this hidden power in a short poem of this sort derives in part from this submerged system of allusion. Where 17th century and modern poets make specific learned allusions to poetic traditions, erudition, or history, Wordsworth, who despised that sort of practice, has another system of allusion operating in his favor. By evoking the archetypes common to *Paradise Lost, Pilgrim's Progress,* and numerous other poems in his own "natural" context, he gets both a psychological and literary power into the poem, the source of which is at first baffling.

Closer to the surface of meaning are the evocations in the words "westward," "wildish," and "heavenly," in connection with the Scottish Highland setting. As late as Wordsworth's day, the Highlands and the "road to the Isles" had a factual sense of remoteness and wildness for the civilized Englishman. Lake Katrine in the west of the lower Highlands is an approach to the western Scottish islands. Even further west were the "wild Irish" of Elizabethan memory and the absolute end of civilization and the sea. So we get the combination, wild people, wild country, land's end, the sea, and the end of the world, leading to heaven, the sky. It is important to remember that part of the special thrill in the greeting "Stepping Westward" and the reply "*wildish* destiny" stems from the situation, carefully noted by Wordsworth in the introduction to the poem, that the travellers exchanged this greeting with two well-dressed women of quality in one of the loneliest parts of the country. The imagination is set in motion by the contrast between civilized and uncivilized, known and remote. The Irish aspect of all this did not enter the English literary imagination until the end of the 19th century, and is evoked fully in the concluding passages in Joyce's "The Dead."

> The time had come for him to set out on his journey westward. Yes, the newspapers were right: snow was general all over Ireland. It was falling on every part of the dark central plain, on the treeless hills, falling softly upon the Bog of Allen and, farther westward, softly falling into the dark mutinous Shannon waves. . . .
> His soul swooned slowly as he heard the snow falling faintly through the universe and faintly falling, like the descent of their last end, upon all the living and the dead.

Here we have the darkness, the living and the dead, the mysticism of the west, in short, the elements invoked by Wordsworth. The spiritual realm, a mingling of the living and the dead, is at the center of both "The Dead" and "Stepping Westward." Wordsworth was the last writer to get this much *wildness* and sense of mystery out of the Scottish landscape, which had been worked over thoroughly in the 18th century, by Collins, Burns and others, and he was certainly one of the last, as I am trying to show in the larger context of this book, to evoke it out of the matrix of Protestant spirituality. Joyce, of course, worked the Catholic vein, still potent in the early 20th century in the English-speaking world, and the power of "West of Ireland," a dominant image in Irish Revival Literature, such as *Playboy of the Western World* and *Riders to the Sea.* The analogy between the two, so far as it goes, is a sound one.

The differences are crucial, too. In "The Dead," cold, silent snow, the graveyard scene and total darkness show that Joyce's dark journey into death is an inferno without sight of a paradise; his rejection of Catholicism had left him a hell if not a God and a heaven. *Ulysses* would later give a new humanistic vision. Wordsworth's landscape is dark behind and at his feet; but ahead is the region bright, the glowing sky at the end of the Puritan spiritual journey, shared with Spenser's pilgrim in *The Faerie Queene* and John Bunyan's in *Pilgrim's Progress.* Cleopolis, the new Jerusalem, and even Yeats' Byzantium are closer analogues to the meaning of Wordsworth's poem, yet in mood and language Joyce and Wordsworth reach depths of feeling the others do not.

There are numerous smaller effects in "Stepping Westward" which contribute to its depth and power, such as the easy complexity of the opening lines with their balance of the hypothetical and the actual, giving a sense of reality to both: "'Twould be ... If we ... were ... the guests of Chance." The travellers are *not* the guests of chance, lost rootless people, yet the poem depends upon this suggestion for its power and spirituality. The verbal ease and suggestiveness of possibilities reminds one of Yeats in his latest and most sophisticated manner, in "Deep Sworn Vow" and "Among School Children." But there is no need to enumerate all these smaller effects. "Stepping Westward" fully evokes the world of the spirit of the living and the dead. Later we will return to "Stepping Westward" to point out more general features of Wordsworth's religious sensibility.

The poems thus far discussed have revealed Wordsworth's interest in the presence of "the Spirit," whether in man or in the world. They show the more optimistic side of his religious sensibility, attuned in vital ways to his earlier philosophical and naturalistic optimism. There is also a darker side to the picture, appearing first in the poems "Nutting," "Peele Castle," and "Resolution and Independence." The darker side is less easily viewed as an aspect of the Calvinist temper than is the optimistic side, even though the symptoms are more obvious and closer to the pattern of other writers. The reasoning which accompanied this darker aspect of Wordsworth finally led him to Anglican orthodoxy and to the account of original sin which makes the existence of evil most understandable to man. In the poems to be discussed, all reasonably early in the canon, such clear-cut recognition and explicitness is not found. The darker religious language, where it appears, is used mainly as metaphor, distanced from dogma as literal truth. In any event, the darker side of Calvinism proved to be useful in a transition period for the expression of his less optimistic states of mind.

"Resolution and Independence" tells the story of despondency, and of despondency corrected. It has four moods of action. The poet first feels the spectre of despair haunting him, rises to ward it off, sinks deeper into despair, and finally is led into a cool and deliberate resolution by the presence of the leech-gatherer. There are various symbols and dramatic vehicles through which the action takes place. It is not our intention to give a full reading of the poem, only to show how the religious sensibility comes into play. The early turns of the poem, and some aspects of the poet's changed personality at the end, while important in the final unity of the poem, lie outside our scope. Our interest begins with the introduction of the leech-gatherer in stanza viii, which is given in deliberately religious language:

> Now, whether it were by peculiar grace,
> A leading from above, a something given . . .

Here there are two clearly Calvinist ideas in the notions of "peculiar grace," and something given" (irresistible grace). Milton used the former in its exact theological context in *Paradise Lost*, III, 183–84: "Some I have chosen of peculiar grace / Elect above the rest." Wordsworth's use is metaphorical and with the same overall purpose of defining a spiritual state, which in this poem is presented through the image of the leech-gatherer.

It will be impossible to present here the full structure and resolution of this complex poem, but I shall try to hint at the full resolution in relating the above lines to the meaning of the central image. The central image appears in the following stanzas:

> As a huge stone is sometimes seen to lie
> Couched on the bald top of an eminence;
> Wonder to all who do the same espy,
> By what means it could thither come, and whence;
> So that it seems a thing endued with sense:
> Like a sea-beast crawled forth, that on a shelf
> Of rock or sand reposeth, there to sun itself;
>
> Such seemed this Man, not all alive nor dead,
> Nor all asleep. . . . (ll. 57–65)

Wordsworth explained the structure of the image of the leech-gatherer in one of his few, justly famous excursions into literary criticism. The movement of perception is from stone (inanimate) to beast (lower animal) to man, but man "not all alive nor dead / Nor all asleep." On the human end of the perception man is emerging into, but not quite into, normal human life. On the "natural" end, the inanimate stone is the threshold to the invisible non-perceptible world, the spiritual dimension. The leech-gatherer blends imperceptibly with the seabeast and the stone, and hence shares in the non-human quality of the pre-physical world beyond the stone and beyond man's perceptions. In stanza xvi,

> The old Man still stood talking by my side;
> But now his voice to me was like a stream
> Scarce heard; nor word from word could I divide;
> And the whole body of the Man did seem
> Like one whom I had met with in a dream;
> Or like a man from some far region sent,
> To give me human strength, by apt admonishment.

"In a dream," "from some far region sent," suggest the "other" world, a world in which the appropriateness of the leech-gatherer's presence suggests the spirit of death as well as of life. It is this straining after another world, having some dim sense of community with our own, "To give me human strength, by apt admonishment," that explains the function and appropriateness of the Calvinist-Puritan language in the poem. "Peculiar grace / A leading from above, a something given" obviously suggests heaven, the other and better world, and also the infusion of power or influence of that world into the actual world. But the Puritan notion of grace also includes the aspects of mystery, irresistibility, and arbitrariness: one person is chosen, many are not. So, in the dramatic structure of the poem the narrator is finally moved by a force he cannot understand emanating from the spectral murmur of the leech-gatherer, a force never explained in the poem, yet made a bit more appropriate by use of this Puritan imagery. Even some of the terror and inscrutability of "peculiar grace" as usually described by 17th century Puritan writers is appropriate to the scene: the *accidental* meeting with the leech-gatherer, his human hideous demeanor and occupation, the unexpected firmness of his mind, and the sudden and inexplicable nature of the narrator's conversion to strength over his former weakness. All these elements are appropriate to the theory of "peculiar grace" described by Puritan theologians from Calvin to Edwards. Wordsworth is using the older theological doctrine metaphorically to set a mood and establish a tone for the acceptance of the "miracle" of his own vision. The residue of moral and metaphysical meaning in the theological terms helps him to do this, but unlike Coleridge, he was not interested in the theological meaning of the words for their own sake.

In contrast to "Resolution and Independence," "Nutting," "Peele Castle," and "Ode to Duty" deal with motivation of feelings and speculation about them. Consciousness of the problem at hand is closer to the surface of the poet's mind. There is not the mystery of unmotivated despair and unexpected recovery of assurance which animates "Resolution and Independence." "Nutting" overtly considers the sense of guilt in an Edenlike setting; "Peele Castle" the relationship of evil and God to appearance and reality; "Ode to Duty" an assertion of morality over aestheticism, occasioned by personal sorrow and an increase of moral awareness. The general theme of all three is the growth of moral awareness, as that of the other religious poems was the exploration of pure consciousness and feelings. These are ethical poems in a general sense and need not be attached to a particular religious spirit, in the absence of definite evidence for this awareness. No specific evidence, such as the play upon "peculiar grace" in "Resolution and Independence" appears in these poems; nor does the general sense of spirit or πνεῦμα which loomed throughout the poems concerning expanding consciousness, "Solitary Reaper," "Stepping Westward," and the Lucy poems. The Eden-fallen world analogy in "Nutting" is clearly a general mythic setting, with the widest possible application. So is the sense of *hubris* which precedes, and of guilt which follows, the spoiling of the trees. In "Ode to Duty" the analogy which comes most quickly to mind is not Christian ethics but Kant. In "Ode to Duty" the intended substitution of ethics for consciousness and imagination could easily be traced to a Kantian source. Yet even in the lack of specific textual evidence there is a militant spirit and mood in "Ode to Duty" which is foreign both to Kantian rationalism and Anglican orthodoxy. The sense of battle cry in the opening stanza would have found favor with many of the 16th century Puritans we have studied. It is this tone and the exclusive appeal to the will which give a slightly fanatical flavour of renunciation and acceptance to the poem:

> Thou, who art victory and law
> When empty terrors overawe;
> From vain temptations doest set free;
> And calm'st the weary strife of frail humanity!

How often, in similar but more specific religious contexts do some of these phrases, "victory and law," "empty terrors," "vain temptations," "weary strife of frail humanity," occur in Puritan literature! What the poet hopes to achieve through reverence to duty is an end common to much Puritan writing and striving of the spirit: assurance amidst humility. In Wordsworth, the Puritan desire for assurance of right conduct and salvation has momentarily been reduced to the former only: here is the rationalist and Kantian influence at work. But the emotional force of being both low and high, a legacy of the Puritans, is still there:

> Oh, let my weakness have an end!
> Give unto me, made lowly wise
> The spirit of self-sacrifice;
> The confidence of reason give. . . .

The weakness of unrealistic confidence in imagination and conscious-ness will be replaced by the strength and confidence of right reason — i.e. knowledge of and adherence to the moral laws. As in the Puritan road to salvation, self-sacrifice and abasement are the price of confidence and glory. One becomes "high" and "low" at the same time. The Miltonic echo in "made lowly wise" (*Paradise Lost*, VIII, 173, "be lowly wise") is appropriate both to the general religious spirit of acceptance and resignation in the poem, and to the more specific Puritan exaltation in this resignation, which Milton knew. Thus, without containing specific Puritan doctrine or even metaphoric usage of religious terms, "Ode to Duty" manages to convey a lingering sense of life in the Puritan tradition in the early 19th century. Wordsworth's poetry may seem to be an odd place to find it, and indeed it is fleeting in his work. Yet it appears in various ways in certain poems.

"Peele Castle" continues the moral education of the poet, but in ways that offer almost nothing of religious sensibility. The major contrast, again, is between the aesthetic-imaginative and the ethical-human, with the poet feeling he has been converted to the latter, "A deep distress hath humanized my Soul." The ethical here is no more than vague, general concern with the actions and problems of humanity, not the specific religious commands and certainties of "Ode to Duty." Were it not for the last stanza one could say that the poem moves toward the unrestricted modern-humanist view of Byron and Shelley, the doorstep to sentimentality and scepticism. But that stanza suggests, without the assertion of anything specific, the general Christian-Stoic viewpoint which has come to be characterized as Wordsworthian:

> But welcome fortitude, and patient cheer . . .
> Not without hope we suffer and we mourn.

The adverse criticism which must be made of this poem is not that it lacks a religious framework, or is sentimental, but rather its superficial distinction of the consciousness-imagination from the ethical-human. Wordsworth's greatest poetry, before and after "Peele Castle," belies such a distinction, and often manages, in certain poems we have called religious, to be all these things — poems of imagination, consciousness, ethics, and humanity at the one time and in the one experience.

To view Wordsworth's poetry as religious may at first seem impertinent, and in some senses obvious, and finally as mysterious and unsatisfactory as any other particularist view. The strength in the view is that it relieves the poetry of a false distinction, prominent both in "Ode to Duty" and "Peele Castle," that the ethical-religious and imaginative-human are somehow mutual opposites. Wordsworth's best poetry belies that view. But the question is complicated by the presence in the Wordsworth canon of purely aesthetic and descriptive poems (most but not all early and some very good), and of poems devoted to moralizing divorced from the usual centers of Wordsworth's strength. These poems have usually been considered as the "religious poems" of Wordsworth and have not been looked upon with critical favor. The greatest example here, of course, is *The Excursion*, which mixes personal aesthetic experience, powerful moralizing on man's ethical life, and general social doctrine. With so vast a poem and so complex an issue this study cannot presume to deal fully although it is hoped that some matters raised here will be helpful in reading *The Excursion*. For our purposes there must be a distinction between the religious and the moralizing poems, just as there is between most of the early poems in the *Lyrical Ballads* and the religious poems. A primary religious context for some poems will presumably not be denied except by the most enthusiastic of "myth" and "visionary" critics.

It is when one turns from such general religious contexts, as in the poems above, to define something more specific that a serious problem arises. The readings given above are exploratory, and must of course carry themselves if they are to have any value. Yet even such tentative explorations raise uneasy questions about what actually is going on in Wordsworth's religious poetry. What can one say of Wordsworth's intention in his deliberate or unconscious evoking of religious associations? If we conclude that these evocations are largely unconscious, what does this lead us to think about Wordsworth as a religious poet?

At the beginning of this chapter it was acknowledged that heretofore the central tradition of religious poetry in English has been seen to run from Donne to Eliot, and to be predominantly "metaphysical" in structure and Anglo-Catholic in content. The prominence of this tradition in literary study today is partly responsible for the critical obscurity surrounding the religious poetry of Wordsworth (and others). The critical tools useful in dealing with Donne or Herbert are largely useless for Wordsworth or the Calvinist poets. A comparison of the poem discussed above, "Stepping Westward," and Donne's "Hymn to God my God, in my Sickness," on the same subject, may help in defining certain differences in religious style and in clarifying the tradition to which Wordsworth belongs.

Stanza three of Donne's "Hymn to God my God" expresses the central theme of "Stepping Westward," in ideas and images that are witty, intellectual, and, in comparison to Wordsworth's, explicit.

> I joy, that in these straits, I see my West;
> For, though their current yield return to none,
> What shall my west hurt me? As West and East
> In all flat maps (and I am one) are one,
> So death doth touch the resurrection.

The use of the East as a symbol for the resurrection and for heaven was traditional in Christian literature, as in the Vulgate's translation of Zechariah 6.12: *Ecce vir, Oriens nomen eius* ("Behold the man, the East is his name"). The West, then, signified the end of life's journey and death. Donne's symbolism more or less states that West (death) merges into East (heaven and resurrection) just as the seeming opposites West and East on flat maps are one on a globe, or, as he says in his sermon on Psalm 6.8−10: "In a flat Map, there goes no more, to make West East, though they be distant in an extremity, but to paste that flat Map upon a round body, and then West and East are all one." We have said that in Wordsworth's "Stepping Westward" the journey into death becomes the journey into light, the heavenly destiny, through the implied contrasts in the imagery alone. The dark land at the poet's feet and the westward direction imply traditional notions of death in a tenuous way; but superimposed, as it were, not juxtaposed, as in Donne, is the image of the glowing sky with its stated meaning of a wildish heavenly destiny. Donne's method and ·Wordsworth's illuminate each other mainly through contrast, yet both writers are in these poems religious poets. Wordsworth fuses more images and middle terms than does the intellectual 17th century poet; religiously speaking, he is the inheritor of the doctrine of the Holy Spirit or πνεῦμα in Christian tradition, while Donne, as Roman Catholic become Anglican, thinks with the central tradition of the Word, Christus, and the human analogy. Donne's tradition has been widely heralded and explicated by recent criticism; Wordsworth's is still largely uncharted ground, partially on account of disinterest in Puritan-Calvinist thought by literary critics, and more so on account of special difficulties in Wordsworth himself, usually called "obscurities." His use of the Puritan spirituality and of religious archetypes, usually several degrees removed from their original or dogmatic appearance in literature and theology, makes it difficult for the critic to call any specific poem or pattern religious. Let us leave for a note an exploration of further possibilities in the journey-westward-eastward image, involving Hilton and Vaughan with "Stepping Westward,"[59] and turn to examples of the religious journey image in Wordsworth's greatest poem, *The Prelude* of 1850.

As this is Wordsworth's most complicated poem, our task will be likewise complex. If patterns as widely separated as Hilton's and Vaughan's are proper parallels for the religious archetype of "Stepping Westward," one can imagine the difficulty of relating the personal-psychological structure of *The Prelude* to the archetypal religious ideas mentioned above. First, something must be said about the structure of *The Prelude* itself, about which so much has been written, not often in agreement.

The narrator in *The Prelude* passes through various stages of self-awareness, or mystical perception, to gain some final view of reality. The first stage is immediate perception of nature (Books I−II), the second of a religious element in nature (III−IV), and the others the stages of imagination, understanding, and finally higher reason. As stages in a personal mystical way we can say that Wordsworth's first stage is pure aesthetic experience of the natural man, the second (religious perception in nature) an awakening or initiation to the personal religion of the mystical life. Wordsworth's recognition of imagination (Bk. VI, Simplon Pass) is a stage of contemplation, a term he uses throughout *The Prelude*, usually carelessly and meaning only meditation of a general sort. Real contemplation begins in Book VI. The fall in Books IX−XI from imagination to understanding, the faculty called by Coleridge and Wordsworth the state of limitation and death, is the first dark night of the mystics, the milder one described so well by Hilton. The final assertion in Books XII-XIV of the restoration of imagination and the vision of the "ontological Other" corresponds by analogy to the state of illumination in mysticism. The stages of mysticism called "dark night" and "union," which appear most often in Catholic practice, have no real correspondence in Wordsworth, though critics have occasionally used these terms carelessly in reference to Wordsworth and Coleridge. Obviously it is well to bear in mind that all these stages are merely convenient analogies for Wordsworth's entirely personal experience. Yet it is clear that the direction of Wordsworth's experience is mystical, although he has experiences that are not mystical and lacks some that are; there is the intention of some sort of communion with forces beyond the natural and psychological, and therefore classical Christian mysticism can be of help in understanding his experience. One may even be tempted by his frequent use of the words "contemplation," "illumination," "prayer," etc., to call his experience classical mysticism, yet there are very few lines in *The Prelude* which allow us to take Wordsworth's use and awareness of the tradition as more than analogy or metaphor.

There are several lines in *The Prelude*, however, which do tempt the critic to stronger language than analogy in dealing with the relationship, as in I, 409—12:

But with high objects, with enduring things —
With life and nature — purifying thus
The elements of feeling and of thought
And sanctifying, by such discipline. . . .

Here it is not the obvious words "purifying," "sanctifying" which alert the reader, as such analogies with Christian devotion and the way of holiness would be obviously available to any poet as metaphor, and are quite commonly though somewhat awkwardly used by Romantic poets. But in saying "purifying thus / The elements of feeling and of thought" Wordsworth echoes a point of all classical mystics, and in a form which appealed to the looser variety of medieval mystics, especially English and German, and to 17th century Protestant mystics such as Böehme and, later, Law. This form of mysticism emphasizes the reform of feeling as primary in the initiation of the whole man into the mystic way. Intellect is important, but follows in course if feeling is reformed. The mystics of the post-Reformation Spanish school emphasize more strongly the intellect and stages of intellect.

Even this remarkably close parallel to the mystical tradition must be viewed with caution in assessing Wordsworth's relationship to specific sources. It has always been easy — too easy — to point out analogies between Wordsworth and other writers. Just as Hartley, Schelling and Coleridge have been mentioned frequently in the past, we could now cite Hilton, Vaughan, Böehme, the Cambridge Platonists, Law and Coleridge as analogues for Wordsworth's religious patterns. The connection between Böehme and Schelling, and relationships among some of the others, could bring the philosophical and religious traditions together. If one were forced to choose the dominant pattern of analogy in Wordsworth this writer would hold that the Puritan-mystical strain in Protestantism prevails over others. Perhaps at this point proving its importance is service enough. What can finally be said is that Wordsworth's personal meditations and certain religious patterns of a definite tradition come close together in certain passages of *The Prelude*.

The two final examples of religious pattern in *The Prelude* to be used here are actually specific symbols of more limited reference than the general patterns mentioned above. One is the emblem of the blind beggar (Bk. VII, London), the other the gibbet and old stone wall appearing in Book XII. Both symbols are called by the narrator mysterious portents from God and the unknown world. But it is not entirely obvious in the contexts how they function in the poem at large.

To do so we shall call upon David Ferry's distinction in *Limits of Mortality* between surface action and the inner drama of *The Prelude*.[60] Put briefly, Ferry believes that *The Prelude* is not drama in the accepted sense because of the distance between the two levels in the poem, and in the primary importance in the poem of the secondary or personal level over that of worldly action and scene. He makes apt illustrations from Book VII, on London. Accepting his distinction, we can say that events such as the Simplon Pass episode, the Mt. Snowdon scene, the appearance of the beggar, the gibbet and stone wall, which all relate to the inner drama or personal story, are more important in the poem than those which color or fill in the external scene. They are portents which appear as a series of events that are not fully explained by cause-effect relationship. No doubt this is the case because Wordsworth felt his life to be mysterious while he was living out the patterns which led to the writing of *The Prelude*. In the published versions of the poem the life is somewhat less mysterious to the extent that he has assigned terms for his experience drawn from a wide variety of sources. Understanding, imagination, reason and fancy are the most famous of these. Also, he has sketched in a series of settings – the Lake Country, Cambridge, London, France – which give some sense of unity and actuality to his experience. Ferry has put his finger on the deceptive quality of this dramatic reality. If Ferry is correct, then the symbols or portents we are discussing must have appeared more mysterious and providential in actuality than the descriptions in the poem would have us believe. Wordsworth familiarizes and humanizes these portents by calling them "spots of time." It may seem far-fetched if we ascribe the sense of providence and mystery in these appearances to a Puritan pattern of thought in Wordsworth's sensibility, but the evidence, like that for "Resolution and Independence," seems very strong. The muted echoes of Puritan thought bespeak themselves once they are pointed out:

> I was *smitten*
> *Abruptly*, with the view (a sight not rare)
> Of a blind Beggar, who, with *upright face*,
> Stood, propped against a wall, upon his chest
> Wearing a written paper, to explain
> His story, whence he came, and who he was.
> Caught by the *spectacle* my mind turned round
> As with the might of waters; an apt type
> This label seemed of the utmost we can know
> Both of ourselves and of the universe;
> And, on the shape of that *unmoving man*,
> His *steadfast* face and sightless eyes, I gazed,
> As if *admonished* from another world.
>
> (VII, 637–49; italics mine)

Any one, or even a couple, of these words would not carry much weight in defining a religious pattern. It is the cumulative effect of them all together in this passage which gives force to the Calvinist-Puritan overtones here of the idea of special providence. It is hard to believe Wordsworth is being deliberate here; rather, it is his characteristic unconscious appropriation of terms and moods of a buried English religious tradition that is going on.

In Book XII there are two episodes called "spots of time." The first, the incident of the gibbet, we will pass over, except to note the same quality of familiarity and mysteriousness, the sense of its having an unknown source, with which Wordsworth invests it:

> It was, in truth,
> An *ordinary sight*; but I should need
> Colours and words that are *unknown to man*,
> To paint the visionary *dreariness*
> Which, while I looked all round for my lost guide,
> Invested moorland waste and naked pool,
> The beacon crowning the *lone eminence*,
> The female and her garments *vexed and tossed*
> By the strong wind.
>
> (XII, 253–61; italics mine)

The second symbol is more complex, containing elements of hubris and despair, a specific sense of providence, and an appropriate, clearly etched pattern. The situation is that of "Resolution and Independence," with the initial structure reversed. The scene here begins in anxiety and hope, not motiveless despair. The outside force is not the elevating leech-gatherer, but rather the sudden death of his own father. Yet the inner pattern is the same in both instances. A false pattern, because superficial (despair, hope), is mysteriously struck down by a Presence, the old Man, or, as here:

> The event,
> With all the sorrow that it brought, appeared
> A chastisement, and when I called to mind . . .
> Yet in the *deepest passion* I bowed down
> To *God*, Who thus *corrected my desires.*

(XII, 309−16; italics mine)

This mysterious force, which has overtones of the Calvinist ideas of election and irresistible grace, creates a deeper pattern. In "Resolution and Independence" it was of hope amidst despair and poverty; here of a deeper courage that follows on superficial hope and callow despair:

> And afterwards, the wind and sleety rain,
> And all the business of the elements,
> The single sheep, and the one *blasted tree*
> And the *bleak music* from that old stone wall . . .
> All these were *kindred spectacles* and sounds
> To which I oft repaired, and thence would drink
> As at a fountain . . .

(XII, 317−26; italics mine)

This is Wordsworth's own version of the search for signs of divine providence and of grace and election in the Puritan tradition, displaced partially into secularity.[61]

A very selective look at some of the Puritan religious patterns which appear in *The Excursion* will close this chapter. The most explicitly religious poems, religious even to the point of partly justifying John Jones' view of the later poetry as the "baptized imagination," poems such as *The White Doe of Rylstone,* are not our concern.[62] *The Excursion* and some short later poems, wherein are found Puritan patterns and other matters of the spirit prominent in Calvinist tradition, might be called the "middle ground" of

Wordsworth's career, and so an appropriate place to end a selective study of Wordsworth's poetry from our perspective.

This is not to suggest a note of triumph in termination in what follows. Like all other approaches to *The Excursion* and Wordsworth's later poetry, the present study must admit the general disappointment that all have felt with this poetry, particularly *The Excursion*, which promised so much.[63] This overall comment can be phrased in a general way: the advance which *The Excursion* promises over *The Prelude* as the long awaited philosophical poem of the age is not achieved, whether in terms of philosophical exposition, style, imagination, or dramatic presentation. Many critics have taken up this strange phenomenon from various angles, and this study will only add another interpretation to the list. *The Excursion* does not fulfill the explicit philosophy promised by Coleridge and Wordsworth, or by the stirring introduction, and what might have been a grand philosophical work in the tradition of *Paradise Lost, The Brothers Karamazov,* and *The Magic Mountain*; it is instead a strangely muffled philosophical work. True, there is dialectic, as all sympathizers with the poem have pointed out, with an extra nod for Wordsworth's stubbornness and courage in not resolving the critical issues between the Wanderer and the Solitary. But no critic, however sympathetic, has successfully countered the simple and obvious point made by the earliest adversaries, that the Solitary and Wanderer are two versions of the earlier Wordsworth, in indirect discourse as it were, which readers were able to find after 1850 in more directly satisfactory forms in *The Prelude*. There is no progression in the religious perspective either, beyond the Puritan patterns, the state of illumination, and the mysterious "signs" of election or regeneration we have noted in *The Prelude*. There are very interesting examples of all these phenomena, to be sure, one of the few reasons no doubt why the poem is not a total loss, so it is of limited interest to observe some of them. It is of greater interest to decide, from this angle of vision, why *The Excursion* does not advance beyond the earlier religious poetry, and also why it does not take a drastic step into another kind of religious writing. This is an important point, because, in fact, it can be argued, despite the efforts of Jones in *The Egotistical Sublime*, that there is always something odd and hesitant about any religious poetry in Wordsworth, even in *The White Doe* and the "Vernal Ode," written during formal Anglican influence, of which Jones made so much. Our argument is that Wordsworth reached his own version of the stage of illumination in the *via mystica* under the strong influence of Puritan patterns and traditions, and did not need a serious "dark night" or union, such was the limiting influence of Puritan traditions. Anglican orthodoxy must come to him easily and, above all, naturally, without the embarrassing struggle in Donne, Crashaw, or later in Hopkins and Eliot, in other words essentially in natural rather than in supernatural forms and sensibility. *The Excursion* is a plateau, a goal achieved from which the poet looks back and takes account of the past, not a new and interesting pattern of the journey developed in *The Prelude*. There are clarifications, in relation to *The Prelude*, and we rejoice that the removing of obscurities supports our thesis; but the rejoicing would have been greater if the poet had really broken new ground. If he had done that, however, many other critics would have anticipated this commentary, and the need now to discuss Wordsworth as a major religious poet would not exist, as it does not about Donne, Crashaw and the others of Anglican-Catholic traditions.

The Wanderer is a dramatic characterization of the successful pilgrim of *The Prelude*. His life has been illuminated by his *via* in nature and by the nuances of the Puritan religious quest for redemption and regeneration. He is even a lowland Scottish peasant, a type much admired by Wordsworth in poetry and in life. The Solitary is the sceptical and unregenerate version of the pilgrim of Books IX–XI of *The Prelude*. The dialogues – and dialectic if one may call it that – of *The Excursion*, Books III–IV, reflect the imaginative, intellectual and spiritual progress of *The Prelude*, and also, with rather devastating effect upon the poetry, the new note of moralism introduced in "Ode to Duty," "Peele Castle" and the preachier poems written between 1807 and 1814. Though the dramatic structure gives the Wanderer the final word, the debate is a stand-off in rational content. The Wanderer's affirmative appeals to experience, nature, imagination and the spiritual or "finer tones" of things do not move the Solitary to the expected μετανοια or change of inner being. Something further is needed to remove this impasse and that, presumably, is what the poet thought he was providing in the character of the Pastor.

By the time of the writing of *The Excursion* Wordsworth had developed a clearer view of the function of poetry than he had held in the 1798–1805 period and in the Preface to *Lyrical Ballads*, and though never the scholar Coleridge was becoming at that time, he managed to articulate his view of the spiritual as it relates to poetry quite adequately in the "Essay, Supplementary to the Preface," printed in 1815. We may take this as one major presentation of the purpose of *The Excursion*, granting that the most explicit presentation is in the splendid introduction itself, the "Home at Grasmere" fragment. If "Home at Grasmere" gives the explicit philosophical intention, this passage from the "Essay" states the importance of the religious theme:

Faith was given to man that his affections, detached from the treasures of time, might be inclined to settle upon those of eternity; − the elevation of his nature, which this habit produces on earth, being to him a presumptive evidence of a future state of existence; and giving him a title to partake of its holiness. The religious man values what he sees chiefly as an "imperfect shadowing forth" of what he is incapable of seeing. The concerns of religion refer to indefinite objects, and are too weighty for the mind to support them without relieving itself by resting a great part of the burthen upon words and symbols. The commerce between Man and his Maker cannot be carried on but by a process where much is represented in little, and the Infinite Being accomodates himself to a finite capacity. In all this may be perceived the affinity between religion and poetry; between religion − making up the deficiencies of reason by faith; and poetry − passionate for the instruction of reason; between religion − whose element is infinitude, and whose ultimate trust is the supreme of things, submitting herself to circumscription, and reconciled to substitutions; and poetry − ethereal and transcendent, yet incapable to sustain her existence without sensuous incarnation.[64]

Symbol as the common element of religion and poetry is also argued in this fashion, expressed more abstractly in many writings of Coleridge, and this was no doubt a major aim for *The Excursion*, given Coleridge's constant urgings on the subject of a major philosophical poem. And even though it lacks Coleridge's metaphysical formalities, we note a directness and surface clarity in the "Essay" of 1815 that is missing from the earlier prose of Wordsworth. Clearly in the introduction of the Pastor we are led to expect a character who will unite with the Wanderer in illuminating the affinity of the spiritual and the imaginative, with enough power and confidence to convey this version of renovation and regeneration to the Solitary.

In the Pastor's earliest appearances in Book V we are not disappointed. Referring to his churchyard flock, he views their mysterious presence in death as a symbol uniting the powers of the cross and of imagination:

To a mysteriously-united pair
This place is consecrate; to Death and Life,
And to the best affections that proceed

From their conjunction; consecrate to faith
In him who bled for man upon the cross;
Hallowed to revelation; and no less
To reason's mandates; and the hopes divine
Of pure imagination. . . .[65]

The fact that this is a dramatic presentation by the Pastor does not lessen the significance of the first serious use in Wordsworth's poetry of this central Christian symbol in an unambiguous context, unlike the sky allusions to such explicit symbols restricted within Catholic culture and tradition in *The Prelude* and other early poems. Here faith, the affections, Christ, the cross, revelation, reason, and pure imagination, as if in obedience to Coleridge's fondest wishes, are asserted as cotemporaneously present in the graveyard, which is the fundamental image of the spiritual presence of the living and the dead. The stage is made ready for spiritual poetry of the greatest and most profound sort. Do we find this in Books VI and VII in the Pastor's soliloquies? Despite this writer's aversion to the tone of Geoffrey Hartman's scoffing treatment of *The Excursion* in *Wordsworth's Poetry*,[66] his humorous notion of the conjuring of the dead from a mass grave and droll allusions to *The Magic Mountain* and Walpurgisnacht are not out of place in criticism. These books are an enormous anecdote, occasionally interspersed with, if not relieved by, preachy sentiments of the Wanderer. When it ends, the Wanderer has the opportunity to preach for two final books, now adding some facets of the social gospel to his earlier views on nature and the spiritual. The Solitary is not separated from his scepticism, nor are readers convinced that they have seen the imaginative and the spiritual at work together in the coterminous symbol promised by the "Essay" and by the opening remarks of the Pastor. For this reason the religious explicitness of *The Excursion* does not advance the movement of the spiritual in Wordsworth's imaginative pilgrimage beyond the stage of *The Prelude*, astonishing as that may seem at first glance.

It has been the ambition of every critic of *The Excursion* to point out the reasons for its failure after the great promise of the Introduction and the opening book. From the viewpoint of this study this can be done rather succinctly, and, perhaps more accurately than ever before. In Book V, "The Pastor," the narrator speaks of renovation, the Wordsworthian term for regeneration of the inner spiritual life, referring to the previous discourses of the Wanderer of Books I and IV:

This, in the lonely dell discoursing, you
Declared at large; and by what exercise
From visible nature, or the inner self
Power may be trained, and renovation brought
To those who need the gift.[67]

The Wanderer's renovation comes through communion with nature and is presented in the early Wordsworthian deistic and pantheistic terms, without any advance into specifically religious and Christian ideas and discourse. It is the Pastor, as we have noted, who introduces Christian symbols and what might still be called the time-honored ethical beliefs of a slightly stoical version of Christian civilization. But in the Pastor himself we see nothing of renovation or inner renewal. He is presented to us as of aristocratic origin, somewhat learned, and firm of faith and piety. Through the symbol of the chapel he is associated with the history of the Church and the state in England. What he has to offer, the Wanderer to some extent, and the Solitary completely, lack, but he shows little sign of the inner struggle of the one or the spiritual growth of the other. Here is the fatal flaw of *The Excursion* as a unified and successful poem: a failure to bring together the meaning of the Wanderer, the Solitary and the Pastor. If *The Excursion* is viewed as a part of something bigger and more complete, there is no problem. But since that final epic never came into being, the problem of failed expectation for *The Excursion* itself remains. There is much in the character and the symbol of the Pastor which reveals the poet's desire to leap beyond his dialectic and organized intellectual growth to the historical and other certainties of Anglican orthodoxy. In a way more fundamentally profound than in Scott's popular images or even Coleridge's intellectual abstractions, Wordsworth's deepest current of feeling in *The Excursion* is aiding the demise of the Calvinist-Puritan spirit and the birth of the Oxford and other orthodox movements, though he never was in the forefront of them or deeply moved by them. For an example of how the intellectual, nature-mystical, and religious imagination could be brought together in the kind of character we must assume Wordsworth was trying to create in *The Excursion*, we need only turn back a few years to the American Puritan Jonathan Edwards, who has been alluded to briefly in the preceding section. Edward's account of his own conversion[68] contains some language startlingly similar to that in Wordsworth's early poetry, and the unity of his experience was what I submit, Wordsworth was striving for unsuccessfully in *The Excursion* in his three main characters.

In Edward's account, the sense of the power of nature, religious depth, and renewal or renovation are deeply one. Only the language that is very close to Wordsworth in Edwards' remarkable little treatise will be mentioned here. Nature is always close to the sensible manifestations of God and Christ:

I was much affected by the discourse we had together; and when it was ended, I walked abroad alone, in a solitary place in my father's pasture, for contemplation. And as I was waking there, and looking up on the sky and clouds, there came into my mind a sweet sense of the glorious *majesty* and *grace* of God. . . .

My mind was greatly fixed on divine things; I was almost perpetually in the contemplation of them. I spent most of my time in thinking of divine things year after year; often walking alone in the woods and solitary places, for meditation, soliloquy, and prayer, and converse with God. . . .

Prayer seemed to be natural to me, as the breath by which the inward burnings of my heart had vent. The delights which I now felt in the things of religion, were of an exceedingly different kind from those before mentioned, that I had when a boy, and what I then had no more notion of than one born blind has of pleasant and beautiful colors. They were of a more inward, pure, soul-animating, and refreshing nature.

On January 12, 1723, I made a solemn dedication of myself to God, and wrote it down; giving up myself and all that I had, to God. . . .[69]

The parallels here with passages in "Tintern Abbey" and *The Prelude* are very strong, and there are many others of the "heart leaps up" and nature visionary variety. In Edward's account, all these moods are integrated by religious belief and the Calvinist account of the way of salvation, leading to the moment of final "awakening," the Puritan equivalent of the inner renovation described at such length by the Wanderer. Of course we do not "explain" Wordsworth or Edwards by this analogy, but it is clear that some of Wordsworth's obscurity and incompleteness in *The Excursion* stems from the failure of the nature and religious mystical experiences in the poem to become one imaginative experience. The reason for this obviously lies in Wordsworth's own experience, where the Calvinist-Puritan urges were muted and in a purely intellectual sense perhaps partly unrecognized. But they account for at least a part of the power of Wordsworth's mysterious moments and looking for "signs" of election in the events and objects of nature.

Despite all the weaknesses and vacillations of viewpoint towards religious things on the part of the various characters and the narrator, *The Excursion* nevertheless does end with at least a surface of religious assertion, this given in diction and images strongly Puritan and deliberately evocative of similar ones in the final books of *Paradise Lost*. It would be unwise to claim more for them than for manifestations of the "rhetoric of the spirit" in the lyrics discussed earlier in this chapter. But at least as much can be claimed, that is, Wordsworth's special sense of the "spirit" and the "spiritual," and of the poet and other special beings as "elect" in some way:

> and as a power
> Is salutary, or an influence sweet,
> Are each and all enabled to perceive
> That power, that influence, by impartial law.
> Gifts nobler are vouchsafed alike to all;
> Reason, and, with that reason, smiles and tears;
> Imagination, freedom in the will;
> Conscience to guide and check; and death to be
> Foretasted, immortality conceived
> By all, − a blissful immortality,
> To them whose holiness on earth shall make
> The Spirit capable of heaven, assured.   (IX, 217−28)

In the final statement of his vision, the Wanderer, surrogate for the poet, remains true to the element of his Puritan heritage which he gradually discovered was a legitimate way to make a bridge between early nature-mysticism and later orthodox Christianity. Spiritual calling and spiritual election appear in partly displaced ways, and make the final statements of the Wanderer a stronger force than is his otherwise mere indirect discourse taken from the more vigorous *Prelude*. Although the poem does not end with the following comment of the Pastor, it might well have been stronger if it had, for what follows after are the long, vague repetitions and codas we are resigned to expect from Wordsworth. The connection between this passage and the points made previously in this chapter will be obvious, and our discussion of *The Excursion* may conclude with it:

> Such as they are who in thy presence stand
> Unsullied, incorruptible, and drink
> Imperishable majesty streamed forth
> From thy empyreal throne, *the elect* of earth
> Shall be − divested at the appointed hour
> Of all dishonor, *cleansed* from *mortal stain*.

> — Accomplish, then, their number; and *conclude*
> *Time's weary course!*   (IX, 628–35)

It will not be necessary to look at any of the other lesser and shorter poems of Wordsworth's later career. Most are of inferior artistic quality and some have been overemphasized in assessing Wordsworth's mind. There is an obvious danger in weighing too heavily a writer's lesser poetry, and in the case of the prolific Wordsworth, this danger is extreme. Jones and Hartman have called attention to the Anglicanism and conservatism of the poet's later years, and with such views there can be no quarrel. The strain we have been following is played out after *The Excursion* and the *Ecclesiastical Sonnets* of the middle years, which were discussed at the beginning of this chapter to introduce the theme of Puritan imagination in Wordsworth's poetry.

The task now is to assess the value and meaning of this varied evidence and the specific readings offered. In this book we are trying to establish a line of metaphor in a religious tradition ranging from the most precise usage (Calvin and the Puritans) to the most free (18th century and Romantic writers) with the gradations falling between. The Puritans, Spenser, Bunyan, Milton, and others have been cited as parallels from time to time with Wordsworth; legitimately, we hope, as part of the same tradition. Some analogies of contrast, Eliot and Joyce, have also appeared in partial clarification and justification of points. Wordsworth belongs, in certain of his moods and poems, to the religious tradition we are defining, albeit in a more tenuous way than Coleridge, Cowper, or Dickinson. Yet we have admitted that certain poems — "Tintern Abbey," the "Intimations" ode, and others — are best described in the older scientific-philosophical-naturalistic language of most Wordsworthian criticism, or in the newer language of general religious myth.[70] Where Wordsworth is expressing the workings of his own mind or his relationship to external nature these are satisfactory explanations. Where he attempts something more archetypal and profound, they are not. The difference can be seen in comparing the pleasant descriptive poem, "To a Highland Girl," which is specific and limited in reference and interest, to "Stepping Westward" and "The Solitary Reaper." For the latter poems and others like them I have tried to point out how Wordsworth falls back implicitly upon an earlier metaphysical view of spirit, the Puritan interpretation of the Christian doctrine of the Trinity, in which the

Holy Spirit or πνεῦμα supplies the ground for the relationship between any two persons in the spiritual community of saints, and also the ground of the human personality itself. This idea of community has earlier precedent in the "I-Thou" language of the Bible, referring both to the relationship of self and God, and to the relations among selves, which has been popularized by Martin Buber in our own century. The Puritans were, of course, even as followers of Trinitarian Christian theology, the most direct inheritors among all the Christian groups of the self-God relationship of the ancient Hebrews. In Trinitarian terms, this relationship deemphasizes the role of the Mediator and stresses that of the Holy Spirit, sometimes to the point of heresy. Wordsworth's use of this idea of community is not explicit or dogmatic, but rather part of a residual Protestant heritage in the Low Church Anglicanism of his own day. The historical passage of 17th century Puritanism into the Low Church Anglicanism of Wordsworth's day is well documented in the history of English religion. A more precise and difficult biographical question is the exact sources of this influence as we find it in Wordsworth. Is it the imbibing of the low Anglican tradition in youth or the product of his own reading? We have voluminous evidence for Coleridge's reading of 17th century Protestant and Anglican literature, but this writer has never been impressed with the numerous source arguments that attribute knowledge of specific items or writings to Wordsworth simply on the grounds that Coleridge read them and informed Wordsworth. In the absence of specific evidence which may be made available by future research, the answer seems to be that the low Anglican–Puritan source of Wordsworth's inspiration is a part of a residual metaphorical heritage which he could call upon in need, to create new and unique spiritual meanings of his own.[71]

Standing back from the idea of a Puritan religious tradition for a moment, it may be that Clay Hunt's final words in his fine book, *John Donne,* apply with changed emphasis to Wordsworth and all great religious poets. When the context is duly restricted to a specific intellectual tradition and time, what Hunt can say about Donne has little relevance for Wordsworth:

And their paradoxical character [of religious ideas] served merely to dramatize, to a medievalized imagination, the incomprehensible mystery of the Wisdom at the heart of things and of the Word which was made flesh, the mystery of a fixed order behind the ceaseless flux of phenomena, of eternity in change, corruption which put on incorruption, and mortal things which could put on immortality.[72]

Wordsworth had little explicit use for paradoxical character, the medieval imagination, even for the Word made flesh. But for the mystery of a fixed order behind the ceaseless flux, and for the Wisdom at the heart of things, he felt a deeper pull. So when Hunt goes on to draw general conclusions about the religious poetical sensibility, they apply with equal force to Donne and to Wordsworth.

But it is not factual, scientific truth which a man contemplates as he stands on the shores of Time and Space and looks out into the opening mysteries of the vast Ocean which is God. These analogies are at least symbolically true, and that truth is now of greater moment: they are traditional imaginative patterns which men have contemplated throughout the ages as they have let their imaginations play, with wonder and delight, over the intricate system of "correspondence" in which was made manifest the great fact of Design in the Nature of Things.[73]

The correspondences and the design were less clear and traditional for Wordsworth and the 19th century than for Donne in the 17th, but still exerted hidden force. The Calvinist-Puritan pattern is one set of religious symbols within the great tradition of western Christianity, the set which had most natural appeal to a man like Wordsworth. For one of Wordsworth's little formal religious training, interest, or knowledge (compared to Coleridge, Arnold, Dickinson, or Hawthorne) it was easy to blend the individualistic insights of his own mind and temperament with blurred patterns of "spiritual Protestantism" into a peculiar religious *gestalt* or form of his own. This, I hope to have shown, is what happened in certain of his major poems.

IV. Byron

It has been a mark of the best recent studies of Byron to question the old dichotomy of Byron the Romantic and Byron the satirist and to provide readings of the major poems which show unity of outlook and accomplishment in them.[74] The Calvinist background has been noted by all these critics and treated in various ways as a contribution to some kind of unity in the poems, but it has not been considered of vital concern in recent studies. It has been seen as one source of satire pushed to the extreme of denying any human goodness, as by Kernan in his reading of *Don Juan*, Book II,[75] or in an extremely secularized form manifested as pure will and as the impetus for the demonic excesses in *Manfred* and *Cain*. Recent criticism has tended to look to more purely literary traditions − classical or modern but with wide diversity among themselves − to unify the satiric and Romantic in Byron and to give counter-arguments for the lack of satisfaction in Byron's poetry as a whole that had set it apart from the reputations of the other major Romantics for several decades earlier in this century. Some of these studies have been quite successful in certain respects, and all improve upon the dichotomy of either satire or Romantic gloom that had been the argument of a previous generation of critics. Yet there still remains a sense of incompleteness of purpose and achievement about the "Romantic" works, in which, interestingly enough, the Calvinist element is most noticeable. *Childe Harold*, *Manfred*, the religious closet dramas, some of the more serious lyrics and certain sections of *Don Juan* have this element. The degree of obviousness and importance of the Calvinist theme varies considerably among these works. This chapter will not claim more for the Calvinist element than the evidence of the texts will bear, or that it is the one missing force bringing Byron's work into unity; but it is much more than merely superficial showing off or unimportant reminiscence from Byron's early Scottish background and upbringing, and makes a contribution to our understanding of Byron that has been ignored by the more fashionable criticism of recent times.

The best recent work on Byron, such as that of Cooke and Gleckner, brings the "satiric" and Romantic poems closer by finding common attitudes among them. The scheme is to demonstrate that the more acceptable – to the modern mind – attitudes of the satires are also those of the tales, plays and narrative poems, beneath the *weltschmertz* and heroic posing acceptable in the 19th century but no longer today. The notions of quiet heroism, resignation, scepticism and acceptance of man's human and tragic fate are stressed over either positive or negative qualities once called Romantic, the Byronic hero or the scoffing jester. This general view, found also in other recent books in less cogent form, is likely to dominate for some time, replacing the stereotyped "Romantic" Byron, and the darker views of Ridenour and Marshall. Ridenour reads *Don Juan* in a Christian context, placing great stress on the patterns of the fall; Marshall assumed a totally despairing situation in Byron's poetry, reviving and modernizing the 19th century continental, particularly German, view of his pessimism. In the fundamental sense the view of this study is aligned to that of Ridenour, and before him to Lovell, whose reading of Byron pointed out the mixing of religious and secular themes and patterns in the poetry. The religious frame of Calvinism accounts more than does Ridenour's perspective for the darker, grimmer elements stressed by Marshall, Cooke and Gleckner.

Our question is whether in Byron's pessimism and final subdued outlook on mankind there is a link or complete break with the religious past, which in Calvinism allowed generously for both pessimism and a kind of restrained optimism opposed to the humanist variety. We cannot expect contemporary critics to show great eagerness for the religious tradition of Calvinism, particularly the implications of the fall, wherever other terminology or viewpoints are available to explain the same phenomena in the poetry. This fact should not deter us from examining the poetry from a religious perspective anew, and particularly from the Calvinist perspective. In doing this, recognition is given to the fact that Byron's poetry stands in a quite different relationship to religious beliefs in literal and cultural terms than does the poetry of the other Romantics discussed in this section, or even of American writers of similar temperament – Hawthorne, Dickinson and Melville – whose explicit rejection of

Calvinism leaves their work closer to the tradition than does Byron's evasiveness on one hand and scoffing on the other. But it is not merely a negative cultural influence, as was the sexual puritanism of the chapel class upon Lawrence. Some sort of coherent Calvinist pattern, within the cultural permutations of the tradition in the 19th century, as is the case with the other Romantic writers, must inform the major poems to some extent or it would be more intelligent to accept the very cogent readings of the pessimistic and sceptical patterns in the poetry given by Cooke and Gleckner.

The evidence for the influence of Calvinism upon Byron's early life is abundant, and has been presented many times.[76] Though not of the class of Scots most directly subject to its influence, the circumstances of his early life forced him under the domination of low servants and Presbyterian schoolmasters, a grim combination in any event and for a young boy as impressionable as Byron a decisive one. His nimble and sceptical mind was quickly bored with the dogmas of Presbyterian Calvinism, as were his body and spirit with its dourness and discipline. But deep psychological reasons led Byron to an emotional attraction for this religion he outwardly abhorred. And Calvinism later furnished him with metaphor and rationale for his own experienced dark view of life and the world. Without the emotional equipment founded on contact early in life with Calvinism he might not have met the gloomy side of the religious views of the Scots at least half-way. Calvinism was a convenient metaphor and analogy to Byron for his own inner turmoils in early youth, and it remained in more disguised and sophisticated forms throughout his life. Characteristically, he shed with literal belief all of the positive and purely spiritual (in the devotional, Christian sense) aspects and values in Calvinism. Ideas such as the elect, the devout life and the joy of the religious spirit he viewed scornfully as cant and hypocrisy. Actual religious practice of the average Scot or believer in any age makes the higher aspects of religious life an easy victim of scorn and scepticism, but the point is that Byron was unlikely to understand and accept that side of the story even if it had been manifest in those around him, because there was little in it which answered to the needs of his emotional nature and later to his darker psychological propensities. On the other hand, the darker side of Calvinism offered a great deal, perhaps too much, to the susceptibility of the in many ways unfortunate young lord.

Byron's conflict with his heredity in the matters of his lameness, emotional instability and susceptibility to violent acts found a plausible explanation in the Calvinist doctrines of original sin, hereditary taint, and ineradicable nature of evil. The rather strong if implicit frowning upon sex as both a source and symptom of this sin and evil in the Augustinian tradition and in Calvinism as presented in Scotland also played easily upon the susceptibilities of one whose sexual temperament was precocious and fated to a disasterous early history. Byron's attitude towards the nature of sexual activity, as toward the nature of mankind and the world at large, was fundamentally ambivalent, wildly oscillating from extreme to extreme, and both were formed in early youth as a result of temperament and experience. The darker side of Calvinism merely provided one manner in which this basic distrust could be expressed, since the mature Byron easily discovered the more sophisticated formulations of philosophical dualism. But the Calvinist formulation was the decisive one, having been present in his earliest and most impressionable years, and he came back to it in a multitude of ways in the course of the mature reflections and writing.

After reading Byron's poetry once again and all of the newer critical responses, some very original and refreshing indeed, this writer must still agree with the general observation made wisely by Lovell during the previous great wave of Byron criticism and scholarship:

His Calvinistic-generated categories of mind and matter, the Catholic sympathies of his later years, and the deistic beliefs which were produced in part by his inability to accept wholly either one of these two great faiths – all these made for him a dichotomy of spirit and matter the only view which he could consistently maintain.

Byron was by no means convinced of the existence of a deity generally benevolent, and for him the evidence of science was just more evidence in favor of a Calvinistically imagined God. [The] last period of his life reveals more clearly than any other his preoccupation with a God who was not only cruel and unjust but even blood-thirsty.

Nature was never self-explanatory for Byron. But he never found the necessary faith to believe, consistently, that the natural order was essentially benevolent to man; and if not, what is then to be said of its Creator? This is the fundamental question which Byron finally stumbled over, and his failure to answer it was a failure in faith. Nothing was more evident to him than that things changed, but was it for good or for ill? And if for ill, what, again, is to be said of the Creator?[77]

Byron's characteristic voice, Lovell goes on to say, shows concern with the personal consequences of irreligion, the voice of unbelief faithfully describing the consequences of unbelief, a voice in quest of a faith to replace the lost but yet decisive Calvinist faith of his background. With these observations we can agree and make them the starting point of this assessment of Byron's use of the Calvinist tradition in poetry.

The great passages of negativism and despair in Book IV of *Childe Harold's Pilgrimage* have been given general application by many critics, from indication of the ruin of the lost paradise to the modern sense of the absurdity of man. There are strong reasons to read the lines in these ways and to resist the idea that a tradition that may seem narrow and parochial to many today is the specific guiding force behind them, namely, the Calvinism of Byron's youth secularized, inverted and generalized beyond any specific religious and Christian context. But it will be possible to show that such is the case by close inspection, and that the import of these lines ranges widely in Byron's poetry beyond their immediate context into the whole of *Childe Harold* and much of the other poetry.

cxxvi

Our life is a false nature — 'tis not in
The harmony of things, — this hard decree,
This uneradicable taint of sin,
This boundless upas, this all-blasting tree
Whose root is earth, whose leaves and branches be
The skies which rain their plagues on men like dew —
Disease, death, bondage — all the woes we see,
And worse, the woes we see not — which throb through
The immedicable soul, with heart-aches ever new.

cxxxiii

It is not that I may not have incurr'd,
For my ancestral faults or mine ·the wound
I bleed withal, and, had it been conferr'd
With a just weapon, it had flow'd unbound;
But now my blood shall not sink in the ground;
To thee I do devote it. . . .[78]

The "hard decree" and the "uneradicable taint of sin" are of course pure Calvin on predestination, election, and original sin. With what we know of Byron's continual scoffing at religious belief in his poems and casual writings our instinct is to take these words, and also the more generally Calvinist ideas elsewhere in the stanzas, metaphorically, as Byron's pungent way of expressing doom and general gloom. Fair enough, at first glance, but, *how* metaphorically? From experience with past criticism it is clear that a very general *initial* reading here leads to various kinds of even more general readings of the larger context, the modernism and absurd we have heard so much about in recent Byron studies. What is the primary and most important context of the metaphor here?

When we turn elsewhere in *Childe Harold* and Byron's poetry, there are many other instances of very specific echoing of Calvinist language. For the moment let us remain within the confines of *Childe Harold's Pilgrimage*, since that poem is the earliest major work by Byron, and the one in which the development of his serious ideas is most readily seen. From the context of *Childe Harold* we can move to other serious texts, some of the lyrics, *Manfred* and a few of the closet dramas.

> If from society we learn to live
> 'Tis solitude should teach us how to die;
> It hath no flatterers; vanity can give
> No hollow aid; alone — man with his God must strive:
> Or, it may be, with demons, who impair
> The strength of better thoughts, and seek their prey
> In melancholy bosoms, such as were
> Of moody texture from their earliest day,
> And loved to dwell in darkness and dismay,
> Deeming themselves predestinted to a doom
> Which is not of the pangs that pass away;
> Making the sun like blood, the earth a tomb,
> The tomb a hell, and hell itself a murkier gloom.[79]

Here is a stark appearance of predestination in a secular, displaced context. The sceptic can yet be doubtful of the Calvinist heritage of this, and we must grant an argument. God seems to be mentioned only for the value of the quick parry with demons, and those demons may perhaps be the familiar furies of the classical tradition which Byron sprinkles throughout his poetry. The last two lines are the kind of unfortunate fustian of which there is all too much in *Childe Harold* and the early poetry. It is exaggeration, but very serious exaggeration, expressing a serious element, the notion of predestined doom for the unusual human spirit, extended to include all humankind before it is completed. What begins as wrestling with personal demons in an almost (some would say complete) solipsistic context gradually comes to include all mankind, from the few "melancholy bosoms" to the grand "Our life" of cxxvi quoted previously. *Childe Harold* dwells primarily upon the self, but the general urge to include all mankind in its doom is never far away.

The passages of gloom and predestined despair in *Childe Harold* have perhaps not been taken seriously enough in a critical climate wherein the poem itself has not won much favor. The recent good work mentioned in this chapter has and will do much to revise that opinion, but it is not necessary to locate this argument exclusively upon the heightened passages in *Childe Harold*. The sense of predestination, demons pursuing, special sin and doom, and other attitudes obviously derived in part from Calvinism in *Childe Harold*, are the themes of all of Byron's best work after the juvenile pieces and before *Don Juan* and the late satires. *Manfred, Heaven and Earth* and *Cain* are major texts; the longer dramas and some lyrics provide insights. The late satires are not necessarily excluded from this kind of pessimism, as most commentators have noted in discussing the shipwreck scene in *Don Juan*, Canto II. But to include extensive discussion of satire would not preserve the direct focus upon Romantic religious imagery in this chapter. For this purpose *Childe Harold* remains the most central text, with other works grouped around it, to examine the peculiar Calvinist sensibility in Byron.

The dominant image of the journey in *Childe Harold* plays an important role in the evolution of Byron's Puritan conception of sin, guilt and predestination, and may legitimately be connected with the general notion of pilgrimage that we have traced from early Puritan and other spiritual writings to Wordsworth. The pilgrim theme in *Childe Harold* has given a great deal of initial trouble to critics because of its openness and abrupt inconclusion. It does not follow the pattern of divine journey in Hilton, Bunyan and Wordsworth, or the humanistic pattern of the *Odyssey* or *Prometheus Unbound*, wherein we would expect a return to life and home, and a humane maturing of the hero. In *Childe Harold* there is no presentation of mature womanhood and love; the Childe grows from sullen, spoiled adolescent into ranting, worldweary Romantic poseur. The agony and aloneness of the narrator, as we leave him gazing at the eternal ocean at the end of Canto IV, makes of *Childe Harold* a spiritual journey of a special kind, one not entirely new at the beginning of the 19th century, but certainly recent, and cut off from the traditional idea of the spiritual journey except by opposition and antithesis. In it the Calvinist-Puritan ideas of sin, guilt and predestination help define the opposition and antithesis to the normal positive pattern of the journey, yet give a special spiritual quality to the opposition. Unexpiated guilt and unforgiven sin impede vision – the Childe's mountaintops do not lead to a heavenly destiny, but to deflation and looking at the eternal sea laughing at man. It is not difficult to understand how Byron's temperament readily found in this extreme perversion of Calvinist doctrine a way of handling religious impulses deeply entwined in his nature, while remaining faithful to the unbelief, scepticism and despair of human nature that permeate *Childe Harold* III and IV. The relationship between predestination as echoed in the passages cited above and the fact of the open, unending journey of no clear consequence is a more obscure and difficult matter. Later in the chapter this issue will be looked at more closely.

Serious attention to these issues in Byron's poetry must also be focussed elsewhere than on *Childe Harold*, although insights from a few more of its greatest passages are ultimately necessary for understanding what is best and most important in Byron. *Childe Harold* sets the problem and points the way to the best poems of Byron's Calvinism. The dark journey, the effects of predestination and the goal of the journey are matters of concern in his other mature works, particularly the closet dramas, *Manfred* and some of the major lyrics. Discussion should begin with the most powerful and direct of these works, also the best, *Manfred*.

The best wisdom we now have on Byron's *Manfred* regards the play as one of his superior achievements, and one of the major achievements of its kind in the Romantic movement.[80] The Faustian, Promethean, and Giovannian myths give the character of Manfred its strength, the Gothic novel provides the trappings of a gloomy setting and a sense of mystery, the approach to true tragedy gives the final scene awesome power. There are two aspects to the powerful effect of *Manfred* which have still to be explored, Manfred as magus in relation to eastern tales, and the play itself as a type of the saint's play, peculiarly inverted in morality to quite different ends than the standard Christian versions. For the former we have *Vathek,* known in general to be an influence upon Byron, as a guide; for the latter a series of saint's plays from *Everyman* through *Samson Agonistes* to *Murder in the Cathedral*. The structural aspects of all saints' plays are quite similar, as Martz has pointed out,[81] and it is to these elements, not the particular content of plays from different ages, that we will turn in the second part of this discussion.

The power in the character of Manfred is manifest if we see it in the light of other Byronic heroes. He has he energy of Lara, the Corsair, and the Giaour without the swashbuckling quality that makes them seem slightly silly to many readers. Like Childe Harold, he broods, thinks intensely, and is subject to melancholia, but not to the Childe's persistent self-pity, his least attractive quality. He shares an Eastern aura with Sardanapolus without that potentate's effeminacy and sensuality. His one affair, though surrounded by hints of violence and criminality, was conducted with the dignity befitting his and Astarte's high station, we may surmise. In seriousness it is true that he is rivalled by the heroes of other closet dramas and by the Foscari and Faliero, but they are all, for different reasons, dull, while Manfred is intensely interesting. One factor contributing to the unusual interest is that he is a magus, a fact little pursued in its implications by critics. That he is a kind of inverted saint, or a saint in his own right, to put the point more neutrally, has not been much acknowledged. Some of his unusual power shows his cousinship with Vathek and Eblis; some of his unusual interest derives from his rather strange, at first thought, closeness to Samson, Becket, Joan, and assorted other saints made memorable in plays.

To establish a meaningful connection between the character of Manfred and the saint's play tradition requires us first to have as firm a sense as possible of the character. As was stated, the mixture of Promethean, Faustian, and Giovannian elements in the character, all very powerful myths of the period, was convincingly presented by influential critics in the past and restated in more contemporary fashion in recent criticism. There has also been a natural and irresistible urge to view Manfred as a modern man, an existential hero, cut off from the past and traditional values, forced to make the free choices which determine his fate. The Promethean and Faustian myths contribute a historical dimension to the existential predicament, so that the reading of Manfred as modern, isolated, solipsistic and doomed to live in his own head-space like the rest of us is not contradictory to the historical perspective. It may be described as philosophical rather than historical in its critical awareness. William Marshall articulated the modern dilemma in Manfred in a decisive way, in an argument that need not be repeated here.[82] To assert his own freedom Manfred chances all, and there is both triumph and barrenness in his victory. So many modern characters in philosophy, fiction, poetry and drama have followed this route that this ground is familiar, perhaps even sacred, holy or terrifying to us, and it would belabor the obvious to describe much of this. If we can move backward to one somewhat neglected aspect of the Gothic tradition, I believe some aspects of the character of Manfred can be clarified and in a way by no means merely a return to antiquarianism, but a rein- forcement of our current attitudes.

Byron's admiration for Beckford and *Vathek* is well known, leaving no need for grounding the next part of the argument in preliminary source study. The character Vathek is an eastern potentate of vast magical powers and at the same time a gross comic buffoon. In him and his mother, Carathis (though less so in her case), the extra- vagance of the magus' powers disgusts, not awes, the reader. Only in Eblis, keeper of the underworld, and in the underworld itself, Istakar, are eastern grandeur, splendor, and sheer size united to western seriousness about the pain, horror and grimness of eternal damnation. Some of the resonances in Manfred's character, which combines eastern power and magic with western alienation and moroseness, derive from Byron's use of Eblis in the creation of Manfred. It is not his whole character, obviously, yet there is a dimension that this eastern source adds to his full nature which we must understand before considering Manfred's peculiar austerity in the light of the saint's play. From study of *Manfred* in the light of the saint's play there is a natural return to the main theme of this study, the Calvinist temper in Byron, which appears in its most extreme and powerful form in this play.

Manfred as magus has powers of conjuring which had been presented in the literature of earlier periods with full seriousness, and in the Romantic age in a mixed way. Byron certainly knew the mixture of seriousness and levity which prevails in Radcliffe, Lewis, Maturin and Beckford. *Vathek* is most helpful for *Manfred* for many reasons. In *Vathek* the seriousness of Eblis contrasts with the wonderful, extravagant eastern powers of Vathek himself and his horrible mother Carathis, providing Byron with material for his purpose in *Manfred* not directly present in the other Gothic novels. Byron intends Manfred's character to be an inverted parallel with Christian sainthood, as we shall see, and manages to preserve seriousness in his magus aspect in various ways, one of which is in allusions to the "eastern" Gothicism of *Vathek*. Manfred's path is predestined by a kind of inverted Calvinism. This requires an "unholy" yet serious note in some scenes.

Most notable in this respect is the ending. The Abbot attempts a charitable interpretation of Manfred's death in the last line, "Wither? I dread to think − but he is gone." But the focus of the final scene falls upon Manfred's last words and their mystery, "Old man! 'tis not so difficult to die!" Dying is not difficult for Manfred because his life, in his terms (barren to the Christian and humanistic perspectives which surround it), has been fully lived. Predestined to "doom" in both the Calvinist and Byron's own sense of that term, within his narrow outward range his experiences were remarkable. He had attained equality with the mountain spirits, the ability, with the help of the underworld, to commune with the shade of his deceased "double," Astarte, and a kind of confrontation and respect from the keeper of the underworld, Arimanes. All these aspects lend meaning to the inverted Calvinist idea of a "predestined path." In his creation of the character and atmosphere of Arimanes Byron of course had access to the various descriptions of the classical Hades which are present in a general way. Yet we cannot help but see in the confrontation of Manfred and Arimanes a raised vision of the conclusion of *Vathek*, where Arimanes' surroundings are much like those of Eblis. Manfred is a doomed man, but not the fool Vathek or wanton criminal Carathis. He has been given a character and destiny worthy of the confrontation, and a will able to check the power of Arimanes in his case. Act iv, scene iv opens as follows:

The Hall of Arimanes − Arimanes on his Throne, a Globe of Fire, surrounded by the Spirits.

The parallel to the first appearance of Eblis in *Vathek* is unmistakable:

An infinity of elders with streaming beards and afrits in complete armour had prostrated themselves before the ascent of a lofty eminence, on the top of which, upon a globe of fire, sat the formidable Eblis. His person was that of a young man, whose noble and regular features seemed to have been tarnished by malignant vapours. In his large eyes appeared both pride and despair.[83]

Arimanes represents the sternness and pride of the ruler of the underworld, as does Eblis, but since Byron's dialectic is different, the shapes of the scenes differ accordingly. Vathek, Carathis and the others are being justly punished, ultimately by the extinction of hope. Manfred has no hope of this naive sort by the time of his descent, only wishing to commune with the spirit of Astarte and to die. Manfred's pride and individuality impress Arimanes, who allows a vision of his phantom double, Astarte. It is clear that Manfred and Arimanes deal in as equal terms as are possible between mortal and immortal, Manfred owing nothing to evil, either allegiance or punishment, in the usual senses. However, he is grateful for the vision of Astarte allowed by a magus greater than himself, since Manfred is, finally, at least partly human, the "dust and deity" of humanity's curse as Byron presents it here and elsewhere. Being human, in some sense, he is capable of being some kind of tragic character, in the framework of inverted Calvinism, as no heroes of the typical Gothic novels can possibly be. Eblis is a spirit, Vathek a ridiculous figure, the characters in *The Monk* partly both. Manfred's relationship to malignant deity is made clear in this scene with the context of *Vathek* as an aid. For an explanation of his relationship with Astarte, and hence of his full tragic nature, the reference of the saint's play must be invoked. But a partial reason for his tragic nature is fully clear in this scene with Arimanes–Eblis. Manfred, though human and therefore potentially tragic, has something about him of a demonic character nobly presented. He is not the double of Arimanes, yet demonic grandeur is reflected in Manfred through the aid of Byron's reading of Eblis in *Vathek*.

The tragic nature of the character of Manfred has now been established. To the well known sources in Promethean, Giovannian and Faustian legend, and their contemporary forms, we have added the aura which *Vathek* contributes to our knowledge of the characters of Manfred and Astarte. But for many reasons the play is not an effective tragedy in the traditional terms. It is different, and better than all except the best of true tragedies. The Calvinist concepts of the dark journey, predestination, and the effects of sin in the fallen world developed in *Childe Harold* remain operative and firm in the closet dramas, *Cain, Heaven* and *Earth* and above all, *Manfred*. The structure of the so-called "saint's plays," inverted in content but not in form to very special uses in *Manfred*, helps to illuminate the nature of the tragic character Manfred and also the Calvinist concepts at work at the center of the play. Some might see a perversion here of the traditional concept of the saint, but this is to look in the wrong area for the special character of *Manfred*. In *Manfred* the peculiar inversion of Calvinism is subtly done, and the simultaneous phenomena – saintliness and inverted Calvinism – lead to a complexity in *Manfred* never before fully explained.

This study has explored Calvinist concepts and their literary relations, inversions and developments in various contexts, leaving no further need for an abstract, except to refer to the opening pages of this chapter on the development of these ideas in *Childe Harold* in their relationship to the seminal ideas of this book in Part One. For the saint's play tradition the ideas in Martz' essay already cited will be briefly recalled. *Manfred* closely follows the general contours of this tradition in its external structure, injecting internally an original content. Saints' plays are essentially one-act plays, no matter how artificially divided, without meaningful action in the sense of interaction between the hero and the other characters. Meaningful action is possibility for change in the present by experience and compromise, as in the traditional tragedy. The saint has had his experiences, has his mind set, listens to his inner voices (or other-worldly ones as he chooses to define them), rather than to the urgings or threats of those around him. The action must then be a series of encounters with other characters drawing sharply the difference between the hero and others. The others are varied from moral adversaries to would-be friends. All are rejected. None can reach the hero where his deepest thoughts are buried, in a past deliberately mysterious, so that after the encounter comes the predestined martyrdom. In plays having traditional orientation the saints – from Samson to Becket – clearly triumph, though irony is allowed its place. Shaw writes about saints in a spirit more like that of Voltaire, and Mann can darken their nature with Germanic gloom, but the structural issue is always the same, the static nature of the saint's play, the need for varied characters to respond to the assured saint from various moral positions, and the inevitable conclusion in sought-for or imposed martyrdom. In either case the conclusion is somewhat predestined by the character, personality and situation in which the saint finds himself. The parallels with the actual historical situation of 17th century Puritan saints are obvious, as a remote source for some saints' plays, but probably not for Byron's. Puritan ideas went deep into Byron's mind in youth, but he was never inspired by a clear Puritan character type; indeed, as we know, the matter was always quite the opposite.

Manfred fulfills the requirements of the external structure of the saint's play, though it is only initially helpful to know this, since the nature of Manfred himself remains the real and clouded matter. His mind is indeed made up as the play opens; he has had his experience – only Astarte could deeply move him, and she is dead. Her relations with him and her death are crucial to his character, but not to the play's action, for she is not alive. Even the living are not real influences upon Manfred. He scorns the "wine, woman and song" philosophy of his father and his servants, respects the Chamois hunter (but is "distant from the Kind" and proud of it, like the Childe on the mountain-top, not Wordsworth of "Elegaic Stanzas"), and longs, really, only to converse with the spirit of the dead Astarte. His rejection of Arimanes' fellowship and then his will comes closer to a true conflict and is the most obscure part of the play. Here the Vathek-Eblis-magus and Calvinist themes are most crucial to the play and character. With the Abbot at the end it is somewhat different. Manfred's relations with the Abbot are warmer than with Arimanes, although their viewpoints are totally alien. We are on familiar ground with the Abbot's Christian absolution and clear view of moral good and evil. *Manfred* can almost be read as a morality play in this section, until we remember his actual character and Byron's dialectics, which are not traditionally Christian. From the outside Manfred seems to be choosing hell in Faustian style, but his own perspective dominates the play, and from that perspective he is simply rejecting another alternative to the firmness of his own dark mind, as he dispensed with the Chamois hunter's humanism. These attractive alternatives are no more compelling than the sensuality of the servants, the sinister will of Arimanes, or the equality offered by the Alps spirits. These points are obvious enough, I believe, not to require extensive quotations for serious readers of the play. Manfred as magus-saint, his predestined path, and his relationship to Astarte are the ideas and themes needing further scrutiny, as the ones which tend to reveal the presence of the Calvinist temper in Byron's poetry.

As a magus Manfred has attained to a portion of the Faustian dream of knowledge. He chose the eastern way of poring over books, deciphering by skill and intelligence the hidden secrets in the manner of Chaldeans and Persians, scorning both the Faustian pact with Satan (here Arimanes) and promised pleasures other than the intellectual. Arimanes lacks control over him or his death. But Manfred in the play no longer takes any pleasure even in intellectual feats except as means to scorn those of others. There is the hint that he once did so in the presence of Astarte before the barrier of the nameless act or crime that caused her death. The "*Kalon*," the beautiful vision granted to Greek sages, is denied him in his last hours except for a moment of equilibrium and perception of its existence. In his peculiarity his magus nature brought with it the asceticism and sensibility of sainthood, not the sensuality and repentance/unrepentance of the various Faust legends. His asceticism is an end in itself, a *contemptus mundi* unframed by the piety and belief which the Christian Abbot represents. Unlike Wordsworth in so many poems of Calvinist implication, there is no heavenly destiny, although one is offered by the Abbot. Manfred is one of the loneliest figures in Romantic literature. He maintains his will and a kind of integrity, rendering unfair the charge by some critics that he is too barren to be a tragic hero of any kind. It is a sad limitation, if not a tragic one, that his only desired communication is with the dead Astarte, and this communication, brief as it is in the play, cannot be "high talk with the departed dead," but is rather a mute experience of grief and guilt, about which only surmise is possible, and such surmise fruitless, no matter what biographical evidence or modern psychological theory is presented as a solution to the problem. Manfred is the dramatized character, and the effects upon him of the meetings with Astarte and Arimanes are immediately apparent. He almost becomes a shade himself before his death. It is great artistry that he dies slowly, imperceptively, a creature really neither of this world nor of another. Modern existential characteristics have been described in Manfred with some justice. It is no less just to view the nemesis of the play as a certain kind of predestined end, the poet projecting an image of himself devoid of theological content and scruple. Calvinism was a hopeful doctrine for the few; in Byron's hands a negative Calvinism issued often in a damnation having the stature of defiance of various manifestations of the Godhead. Beyond that is the nothingness of Manfred's life and death, which a critic may view as the bitter culmination of a religious tradition, or as the beginning of one of modern man's most gloomy but persistent beliefs about his destiny. In either case, Manfred has chosen in his own way, and has his own special sort of "election."

Cain: A Mystery and *Heaven and Earth* are not so profound as *Manfred*, though by invoking the religious mysteries directly the Calvinist influence appears in them in more manifest form. They show us once again that Byron's contact with religious tradition occasioned neither settled belief nor mere indifference. He did not *have* to write on such subject matter, even if sceptically. This continual preoccupation with traditional beliefs is evidence of continual inner conflict. Despite his bold scoffing in some poems and many letters, religious uncertainty was a constant source of inward distress and suffering to him. In both these plays he concerned himself with divine sovereignty and predestination in the Calvinist sense. In other works we have seen his disposition to believe in predestination to evil, with little interest in divine grace and eternal life. In these plays the same disposition prevails, yet surrounded by some religious awe occasioned by choice of subjects. The divinity behind both plays is treated without levity or rationalistic disrespect, but without belief either. In both plays a vast gulf between God and the world emerges, consonant with the Hebraic source material and Calvinist interpretations of these materials.

Yet there is the usual difference. Calvinist emphasis upon original sin agreed with Byron's experiences in life, but even the limited redemption granted by Augustine and Calvin had no place in Byron's scheme of justice. If some survive, it is totally arbitrary, the act of an arbitrary being, or worse. Upon Byron's fundamentally religious youthful mind had been implanted the idea of the wrathful arbitrary God, yet in such a way and with such a reception that orthodox piety was not an alternative for him. Still he continued to concern himself with a possible supernatural order, and to impose upon traditional beliefs his own interpretations, extreme extensions or twisted inversions of Calvin's teachings. Since Byron's moods of misanthropy were entirely in accord with the doctrine of original sin, and man's resultant depravity, subjects such as Cain and the flood had intrinsic appeal for him. By choosing early Hebraic subjects he was also able to overlook (in fact, reject) the positive and redemptive elements in Christianity. Byron's religious characters are insignificant unless they look for support within themselves, in Manfred-like fashion. Cain is preferred to Abel, the impious daughters to the dutiful Japhet. Submission to a wrathful God is of no use in final travail, unless it suits the arbitrary will. These plays have been called "Hebraic" as opposed to Christian by some critics. This is not so. Only the material is Hebraic. The Hebraic submission to God's will is not given approval in the context of the plays. The plays work towards a conclusion in which God's will is arbitrary and election as a fact even more arbitrary. It exists. The wrathful God saves some in each play, for his own good pleasure, without that pleasure having the stamp of Hebrew or Calvinist positive belief. The redemptive acts in the conclusions (except Cain's rather humanistic one) remove no blame from the arbitrary God. God's will is done without raising his chosen ones from abject humiliations. Nor does the naturalism of modern scientific speculation, called upon to give the subject matter respectability for Byron's audience, have much interest for the real drama in each play.

That naturalism, like the 18th century theories concerning the flood, number of worlds, nature of angels and others, is sadly dated. What is still of interest is the raw religious side of Byron's mind in its sometimes ferocious quarrel with the wrathful God of predestination he could never seriously reject from his mind or poetry. Though Cain and the Daughters of Men defy God in ancient parables equivalent to *Manfred,* the power and presence of the ancient God, as in *Manfred,* are not thereby removed.

To be more specific about the plays, neither *Cain* nor *Heaven and Earth* has the unity, brillance and originality of *Manfred,* though they have not deserved the slighting thus far received as serious poems even by critics who read Byron's non-satiric poetry with respect. Perhaps the sophistication attending the attempts to deal seriously with the non-satiric poetry has led to avoidance of direct religious subjects such as *Cain* and *Heaven and Earth.* Some critics have called into question Byron's seriousness about them. These plays are certainly not the best or most serious of Byron's works, yet to approach them lightly is to minimize seriously Byron's religious inclinations, his peculiar combination of scepticism and belief and the underlying Calvinist sources.

The characterizations in the plays are not new. Cain and Aholíbamah have the pride and immovability of Manfred; Japhet shows the semi-humanistic rebellion, perhaps somewhat sentimentalized, against power and deity characteristic of Sardanapalus and some heroes of the Tales. The pious characters are not drawn favorably: only context makes Japhet ultimately pious; Abel is given a weak, soft character; while Noah has an obtuse hectoring disposition. The pious women are not regarded for their piety but for capacity to love, a recurring idea in Byron's poetry. Except for Adah's close questioning of Lucifer in Act One of *Cain,* little intellectual power or motivating force in the plays resides in the female characters.

The specific biblical settings create differences and restrictions not present in the more general, open and metaphysical context of *Manfred,* most obviously in the biblical stories themselves and the rabbinical-Christian commentary surrounding them which Byron accepted, at least for the sake of the plays. Despite the levity of his introductions, there is a core of meaning in both plays almost as serious as in *Manfred,* though less successfully presented. The attitudes of Cain, Samiasa, Azaziel and Aholíbamah are Manfred-like in a religious setting. They are rebellious characters. Anah is softer in character yet also chooses to defy God at the final moment. The existence and power of God in both plays are without question, not ambiguous as in *Manfred*, where ultimate destiny is fate and man is forced to fall back upon his inner self. In these plays the rebels hate their "dust," but accept it, and also assert a share of deity and of the supernatural on their own, echoing Byron's theme of dust and deity in the lyrics, *Childe Harold* and *Manfred*. The supernatural assertions of the wayward angels, the "daughters of Cain" and of Cain himself may well be delusions in the contexts of the plays — the fate of all but Cain is deliberately left ambiguous. It is the assertions against deity which matter, not the reality. In choosing to defy God and his will, these characters become partly heroic, usurping the biblical reverence for Adam, Noah and other submissive ones.

In both plays God's power and arbitrary will are acknowledged by all (a departure from *Manfred*) but the justice of this power by the meek and pious only. No character questions predestination; whether it is for the good of anyone except God is the heart of the quarrel between the pious and the rebellious. The rebellious are partly "humanist" in a guarded Byronic, not Enlightenment, way. They accept being dust, but yearn for immortality on their own terms, not Judeo-Christian ones. Since Byron is an inverted Calvinist, part sceptic, part believer, not an Enlightenment man, no serious counter-myth is invented, as in Blake. (In turning Calvinism inside out Blake did not completely elude predestination and other major doctrines, as we have seen.) Some of the characters are "Satanic" in their opposition to God's plans for the world and for them, and the character of Lucifer is decidedly favorable, though not unqualified. From a certain point of view he is freeing Cain from ignorance, yet the cold fact remains that he also lies, and the influence of these lies precipitates the tragic destiny for Cain and his race, a destiny quite far along in Cain's brooding as the play opens. The final disposition of the rebels in *Heaven and Earth* is left moot. Like Cain, their assertion is of endurance, allowing God's plan, power and predestination while despising them.

Byron seems to be accepting God's plan and power too, even if we allow for the conventions of the plays. These biblical conventions do not conflict with the more open speculations and assertions in *Manfred* and *Childe Harold*. There is the accustomed bitterness in his resolutions to these two plays, the Byronic element not present in Blake's transformations or Wordsworth's resignations. His refusal of transformation can be called "thinking like a child," and his refusal of piety and acceptance blasphemy in his day, or petulance, false negative heroics, by a more sophisticated era. These judgments are unfair to Byron's historical place and personal situation. All these factors are merely further aspects of his inner turmoil of scepticism and belief, the Calvinism inverted but not discarded. To have respect for this aspect of Byron, we must have respect for the power of Calvinist theology in his development. His willingness to partly believe in what he mostly hated may seem perverse, but this is a deeply important aspect of Byron's creative power deserving more attention than has been given in the recent critical past.

Few of Byron's lyrics before 1816 have a seriousness of intention that would make them of interest for this study. They are of interest for development of Byron's ability in formal techniques, such as versification, and for his use of self as material for themes. In the poems of 1816, after the exile, there is a deepening of thought and power in the lyrics, which continues in some of the occasional lyrics of the following years. (He also continued to write vituperative and facetious verses in his earlier style, and serious poems which are primarily personal and autobiographical, neither type of primary concern for this study.) The serious poems of 1816 and after of interest for the Calvinist temper are ones reflecting the themes and interests in *Childe Harold, Manfred* and the later long poems. Three of these poems stand out for consideration, the "Epistle to Augusta," "Darkness" and "Prometheus." The involvement with the Calvinist temper is less direct in the lyrics than in the longer poems, but certain themes and patterns in these lyrics echo similar ones in the longer poems where the religious element is open and plays a stronger role. The sense of destiny and predestined doom of *Childe Harold* pervades "Epistle to Augusta." "Darkness" in a naturalistic setting hints at an irresponsible God and victimized humanity. "Prometheus," after the familiar Romantic paean to that hero, turns to the view of man in *Manfred* as a victim of conflicting dust and deity. A personal-auto-biographical interpretation can be given to all these poems, or a modern psychological one concerned with the problem of "identity," and certainly a classical interpretation centering on the use of the words "will" and "fate," or in other words the interpretations given to the major poems by modern critics. Our interest is to define the relationship between these lyrics and the major poems in the light of the Calvinist heritage in Byron.

In the "Epistle to Augusta" the poet speaks freely and biographically of the themes partly hidden by generality and persona in *Childe Harold*. This openness is a mixed blessing, displaying frankness to those who admire that quality in Byron, or sentimentality to those put off by directness in lyric poetry. It is the most powerful and accomplished of the Diodati poems, a miniature of *Childe Harold* III and IV in its compression of key words and themes into personal utterance. The "destiny," the "strange doom," the struggle between fate and will, between dust and fame, and the outcome of cold despair are all familiar and all there. Lines 26−30 contain the elements in the familiar struggles of Byron's tortured life and mind:

> My whole life was a contest, since the day
> That gave me being, gave me that which marr'd
> The gift, − a fate, or will, that walk'd astray;
> And I at times have found the struggle hard,
> And thought of shaking off my bonds of clay. . . .

Contemporary critics who have located the central dilemma in Byron's poetry in these lines and their many variations in other poems view the doctrine as Greek − he is fated because a will such as his was given him without his asking, but he has will because the fate is so closely shaped to the qualities of the will. But their inclination is to translate the dilemma into what we may call modern or "existential" terms:

Freedom is experienced as both personal necessity and intolerable burden, determination as a necessary guarantee of the value and meaning of the individual life and as a force to be resisted in the name of the freedom which is equally indispensable. The dilemma is handled by pushing both terms as far as they can go, so that the play is an enactment of a will to radical freedom and to radical determination.[84]

The categories of religious orientation from Lovell may apply with equal force to these lines and hence to this central thematic complex in Byron's poetry, as all agree. (Critics now assume that the personal themes in the Augusta poems and others of the 1816 period are related closely to the life, as has been demonstrated by Marchand and other biographers.) To repeat Lovell, more briefly than in an earlier reference:

His Calvinistic-generated categories of mind and matter . . . made for him a dichotomy of spirit and matter the only view which he could consistently maintain. . . . Byron was by no means convinced of the existence of a deity generally benevolent, and for him the evidence of science was just more evidence in favor of a Calvinistically imagined God.[85]

Lovell's full text makes allowance for a susceptibility to Catholiscism in the later years which is irrelevant to introduce here, since this susceptibility is to sensuality and popular mythology in Italy. Lovell also gave great weight to deistic beliefs inherited by Byron from the 18th century, a fact certainly in the satires, yet his further statement, that the last period of Byron's life reveals more clearly than any other his preoccupation with a God not only cruel and unjust but even bloodthirsty, makes it evident that Lovell has given greatest weight and priority to the "Calvinistic-generated categories of mind and matter," that is, to the assertion of this study, that the primary mental origins of Byron's dilemmas are in the Calvinist background. Sound scholars such as Marchand have acknowledged this point but have not worked out the implications critically, while the modern tendency has been to look to existential or visionary areas seemingly more in the Romantic or modern tradition of criticism. With some critics of Byron (as of Blake) the terms are interchangeable as Romantic critics claim Romanticism as modern by viewing the historical movement in contemporary perspectives. From the Greek terms "fate" and "will" to existential terminology to "Romantic" vision is often a short, sometimes almost indiscernible critical leap. The point of this critical conflation of views on these central lines is not to stress the wrongness of others, nor the originality of the Calvinist perspective (it is not original), but to insist upon the historical orientation and real differences from the dominant modern Byronists, excellent as some of them have been. A full reading of "Epistle to Augusta" is not needed in this context, since the main import of the poem is biographical, personal, and not philosophical. The allusions to destiny and doom, fate and fault, which intertwine the personal and philosophical, lead quickly to the central lines discussed. After the fifth stanza personal matters occupy most of the remainder of the poem, occasioned by the situation in 1816. In the earlier lines where the poet has sought out the deepest sources of his predicament, the answer seems to lie in the inscrutable destiny of the Byron family, in Calvinistically predestined doom secularized and personalized, yet not, as in the longer poems, generalized beyond his own case.

"Darkness" is a kind of early science fiction, as has been pointed out. It was part of a popular vogue, which includes *Omegarus and*

Syderia (1806) and Hood's "The Last Man." Its secularity and scientism are apparent and uninteresting. The end of the sun is not caused by divine order nor by breakup of divine order. Lovell's discussion of Byron's view of nature is apropos here:

Nature was never self-explanatory for Byron. But he never found the necessary faith to believe, consistently, that the natural order was essentially benevolent to man; and if not, what is then to be said of its Creator?[86]

The parallel derogatory view of human nature is in keeping with Byron's most pessimistic moods, his Calvinist fallen man generalized everywhere and to all times, without election or redemption. Blake reversed Calvin by making everyone elect and redeemed ultimately. In this poem and others like it, Byron dooms all men and the natural universe as well in a drastic application of the most potentially sinister aspects of the Calvinist sensibility unmoored from the theological underpinnings of the religious tradition. For religious Calvinists, God remained inscrutable *and* believed in as the ultimate good. Byron's perception of this is described well by Lovell's statement that if nature revealed God, it was a God not only cruel and unjust but even blood-thirsty, as was also man his creature. This horrible God is the missing element which would have made "Darkness" more interesting, not merely a naturalistic tract. But his malignant existence is implied throughout.

"Prometheus" primarily is about the god also praised by Shelley and later Romantic minds. At line 45 the god becomes "a symbol and a sign" for man's fate, a return to the lines of meditation we have discussed in "Epistle to Augusta." In "Augusta" the emphasis was upon his own doom and hereditary taint; "Darkness" contemplated the wickedness of the universe looked upon naturalistically, and man's deserved evil portion. In the final lines of "Prometheus" man's fate is generalized, perhaps out of the poet's personal experience, by implication, but in the structure of the poem after Romantic contemplation of the role of the Titan in Greek mythology:

A troubled stream from a pure source,
And Man in portions can foresee
His own funereal destiny;
His wretchedness, and his resistance,
And his sad unallied existence:
To which his Spirit may oppose
Itself — and equal to all woes,
    And a firm will, and a deep sense,

Which even in torture can descry
Its own concenter'd recompense,
Triumphant where it dares defy,
And making Death a Victory.   (ll. 48–59)

As with the references to himself in "Epistle to Augusta," a modern existentialist attitude might easily be imposed upon the Greek ideas here. The funereal destiny, "fate," is inexorable, yet Spirit, and a firm will, allow a triumph in suffering, the stoic control over pain giving man his "victory." These views are very close to the dramatization in *Manfred*. The implied connections of this fate-will struggle with Byron's displaced, personal, twisted Calvinism has been discussed above with regard to *Manfred*. These lines from "Prometheus" and the theme of *Manfred* are linked by a process we have analysed to the overt Calvinist terminology of *Childe Harold* with which this chapter opened. The process in Byron never includes a stage of belief (naïveté) in the divine order. It begins with inversion of religious ideas and terms, a technique widely practiced in the Romantic period, in his case Calvinist ones, and moves through stages of naturalism and exaltation of man, of joy in life in *Childe Harold* I and II to the acceptance of universal doom, with the triumph in the sheer perversity of the struggle. Calvin's insight into the nature of God's majesty, or Edwards' fiery sermon on the spider and the flame differ from Byron in only one major respect. It is not the perversity of fate or predestination, or the weakness and vileness of most men which constitutes the difference, for predestination without God is blind fate, and in Byron only the strong, his "elect," are equal to the struggle to maintain some human dignity against destiny. The difference obviously is the ultimate one: the gloomiest Calvinists believed in the rightness of God's world and power, while Byron could accept the grimmest analysis of the universe and of man's fate, but not God's rightness and proper triumph, nor man's either through the human imagination, as did Shelley in full and Blake in part. These lines in "Prometheus" put forth the same eternal struggle and failure as was dramatized in *Manfred*. Man's dignity lies in the fact that a few like Manfred can follow the mythic example of the Titan, succumbing finally from without, not from within.

In a perceptive book on Puritan literature alluded to early in this study, U. Milo Kaufmann gives an insight into the Puritan consciousness, useful for understanding the structure of Puritan literature:

The Puritan unquestionably assumed that his life was a tightly knit fabric of providences (with the consequences, noted above, that he saw his life as a divinely ordered and rational whole), and the divine providences which the individual discerned in his past constituted the most important single topic for meditation in this tradition.[87]

With some necessary rearrangements and inversions the same consciousness is unquestionably present in the best of Byron's lyrics, in *Childe Harold*, the religious plays and *Manfred*. Byron's sense of his destiny leads to belief in a tightly knit fabric of providences, to constant meditation upon his past as a revelation of divine providence, but not, naturally, to belief in his life as a divinely ordered and rational whole. Despite his persistent denials of belief in a good and rational providence, some sense of predestination remained, and helped to order his perceptions while also giving a special sense of structure to his work. As life was a holy journey for the Puritan it became a doomed and fated one for Byron, yet a journey, and a predestined one, as in Puritan tradition. The structure and meaning of *Childe Harold* and much of the meaning in his other serious works bear this stamp. The interactions between *Childe Harold* and some of the other works of similar mood and idea are interesting to look at in this light of Calvinist influence upon Byron's mind as a whole.

In the opening pages of this chapter the most famous direct presentations of Calvinist themes in *Childe Harold* were quoted, ones in which the doctrinal terms appear explicitly in Byron's own kind of special inversion of ultimate aims. The Puritan idea of the journey and predestination are also present throughout *Childe Harold* in more indirect ways, in imagery and in implicit assumptions that are at times below the level of the primary discourse. The opening sixteen stanzas of *Childe Harold* set the pace for Byron's constant meditations upon Puritan themes, his scrutiny of himself in relation to a destiny partly imposed from without (predestination) and partly from within (his version of original sin in the individual), which Gleckner calls the general fall from Paradise in all of Byron's serious work. Byron's primary interest in *Childe Harold* was, for better or worse, "his own dark mind"; where the canvas is wider in the travelogues it is seldom interesting except for a few bright spots when the internal, meditative interest mingles with some object of contemplation. The historical musings, *laudator temporis acti*, give greater occasion than the travelogues for such interaction. In the first sixteen stanzas the interaction is between the character and his own fate, as the narrator slowly gets the new canto underway. It is unlikely that Byron's knowledge of Calvinism was more than general, a mental atmosphere inherited from schoolmasters and his mother's ancestors. Part One of this book cited a famous passage on journey and shipwreck in Calvin's *Institutes*. Though there is little likelihood that Byron knew the passage it is interesting to recall it in looking closely at similar themes in the opening stanzas of Canto III. The analogues of the journey and shipwreck are legion, of course. Byron's peculiar instincts are Calvinist, having a parallel in intensity to the thoughts of Calvin on this otherwise very general subject:

Therefore, if we dread shipwreck, let us anxiously beware of this rock, on which none ever strike without being destroyed. But though the discussion of predestination may be compared to a dangerous ocean yet, in traversing over it, the navigation is safe and serene, and I will also add pleasant, unless any one freely wishes to expose himself to danger.[88]

No one more than Byron wished to expose himself to the dangers that make the journey in relation to predestination a dangerous one. The ocean metaphor in all of its forms is most apt for his inverted, fated, yet meditative Calvinism in the Puritan tradition. His use of the ocean image in *Childe Harold* III, apart from literary commonplace and naturalism, is also a felicitous hereditary instinct, no matter how little he may have known of Calvin's own writings. The ocean journey allows him to meditate in the Puritan tradition on his own terms, the religious ideas brought up to date and spiced with Byronic perverseness.

 Canto III opens with the idea of the journey that dominates all of *Childe Harold*, the image of the ocean as a vast uncertainty willingly entertained, and of a fate (predestination) met more than half-way by force of the will. The language of the journey is not explicitly religious. "I depart / Whither I know not. . . ." "Once more upon the waters! Swift be their guidance, whereso'er it lead!" When the narrative contemplates the reasons for the departure in the necessities of "the wandering outlaw of his own dark mind," the Calvinist relationship between sin, guilt and the necessary, predestined journey begins to emerge: "the journeying years / Plod the last sands of life." Inward and outward hopelessness are equated again and again by Byron, the inward Calvinist cause of sin transferred secularly to an attitude of hostility towards the world in which the pilgrim is always a transient fated figure. Fate or predestination is not made the grounds of injustice in this situation, as a more superficial or self-pitying observer might have been inclined to have done. The narrator proclaims, "My Springs of life were poison'd," but his finger is not pointed at any person or single situation. Those familiar with Byron's life know that he often pointed to many culprits, as he does also in lesser poems and is tempted to do here as thoughts of his wife and daughter cross his mind. For purposes of the fiction he is willing only to assign a hereditary taint, ancestral, personal, and environmental, summed up later in one of the great climatic passages as the process of a general predestination, his inheritance of Scotch Presbyterian tradition in his own way. These passages were quoted earlier by means of introduction to the subject of Calvinism in Byron. Stanza vi stands in some contrast to the main drift of this opening, one of Byron's few contemplations of aesthetic creation as an act valid in and for itself, also one of his last thoughts at the end of Canto IV and thus not merely an isolated whim. But this commonplace of German and English Romantics is very rare in Byron's poetry. It is significant here as an alternative to the more literal, Calvinist and existential musings which dominate the opening stanzas and the poem. Stanzas x—xvi merely reiterate the familiar picture of Harold in tones somewhat blacker than in Cantos I and II, as befits the hero of this new journey. Then begins the scenic tour of battlefields, beautiful places and encomia of famous men, interspersed by attempts at nature meditation in the manner of Shelley and Wordsworth. Of all this, only stanzas lxxiii and cviii have interest for the Calvinist religious theme. This theme becomes more open and important in Canto IV in the stanzas discussing sin and predestination.

In lxxiii Byron is brought back to his sole self from one of his strongest nature flights ending on the halcyonic "And thus I am absorbed, and this is life." As Keats was drawn away from the nightingale by the word "forlorn," a single word also ruins Byron's reverie, the word "sin," or more exactly, "Where, for some sin, to sorrow I was cast. . . ." He manages to soar again, temporarily, in the stanzas that follow, but not until the idea of sin has cast its shadow across his happier musings. The lines

I look upon the peopled desert past,
   As on a place of agony and strife. . . .

bring together again the ideas of sin-guilt and the fatal predestined journey from which the imagination can escape only temporarily. This "some sin" is the one referred to constantly in the canto and elsewhere, that combination of hereditary taint and personal will in his nature which Byron looked upon as his lack of election, usually phrased in contemporary descriptive language as "demonic." Byron tried later in life to convince some of his friends that he took these religious ideas seriously. Some believed him, others not, and the argument perhaps rests fairly in that uncertain modern appellation of Byron as sceptic and believer. More recent criticism has stressed the sceptic, the cynic and the artist. Yet when the poet goes on to say at the end of the nature reverie, "But this is not my theme," he is essentially correct, even if other reveries will occur throughout the poem. Stanza cviii in particular should be read as a corrective to some recent negligence of the element of belief in Byron. Without that element the power of the persona's suffering would disappear; he would be a mere poseur. There is some posing in *Childe Harold* and in *Don Juan*, yet what serious critic of Byron can admit that the source of all of this lies in mere play-acting? Byron has been rescued from this charge by recent criticism without the point having been driven hard enough. Stanza cviii is an indication of Byron's seriousness about religion, for it points out sharply something only implied or handled with humor (and therefore open to question and misinterpretation) in many other passages of *Childe Harold* and *Don Juan*. The source of the power of his poses lies in the conflict between scepticism and belief in deity with its attendant retribution:

> Yet, peace be with their ashes, − for by them,
> If merited, the penalty is paid;
> It is not ours to judge, − far less condemn;
> The hour must come when such things shall be made
> Known unto all, or hope and dread allay'd
> By slumber, on one pillow, in the dust,
> Which, thus much we are sure, must lie decay'd;
> And when it shall revive, as is our trust,
> 'Twill be to be forgiven, or suffer what is just.

For Byron scepticism means the usual dust and eternal slumber of classical tradition. Belief, "as is our trust," will bring an eternal choice, as in orthodoxy. This stanza is about Voltaire and Rousseau and so does not indicate the nature of the eternal choice for the narrator, a choice abundantly clear elsewhere as predestined damnation. The fact is that this stanza proves the existence of a rock-bottom belief, as strong as is possible in any thinking, sophisticated person, a belief which Byron usually twists to his own damnation. Calvin had asserted that the ocean journey might be serene for the elect. Shipwreck is possible for many, but not for those who cling to belief in election through the church. Childe Harold's bark, and later also Don Juan's, is always at the point of shipwreck, Don Juan's bark being actually engulfed in one instance. The shipwreck and engulfment metaphor is a true signal of Byron's conditional belief in damnation by his own interpretation of predestination. The jokes and posings cannot hide the same terror noted by everyone in Byron's fellow Calvinist and castaway, William Cowper. The reluctance to view terror as a dominant aspect of Byron's poetry is understandable. No two poets could differ more than the shy, reclusive, literal minded (on religious matters) Cowper and the worldly, scoffing, fanciful Byron. On this most fundamental matter under their different surfaces they were much alike, struck by the same terror of Calvinist heritage misapplied. Blake avoided a morbid Calvinist humor by revision, Coleridge by piety in later life and Wordsworth by cheerfulness and occupation with light and a heavenly destiny. Horror of life is at the heart of *Childe Harold* III and IV, spreading from there to include all the works of his maturity that modern readers still find of interest.

Canto IV is the culmination of Byron's commitment to belief and predestination to doom. It may be viewed as the centerpiece of his poetry. Direct presentation of these themes appears in *Cain* and *Heaven and Earth*, where hatred of an unjust yet all powerful God determines the theological twistings of the biblical materials. Byron's sympathy, a mixture of sentimentality and defiance, is obviously with those who lose out in God's plans for man, while his awe and fear, and primary reason for writing the plays, is with the idea of the indisputable and unjust decrees of God for most men.. The minimal success of these works is a mark of his inability to sort out his thoughts and emotions on these matters. In the 1816 divorce and Diodati poems Byron's concentration fell upon the dust and deity conflict in his own nature, a nature implicitly condemned by the implied inverted Calvinism of *Childe Harold* III and IV. *Manfred* is more problematic in these respects. The defiance and doom of the individual will may have the same source in Byron's Calvinist obsessions — nowhere in the dramatic action is the existence of an all powerful malign deity denied. Traditional Christian heaven and classical Hades are played off against each other, without their relationship to something more ultimate brought into focus. The denial of the power of traditional forces by Manfred need not preclude the shadowy presence of the ultimate, greater, inscrutible being. As in the drastic naturalistic poem "Darkness" the higher power is not explicit in the final reckoning. Manfred's concern with the autonomy of his own will and choice as the basis of his life and dignity admits the modern term "existential" into discussion of the play as more than a mere critical fad. Yet what Byron seems to admire in the will of Manfred, its autonomy and static defiance of all outside forces, is, we must remember, a different quality than that emphasis upon action and the need for action as the determinant of character and identity in the godless world of Sartre and others. Manfred may be static in the unseen presence of some unstated determining force, a *deus absconditus* not forgotten, forgiving or forgiven. Admittedly this is critical speculation, on a plane with the surmises of other critics coming to terms with the difficult ending of the play, in a less worldly direction than has been fashionable recently. *Don Juan* as a full poem lies outside the scope of this chapter. Yet I will venture that its inner meaning is not so far from that sketched here for *Childe Harold* III and IV. The best alternatives recent critics have had to offer − that it is an elaborate joke, or terminal irony, or an elaboration of the myth of the fall, or a renewal of humanism and man's dignity and belief in liberty − seem unsatisfactory. There is evidence in such a vast and unfinished poem for all these views[89]. From the perspective of this book the essential theme seems to be that pointed out by Marshall, the gradually darkening corridor and grimness as the poem progresses, and the uneasy, threatening quality of the entire poem. The blood thirsty God of the shipwreck and battle scenes has been noted by Lovell and acknowledged to a point by every serious critic. No one has recently made the point, in deference to sophisticated scepticism, that it is the malign influence of Abraham's God without his Covenant, otherwise recognizable as Calvin's God without the dogmatic peculiarity of election for the few, which gives the special hideous quality to the total poem, a poem whose parts are variously funny, worldly, cynical, even at times Romantic and benign. The critical confusions and cautions arise from the refusal of the critics to see deity as Byron saw it, as belief without hope, and Byron as a Calvinist *malgré lui* in his thought and works of serious purpose.

To return to Canto IV and the elaboration of the Calvinist theme in the context of the complete poem. Canto I tends to justify the medley of themes and various structures in the previous three cantos. This justification of *Childe Harold's Pilgrimage*, except for the important ways in which the understanding of the Calvinist question also reveals some unity in the total poem, is a matter of secondary interest to the purpose of this chapter. The work of Ridenour and Gleckner is most helpful on the question of unity and value in the poem, and will be drawn freely upon, although this writer does not share their sanguine views of Byron's full success on the structural level.[89] They in turn have not very much interest in Byron's Calvinism as such. Yet to a point their structural views of *Childe Harold* and this argument complement each other quite happily.

Through Cantos I–III it is reasonable to accept the idea of some separation between the narrator-poet and the character Childe Harold. This separation is not necessarily as elaborate and consistent as Gleckner and Ridenour try to hold, to justify the structure of the entire poem. The poem is very powerful and successful, even if flawed in minute execution. Harold is prematurely doomed from the start, a victim of personal and hereditary traits. The few allusions to predestination and Calvinism in the early cantos apply to him, not to the poet or the scope of the cantos. The poet-narrator delights in travel, in events and in moralizing in Cantos I and II, and some of this attitude persists into the darker atmosphere of III. The moralizings in particular are quite positive, especially on the subjects of liberty and Mediterranean decadence. Presumably Harold is in no position to share such views and joys. In Canto III the moralism becomes less sure, and there is a deepening gloom, without however a complete merging of poet and character. Travels and events are still pursued with interest by the poet-narrator, and a new interest, in the process of creation, enters the poem at the point at which interest in travel and events begins to flag. The most magnificent parts of Canto III are the attempts to find redemption in Wordsworthian-Shelleyan nature, the metaphysical rather than the landscape approach to nature, and the failure of that aim. During this misadventure the minds of the pilgrim and the poet grow closer, as the later loses further hope in things of the world. The poet becomes more like Harold as his various hopes wane, but he has not as yet been restricted to the doomed Calvinist sense of life as his only course.

Canto IV radically alters this situation. Belief in travel, event and positive values disappears. Only the belief in the visions of art, introduced in Canto III, remains as a counterforce to the prevailing

Calvinist gloom. The general sense of doom and fate finally becomes identical with Harold's personal doom in Canto IV. That is why we find both personal, restrictive Calvinist passages and large general ones as Canto IV progresses. The fate of Harold has become the fate of the poet, and that in turn the fate of the world at large. Therefore the disappearance of Harold as a separate character in Canto IV has perfect logic; as predestination overtakes the poet and his poem, travel becomes mere vacancy, a mental removal from reality, and events, formerly exciting, are now only static meditations upon the graves of the great, or upon the ruins of ancient Rome and later Christian civilization. Civilization itself, and man's life in it, is merely a cycle of despair from the viewpoint of time:

> There is the moral of all human tales;
> 'This but the same rehearsal of the past,
> First Freedom, and then Glory — when that fails,
> Wealth, vice, corruption, — barbarism at last. (cviii)

The viewpoint of time is not the poet's final interest. From the viewpoint of eternity, or of "the pilgrim of eternity," man's fate becomes predestination, as secularized in the great metaphors of the Calvinist tradition quoted in the beginning of this chapter, surely the most powerful passages in Canto IV. The journey image remains central, and an important irony. Pilgrimage to secular shrines, the graves of Voltaire, Rousseau and Dante, brings no hope, yet the religious shrines of the believing past, Rome or Canterbury, are unavailable in any real sense, except as lessons in despair. The eternal ocean at the end represents eternal power, as Shelley's Mont Blanc, a power unknown, unrelated, and unfriendly to man. God exists, as an absolute other, indifferent or malicious, always there in the manifest power of the ocean. Many writers have come to this conclusion, a rather commonplace one since Byron's time. Byron used the metaphors of his Calvinist heritage to express it, first restricted to a character somewhat like his younger self, Childe Harold, then his larger self, finally the entire universe. The visions of artists, the need to create and to live through works of art, a need as old as Horace and as contemporary as Wordsworth, provide the one counterforce against the negative tidal wave at the end of Canto IV, expressed in Calvinist terms. This element is relatively weak in Byron, as he is confronted by an intellect which tells him that all works of man are foredoomed to atrophy. Imagination urges man to creations and permanence, an urge Byron shared with his fellow Romantic poets. His emotions, the personal ones expressed through the character of Harold, tracing the peculiarities of Byron's Calvinism, place final responsibility on God, the Calvinist God who is real and powerful, not good and true to man. This is twisted Calvinism, as has been said above, yet an element in Byron's poetry giving special flavor and direction. This unique conflict — for an English Romantic poet — gives his works at their best the affinity some have noted with the most serious 19th century American Calvinists, Hawthorne, Melville and Dickinson. No other Romantic poet was so deeply affected by the dark and negative side of Calvinist thought and tradition.

Epilogue

It remains now only to consider some of the reasons for the break-down of the Calvinist-Puritan tradition in English poetry. The reasons for England and America are somewhat different, though the under-lying cause is the same. That was the loosening of the hold of religion upon the mind of modern man in all countries of the western world. Considering the force of this phenomenon, the fact of religious poetry and literature, which continues to this day in various traditions, is a major event in itself and not easily explained. Calvinist-Puritanism is not one of the viable religious traditions of today, so it would seem, and all the factors in its disintegration can be found in the lifetimes of Dickinson in America and Ruskin in England.

In England there was a positive transference from the Calvinist-Puritan mode of religious thought to others in the decline of the Romantic movement. No one kept up the interest of Coleridge and Wordsworth in Puritan religious patterns. The Tractarian, Oxford and High Church movements claimed the most illustrious religious minds of the Victorian period. Ruskin, of Puritan origins, was an exception, but he abandoned the interests of his ancestors for an aesthetic view of art and culture, creating the tradition of Pater, Wilde and the Aesthetes. Calvinist-Puritanism comes back into this work as no more than a vague yearning, and is explicitly rejected. Ruskin's important and justly famous comment on *The Faerie Queene* as symbol and allegory might be considered a final strange flourishing of Puritan thought in the English tradition.

The successes, failures, and continuities of the Oxford movement, and the later revival of Roman Catholic writing in England, are not our concern here. Suffice it to say that it is in these two forms that religious literature led its life, powerful in the early third of this century, a waning yet important influence since the Second World

War. Waugh, Chesterton, Greene and Belloc are still names to take seriously, not easily dismissed even by the various types of "liberal" academic criticism. There have been other revivals of older traditions in twentieth century English literature, rivals of the prevailing cosmopolitan and sophisticated European models of literary culture. The ethnic revivals of Irish, Scots and Welsh literature have had a few major, and many minor, successes. There has been no similar revival of the traditions of the Calvinist-Puritans, despite the fact that this tradition, as we have now seen, is one of the most central and enduring of the English past since the Reformation. Though the religion of the sectarians seemed to have died as a cultural force with the loss of faith of Ruskin, a kind of secular sectarianism does live in the working-class novelists of the 20th century. A consideration of dying faith in Ruskin and dead religion, hatred of religion turned to social goods and the cult of sex in Lawrence, will conclude this necessarily brief postscript of Calvinist religion and literature in modern England.

Before this glimpse at Ruskin and Lawrence, a look at the situation and decay of Calvinism in America in the 19th century will not be out of place. In the second section of this book, on the 17th century, an argument for including Edward Taylor was given. He was born in England, his interests were mainly in the moral and intellectual sides of Puritanism, and his life was spent mainly as a curé of souls. Not affected by the evolutionary movement of Puritanism in New England about which Perry Miller and his school have written so well,[1] the inclusion of Taylor in a book on English Puritanism is fair. This cannot be said for any later American writer, even those deeply influenced by Puritan thought. The American situation created vital changes in Puritanism, even in Dickinson, Melville and Hawthorne, the spiritual heirs of Edwards and the 17th century. Our point, then, in glancing at the American tradition will not be literary analysis as such, considering the many fine studies available on American writers. The only point is to provide a skeletal cultural contrast for the English situation after the Romantic period.

The case of Edwards is crucial as we approach early 19th century New England literary figures, for we cannot hold up the rather comforting theory of anachronism that allowed Taylor to be looked upon as an English poet. Edwards is the complete American Puritan. The inner life of Puritanism and its artistic sensibility came to him from the 17th century, and he passed it enriched to Dickinson, Hawthorne and Melville. This is not to deny that there were enormous outside influences upon the truly Puritan writers, including the influence of Emerson and Whitman, nor that the majority did not follow the paths charted by Miller and Feidelson, from Puritanism to federal theology to rationalism to transcendentalism. But the great Puritan writers did not follow that path, though they were aware of all the dominant trends. Biographical facts give a partial explanation, but this writer is willing to hazard the deeper explanation that the moral and metaphysical concerns of the best artists were more in harmony with the somber and at times tragic explanations of man's destiny which Puritanism was capable of sustaining, than with the optimistic and cheerful views of man and society that became their official replacement in the 19th century transformation of Calvinist-Puritanism into transcendentalism-democracy. Calvinist-Puritanism in America remained viable through the lifetimes of Dickinson, Melville, and Hawthorne. These Puritans have more in common with Coleridge, Wordsworth, Byron and Cowper than either set of poets, English or American, had with compatriots who marched to more secular and optimistic drums. That these are the better writers for their deep religious sense of life with its tragic implications is also true, but not a point that can be dealt with directly in this epilogue.

Edwards, like Baxter and Law, a writer of powerful prose, is outside the formal limits of this study. He is the crucial intellectual figure in America, more important as a single figure than Baxter or Law to England. His presence, intellectual power, and choices ensured the continuance of some form of genuine Puritan thought and belief into the early 19th century, as counterbalance to federal theology, Unitarianism, and transcendentalism. That course was long delayed by Edwards and was never inevitable. On the thorny problem of a decisive New England view emerging towards the end of the 17th century, all serious students defer to Miller's work, though there are important qualifications which the case of Edwards fully proves. Norman Pettit's *The Heart Prepared* has pointed out the continuities between English and New England thinking on that subject, so vital for an understanding of the place of devotion in Puritan thought and thus the grounds for a certain kind of Puritan poetry[2]. Among other things carefully documented by Pettit are the struggles between preparationists and believers in instant election, and the irony of Edward's reversal of what might be called the more liberal trend of his grandfather Stoddard. From our distance and standpoint both positions fall within the range of genuine Calvinist experience. It was the more dramatic or terrifying style of conversion that was urged on Emily Dickinson, to no avail.

This may also be the place to mention some of the poetic qualities of Edwards' Puritan mind and literary style, for these, solidly within the mainstream of Puritan tradition, certainly provided a strong influence upon early 19th century Puritanism, and helped to keep alive the more authentic varieties. There is no exact way that this influence can be documented, beyond the fact that Edwards was read by many important 19th century writers, including Dickinson. By their day most of Edward's theology was found abhorrent, Chauncy and the Liberals having won the public mind, but the deep impression of Edwards' conservative Calvinism upon Hawthorne, Dickinson and Melville is obvious, for they were in reaction to the optimism and rationalism against which Edwards had fought his last rear-guard action. Denying belief in literal Puritan doctrine, none of these writers could have found Edwards' theology of conversion experience attractive, but they were drawn to his intensity and intellectual superiority over his adversaries, as we are. His fusion of Lockean language theory and the old Puritan doctrines of the patterns of salvation created a style that tried to render the thing, the idea and the word as one, creating awesome visions of ecstacy or terror. The famous "Sinners in the Hands of an Angry God" and its image of the spider wriggling over the flame is an example of a kind of work that the 19th century Puritan descendants, still disciplined and sensitized to the physical reality implied by such words in the Puritan drama of salvation, responded to powerfully. The intensity of scene and words in Hawthorne and Melville owes much to Edwards. His influence upon major poetry is more limited in the late 18th and early 19th centuries. Not many serious literate and intellectual people were then eager to read *Religious Affections* or *A Faithful Narrative of the Surprising Work of God*. The ideas, patterns and power of these works are a part only of the poetry of Emily Dickinson, among major writers. Finally Edwards, like so many of the best Puritan writers before him, has to be called a poet in prose, at least in regard to his greatest flights of imagination expressing Puritan doctrine and idea. It is a pity to find so few poets among the most gifted Puritans, a situation for which obvious reasons are available and yet do not explain why Taylor and Dickinson could turn to poetry as a means of expression, while Edwards, the most intense and palpable Puritan of all, inventing his Lockean-Puritan

amalgam of "taste," "excellency" and "relish" to express the spiritual
life, presumably found it trivial or inadequate. No one of sufficient
merit until Dickinson arose to adopt his new patterns to poetry, which
is only better than having a series of inadequate followers. Dickinson
used an Edwards transformed to her own original purposes, a transformation in which many other influences are involved, as we expect
in the influence of one original mind upon another.

Before leaving the subject of Edwards and his influence we must
admit that not too much comfort can be extracted from it, only
enough to encourage the thought of important influence upon 19th
century poetry. Though Edwards on occasion has poetic sensibility,
and first-rate Calvinist-Puritan sensibility at that, his influence should
not be overrated in reaction to the ministrations of the Miller school.
We have discussed the only poet of note in American 18th century
Calvinism, the rather conventional Samuel Davies. Edwards' own
thought on beauty and its place in the divine scheme of the Trinity is
so abstract as to constitute a branch of ontology and metaphysics,
on the Augustinian or Aquinian model, and hardly one by which
poets were to be deeply moved.[3] On the other hand, since we have
made and must accept the distinction between personal and social
Calvinism, there is abundant evidence that Edwards' social doctrines
had transformational and even revolutionary effects upon Calvinist
thinking in the aftermath of the Great Awakening, leading despite his
own inclinations to a more worldly and secular view of man and
society.[4] A mind like Edwards' inevitably has enormous influence in
all areas, many contradictory with others, as the historians of the
American mind have pointed out. In strictly literary terms he did not
himself attempt much, but one tendency of his writings was to
preserve and transfer the power in the doctrines of Calvinism to later
generations, a thing that without him would no doubt have been
impossible. This is his contribution and importance for the study of
Puritanism and literature.

In the Deerfield valley the religious tradition of Stoddard and
Edwards survived vigorously into the middle of the 19th century. For
the childhood and adolescence of Emily Dickinson the traditional
ideas, and more importantly, the feelings attached to them, of calling,
election, grace and joining the church in a profession of Christ as a
visible sign were *the* way of life, almost as hard, stern and unbending
as in the earliest New England or English traditions. All biographers
and critics of Dickinson agree that the poet outgrew the original,

literal Calvinism, and point to the fact of her inability to make public profession of Christianity and to accept election. A long series of poems revealing the crisis in a spiritual, mental warfare with the self is accepted by all readers of Dickinson as an extraordinary revealing of the Calvinist temper somewhat secularized. Her Calvinist feeling was removed to pattern, analogy and metaphor. In her mature writing there is certainly evidence of wide reading outside of the Calvinist tradition, with no indication that Calvinism was decisively repudiated or transcended. She read and absorbed Emerson and the American agnostics as adeptly as Joyce did all of the currents of European thought before and after leaving Ireland. Yet as Joyce's writings are grounded in Irish Catholicism, as even liberal critics are willing to understand, so Dickinson's are based in the authentic Calvinism of her environment, not because of fate or her lack of cleverness in transcending the background, but rather because the background offered her more than did anything from the outside to deal with her problems, her poetic gift, and her world.

The general elements of this spiritual Calvinism are located easily in her poetry. It is true that some of these elements may seem so general as to be the constituents of any good poetry, in which cases Calvinism merely adds intensification. Others are directly the result of the process of secularization of Calvinism in aesthetic impulses, and are of more immediate interest in understanding the poetry. In the first group fall intense introspection, heightened sense of the self and of self-consciousness, and painstaking attention to detail. The second certainly includes secularized usages of such ideas as predestination, renunciation, election, calling, and sanctification, applied to nature and other elements of life in this world. The sense of guilt and sin appears in many disguises, and perhaps more dubiously, the Puritan occupation with glorification and last things in her obsession with death. This last point is more dubious than the others because Dickinson's usages of death are so very dramatic and theatrical and many times dwell intensely upon physical elements of no spiritual value. At their best, though, the death poems hint at the impending revelation that the hours before death are supposed to bring in Puritan tradition, that sense of being one of the the saved or elect which in Dickinson's poems becomes the possibility for some mysterious secular revelation that is never named because untransferable from the dying to the living.

Dickinson, like the other great Puritan writers of the early 19th century, Hawthorne and Melville, is more at ease with nature and the world, and even with writing as a vocation than were the earlier Puritan poets. The later poets are less at ease with the theology, though attempts to bury it merely reveal its hidden powers. Perhaps Jonathan Edwards' great struggle in the previous century with the place of beauty in the theology of Calvinism, with its final assertion of the concept of beauty over that of power in the Calvinist Godhead, was the turning point in making aesthetics easier within Calvinist-Puritanism, even though Edwards' rarified intellectual world of ideas could have had little direct effect. Indirectly, through Emerson and popularizers of Emerson among the clergy, Edwards' austere struggle with and final acknowledgement of the primacy of beauty in the manifestation of God in the world reached Emily Dickinson through her reading. But not even Edwards' great intellect could stem the forces of decay leading to the demise of literal belief in Calvinist theology among the educated class in the 19th century, and Emily Dickinson's case history in this respect was unique only by virtue of her great gifts of imagination and sensibility. Many others travelled the path from doubt and emotional acceptance of the system to the new destination of pure scepticism and emotional withdrawal, rather than to the assurance and serenity which earlier generations of Puritans were led to expect and found. Dickinson's case was unusual in her early clarity and obstinacy in refusing to submit herself to the conversion experience at all.

Her situation with respect to both religion and poetry corresponds closely to that of the English poets Coleridge and Wordsworth, and even more exactly, in the decisive influence of the Calvinist strain of religious influence, with those of Byron and Cowper as described in this book. Apart from this brief description of its Calvinist contours, however, this is not the place for extensive analysis of Dickinson's poetry.

The final American Calvinist figures in the 19th century are Hawthorne and Melville. The Calvinist strain in both has been fully discussed many times. In our introduction to the English 19th century something was said of Hawthorne's Calvinism, and we noted a curious analogy between Coleridge and Melville in a later part of that section. Again the major point brought out is the general similarity of English and American writers in this tradition, an unavowed or unknown cousinship in most instances. The decay of Calvinism in America was delayed by the magnificent writings of Hawthorne, Melville and Dickinson, yet there is no doubt that they were living in its final phase of power, the literary power that often follows the intellectual. As a serious system of thought, Calvinism had decayed sadly from the time of Edwards to that of these great writers. Emerson, Thoreau, and Whitman represent and lead to different ideas and traditions, the triumph of the transcendental, the democratic, the non-tragic sense of life and the irrelevance of spiritual religion. American literature was to return to the tragic vision in the twentieth century, though not to its Calvinist form. Many writers and poets were to be haunted by the image of Ahab ineluctably predestined to sink into the ocean with Moby Dick, or of Ethan Brand leaping into the lime kiln. Religiously based terror and tragedy were not to be revived. The 19th century writers were remote from Calvinist belief, but not sensibility; after about fifty years of optimism, tragedy returned to American literature, while Calvin and his American progeny, the Puritans, remained remote and inaccessible on the shelves of libraries, except for the enthusiasm of scholars, critics, and a few southern writers.[5]

The most eloquent and greatest Puritan witness in 19th century England after the Romantic period in the literary world was John Ruskin. His evangelical background, crisis of faith, period of disbelief and return to a general Christian faith have been closely documented, most recently by Leon and Landow.[6] Such a crisis for a brilliant and pious person was inevitable in the mid-19th century. Ruskin's was prolonged throughout most of his life, beginning with his refusal to take orders upon graduation, to a later more serious crisis of despair brought on by personal problems, then a long period of agnosticism and seeming indifference to religious problems, and finally a return to modified faith. Ruskin's return to general Christian faith is more surprising than its loss. The more likely alternatives were to lose faith completely, or undergo a drastic conversion experience, as happened variously to Manning, Newman, Darwin and Tennyson, and countless other intelligent people of lesser note. Ruskin is most significant because his early belief was in the Puritan-evangelical tradition, engrained and familial, combined with an unusually precocious artistic temper. His Puritan displacements in literary guise, such as the famous commentary on *The Faerie Queene*'s allegorical meaning, give an idea of the potential be might have had as a religious writer. But his ultimate commitment was to be to art, not to religion, and an association of the liberation of the imagination with art and literature. The later, genuinely Christian Ruskin in faith and act disavowed his early sectarian origins and preferred to express his views in aesthetic and literary terms. In doing so, Ruskin stands for the death of Puritan-evangelical sensibility in literature. Though not primarily an aesthete, he bequeathed aestheticism, not religious sensibility in literature, to the next generation of writers and critics who did not share his anguish over faith and belief. The words of Leon are appropriate here, though we need not share his certainty about the rightness of the outcome:

> But Ruskin's real communion, throughout his life, was the communion of the artist and poet: his *panis supersubstantialis* those rare moments of fully awakened consciousness when the mind is detached and deliberately at rest; when . . . the emotional faculties, cleansed of all human desire and sorrow, respond in serenity and joy to the mystery and beauty of the external world.[7]

Generations of earlier evangelicals and Puritans, Ruskin's ancestors, had such moments within certain faith; some were literary artists, as we have seen. The crucial point about Ruskin was not that he lost and regained his faith, but that he did both largely apart from his literary activity. Religion was seldom a matter of poetry or imagination for him, though it was a genuine burden. He found final artistic serenity elsewhere, and solace in the practical aspects of Christianity, for which he is justly famous and admired. Ruskin is the end of the Puritan line in positive literature. George Eliot was another evangelical who underwent crisis, threw off her background completely, and went on to view it with the cold eye of satire. Ruskin is somehow authentically evangelical-Puritan to the end, even in his abandonment of the tradition as useless for artistic purposes in his time. There was no more that could be said, seemingly, through it, and though he felt great agony over the outcome, with Puritan seriousness he was willing to abandon Puritanism as a serious element in the English literature of the present and future, only able to respond to it when thinking of the past, and then once greatly, in his exposition of Puritan allegory in *The Faerie Queene*.

Calvinist religious tradition is still alive in the early work of D. H. Lawrence, especially *Sons and Lovers*. The viewpoint toward religion in that book will stand here for all the authentic working-class novels of the early 20th century, and books about the working class written from a sympathetic but superior perspective. The common denominator in these works is that sectarian religion is an aspect of the degradation and poverty of the miners, factory workers, others forced to do the hard work in the new industrial era. The men, sodden and bitter, despise the chapel. For the women it is a consolation for their burnt-out lives, and a source of friction with the men as marriages sour in grinding poverty. The chapels and their dreary services provide no imaginative or emotional relief from the bitterness of actual life. For Blake's chimney sweeps imagination transformed the services from perfunctory rituals into a temporary vision of perfect joy and peace. In Lawrence and the others, parsons persuade the poor to accept and to remain in their place, willing tools of the state and the industrial system. The message of Christ and salvation, presented in the bleak Calvinist way, plays into the hands of the rich and powerful, leaving the poor in despair. What was once a force for individualism, dignity and imagination is now a tawdry rationalization of the dismal fate of the downtrodden, helping them to accept what they must expect throughout their lives. God has chosen them to remain poor, miserable and ignorant. This is how the ineradicable decree of fate, the sublime doctrine for all men, was parsed for the flock by complacent clergymen. Paul Morel, and the many others like him – young, imaginative, enlightened by reading – reject this version of fate, tainted by association with family, poverty, degradation. Whether explicitly Marxist or not, young literary rebels of the early 20th century viewed all protestantism, especially Calvinism, as a system repressing the individual's personality and instincts, while also forcing life into a pattern suitable to industrial capitalism. This is the well known Tawney thesis. Its validity is not our interest here, but the wholehearted imaginative acceptance of this viewpoint by the bright scions of the non-conformist poor meant that hatred and rebellion would replace Ruskin's more pious and resigned indifference to the decline and failure of the Calvinist tradition. In the 20th century the ridicule and hatred come from the individual within the tradition joining the forces hostile to Calvinism since the 17th century. Also widely accepted is the theory that the extreme sexual rebellion of Lawrence and lesser versions of it in others can be viewed as some twisted Calvinism in reverse, sex having always been the primary symbol of repression in the narrow, dreary unimaginative pastoral practice of the 19th century. The preachers were perceived not only to have connived at the oppression of man's body by industrialism, but also to have oppressed his spirit needlessly with guilt feelings about one of the few natural pleasures given even to the very poor. It was a manifest duty of young rebels like Paul Morel to reject all religion, especially dour non-conformist Calvinism, to equate it with capitalist exploitation of the poor, to contrast it with humanism and socialism, and find in sexual experience and the imagination it released, the salvation offered by earlier generations of Calvinist preachers through the religious joy of the Word, not as interpreted by the cold logic and stern light of Calvin himself, but by his many exegetes in the Puritan heyday of the 16th and 17th centuries. On this note we must end our study, for since the early 20th century there has been no more to add of literary merit in England. Even the softer and more popular religious traditions have come to be ignored by the most sophisticated critical circles on both sides of the Atlantic, though they are probably going to remain strong influences upon the writing of novels, poetry and drama for some time to come. Calvinism was resolute. Its most distinguished sons deserted it when they could not live by and through it. These distinguished progeny, from Carlyle to Lawrence, became the most violent and methodical detractors of religion, and at pains to separate religion and literature forever. But that is another story. We have finished the one chosen to tell in this book.[8]

Notes

Notes to Part One

1 John T. McNeill, *The History and Character of Calvinism* (New York, 1954).
2 William Haller, *The Rise of Puritanism* (New York, 1938).
3 Perry Miller, *The New England Mind: The Seventeenth Century* (1939; rpt. Cambridge, Mass., 1954).
4 The place of the sacraments, and especially the Eucharist or Lord's Supper, was in Calvin's system, and still is among his commentators, a subject of great dispute. In later sections of this study we shall see the practical consequences of this troublesome problem in the disagreements among students of piety and literature such as Martz and Wakefield about the importance of Eucharistic worship in the Calvinist tradition. In Francois Wendel, *Calvin, The Origins and Development of his Religious Thought* (New York, 1963), pp. 312−55, there is a succinct and lucid explanation of the place of the sacraments in Calvin's system. On the Lord's Supper Calvin insisted upon more than mere "spiritual" presence, as in Zwingli, but less than in the bodily or real presence of Luther or the Catholics. The distinctions made by Calvin are subtle and at times only verbal, as Wendel shrewdly points out. The place of the sacraments must be ambiguous in a system with the center in the Word, the Gospel, and elsewhere, as was Calvin's. Calvin's ambiguity between "spiritual" and "actual" presence led to important conclusions for the history of doctrine and worship in Calvinism. There was bound to be a range of belief and practice from empty "sign" on the left to actual, though not bodily, presence on the right of Calvinist worship and piety. The simple either / or solutions of modern literary commentators miss this fact. But one thing is clear in Calvin, as Wendel stresses, and that is the need of the believing subject to partake in the sacramental act for it to take place, in order that the Work and the promises may be joined to the physical symbols of bread and wine. There is no sacrament without this conjoining, as in Catholic belief, and theoretically at least, in Lutheran and Anglican. Such shared belief of all Calvinists later led in the seventeenth century to a decisive type of Calvinist sacramental meditation, as we shall see in the poetry of Edward Taylor. The sacrament of the Lord's Supper was not a mere memorial or empty sign in Calvin's teaching or in the main line of Puritan devotion, at least in the English speaking world. The relevant passages in Wendel are as follows:

"According to Calvin, the spiritual reality of the body and blood of Christ does not identify itself with the material elements nor find itself in any way included in them. It is given at the same time as they were. This is neither the Roman transubstantiation nor the Lutheran consubstantiation, but neither is it the symbolization of Zwingli" (p. 339). "In fact, though Calvin always rejected the transfusion of the natural substance of the body of Christ, he did affirm, on the other hand, the communication by faith of the Christ and his benefits, considered as the spiritual substance of the body of Christ in the Supper. . . . He . . . could affirm the existence of a union with the substance of the Christ; but only by giving this term the meaning of a spiritual substance comprising the Christ himself and the benefits that he has won for us" (pp. 342–43). "The whole conflict upon this point can be shortly summed up thus: Union between the Christ and the Eucharistic elements meant, according to the Lutherans, that there was a real contact between the body and the blood on the one hand, and the bread and the wine on the other: according to Calvin, it meant only that the believer received the body of Christ when he consumed the consecreated bread. . . . The Lutherans therefore maintained that there was a direct relation between the Christ and the elements; Calvin, on the contrary, put the Christ and the elements separately into direct contact with the believer" (p. 344).

"The Eucharist, then, is a means of sanctification for the elect who are already incorporated in Christ. It is an instrument that the Holy Spirit uses to confirm our faith and deepen it, by giving us the ever-renewed certitude of our union with Christ, and by reinforcing that "holy union that we have with the Son of God. . . ." It serves to complete or to double the action of the Word, with the aid of material or corporeal means appropriate to our frailty" (p. 354).

5 This brief note presents only the books the writer has found useful, and is by no means intended as a complete bibliography. Francois Wendel's *Calvin* is the best recent comprehensive study; an historical account is found in McNeill's *History and Character of Calvinism*. For accounts of the *Institutes* and doctrines in general, see A. Mitchell Hunter, *The Teaching of Calvin*, 2nd ed. (London, 1950); Geddes MacGregor, *Corpus Christi* (London, 1959); Wilhelm Niesel, *The Theology of Calvin* (Philadelphia, 1956); and T. H. L. Parker, *The Oracles of God* (London, 1947). On specific doctrinal and theological points, see Heinrich Quistorp, *Calvin's Doctrine of the Last Things* (London, 1955); T. F. Torrance, *Calvin's Doctrine of Man* (London, 1949); and two books by Ronald S. Wallace, *Calvin's Doctrine of the Christian Life* (Edinburgh, 1959) and *Calvin's Doctrine of the Word and Sacrament* (Edinburgh, 1953).

6 John Calvin, *Institutes of the Christian Religion*, trans. John Allen, 2 vols. (London, 1838); all citations given hereafter in the text are from this edition; references are to book, chapter, and section number. Also consulted was the Westminster edition, trans. F. L. Battles and ed. J. T. McNeill, 2 vols, Vols. XX and XXI of *The Library of Christian Classics* (Philadelphia, 1960).

7 William Perkins, *A Discourse of Conscience Wherein is set down the nature, properties, and differences thereof* . . . in *The Works of William Perkins*, 2 vols. (Cambridge, 1608), I, 510.

8 Haller, *The Rise of Puritanism*; Louis L. Martz, *The Poetry of Meditation* (New Haven, 1954); Gordon Wakefield, *Puritan Devotion* (London, 1957); Malcom M. Ross, *Poetry and Dogma: The Transformation of Eucharistic Symbols in Seventeenth Century England* (New Brunswick, N. J., 1954). The ideas of Martz, Wakefield, and Ross will enter the discussion more fully below.

9 Walter Hilton, *The Scale of Perfection*, trans. Dom Gerard Sitwell (London, 1953), p. 222. Hilton also uses other terms which became central in Puritan thought, including "election to faith" in many chapters and "the secret operation of the Holy Ghost" in II, viii. But the use is always within the Catholic and medieval concepts of faith, and of penance and other practices rejected by the Reformation. On the whole it is fair to state that the chapter from which the quotation in the text was taken (II, xxviii, "The work of our Lord . . . the call, justification, exaltation, and glorification") finely indicates the degree of difference and similarity between Hilton and the Puritans. The Pauline language used there

by Hilton to describe a special mystical way of the religious contemplative life was later applied by the Puritans to the lives of all Christians without distinction in the world. The journey image and the way to Jerusalem will be of interest again in the chapter on Wordsworth (see note 59 to Section Four).

10 Augustine, *De Magistro*, as quoted in Louis L. Martz, *The Paradise Within* (New Haven, 1964), p. 169.

11 The *Confessions* and The *City of God* are referred to in the text by generic divisions, so that the reader may consult any good edition.

12 For excellent lists of the major Puritan writers of the sixteenth and seventeenth centuries, see Haller, pp. 405–40; John E. Smith, Introduction to Jonathan Edwards' *Religious Affections*, Vol. II in *The Works of Jonathan Edwards*, gen. ed. Perry Miller (New Haven, 1959), pp. 1–72; Wakefield, *Puritan Devotion, passim*.

13 John Flavel, *Husbandry Spiritualized* (London, 1669), for example.

14 Harry Berger, Jr., *The Allegorical Temper* (New Haven, 1957); U. Milo Kaufmann, *The Pilgrim's Progress and Tradition in Puritan Meditation* (New Haven, 1966); and Hyatt Waggoner, *Hawthorne: A Critical Study* (Cambridge, Mass., 1955) are fine examples of literary studies of aspects of Puritan tradition. See also note 8 to the epilogue of this book.

15 Edwards, *Religious Affections* (1746); the edition and notes by John E. Smith (see note 12 above) are used throughout this study.

16 Evelyn Underhill, *The Mystic Way: A Psychological Study in Christian Origins* (London, 1913) and *Mysticism: A Study in the Nature and Development of Man's Spiritual Consciousness* (London, 1911); William Inge, *Christian Mysticism* (London, 1932).

17 William Holden, *Anti-Puritan Satire, 1572–1642* (New Haven, 1954).

18 See Section Four, chapters one and three for further discussion of these points.

19 S. T. Coleridge, *Biographia Literaria*, ed. J. Shawcross, 2 vols. (Oxford, 1907), I, ix.

20 Martz, in *The Poetry of Meditation*, and Ross, in *Poetry and Dogma*, accept and perpetuate the cliché that Puritan doctrines and aestheticism are antithetical. John E. Smith, in the introduction to *Religious Affections*, and Gordon Wakefield, in *Puritan Devotion*, point out the injustice of this view with positive examples. More recent work, such as Lawrence Sasek's *The Literary Temper of the English Puritans* (Baton Rouge, La., 1961) and Kaufmann's *The Pilgrim's Progress* (1966) have done much to dispel this cliché.

21 Ross, *Poetry and Dogma*. Ross' case is based on the premise that the doctrine of the Real Presence is the true one, all others either approximations or errors. From this premise he notes the decline of fervor in sacramental poetry, culminating in the frozen dogma of Milton's *Paradise Lost*. But the decline of religious fervor was a cultural phenomenon in all religious groups, a change in religious style towards the close of the seventeenth century. Before that point the Puritans were as fervent in beliefs and devotions as the others, expressing them in Calvin's framework. Ross assigns the wrong cause to explain accepted facts, and thus his attack upon Milton is both unfair and misleading.

22 Cleanth Brooks and William K. Wimsatt, Jr., *Literary Criticism: A Short History* (New York, 1957), pp. 723–55. William Lynch, S. J., "Theology and the Imagination," *Thought* 29 (1954), 61–86 and 529–44; 30 (1955), 18–36.

23 Charles Feidelson, *Symbolism and American Literature* (Chicago, 1953), presents the standard view of historians of nineteenth-century American intellectual history, reinforced by the later writings of Perry Miller. The problem is that this view explains the majority, including such writers as Emerson, Whitman and James, but not Dickinson, Hawthorne, Melville, or their English counterparts.

24 Haller, *The Rise of Puritanism*, p. 93.

25 Haller, p. 95.

26 Haller, p. 96.
27 Haller, p. 97.
28 Haller, pp. 99–100.
29 Extensive and convenient bibliographical notes are given by Miller, Haller, Smith, Wakefield; and by M. M. Knappen, *Tudor Puritanism* (Chicago, 1939).
30 Wakefield, in *Puritan Devotion*, was the first to devote a great deal of space to Bayly as an exemplar of sixteenth-century Puritan piety, in refutation of the standard views accepted and passed on by Martz and others. But others have pointed out that extensive use of Bayly is questionable; though he was of the Puritan party in the Church, his theology was not decisively Calvinist-Puritan, as was the case with the Cambridge group.
31 Baxter will be quoted from the collected works, *The Practical Works of the Rev. Richard Baxter*, ed. Rev. William Orme, 23 vols. (London, 1830).
32 See Murray Roston, *Prophet and Poet: The Bible and the Growth of Romanticism* (Evanston, Ill., 1965) on this point.
33 Henri Talon, *John Bunyan: The Man and His Works* (London, 1951).
34 Talon, pp. 29–30.
35 Talon, p. 88.
36 Talon, p. 89.
37 Talon, p. 93.
38 Talon, p. 91.
39 Calvin, *Institutes* (trans. Allen), I.I.I. and I.I.II.
40 Perkins, *A Golden Chaine: or the description of Theologie* in *Works* (1608), I, 15.
41 *Two Elizabethan Puritan Diaries*, ed. M. M. Knappen (Chicago, 1933).
42 Helen C. White, *English Devotional Literature 1600–1640* (Madison, Wis., 1931), pp. 53–56.
43 Edwards, *Religious Affections* (ed. Smith), p. 84.
44 John Preston, *The New Covenant or the Saints Portion* (London, 1634), p. 13.
45 Published as *Armilla Aurea*, 1590, and separately in English in 1595, this evidently was Perkins' first important work and one of the most popular. Quoted here from *Works* (1608), I, 11–118.
46 Hugh Barbour, *The Quakers in Puritan England* (New Haven, 1964).
47 William Ames, *Conscience, with the Power and Cases thereof . . .* (London, 1639), p.v.
48 Ames, p. vi.
49 Perkins, *A Case of Conscience, the greatest that ever was . . .* in *Works* (1608), I, 421–37; and *A Discourse of Conscience . . .* in *Works* (1608), I, 510–48.
50 Ames, *Conscience, with the Power . . .*, p. 2.
51 Ames, p. 26.
52 Ames, pp. 21–22.
53 Ames, p. 27.
54 Ames, p. 30.
55 Perkins, *A Case of Conscience, Works*, I, 427.
56 Perkins, I, 430.
57 Perkins, I, 431.
58 Perkins, I, 436.
59 Perkins, I, 432.
60 Richard Sibbes, *The Bruised Reede and Smoaking Flax* (London, 1635), preface, unpaginated.
61 Sibbes, p. 16.
62 Sibbes, pp. 39, 40.
63 Calvin, *Institutes* (trans. Allen), III.XXI.I and III.XXI.V.

64 Lawrence Thompson, *Melville's Quarrel With God* (Princeton, 1952); also Feidelson, *Symbolism and American Literature*, ch. V, "The Fool of Truth."
65 Calvin, *Institutes* (trans. Allen), III.XXI.VII.
66 Perkins, *A Treatise Tending unto a Declaration, whether a man may be in the the estate of Damnation, or in the estate of grace* in *Works* (1608), I, 356.
67 Perkins, I, 357.
68 Perkins, I, 358.
69 Perkins, I, 359.
70 Perkins, I, 362.
71 Perkins, I, 365.
72 Perkins, I, 365.
73 Perkins, I, 366.
74 Perkins, I, 367, 368.
75 Perkins, I, 368.
76 Martz, *The Poetry of Meditation*, pp. 153–75.
77 Perkins, *Treatise Tending unto a Declaration*, *Works*, I, 374.
78 Sibbes, *The Bruised Reede*, pp. 50–51.
79 Sibbes, pp. 98–99.
80 Sibbes, pp. 102–03.
81 John Preston, *Four Godly and Learned Treatises*, 3rd. ed. (London, 1633), pp. 60, 61, 62.
82 Preston, *The New Covenant*, p. 228.
83 Preston, p. 235.
84 Sibbes, *The Soules Conflict with it selfe, and Victory over it selfe by Faith* (London, 1635), pp. 514–16.
85 Preston, *The New Covenant*, pp. 334–35.
86 John E. Smith, Introduction to *Religious Affections*.
87 Martz, *The Poetry of Meditation*, chapter one, "The Method of Meditation."
88 Perkins, *A Golden Chaine*, *Works*, I, 84.
89 Perkins, I, 86.
90 Perkins, *The Whole Treatise of the Cases of Conscience, Distinguished into Three Books*, *Works*, II, 5.
91 Sibbes, *The Soules Conflict*, pp. 107–08.
92 Sibbes, p. 178.
93 Sibbes, p. 205.
94 Sibbes, pp. 217–18.
95 Sibbes, pp. 618–19.
96 Preston, *The New Covenant*, p. 248.
97 Preston, *Sinnes Overthrow: or a Godly and Learned Treatise of Mortification* (London, 1635), p. 40.
98 Preston, p. 69.
99 Preston, p. 79.
100 Preston, p. 114.
101 Horton Davies, *The Worship of the English Puritans*, (Philadelphia, 1948).
102 Miller, *The New England Mind: The Seventeenth Century*.
103 Perkins, *A Case of Conscience*, *Works*, I, 422.
104 Perkins, *The Whole Treatise of the Cases of Conscience*, *Works*, II, 64.
105 Perkins, II, 65.
106 Lewis Bayly, *The Practice of Pietie Directing a Christian how to walk that he may please God*, 21st ed. (London, 1628). Earliest edition in STC is the third, 1613.
107 Bayly, p. 243.
108 Bayly, p. 325.
109 Bayly, p. 340.

110 Bayly, p. 469.
111 Bayly, p. 482.
112 Wakefield, *Puritan Devotion*, pp. 44–52.
113 Calvin, *Institutes* (trans. Allen), IV.XVII.
114 *Institutes*, IV.XVII.
115 *Institutes*, IV.XVII.
116 Geoffrey Nuttall, *The Holy Spirit in Puritan Faith and Experience* (Oxford, 1946), p. 92.
117 Wakefield, pp. 48, 49, 50.
118 Bayly, *Practice of Pietie*, p. 522.
119 Bayly, p. 546.
120 Bayly, p. 551.
121 Bayly, p. 579.
122 Bayly, p. 601.
123 Bayly, p. 605.
124 Perkins, *The Whole Treatise of the Cases of Conscience, Works*, II, 84.
125 John Dodd, *Ten Sermons tending to the fitting of men for the Lords Supper. The six first by J. Dodd* (London, 1610). p. 108.
126 Dodd, p. 130.
127 Dodd, p. 135.
128 Dodd, pp. 159–60, 164.
129 John Preston, *The Breast-Plate of Faith and Love*, 5th ed. (London, 1634), pp. 73–74.
130 Preston, p. 73.
131 Preston, *Three Sermons upon the Sacrament of the Lords Supper*, n.d., p. 316.
132 Preston, p. 319.
133 Preston, p. 279.
134 Preston, pp. 281, 290.
135 White, *English Devotional Literature 1600–1640*, pp. 197–98.
136 John Preston, *A Heavenly Treatise of the Divine Love of Christ* (London, 1640), pp. 21–22.
137 Preston, p. 23.
138 Preston, p. 28.
139 Preston, p. 91.
140 Preston, p. 94.
141 *The Saints Everlasting Rest* in *Works*, ed. Orme (London, 1830), Vols. XXII–XXIII.
142 Martz, *The Poetry of Meditation*, pp. 153–75.
143 Baxter, *The Saints Everlasting Rest, Works*, XXIII, 283–84.
144 Baxter, p. 305.
145 Baxter, pp. 365–66.
146 Baxter, pp. 385–86.
147 Baxter, p. 409.
148 Baxter, pp. 420, 423, 432.
149 *Two Elizabethan Puritan Diaries*, ed. Knappen (Chicago, 1933), pp. 2, 3.
150 *Diaries*, p. 4.
151 *Diaries*, pp. 7–8.
152 *Diaries*, pp. 8–9.
153 White, *English Devotional Literature 1600–1640*, pp. 53–56.
154 *Diaries*, p. 105 (Ward, May 25, 1595).
155 *Diaries*, p. 105 (Ward, May 28, 1595).
156 *Diaries*, pp. 106–07 (Ward, June 8, 1595).
157 *Diaries*, p. 59 (Rogers, Sept. 2, 1587).

158 *Diaries*, p. 59 (Rogers, Sept. 12, 1587).
159 *Diaries*, p. 61 (Rogers, Oct. 30, 1587).
160 *Diaries*, p. 67 (Rogers, Nov. 29, 1587).
161 Bayly, *The Practice of Pietie* (London, 1628), pp. 694, 697, 717.
162 Bayly, pp. 714–15.
163 Bayly, p. 716.
164 Miller, *The New England Mind: The Seventeenth Century*, chs. xiii–xvi.
165 See Davies, *The Worship of the English Puritans* (Philadelphia, 1948).
166 Lawrence Sasek, *The Literary Temper of the English Puritans* (Baton Rouge, 1961); Walter J. Ong, S. J., *Ramus: Method, and the Decay of Dialogue* (Cambridge, Mass., 1958); Louis L. Martz, Introduction to *The Poems of Edward Taylor*, ed. Donald Stanford (New Haven, 1960), pp. xiii–xxxvii.
167 Lily B. Campbell, *Divine Poetry and Drama in Sixteenth-Century England* (Berkeley, 1959).
168 Sasek, ch. v, "As the Heathen Man Sayeth."
169 Ong, ch. xii, "Ramist Rhetoric," pp. 270–92.
170 Preston, *The New Covenant* (London, 1634), pp. 61–2, 71, 133. Italics mine.
171 Preston, *Four Godly and Learned Treatises* (London, 1633), p. 126 Italics mine.
172 Preston, *Three Sermons upon the Sacrament*, n.d., p. 314.
173 Miller, chs. xiii–xvi.
174 Barbour, *The Quakers in Puritan England* (New Haven, 1964), pp. 127–159.

Notes to Part Two

1 Harris Fletcher, *The Intellectual Development of John Milton* (Urbana, Ill., 1961), Vol. II, Part I, ch. 5 and Part II, ch. 8.
2 William Haller, *The Rise of Puritanism* (New York, 1938); M. M. Knappen, *Tudor Puritanism* (Chicago, 1939).
3 Lawrence Sasek, *The Literary Temper of the English Puritans* (Baton Rouge, 1961) provides an outstanding exception.
4 Louis Martz, *The Poetry of Meditation* (New Haven, 1954).
5 Lily B. Campbell, *Divine Poetry and Drama in Sixteenth-Century England* (Berkeley, 1959).
6 Warren Chernaik, *The Poetry of Limitation: A Study of Edmund Waller* (New Haven, 1968).
7 Haller, *The Rise of Puritanism*; Knappen, *Tudor Puritanism*.
8 U. Milo Kaufmann, *The Pilgrim's Progress and Traditions in Puritan Meditation* (New Haven, 1966).
9 A. O. Lovejoy, *The Great Chain of Being* (Cambridge, Mass., 1936); Basil Willey, *The Seventeenth Century Background* (London, 1934); E. M. W. Tillyard, *The Elizabethan World Picture* (London, 1960, c. 1943).
10 William Haller, *The Elect Nation: The Meaning and Relevance of Foxe's "Book of Martyrs"* (New York, 1963).
11 *The Saints Everlasting Rest* (London, 1650) is conceded by all students of Puritanism to be one of the movement's most crucial works.
12 See C. F. Allison, *The Rise of Moralism: The Proclamation of the Gospel from Hooker to Baxter* (London, 1966) for documentation of the substitution of Arminianism for early Reformation doctrine in the Church of England after 1660.
13 Charles H. and Katherine George, *The Protestant Mind of the English Reformation* (Princeton, N. J., 1961).
14 William H. Halewood, *The Poetry of Grace* (New Haven, 1970).

15 John New, *Anglican and Puritan* (Stanford, 1964).
16 Norman Pettit, *The Heart Prepared: Grace and Conversion in Puritan Spiritual Life* (New Haven, 1966).
17 Haller, *The Elect Nation*.
18 Northrop Frye's *Anatomy of Criticism: Four Essays* (Princeton, N. J., 1957) has had a powerful influence upon the nomenclature of criticism, preferring myth to allegory. But Angus Fletcher in *Allegory: The Theory of a Symbolic Mode* (Ithaca, N. Y., 1964) has helped to restore the balance.
19 Helen White, *English Devotional Literature 1600–1640* (Madison, Wisc., 1931), pp. 53–56.
20 Harry Berger, *The Allegorical Temper: Vision and Reality in Book II of Spenser's Faerie Queene* (New Haven, 1957).
21 Cedrie H. Whitman, *Homer and the Homeric Tradition* (Cambridge, Mass., 1958).
22 Along with Berger's important book (*The Allegorical Temper*), there recently have been: Thomas P. Roche's *The Kindly Flame: A Study of the Third and Fourth Books of Spenser's Faerie Queene* (Princeton, 1964); and Donald Cheney's *Spenser's Image of Nature: Wild Man and Shepherd in The Faerie Queene* (New Haven, 1966). Since this study is not primarily concerned with contemporary views of Spenser, there is no need to write a complete bibliographical note on recent "myth" criticism of Spenser.
23 *The Works of Edmund Spenser: A Variorum Edition*, ed. Edwin Greenlaw, et al. (Baltimore, 1932–57).
24 D. Douglas Waters, *Duessa as Theological Satire* (Columbia, Miss., 1970).
25 All quotations from *The Complete Poetical Works of Spenser* (Cambridge, Mass., 1908). Italics mine.
26 Berger, *The Allegorical Temper*, p. 218 and p. 219 (where Berger quotes Aquinas, *Summa Theologica*).
27 Richard Baxter, *The Saints Everlasting Rest*, Vol. xxii–xxiii of *The Practical Works of the Reverend Richard Baxter*, ed. Rev. William Orme (London, 1830), pp. 234–35; p. 302.
28 See the various arguments and interpretations of allegory in Greenlaw, et al., ed., *Spenser . . . A Variorum Edition*.
29 C. S. Lewis' *The Allegory of Love* (Oxford, 1936), referred to earlier in this chapter as a major influence upon the modern study of Spenser.
30 Louis L. Martz, *The Poetry of Meditation* (New Haven, 1954); U. Milo Kaufmann, *The Pilgrim's Progress and Tradition in Puritan Meditation* (New Haven, 1966).
31 Kaufmann, p. 94.
32 Kaufmann, pp. 112–13.
33 Kaufmann, taking the hint from Martz, further separates imagination and meditation from Calvinist-Puritan thought throughout the book. A sharp distinction is drawn between the abstract *logos* tradition of most Puritans and the more imaginative practice of Baxter and Sibbes, leading to Bunyan's free literary imagination. The result is the kind of comment quoted above, of mixed praise and blame for the literary results. While it is true that all Puritan commentators did not march in lockstep, a basic continuity existed by virtue of their acceptance of the same fundamental theology. Yet Kaufmann remains the best recent commentator on the relationship between Puritanism and literature when his focus is not too exclusively literary, as for instance, the place of predestination, emphasis upon sin, importance of personal experience, and the aural nature of the Puritan response to Scripture. On this last point he quotes (p. 244) a fine passage from Baxter's *Saints Rest* which is illuminating for the entire area of Puritan dogmatics and literature, not merely the "special qualities" in Baxter, Sibbes, and Bunyan, which Kaufmann, following Martz, separates from the dry rationalist Puritan main stream:

Rest! How sweet a word is this to mine ears! Methinks the sound doth turn
to substance, and having entred at the ear, doth possess my brain, and thence
descendeth down to my very *heart*; methinks I feel it stir and work, and that
through all my parts and powers. . . .

The viewpoint of this study is that on all these great fundamental issues of Puritan
doctrine there is continuity from the theologian to the commentator to the more
creative writers and then the poets, so that Baxter can be used to illuminate Taylor, but also perhaps the reverse, and Calvin remains the center of understanding
for the entire range of Puritan writers in prose and poetry.

34 See Joseph Mazzeo, "Cromwell as Machiavellian Prince in Marvell's 'An Horatian
    Ode,'" *Journal of the History of Ideas*, 21 (1960), 1–17; and "Cromwell as Davidic
    King," in Mazzeo, ed., *Reason and Imagination* (New York, 1962), pp. 29–55.
35 Harold E. Toliver, *Marvell's Ironic Vision* (New Haven, 1965).
36 Pierre Legouis, *André Marvell: poète, puritain, patriote* (Paris, 1928).
37 "Articles Concerning Predestination" in *Calvin: Theological Treatises*, ed., J. K. S.
    Reid, Vol. XXII, Library of Christian Classics (Philadelphia, 1954), p. 180.
38 Ibid., p. 179.
39 Lines 131–148; all quotations from *The Poems and Letters of Andrew Marvell*, ed.
    H. M. Margoliouth (2nd ed., Oxford, 1952).
40 "Articles Concerning Predestination," *Calvin: Theological Treatises*, p. 127.
41 Dante, *Paradiso* I.88: "*Tu stesso ti fai grosso / col falso imaginar, si che non vedi /
    ciò che vedresti se l'avessi scosso.*" Coleridge was later to cite this same passage
    with similar purpose in the conclusion of his *Church and State* (1829).
42 Toliver, p. 8.
43 Toliver, p. 56.
44 Toliver, p. 12.
45 Toliver, p. 24.
46 Toliver, p. 4.
47 Toliver, p. 34.
48 See Martz, *The Poetry of Meditation* and *The Paradise Within*, for use of the
    creatures in various medieval and Renaissance Catholic traditions.
49 Toliver, p. 56.
50 Allison's *The Rise of Moralism* documents the rise of Arminianism in seventeenth-
    century Anglicanism. It is interesting that Allison also notes Coleridge's disapproval
    of this trend in the latter's comments on Jeremy Taylor (p. ix). This point has been
    presented in my *Coleridge as Religious Thinker* (New Haven, 1961; pp. 37–64),
    and is one of the many important links between seventeenth-century Puritan tra-
    dition and the Romantic poets to be studied in this book.
51 *Poems of Edward Taylor*, ed. Donald Stanford, foreword by Louis Martz (New
    Haven, 1960); all quotations from this edition.
52 *Poems of Edward Taylor*.
53 Perry Miller, *The New England Mind: The Seventeenth Century* (Cambridge, Mass.,
    1954, c. 1939), chs. I–IV.
54 Hyatt Waggoner, *American Poets from the Puritans to the Present* (Boston, 1968),
    pp. 16–24.
55 Interest in Taylor's style and diction has been marked in recent years. See William
    J. Scheick, *The Will and The Word* (Athens, Ga., 1974), ch. V, particularly the
    notes to pages 129, 135, and 147, which give references to the many diverse com-
    mentaries on this subject since the appearance of Taylor's major poetry.
56 Scheick approaches the entire corpus of Taylor's poetry in this way, as having its
    basis in general Christian tradition, particularly Augustine. Though he acknowl-
    edges that Taylor was a modified Calvinist and orthodox Puritan (not one of the

Boston rationalists described by Miller), this aspect is not stressed in his reading of the poetry. There is little sense of the actual Puritan content of the poetry. Thus his reading is most effective on the total spectrum of Taylor's poetry, and particularly on the generally Christian poems which occupy so much space in both Series. In this chapter little attention is devoted to such poems. Stressing of Calvinist-Puritan doctrines and poems provides a balance, not a contradiction, to Scheick's book and also to the recent general study by Norman Grabo, *Edward Taylor* (New York, 1961).

57 See "Edward Taylor's 'Spiritual Relation,'" ed. Donald E. Stanford, *American Literature* 35 (1964), 467–75.

58 See Section One, note 40, et seq.; and, on Preston's *The Breast-Plate of Faith and Love,* Section One, note 129.

59 Scheick, pp. 113–14.

60 The term "sanctifying grace" was used by other Puritans in the seventeenth century. In reference to the sacrament Taylor's favorite term is "Lord's Supper," which he regards in a "spiritual" way. He also uses the term "sacrament" and the Calvinist ones, "Seale of the Covenant" and "Spiritual Ordinance."

61 Thomas Greene, *The Descent from Heaven: A Study in Epic Continuity* (New Haven, 1963); William Empson, *Milton's God* (London, 1961).

62 Greene, p. 417–18.

63 Greene, p. 408.

64 Fyodor Dostoyevsky, *The Brothers Karamazov,* trans. C. Garnett (New York, 1950), p. 255.

65 Empson, p. 120.

66 Empson, p. 128.

67 I. G. MacCaffrey, *"Paradise Lost" as Myth* (Cambridge, Mass., 1959), p. 21.

68 Fletcher, *The Intellectual Development of John Milton,* Vol. II, Part I, ch. 5, "Religious Instruction and Knowledge of the Bible."

69 Book XII, 393–429; all quotations from Helen Darbishire, ed., *The Poetical Works of John Milton,* 2 vols. (Oxford, 1952). References will be incorporated into the text.

70 Joseph Summers, *The Muse's Method* (London, 1962), p. 220.

71 Summers, p. 224.

Notes to Part Three

1 Malcolm M. Ross, *Poetry and Dogma: The Transfiguration of Eucharistic Symbols in Seventeenth Century English Poetry* (New Brunswick, N. J., 1954).

2 For a good study of the decline in Puritan fervor after 1688, see Gerald Cragg, *From Puritanism to the Age of Reason* (Cambridge, UK: Cambridge U. Press, 1950).

3 David Morris, *The Religious Sublime: Christian Poetry and Critical Tradition in Eighteenth-Century England* (Lexington: Univ. Press of Kentucky, 1972).

4 William Law, M. A., *The Spirit of Prayer* and *The Spirit of Love,* 3rd ed. (London 1752). Law was strictly speaking in the Anglican tradition. But his earlier and most popular works, *A Practical Treatise upon Christian Perfection* (1726) and *A Serious Call to a Devout and Holy Life* (1729) displayed the Puritan emphasis upon serious vocation in this world which had earned ridicule for the Puritans in the previous century, and ridicule for Law among the wits of his own time. His work was influential among the Methodists in its high religious seriousness, from which 18th

century Anglicanism for the most part turned a deaf ear. Law remained in the Established Church even in his later mystical phase. Religious spirits such as Smart and Cowper were certainly influenced by Law, as later was Coleridge.

5 Isaac Watts, Preface to *Horae Lyricae* (Boston: Little, Brown, 1864), pp. lxxxviii–xc.

6 Watts, Preface, pp. xcvi–xcvii.

7 Samuel Johnson, "Watts," *The Lives of the Poets* (Everyman edition), II, 298.

8 Hoxie Neale Fairchild, *Protestantism and the Cult of Sentiment*, Vol. I of *Religious Trends in English Poetry* (New York: Columbia Univ. Press, 1939), and *Religious Sentimentalism in the Age of Johnson*, Vol. II of *Religious Trends in English Poetry* (New York: Columbia Univ. Press, 1942).

9 *Coleridge as Religious Thinker* (New Haven: Yale Univ. Press, 1961).

10 *Protestantism and the Cult of Sentiment*, pp. 123, 129–30.

11 *Religious Sentimentalism in the Age of Johnson*, pp. 140, 148.

12 Original edition in 1737. The Boston edition of 1831 was the one consulted as adequate for this purpose.

13 Samuel Davies' works most recently appeared in *Collected Poems of Samuel Davies*, ed. Richard Davis (Gainesville, FL: Florida Univ. Press, 1968).

14 As a cultural phenomenon Davies is important in giving one more example of the closeness of English and American Calvinist-Puritan tradition in the 18th century. Davies was a Presbyterian minister who lived along the Virginia frontier. He later became President of Princeton after the death of Edwards and travelled in England looking for funds for the new school. His poetry was highly considered by Puritans in both countries as a finely articulated form of the Calvinist-Puritan experience of the day. In the Preface to the published poems he reveals a highly sophisticated view of the function of the Calvinist-Puritan poet. Though reverence for the classics, Pope and Addison is evident, his special poetical precepts derive from Milton and Watts. His discussion of the Muse as the "sacred fire" seems to derive from the Introduction to *Horae Lyricae*, with the example of Milton as supreme poet mentioned often. As Watts had stated, the sacred scriptures and Christian doctrine provide endless material for the imagination and meditation of the poet, and a proper poetic presentation of these materials must draw the reader to them and away from the lewd productions of the worldly imagination. A strong moral reason, as well as metaphysical-religious rationale, exists as incentive for writing of sacred poetry, as we may expect from a good Puritan. Davies defers to Edwards as the first in Puritan intellect, and views his role merely as a necessary substitute for fine intellect and taste on the frontier. This deference may account for some disappointment with his verse, which suffers like that of Watts from occasional tepidity, but he may have kept his imagination under firm reign with the limited purposes of piety and propriety in mind. He does have moments and occasionally whole poems of real poetic merit.

15 The edition of Watts used for quotation was reprinted from the Quarto edition of 1753, with the Memoir of Robert Southey (Boston: Little, Brown, 1864). With our hindsight concerning the great popularity of 17th century religious poetry since World War I, this apologetic note to the *Divine Poems* section of *Horae* is instructive on the question of changes in taste.

16 Arthur P. Davis, *Isaac Watts* (London: Independent Press, 1943); Harry Escott, *Isaac Watts, Hymnographer* (London: Independent Press, 1962).

17 There is no need for a note on the life of Smart for our purpose, since Smart was never formally connected with 18th century Puritanism. Smart has had sympathetic biographers from Dr. Johnson through the editor Norman Callan to the more recent general volume on the life and work, Moira Dearnley, *Poetry of Christopher Smart* (London: Routledge and Kegan Paul, 1969).

18 For the *Jubilate* text, the MS. as printed in W. H. Bond's *Jubilate Agno* (London: Rupert Hart-Davis, 1954) is followed, rather than the older editions. The internal markings of the MS. are given, not pages in the Bond edition.

19 See Dearnley, *Poetry of Christopher Smart*; Arthur Sherbo, *Christopher Smart, Scholar of the University* (East Lansing: Michigan State Univ. Press, 1967); and Robert Brittain, ed., Introduction to *Poems by Christopher Smart* (Princeton: Princeton Univ. Press, 1950). Also of course the comments in the Bond and Callan editions. All quotations except for *Jubilate Agno* are from *The Collected Poems of Christopher Smart*, ed. Norman Callan, 2 vols. (London: Routledge and Kegan Paul, 1949).

20 Since there has never been a special study of Cowper from this point of view, there is need here to cite only the most useful of the general works on the poetry and life. All the studies take up the subject of Calvinism in some way, either personal or in relation to some of the poems, and my debts to these studies will be obvious to readers of Cowper. David Cecil, *The Stricken Deer* (London: Constable, 1929); Norman Nicholson, *William Cowper* (London: John Lehman, 1951); Maurice J. Quinlan, *William Cowper: A Critical Life* (Minneapolis: Univ. of Minnesota Press, 1953); Charles Ryskamp, *William Cowper of the Inner Temple, Esq.* (Cambridge: Cambridge U. Press, 1959). In addition, I have consulted J. G. Frazer, ed. *Letters of William Cowper* (London, Macmillan, 1912), and Brian Spiller, ed. *Cowper, Poetry and Prose* (London, Hart-Davis, 1968). It is accepted by all biographers of Cowper that he received the evangelical revival in the Calvinist-Methodist form, even though Newton and Cowper remained within the Established Church at Olney. This Evangelical branch of the Anglican Church was later led by Wilberforce. Cowper's religious life diverged from the Anglican norm of the time in the crucial respect of his conversion experience, and from the Wesleyan branch of the Methodist revival in his acceptance of the Calvinist viewpoint of Whitefield and Newton. The nature of conversion in the *Memoir of the Early Life of William Cowper, Esq.*, composed in 1766 or 1767 and published after Cowper's death is certainly in general "evangelical." After his conversion the form of his religious experience was determined by the Calvinist doctrines of those around him, which accounts for the decidedly Calvinist religious language of the *Memoir*.

21 *The Poetical Works of William Cowper*, ed. H. S. Milford, 4th ed. (London: Oxford Univ. Press, 1950). All quotations from this edition.

22 The distinction between the "inner" poetic Puritan and the "outer" militant one was made early in the book. The "outer" flourished during the Commonwealth, and in Scotland, and were overwhelmingly non-writers, at least in the literary sense, and quite willing literally to buckle on the armor and breastplate of the Lord to combat the evil of the world. Some were meditative men, like Cromwell, most were not, and a few were the ranting hypocrites of anti-Puritan folklore. Only Milton seemed to have the wordly drive and the inner psychic energy to play both roles in the most heightened way. By the 18th century, history having rejected the claim of sovereignty of Calvinist-Puritanism in the world, the struggles were mainly inward in England, and mixed in the Colonies, as the writings and outwards struggles of Edwards in Northampton make poignantly clear.

23 This is a value judgment on a moot point. "The Castaway" is a great poem, but the larger scope of Calvinist themes in *The Task* leads to the relative placement of the poems in considering the general subject of the Calvinist temper in this study. *The Task* is the more important poem in this respect, however differently the poems may be related to the poet's biography. Students of Cowper have discussed this problem in relation to Cowper's *Memoir of the Early Life of William Cowper, Esq.*, written in 1766 or 1767, a work known by his early biographers but not published in his lifetime. It was interpreted by the biographers in the 19th century as a traditional

account of the "conversion" experience. Later biographers, such as Ryskamp and Quinlan, stress the insights it gives into Cowper's psychology at the time of his near suicide and recovery. More recent students have considered the *Memoir* as an instance of the problem of reliability of the narrator in autobiography. (See Frank McConnell, *The Confessional Imagination* [Baltimore: Johns Hopkins, 1975] and Patricia Meyer Spacks, "The Soul's Imaginings: Daniel Defoe, William Cowper," *PMLA*, 91 [1976], 420−35.) McConnell takes a sophisticated approach without doubting the traditional categories. Spacks considers the framework of conversion as an outside frame in conflict with Cowper's individuality and imagination. Such a view forecasts the inevitability of "The Castaway" as Cowper's true will and testament. Even if this view is accepted, *The Task* remains the greater poetic achievement, written after the conversion experience and only possible with that experience as temporary guarantee of faith, stability and sanity.

Notes to Part Four

1 Hyatt Waggoner, *Hawthorne: A Critical Study* (Cambridge, Mass., 1955).
2 Waggoner, p. 260.
3 Earl R. Wasserman, *Shelley: A Critical Reading* (Baltimore, 1971); and M. H. Abrams, *Natural Supernaturalism* (New York, 1971).
4 Harold Bloom, *Blake's Apocalypse* (New York, 1963); Alfred Kazin, *The Portable Blake* (New York, 1946); Geoffrey Hartman, "Blake and the Progress of Poesy" in *William Blake: Essays for S. Foster Damon*, ed. Alvin Rosenfeld (Providence, 1969), pp. 57−68; E. D. Hirsch, *Innocence and Experience* (New Haven, 1964).
5 *William Blake*, ed. A. Rosenfeld (1969).
6 James D. Boulger, *Coleridge as Religious Thinker* (New Haven, 1961), ch. I.
7 Boulger, *Coleridge as Religious Thinker*, ch. I.
8 Bloom, *Blake's Apocalypse*, pp. 371−72.
9 Kathleen Raine, *Blake and Tradition* (Princeton, 1968); George M. Harper, *The Neoplatonism of William Blake* (Chapel Hill, N.C., 1961). Also S. Foster Damon's original *William Blake: His Philosophy and Symbols* (Boston, 1924) described the later Blake as a mystic of fundamental Christian type. It has not, of course, been necessary to go so far afield in searching for religious sources of Blake's inspiration. Aside from the special Swedenborgian and Evangelical, critics such as Fairchild and Morris, cited in our previous section, have pointed out interest in the religious sublime ranging from Dennis early in the century, through Lowth to Cowper and Blake's contemporaries. An argument for *Milton* and *Jerusalem* as culminating poems in this tradition since *Paradise Lost* might easily be made, including elements of theme, style and derivation. Such an argument is more general and inclusive than the one focused on in this study.
10 Northrop Frye, *Fearful Symmetry: A Study of William Blake* (Princeton, 1947), p. 346.
11 Frye, p. 334.
12 Frye, p. 340.
13 Frye, pp. 337−38.
14 Boulger, *Coleridge as Religious Thinker*; Thomas McFarland, *Coleridge and the Pantheist Tradition* (Oxford, 1969). Both books discuss this area of Coleridge's thought at length.
15 *The Ghost of Abel*, etched 1822. Except for the intra-Calvinist connection with Byron, as a response to his *Cain*, the poem is not directly important for this chapter.

Cain will be studied in the chapter on Byron as one of the fundamental Calvinist poem's of Byron's Calvinism — more direct than Blake's and rebellious in different ways.

16 Frye, pp. 387–89.

17 *Coleridge as Religious Thinker* and Introduction to *Twentieth Century Interpretations of "The Rime of the Ancient Mariner"* (Englewood Cliffs, N.J., 1969), pp. 1–21.

18 "Imagination and Speculation in Coleridge's Conversation Poems," *Journal of English and Germanic Philology*, 64 (1965), 691–711; and "Christian Skepticism in 'The Rime of the Ancient Mariner'," in *From Sensibility to Romanticism*, ed. Frederick W. Hilles and Harold Bloom (New York, 1965), pp. 439–52.

20 *Coleridge as Religious Thinker*, pp. 94–195; Paul Deschamps, *La Formation de la Pensée de Coleridge* (Paris, 1964).

19 *Coleridge as Religious Thinker*; J. Robert Barth, *Coleridge and Christian Doctrine* (Cambridge, Mass., 1969); McFarland, *Coleridge and the Pantheist Tradition*.

21 All quotations of poems from *The Complete Poetical Works of Samuel Taylor Coleridge*, ed. E. H. Coleridge (Oxford, 1912).

22 Notebook 36, folio 65.

23 Notebook 27, folio 24.

24 *Coleridge as Religious Thinker*; also, S.T. Coleridge, *Coleridge on the Seventeenth Century*, ed. Roberta Brinkley (Durham, N.C., 1955), and McFarland, *Coleridge and the Pantheist Tradition*.

25 *The Collected Works of Samuel Taylor Coleridge*, Kathleen Coburn, general editor (London and New York, 1968, 1969 et seq.).

26 Humphry House, *Coleridge* (London, 1953).

27 Hoxie N. Fairchild, *Romantic Faith*, Vol. III of *Religious Trends in English Poetry* (New York, 1949).

28 McFarland, *Coleridge and the Pantheist Tradition*; Deschamps, *La Formation de la Pensée de Coleridge*; and John Beer, *Coleridge the Visionary* (London, 1959).

29 *Coleridge as Religious Thinker*, pp. 37–64: especially Coleridge's comment on the doctrines of justification and grace held by the severe Arminian divine, Jeremy Taylor:

> But, confining my remarks to the doctrines and the practical deductions from them, I could never read Bishop Taylor's Tract on the doctrine and practice of Repentance, without being tempted to characterize high Calvinism as (comparatively) a lamb in wolf's skin, and strict Arminianism as aproaching to the reverse. . . . And it so marvellous, such a hungry dry corrosive Scheme of a monachomanichaean Ethics in so rich, so genial, so tender a Soul as Bishop Taylor's! That he should have strangled the philosophy of Love by the parasite method of rank weeds, the Logic of Casuistry. . . .

30 George Ridenour, "Source and Allusion in Some Poems of Coleridge," *Studies in Philology* LX (1963), 73–95; McFarland, *Coleridge*; and J. D. Boulger, "Marginalia, Myth-Making, and the Later Poetry," *Studies in Romanticism* 11, 4 (Fall 1972), 304–19.

31 Ridenour, "Source and Allusion in Some Poems of Coleridge."

32 *Inquiring Spirit*, ed. Kathleen Coburn (London, 1951), p. 142.

33 *Coleridge as Religious Thinker*, pp. 94–195.

34 For instance, in a letter to Thomas Clarkson in 1806, *Collected Letters of Samuel Taylor Coleridge*, ed. E. L. Griggs (Oxford, 1956 et seq.), II, 1193–99.

35 This reminds one of the early letter to Poole (March 23, 1801, in *Letters of Samuel Taylor Coleridge*, ed. E. H. Coleridge [London, 1895], I, 350–52) in which Coleridge alleged that Newton made mind a mere lazy onlooker in nature.

36 Some of the poems we call later poems are fragments and scattered pieces collected by E. H. Coleridge for his edition of 1912. Coleridge himself had never prepared them for publication. "Limbo" and "Ne Plus Ultra" appear in *Sybilline Leaves*, but most remained in notebooks; other poems grace philosophical treatises. The converse of this, as we shall note shortly, is the extremely poetic nature of much of Coleridge's later religious and philosophical prose, a point missed by many commentators on the subject.

37 Marginal note to Edward Irving, *Sermons, Lectures, and Discourses*, 3 vol. (London, 1828), II, pp. 333–49.

38 Marginal note to Joseph Hughes, *The Believer's Prospect and Preparation* (London, 1831), pp. 13–23.

39 Herman Melville, *Pierre, or, the Ambiguities* [1852], ed. Henry A. Murray (New York, 1949), p. 244.

40 Melville, *Pierre*, p. 247.

41 *Specimen of the Table Talk of Samuel Taylor Coleridge*, Vol. VI of *The Complete Works of Samuel Taylor Coleridge*, 7 vols., ed. W. T. Shedd (New York, 1860), p. 416.

42 *The Notebooks of Samuel Taylor Coleridge*, ed. Kathleen Coburn (Princeton, 1957 et seq.), Vol. II, entry 2661 and note to that entry.

43 *Anima Poetae*, ed. E. H. Coleridge (London, 1895).

44 For Coleridge's later writings as Christian idealism, see Boulger, *Coleridge as Religious Thinker* and McFarland, *Coleridge and the Pantheist Tradition*.

45 In the Hendricks House edition Henry A. Murray lists many possible sources for the Plinlimmon section and pamphlet, and also gives an interpretation of the section in the light of the novel as a whole (pp. lxix–lxxix and 475–77). The interpretation is not wholly relevant to what has been presented here, except in also pointing out the ambiguity in the use of the image of the Greenwich chronometer. As sources Murray lists some obvious ones – Carlyle, Plato, St. Paul, and possibly Emerson and Hawthorne – as models for the character of Plotinus Plinlimmon. More helpful and specific are Pascal's *Pensées*, no. 294: "we see neither justice nor injustice which does not change with climate. Three degrees of latitude reverse all jurisprudence; a meridian decides the truth"; and also Sir Thomas Browne on the word "horologe" for earthly time, in *Pseudodoxia*, 5, 18: "It is not to be denied that before the daies of Jerom there were horologies, and several accounts of time; of later years there succeeded now inventions, and horologies composed by Torchilick on the artifice of wheels."

   From this it would seem that Melville created his figure from a conflation of "idealist" and "practical" moralist sources, and perhaps he did, though this writer still believes that the striking similarity with the figure in Coleridge suggests a common and succinct source that brings the elements of the figure together.

46 Of the voluminous literature on the subject of the sources of Wordsworth's thought, several recent works should be mentioned: E. D. Hirsch, *Wordsworth and Schelling* (New Haven, 1960); H. W. Piper, *The Active Universe* (London, 1962); John Jones, *The Egotistical Sublime* (London, 1957); and Jane W. Smizer, *Wordsworth's Reading of Roman Prose* (New Haven, 1946). All quotations of the poems and prose are from *The Poetical Works of William Wordsworth*. ed. E. de Selincourt and H. Darbishire, 5 vols. (Oxford, 1940–49).

47 G. F. Nuttall, *The Holy Spirit in Puritan Faith and Experience* (Oxford, 1946), p. 32, cites Richard Baxter (*Works*, ed. Orme, 1834; V, 559):

> We must try the Scriptures by our most spiritual apprehension but our apprehensions by the Scriptures: that is, we must prefer the Spirit's inspiring the apostles to indite the Scriptures, before the Spirit's illuminating of us to understand them, or before any present inspirations, the former being the more

perfect. .... This trying the Spirit by the Scriptures, is not a setting of the Scriptures above the Spirit itself; but it is only a trying of the Spirit by the Spirit; that is, the Spirit's operations in ourselves and his revelations to any pretenders now, by the Spirit's operations in the apostles, and by their revelations recorded for our use. For they and not we are called foundations of the church.

48 See Nuttal; Barbour, *The Quakers in Puritan England* (New Haven, 1964).
49 See Nuttal, pp. 141−47; Boulger, *Coleridge as Religious Thinker*, pp. 140−42.
50 W. K. Wimsatt, Jr., "The Structure of Romantic Nature Imagery," in *The Verbal Icon* (Lexington, Ken., 1954), pp. 114−15.
51 See S. F. Gingerich, *Essays in the Romantic Poets* (New York, 1924), ch. II; and, more recently, Piper, *The Active Universe*, esp. ch. III, "Wordsworth and the Religion of Nature," pp. 60−84.
52 Wimsatt, pp. 103−16; Geoffrey Hartman, *The Unmediated Vision* (New Haven, 1954), ch. I.
53 Calvin, *Institutes* (trans. Allen), I.XII.IV−V.
54 See Wimsatt, p. 80; F. A. Pottle, "The Eye and the Object in Wordsworth's Poetry," in *Wordsworth Centenary Essays*, ed. G. T. Dunklin (Princeton, 1951), pp. 40−41; and Florence Marsh, *Wordsworth's Imagery* (New Haven, 1952), p. 59.
55 See Hartman, *The Unmediated Vision*, ch. I, for an analysis of "Tintern Abbey."
56 Boulger, "Keats' Symbolism," *ELH* 28, 244−259.
57 Wimsatt, "The Concrete Universal" in *The Verbal Icon*, p. 80ff.
58 See, for instance, R. A. Durr, *On the Mystical Poetry of Henry Vaughan* (Cambridge, Mass., 1962), where the implications of the journey image are worked out in full.
59 At the risk of seeming to multiply analogues indefinitely, let me cite one more seventeenth century text in relation to "Stepping Westward" − a short passage in Vaughan's *The Mount of Olives* (in *Works*, ed. L. C. Martin [Oxford, 1957]):
    The first man that appeared thus, came from the *East*, and the *breath of life* was received there. Though then we travel *Westward*, though we embrace *thornes* and *thistles*, yet the businesse of a *Pilgrim* is to *seek his Countrey*. But the *land* of *darkness* lies in our way . . . (p. 169).
The basic pattern here is strikingly similar to that in Wordsworth and Donne, perhaps closer to Donne's traditional form without the wit. The "westward" idea of the journey into death, and of West becoming East, or eternal life, closely follows Donne's image in "Hymn to God my God." One element, "the *land of darkness* lies in our way," is common to Vaughan and Wordsworth, but not Donne. Vaughan knew the medieval tradition and Donne, so the appearance of this passage in his prose raises no special issue, except to lead into a common medieval source for the image. For instance, an English example of some interest here would be Walter Hilton's *The Scale of Perfection*, where the version of the journey along the *via mystica* contains three elements important in "Stepping Westward": the journey itself as a spiritual metaphor, the darkness or night through which the soul must pass, and the light at the end of the journey connected with Jerusalem and the East:
    Jerusalem is, as much as to say, a *sight of peace*, and betokeneth contemplation in perfect love of God; for contemplation is nothing but a sight of God, which is very peace. Then if thou covet to come to this blessed sight of very peace, and be a true pilgrim towards Jerusalem, though it be so that I was never there, nevertheless, as far forth as I can, I shall set thee in the way towards it. (*The Scale of Perfection*, trans. Sitwell [London, 1953], p. 194)
    But in this medieval archetypal image there is no sense of westward direction towards death in contrast to the eastward spiritual motion. The contrast is probably a Renaissance addition. In any case, we see the complexity and age of the pattern

with which Wordsworth is working in "Stepping Westward." Our critical interest ought to remain centered on the point of Wordsworth's creative ability to link his own personal and literal experience with a symbolic commonplace of the western religious tradition without seeming to have that intention in mind. It is an authentic example of the religious archetypal imagination at work.

As Wordsworth grew older his awareness of using such patterns of religious type became more explicit, perhaps as the result of his reading (a point we are not trying to prove). But his explicit awareness of working within these patterns and his accepting their antiquity with reverence should inject a note of caution into many recent claims that his imagination was completely naturalistic and apocalyptic in tendency. In his later "Essay on Epitaphs" there is an explicit use of the east-west image in relation to the journey of the soul, with a slightly different twist. More important than the difference is his specific and full rational awareness of using the traditional images, as opposed to his more artistic imaginative gropings in the poem:

As, in sailing upon the orb of this planet, a voyage towards the regions where the sun sets, conducts gradually to the quarter we have been accustomed to behold it come forth at its rising; and, in like manner, a voyage east, the birth place in our imagination of the morning, leads finally to the quarter where the sun is last seen when he departs from our eyes; so the contemplative Soul, travelling in the direction of mortality, advances to the country of everlasting life; and, in like manner, may continue to explore those cheerful tracts, till she is brought back, for her advantage and benefit, to the land of transitory things — of sorrows and of tears. (*Works,* V, 447—48)

Some of these problems regarding Wordsworth's relationship to the past can only be settled by careful study of his prose and his readings, attention to which has not reached the level of that given to other Romantics. The startling similarities between the "Intimations Ode" and poems by Vaughan and Traherne have been noted by de Selincourt and Darbishire. Hilton's sections on darkness and the false and true lights (Bk. II, chs. 24—26) are also close to the imagery on that subject in the Ode. Whether this is a source or a general similarity in mystical expression of difficult, but perennial, moods is still moot.

60 David Ferry, *The Limits of Mortality* (Middletown, Conn., 1959).
61 At this point Geoffrey Hartman's important book, *Wordworth's Poetry, 1787–1814* (New Haven, 1964), should be mentioned. The reader will note similarities in our respective approaches, especially the use of religious analogy to explain structure in Wordsworth. Both studies wish to examine what is behind the loco-descriptive and literal nature poetry of Wordsworth. In doing so, important differences are also to be noted. Hartman's complete study naturally entertains a wider range of sources and influences upon the poet than does this chapter. More centrally, Hartman views the religious analogies as generally leading to something more significant than the locus of the religious poetry itself, the creation of a modern secular or apocalyptic imagination. Thus he handles his adopted spiritual terminology — the *via naturaliter negativa* from medieval mysticism, and *akedah-akedot* from Jewish mysticism — as means to this other end. We have tried to view the implied religious patterns in Wordsworth's major poetry in the context of traditional habits of thought, of which Wordsworth was more likely to be aware than of modern mythic theories. Consideration of Wordsworth's importance in English literature and his place on the stage of intellectual history should lead a reader to conclude that these different emphases are not necessarily contradictory. This writer agrees that in many ways Wordsworth is a "modern imagination" (as A. N. Whitehead said years ago), while Hartman allows the radical Protestant origins of many of his attitudes. Among his many allusions to this is a fine statement on Wordsworth's Puritan ancestry:

I call this aspect of Wordsworth's poetry spiritual because its only real justification (which few of his contemporaries were willing to entertain) was that it carried the Puritan quest for evidences of election into the most ordinary emotional contexts. Wordsworth did not himself talk of election and salvation, but, as we shall see, of renovation (regeneration), and he did not seem to be directly aware of his Puritan heritage, although the *Poems* of 1807 . . . shows a heightened intimacy with seventeenth-century traditions. (p. 5)

This is a fair enough appraisal for the early Wordsworth and the poetry of Hartman's major interest. But as we shall see in looking into the later and more explicitly religious poetry, Wordsworth's awareness of his Puritan heritage also became more explicit. For other corroboration, see footnote 71 below on the work of Leslie Chard.

62 Jones, *The Egotistical Sublime*, pp. 144–153.
63 See Judson S. Lyons, *"The Excursion": A Study* (New Haven, 1950); Hartman, Part III, chapter nine; and Jones, pp. 143–53.
64 "Essay, Supplementary to the Preface," *Works*, II, 412; see also Coleridge, *Works* (ed. Shedd), I, 436 ff. (*The Statesman's Manual*) on religious symbols.
65 *The Excursion*, V, 903–10.
66 Hartman, pp. 292–323.
67 *The Excursion*, V, 582–86.
68 Edwards, *A Faithful Narrative of the Surprising Work of God* . . . (Boston, 1831).
69 Edwards, pp. 121, 123, 126.
70 M. H. Abrams, *Natural Supernaturalism*; Harold Bloom, *The Visionary Company* (Garden City. N. Y., 1961); Hartmann *Wordsworth's Poetry*.
71 A recent book by Leslie Chard, *Dissenting Republican* (The Hague, 1972), partially answers the question of Wordsworth's connection with the Puritan and republican dissenting traditions from a biographical point of view. He points out that Wordsworth associated with the political heirs of the tradition in London in the 1790's, and that he might have learned the intellectual and religious heritage of the seventeenth century from them. Much of Chard's evidence for the earlier connection is unfortunately weak, since his main interest is with the dissenter of the 1790's. His book nevertheless builds a bridge in the direction of Wordsworth's spiritual Puritan heritage without taking up the subject directly. One hopes that a further source study can track down the ways by which Wordsworth learned the specifics of the Calvinist-Puritan tradition, for it seems clear, though indirectly so, from his poetry, that he knew and had a great affinity for this tradition.
72 Clay Hunt, *Donne's Poetry* (New Haven, 1954), p. 108.
73 Hunt, p. 108.
74 George Ridenour, *The Style of "Don Juan"* (New Haven, 1960); Robert Gleckner, *Byron and the Ruins of Paradise* (Baltimore, 1967); Paul Elledge, *Byron and the Dynamics of Metaphor* (Nashville, Tenna., 1968); Michael Cooke, *The Blind Man Traces the Circle* (Princeton, 1968).
75 Alvin B. Kernan, *The Plot of Satire* (New Haven, 1965), pp. 172–222.
76 Leslie A. Marchand, *Byron: A Biography*, 3 vols. (New York, 1957). Marchand gives the details of Byron's early Calvinist upbringing and training, and in the more general sense has this to say:

Like many of his contemporaries in the nineteenth century, he had escaped rationally but not emotionally from the fear-inspired religious training of his youth. The Calvinistic sense of sin haunted his subconscious mind, a ghost that could never be completely exorcised. But that fatalistic conception of human depravity blended with his own weakness to drive him on to further violation of the inhibitions of his own mind. (Vol. I, 404)

The classic work on the subject of Byron's religious beliefs is still E. W. Marjarum's *Byron as Skeptic and Believer* (Princeton, 1938). Stressing the intellectual content of Byron's Calvinism more than does Marchand, it is one groundwork for the viewpoint of this chapter.

77 Ernest J. Lovell, *Byron: The Record of a Quest* (Austin, Texas, 1949), pp. 192, 214, 226.

78 Canto IV, cxxvi, cxxxiii. All quotations are from *The Poetical Works of Lord Byron*, ed. John D. Jump (Oxford, 1970).

79 Canto IV, xxxiii, xxxiv.

80 This short list is not meant to be invidious, merely to establish the consensus among some of the best contemporary critics: William Marshall, *The Structure of Byron's Major Poetry* (Philadelphia, 1962); Gleckner, *Byron and the Ruins of Paradise*; Cooke, *The Blind Man Traces the Circle*. These recent critics agree upon the importance of *Manfred* in Byron's work and upon essential points in the character, though not necessarily about details of structure and meaning in the play.

81 Louis Martz, "The Saint as Tragic Hero: Saint Joan and Murder in the Cathedral," in *Tragic Themes in Western Literature*, ed Cleanth Brooks (New Haven, 1955) pp. 150–178.

82 Marshall, pp. 98–110.

83 *Three Eighteenth Century Romances*, ed. Harrison Steeves (New York, 1931), p. 234.

84 Paraphrase and citation from George Ridenour, "Byron in 1816: Four Poems from Diodati," in *From Sensibility to Romanticism*, ed. Hilles and Bloom (1965), p. 454. This is an admirably succinct modern view of Byron, and fairly typical. As mentioned above, the view of Byron in this book is closer to Lovell, Marjarum, and Marchand than to the more contemporary studies. Perhaps the fact that Ridenour moved from the more traditional views in his earlier *The Style of "Don Juan"* to this "modern" position is an indication of how difficult it becomes not to describe Byron in ideas deriving from existentialism.

85 Lovell, pp. 192, 214.

86 Lovell, p. 226.

87 Kaufmann, *The Pilgrim's Progress and Tradition in Puritan Meditation* (New Haven, 1966), p. 210.

88 Calvin, *Institutes* (trans. Allen), III, XXIV, IV.

89 Gleckner, *Byron and the Ruins of Paradise*; Ridenour, "Byron and the Romantic Pilgrimage: A Critical Examination of the Third and Fourth Cantos of Lord Byron's *Childe Harold's Pilgrimage*," Diss. Yale University, 1955.

Notes to Epilogue

1 Perry Miller, *The New England Mind: The Seventeenth Century* (Cambridge, Mass., 1939).

2 Norman Pettit, *The Heart Prepared* (New Haven, 1966).

3 Roland Delattre, *Beauty and Sensibility in the Thought of Jonathan Edwards* (New Haven, 1968). The poetry of Davies was described briefly in Section Three as a parallel to his English contemporaries.

4 Alan Reimart, *Religion and the American Mind* (Cambridge, 1966).

5 A great amount of writing has been done on the general cultural influence of Calvinist residue upon twentieth-century Southern writers, particularly Faulkner, Robert Penn Warren, and Flannery O Connor. For more general influence upon

contemporary writers, see my article, largely speculative in nature, "Puritan Allegory in Four Modern Novels," *Thought* 44 (1969), 413–32.

6 George Landow's *The Aesthetic and Critical Theories of John Ruskin* (Princeton, 1971) contains a definitive account of Ruskin's spiritual crisis in relation to his evangelical faith and vocation as a writer.

7 Derrick Leon, *Ruskin, the Great Victorian* (London, 1949), p. 569.

8 Two more recent works in this same historical tradition may be cited here: Donald Davie, *A Gathered Church: The Literature of the English Dissenting Tradition, 1700–1930* (New York, 1978); and Barbara K. Lewalski, *Protestant Poetics and the Seventeenth-Century Religious Lyric* (Princeton, 1979).

Index

ISBN 90 279 7926 X

James D. Boulger

The Calvinist Temper in English Poetry

Mouton Publishers
The Hague · Paris · New York

DE PROPRIETATIBUS LITTERARUM

Series Maior 21

edenda curat

C. H. van Schooneveld

Indiana University

Boulger, The Calvinist Temper in English Poetry